add.

GARDENING

PLATE I. A WELL-PLANNED GARDEN

GARDENING

A COMPLETE GUIDE
TO GARDEN MAKING

including FLOWERS AND LAWNS, TREES
AND SHRUBS, FRUITS AND VEGETABLES,
PLANTS IN THE HOME AND GREENHOUSE

BY MONTAGUE FREE

STAFF HORTICULTURIST, "THE HOME GARDEN"
FORMERLY HORTICULTURIST, BROOKLYN BOTANIC
GARDEN; GRADUATE OF THE ROYAL BOTANIC GARDENS, KEW

with 73 halftones & 125 line drawings

REVISED EDITION 1947

HARCOURT, BRACE AND COMPANY, NEW YORK
AND
THE AMERICAN GARDEN GUILD

635.9
F85392
c.2

PREFACE

This volume, the outcome of many requests for a gardening book which is comprehensive yet not too long, has been designed to meet the needs of the average gardener. Although it is simple enough to be easily understood by the novice, I believe that more advanced gardeners will also find it useful. In it I have tried to supply the answers to the problems which have proved puzzling to both amateur and professional gardeners, as revealed by the questions I have been called upon to answer for more than twenty years in the classrooms and correspondence of the Brooklyn Botanic Garden, and for the past five years in the thousands of letters addressed to the "Garden Guide" department of the *New York Sun*.

Since it is in the main a practical book, I have gone into detail in telling how the operations in gardening are performed. At the same time I have endeavored to give the reason back of every practice; and in a few instances—for example, in the pruning chapter—I have emphasized the principles rather than given concrete directions.

The majority of the plants in the descriptive lists are kinds which have proved their worth for general planting, with a few outstanding lesser known species and varieties included. The nomenclature is based on *Hortus*. Selections of named garden varieties are mentioned with misgivings, knowing that in some cases they will soon be superseded by new introductions. But the novice is so apt to be bewildered by the multiplicity of varieties listed in catalogs that it seemed desirable to extend a helping hand in this direction.

While the book is newly written, I have occasionally included excerpts from my previously published articles. I am indebted to the *American Rose Society*, the *Brooklyn Botanic Garden*, *Better Homes and Gardens*, the *Gardeners' Chronicle of America* and the *New York Sun*, for permission to draw upon material which they have published. The chapter ROCK AND WALL GARDENS is adapted from an article contributed by me to *The Garden Dictionary* and is included here by permission of the Houghton Mifflin Co.

My thanks go to Miss Carol H. Woodward for editorial assistance

v

in preparing the manuscript, and to my colleagues, Dr. C. Stuart Gager and Dr. Arthur Harmount Graves, for critically reading the manuscript and making numerous suggestions. I am grateful to Dr. George M. Reed, Plant Pathologist of the Brooklyn Botanic Garden, for writing the section "Some Diseases of Plants" in Chapter XXIX. Miss Barbara Capen and Mr. S. R. Tilley have been of immense service in verifying formulas and in the preparation of the index. Professor R. H. Clark of the New Jersey Agricultural Experiment Station aided by making suggestions regarding the fruit garden chapter; and Mr. Howard R. Sebold, Landscape Architect, kindly criticized the chapter on planning and contributed two plans.

Much of the value of this type of book depends upon illustrations. I feel I was fortunate in having the services of Miss Maud H. Purdy, staff artist of the Brooklyn Botanic Garden, who made all the line drawings with the exception of Figs. 107, 109, 110, 112, 114, and 115, which were done by the late Violette T. Free, and those of greenhouses, which are by the courtesy of the Lord & Burnham Co.

Most of the half-tones are from photographs made in the Brooklyn Botanic Garden by Mr. Louis Buhle, staff photographer, and I am indebted to the Garden authorities for permission to use them.

Montague Free

Brooklyn, N. Y.
February, 1937

PREFACE TO THE SECOND EDITION

So far as garden operations are concerned only a few minor changes seemed to me to be necessary.

All of the lists of garden varieties have been checked carefully and the least desirable of the older introductions removed to make room for newer, improved forms.

The section pertaining to garden enemies needed much revision to take into account the flood of new material and new methods of fighting pests and diseases.

M. F.

Hyde Park, New York
April, 1947

CONTENTS

CONTENTS

LIST OF PLATES

LIST OF PLATES

GARDENING

I. SELECTING AND PLANNING
THE PROPERTY

Planning the garden begins ideally with the selection of the property. If the site is to be in the city, the deciding factor is likely to be the size of the plot or the character of the neighborhood; if in the country, it may be a brook, a pond, a rocky bank, a view, or an excellent depth of topsoil that determines the choice. In the country there are also severely practical aspects to note, such as water supply both for house and garden use, availability of sewers, or, lacking these, other means of sewage disposal. If one is to use the place as a year-round residence, it must be adjacent to a road that is kept open all winter.

Locating the house. Before the garden can be planned the house must be located. As a general rule it should not be set in the middle of the plot, for if it is (unless the property is large), the space left for gardens is too small for effective treatment. The house is best placed on a gentle rise of ground, so that there is efficient outward drainage of water on all sides, yet it should be accessible without steep grades.

When trees are already standing on the property, their uses for shade and shelter, for ornament, for shutting off unsightly views, and for framing vistas offer endless possibilities which may affect the entire layout of the grounds. Whenever practical, the house and property should be so arranged that the windows of the important rooms overlook the best views. The direction of the prevailing winds is another important factor. Protection by a low hill or by trees and shrubbery on north, northeast, or northwest will mean greater comfort in winter for plants in the garden as well as for the occupants of the house. More than anything else, the house should be placed and surroundings designed for maximum comfort and convenience. When making a home and contriving a garden to enjoy for many years, it is wise to remember that as one grows older, inconveniences tend to become more irksome and comforts are increasingly appreciated.

Save the topsoil! When the excavation for the house is being made, it is important to save the topsoil and to deposit the coarse subsoil where it will do the least harm to the grounds. These points will receive scant thought from the building contractor unless brought to his attention.

Even then, there is always debris left around the house when the last workman has packed his tools and departed. The owner surveys his new property with a feeling of despair, for the grounds at this stage resemble anything but an ideal garden spot, and the garden maker wonders how and where to begin.

Who shall make the plan? If the property is large and if elaborate planting is desired, or if one's personal time is limited, by all means call in a landscape architect. To him the upheaval around the house will not look so discouraging. He is trained to see through the debris to the fine green lawn that will follow it. He knows at a glance where the trees belong to provide shelter, shade, and vistas. He envisions a flowering hedge or a screen of evergreens where the land abuts on adjoining property; and he knows where the gardens of different types will flourish best and present the most charming views from the windows and walks. He is experienced in laying out grounds for both beauty and convenience, and can create a well-designed property based on ideas which express the owner's personality. All that needs to be done when the design for the grounds is finished is to turn it over to a landscape contractor for execution.

On the other hand, when the house is finally constructed, one may wish to make the garden plan and do the work oneself. In that case, it is hoped that this introductory chapter will point the way for the home-owner who wants to develop his property into the beauty-spot of which he has dreamed.

Preliminaries to gardening. The first job is to clean up the rubbish around the house. Burn what you can, but save brickbats and stones, as they may be handy later to serve as foundations for walks and such features. Then take time out for thoughtful deliberation, to avoid doing things that will have to be changed later on. Remember, it is bad practice to undertake more than can be handled. A square rod properly kept is better than an acre in which the flower beds are cluttered with weeds and the trees and shrubs are dying from lack of care. The amount of time and money available for upkeep is a prime consideration. A garden does not take care of itself: the lawn must be mowed, the trees pruned, the borders dug, the pests destroyed, the annuals planted, perennials transplanted, and the bulbs set out and later dug up—these and many other tasks demand the gardener's time and cash.

The type of development that looks best with a minimum of expense for maintenance consists mainly of lawn with trees and shrubbery growing informally. The cost is increased when there are hedges to clip several times a year, pergolas and arbors to paint, and ornamental vines to train. Flower borders add considerably to the cost of upkeep; but most expensive of all is the formal garden which demands a display of spring bulbs and carpeting plants, followed in summer by tender bedding plants. These factors must be kept in mind while making the plan. One may not feel able at first to have more than the simplest design; yet it is wise to draw up a comprehensive plan, even though it is years before it can be carried out in its entirety.

First examine the existing features and make full use of them. Consider the trees from every angle before cutting any down; it takes a long time to grow an enduring tree. If part of the property consists of woods, think over the possibility of judiciously thinning the trees, clearing away weedy underbrush, and making a woodland garden furnished with shade-loving flowers, rhododendrons, and ferns.

Before blasting out a rocky bank to make a level greensward, ask yourself whether, at some time later, you may be wanting to make a rock garden there, and wishing you had not eliminated the bank.

If there is a decided depression on part of the property, it might be converted—if and when water is available—into an attractive pond, the home of gorgeous waterlilies and goldfish, with Japanese irises and other water-loving plants along its banks.

Now make a list of features commonly found in gardens and decide which of them seem immediately essential and which will be most desirable when you have time and money to install them. Among the essentials are lawn, trees, shrubs, and walks. Desirable features include a flower garden, which may be in the form of borders, beds, or formal garden; a fruit and vegetable garden; a rose garden; rock garden; waterlily pool; pergolas and arbors; area for tennis or other games; play area for children; drying ground; service yard; and possibly other pet features that you have in mind.

You can already see how some parts of the design must be laid out with direct reference to others. Grading and walks, for instance, must be planned in correlation; the terrain and the view from the principal windows together determine the site of the flower beds; the service yard, drying ground, and vegetable garden ought to be near the kitchen. The property that is developed in an orderly, logical manner, with strict regard for convenience and appropriateness, is likely to be the one that gives the most satisfaction, both to the owner and to his visitors.

Making a plan. In order to keep all these details and many others in mind, it is quite necessary to put one's scheme on paper. The first step is to make a plan of the area showing the boundaries, the position of the house, the lines of view from the windows, and the important existing features, such as trees, outbuildings, hills, and hollows. Then superimpose the features that you hope to develop. The plan should be made to scale—1 inch equaling 8 feet is workable if the property is not too large.

Grading. If the topography of the plot is rugged, some grading will be necessary, if only to take care of walks and drives. A level surface over the whole plot is not necessarily ideal, although many home-owners seem to think that it is. But around the house a level area which extends down toward the lawn with a gentle slope is of sufficient advantage to warrant a certain amount of grading. It is sometimes essential also to cut and fill in order to make a formal garden, to secure an easily cultivated area for the kitchen garden, or to overcome grades that are too steep for driveways and walks. But it is important to try to utilize most of the land as it is, rather than to tear the whole plot to pieces.

When the necessary grading has been accomplished, it is time to make provision for supplying water to the garden; and also for removing it if the land is badly drained. These points, as well as details of grading, will be presented in later chapters.

Locating walks. Primarily, walks should "go places and do things." That is to say, they should facilitate one's getting somewhere, such as from the street to the house, from the house to the arbor or sundial or whatever point of interest there is at the end of the garden. They should enable one to get around conveniently both to enjoy the beauty of the flowers and to trundle a wheelbarrow with manure for the vegetable garden. Generally speaking, walks should be strictly utilitarian and achieve their objects in the most direct way, because there is nothing more exasperating than to have to take a devious course when a more direct line would be better. This does not mean that a curved walk is unallowable, but that a curve without reason is unjustifiable. It is entirely proper to curve a walk on a steep grade, to avoid cutting across an expanse of lawn, or to get around a jutting rock, a clump of trees, or shrubbery. But curves, when used, should be bold and sweeping and never insane wriggles.

With grading and walks at least tentatively plotted, it is now the appropriate time to begin to think about the planting.

Trees. If I were making a garden on treeless property, the first thing I should do after the grading had been accomplished would be to plant trees if it were the right time of year, even if everything else had to wait. Because trees are—or should be—the most permanent features of the place, careful forethought must be given to placing them correctly. Proportion and balance (not necessarily symmetry) are among the important principles to strive for in making a garden; thus when the area is small, the number of trees that may be used is severely restricted—possibly to one or two. Such giants as American elm, tulip tree, and sugar maple must usually be avoided, and smaller-growing subjects such as the scarlet thorn, flowering dogwood, flowering crab-apple, and Japanese cherry used instead.

As a general rule, one should leave the center of the grounds open, massing the trees and shrubbery around the borders, not in regular rows but in bold promontories and bays. The largest trees should be used in the promontories, the small trees and shrubs where the planting is narrower. Thus a monotonous skyline is avoided. Still more variety may be introduced by associating spire-like and columnar trees with those having a broad rounded outline. Lombardy poplars, for instance, in groups of three or five, have value as accent points in the composition.

Trees for shade. On the south, southeast, or southwest side of a house, one or two trees may be planted to give shade. For a small property, suitable subjects are flowering dogwood, downy hawthorn, English hawthorn (double-flowered forms in scarlet or white are especially good), Washington thorn, red buckeye, tree lilac, and Japanese cherry. These trees should stand at least 10 feet away from the house. Where there is room for a larger tree, which can be set 20 feet or farther away, a sugar or red maple, black or red oak, or an American elm may be chosen. If, however, a tree when placed to greatest advantage for shade would shut off a pleasant view, one must decide which is preferable—shade or scenery.

Often it is desirable to frame the house with trees to enhance its architecture and to provide a proper setting. Near the house, the majority of such trees should be deciduous, because in the temperate zone we want our windows exposed to the winter sunshine. But at a little distance from the dwelling, evergreens may be used effectively. They must be chosen with an eye to their future size and shape, as well as to their vigor in that climate and situation. For a majestic note in the framing of the house, the white pine is perhaps the finest evergreen. For picturesqueness, choose a sturdy Scotch pine. If a spire-like effect is required, select from among the firs and spruces. (See the section on SELECTING TREES AND SHRUBS in Chapter VII.)

Windbreaks. In climates where the house needs to be shielded from northern gales, a windbreak should be planned and planted at once. Tall trees may be used only where there is sufficient space to set them at least 50 feet away from the house. The influence exerted by a windbreak extends horizontally twenty times its height.

The trees selected for windbreaks should be the hardiest kinds of evergreens. The red pine and the Scotch pine (especially the Riga variety) are desirable in light sandy soil. In sandy loam, the white pine, Douglas fir, and Norway spruce may be used. In heavy soils, white spruce, arborvitae, and balsam fir are preferable. When the windbreak is designed to serve the dual purpose of shelter and ornament, and there is sufficient room, the trees should be set so as to form a natural-looking planting, as indicated in Fig. 1.

In the case of small properties where there is no room for a large windbreak, a tall evergreen hedge of arborvitae, Japanese yew, red cedar, or white pine will serve to shelter the garden and, in part, the house.

Screen planting. The trees used to shut off an undesirable view should be evergreen to be effective throughout the year. In northern regions the white pine is excellent for this purpose, or, if a spire-like tree would be more effective, spruce or fir. In regions having a favorable winter temperature, it is possible to select from a large variety of broad-leaved evergreens such as live oak, magnolia, and eucalyptus.

When planting is necessary to shut off the service yard, drying ground, or compost pile, it is not necessary to use such large-growing material. A hedge of evergreens such as Japanese yew, white pine, or hemlock, which may be restrained at the desired height, or a group of shrubs is usually all that is necessary. If space is limited the screen may be a trellis clothed with vines or roses.

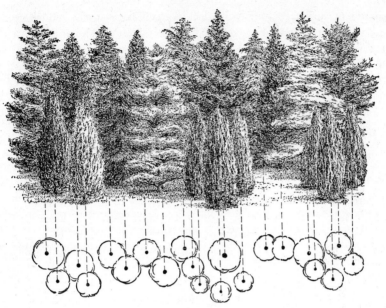

Fig. 1. Windbreak

Planting between house and street. The type of planting between the house and the street is dependent on the amount of space available, the character of the terrain, and whether the garden is to be located in that area. If it is, and if the owner wishes to enjoy his flowers without being exposed to the gaze of every passer-by, a screen planting is essential. When room is limited, a dense evergreen hedge is most suitable; otherwise the screen may consist of trees and shrubs irregularly grouped along the street boundary with the heaviest planting concentrated at the corners and on either side of the entrance. It is probably unnecessary to remind anyone that when the entrance is designed for automobile traffic, it is essential that a free view of the street be afforded to drivers. This may be accomplished by broadening the approach or by setting the entrance posts back from the street and using low-growing plants between them and the sidewalk (Fig. 2).

Sometimes the house is so near the street line that it is impossible to secure privacy without shutting out light and air from the windows. In such cases one must accept the inevitable, restricting the border planting to a low hedge.

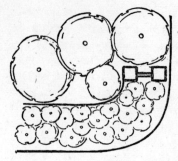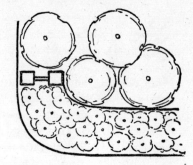

FIG. 2. Planting at entrance gates

Simplicity, in general, should be the keynote of the planting on the street side of the house. If dictated by usefulness, it is likely to be pleasing too. The service driveway, if there is one, should be screened by planting. A flower border on either side of the entrance walk is usually permissible, and so is a low hedge of boxwood, dwarf spreading Japanese yew, or similar material. Landscape architects frown, with justice, on the practice of planting specimen weeping mulberries, blue spruces, and beds of geraniums and cannas in the center of the grass plot.

Framing a vista. When trees or shrubs are planted for the purpose of framing a vista they should be unobtrusive in character—of such a nature that they merge with their surroundings and do not call attention to themselves at the expense of the view they frame. This rules out flowering trees and those with conspicuous foliage, such as the purple beech and the tropical-appearing *Ailanthus.*

Specimen trees. Trees intended to serve as specimens must be planted with sufficient space around them to keep them free from competition with other trees and shrubs. This is possible only on properties of considerable size. They should not be scattered indiscriminately over the lawn; for, in the main, its center should always be kept clear. Specimen trees show off to most pleasing advantage when they are set fairly near to, yet entirely free from, the border planting.

Other elements of the design. With trees for every purpose allotted to their proper places, shrubs and other features of the layout may be considered. In later chapters the development of many different types of plantings—annuals and perennials, fruit and vegetable gardens, rose gardens, rock and wall gardens, water, herb, and wild gardens and foundation planting—is presented in detail. Here, only those plantings which will particularly affect the original design of the property are briefly mentioned in order that they shall be included from the beginning.

Shrub planting. Shrubs, apart from intrinsic beauty of form, flowers, and foliage, are of value for providing backgrounds, enclosing the garden and thus securing a measure of privacy, and for giving food and shelter to birds. They should be grouped around the margins, not spotted hither and yon throughout the whole area. As with trees, specimen shrubs are permissible only if thoughtfully placed and used in moderation.

Before allotting too extensive an area to shrubs, the location of other necessary features should be decided, because many of these will require shrubs for background, border, screen, or accent.

Flower garden. Ordinarily the flower garden should be made close to the house to be seen from the windows of the most used rooms. It may consist of flower borders on one or both sides of the main walk, in which case a shrub planting often looks well as a background for the border nearest the boundary line. Or the flower garden may be formal in character and consist of a series of beds of simple geometrical shapes laid out in a coherent design. (See Chapter XI, FLOWER BEDS AND BORDERS.) Such a treatment usually calls for a planting of shrubs to enclose it and to separate it from the less formal parts of the grounds. These shrubs may be varied or may consist of a single species sheared to a formal outline, their character depending on the style of the garden and the taste of the owner.

Vegetable garden. Although there are those who see great beauty in the vegetable garden (their perception perhaps being colored by thoughts of gastronomic delights), usually it is desirable to place it in a somewhat sequestered spot, not too far from the kitchen. Here again, shrubs serve the utilitarian purpose of a screen. On a small property, however, the screening off of a fair-sized portion of ground for vegetables will result in greatly reducing the apparent size of the place. This effect may be overcome, in part, by skillful handling of the shrubbery screen and by planting a few ornamental trees and shrubs in such a way that the kitchen garden seen from a little distance will appear to be an extension of the flower garden. The vista of a flower-bordered walk in the kitchen garden, visible through an opening in the shrubbery screen, will add to the desired illusion.

The vegetable garden should be a fairly level area with a good depth of rich soil. It should be accessible so that manure can be delivered to it without too much inconvenience. I know of a large estate with an enormous vegetable garden where every bit of manure has to be carried in by hand-baskets because the only access to the garden is by means of long steep flights of steps!

Game grounds. The area devoted to games also demands a level spot. If the backstops required for tennis make it difficult to work the court in as a part of the garden composition, it is usually best to locate it in a place apart. This is especially true if other than a grass court is used. On the other hand, when providing for less strenuous games, such as croquet, there is no reason why the playing area should not be laid out on the lawn without detriment to the appearance of the garden.

Play space for children. The play space allotted to children should be chosen thoughtfully. Both sun and shade should be provided, and there should be a definite demarcation between this area and the rest of the property. This will help in protecting the garden and in keeping the sandpiles, toys, and miscellaneous collections of things that boys and girls acquire from being scattered over the lawn, to the detriment of the mower and the temper of the garden-maker.

Service yard. The service yard and drying ground should, when possible, be located out of the direct view of the living rooms of the house, and should be convenient to the kitchen and laundry. These portions of the layout should either be paved or situated on thoroughly drained ground with a surface covering which dries rapidly after rain.

In order that a clear picture might be obtained of the many elements that enter into the making of a garden landscape, I have attempted above to outline the planning of a property development as a series of progressive steps. Actually, the making of a plan cannot be divided into differentiated items; each component has a bearing on some other part and, if each were considered separately without relation to the rest, the final result would quite likely be a hodge-podge. That is why a comprehensive plan of the development is necessary from the very start.

Specimen plans. I am indebted to Mr. Howard R. Sebold, Landscape Architect, for the two plans (Figs. 3 and 4) which follow on pp. 14 and 15, together with his suggestions accompanying them.

PLATE II. *(upper)* IN THIS CALIFORNIA GARDEN A PICTURESQUE PEPPER TREE IS THE CENTRAL FEATURE. *(lower)* A PATIO GARDEN, SANTA MARIA INN

PLATE III. (*upper*) EUROPEAN WEEPING BEECH, *Fagus sylvatica pendula*. SUMMER. (*lower*) EUROPEAN WEEPING BEECH, *Fagus sylvatica pendula*. WINTER

FOR A LOT 50 X 100 FEET

1. With a lot as small as this one, it is not possible to have many different areas. The owner must choose the type of development he likes best and carry it out to the exclusion of a more varied type. If he is most interested in flowers, he might omit the shrubs and trees at the back, and devote the entire area to flowers. On the other hand, the writer feels that for a year-round effect, the shrubs and trees as seen from the living room would give a more continuously pleasing effect.

2. If no laundry yard is wanted, and if there are no children in the family, either or both of these areas might be devoted to vegetables or flowers for cutting.

3. The small trees in the garden area at the back of the house might be flowering dogwoods, crab-apples or the like. Spring bulbs and shade-loving herbaceous plants might be planted underneath these small trees. Perennials could be used in front of the shrubs in this same area, although it is pointed out that from the horticultural standpoint this is not the best practice because of eventual shade and root competition offered by the shrubs. Also, it might be noted that perennials are only shown in bays in the shrubbery and are not to be planted as a continuous edging.

4. Vines might be used at intervals along the property line on the fence; that is, if a fence is used. The writer feels that it would be desirable to have one. It might be of any of the available wooden kinds preferably, with the possible exception of the woven wood fence which is much too rustic for the usual suburban development.

5. The stepping-stones across the front of the house may be omitted. They were used so that there would not be a worn path across the lawn from the garage to the front door.

FOR A LOT 100 X 175 FEET

1. A property of this size allows a greater variety of areas. A lawn is seen out of the living-room window. The perennials are kept at the sides so as not to be too conspicuous in the winter. The shrubs immediately back of the flowers were thought of as lilacs of various kinds. At the far end of the lawn an open arbor is placed. This, with the tall shrubs at the sides, tends to enclose the lawn area. At the same time, however, the arbor is open and a feeling of something beyond will be gained by one looking out from the house. The color of the roses would be visible, but not their usual bare stems and branches. Their ugliness in winter would not intrude upon the people in the house. These are the reasons why the rose garden is not put directly adjacent

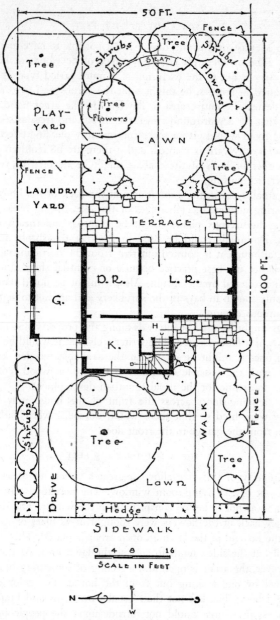

Fig. 3. Plan for a lot 50 x 100 feet

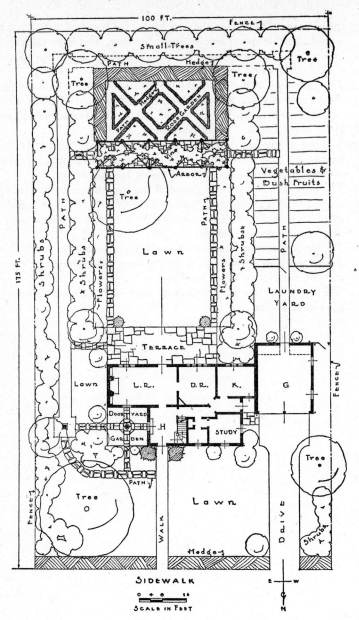

FIG. 4. Plan for a lot 100 x 175 feet

to the house. The beds in the rose garden are bordered with some low edging, such as dwarf box or dwarf barberry. The three sides of the garden are then surrounded by some taller-growing hedge to about the height of 3 or 4 feet.

2. The long walk at the left of the lawn area is bordered on one side by shrubs such as lilacs, and on the outer side by various kinds of flowering shrubs. Between the path and the shrubs themselves, different kinds of wild flowers might be planted.

3. The row of small trees at the back of the lot were thought of as dwarf fruit trees. Other small trees on the plot might be crab-apples, Japanese cherries, hawthorns, flowering dogwoods, laburnums, etc.

4. The little dooryard garden shown at the front might be planted to a few shade-loving evergreens, such as *Taxus, Pieris,* etc., with a ground-cover such as *Vinca.* Then various kinds of spring bulbs could be planted to come up through the ground-cover.

5. The black spots shown at the intersection of the paths in the dooryard garden and also outside of the little garden were thought of as locations for features such as a sun-dial.

6. The hedge in front of the property may be eliminated, as may the fence on the sides.

II. GRADING

Preliminary thought applied to grading will save time and money, improve the property with a minimum of labor, and enable better provision to be made for the growth of plants.

When grading is necessary, it should be done with a view to making the house and the garden features conveniently accessible, avoiding steep slopes in walks and driveways; leveling areas for flower gardens, tennis court, and such specialties; and developing contours which are pleasing to the eye.

When possible, grades should be such that surface water is conducted away from walks and drives as well as the house; otherwise drains must be constructed.

Topographical survey. On a large place where extensive grading is necessary, it is wise to have a topographical survey made by someone who is skilled in this work. The existing contour lines should be marked on the plan; then the proposed contour lines will be added and a scheme worked out on paper to ensure the most economical method of handling the soil. On small plots the required cutting and filling may be estimated with the eye.

For economy's sake as well as for distinctiveness of design, existing contours should be studied for their adaptability before any plans for extensive grading are made. There should be no objection whatever to a rolling terrain, for a lawn with graceful slopes may be far more pleasing than one that is perfectly level. If there happens to be a depression suitably placed, it might be developed charmingly as a sunken flower garden; or a small hill might be left to be topped by a shelter overlooking a view.

Utilizing the topsoil. It is important to save the topsoil from every inch of the ground from which it is removed. Especially where the topsoil is poor and scanty is this desirable; but even where it is plentiful a gardener can always find uses for an extra supply. Therefore, the topsoil should first of all be stripped from the site of the building and from a space about 20 feet beyond the lines of the walls. Also, the topsoil from areas to be used as drives, walks, service yard, and drying ground should be salvaged as well as from the tennis court except where a grass court is to be used; and from all sections whose levels are to be changed.

After the topsoil is removed from the areas to be lowered or raised, the subsoil may be graded to the proposed height by cut or fill; then the topsoil may be put back in place. If the area is to be used for planting of any kind, the level should be made below the finished grade to allow for adding the proper depth of topsoil. If the subsoil removed while excavating for the cellar can be dumped directly into a hollow from which the topsoil has been stripped, the labor of handling the excavated soil a second time is avoided.

When topsoil is plentiful there is always the temptation to fill in the hollows with it rather than first to grade the subsoil. The error of this bad practice will be disclosed later by a patchy-looking lawn, the growth being more vigorous where the topsoil is deeper. This condition would show itself particularly during a drought.

For a lawn a depth of 6 inches to 1 foot of good topsoil will be sufficient, but for flower borders and tree or shrub planting a depth of 2 feet is desirable. When the topsoil is thin in the garden, it is often a good plan to remove a foot or two of subsoil and use it elsewhere for fill, replacing it with the good topsoil saved from other parts of the grounds. At the time this may seem like a great deal of trouble, but when the permanency of the garden and the welfare of the plants are considered, it will be found to pay in the long run.

Terrace banks. Whenever conditions permit, the level ground around the house should be made to fall away in a continuous, gentle slope towards the boundaries of the property, rather than in an abrupt declivity (Fig. 5). But in many cases there is insufficient room and some provision must be made to hold up and prevent erosion of the terrace. A sloping bank of 45 degrees or less, planted to prevent erosion, or a wall of brick or stone may be used.

Skimping on topsoil is a serious mistake when building the terrace bank. It is always difficult to maintain a planting on such a slope because much of the water runs off immediately. The consequent droughty condition is intensified if the topsoil is thin. The usual method of treating a terrace bank is to attempt to grow turf. But grass does not do well in such situations when it is dry and mowing

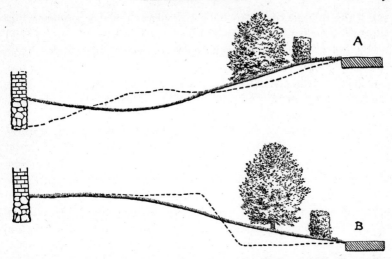

Fig. 5. Grading: *A*. When house is lower than street. Broken line represents original grade. The new grade conducts water away from the house. *B*. When house is higher than street. The gradual slope is preferable from the standpoint of easy maintenance.

on a steep slope is always difficult. My solution would be to plant something that does not require mowing and that has sufficiently dense growth to discourage weeds, and a root system extensive enough to hold the soil in place. Good subjects for this purpose are rambling roses such as *Wichuraiana* or Max Graf; dwarf spreading cotoneasters such as *C. horizontalis;* creeping junipers like the Bar Harbor variety; or Japanese honeysuckle. Such a treatment is infinitely preferable to a moth-eaten turf on the score of appearance, interest, and ease of maintenance. In the case of steep banks there still remains the problem, in regions subject to heavy rains, of preventing erosion until the time when the soil-holding plants have become established. I have solved it to my own satisfaction, in the case of roses and similar furnishing plants, in the following way:

First, make the soil on the slope quite firm by tamping. Then sod the bank with turves cut from a pasture or meadow, holding them in place with wooden pegs, 6 to 8 inches long, driven through the sods into the bank. The sods do not have to be of first-class quality because they have only a temporary rôle. If the bank is sodded in the spring, by the time autumn arrives the roots of the grasses will have pene-

trated the soil sufficiently to hold it in place, and the permanent occupants of the bank may then be planted.

Dig holes, just large enough to accommodate their roots, 3 feet
apart in straight lines parallel to the top of the bank. The first line
should be 18 inches from the edge, and subsequent lines 2 feet 10 inches
apart. Set the plants in place and pack the soil firmly about their roots.
Now comes the essential part of the plan:

Cover the whole of the planted area with mulch paper, starting
with an 18-inch width along the top and following this with 3-foot
widths to the bottom of the bank. The lower edge of each strip should
lie underneath the upper edge of the width below—just opposite from
laying shingles—to allow water to reach the soil from above. Slits must
be cut every 3 feet so that the paper fits snugly around the planted
shrubs. The mulch paper serves a triple purpose: it conserves moisture
by preventing evaporation, it smothers the grass, and prevents the
growth of weeds. By following this procedure the bank is never left
unprotected against erosion, for, by the time the grass roots have
decayed, the roots of the permanent planting have grown enough to
hold the soil.

Another method of preventing erosion on a terrace is by facing
the bank with irregularly placed rocks, thus making a semiformal
rock garden which should be planted with vigorous rock plants. When
the surroundings demand it (and if the pocketbook can stand it), a
formal wall of brick or stone may be erected. If stones which can be
laid without mortar are available, a wall garden may be appropriate.
These types of planting are discussed more fully in Chapter XVI,
ROCK AND WALL GARDENS.

Laying out level areas. When laying out small areas which must
be absolutely level (for example, a tennis court), the job may be done
with the aid of a spirit level and a straightedge, which any good
carpenter can make by planing an 8-foot board to perfect evenness.

The ground is first graded as nearly level as possible with the eye.
Pegs are driven into the ground at about 8-foot intervals, leaving
them projecting 3 or 4 inches above the surface. Start at the peg which
seems to be at the lowest point and support the straightedge on it and
the nearest peg. Apply the spirit level to the straightedge and hammer
down the second peg until it is seen to be level with number 1. Then
proceed to the next peg and drive it down to correspond to the second
peg, and so on over the whole plot. If the work has been well done

the tops of all the pegs will be on the same level and will serve as guides in distributing soil to make the final grade.

Technique of grading. In all grading operations, remember that disturbed soil occupies more space than undisturbed soil, so it is necessary either to allow for settling or to compact the soil as it is put in place.

The technique followed in moving the soil from place to place is dependent on the amount that has to be moved, and on the distance it has to be transported. On small jobs a pick and shovel and possibly a wheelbarrow may be the only tools required; on larger areas horse- or tractor-drawn scrapers may be the most efficient equipment to use; while in the case of operations which involve the transportation of thousands of tons of earth a steam shovel and motor truck, or a bulldozer, may be most economical.

Considerable hand work is necessary for the finishing touches. The man with the shovel follows the scraper or dump truck, and he in turn is followed by the man with the rake.

Labor-saving method. Economies in grading may be instituted by exercising forethought. For example: Supposing there is an area of 40 x 100 feet where the grade is to be lowered and a similar area where it has to be raised. Instead of stripping all the topsoil from both areas at one time, remove it from a space of 20 x 20 feet on each piece and place it to one side. Then correct the subgrade by transferring subsoil from the high to the low area. When this has been done the topsoil from the adjacent plots of 20 x 20 feet can be placed on the newly graded areas. Proceed along these lines until the last two 20 x 20-foot areas are reached, then bring the topsoil removed from the first two areas to finish the grade. By following this method nine tenths of the topsoil has to be moved once only, whereas if the whole of the two areas of 40 x 100 feet had been stripped at one time, *all* of the topsoil would have had to have been moved twice.

Drainage and irrigation. When grading has been completed it is necessary to think about the installation of underdrainage and irrigation pipes.

On most properties underdraining will probably be quite unnecessary, but if there are any swampy areas, or places where water stands in puddles for several days after a rain, draining is essential unless the owner contemplates the establishment of a swamp or bog garden. If he does, a reminder is in order that mosquitoes are bothersome.

Draining is discussed and the methods of laying the drains are described in Chapter IV, soil improvement. It is mentioned here because if it is necessary to install drains it should be done early in the game to avoid the inconvenience and unsightly disruption that are caused by putting them in after planting has been done.

Irrigation pipes should be laid so that all points likely to need artificial watering may be reached by attaching a 50-foot length of hose to the faucet. The faucets, to be inconspicuous, should project only a few inches above the surface. Whenever conditions permit they should not be located on lawns because of the difficulty of mowing around them. Of course, where large lawns are concerned, it may be impossible to avoid this. The faucet should be horizontal, to allow the hose to be easily attached. When the opening points downwards, a hose is difficult to attach, and, because of the angle formed near the point of attachment, the hose quickly wears out at this point.

The ideal is a complete network of pipes with a sufficient number of risers, fitted with spray heads flush with the soil surface, so that the whole garden may be watered if necessary by merely turning a valve. Such a system, however, is expensive to install.

Whichever system of irrigation is adopted, there should be a shut-off valve at the intake, and all pipes should slope to the lowest point to a drain valve for draining water from the pipes before freezing weather comes. This obviates the bother of having to protect the water from freezing in the risers and does away with the necessity of burying the pipes below the frost line.

III. WALKS

This chapter is concerned with the practical aspects of walk construction.

Layout and foundation. In the first place one must decide which are the most convenient routes for reaching the flower borders, vegetable garden, or other points from the house or from the different parts of the grounds. Then plan direct pathways, using straight lines wherever they are advisable, employing curves only when the scheme of the garden demands them. The purposes of the paths will thus determine their layout. The material of which they are made is also contingent on their use. Those that will be much traveled or that will carry heavy wheeled traffic must be more durably built than those meant for only occasional strolls.

Likewise, the width of walks depends in part upon their use, and should also be in keeping with the size of the property. Except in small gardens, such as those in a city back yard, 3 feet should be looked upon as a minimum width. In small formal gardens the auxiliary walks dividing the beds may be as narrow as 2 feet, but even here the main walks should not measure less than 3 feet.

Staking out the walks. The lines of the walks should first be staked out in order that one may visualize their final appearance in relation to the other garden features. When a straight walk is to be made, stretch guide-lines so that it will be really straight. When curved walks are being laid out, a garden hose is the most effective aid in securing the curve desired. A hose is flexible enough to be handled easily, stiff enough to be laid in graceful lines, and large enough to be seen at a distance. A rope, which is often recommended for this purpose, is likely to be flabby and to lie in awkward bends.

Preparing the foundation. After the course of the walk has been determined and staked, the fertile topsoil is removed and saved for some other part of the garden. (See Chapter II, GRADING.) If the topsoil is only 6 inches or so in depth, the next step depends upon the character of the subsoil. If water passes through it with difficulty, it should be dug out to allow a total depth of 1 foot for foundation and surface. The foundation should then consist of 9 inches of coarse material, such as broken bricks, crushed rock, or small stones. This will afford a firm base for 3 inches of surfacing material, ensuring a walk that will stand up under traffic and that will come through the winter unscathed. Roll the foundation and apply whatever surfacing is desired.

If, however, the subsoil is sandy or gravelly and readily permeable by water, no further excavation is necessary. Crushed stone may be laid to within 3 inches of the grade, then firmly rolled and covered with almost any type of surface. I am acquainted with roads, even, made by merely rolling the subsoil with a heavy roller and then applying 3 inches of crushed stone, using a binding of tar for the surface. After a few years heaving from frost makes patching necessary, but otherwise this kind of road works fairly well.

Types of surfacing. Gravel of a binding type is excellent if a deep foundation is first established. Brick is appropriate for straight, formal walks. Concrete is most durable, but not always suitable. If cinders, ashes, or clinkers are used, they are best treated with a bituminous binding and surfaced with crushed stone. Flagstones, either the squared or irregular ones, may sometimes be laid without a special foundation. Tanbark is delightful to walk upon and is especially effective in informal gardens. Where walks are infrequently used, broad lanes of grass between beds of flowers are beautiful.

Details of construction of each of these types of walks are given in the following paragraphs.

Gravel walks. I have a predilection for walks of gravel because of the pleasant appearance of old moss-covered gravel walks common in many English gardens. But unless a good foundation is laid, such walks are apt to be muddy in wet seasons, and when the frost is coming out of the ground in the spring, they are unfit to walk on. Weeds in them may be controlled by annual applications of a weed-killer.

To make a gravel walk, an inch or two of clinkers or coarse ashes should be placed on the foundation and shaped to present a convex surface, allowing a rise of 1 inch to 1½ feet of width. After the ashes have been graded, roll and then apply 2 or 3 inches of gravel, which must be of a type which binds when rolled. Pay particular attention to getting the surface true by raking, making sure that the crown or highest point is centered throughout the whole length. Then water

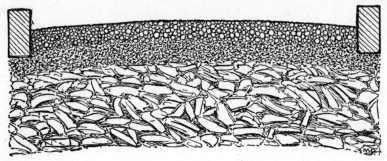

FIG. 6. Gravel walk (section)

thoroughly and roll with a heavy roller. If the gravel is of the right consistency and the job properly done, the surface will be almost as compact as if concrete were used (Fig. 6).

Brick walks. Porous red bricks are excellent for walks wherever they can appropriately be used—which is for straight paths and on the comparatively small place. Their inflexibility makes them unsuited for sharp curves. A

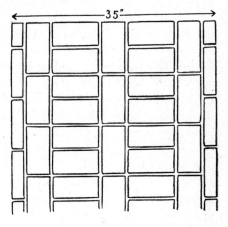

FIG. 7. Simple pattern for a brick walk

width of 3 feet will take seven rows of standard bricks laid flat, plus two outer rows laid on edge for a raised border, with half-inch interspaces.

The foundation should be prepared as previously described, bringing it up to within 5 inches of the surface. Place on this about 2 inches of ashes, consolidate by rolling, then apply 1 inch of builder's sand. The American standard bricks are 2 x 4 x 8 inches, so if they are laid flat the surface will be at the correct level.

Set the bricks first along the sides of the walk. Any simple pattern (Fig. 7) may be used in laying the bricks so long as it allows the joints to be broken. But a design which involves much cutting of the bricks should be avoided, because of the labor and because of the

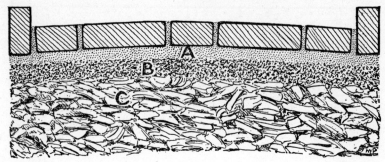

Fig. 8. Brick walk (section). *A*. 1 inch sand; *B*. 2 inches coarse ashes; *C*. 6 inches brickbats, etc. If subsoil is porous, *C* may be omitted.

less stable surface of the halves. The bricks should be firmly laid with the concave side (if any) downward and the tops flush and level. Then fill the interspaces with sand, water thoroughly to settle it, and then apply more sand to make good any depressions caused by subsidence. Brick walks are sometimes grouted with cement but such walks are not so attractive and they usually require special provision for the disposal of surface water (Fig. 8).

Concrete walks. Concrete has the merit of being about the most durable material possible to use in walk construction, but it is not always suited to garden use because of its hardness and its unsatisfactory color. It must be laid with a good foundation to lessen the chances of being cracked by frost, and provision must also be made to prevent buckling from expansion in hot weather.

The color objection may be overcome by adding pigments while the concrete is being mixed. But first, make up several samples to get the color which is most pleasing, and make careful note of the proportion and kind of pigment used in each, so that the color selected may be repeated accurately when the walk is laid. When pigment (obtainable from paint stores or builders supply concerns) is used, preferably not more than 5 pounds to 100 pounds of cement should be included because of the danger of weakening the concrete. Only best grades of mineral pigments should be accepted.

There is also a patented process for staining concrete by chemical means, creating, it is said, lovely duotone effects. The appearance of tile may be obtained by marking off squares before the cement is set. Another variation comes from embedding small colored stones in the

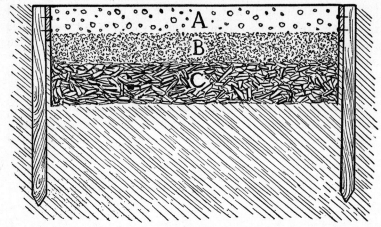

FIG. 9. Concrete walk (section). *A.* 3 inches concrete; *B.* 3 inches ashes; *C.* 3 to 6 inches brickbats, etc. If subsoil is porous, *C* may be omitted.

surface of the concrete so that little of the matrix is visible. These may be 1-inch gravel or angular crushed stones.

In making a concrete walk (Fig. 9) the foundation is prepared as previously described, or half as deep if the subsoil is porous. The walk is outlined with boards 3 or 4 inches high, rigidly fastened to stakes so that they will not spread. The upper edges of the boards should follow the completed grade of the walk so that they may be used as guides when finishing the concrete surface. A 3-inch layer of concrete (made of cement, 1 part; sharp clean sand, 2 parts; and crushed stone or gravel, 3 parts) is poured over the foundation. The mixture should be wet enough to be easily worked without being too sloppy. Pour or shovel it into place and work down to correct grade by sliding a straightedged board back and forth, and forward, pushing the surplus concrete ahead of it. When the concrete has partly set, finish it by troweling with a wooden float, which will give a slightly rougher surface than a steel trowel. A rolled edge may be given to the walk by the use of cement worker's edger, and the surface may be divided into sections with a jointer. To prevent buckling during hot weather, expansion joints should be furnished every 15 feet, made by placing a half-inch board between sections.

Bitumen-bound walks. The ordinary walk of cinders, ashes, or clinkers is an abomination. But if it is properly made, treated with a binding bituminous emulsion—a cold asphaltic binder obtainable (under various trade names) from a builders supply house—and surfaced with crushed stone, it may be durable, pleasant to walk upon, and not unsightly.

A method that will work if the subsoil is fairly open is first to lay down 4 inches of clinkers or hard ashes. On top of this place a 2-inch layer of finer clinkers or ashes with every piece larger than ¾ inch and smaller than ¼ inch sifted out. Grade to a slightly convex surface to shed rain. Water thoroughly and roll until there is no further subsidence. Make good any inequalities and roll again. While it is still wet, grout it with emulsion at the rate of 1 to 1½ gallons per square yard. Immediately apply crushed stone of suitable color. This stone should be *free from dust* and should range in size from ¼ to ¹⁄₁₆ inch. Roll it thoroughly and then brush off loose material. A better job is obtained if this is followed by applying a sealing coat of emulsion at the rate of 1 gallon to every 5 yards, followed by another dressing of stone chips and another rolling and brushing. The surface must be brushed free from dust and loose material before the second coat of emulsion is applied. In order that the edges may be trim, board forms should be used as for concrete.

Flagstones. There are some who object to flagstones for walk construction because they are reminiscent of dusty streets and because of their often unpleasing color. But stone flagging is obtainable in various hues and if random sizes are carefully laid there need be no suggestion of a sidewalk. A pleasing pattern made with rectangular stones of varying size is shown in Fig. 10. Instead of squared stones the irregular ones which make up "crazy" paving are sometimes used. For good appearance, these must be fitted with interspaces as uniform as possible, as indicated in Fig. 11.

The technique followed in laying flagstone walks varies in accordance with their uses. I have seen fairly satisfactory walks made without a foundation; merely sufficient soil was cut out to admit of setting the stones flush with the surrounding grade. Ordinarily, better results are obtained when a 6- to 12-inch foundation of rough material is provided, surfaced with 1 inch of builder's sand. The flags are bedded on the sand and the joints grouted with cement mortar if a fixed and immovable job is required. If the interspaces are to be set with dwarf plants, however, the joints should be filled with earth instead of cement, and the foundation material, though porous, must be such

that it holds some moisture
and is not too inhospitable to
the roots of plants.

Tanbark walks. Delightful
to walk upon are paths surfaced with tanbark. Such
walks are most appropriate in
informal gardens, and are admirably in keeping when
planted on either side with
wild flowers in a woodland
scene. As with other walks, a
foundation of hard, rough,
porous material must be provided so that no puddles form
during wet weather. Then an
inch or two of tanbark is
spread on the foundation and
raked level. An edging of
some kind is necessary to prevent the bark from scattering.

Grass walks. Turf walks are

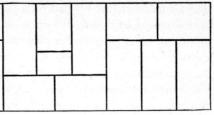

Fig. 10. Pattern for walk of rectangular
flagstones

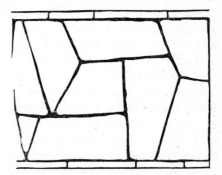

Fig. 11. Walk of irregular flagstones.
Border of flagstones set on edge.

excellent in appearance and satisfactory for foot traffic (except in wet
weather) in situations where they are lightly used and where it is possible to make them broad enough to distribute the traffic and thus
avoid the moth-eaten appearance given by worn spots. The minimum
width for this type of walk is 6 feet, and greater width is desirable.
Often pleasing effects may be gained by using stepping-stones in combination with the turf. These need to be laid with care both for esthetic
and practical reasons. They must be set exactly flush with the soil of
the lawn, for if too high, they will interfere with the lawn mower, and
someone will be forever stubbing his toe, while if they are set too low,
they will collect the very water which they were designed to keep from
the gardener's feet. To judge the distance to allow between the stones,
the stride of the person who uses the garden most may be used as a
guide.

Edgings for walks. Often it is desirable to provide some kind of
edging to serve as a barrier between walk and lawn or walk and
flower border. In England, dwarf boxwood is used for this purpose,

and I remember that we had little portable bridges so that the wheel-barrow could be trundled from walk to border without injuring the boxwood. (I also remember that we used the edging as a brush to clean mud from our shoes—if the head gardener was not around!) In sections where boxwood will thrive it is a valuable edging plant when the true dwarf variety is used. Even then, considerable trimming is needed to keep it low, and once in a while one must take it up and replant it more deeply.

There are other plants available for providing living edgings, such as common thrift (*Statice Armeria*), the creeping evergreen sedum (*Sedum hybridum*), and the dwarf Japanese barberry (*Berberis Thunbergii minor*). Their maintenance in good condition, however, is often a chore, and they do not always prevent the commingling of walks and borders.

An effective and delightful way of providing a barrier between a flower border and a gravel walk was seen by the writer a few years ago on one of the large estates in England. It consisted of an edging of rocks from 6 to 18 inches wide, sunk rather deeply in the ground and interplanted with rock plants. These plants nearly covered the rocks, making them unobtrusive, and while some of them sprawled over onto the path they did not impede traffic.

When the lawn comes up to the edges of a gravel walk, it is a difficult and onerous task to maintain a trim line unless a barrier is used. One of the neatest and most effective consists of strips of metal about 3 inches high and ⅛ inch thick sunk firmly in the ground with the top at the same level as the soil—that is, about 1 inch above the edge of the walk. If for any reason the metal strip has to project higher, anchoring stakes should be used every few feet. Zinc strips of varying weight are designed especially for this purpose and are supplied with supporting metal stakes. Iron or steel is cheaper but of course will eventually rust.

Concrete and bituminous walks if properly made do not require any special edging. When the walk is of brick or flagstone, an edge, if it is used, should be made of the same material, setting it an inch above the general level. If the edging pieces are not quite rigid, they may be bolstered with cement mortar, applied along the outside just below the level of the soil.

Surface drainage. In the case of walks that are impervious to rain, unobtrusive catch-basins should be made at the lowest point to carry away surface water. These should be provided with a trap to catch sediment, which must be removed from time to time. A good method is to sink a sewer pipe vertically in the ground and rest a grating on it. The pipe may be 3 feet long, 1 foot in diameter, and have an opening on the side about halfway up. To this opening is attached the underground pipe which will carry away the surplus water. This pipe may be connected with the sewer (if a trap is installed to prevent sewer gas from backing up) or with the drainage system; or, if the subsoil is porous, a few lengths of tile drain laid with open joints will be sufficient. Another method of handling the surface water is simply to make a sink-away drain by digging a hole 3 or 4 feet deep and 2 or 3 feet wide and filling it with stones.

IV. SOIL IMPROVEMENT

Drainage. The first question in any scheme of soil improvement is whether or not underdrainage is necessary. The chances are that no artificial drainage will be required, for most soils have a subsoil that allows of natural drainage. But when the subsoil is so impervious that water stands in puddles for several days after a rain, artificial underdraining is necessary if the general garden crops—vegetables, flowers, shrubs, and trees—are grown. There are, of course, many kinds of plants which will grow in waterlogged soil, but mainly they are not the kinds most valuable to the gardener.

Why garden soils need drainage. A soil that is waterlogged is slow to warm up in the spring; thus the plants that are growing in it get a later start. Also, because of its wetness, tillage operations cannot be started as early as on similar but well-drained soil.

Plants on poorly drained soils are likely to suffer from drought in dry summers, because their roots are not able to penetrate deeply into the ground when the water table is near the surface.

Since waterlogged soils are not well aerated they are unhealthy for the roots of most kinds of garden plants. Moreover, they do not provide the right kind of home life for those beneficial bacteria which, by breaking down organic matter, make the nutrients it contains available for the use of higher plants. Again, poorly drained soils are liable to erosion because in times of heavy rains the water, instead of percolating gently to the lower levels, runs off in a surface flood carrying with it much of the finer and more valuable particles of soil.

Underdrainage increases the amount of water available in the soil for the use of plants, and their root range is extended by the increased depth of congenial soil. A well-drained soil warms up quickly in the spring. For these reasons, unless the cultivation of special plants is contemplated, drainage should be carried out whenever it seems necessary.

Methods of draining the soil. Drainage may be accomplished by open ditches, but the most satisfactory way is by means of covered drains consisting of unglazed tile pipes, 2 to 5 inches in diameter, laid from 2 to 4 feet below the surface.

The lay of the land must be carefully examined before staking out the lines for the drains. A series of parallel lines, each having a separate outlet, is preferable to having several drains connected to a trunk line, because of the danger of silt clogging the system at the junctions. When laterals must be connected with a main line they should enter at an acute angle to lessen the danger of clogging.

Disposal of drainage water. The disposal of the water from the outlets is dependent on local conditions. Either a nearby stream or sewer system might be used, but if neither of these solutions is practicable the drain line may be carried to a point where a "sink-away" of stones as described in Chapter III, WALKS, will do the trick. The outlets to tile drains should always be screened to prevent the entrance of animals which might set up housekeeping or even die in the pipe, thus eventually stopping the flow of water.

Depth to lay the drains. The depth and distance apart to lay the drains is dependent largely on the character of the subsoil. Where it is a tenacious and sticky clay it may be necessary to have the lines as close as 20 feet, whereas in more permeable soil a line every 200 feet may be sufficient. The depth may vary from 2½ to 4 feet. In general, the nearer they are to the surface the closer the lines should be. In heavy clay soils, the drains should be not much deeper than 2½ feet. Also, if the water causing the trouble comes from above, comparatively shallow drains are in order, but if the water rises from lower levels in the soil the pipes should be laid as deep as 4 feet.

Amount of pitch. So far as possible the drains should be laid in a continuous uniform slope of not less than 6 inches per 100 feet. When digging the trenches avoid disturbing the soil any deeper than necessary, so that there is a solid base of natural soil to support the pipes. If they are laid on recently loosened soil there may be sufficient subsidence later to force them out of alignment.

Prevention of clogging. The tiles should be laid in lines as straight as the character of the terrain permits with about ⅛ inch of free space between them. To prevent the covering soil from sifting into the pipes the upper half of each joint is covered with a tile collar or with tarred building paper. If small stones or coarse ashes can be filled in around and over the tiles to a depth of 6 to 12 inches, they will help to promote more efficient drainage. When the soil removed in making the trench is returned, the job, barring earthquakes, landslides, and inefficient workmanship, is done forever.

Breaking up the hardpan. If the waterlogged soil is due to the formation of a hardpan, an impervious layer just below the topsoil, it may be possible to break it up enough to secure underdrainage by the use of dynamite. In some cases where the hardpan is quite shallow, with porous earth beneath, the use of a subsoil plow (Fig. 118) may achieve the desired result.

Organic matter. The next question to be decided is whether the soil contains sufficient humus. If you are in doubt the submission of a sample to your State Agricultural Experiment Station will probably inform you on this point. Humus is partly decomposed organic matter from plant and animal residues.

Importance of humus. The presence of considerable quantities of humus darkens the color of the soil and helps it to warm up more quickly in the spring. It also helps to prevent soluble plant foods from leaching from the soil. Partly decayed organic matter, by acting as a sponge, greatly increases the water-holding capacity of the soil and thus is indispensable in sandy soils which lose their moisture quickly. In heavy clay, also, coarse organic matter such as strawy stable manure and peatmoss improves the physical texture by opening up the soil so that it becomes aerated and more permeable to water.

Organic matter contains potential plant nutrients and by its decay into humus it liberates compounds. which, in contact with mineral particles, help to set free otherwise insoluble plant foods.

Concentrated fertilizers give best results when the soil is bountifully supplied with humus.

Sources of humus. Sources of humus are: organic manures; tree leaves, partly or fully decayed; peaty products in various stages of decomposition such as peatmoss, sedge peat, commercial humus; plant debris such as grass clippings and tops of herbaceous plants; and, in moderation, sawdust or wood shavings. Usually coarse organic matter should be at least partially decomposed before adding it to the soil. This can be done via the compost pile. One method of making this almost indispensable adjunct to the garden is to dig a pit 6 to 8 inches deep, 4 to 5 feet wide, and long enough to accommodate the material in a pile 3 to 4 feet high. Start by putting in a 6-inch layer of organic matter, then add in succession an inch or two of horse or cattle manure (or a smaller quantity of chicken, sheep, or rabbit manure) and an inch of topsoil sprinkled with wood ashes or ground limestone. Continue in this way until you have a flat-topped pile 3 to 4 feet high. If the vegetable matter is dry, thoroughly moisten each layer. After two or three months the heap should be turned bringing the sides and top towards the center. If animal manures are not available as activators, dried blood, tankage or a commercial fertilizer rich in nitrogen may be lightly sprinkled on each layer. A compost pile made in this way in the spring and turned once or twice during the summer will be in good condition for incorporating with the soil in the fall or the following spring. Several of the Agricultural Experiment Stations have experimented with methods of accelerating the decay of straw, etc., and have published their findings and formulae in bulletins.

How much organic matter? It is almost impossible to make specific recommendation concerning the proper amount of organic matter to add to the soil, because of the variable character of the materials. When they are loaded with water, 30 tons per acre could be applied to advantage to some soils, whereas if dry, one fifth of this amount might supply an equal amount of humus-forming material. Perhaps the best method of estimating the quantity to apply is on the basis of the depth of the layer. Excluding animal excrement (see Chapter V, MANURES AND FERTILIZERS) this may be about 1 inch if the material is in a fine state of decomposition, or up to 3 inches if the material is coarse. The character of the soil, the kinds of plants to be grown (rhododendrons and allied plants delight in a soil rich in humus) and the existing content of humus are other factors which should influence a decision concerning the proper amount to supply.

Handling different soils. Each type of soil, outside of one that is already in good physical condition and rich in essential substances, requires special treatment to make it productive of good plants.

Clay soils. Stiff, heavy soils make gardening laborious, for, while they retain plant foods and moisture, they are difficult to work and they warm up slowly. Improvement may be effected by the addition of organic matter, sand, coal ashes, and lime, but correct tillage is perhaps even more important.

By plowing clay soils in the fall and leaving them rough through the winter, they are more easily worked in the spring. The water held in the soil expands on freezing, forcing the particles of earth apart, thus making the soil more friable. Also, the soil dries out more rapidly in the spring because of the increased area exposed to evaporation.

The application of lime on soils of a sticky nature likewise makes the soil more friable by flocculating the clay. This granular and porous condition also enables the plant roots to penetrate more readily and facilitates the movement of soil water.

Quicklime (calcium oxide) and hydrated lime (calcium hydroxide) are more efficient in flocculating clay soils, and should be used in preference to the carbonates of lime, which are better adapted for use on light sandy soils. The initial application of hydrated lime (which usually is easily obtainable and more convenient to apply than quicklime) may be at the rate of 1 to 2 tons to an acre (2 to 4 pounds to 40 square feet) of clay soil if the soil is distinctly acid. Subsequent applications of about one quarter of this amount may be made once in from 3 to 5 years.

Quicklime contains from 90 to 98% of lime and magnesia; slaked or hydrated lime from 65 to 70%; and ground limestone from 48 to 52%. These figures must be taken into account when estimating the acid-neutralizing value of various forms of lime when applied to the soil.

Usually it is better to apply lime after plowing or digging, and then cultivate it into the surface soil.

The chemical action of lime in soil is discussed later in connection with fertilizers in general.

Sand and sifted coal ashes may help to open up clay if they are applied in sufficient quantity, but this usually means a layer 3 inches thick, which is impractical on large areas.

The coarser forms of humus-forming materials (organic matter) are more efficient than fine material in improving the texture of heavy soils.

Sandy soils. Sandy soils warm up quickly, are easy to work, but are not retentive of moisture. They may be improved by the addition of humus-forming materials and lime and, when practicable, clay.

In applying humus to light, sandy soils those kinds should be used in which the processes of decay are advanced and are in consequence more cohesive. These soils may be made more compact and their acidity neutralized by the addition of lime. It is believed that smaller quantities more frequently applied are desirable on sandy soils. Finely pulverized limestone, chalk, or oyster shells (in which the lime is in the carbonate form) may be applied at the rate of about 1 ton per acre.

Sandy soils, which tend to lose soluble plant foods by leaching, should not be plowed in the fall unless they are immediately planted to a cover-crop. This takes up and holds much of the soluble foods, and helps to prevent surface leaching. It is good garden practice to make use of winter cover-crops in unoccupied parts of the sandy-soil garden (for example, the vegetable plot) both for the reason just mentioned, and because it affords an opportunity of economically adding humus-forming materials.

Peaty soils. Except when rhododendrons and allied plants are to be grown, peaty soils and acid muck soils are benefited by lime in large amounts equal to those applied to clay soils. Also, they should receive liberal applications of commercial fertilizer rich in phosphorus and potash.

General programs of soil improvement. Below are outlined three practical methods of improving soil. Which one is chosen will depend on the condition of the property and on the effort one can or is willing to spend.

Method No. 1. The simplest way is to plow in 15 to 20 tons of rotted manure, leaf mold, or compost to every acre in the spring. Then apply commercial fertilizer, analyzing about 5% nitrogen, 10% phosphoric acid, and 5% potash, at the rate of 1,000 pounds to an acre; harrow or rake thoroughly, and proceed with lawn-making and planting of all kinds. In north temperate climates, fall is a better time to start a lawn, but considerable effective work can be done in spring.

Method No. 2. Apply 15 to 20 tons of rotted manure to the acre early in August. Then go over the ground thoroughly with a disk harrow for the purpose of incorporating the manure with the soil. Afterwards plow deeply whenever the soil is sufficiently moist to allow of a workmanlike job. Apply lime if the soil is acid and cultivate it into the surface. Harrow at intervals to kill weed seedlings and shoots that spring up from perennial weeds. Prior to planting, apply commercial fertilizer as suggested in Method No. 1.

Following this program, evergreens may be planted in late August and early September; the lawn in early September; and hardy deciduous trees and shrubs, perennials and spring-flowering bulbs from October up to the time the ground freezes.

Method No. 3. When it is desired to do a thorough job of soil preparation on poor, run-down land, or on land that is covered with sod, the work outlined below will give excellent results.

If the soil already supports a vigorous growth of weeds and grasses, the chances are that it is reasonably fertile, so if it is properly handled it will provide a basis for a splendid garden. This growth, however, will cause considerable trouble unless the perennial vegetation, which forms its principal part, is killed off before planting commences. Although this will take time and labor, it will greatly improve the soil.

August is a good time to start if the ground is sufficiently moist to be plowed. The earth is warm then and the bacteria and fungi which are responsible for the breakdown of vegetation are active; thus the desired decay of the sod is rapidly brought about.

If manure is available, spread it at the rate of 15 to 20 tons per acre. If it is partly decayed, so much the better, though fresh manure may be used if none other is obtainable. Run a disk harrow over the ground several times and then plow 6 to 8 inches deep, turning under the sod and manure. If there is a hardpan underneath the surface soil, follow the furrow made by the turning plow with a subsoil plow which, by breaking up the subsoil, will allow water both to enter and drain away from the soil. The reservoir thus created through the improvement of the soil's water-holding capacity, increases the range of roots and gives the plants moisture to draw upon in times of drought.

If the soil is sour, apply lime to correct the acidity. Whether or not lime is needed may be determined for practical purposes by means of a cheap testing kit, obtainable at any large seed store. Finely ground limestone may be applied at the rate of 2 to 3 tons to the acre or hydrated agricultural lime at half this rate.

Caustic lime, however, must not be added in contact with manure, because it releases nitrogen from the manure in the form of ammonia, thus depriving the fertilizer of much of its value. Neither should lime be put on soil intended for acid-soil plants such as rhododendrons, mountain laurel, and blueberries.

After the soil has been plowed, harrow it thoroughly and sow a cover-crop to be turned under the following spring as green manure. Fifty pounds of hairy vetch or 120 pounds of rye may be sown per acre; or the two crops may be planted together, using half the quantity of each. Of the two, the hairy vetch is more valuable if a good stand is obtainable, because it belongs to the group of plants which add nitrogen to the soil. But it has been my experience that rye is a more certain crop, so if there is any doubt as to the success of the vetch, it is perhaps better to plant either rye alone or a mixture. Planting is accomplished by scattering the seed broadcast with a sweeping motion of the hand after the soil has been harrowed. It is then harrowed again to cover the seed, and rolled to bring it in close contact with the seed. To secure an even distribution it is a good plan to divide the seed into equal portions—sowing half when walking east and west and half when walking north and south.

In the spring, plow under the cover-crop. If lime was wanted but was not put on the preceding fall it may be applied just before turning under the cover-crop. After the ground has been plowed apply a complete commercial fertilizer, analyzing about 5% nitrogen, 10% phosphoric acid, and 5% potash, using it at the rate of ½ ton to an acre.

What to do next depends partly on the condition of the soil and partly on the patience of the owner. If the soil is still poor and lacking in humus and if he wishes to "go the whole hog," another cover-crop will be planted, such as buckwheat, 1 to 1½ bushels per acre; Canada field peas, 2 bushels per acre; soy beans, 2 bushels per acre; or whatever cover-crop has proved successful locally. When this has attained its maximum growth, it is plowed under and the surface kept cultivated by harrowing at intervals until late August or early September.

If this program (admittedly a long one) is followed, lawn seeds may be planted, and trees, shrubs, and perennials set out with assurance that the soil is in excellent condition and that most of the weeds have been killed.

The above methods are applicable to properties sizable enough to allow manoeuvering with a plow. On smaller places the same practices may be followed except that they are carried out with the aid of spade, spading-fork, and rake. (See Chapter XI, FLOWER BEDS AND BORDERS.)

Importance of correct tillage. The importance of correct tillage cannot be too greatly emphasized. Soil should never be worked when it is wet, because of the danger of "puddling" it so that it becomes putty-like with its texture destroyed. This is particularly true of clay soils and those which are of a sticky nature. The wise gardener watches weather and soil conditions closely so that the land may be plowed or dug at a time when earth particles tend to fall apart when disturbed. When preparing soils for immediate planting, it is important not to let the plowing get too far ahead of the harrowing or raking; for, if the plowing is done on a bright, windy day, the overturned soil quickly bakes into hard, intractable lumps unless it is broken down before it becomes thoroughly dried. The soil should be free from lumps for the whole depth that is turned by plow or spade. Thoroughly working the soil with a disk harrow before plowing is an aid in bringing this about.

The physical condition of the soil is one of the fundamental factors in the maintenance of soil fertility. As we have seen, it is influenced by the application of humus-forming materials which render clay soils more open and increase the water-holding capacity of sandy soils; by lime which flocculates clay soils, bringing about a more granular and porous condition and making them easier to work; by chemical fertilizers, some of which under certain conditions may be inimical to the soil structure (see p. 47); and by tillage, which if well done may greatly improve the soil, but if badly done, results in rendering it almost entirely unfitted for plant growth.

The particular problems of soil improvement in a city yard are handled in Chapter XVIII, CITY GARDENS.

V. MANURES AND FERTILIZERS

The terms "manure" and "fertilizer" are often loosely applied, and if used without qualifying adjectives, one is often in doubt as to whether bulky organic manures are in question or concentrated commercial fertilizers. Generally speaking, the term manure is more often applied to animal excrement, although some of the more finicky lady gardeners seem to consider "fertilizer" more euphemistic. English gardeners make a distinction by calling animal excreta "manure" and the more concentrated, manufactured products "artificials," "artificial fertilizers," or just "fertilizer." It would seem well to retain the term manure in the sense that it is used in England and use the word fertilizer for the concentrated products of the factories. In America "chemical fertilizer" is a name in frequent use and we often hear the term "commercial fertilizer," but all fertilizers may be said to be commercial because practically all are handled commercially.

Elements necessary for plant nutrition. There are many elements necessary for plant nutrition, but those that are most likely to be deficient in the soil are nitrogen, phosphorus, and potash.

Nitrogen is largely concerned in the production of leaves and stems. An excess of it, especially if in combination with a deficiency of phosphorus and potash, is undesirable because it may result in strong vegetative growth at the expense of flowers and fruit. Furthermore an excess of nitrogen is believed to cause a flimsy development of cell walls so that fungous pests find easy access. Whether or not this is so, plants exhibiting a sappy growth, characteristic of over-abundant nitrogen, seem to be far more susceptible to disease and, in some cases, to insect attacks.

Phosphorus is believed to be largely concerned in the production of fruits and seeds. It induces strong root development and hastens maturity; whereas nitrogen may be a factor in delaying maturity. Phosphorus is also of value in stiffening plant stems and making them more woody.

The rôle of potash is to aid in the production of starches and sugars.

It also has a stiffening influence on the stems of some plants and it is believed to be an important factor in enabling plants to resist the invasions of disease. Like phosphoric acid it helps to overcome the rankness of vegetative growth induced by over-abundance of nitrogen.

A balanced ration is as necessary for plants as it is for animals; and the wise gardener is as chary of feeding his plants exclusively on nitrogen, for example, as he is of feeding his children nothing but sugar.

Manures and fertilizers which contain nitrogen, phosphorus, and potash are said to be "complete," even though their proportions of these elements are not necessarily suited for the crops to which they are applied. Although I have already been guilty of recommending fairly specific fertilizer formulas, it should be clearly understood that no one formula can be of universal application. Soils vary in their composition, hence it is important to discover which elements in one's soil are deficient, then supply them in the fertilizer program. The State Agricultural Experiment Stations usually are able to recommend soil treatment for each section of the state. Another way of finding out the fertilizer requirements of any particular soil is to make a test by applying nitrogen, phosphorus, and potash alone and in various combinations to groups of plants and carefully note the results.

A simple program. Plants will, of course, grow even though nothing in particular is done to the soil. At the Rothamsted Experiment Station in England there is a plot which has grown crops of wheat continuously between 1839 and 1911 (and possibly later) without having any manure or fertilizer during all that time. The average soil is a vast storehouse of plant food which is continually going into solution because of the decomposition of the soil particles. But to get the best results in the garden it is necessary to hasten this decomposition by adding organic matter and by tilling the soil. Still further improvement is effected by adding plant nutrients.

As a simple program for the average garden, therefore, I would suggest the application of a 1- to 2-inch layer of manure or compost annually, to be dug into the soil of the cultivated areas. Then, in the spring, apply a complete fertilizer (obtained from a dealer in horticultural supplies), analyzing about 5% nitrogen, 10% phosphoric acid, and 5% potash, at the rate of 25 pounds per 1,000 square feet and thoroughly cultivate it into the surface soil.

The above schedule will give the beginner a good start toward creating productive soil and keeping it in prime condition. The gardener who wishes to do a more specialized job of soil enrichment, delving into the source and effect of each kind of fertilizer, will find the information in the remaining pages of this chapter. It is well for the beginner, however, even though he ignores such products as dried blood and cottonseed meal, to understand thoroughly the use of barnyard manure, as explained in the paragraphs immediately following.

Organic fertilizers. Any plant food derived from living matter or from matter that has once had life, in contrast to inanimate chemicals or minerals, is designated as an *organic* fertilizer. Most important is barnyard manure which, because it contains nitrogen (about 0.5%), phosphoric acid (about 0.35%), and potassium (about 0.5%), is a complete fertilizer. Other types of manure vary in these proportions, but all of them contain the three essential elements.

Some organic fertilizers, however, are incomplete, hence are suited only for special purposes. These include cottonseed meal, castor pomace, bonemeal and other products of slaughter houses.

Manures and their functions. As an all-around garden fertilizer, BARNYARD OR STABLE MANURE is considered the best. Although the proportions of its important elements vary with the kind of feed and the type of bedding given the animals, it will produce satisfactory results even if no other fertilizers are used. Because of its rather low phosphorus content, however, plants will be benefited by the addition of material rich in phosphorus, such as superphosphate or bonemeal. Also, supplements of concentrated plant nutrients may be desirable for special crops, such as potatoes and beets, which require much potash; leaf vegetables which are benefited by ample supplies of nitrogen; and roses and turnips which respond remarkably to phosphates.

In addition to the plant nutrients contained in bulky animal manure, organic matter—the value of which already has been discussed (page 34)—is supplied in considerable quantities. Experience has shown that in order to get best results from concentrated fertilizers it is necessary that the soil be well stocked with humus-forming materials, and manure is probably the best source of these. When the humus supply is derived from peatmoss, leaves, etc., in which the supply of plant nutrients is lower even than in barnyard manure, it becomes desirable to add plant foods in the form of fertilizers of some kind.

Much of the fertilizing value of manure is lost if it is not properly handled prior to its application to the soil. Manure stored in the open and exposed to rain may lose, by leaching, etc., more than 40 percent of its nitrogen in three months. The best way to handle manure to conserve as much as possible of its fertilizing value is to spread it on the land as soon as it is made; but this, of course, is usually impossible. Composting it with soil and keeping it under cover is another method of saving the fertilizing constituents, but this again is usually impractical and uneconomical because the cost of handling more than counterbalances any saving of plant nutrients. The most practical way of conserving the nitrogen content would seem to be to store it packed down closely, under cover. Experiments conducted at Rothamsted, England, showed that by using this system only 4 percent of the nitrogen was lost in three months.

The time of application is dependent upon the character of the soil and the condition of the manure. On heavy clay soils, coarse and strawy manure may be applied in the fall and plowed under. When dealing with sandy soils it is better to use decayed manure and put it into the soil in the spring. Fresh, undecayed manure should not be so used that it comes in contact with plant roots. Gardeners prefer to use decayed manure whenever possible because it contains immediately available plant foods, and because there is less danger of causing damage by its use. It should be remembered, however, that although decayed manure may be richer in plant foods than fresh manure, ton for ton, it takes about 2 tons of fresh manure to make 1 ton of decayed manure and that some of the fertility is lost during the processes of decay.

"Use as much manure as you can get," is sometimes advised, but it *is* possible to apply it with such lavishness that it becomes uneconomical. A moderate amount is 15 tons per acre—equivalent to about 750 pounds to 1,000 square feet; but five times this amount may be appropriate for special crops or certain types of soil.

In SHEEP MANURE the plant nutrients are more concentrated. Dried and pulverized, it contains about 2.38% nitrogen, 1.28% phosphoric acid, and 2.16% potash. It quickly becomes available in the soil and is useful as a top-dressing after crops are up, spread at the rate of about 100 pounds to 1,000 square feet. It does not contain sufficient bulk to be of much value in improving the texture of the soil, but when other humus-forming materials are unavailable it may be incorporated in more liberal amounts. For example, it could be used at the rate of 200 pounds per 1,000 square feet if thoroughly mixed with the topsoil prior to planting. As its phosphorus content is comparatively low, it should be supplemented by a phosphorus carrier such as superphosphate.

POULTRY MANURE, when dry, contains about 4.41% nitrogen, 2.24% phosphoric acid, and 1.48% potash. As the plant foods it contains are quickly available it should be applied in the spring as a surface dressing at the rate of 50 pounds to 1,000 square feet and afterwards cultivated into the surface soil. Its phosphorus and potash content is low in comparison with nitrogen, therefore the supplementary use of superphosphate plus unleached hardwood ashes (or some other potash carrier) would probably prove beneficial in most soils. But wood ashes must not be mixed with the poultry manure *before* application, for loss of nitrogen would result.

Incomplete fertilizers of organic origin. Other materials of organic origin which are widely used for the purpose of adding plant foods to the soil are as follows:

DRIED BLOOD is a product of slaughter houses. Good samples contain about 12% nitrogen. It decomposes rapidly when placed in the soil so that its nitrogen quickly becomes available. Some gardeners believe that it has special value when used as the source of nitrogen for roses. About 10 to 15 pounds to 1,000 square feet is the usual application.

TANKAGE, also a by-product of slaughter houses, contains all the refuse (bones, lungs, intestines, tendons, etc.) that cannot be utilized in other ways. Cooked, pressed, dried, and ground, it lacks potash but contains 4% to 8% nitrogen and 7% to 14% phosphoric acid, the proportion depending on the relative amounts of blood and bone. It is applied at the rate of 30 to 40 pounds to 1,000 square feet.

COTTONSEED MEAL is what remains after the oil has been expressed from cotton seeds. Sometimes used as feed for livestock, it is also applied directly to the soil as a fertilizer. It contains about 7% nitrogen which is less quickly available than that, for example, in nitrate of soda. It is a common practice when making up a complete, concentrated fertilizer to utilize both cottonseed meal and nitrate of soda, so that part of the nitrogen is immediately available and part in a form that is liberated over a longer period. It may be used at the rate of about 30 pounds to 1,000 square feet.

CASTOR POMACE is a similar product, containing about 5% nitrogen, used at the same rate or a little higher.

The above fertilizers, with the exception of tankage, are considered mainly as sources of nitrogen. BONES in various forms are looked upon as a source of phosphorus. The rate of availability of the phosphorus is dependent upon the fineness to which the bones are ground, and whether or not they are treated with acid to convert part of the phosphorus to a soluble form. When it is desired to have the phosphorus liberated slowly over long periods of time, as, for instance, for vine borders in greenhouses, half-inch bones are liberally mixed with the soil. The usual practice, however, is to use bonemeal or bone flour —and the finer it is ground the more quickly does it become available. Bonemeal should contain about 2% to 4% nitrogen and 20% to 30% of phosphoric acid. Bones which have been ground and treated with sulphuric acid contain only from 12% to 14% phosphoric acid because the acid used to dissolve the bones is about equal in weight to that in the bones; thus the percentage is reduced about one half. Bonemeal is considered safe to use because its fertilizing constituents become so slowly available. It is a favorite source of phosphorus for roses. It may be used at the rate of 30 to 60 pounds per 1,000 square feet.

Inorganic fertilizers. So far, the fertilizers mentioned have been derived from living matter. Often they need the addition of inorganic substances to make their work in the soil more effective. Often, too, inorganic fertilizers can be made to supply all the nutrients necessary, as long as there is a plentiful supply of humus in the earth. The principal elements of inorganic fertilizers, as of organic ones, are nitrogen, phosphorus, and potash.

Inorganic nitrogen. In addition to the nitrogenous fertilizers of organic origin mentioned above, there are some of inorganic origin which are highly important.

NITRATE OF SODA occurs in deposits in the rainless regions in the north of Chile. After it is prepared for commercial use it contains about 15% nitrogen. The nitrogen, in the form of nitrate, is soluble in water and is immediately available for the use of plants. It has the quickest action of any fertilizer and its effects on plant growth are evident within two or three days after application—assuming, of course, that sufficient soil moisture is present to ensure its diffusion about the plant roots. The residue after the nitrogen has been used, or lost by leaching, has the effect of releasing potash from insoluble compounds of potassium, thus making them available for the use of the plants. Unfortunately, the residue also has the bad effect of deflocculating clay, and on heavy soils may result in considerable detriment to the physical texture. To prevent this, either apply lime or reduce the amount of nitrate of soda and make up the needed nitrogen with sulphate of ammonia.

While an extremely valuable fertilizer, nitrate of soda must be used with considerable discretion. It must not be applied so as to come in contact with the foliage, for it will injure it; neither should heavy applications be given at any one time, partly because of the danger of "burning" the roots, and partly because, owing to its easy solubility, much of it may be lost by leaching. As previously noted, the unbalanced use of nitrogen may result in excessive vegetative growth and susceptibility to disease. These dangers are perhaps accentuated when a fertilizer as quick in its results as nitrate of soda is used. The slogan when using this fertilizer should be "little and often." Apply it only when the plants are growing and able to use it. It is safer not to apply it in amounts exceeding 5 pounds to 1,000 square feet.

NITRATE OF LIME is manufactured by a series of processes which convert atmospheric nitrogen into nitric acid; this is then neutralized with limestone to form calcium nitrate. It is similar in its action to nitrate of soda, and is said to be free from the disadvantage of injuriously affecting the physical texture of the soil. As it is deliquescent, if it is not used immediately it forms a pasty mass which is difficult to spread.

SULPHATE OF AMMONIA, another source of nitrogen, is a by-product in the manufacture of coal-gas, etc. It contains about 20% of nitrogen, which becomes rapidly available when dissolved in the soil water. In its effect on plant life it is quite similar to nitrate of soda; but in its effect on the soil it differs considerably. Through a series of somewhat complex chemical changes, calcium carbonate is removed from the soil with the result that the sulphate of ammonia leaves an acid residue which may be detrimental to certain lime-loving plants if the lime content of the soil is low. Sulphate of ammonia is considered an excellent fertilizer to increase the acidity of soils: for example, to favor the growth of certain bent-grasses in putting-greens or lawns. It has already been mentioned that its use in combination with nitrate of soda neutralizes the deflocculating tendency of the latter; at the same time, nitrate of soda neutralizes the tendency of sulphate of ammonia to make the soil acid. The rate of application is up to 4 pounds to 1,000 square feet.

Phosphorus. An important source of phosphorus is the phosphatic rock mined in the southeastern states. It usually is treated with sulphuric acid to render part of the phosphoric acid content soluble and thus available for the use of plants. The treated rock is known as superphosphate or acid phosphate. It is variable in composition—samples containing about 15% phosphoric acid may be used at the rate of 15 to 25 pounds per 1,000 square feet. Unlike some of the chemical fertilizers, its use does not adversely affect the texture of the soil.

Potash. The Stassfurt mines in Germany formerly were the chief source of potash fertilizers which appear on the market mostly in the form of sulphate of potash and muriate of potash, in both of which the potash amounts to about 50%. In recent years much potash has been obtained in this country from sources in California, Utah, Texas, New Mexico, and other states.

Potassic fertilizers are likely to give good results when applied to light sandy soils or to peaty soils. They are especially valuable for crops in which there is considerable formation of starch or sugar—for example, potatoes, sugar beets, fruits.

Sulphate and muriate of potash may be applied at the rate of 3 to 5 pounds to 1,000 square feet.

Wood ashes are another source of potash, the amount present varying between 2% and 10% according to whether they are produced from soft or hard woods, and whether they have been exposed to rain. The usual application of wood ashes is 50 to 70 pounds to 1,000 square feet. Wood ash may contain about 40% lime and the suggestion has been made that the beneficial results following an application of wood ashes may be due just as much to the lime as the potash.

Lime. In itself, lime is a direct plant food, but it seldom, if ever, is necessary to apply it as such. Its chief horticultural and agricultural use is for the indirect benefits it confers on the soil. We have already seen (Chapter IV, soil improvement) that it is of value in modifying the physical texture of soils. Its application also gives rise to chemical reactions, one of the most important of which results in the liberation of otherwise unavailable plant foods. It acts on potassium compounds and sets the potash free in a form that may be absorbed by the roots of plants. It aids the decomposition of organic matter and thus liberates nitrogen so that it may be utilized by plants. Its presence in the soil encourages the growth of the beneficial bacteria which are active in rendering available for plant use the stores of food locked up in organic matter. The use of lime in neutralizing soils that are too acid has been briefly mentioned in Chapter IV, SOIL IMPROVEMENT.

Most garden plants are tolerant of a fairly wide range between acidity and alkalinity, with the exception of a few groups with distinctly alkaline preferences (snapdragon, celery, asparagus, most crucifers, Japanese anemone), which require extra lime, and some with acid preferences (rhododendron, mountain laurel, most hardy orchids, sand-myrtle, etc.), which must be kept absolutely free from lime. In general, therefore, it is well to maintain the garden soil near pH 6.5— slightly below the neutral point. Plants with special preferences should be grouped together so far as possible without doing violence to the general layout of the grounds.

Caustic lime should not be applied in direct contact with organic fertilizers, or with chemical fertilizers containing ammonium salts, because through its chemical reactions it will cause the loss of ammonia nitrogen.

It may be applied in fall or spring, after the ground has been dug or plowed, and cultivated into the surface soil. The amount to use is dependent on the degree of acidity it is intended to counteract. A usual application is 50 pounds of hydrated lime to 1,000 square feet, or double this amount of ground limestone.

Again, let it be emphasized that, to get best results from the use of manures and fertilizers, they must be used intelligently. In most cases the amounts that may be supplied have been indicated, but they are intended merely as a rough guide. In general, so far as chemical fertilizers and the richer organic manures are concerned the rates of application are lower than those usually recommended. I believe it is better to err on the side of using too little rather than too much— more can always be added if necessary. Inorganic fertilizers should be used to supplement rather than to supplant bulky organic manures. The important thing is to find out if possible the elements most lacking in the soil and govern accordingly the program for fertilization.

VI. THE LAWN

If the preliminary work of soil improvement has been accomplished before the end of summer, the remaining months will give ample time to start a lawn, plant trees and shrubs, and begin work on flower borders. How much can be done depends upon the funds and the labor available.

While trees and shrubs are of first importance, because they provide the framework of the place and because they require the longest time to reach maturity, one would be justified in beginning by planting a lawn, especially if the work can be done in August or September. Evergreens may be set out at the same time, while the planting of deciduous trees and shrubs may be deferred until late fall or the following spring. If funds are limited, the making of flower beds and borders may also be postponed.

Creating a lawn. Even if flower gardens are to be made the first season, they need not interfere with the planting of the lawn, for they can be outlined with sod immediately. A better scheme, however, if one is willing to wait until spring, is to sow the entire lawn in early fall, then in the spring cut out the turf where the beds and borders are wanted, and use it for patching spots where the grass did not catch, for covering terrace slopes, or, dug into the soil, for increasing the humus content. This is the more economical plan of the two, because sods are expensive to buy and they require considerable labor to lay. Moreover, if imported sods are of a different texture from the surrounding lawn which is seeded, they will detract from the beauty of the grounds.

Time of planting. In the northern states late summer or early fall is the best time to seed the lawn because the grasses best adapted for lawn culture make their most vigorous growth during comparatively cool weather. If planting the lawn is deferred until spring, the grass seeds germinate slowly because the ground is cold; the young grass has to fight weed seedlings; and hot weather comes before the young roots are established in the soil. But in early September the seeds have the

50

benefit of a soil that is warm and usually fairly moist, so that germination is rapid. The fall rains and cool nights ensure a healthy growth that will pass through the winter without injury and be ready for a good start the following spring. Competition from seeds of weeds is largely eliminated by fall planting, because most of them do not germinate until the following spring.

The exact date of planting the lawn in the fall depends upon location and weather. If the seeds are sown from six to eight weeks before cold weather comes the seedlings have a chance to get through the winter without injury. Watching out for favorable conditions, one should plant when the soil is moist and when there is prospect of rain. If the soil is dry and rain seems far away, seeding should not be attempted unless it is possible to water the ground with a fine spray every day or two.

Preparing the soil. A good lawn can be made by preparing the soil to a depth of only 6 inches, but 8 to 10 inches is preferable. The general methods outlined in Chapter IV, SOIL IMPROVEMENT, are applicable to the lawn as well as the garden. A method which requires the use of a cover-crop is desirable because such a planting helps to get rid of weeds and adds humus-forming materials to the soil. Humus should be incorporated with the soil before the lawn is seeded, for the only way it can be done later is by remaking the lawn, or by the makeshift method of periodically adding it to the surface.

Assuming now that the soil has been improved by the proper addition of fertilizers and humus, with lime if it was needed, and that it has been either plowed or dug, then harrowed or raked smooth, we must next fit the soil for the reception of the grass seed. This step involves the removal of stones and the fining of the surface. If an acre or more needs attention, it will pay to borrow or buy a smoothing harrow (Fig. 119), which consists of several close-set rows of revolving disks, which cut and break the lumps as it is drawn along. The surface is leveled and the earth made still more fine by an attached board set at an angle which permits it to slide over the ground. With this implement the surface is put into such a fine tilth that the amount of hand raking necessary is negligible.

If the plot is too small to admit of the use of horse-drawn implements, a small motor-driven cultivator might be used to advantage for a great deal of the rough work, but for the removal of stones and for the finishing touches, hand raking is necessary.

. On still smaller plots all the work may be done with an iron-toothed rake, which is pushed and pulled back and forth until all the lumps are broken and inequalities smoothed out.

Usually the tramping to which the soil is subjected in fining the surface is enough to consolidate it sufficiently for the reception of seeds. If, however, when walking over the plot the feet sink into the soil more than half an inch, further consolidation is necessary. This may be accomplished by using a roller, or by further tramping.

Sowing the seed. A calm day should be chosen for sowing, otherwise many of the seeds will find their way into the next lot. Very often the air is quiet in the early morning hours, and the lawn-maker who can force himself to get up before sunrise will have a new illustration of the benefits of early rising.

Figure on using seed at the rate of 150 pounds per acre, or 3¾ pounds to 1,000 square feet. When a large plot is to be seeded and the operator is not accustomed to the work, it is a good plan to divide the plot into a number of parts of equal size, marking the divisions with strings. Then divide the seed correspondingly. Further divide in half each lot of seed. Take one portion and scatter it as evenly as possible over one division. Then take the other half and scatter it by walking at right angles to the initial line of travel, to ensure an even distribution of the seed. When all the divisions have thus been sown, rake the surface lightly to cover as much of the seed as possible, then roll the ground to bring the soil in close contact with the seed and to help moisture from the soil below to rise to the surface where the seeds are lying.

Treatment after planting. If the weather is dry, watering will be necessary. When the grass is nearly long enough to be mowed, run a light roller over the lawn to firm the soil about the grass roots. The next day cut the grass with the blades of the lawn mower set about 2 inches high. Cut as often as needed until growth is stopped by cold weather. In climates similar to that of Long Island, N. Y., it is not necessary to protect a new lawn against winter, but in more rigorous climates a light mulch of manure, so thoroughly decayed that all weed seeds are destroyed, may be advantageously applied.

Making a lawn with sods. If a lawn sufficiently tough to be used for games is required in a hurry, one may resort to sodding. The ground may be prepared as if for seeding except that it is not so important to remove every stone from the surface. The sods should be carefully inspected before they are purchased to make sure that they consist of lawn grasses rather than weeds. They should be of a uniform thickness—1 to 1½ inches—and should be square so they will fit snugly when laid. They are more neatly cut by machine than by hand. If they are of varying thickness, either remove or apply soil as needed underneath them as they are placed. Scatter screened soil over them after they are laid, and work it into the crevices by means of the back of a rake, by brushing with a besom broom, or by swishing back and forth a long flexible bamboo pole known as a whipping-stick. Then roll with a fairly heavy roller. On small areas, if a roller is not available, the sods may be knocked into close contact with the earth by hitting them with a tamper or the back of a spade. A tamper consists of a section of plank 2 x 12 x 12 inches to which a 4-foot handle is attached—either vertically or at an angle of about 45 degrees (Plate XXXII). If the ground is very dry, water thoroughly.

Making a lawn by sodding has its good points when immediate results are required. If the existing soil is poor it may be the means of adding an inch or two of good topsoil. Often it is the only method of obtaining a good growth of grass on steep terrace banks. The drawbacks to the use of sod are the expense; the difficulty of obtaining really good sods; and the possibility that the grasses contained in them are not adapted to growth in the soil to which they are transplanted.

Making a lawn with stolons. Another method for starting a lawn is by planting stolons, which are prostrate shoots formed by certain strains of bent-grass which creep along the surface of the ground and root as they go. Stolons about 1 inch long may be purchased in bulk at large seed stores or from lawn grass specialists.

The technique of planting begins the same as when sowing seed. The cut stolons are scattered over the surface of thoroughly prepared soil at the rate of about 100 pounds per 1,000 square feet. They are then covered with ½ inch of sifted topsoil, or topsoil previously composted with manure. This is made even with the back of a rake, care being taken not to disturb the stolons. Frequent waterings are necessary, especially during dry weather, for the stolons must not be allowed to become dry either before or after planting. Top-dressings of screened compost which are worked into the soil with whipping-sticks are part of the regular routine in caring for lawns of stoloniferous bent-grasses, whether started from stolons or seeds.

Lawn grasses recommended. Of the thousands of grass species known, there are only a dozen or so that fulfill the requirements of a good lawn grass—the ability to thrive under close cutting, to endure traffic, and to make a close, fine-knit turf.

The kinds of grasses to use in making a lawn are dependent on the purpose in view—whether a closely mown lawn of the putting-green type with the grass kept cut to ¼ inch is desired, or whether the inch and a half or 2-inch height of the normal lawn will be satisfactory. The character of the soil and climate should also be considered when choosing the composition of the seed mixture. No one grass seed formula can be expected to thrive on all soils and under all conditions. For fairly good, non-acid soils in the northern part of the country, Kentucky blue-grass is favored to form the major part of the mixture. Where the soil is naturally acid, particularly in many sections of New York and New England, and the western parts of Oregon, Washington, and northern California, the bent-grasses may be used with success. Before deciding on any mixture it would be well to get the opinion of the local State Agricultural Experiment Station. Whatever type of mixture is used, it should be of the best quality, and usually this is to be obtained from a seed store rather than a hardware store. The following notes on the characteristics of some of the more important lawn grasses may be of value in helping to make a selection.

Kentucky Blue-grass is one of the best lawn grasses for fairly good loamy soils, particularly where they have an alkaline or neutral reaction. It is rather slow in forming a sod, and for this reason is commonly used in association with quick-growing but less permanent grasses such as redtop and perennial rye-grass. In lawns where blue-grass is intended to be the dominant grass, it should form 50 percent of the mixture.

Redtop comes up quickly and adapts itself to poor soil conditions. It forms a rather coarse turf, therefore is used primarily as a sort of nurse crop in combination with finer grasses such as Kentucky blue-grass and the bents. It should form about 20 to 25 percent of the mixture.

South German Mixed Bent forms a desirable component for a general purpose lawn. It blends well with Kentucky blue-grass, and can form from 25 to 30 percent of the mixture when used with blue-grass and redtop.

Perennial Rye-grass is rapid-growing, but short-lived under lawn conditions. It is used to make a quick showing in conjunction with the more permanent but comparatively slow-growing species. It should not form more than 10 to 15 percent by weight of the mixture.

Chewing's New Zealand Fescue has tough, wiry blades which are difficult to cut, but it stands hard wear and will grow in poor or sandy soils. It also endures shade fairly well, and is acid-tolerant. While it does not form a rich-looking turf and does not blend well with the better lawn grasses, it should be used up to 35 percent in mixtures designed for poor soils or shaded areas.

Rough-stalked Meadow-grass is also valuable for its tolerance of shade. It is similar in appearance to Kentucky blue-grass, and should be the principal ingredient in shade mixtures.

Those who enjoy seeing clover in the lawn may use white clover seed to the extent of 5 percent by weight of the mixture. Through the nitrogen-fixing bacteria in the nodules found on its roots, clover gathers nitrogen, which adds to the fertility of the soil. It is therefore valuable in many lawn mixtures.

Grass mixtures for different conditions. Some typical formulas for lawn seed mixtures are given below.

For naturally acid soils. Rhode Island bent or South German mixed bent may be used. In general, bent-grass lawns require more care than those made up mainly of Kentucky blue-grass.

For good soils not acid in reaction. Kentucky blue-grass 40%, South German mixed bent 25%, redtop 20%, perennial rye-grass 10%, white clover 5%. If clover is not desired, use 5% more redtop.

For poor or sandy soils. Chewing's New Zealand fescue 35%, redtop 25%, perennial rye-grass 15%, Kentucky blue-grass 20%, white clover 5%.

For shade. Rough-stalked meadow grass 35%, Chewing's New Zealand fescue 30%, Kentucky blue-grass 20%, redtop 15%.

In the South. Where the northern grasses will not thrive, Bermuda grass is largely used, the lawns being started with either seeds or stolons. About 100 pounds of stolons cut into inch-length pieces are used to 1,000 square feet. As Bermuda grass is likely to look rather shabby during the winter, it is a common practice to cut it closely in the fall, scarify the surface soil with a rake, and plant Italian rye-grass, topdressing the lawn immediately after.

Still further south, in Florida, the coastal regions of North and South Carolina, and the southern parts of the tier of states extending west to Houston, Texas, centipede grass and St. Augustine grass are largely used. The latter thrives in both sun and shade. Both kinds have to be started from stolons.

Substitutes for grass. In some parts of the Southwest, *Lippia canescens,* a low creeping plant related to verbena, is used as a substitute for lawn grass.

It is practically impossible to form a satisfactory lawn in the dense shade cast by trees such as Norway maple. Under such circumstances, instead of hopefully planting grass seeds each fall or spring, the better plan is to plant a ground-cover of a nature known to thrive under these adverse conditions. For the North, in soils which are inclined to be acid, the Japanese pachysandra is the most desirable. This forms a dense evergreen covering 6 to 8 inches high. The ground should be prepared as for a lawn and plants set out 6 inches apart each way. Planting so closely runs into money; but pachysandra appears to yearn for close companionship of its congeners and, if sparsely planted, either fails to thrive as it should, or takes an unconscionable time to form the close mat which is desired. It has the reputation of being unaffected by insect or fungous pests, but in recent years I have noticed that it is subject to attacks by the oyster-shell scale or a similar species. This should not deter anyone from planting it, however, as the chances are that the pest may be controlled by spraying the plants with miscible oil, 1 to 25, when they are dormant.

For soils in northern gardens which are on the alkaline side, periwinkle, or trailing myrtle, is available as a ground-cover. It will also grow in slightly acid soils. This also makes a mat 6 to 8 inches thick, the slender shoots being clothed with small shiny leaves. Its flowers of periwinkle-blue in early spring are an added attraction. The plants may be set from 9 inches to 1 foot apart.

In sections where the climate is not more rigorous than that of New York City, English ivy will form a delightful ground-cover. It is usually at its best in shade but will also thrive in full sun. The size of plants determines the distance to set them apart. Cuttings 8 inches long inserted in sandy soil in the fall and placed under greenhouse benches to root during the winter will form plants which, if set 9 inches to 1 foot apart in the spring, are capable of covering the ground before the summer is past. If plants with shoots from 2 to 3 feet long are used, they may be planted 2 to 3 feet apart, the streamers pegged to the ground to achieve all the coverage possible.

Care of the lawn. The care of the lawn consists of mowing and watering when necessary, the maintenance of fertility, and the elimination of weeds.

Ordinarily, mowing should be sufficiently frequent so that the clippings may be allowed to remain, thus returning fertility to the soil and helping to maintain the humus content. During warm, wet weather in late spring and early summer the grass may grow so vigorously that it gets ahead of the mowing. The clippings may then be so heavy that if left on the lawn there is danger of their matting down and injuring the grass below. In such cases the clippings should be raked off, or the mower should be equipped with a grass catcher. The shortness of cut is dependent on the kinds of grasses composing the lawn and the preferences of the owner. Bent-grasses such as are used for putting-greens may be kept closely shaved down to $\frac{3}{16}$ of an inch. For ordinary lawns $1\frac{1}{2}$ to 2 inches is usually preferred.

Fertilizers and weeds. The maintenance of fertility and the elimination of weeds are partially interlocking problems. One of the most important factors in weed control in lawns is the encouragement of a thick vigorous turf in which weeds find it difficult to obtain a foothold. This involves the application of fertilizer at the most favorable season for the growth of grasses and ample watering whenever the grass needs it. Established grass makes its most vigorous growth early in spring and again early in the fall. It is at these periods, therefore, that the bulk of the fertilizer should be applied. Use a complete fertilizer analyzing about 5% nitrogen, 10% phosphoric acid, and 3% to 5% potash, at the rate of 20 pounds to 1,000 square feet. The nitrogen content, preferably, should be partly in soluble form so as to be immediately available and partly of organic origin so that it will become available over a longer period.

In addition to the complete fertilizer, two or three applications of sulphate of ammonia during the growing season at the rate of 2 to 3 pounds to each 1,000 square feet will probably prove beneficial. During very hot spells the dosage should be halved or the application omitted entirely. To distribute the sulphate of ammonia evenly so that the grass will not be injured by burning, mix the fertilizer with soil before spreading it. Thoroughly watering the lawn immediately after application is a further insurance against injury to the grass blades.

A few years ago we heard a great deal about the desirability of maintaining the soil in an acid condition to discourage the growth of weeds. Free use of sulphate of ammonia was recommended because it leaves an acid residue. Now the opinion of the turf specialists seems to be veering slightly. It appears that an excessively acid soil does not

necessarily discourage weeds and that an acid soil combined with
liberal amounts of nitrogenous fertilizers favors the development of
"brown patch" and "dollar spot," two bad diseases of bent-grass turf.
It also has been found that even bent lawns, which are supposed to
thrive best in acid soil, may under some circumstances be improved by
the application of lime at the rate of 25 to 50 pounds to 1,000 square
feet.

If a lawn is not thriving, and if one is reasonably sure that its poor
appearance is due neither to nitrogen deficiency nor to drought, it is
worth while to try the application of lime on a strip of, say, 10 x 20
feet, and note the results. If they are favorable then the rest of the lawn
may be limed. This method is preferable to relying on an acidity test
for determining whether lime should be given, because in some instances lawns in which the soil showed an alkaline reaction have been
improved by liming.

Crab-grass. One of the worst weeds in lawns is crab-grass and, so
far as is known, there is no royal road to its extinction. The common
practice of starting the lawn in the spring, with the result that the
lawn grasses do not become established before the crab-grass gets on
the job, is one reason for the prevalence of this weed. Crab-grass is an
annual, so if it is prevented from seeding the infestation is lessened
the following year. But it has the habit in lawns of producing some
of its flowering stems in an almost horizontal position so that they
escape the lawn mower. If the lawn is raked before each mowing so
as to make these stems stand erect enough to be cut, dispersal of
ripened seeds will largely be prevented. Such mowing, combined with
sowing of mangy spots with good seed in the fall, plus adequate fertilization will ultimately conquer this pest.

A heroic method of combating crab-grass is to dig up the lawn in
July after all the crab-grass seed has germinated but before the young
plants have had a chance to form seeds. The surface is kept cultivated
(to kill any weed seedlings) until early September, when lawn grass
seed is planted. If you can endure the sight of bare ground for two
months and if you can find anyone willing to dig up a lawn during
the heat of July, this is a good plan.

Hand weeding. In England I once heard of a gardener who used to
take up his lawn every winter, a small section at a time, and carry it
into the greenhouse where, seated in comfort, he could remove the
perennial weeds! This, of course, is preposterous for most of us. Our

weeding must be done in a prayerful position out-of-doors. Weed-killers containing 2-4-D (2,4-dichlorophenoxyacetic acid), applied according to directions on the container, are effective against most broad-leaved weeds and, properly used, do not injure the grass. These weed-killers eliminate most of the hard work but, even so, a certain amount of hand weeding is almost sure to be necessary.

Insect pests. In regions where trouble may be expected from attacks on the grass roots by grubs of various insects such as the Japanese beetle, the lawn should be grub-proofed by the application of lead arsenate at the rate of 10 pounds to 1,000 square feet. To prevent the lead arsenate from blowing during application and to aid in even distribution, it should first be mixed with moist sand or soil. If the lawn is to be top-dressed, the compost and arsenate may be mixed together; otherwise use a bushel of sifted soil or sand to each 5 pounds of lead arsenate. This treatment also makes the soil an unsuitable habitation for earthworms. Lead arsenate seems to have no deleterious effects on most lawn grasses with the possible exception of annual blue-grass (*Poa annua*), which in any case many consider an undesirable component of the lawn. Lead arsenate is a deadly poison and must be handled with care. Children and animals must be kept entirely away from the lawn until the lead arsenate has been thoroughly washed from the grass blades by abundant rain or artificial watering.

Top-dressings. Periodical top-dressings with sand or soil, a mixture of sand and soil, or compost are a necessity for lawns composed mainly of stolon-forming bent-grasses, and in lesser degree are desirable for all lawns. Since stolons are shoots which creep along the surface and root as they go, the chief object of top-dressing them is to keep them covered to prevent their forming a mat on the surface.

The type of soil used for top-dressing is determined partly by the nature of the topsoil. When the soil is quite sandy, a fine-textured top-dressing is preferable; if it is clayey, or a heavy loam, considerable sand should be used. If the lawn soil is deficient in humus the material used for top-dressing should consist largely of thoroughly rotted and screened manure, leafmold, or peatmoss. I am not much in favor of using peatmoss alone as it has a tendency to form a kind of felt on the surface, which, when it becomes thoroughly dry, is almost impermeable to water.

A good compost for lawns is obtainable by making multiple-decked sandwiches of soil and manure—6 inches in each layer—in flat-topped piles so that rain is absorbed and not shed. These piles should be about 2 feet high and of any convenient size. The compost pile should be cultivated just as carefully as the vegetable garden. It should be turned over and mixed several times in the course of the year, to aid in the decomposition of the manure, to destroy weeds, and to bring previously buried weed seeds near the surface so that they may germinate and be killed the next time the pile is turned over. To make doubly sure that weed seeds will not cause trouble in the lawn, sterilize the compost with steam before applying it. This, however, usually is not convenient on small places, so that the next best thing is to be faithful in frequently turning the pile, thus getting rid of most of the weeds.

Before applying the compost it should be sifted by passing it through a half-inch screen. In applying it, use 4 or 8 bushels to 1,000 square feet. Closely shaven bent-grass lawns will take the smaller amount. Lawns of blue-grass which are allowed to grow 1 inch or longer may receive the larger amount two or three times a year. Scatter as evenly as possible and work it into the surface by raking with the back of a rake, by dragging with a steel door mat, or by swishing back and forth with a long flexible bamboo pole. The stoloniferous bent-grasses should be top-dressed every month or six weeks during the growing season.

Just as soon as the frost is out of the ground in spring, the lawn should be rolled to smooth the surface and compact the soil after the heaving due to frost. A motor lawn mower with a drive roller is good for this purpose if a regular roller is not available. If the soil is heavy, care should be taken not to roll too freely or with too heavy a roller.

Watering. One of the chief factors in maintaining a good lawn is an ample supply of water at the roots during the growing season. The ideal way to supply this water is to have the lawn piped, with sufficient spray heads set flush with the surface to allow the whole lawn to be watered at once. Light daily sprinklings are not advisable. Water the lawn thoroughly so that the ground is wet 1 foot deep, then do not water again until the lawn is dry. Too much water is just as injurious as not enough, and particular care should be taken to avoid over-watering if there is any suspicion that the underdrainage is sluggish.

VII. TREES AND SHRUBS

THE TECHNIQUE OF PLANTING AND TRANSPLANTING

Soil preparation. The general soil preparation previously described (Chapter IV, SOIL IMPROVEMENT) will be ample for most tree and shrub planting. But there are times when a hard and infertile subsoil, or the necessity of planting in areas under sod, demands some special treatment before planting; the object of which is to ensure that the tree or shrub finds congenial conditions at its roots, at least during the beginning of its career.

If planting is to be done in sod-covered, deep topsoil, it is unnecessary to do more than to dig a hole wide enough and deep enough to accommodate the roots comfortably and provide room for the layer of sods, which are chopped up and placed in the bottom of the hole.

If subsoil is infertile. When planting trees in thin topsoil which overlies infertile subsoil, the following method should bring success.

First mark a space of sufficient size to allow from 1 to 3 feet (depending on the ultimate size of the specimen) between the ends of the roots and sides of the hole. Then cut off the sod in a layer 3 inches deep and place it aside. Next, dig out the topsoil and place it in a pile. Then remove the subsoil until the hole is 2 feet deep. Now place the sods in the hole, roots up, chopping them into fairly small pieces with a spade. Add a half-and-half mixture of subsoil and topsoil, with some thoroughly decayed manure, to bring the bottom of the hole nearly to the level on which the tree roots will rest. Tramp it down firmly, add 2 or 3 inches of topsoil, and set the tree in place. Then fill in around the roots with the remaining topsoil, placing the subsoil on top until the hole is filled.

The advantages of this method are: (1) It does not necessitate bringing in new topsoil; (2) the subsoil is improved by the admixture of topsoil and manure; (3) nothing but topsoil is in actual contact with the roots; (4) much of the subsoil is brought to the surface where it is accessible for improvement.

If hardpan must be broken. Sometimes the tree planter is confronted

61

by an almost impenetrable hardpan a foot or so beneath the surface. This, of course, must be broken up if the shrub or tree is to have proper drainage. Whether this is done with the aid of a pick or by means of dynamite is dependent on local conditions and the number of trees to be planted. Booklets describing in detail the use of dynamite are obtainable free from the Du Pont de Nemours Company, 350 Fifth Avenue, New York; the Atlas Powder Company, 60 East 42nd Street, New York, and the Hercules Company, Wilmington, Delaware.

If rocks stand in the way. In some regions, the planter is likely to find a large boulder just beneath the surface where he would like to plant a tree. The easy way out is to change the location of the tree, but if the tree is wanted in that particular spot, the boulder must be removed. If it is so large that it cannot be moved unbroken except with the aid of mechanical equipment, it is better to break it up and take it out piecemeal. Some rocks are easily broken by first heating, then suddenly cooling them. To do this, expose the boulder by removing the soil from around it. Then build a roaring bonfire on and around the rock. (Great fun on a winter morning!) When the rock is thoroughly heated let the fire die down, then throw a few pailfuls of cold water on the rock. Usually this develops enough cracks so that a few taps with a sledge-hammer will break it into pieces small enough to be easily handled. Meanwhile, a grand job of soil preparation has been done; for the ashes from the fire, and the necessity of breaking up the ground to a considerable depth, are factors which will make for the future success of the planted tree. Be sure the loosened soil is packed firmly in the bottom of the hole before planting.

Methods of handling trees and shrubs. The way in which trees and shrubs are handled from the time they are dug until they are set in their permanent locations has an important bearing on their success or failure. They should be dug in the proper manner, the roots must not be allowed to become dry, and the sooner they are replanted after being removed from the ground, the better it is for their future growth. The season in which certain plants are dug also exerts an influence on their health.

Getting specimens from a nursery. Trees and shrubs are shipped from the nursery either with bare roots, which are covered with moist material to prevent their drying in transit, or they are "balled and burlapped."

The bare-root method is used with most deciduous subjects, although there are some exceptions, such as Japanese maples, azaleas, some varieties of birch, varieties of flowering dogwood, beeches, and magnolias, which, because of their value or because they are difficult to transplant, are balled and burlapped. This last-named method is almost universally used with evergreens. The reputable nurseryman digs them up so that a ball of earth remains attached to their roots. This is securely wrapped with burlap and tied. When this operation is properly carried out, the plants have a better chance of survival than bare-root plants because the roots within the ball do not lose their contact with the soil and there is less danger of their becoming dry. An unscrupulous nurseryman, in order to save time, may, instead of digging the plants with a ball, carelessly dig them with bare roots. He then sets them on a square of burlap, covers the roots with a shovelful or two of soil, ties up the burlap and sells the product as a balled and burlapped plant. This is bad practice because the chief value of balling (that of undisturbed roots) is lost and the purchaser has to pay freight on weighty soil, when, under the circumstances, the roots could have been kept moist just as well by packing them with light, damp moss.

When stock is obtained from a nursery, the purchaser has little control over the way it is handled except by buying from reputable nurserymen who may be counted on to dig a specimen with the greatest amount of care consistent with making a reasonable profit.

When living plants are received from the nursery, they should at once be unpacked and, preferably, planted immediately. Otherwise, they must be cared for to prevent the roots from drying. Balled and burlapped stock should be stood upright as closely together as possible in the shade and the balls should be soaked with water. Bare-root plants should be "heeled in" by placing the roots close together in a trench with the tops all slanting in the same direction, and throwing moist soil between and over the roots, packing it down so that it is in close contact with all of them. If through any mishap, such as improper packing or delay in transit, the bark is dry and shriveled on arrival, it is a good plan to bury the plants completely, roots and tops, in moist earth for a week or more before they are planted. This treatment enables the bark to absorb moisture and greatly increases the chance of survival; but of course it is not practicable with very large stock.

Even when trees and shrubs are planted directly from the packing case or the "heeling-in" trench, the roots must be kept moist until they are finally set in the ground. This may be done by wrapping them in wet burlap, or by carrying them in a tub of water transported on a wheelbarrow or truck. It is sometimes recommended to "puddle" the roots by dipping them in a creamy mixture of clayey soil and water. Personally, I am not much in favor of this method because it is messy and because fibrous roots become matted together, whereas it is desirable to distribute them evenly when planting.

Transplanting on one's own grounds. When moving trees and shrubs from one part of the home grounds to another, it is possible to transfer them with little or no set-back by taking precautions not to injure the roots.

Digging deciduous trees and shrubs. In the case of large deciduous trees or shrubs which cannot be dug up by thrusting a spade into the ground on one side and levering them out, the first step is to dig a trench around the tree sufficiently deep to make it possible to obtain most of the roots. The trench should be started as far away from the trunk as the widest spread of the branches, and even farther in the case of trees of fastigiate habit. Having made the trench, dig in towards the trunk with a digging fork, taking care to avoid breaking roots. The loose soil which falls to the bottom of the trench must from time to time be shoveled out. When nearing the trunk, it is usually possible to undermine the tree and, by the leverage exerted by two or more spades, pry the tree loose from its anchorage. If it is a large tree and the time occupied in digging it is prolonged, the roots exposed must be kept from becoming dry by wrapping them in moist burlap. This is the method adopted in the case of most deciduous trees and shrubs.

Digging evergreens. Evergreens, also deciduous trees which are difficult to transplant, are dug up with a somewhat different technique in order to get a ball of earth about their roots. In the case of small trees, a circle is described by thrusting a spade into the ground in a continuous line around the tree. Thus any roots which extend outside the proposed ball of earth are severed. Then by sticking one or more spades deeply into the ground on two or more sides (depending on the size of the specimen), it is possible, by bearing down on the handles, to lift the tree out of the ground. If it is to be planted at once and the ball of earth is solid, it may not be necessary to burlap it. Simply slide it onto a board (the removable side of a wheelbarrow will serve excellently) and carry it over to its planting place. If, however, the ball is loose, it is better to tie it in a burlap square.

Large evergreens are lifted by first digging a trench around them.

Then the ball of earth is shaped up and wrapped with canvas which is lashed securely in place. If the tree has to be taken with a ball more than 2 feet in diameter, the usual practice is to tilt the ball and slip a wooden platform underneath. With trees of large size, it usually is better to let a professional dig them.

ROOT-PRUNING BEFORE TRANSPLANTING. In the case of large and valuable trees and shrubs which have been a long time in one location, it is advisable to root-prune them a year ahead of the time when it is proposed to move them. This is done by digging a trench around the tree at a suitable distance from the trunk, severing all the roots encountered, and then replacing the soil after it has been fertilized by the addition of thoroughly decomposed manure. This results in the production of a mass of fibrous roots which add greatly to the chances of a successful operation when the tree is finally transplanted.

Planting and after-care of trees. Proper care of trees during planting and later involves suitable preparation of the soil, correct digging of the specimens, and assurance that the roots are kept constantly moist, as explained above, besides such elements of care as mulching, pruning, supporting of trunks, protection from sunscald, and later watering and fertilizing, as explained below.

When to move trees and shrubs. There are certain seasons when plants may be moved with less trouble than at others and with greater assurance of success. For deciduous trees and shrubs, these seasons are spring and fall when the trees, denuded of their leaves, are practically dormant. With some trees (for example, oaks, magnolias, and birches) better results are usually obtained in the spring rather than the fall. Generally speaking, however, trees and shrubs which are winter-hardy in the location to which they are being moved may be transplanted to advantage in the fall. Subjects which are on the borderline of hardiness are preferably transplanted in the spring in order that their roots may become thoroughly established in the new soil before winter comes.

The best time for transplanting most evergreens is in late April or May, just before growth commences; or in late August or early September, when the new growth has hardened and while the soil is still warm enough to induce new root formation before winter. Spring planting is preferred for rhododendrons and allied plants in the climate of New York.

Hardy deciduous trees and some evergreens may be transplanted during the winter, if more convenient, provided there is not too much

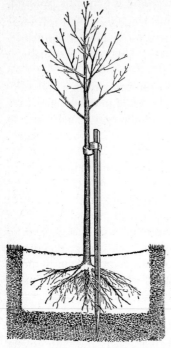

FIG. 12. Method of planting a tree

snow on the ground to hamper the work. To ensure unfrozen soil, the ground about the trees to be moved and at the place where they are to be planted should be mulched deeply in the fall with manure, straw, or hay.

The hardier evergreens, such as red cedars, are sometimes moved during the winter with a frozen ball of earth. Before the ground freezes in the fall a trench is dug around the tree, leaving a ball of earth of adequate size about its roots. At the same time a ramp is dug down to the base of the ball. When the ball has frozen solid it is pried loose, loaded on a stone-boat and pulled up the ramp by team or tractor. The advantages of the frozen-ball method are that the work can be done during the slack season; there is no necessity to burlap the ball of earth; and there is absolutely no disturbance of the roots contained in the ball. The same precaution of mulching the ground where the tree is to be planted should be followed as mentioned in the preceding paragraph.

How to do the planting. If large trees or shrubs with bare roots are to be planted, the soil should be prepared and holes dug prior to the receipt of the trees in order to avoid delay. If the trees are to be mulched after planting (see p. 67), set them in the hole so that, when the soil is filled in, the trees will be at the same depth (as shown by the soil line) as they were when growing in the nursery. If mulching is not contemplated set them 1 inch deeper (Fig. 12). If the subsoil has been disturbed, consolidate it by tamping before setting the tree in place. Spread the roots in the hole as naturally as possible and scatter fine topsoil in among them. It is important to make sure that there are no air spaces about the roots, and that the soil is packed firmly by tamping with the feet or with a piece of two-by-four. Under some circumstances (when the roots criss-cross so that it is difficult to get soil between them) the most efficient method is hydraulic planting, if there is a hose attachment near by. While the soil is being shoveled onto the roots, it is washed between them by a stream of water which is kept continuously flowing until all the roots are covered. Then, as soon as the free water has drained away, the planting may be finished by adding the remainder of the soil. When shaping up the surface make a saucer-like depression to extend a little beyond the spread of the roots. This is to facilitate absorption should a droughty season make watering necessary.

When planting balled and burlapped material avoid disturbing the ball more than is absolutely necessary. Place the tree in the hole without removing the burlap. When you are sure that you have set it at the correct depth unfasten the burlap and tuck it in the bottom of the hole. If it seems to be too bulky cut some of it off but do not disturb the ball. Then shovel in soil, tamp firmly, and leave a depression on the surface as recommended for bare-root trees.

Mulching. If circumstances are such that it is impossible to water trees artificially, by all means apply a 3- to 6-inch mulch to conserve the natural supply of water in the soil. The mulch may consist of strawy manure, straw, partly decayed leaves, peatmoss (which should be neutralized with ground limestone if the plant is a lime lover) or salt hay, which is a baled product of salt marshes of the eastern seaboard. Mulch paper also may be used to conserve moisture. Lay it so that rain is conducted toward the roots of the plant and anchor it to the ground by placing a layer of soil around the edges, by stones, or by means of pegs and wires.

Mulching is most necessary when it is not possible to cultivate the surface soil over the tree or shrub roots. Properly applied, it not only conserves moisture but also smothers weeds. The maintenance of a mulch or the cultivation of the surface soil is almost indispensable the first year or two after transplanting. After the tree has become thoroughly established it is permissible to allow the lawn to extend to within 6 inches of the trunk, but not closer, because of the danger of scarring the bark when the lawn mower is used.

Pruning. It is practically impossible to dig up a tree or shrub without root injury, even if you do the work yourself. In some cases half or even more of the roots will be left behind. To compensate for the loss of roots, it is wise to remove some of the top of the tree. The theory is that the depleted root system will be able to supply the necessary moisture to a reduced top, whereas it might fail if all the top growth were left on. No hard and fast rule can be laid down regarding the pruning necessary when a tree or shrub is transplanted. Plants vary in their ability to recover from the shock of being moved, and much depends on the care with which they are dug and upon their treatment immediately before and for some time after transplanting. If most of their roots have been saved; if they are transplanted immediately so the roots do not become dried; and if they are plentifully supplied with water during the first growing season, only a little pruning will be necessary. Nursery-grown trees and shrubs may be moved with greater assurance of success than those dug from the wild, because the frequent transplanting practised in good nurseries results in the production of a compact and fibrous root system, which may be removed almost intact, and consequently with little shock to the specimen when transplanting. Generally speaking, young material may be transplanted more successfully than older plants of the same species, partly because, in digging them, the roots suffer less damage.

Bearing the above considerations in mind, one may safely prune a tree or shrub at planting time to improve its shape or to remove any branches which cross and rub. Furthermore, for the welfare of most trees, it is wise to cut off two thirds of the length of the growth of the preceding year (in spring) or of the growth of the current year (in the case of fall planting). If a tree has a distinct leader, it should usually be left unpruned. My experience has been that, with subjects which have a very fibrous root system, such as spindle-trees, the tree will thrive with little or no pruning; whereas with the more difficult species of oak it is a good plan to cut back so severely that little more than a bare pole is left.

Because evergreens are usually dug with greater care, and because the ball of earth about their roots prevents them from becoming dry, it is not customary to prune them when they are transplanted. However, it will do no harm and may prove beneficial to practise corrective pruning at this time. If a few weeks after planting the tree shows signals of distress, such as the drooping of the "candles" in pines, or wilting or browning of the new growth of other evergreens, it is advisable to lessen the strain on the roots by a reduction of the top growth. This may be accomplished by pinching off two thirds of the length of the pine "candles" and of the new shoots of fir and spruce.

Evergreens of the feathery type, such as retinospora and arborvitae, may be lightly sheared.

It is commonly recommended that all broken and mangled roots be cut back to sound tissue and that the jagged ends, at least, of the larger roots be trimmed smooth. A clean cut, presumably, heals more quickly and absorbs water with greater facility than a jagged one; and injured roots, because of their inability to produce new ones, are likely to die and decay, perhaps letting decay organisms extend into healthy tissue.

Supports. While evergreen trees do not ordinarily need bracing if they have been properly dug with a ball and carefully reset, large trees of any kind, especially in windy locations, should be firmly supported when transplanted. Do not attempt to drive a stake into the ground alongside the trunk because you will damage the roots and cannot drive it deeply enough to fix it securely in the ground. Instead, place three guy-wires at even distances around the tree. Bend each wire into a loop at one end and thread it through a length of rubber hose a little longer than is sufficient to pass around the trunk at the point of attachment. This is to prevent the wire from cutting into the bark. Fasten the hose-covered wires securely around the trunk. At the other end of each wire attach a stout stake 2 feet long, notched to prevent the wire from slipping. Drive the stakes into the ground at equal distances around the tree until the wires are taut enough to hold the top in place (Fig. 13). While this is the accepted method for all trees more than 3 inches in diameter, on a lawn it has the drawback of the wires and projecting stakes getting in the way of the lawn mower.

For smaller deciduous trees a stout stake long enough to reach to the first branch may be used for support. It should be firmly driven into the bottom of the hole *before the tree is set.* If the stake is placed after the tree is planted there is danger of breaking roots when driving it and, because of the difficulty of making it rigid, the tree may support the stake rather than the stake support the tree. Place the tree on the north side of the stake to take advantage of the opportunity of partly shading the trunk, and fasten the tree to the stake in such a way that the bark is not abraded by rubbing when the wind blows, and that the trunk will not be constricted when it increases in size. A good method is to make use of old garden hose. Cut a piece long enough to pass around both trunk and stake with 3 or 4 inches over and split it lengthwise. Now take a piece of unsplit hose about 2 inches long

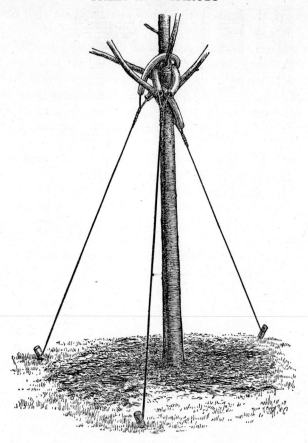

FIG. 13. Tree supported by guy-wires

and place it between the trunk and stake. Pass the strip around the
trunk and stake tightly enough to hold the cylindrical piece in place,
and nail it to the side of stake farthest from the tree. This will prevent
abrasion and allow for expansion of the trunk (Fig. 14). Another
method is to pass the strip around the trunk and cross it before putting
the ends around the stake where they are nailed (Fig. 15).

Protecting from sunscald. High-headed trees whose trunks were
shaded because of close planting in nursery rows may suffer from sunscald when planted in the open. To overcome this, some method of
shading the trunks must be adopted until they have become acclimated,

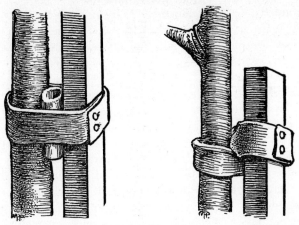

FIGS. 14 and 15. Two methods of fastening tree to supporting stake

or until the head has developed sufficiently to shade the trunk. Shading may be accomplished by nailing two boards lengthwise at right angles to each other and placing them close against the trunk on the south side of the tree (Fig. 16). Another method is to wrap the tree with a piece of burlap or to wind puttee-like strips of burlap around the trunk. Perhaps the boards are to be preferred because they are easy to remove for the purpose of examining the condition of the trunk, and they do not offer so many attractions to domestically inclined insects.

Later attention to transplanted trees. The after-care of transplanted trees consists of ensuring an adequate supply of water at the roots; the cultivation of the soil over the roots of unmulched trees; the prompt removal of any branches which die back; and a close watch to make sure that trunk and branches are not constricted by fastenings used to support the tree.

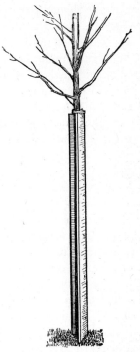

FIG. 16. Tree trunk shaded by two boards nailed at right angles

The routine care of established trees consists of pruning whenever necessary (Chapter XXVII, PRUNING ORNAMENTAL TREES AND SHRUBS); spraying for control of insect and fungous pests (Chapter XXIX, GARDEN ENEMIES); and watering and fertilizing as needed.

Watering. Whenever it is considered necessary to water an established tree of any size it should be remembered that the roots are usually deep in the ground, and in consequence driblets of water applied to the surface are useless. The hose or sprinkler should be left running long enough to enable the water to penetrate the soil to a depth of 2 feet. Remember that the roots usually extend horizontally at least as far as the branches. If the surface is baked hard it is a good plan to loosen it here and there with a digging fork to facilitate the penetration of the water.

Fertilizing. Trees growing in sod land or on lawns may sometimes fail to make satisfactory growth if the soil is naturally poor. Partly brought about by the grass robbing the trees of both food and moisture, this poor growth may be remedied by adequate watering and the application of fertilizer. We still have a good deal to learn about the kind and amount of fertilizer to use, the best time to apply it to the trees, and methods of application. I believe the best method is to strip the sod from an area all around the tree, extending from 2 or 3 feet beyond the periphery of the outermost branches (more in the case of columnar trees) to within 3 feet of the trunk. Stable or barnyard manure should be spread 3 inches thick on this area and dug into the ground deeply enough to be in proximity to the tree roots and inaccessible to the grass roots. Firm the loosened soil by tramping, rake it level, and return the sods. All this involves a good deal of work, but it does bring results.

A method of easier application is to punch holes with a crowbar 2 or 3 feet apart and about 18 inches deep, extending over an area comparable to that described just above. Pour into each hole a handful of complete commercial fertilizer; or a heaping handful of dehydrated poultry manure; or a double handful of sheep manure. The commercial fertilizer (of about 5% nitrogen, 6% phosphoric acid, 3% potash) should be made up, in part, of slowly available ingredients such as bonemeal, tankage, and cottonseed meal. (See Chapter V, MANURES AND FERTILIZERS.) It is sometimes suggested that the amount of fertilizer for each tree be computed by allowing 1 pound of fertilizer for each inch of circumference of the trunk.

The object of making holes is to get the fertilizer down where it will reach the tree roots. It is claimed that if broadcast on the surface most of it is likely to be absorbed by the grass roots, and it will encourage the tree roots to come to the surface where they will be in danger during periods of drought. But many authorities say that this is a danger that can be ignored.

Probably the best time to fertilize most trees is in the spring just as soon as the ground is workable and before new growth starts.

Spacing of trees and shrubs. It is impossible to lay down any hard and fast rules to govern the spacing of trees and shrubs, because there are too many factors involved. These include the character of the plants, soil, and climate; and whether the trees and shrubs are part of a mass planting or intended to stand out as isolated specimens. But one sees so many overcrowded plantings that some kind of a rough guide seems desirable.

The following records of the growth of some representative trees and shrubs at Ottawa (Bulletin No. 89, New Series, Dominion of Canada, Department of Agriculture, 1927) and of specimens growing in the Brooklyn Botanic Garden will give an inkling of the spacing required to allow room for their development without competition.

RATE OF GROWTH RECORDED AT THE DOMINION CENTRAL EXPERIMENTAL
FARM, OTTAWA, CANADA

TREES	Height in feet	Spread in feet	Time after planting in years
Acer platanoides, Norway Maple	44	43	35
Acer saccharinum, Silver Maple	66	56	37
Betula alba laciniata, Cut-leaf Birch	48	38	38
Cercidiphyllum japonicum, Katsura-tree	44	43	35
Cladrastis lutea, Yellow-wood	32	23	35
Crataegus Crus-galli, Cockspur Thorn	25	23	35
Elaeagnus angustifolia, Russian Olive	30	31	35
Gymnocladus dioica, Kentucky Coffee-tree	37	24	35
Malus baccata, Siberian Crab-apple	28	40	35
Quercus borealis (*rubra* of catalogs), Red Oak	49	53	35
Sorbus Aucuparia, Mountain Ash	38	40	35
Syringa japonica, Tree Lilac	21	24	35
Ulmus americana, American Elm	72	70	38

RATE OF GROWTH RECORDED AT BROOKLYN BOTANIC GARDEN, BROOKLYN, NEW YORK

Average nursery stock was planted, the sizes ranging from 3 to 6 feet. In some cases—*Populus,* for example—the trees may have been up to 10 feet high when planted.

TREES	Height in feet	Spread in feet	Time after planting in years
Ailanthus altissima, Tree of heaven	25	20	17
Cladrastis lutea, Yellow-wood	15	15	20
Koelreuteria paniculata, Goldenrain Tree	17	23	17
Malus atrosanguinea, Carmine Crab-apple	16	29	21
Pinus excelsa, Himalayan Pine	18	16	12
Populus canadensis, Carolina Poplar	60	37	22
Populus nigra italica, Lombardy Poplar	45	9	22
Prunus Amanogawa, Japanese Cherry	12	3½	8
Prunus Fujizan, Japanese Cherry	15	20	8
Robinia Pseudoacacia, Locust	40	30	24
Sophora japonica, Pagoda Tree	25	20	20
Tilia vulgaris, Linden	32	35	24

SHRUBS	Height in feet	Spread in feet	Time after planting in years
Exochorda racemosa (*grandiflora*), Pearl-bush	14	18	20
Kolkwitzia amabilis, Beauty-bush	10	12	11
Lonicera fragrantissima, Winter Honeysuckle	9	14	12
Lonicera Maackii podocarpa	12	22	24
Spiraea Vanhouttei	8	11	14
Syringa vulgaris varieties, Lilac	12	16	21
* *Viburnum tomentosum*	15	12	26

* Grown in a mass planting. The spread probably would have been greater if the bush had been standing free.

Using the foregoing records as a guide, one could suggest that the "large" trees in the classified lists at the end of this chapter be spaced at least 50 feet apart; the "small" trees at least 30 feet; the "large, narrow trees" 20 feet; the "large" shrubs at least 15 feet; the "medium" shrubs 10 feet; and the "small" shrubs 3 feet.

I must emphasize the fact that the above is merely a rough guide and that adjustments must be made to accommodate the exceptions. For example: *Cotoneaster horizontalis,* which is listed among the "small" shrubs, is capable of spreading 10 feet or even more, while it is doubtful if *Calluna vulgaris* could ever attain a diameter of 3 feet.

The best way to ensure room for the development of specimens and, at the same time, avoid a sparse appearance, is to set out each plant with plenty of room, then plant fillers in the vicinity, the fillers to be removed as soon as they enter into competition with the specimens.

When planting with a view to obtaining mass effects, the spacing may be about one half that which is allowed for specimens.

SELECTING TREES AND SHRUBS

When choosing trees and shrubs, several considerations should be kept in mind. First and foremost (unless you are an experimenter) select subjects which are known to thrive in your locality. It is a big mistake to plant a tree of dubious hardiness in an important position, or to try to make trees or shrubs happy in poor dry soil when they naturally demand rich moist locations. People who live in limestone regions should remember that mountain laurel, rhododendrons, and other acid-soil plants can be made to thrive only with much effort to make the soil congenial.

It is preferable to choose plant material on the basis of its year-round appearance rather than on its floral display alone. Trees and shrubs which have good foliage throughout the growing season should be selected. The beautiful tracery of the branches of some deciduous trees and shrubs and the color and character of their bark in winter should (other factors being equal) lead to their selection in preference to others.

Whenever possible, trees and shrubs should be chosen which are not especially subject to attacks by insects and diseases, for much of the enjoyment of gardening is lost if one has to spend every spare minute in operating the spray barrel or dust gun.

They should fit the locations assigned them both in size and habit of growth. In situations where the tree or shrub must not exceed a limited size, plants which do not naturally exceed those limits, or those which, by pruning, can be kept within bounds, should be used. When a tree or shrub of massive proportions is called for, plant one which is capable of filling the bill. In situations which call for trees of symmetrical habit, avoid planting those which, when mature, develop gnarled and ungainly branches.

If you are not familiar with plant material, by all means visit some nurseries and look over the growing plants before trying to make a selection. Take advantage of any opportunity to visit a botanic garden or a public park where labeled collections are maintained, to gain knowledge of the appearance of mature trees and shrubs.

Descriptive lists. Below there is given a selection of trees and shrubs of different types, with notes on their characteristics and preferences. Following this descriptive list are tables containing names of many more subjects, classified according to their size, their manner of growth, and requirements of sun and soil.

CONIFEROUS EVERGREEN TREES

North of New York City (except in coastal regions) the only evergreen trees which are reliably hardy are the cone-bearers.

ABIES, **Fir.** The firs in youth are handsome, with symmetrical pyramidal or cone-shaped silhouettes. When aged (more than 50 years) they become bedraggled-looking, without compensating picturesqueness. They need a moist, well-drained soil, well supplied with humus.

A. concolor, **White Fir.** Striking silvery-blue coloration. Endures heat and drought and city conditions if not too intense. Colorado form preferable to the one from Pacific Coast for northeastern states.

A. homolepis, **Nikko Fir.** Needles dark green above, silvery beneath. Pyramidal when young, becoming round-topped with age. Endures city conditions when young.

A. Nordmanniana. Lustrous dark green and silver needles. Hardy in southern Ontario. Does well in the central states.

Cedar, see CEDRUS and JUNIPERUS.

CEDRUS, **Cedar.** The true cedars are native to northern Africa, Asia Minor and the Himalayas. They are doubtfully hardy north of Long Island, N. Y., although a strain of *C. libanotica* (*libani*) introduced by the Arnold Arboretum is said to be hardy in the vicinity of Boston. They are handsome both in youth and age. A rich, well-drained soil and, in the North, a sheltered location are desirable.

C. atlantica, **Atlas Cedar.** Needles bluish green. Variety *glauca* has silvery needles. Considered the hardiest forms until the introduction of the hardy race of *C. libanotica.*

C. Deodara, **Deodar.** The most graceful of all cedars. Thrives beautifully on the Pacific Coast; not hardy in the northeastern states.

C. libanotica, **Cedar of Lebanon.** Longer needles of rich green. Worth planting for its historical associations alone in any region where it may be expected to thrive.

CHAMAECYPARIS. Characterized at normal maturity by flat, scalelike leaves on fan-shaped branches, similar to those of *Thuja* (**Arborvitae**), some species and varieties of *Chamaecyparis* (and sometimes of *Thuja*) are best known under the name of **Retinospora,** applied to them when their needle-like juvenile foliage is retained throughout their life.

This occurs when the juvenile forms are propagated by cuttings or grafting and the character of the foliage thus is permanently retained. In the United States retinosporas seldom exceed a height of 40 feet, although in their native country (Japan) some species of *Chamaecyparis* may attain a height of 100 feet. There are innumerable garden forms, most of them of great merit. Many dwarf forms are offered by nurserymen. (See Chapter VIII, FOUNDATION PLANTING.) Moist, well-drained, sandy loam suits *Chamaecyparis*.

C. obtusa, **Hinoki Cypress.** Dark green, lustrous, scale-like leaves on flat branchlets. Grows 15 to 20 feet here. Hardy in New England. Varieties much used by the Japanese in production of dwarf trees.

C. pisifera, **Sawara Cypress.** Branches horizontal, leaves lighter in tone than *C. obtusa.* Branchlets fan-like and somewhat pendulous. May attain 35 feet. Hardy in southern Ontario.

JUNIPERUS, **Juniper.** Only two of the junipers commonly offered by nurserymen will attain the stature of trees in the northeastern states—the **Chinese Juniper** and the so-called **Red Cedar.** Neither is fussy in its soil requirements. In common with *Chamaecyparis,* this genus has juvenile foliage which is quite different from that of adult specimens.

J. chinensis, **Chinese Juniper.** Thoroughly hardy. Fruit brown. Great variety in color of needles and form of tree in its many horticultural forms.

J. virginiana, **Red Cedar.** Native from Maine to Florida, flourishing in limestone regions but also occurring elsewhere. Berries bluish. Many horticultural forms.

PICEA, **Spruce.** Spruces in general retain their lower branches for a longer period than the firs and are therefore of greater value when tall isolated specimen trees are desired. They like moist, well-drained loam. Branchlets of spruces are commonly drooping.

P. Abies (*P. excelsa*), **Norway Spruce.** Quick-growing but, in this country, comparatively short-lived. Many forms. Useful for temporary effects.

P. glauca (*P. canadensis* or *P. alba*), **White Spruce.** Ranges as a wilding from Labrador to Alaska and southward to Montana and New York. Needles bluish-green, strongly aromatic.

P. orientalis, **Oriental Spruce.** Graceful, with shining, dark green, crowded needles. Naturally tall, but slow-growing under cultivation.

P. pungens, **Colorado Spruce.** In its garden forms, probably the most popular. Variety *glauca* with steel-blue needles and *Kosteriana,* silvery-blue, in great demand in the East, to the annoyance of those who contend that their striking coloration has no place in the eastern landscape.

PINUS, **Pine.** Most of the pines will endure drought and thrive on poor, sandy, or gravelly ground. Usually they are symmetrical and conical as young trees, becoming spreading and picturesque with age.

P. excelsa, **Bhotan** or **Himalayan Pine.** One of the handsomest of pines, with needles like those of our own white pine, but often twice as long. Not reliably hardy north of Long Island, N. Y., and even there sometimes subject to winter injury.

P. nigra, **Austrian Pine.** Rather somber in appearance, with thick, heavy, dark green needles. The only pine which seems fairly happy under city conditions.

P. resinosa, **Red Pine.** A grand tree, especially for northern gardens; also largely planted as a timber tree.

P. Strobus, **White Pine.** Perhaps the most useful of all; adaptable to a variety of conditions; quick-growing and symmetrical when young, picturesque in age. Needles presenting a mass of soft bluish-green.

P. sylvestris, **Scotch Pine.** Endures poor soil and low temperatures. Needles shorter than any previously mentioned. Not handsome as a young tree, but when aged becomes gnarled and picturesque, with cinnamon-colored bark.

PSEUDOTSUGA. This genus of tall handsome evergreens with large drooping cones is best known horticulturally through *P. taxifolia,* the **Douglas Fir.** This is one of the noblest trees on the Pacific slope, where it may attain a height of more than 200 feet. It is quick-growing under cultivation, but not happy under city conditions. Trees propagated from seeds gathered in Colorado are best adapted for exposed locations and for northern regions in the East.

TAXUS, **Yew.** Both English and Japanese yews are capable of making trees up to 60 feet tall; but in this country are usually seen as tall shrubs.

Taxus cuspidata, **Japanese Yew** is the strongest-growing species in the northern states.

THUJA, **Arborvitae.** The fan-shaped sprays of foliage of these spire-like trees are pleasantly aromatic when bruised. The roots prefer a moist soil.

T. occidentalis. In the wild, ranges from New Brunswick to North Carolina, and west to Illinois and Manitoba. Ordinarily small, but may reach a height of 60 feet.

TSUGA, **Hemlock.** By many the hemlock is considered the most beautiful evergreen tree of northeastern America. At its best in a grove with others of its kind. It prefers a moist soil.

T. canadensis. Hardy north to New Brunswick; occurs as a wilding south to Alabama. Of graceful habit in contrast to the stiffness of some of the spruces. May reach 100 feet.

T. caroliniana. Hardy to Ontario. Not as large as *canadensis* but rather a handsomer tree; it is rather difficult to transplant.

BROAD-LEAF EVERGREEN TREES

It has already been hinted that northern gardens must get along without broad-leaf evergreen trees. The hardiest is the American holly which, however, does not make much of a tree in climates more severe than that of Long Island, N. Y.

ILEX, **Holly.** The spiny-leaved English and American species are the best evergreen subjects in the group.

I. Aquifolium, **English Holly.** Magnificent tree of conical outline, clothed to the ground with shiny,. spiny foliage in climates adapted to its growth. Can survive (with occasional killing back) on Long Island, but really requires a climate similar to that of England and the Pacific Northwest.

I. opaca, **American Holly.** May reach a height of 40 feet in favorable situations, but not adapted for planting far inland. Extends as a wild tree north to Boston on the coastal plain.

MAGNOLIA, *M. grandiflora,* **Southern Magnolia.** Sometimes manages to exist for a period of years as far north as Long Island, but should not be planted in the expectation that it will permanently thrive north of Washington, D. C. (For other magnolias, see DECIDUOUS TREES.)

DECIDUOUS TREES

ACER, **Maple.** These are among the most valuable trees for landscape effects. The sugar maple and red maple are gorgeous in their fall coloring. (See also DECIDUOUS SHRUBS.)

A. platanoides, **Norway Maple.** Good for city planting, forming a broad, low-branched, rounded head 80 feet high or more. Variety *Schwedleri* purple-foliaged in spring, turning to a not-very-attractive bronze. Sugar maple preferable where it will thrive.

A. rubrum, **Red Maple.** Useful for wet situations; will also grow in well-drained but moist soil. Among the first trees to show evidence of new life in spring, with red flowers on leafless branches. Capable of reaching 120 feet.

A. saccharinum (dasycarpum), **Silver Maple.** Graceful and quick-growing, reaching 100 feet or more. Should not be used as a street tree because of the tendency of its limbs to decay and break. Needs rich soil, as it is a voracious feeder. Variety *Wieri* is a cut-leaved form. Not to be confused with *A. saccharum.*

A. saccharum, **Sugar Maple.** Tall (to 120 feet), with a well-proportioned oval head of handsome foliage. Leaves turning scarlet and yellow in autumn. Needs a fairly good, well-drained soil. Does well in calcareous regions.

AESCULUS, **Horsechestnut, Buckeye.** The common horsechestnut is much beloved by children for its glossy, mahogany-colored seeds. Although it will thrive as a street tree, it is not recommended because of the temptation it offers to boys to hurl stones to dislodge the nuts. The double-flowered form is innocuous in this respect because it produces no fruit. (See also DECIDUOUS SHRUBS.)

A. carnea, **Red Horsechestnut.** Beautiful with flowers of varying tones of red in panicles at tips of branches. Leaves less liable to turn brown at edges than those of common horsechestnut. May grow to 40 feet high.

A. glabra, **Ohio Buckeye.** Worth-while tree of medium size, about 30 feet high when mature, hardier than common horsechestnut but flowers not so showy. Especially attractive in early spring with developing growth buds rosy in color.

A. Hippocastanum, **Common Horsechestnut.** Valuable when dense shade is required. Spectacular in bloom. Grows to 80 feet. Unfortunately the leaves "scorch" in hot, dry situations, and are attacked by a fungous disease. Many garden forms, some differing in habit of growth; some double-flowered, some with laciniated leaves.

AILANTHUS, *A. altissima,* **Tree of Heaven.** By many considered a weed, but it is the most enduring tree for city conditions. It has long pinnate leaves and grows up to 60 feet. The flowers of the male tree have an offensive odor—the fruits of the female are decorative.

Beech, see FAGUS

BETULA, **Birch.** The birches in general are characterized by their gracefulness. There is some risk in planting them because they are liable to be attacked by the bronze birch borer, for which there is apparently no cure beyond the removal and destruction of infected trees. Spring planting should be practised.

B. alba, **European White Birch.** One of the most desirable of specimen trees for the lawn, especially when seen in winter against a background of somber evergreens. Grows up to 60 feet and has drooping branchlets and white bark. Several horticultural forms available.

B. papyrifera, **Canoe Birch.** Beautiful, and of great interest because of its association with Indian life. Grows to 80 feet.

B. populifolia, **Gray Birch.** Similar to *B. alba* but smaller. Will grow in poor dry soil.

Birch, see BETULA.

CATALPA. *C. speciosa* is a quick-growing but rather short-lived tree, characterized by bold, tropical-looking foliage and panicles of large white flowers, purple marked, in late May or early June. Leaves appear late in spring and are shed early in the fall. It may reach a height of 100 feet, and is not particular as to soil.

PLATE IV. (*upper*) FLOWERING CRAB-APPLE TRAINED BY PRUNING. (*lower left*) SPRING CHERRY, *Prunus subhirtella*. (*lower right*) MAIDENHAIR TREE, *Ginkgo biloba*

PLATE V. (*upper*) JAPANESE CHERRIES, VARIETY KWANZAN. (*lower*) *Vitex Agnus castus, V. Negundo incisa, Clerodendron trichotomum*

CERCIDIPHYLLUM, **Katsura-tree.** *C. japonicum* is an interesting and "different" tree of great beauty, with large, soft, heart-shaped leaves. It usually develops several trunks, which give it, when approaching maturity, the appearance of a gigantic symmetrical bush. It seems to be rather fastidious and is not certain to thrive in all gardens. Demands rich, moist soil. It grows to 80 feet.

CLADRASTIS, **Yellow-wood.** *C. lutea* is a native tree of great merit, but, for some obscure reason, it is often neglected by planters. It can be used to advantage as a specimen lawn tree. Its panicles of white pea-like blooms droop like those of laburnum. It is rather slow-growing, but is capable of reaching 50 feet.

CORNUS, **Dogwood.** Among the most beautiful of flowering trees, the dogwoods are especially valuable for planting on the fringes of woodland or as lawn trees, preferably where they get partial shade. (See also DECIDU-OUS SHRUBS.)

C. florida, **Flowering Dogwood.** Native tree with branches completely clothed with white-bracted flowers before the leaves appear in May. Red berries and red leaves in autumn. Spring planting recommended, preferably with a ball of soil. Variety *rubra,* with pinkish to red bracts, propagated by grafting on seedlings of the species.

C. Kousa, **Japanese Dogwood.** Variety *chinensis,* with inflorescences sometimes 5 inches in diameter, preferable to species. Fruits strawberry-like. Both bloom later than native dogwood. Not easy to grow.

C. mas, **Cornelian Cherry.** One of the first trees to bloom in the spring. Flowers small and yellow in dense clusters. Grows about 20 feet high with a compact and twiggy habit.

C. Nuttallii. Western species, best for planting on the Pacific Coast.

CRATAEGUS, **Hawthorn.** There are hundreds of species of hawthorn, only a few of which are handled by nurserymen. They are specially adapted for mass planting and are useful for providing cover and food for birds. Three distinctive types are mentioned here. Garden varieties of the English hawthorn are excellent lawn trees in regions where they thrive.

C. Lavallei (Carrierei). A hybrid with large, gorgeous, orange-colored haws produced on a spreading tree about 20 feet high, with handsome foliage and formidable spines.

C. Phaenopyrum (cordata), **Washington Thorn.** Native tree about 30 feet high, with rather small but freely produced bright scarlet, shining haws.

C. Oxyacantha, **English Hawthorn.** Planted primarily for its floral display. Double-flowered forms in white, pink, and scarlet are available.

Dogwood, see CORNUS.

ELAEAGNUS, **Russian Olive.** *E. angustifolia* is a small spreading tree of picturesque habit, with narrow, silvery leaves which make it stand out conspicuously against trees with dark green foliage. It is hardy North and attains a height of about 35 feet.

Elm, see ULMUS.

EUONYMUS. This genus contains several small trees grown mainly for their decorative fruits. Because they are susceptible to attacks by scale insects, many knowing gardeners are reluctant to plant them. See also DECIDUOUS SHRUBS (p. 95) and list of vines in Chapter IX.

E. atropurpureus, **Wahoo, Burning-bush.** Native tree about 20 feet high, hardy in Ottawa. Fruit crimson.

E. Bungeanus. Has pinkish fruits which open and disclose the orange seeds. A shallow-rooted tree, which wilts during droughty periods.

FAGUS, **Beech.** Beeches are lofty trees, usually symmetrical, character-ized by smooth bark; light gray in the native species, darker gray in the European. They do not transplant easily. Well-drained, sandy, calcareous loam is preferred for them.

F. grandifolia (americana). One of the handsomest of native forest trees. Grows to a height of about 100 feet.

F. sylvatica, **European Beech.** Less tall but, if anything, more beautiful than the native beech. Horticultural forms with colored or laciniated foliage in great demand as specimen trees for lawn planting. Also a pendulous form which, though grotesque in youth, can be strikingly beautiful when mature. (See Plate III.)

GINKGO, **Maidenhair-tree.** The common name of *G. biloba,* the only species existing, comes from the resemblance of its leaves to the leaflets of the maidenhair fern. In its adolescent stage it is likely to be awkward in appearance, but aged specimens usually achieve a fair amount of symmetry. There is a narrow, more or less cylindrical form—*G. biloba fastigiata.* The ginkgo is not troubled by insects, and is able to thrive in congested areas, sometimes attaining a height of 80 feet. The foliage changes to a clear yellow in the fall. The female tree produces evil-smelling, "gooey" fruits. Where these would be objectionable, only male trees should be planted.

GYMNOCLADUS. *G. dioica,* **Kentucky Coffee-tree** is a sparsely branched tree up to 100 feet high, with twice-pinnate leaves which may be up to 3 feet long. The greenish-white flowers are not showy. It may be used as a street tree.

KOELREUTERIA, **Goldenrain-tree.** *K. paniculata,* a 30-foot tree, has much divided, compound leaves and small yellow flowers in large panicles in July, followed by conspicuous bladder-like fruits. It endures drought, heat, and poor soil, but is likely to be killed back in severe winters north of Long Island, N. Y.

LABURNUM, **Golden Chain.** A distinctive and beautiful small tree in climates similar to that of England. It does well in calcareous soils and grows on Long Island, but far from convincingly. The yellow pea-like flowers are produced in long drooping racemes.

L. vulgare is the common species. *L. alpinum* is said to be the hardier.

Lilac, see SYRINGA.

LIQUIDAMBAR, **Sweet Gum.** *L. Styraciflua* is famous for the brilliancy of its fall coloring. The leaves in outline resemble a conventional star. The tree is of pyramidal habit, attaining a height of over 100 feet. It prefers moist, rich soil and is hardy North to Massachusetts.

LIRIODENDRON, **Tulip-tree.** Although the flowers of the tulip-tree (*L. Tulipifera*) are large, their greenish-yellow coloring is not conspicuous and they often pass unnoticed. This is a handsome tree with distinctive foliage, each leaf being notched at the apex. As a forest tree it may develop a trunk free of branches to a height of about 100 feet, and the entire tree occasionally reaches 200 feet. It is not easy to transplant; spring is the best season. A rich, moist soil is preferred for it.

MAGNOLIA. Though many magnolias bloom so early that sometimes the flowers are injured by late frosts, they are among the most conspicuous of flowering trees, with large, often leathery leaves and similarly large flowers. Some species are evergreen. Magnolias are tolerant of city conditions in residential areas. Care is recommended in transplanting, which when necessary should be done (balled and burlapped) in the spring. A well-drained soil is essential.

M. denudata (*conspicua*). Fragrant white flowers 6 inches in diameter. A spreading tree up to 50 feet high, often without a well-defined, central trunk.

M. Soulangeana. A hybrid with large pinkish flowers suffused with purple on the outside, deservedly the most commonly planted of all magnolias. Many garden varieties available, including *Lennei,* more or less shrubby, with reddish-purple flowers which appear later in spring than in others of this group, and often occur again in the fall.

M. stellata, **Starry Magnolia.** Shrubby, but may form a small tree. Blooms when quite small, and very early, so that the flowers seldom escape injury, but one year of perfect bloom makes up for the dozen when the flowers are browned by severe weather.

M. tripetala. Native species; one of the most tropical-appearing trees hardy in north temperate regions. Leaves may be up to 2 feet in length. There is a fine specimen growing in a front yard along a Brooklyn residential street busy with motor traffic.

M. virginiana (*glauca*), **Sweet Bay.** Small native tree of distinctive appearance, evergreen in the South but deciduous in the North. Fragrant white flowers 2 or 3 inches in diameter. Should be more freely used, especially in damp soils.

MALUS (PYRUS). The flowering crab-apples, because of their hardiness, adaptability to a variety of conditions, ease of transplanting and their beauty in spring when loaded with blossoms, are the most valuable of flowering trees. They flower when quite young, and many varieties also produce ornamental fruits in the fall. They may be used as lawn specimens or for mass planting. The nomenclature of the crab-apples sold for ornamental planting is so confused that the safest thing to do is to select from blooming or fruiting varieties growing in a nursery.

M. atrosanguinea. Somewhat taller than *M. floribunda Arnoldiana* (see below). Carmine flowers freely produced; red fruits.

M. baccata, **Siberian Crab-apple.** Ornamental in flower and fruit. About 30 feet high, spreading to 40 feet in diameter.

M. floribunda Arnoldiana. Originated in the Arnold Arboretum as a seedling of *M. floribunda* (*pulcherrima*). Probably many of the plants sold under this name are in turn seedlings and different from the parent. Tree rather bushy, about 12 feet high; flowers semi-double, pink; fruit yellow. *M. floribunda Scheideckeri,* semi-double pink flowers and a pyramidal habit of growth.

M. ioensis plena, **Bechtel's Crab.** Said to be a development of the prairie crab-apple. Double pink flowers resembling small roses. Very susceptible to apple rust, hence should not be planted where red cedars abound. (Red cedar is the alternate host for the fungus causing apple rust.)

M. Niedzwetzkyana. As remarkable as its name. Roots, wood, leaves, flowers, and fruit all tinged with reddish-purple. Poorly shaped when young.

Maple, see ACER.

OXYDENDRUM, **Sorrel Tree.** *O. arboreum* is a small tree not commonly planted, but useful for acid-soil areas in partial shade. Small greenish-white flowers are produced in late summer in clusters on one-sided racemes at the tips of the branches; colors beautifully in the fall.

PLATANUS, **Buttonball, Plane Tree, Sycamore.** These are handsome, quick-growing trees, with leaves resembling maple. The London plane is much used for street planting. The smooth bark which peels off in sheets during late summer is characteristic; though the phenomenon is sometimes productive of frantic appeals from the uninitiated who think something is wrong with their trees.

P. acerifolia, **London Plane.** The one sold in greatest quantity—usually under the name *P. orientalis.* Supposed to be a hybrid between *P. orientalis* and *P. occidentalis.* Grows to 100 feet and is most tolerant of city life.

P. occidentalis. Capable of forming a massive tree up to 170 feet high. Hardy north to Ottawa but, unfortunately, is subject to a disfiguring disease.

POPULUS, **Poplar, Cottonwood.** Fast-growing trees, seldom particular as to soil, the poplars and cottonwoods are useful and decorative, but not always desirable as permanent subjects.

P. alba pyramidalis (Bolleana), **Bolle's Poplar.** Variety of the white poplar with fastigiate or columnar habit similar to that of the better-known Lombardy poplar. Leaves shining and green above, silvery below.

P. balsamifera (deltoides), **Cottonwood.** Native over much of North America, from Quebec to Maryland and west to the great plains. Grows into a large tree with tremulous leaves, but often becomes a nuisance because of the masses of cotton shed from the pistillate flowers in early summer.

P. nigra italica, **Lombardy Poplar.** Much used to provide accent points in landscape composition. A quick-grower, a soil robber, and subject to disease.

PRUNUS. The flowering cherries, plums, and peaches belong to this genus. The Japanese cherries are among the most attractive of flowering trees. Some varieties may suffer injury to flower buds if exposed to much sub-zero weather. The varieties **Kwanzan** and **Shirofugen** are among those recommended by the late E. H. Wilson for planting in northern New England. The soil must be well-drained. Height is variable according to variety.

P. cerasifera Pissardi, **Purple-leaf Plum.** Grown mainly for its foliage. Forms a tree 15 or more feet high; seems to do best in calcareous soils.

P. Persica, **Peach.** Double-flowered varieties, obtainable in white, pink, and crimson, of great value for garden display. White form especially free-flowering and charming.

P. serrulata, **Japanese Cherry.** Large-flowered forms. Many garden varieties, nearly all of them worth growing. Following are all good. **Amanogawa:** Narrow, upright habit of growth; useful for accent where a small tree is desired; upright branches laden with clusters of large, fragrant, semi-double pink flowers; in full bloom May 4 in Brooklyn, N. Y. **Kwanzan** (also known as **Fugenzo** and as **James H. Veitch**): Large, double, rose-pink flowers; also in full bloom about May 4. (If I were restricted to one Japanese cherry I think I should choose this one.) **Fujizan:** Large, snow-white, semi-double flowers in mid-April. **Naden:** Semi-double, pink, free-flowering; full bloom about April 20; young leaves reddish; strong grower. **Ruth Wohlert:** Semi-double, pink, free-flowering; in full bloom May 4; a vigorous, upright grower. **Shirofugen:** Double flowers, pinkish-white; a strong grower, blooming late.

P. serrulata sachalinensis (P. Sargentii). A handsome variety, capable of reaching 80 feet in its natural habitat. Flowers single, pinkish, more than 1 inch across.

P. subhirtella, **Spring Cherry.** A slender-twigged tree, smothered with comparatively small pink flowers which appear in advance of the leaves in early spring (Plate IV). Variety *autumnalis* blooms in the fall as well as in spring; variety *pendula,* a weeping form obtainable either as a "standard" grafted upon a straight stem 4 to 6 feet high, or grafted low so that it forms a more or less pyramidal weeping tree—the latter preferable except for special purposes where a standard is wanted. *P. subhirtella* and its varieties all attractive.

PSEUDOLARIX, **Golden Larch.** *P. amabilis (Kaempferi* or *Fortunei)* is the only species of this Chinese tree which, though a conifer, sheds its long needles in autumn. It is a handsome tree, sometimes reaching more than 100 feet, well adapted for planting as a specimen. It requires a moist, well-drained soil in an open situation and is hardy in Massachusetts.

QUERCUS, **Oak.** Mainly large and long-lived trees. Contrary to a popular impression, most of the oaks planted are not slow growers once they have become established. They should be set out in the spring, preferably with a good ball of earth about their roots.

Q. alba, **White Oak.** Thrives in a calcareous soil. Of rugged appearance, the branches widely spreading. Needs plenty of room for its best development. Grows up to 100 feet.

Q. coccinea, **Scarlet Oak.** A round-headed tree which grows to 80 feet, thriving in the rather sandy soils of Long Island. Brilliant in the fall with its scarlet leaves.

Q. palustris, **Pin Oak.** One of the easiest to transplant; endures city conditions. Forms a pyramidal head with the lower branches gracefully drooping. Prefers a moist soil and grows to 100 feet.

Q. Phellos, **Willow Oak.** A fine tree for the Southeast. Young branches may be killed back in severe winters on Long Island. Long, willow-like leaves, not lobed as in most oaks. Prefers moist soil and grows to about 60 feet.

ROBINIA, **Locust.** *R. Pseudoacacia,* while it has beautiful and highly fragrant flowers, handsome foliage (except just after the first frost of autumn) and a picturesque habit when aged, is anathematized by many because of its habit of suckering and seeding. Other defects are the brittleness of its young branches, which litter the ground after a summer storm; the poisonous nature of its bark, etc., and the fact that it is attacked by borers. On the other hand, it is quick growing, produces excellent lumber for fence posts, will thrive in poor soil, is hardy far north, and does not inhibit the growth of lawn grasses in its shade. It grows to about 80 feet. There are many varieties of this species.

SALIX, **Willow.** Trees especially suitable for wet soil or for waterside planting are to be found among the willows. They are easily transplanted, and branches merely pushed into moist soil often will grow.

S. alba, **White Willow.** A large, quick-growing tree (to 75 feet) which does not demand an especially moist soil. A form called variety *sericea* (or *splendens* or *regalis*), has leaves which are even more silvery-white than those of the type.

S. babylonica, **Weeping Willow.** Useful for waterside planting. Reaches 40 feet. Several garden forms, among them variety *crispa* or *annularis* with curly leaves.

S. discolor, **Pussy Willow.** Grows well in city back yards, forming a shrub or small tree up to 20 feet. Attacked by boring insects.

S. elegantissima, **Thurlow's Weeping Willow.** Larger than *S. babylonica* and said to be hardier.

S. pentandra, **Laurel-leaf Willow.** Ornamental tree about 50 feet high, with shining, dark green leaves; valuable for planting in wet ground.

SOPHORA, **Pagoda Tree, Chinese Scholar-tree.** *S. japonica,* the best known species, growing to 60 feet, ought to be planted more freely, for it endures smoke and dust and seems to be untouched by insects. It has clean, glossy, pinnate leaves and small, yellowish-white, pea-shaped flowers in large panicles during summer. There is a pendulous variety with tortuous branches.

SORBUS, **Mountain Ash.** This group includes several hardy American, Asiatic, and European trees grown for their ornamental fruits which are much favored by birds.

S. Aucuparia, **Rowan, European Mountain Ash.** A handsome tree, about 40 feet high, with pinnate leaves and beautiful clusters of glossy red berries at the tips of the branches. Especially valuable for planting in cold climates; has also been used with striking results as a street tree in a London suburb, but has not thriven in the Brooklyn Botanic Garden. Should be planted in preference to the native species in regions where it will grow. Many horticultural forms, differing in habit of growth, color or fruit, etc.

S. decora. Most showy of the native mountain ashes, forming a tree about 40 feet high; similar to the preceding. Occurs as a wilding as far north as Labrador.

S. hybrida. A natural hybrid between *S. Aucuparia* and *S. intermedia,* sometimes listed in catalogs as *S. quercifolia* (referring to the oak-like leaves). Gives promise of being more amenable to cultivation than *S. Aucuparia.* Upright habit of growth; holds its fruits into November.

STYRAX, **Snowbell, Storax.** *S. japonica* is the hardiest species, though it may be killed back on Long Island, N. Y., by abnormally severe winters. In mild climates it can be trained into a tree capable of reaching a height of 30 feet; charming when covered with its pendent, snowdrop-like flowers in June and July.

SYRINGA, **Lilac.** *S. japonica,* **Japanese Tree Lilac,** which is hardy in Ottawa, blooms in June with abundant creamy-white flowers in panicles.

It may need encouragement, in the way of removing the lower branches, to make it assume a tree-like form, when it may reach 30 feet in height. (See also DECIDUOUS SHRUBS.)

TILIA, **Basswood, Linden.** These are handsome symmetrical trees which, however, are not recommended for hot dry situations. They transplant easily even as large trees. Leaves are heart-shaped and toothed; flowers, though inconspicuous, are fragrant in early summer.

The first three lindens listed below are more tolerant of drought than some, and usually may be depended upon to retain their leaves all summer. This is more than can be said for the American linden (*T. americana*), which is liable to lose its leaves in August, especially when grown in a hot dry city.

T. cordata, **Small-leaved Linden.** European species which may reach 100 feet. May be clipped to formal shapes.

T. petiolaris, **Weeping White Linden.** Branches somewhat drooping; undersides of the leaves white and woolly.

T. tomentosa, **White Linden.** Similar to *T. petiolaris,* but with upright branches. Nectar of these two species said to be poisonous to bees.

T. vulgaris. A hybrid, said to be one of the best for general planting and for a street tree. Reaches a height of more than 100 feet.

ULMUS, **Elm.** The elms are among the most popular of shade trees, although they are not by any means free from insect and fungous pests. The American elm seems to be particularly unfortunate, being subject to the elm leaf-beetle, canker worm, and, in recent years, the Dutch elm-disease. In many regions the native elms are unsightly by midsummer, owing to attacks by a lace-bug similar to that which attacks rhododendrons. Some of the exotic species are favored hosts of leafhoppers. No one disputes the beauty of a healthy American elm, but under the circumstances one feels hesitant about recommending it for planting.

U. americana, **American Elm.** Famed for its graceful shape and for the great age which a healthy specimen may attain. Transplants easily. (I have known trees of 4- or 5-inch caliper to survive transplanting when pulled out of the ground by a team of horses, after the ground had merely been sketchily loosened around their roots.) Requires moist, rich soil to be at its best. Many different forms of American elm recognized.

U. campestris, **English Elm.** Not so handsome a tree as the American elm, but holds its leaves longer in the fall. Considered in England a dangerous tree in congested areas because of its habit of dropping large limbs without warning. Grows more than 100 feet high.

U. glabra, **Scotch Elm.** A handsome tree which grows to more than 100 feet. Many varieties, the best known of which is the **Camperdown Elm,** a pendulous form which usually is grafted to form a high head.

U. pumila, **Siberian Elm,** sometimes called **Chinese Elm.** The alleged beauty of this tree leaves me cold. It has its uses, however, especially if it lives up to the reputation given it by some nurserymen who claim that it will thrive in any kind of soil from Saskatchewan to Arizona. Apparently there are two kinds sold under the name Chinese elm—*U. pumila* and *U. parvifolia.* Rehder applies the name Siberian elm to *U. pumila;* and Chinese elm to *U. parvifolia.* Apart from other differences, the flowers of *U. pumila* appear in the spring before the leaves, while those of *U. parvifolia* are produced in the fall. *U. pumila* is the species which makes rapid growth. There is a record of a 5-foot "whip" (in Pennsylvania) growing to 40 feet high, with a 40-foot spread in 16 years.

EVERGREEN SHRUBS

ARCTOSTAPHYLOS, **Bearberry.** *A. Uva-ursi* is a valuable ground-cover for sandy soils on the acid side, though it is difficult to establish.

Azalea. See RHODODENDRON.

BERBERIS. Some of the evergreen forms are not reliably hardy north of Long Island, N. Y. (See also DECIDUOUS SHRUBS.)

B. Julianae. Shining, narrow, spiny leaves and small yellow flowers in clusters. About 5 feet high.

B. verruculosa. One of the best of the evergreen barberries, usually not exceeding a height of 3 feet, dense of growth, with small, glossy, spiny leaves. Flowers fragrant.

BUXUS, **Boxwood.** The common box is a European tree with hard, almost grainless wood used in making woodcuts. The famous boxwood of southern gardens is a shrubby form of the above. Box has a distinctive odor, pleasing to some, objectionable to others, and to some non-existent!

B. microphylla, **Korean Box.** Hardier than the type but not so ornamental.

B. sempervirens, **Common Box.** Not much grown in this country.

B. sempervirens suffruticosa, **Dwarf Box.** The kind which makes the dense billowy masses of foliage at Mt. Vernon. The best plant for edging beds and walks in regions where it will thrive. Winter protection desirable in vicinity of New York.

CALLUNA, **Heather.** *C. vulgaris* is a typical plant of the moors of northern Europe. In Massachusetts it has become sparingly naturalized. It requires a sunny situation and an acid, sandy, well-drained soil, bountifully supplied with humus. It ordinarily has purplish flowers in August. There is only one species, but it exists in many garden varieties which are valuable for planting on sunny banks if soil conditions are right. Variety *alba* is a white form. The dwarf kinds are suitable for rock-garden planting.

DAPHNE. *D. Cneorum,* **Rose Daphne,** is a handsome shrub about 15 inches high with clusters of sweetly scented rose-pink flowers in the spring and fall. It is as temperamental as a prima donna—thriving like a weed in some gardens and sulking in others. An open, well-drained soil seems to suit it best. *D. Burkwoodii,* sold as Daphne "Somerset," is a hybrid of *D. caucasica* and *D. Cneorum.* It grows to about 3 feet high, has fragrant, blush-pink flowers, and is evergreen in mild climates. It is one of the most valuable introductions of recent years.

ERICA, **Heath.** While few of the heaths are hardy, they thrive, in general, under the same conditions accorded heather. Some species are happiest under semi-boggy conditions. *E. carnea,* **Alpine Heath,** is one of the most ornamental hardy species, growing about 9 inches high and bearing small narrow leaves somewhat like the needles of the hemlock, with pink flowers in early spring. There are many improved garden varieties, useful in the foreground of rhododendron plantings (in the sun) and in the rock garden.

EUONYMUS. This ornamental genus of woody plants contains trees, shrubs, and vines, some evergreen, others deciduous. Climbing evergreen species of *Euonymus* are mentioned in Chapter IX, VINES.

E. japonicus. An upright shrub, much used in England for hedges, but not reliably hardy even on Long Island, N. Y. Variegated-leaved forms available but (in my opinion) less handsome than the type, which has shining dark green foliage.

E. japonicus microphyllus. A shrublet with tiny leaves, useful in the rock garden. Were it not subject to scale, and could it be relied upon to survive severe winters, it would be a valuable plant for edgings.

ILEX, **Holly.** Some of the shrubby evergreen hollies are excellent under the proper conditions. (See also EVERGREEN TREES, p. 79.)

I. crenata, **Japanese Holly.** Grows into a large shrub 10 feet or more high in vicinity of New York, though branches are likely to be killed back 2 or 3 feet in severe winters. Constantly confused with boxwood, because of its appearance. Black berries not ornamental. Variety *convexa* (*bullata*), a dwarf form (about 4 feet) with rounded leaves, still more boxlike; reputed to be hardier. Variety *microphylla,* smaller leaves and lower stature, also hardier.

I. glabra, **Inkberry.** Glossy, dark green leaves, black berries. If possible to propagate easily by means of cuttings, might become a popular hedge plant for northern planting. Seedlings exhibit too much variation in habit of growth. Will thrive in shade, and needs an acid soil.

I. Pernyi. A dwarf shrub with spiny leaves smaller than those of English holly. Will thrive within the same range as the English holly.

KALMIA, **Laurel.** Growing in rocky, acid-soil mountains of eastern United States, *Kalmia latifolia,* the American **Mountain Laurel** (which bears no relation to *Laurus nobilis,* the laurel of Europe) is one of the handsomest of flowering evergreen shrubs. It bears large clusters of pink flowers against shining green leaves in June. In some regions it becomes tree-like. Beside it, the other species occasionally grown, *K. angustifolia,* **Sheep Laurel or Lambkill,** is an insignificant low shrub, bearing small narrow leaves and purplish-rose flowers. To eat it is poisonous to farm animals, and honey made from the nectar of either is poisonous to humans. Cultural needs of *Kalmia* are the same as for *Rhododendron.*

MAHONIA. While the most frequently planted species of *Mahonia* are considered hardy in the East, they thrive better on the west coast, where they are native, or in a climate like that of England. The name **Oregon Grape,** which especially designates *M. nervosa,* is often applied to others in the genus.

M. Aquifolium, **Holly Mahonia, Holly Barberry.** Hardy evergreen shrub about 3 feet high with handsome foliage which, however, is scorched by winter sunshine in severe climates. Should therefore be planted in shady location. Young shoots admirable as Christmas decorations; should be cut freely to keep the bush compact and shapely. Try in a limy soil.

M. repens. Low-growing shrub (1 foot high); foliage less apt to brown in winter.

OSMANTHUS. *O. ilicifolius* is a shrub or small tree up to 20 feet high, with spiny lustrous leaves which resemble those of English holly. It endures city conditions but is not reliably hardy in and about New York City.

PACHYSANDRA, **Japanese Spurge.** *P. terminalis* forms a dense evergreen ground-cover. It will grow in sun or shade and is useful for clothing the ground beneath trees where grass will not thrive.

PIERIS, **Andromeda.** These shrubs require the same conditions as *Rhododendron.* The flower buds are formed in the fall and open the following spring.

P. floribunda. Native species, 3 to 4 feet high, hardier but perhaps not quite so attractive as its Japanese cousin. Spikes of small white flowers more boldly displayed than those of the following.

P. japonica. Taller and more tolerant of city conditions than native andromeda. Foliage glossy and handsome, assuming reddish and bronzy tints in winter. Injured if long exposed to sub-zero temperatures.

RHODODENDRON. The botanists now include *Azalea* in the genus *Rhododendron,* but it is likely that for many years gardeners will continue to think of them as two separate groups—*Azalea* containing the deciduous kinds and the comparatively small-leaved forms offered under the names

A. amoena, A. ledifolia, A. Hinodegiri, etc., and *Rhododendron,* the large-leaved evergreen kinds.

Generally speaking, azaleas and rhododendrons require much the same cultural conditions. While they will thrive in the sun, both groups, especially rhododendrons, are more appropriately placed in partial shade, and look happiest when the shade is provided by thin woodland.

Soil. A limy soil is anathema to the azaleas and rhododendrons which are commonly cultivated in this country, and it is useless to expect them to grow in such a soil. Unless it is definitely known that the soil is acid, its condition should be determined with a soil-testing outfit (obtainable from any large seed store) or with litmus paper before planting is begun. If it is not too calcareous, it may be fitted for rhododendrons by mixing with it, in liberal amounts, acid humus-forming materials such as peat-moss or partly decayed oak leaves; or by applying flowers of sulphur—making the initial dressing at the rate of ¼ pound to a square yard. Under some circumstances it may be desirable to apply both remedies. If, after the plants are set out, they do not appear to be thriving, or if the leaves are yellowish, test the soil again: it may be that it has reverted to a condition approaching alkaline and that it needs more attention.

The texture of the soil for rhododendrons should be loamy, and it should be liberally supplied with humus, especially in the upper 6 to 9 inches.

Protection. Evergreen rhododendrons should be protected from winter winds and, to some extent, from winter sunshine. They are therefore best planted on the north side of a dwelling with a windbreak of pines or other coniferous evergreens. If they are planted in the open, or on the south side of the house, artificial shade and shelter may be provided by placing ever-green boughs about them. When there is a glut in the Christmas-tree market, ideal material for covering usually can be obtained on December 26, merely for the cost of hauling the trees. It is not too late to apply the protective covering around Christmas time, because most of the damage is brought about by the strong sun of early March causing evaporation of moisture from the leaves at a time when the roots are unable to replenish it because of the frozen ground.

It is a good practice to mulch the soil with 6 inches to 2 feet of newly fallen leaves, which will conserve moisture and prevent the soil from freezing so deeply. Oak leaves are preferable, as they decay slowly, and tend to increase the acidity of the soil. If leaves such as maple or linden must be used it is well to use acid peatmoss as part of the mulch. When the winter mulch is quite thick, most of it should be removed in the spring, leaving only from 4 to 6 inches, which should be retained throughout the whole year to smother weeds, conserve moisture, and shade the soil. Rhododendrons are surface rooters and if the ground is cultivated in the usual way many of their roots will be cut off with the hoe. The decay of the mulch will help to provide the nutrients which the plants need.

Fertilizers for rhododendrons. If the leaves are yellowish and the cause is not an alkaline soil, lack of moisture, or poor underdrainage, the fault may be a lack of proper plant food in the soil. A mixture of rotted cow manure and acid peatmoss, half-and-half, applied in a layer 3 inches thick, may correct the deficiency. Dr. C. H. Connors of the New Jersey Agricultural Experiment Station suggests the formula used for the cultivated blueberry: Sulphate of ammonia, 17 pounds; dried blood, 23 pounds; steamed bone, 34 pounds; raw ground phosphate rock, 34 pounds; 28-percent potash, 17 pounds, or 40- to 50-percent potash, 10 pounds. This is to be applied at the rate of 1 pound to 72 square feet. Before making up this rather complicated mixture I would suggest trying an application of cottonseed meal or tankage at the rate of ½ to 1 pound to 20 square feet. In some soils rhododendrons are benefited by the application of magnesium sulphate (Epsom salts), 1 pound to 200 square feet.

Pruning. Pruning is seldom necessary for rhododendrons except that, in the case of hybrids, any shoots which originate beneath the ground from the understock on which hybrids are commonly grafted should be cut off. If for any reason it is necessary to cut back rhododendrons it may be done without fear that buds will not arise from old wood. Many of the plants collected from the mountains in the South and sold for northern gardens are old bushes which have been pruned to the ground by forest fires and have started up again from basal shoots. If rhododendrons exceed the space assigned them, the best time to prune them is in the spring just before the new leaf growth starts. In some varieties this may mean the sacrifice of a display of blooms for one season if the new growth starts before, or simultaneously with, the opening of the flowers.

If time is available, the flowers should be removed when they have faded, to prevent the formation of seeds. This conserves the plant's energies.

Pests. Rhododendrons and azaleas, especially those which are growing in sunny situations, are subject to attacks by related species of lace bugs. The eggs of the rhododendron lace bug hatch early in May and the eggs of the azalea lace bug hatch toward the end of May. These pests feed on the underside of the leaves by puncturing the tissue and sucking the sap. Both kinds may be controlled by spraying them with nicotine sulphate and soap —½ ounce of the former and 2 ounces of soap flakes to 3 gallons of water. Repeat in about 2 weeks.

Selection of species and varieties. There are three native species of *Rhododendron* which are commonly grown in gardens:

R. carolinianum, from the mountains of North Carolina, is capable of attaining a height of 6 feet, but in gardens is usually seen as a bush 2 to 3 feet high. The flowers are in clusters, pale rose in color, produced in late May. It is valuable for planting in the foreground of large rhododendrons. Young plants are effective in the rock garden but ultimately are apt to grow too tall except for gardens of great size.

R. catawbiense, found growing wild in the mountains from Pennsylvania to Georgia, is a stronger grower, with larger (3- to 6-inch) leaves. The flowers are purplish.

R. maximum, with large clusters of pink flowers, occurs as a wilding from Nova Scotia and Ontario to Georgia. It is capable of attaining a height of 30 feet when planted in a favorable location. Both *R. catawbiense* and *R. maximum* are excellent in thin woodland where they will take care of themselves without much attention from the gardener. *R. maximum* is sometimes inclined to be a shy bloomer, but is worth growing for the beauty of its foliage.

Many of the most handsome hybrid rhododendrons are unsatisfactory in the northern states because of their lack of winter hardiness. The following, which are among the hardiest varieties and hybrids, are known to thrive in the vicinity of Boston.

White—*album elegans,* Boule de Neige, *catawbiense album.*
Purple—*purpureum elegans, Everestianum* (lavender).
Pink—Abraham Lincoln, Lady Armstrong, Mrs. C. S. Sargent, *roseum elegans.*
Red—*atrosanguineum,* Caractacus.

The following which bloom in early spring are good forms of the evergreen or semi-evergreen types with comparatively small leaves, usually listed by nurserymen under Azalea:

Hinodegiri, vivid carmine; one of the most popular kinds;
Hinomayo, similar to the above but with soft pink flowers;
mucronatum (ledifolium of nurseries), pure white, strong grower;
obtusum Kaempferi, salmon red to orange red; upright habit;
lilacina, large single lilac-colored blooms;
yedoense (yodogawa), light purple. Good when planted alone. Its color makes it difficult to associate it with other flowering plants.

The Japanese Kurume azaleas are delightful in regions where the winters are not too severe. We have experienced trouble in the attempt to establish them in the Brooklyn Botanic Garden.

There are numerous species of alpine rhododendrons of inestimable value for rock garden planting. These will be in great demand when they become better known, if the specialists will tell us how to treat them to make them thrive. For deciduous azaleas, see Rhododendron, page 102.

SANTOLINA. *S. Chamaecyparissus,* **Lavender-cotton,** is a shrub about 2 feet high, grown mainly for the beauty of its silvery-gray foliage. It seldom survives the winter outdoors on Long Island.

Dwarf evergreen conifers (see Chapter VIII).

DECIDUOUS SHRUBS

ABELIA. *A. grandiflora,* although it is an evergreen in favored climates, is deciduous on Long Island, N. Y., and may be killed to the ground in severe winters. It has small glossy leaves and little shell-pink flowers produced throughout the summer.

ACER. *A. palmatum.* **Japanese Maple.** There are many garden forms of this species, usually shrub-like in habit, though occasionally they develop into small trees. These maples exhibit great variation in foliage characters. In the variety *dissectum* the leaves are so divided as to be almost thread-like. It is a good plan when purchasing them to select desirable forms in a nursery rather than from catalog descriptions.

AESCULUS (PAVIA). *A. parviflora,* **Dwarf Buckeye,** apart from its intrinsic merits, is of great value because of its blooming in July when flowering shrubs are scarce. It makes a clump broader than high (6 feet), with horsechestnut-like foliage and 12-inch spikes of white flowers.

ARONIA, **Chokeberry.** *A. arbutifolia,* **Red Chokeberry,** is a native shrub about 6 feet high grown for its decorative fruits. Moist soil is preferred.

Azalea, see RHODODENDRON.

BERBERIS, **Barberry.** There are scores of species of *Berberis,* and many hybrids raised mostly by English growers. Some species, especially *vulgaris,* are taboo in wheat-growing regions because they carry one stage of the wheat rust. Most barberries are grown mainly for their autumn foliage and the display of berries in fall and winter. (See also EVERGREEN SHRUBS.)

B. aggregata Prattii. Up to 10 feet, with salmon-red berries in drooping clusters.

B. Thunbergii. Much used as a hedge plant; especially beautiful in early spring, when the red berries (which usually hang on all winter), pale yellow flowers, and opening growth buds may be seen together. Slowly forms a dense, spiny bush about 6 feet high and 8 feet through. Variety *atropurpurea* has reddish foliage; variety *minor,* **Box Barberry,** kept less than a foot in height by clipping, sometimes used as an edging shrub; variety *pluriflora* (*erecta*), **Truehedge Columnberry,** has dense, upright growth. *B. mentorensis* is a hybrid of *B. Thunbergii* and *B. Julianae;* compact and almost evergreen.

B. Vernae. Graceful shrub, up to 6 feet high and 12 feet in diameter; small yellow flowers in June and a wealth of salmon berries in the fall.

B. Wilsonae. Not reliably hardy on Long Isand, but farther south should be valuable both as a specimen and for hedges. One of the most graceful and has handsome foliage.

BUDDLEIA, Summer-lilac, Butterfly-bush. Most of the buddleias grown outdoors in the North are varieties of *B. Davidi* (*variabilis*), which usually is killed nearly to the ground after zero temperatures. This habit, however, does not affect its value as a garden plant, because the new shoots from the base produce flowers in terminal panicles 6 inches or more long during the current season. A more recent introduction is the hardier *B. alternifolia,* which displays its flowers in short clusters along the branches of the preceding year. The name "butterfly-bush" is applied because during daylight hours butterflies may almost always be seen around the bushes.

In localities where the tops freeze back, the roots and lower parts of the branches should be protected by a mulch of straw or hay.

B. alternifolia. May grow to 12 or more feet high; a handsome, comparatively small-leaved shrub with small lilac-purple flowers.

B. Davidi (*variabilis*). An extremely variable species, its height determined largely by the character of the winter. If not killed back, may grow to 16 feet or even more. Flowers usually of some tone of lilac with an orange throat. Variety *Veitchiana,* strong grower, early-blooming, with mauve flowers; *magnifica,* rose-purple flowers. **Fascinating,** cattleya pink; and **Flaming Violet,** brilliant purple, are newcomers. **Ile de France** is a compact variety good for small gardens.

CALLICARPA, Beauty-berry. *C. japonica* is one of the best species in this genus. It is grown mainly for its lavender-blue berries, which are produced in bunches along the shoots of the current season. Thus, even if killed to the ground in a severe winter, it will bear flowers and berries the following summer.

CARYOPTERIS. *C. incana,* **Blue Spirea,** is not a spirea and is not true blue. It is valuable because of its time of blooming—September and October. On Long Island it kills to the ground in severe winters and therefore should be given a sheltered situation. The flowers are small and lavenderish in color, the leaves gray-green.

CHAENOMELES (CYDONIA), Flowering Quince. Although recognized by botanists as the genus *Chaenomeles,* the flowering quinces are generally listed in catalogs as *Cydonia.* These hardy shrubs with rose-like flowers usually in tones of scarlet bloom in early spring before the leaves appear. Often on warm winter days they will also open their buds. They may be trained as wall shrubs, used for mass planting in shrubbery, or set out as specimens on the lawn.

C. lagenaria (*Cydonia japonica*), **Japanese Quince.** Grows to about 6 feet. Flowers orange-scarlet, the size of apple-blossoms. Color forms available in white, salmon, red, pink, and variegated. Variety *Simoni,* larger flowers of dark crimson. (I have seen this in bloom on November 15 after the leaves were gone.)

C. *japonica* (*Cydonia Maulei*), **Dwarf Japanese Quince.** Grows to about 3 feet, bearing clusters of orange-scarlet flowers. Variety *alpina,* more or less prostrate with much smaller leaves.

CLETHRA, **Sweet Pepper-bush.** C. *alnifolia* has sweet-scented white flowers in erect racemes, from July to September. It grows about 6 feet high, preferring moist soil and some shade.

CORNUS, **Dogwood.** Several of the native dogwoods are useful for mass planting. C. *stolonifera* is also valuable for the winter effect given by its red twigs. Variety *flaviramea* (*lutea*) has greenish-yellow twigs. The species usually grows to about 6 feet; its variety a little lower.

COTINUS. C. *coggygria* (*Rhus Cotinus*), the **Smoke-tree,** is conspicuous when covered with the hairy fruit clusters, which have a smoky appearance. It grows about 15 feet high and needs well-drained soil.

COTONEASTER. A chapter could be written dealing with the coto-neasters. Some species, such as *adpressa, horizontalis,* and *microphylla,* are evergreen or semi-evergreen in favored situations. Others, such as *Dielsiana* and *hupehensis,* are definitely deciduous. They all need a sunny position and a well-drained soil.

C. *adpressa.* Creeping, semi-evergreen, with large scarlet berries.

C. *Dielsiana.* A graceful shrub about 8 feet high, with small glossy leaves.

C. *horizontalis.* Grows 2 to 3 feet high and expands laterally almost in-definitely. Beautiful at all seasons, holding its small roundish leaves until late; especially handsome when sprinkled with scarlet berries.

C. *hupehensis.* Small showy white flowers and bright crimson fruits on a bush about 5 feet high.

C. *racemiflora songarica.* Broadly-spreading shrub about 6 feet high with grayish foliage and coral-red berries.

C. *Zabellii miniata.* Grows 6 to 8 feet, with slender branches weighted with bright orange-scarlet berries together with yellow foliage in the fall. A showy variety hardy in southern New York.

CLERODENDRON. C. *trichotomum* is an attractive shrub which pro-duces its fragrant flowers over a long period in summer and early fall. The white petals are conspicuous against the reddish calices. If zero weather is experienced the bush may be killed to the ground, but usually the roots survive and send up new shoots the following spring. (Plate V.)

CYTISUS, **Broom.** In general, the brooms are floriferous shrubs with pea-like flowers, and are excellent for planting in poor sandy soil in dry sunny situations. Unfortunately, they are not resistant to severe winters. Those listed below are among the hardiest of the upright shrubby varieties.

C. *nigricans.* Usually about 3 feet high with long slender racemes of yellow flowers in June and July. Hardy on Long Island, N. Y.

C. praecox. A hybrid form, almost leafless, with creamy-white flowers freely produced in May. Variety *albus* has white flowers, and the growth is dwarfer and not so dense. *C. praecox* and its varieties safest with winter protection wherever zero weather may be experienced.

C. scoparius, **Scotch Broom.** Behaves peculiarly in respect to winter hardiness. Has become naturalized in parts of Nova Scotia, and survives the winter without protection at Poughkeepsie, N. Y., which experiences much lower temperatures than Brooklyn, where it is killed back unless carefully protected. May grow to a height of 10 feet and becomes "leggy" with age. Flowers yellow, usually produced singly all along the almost leafless branches of the preceding year. Variety *Andreanus* less hardy; has dark crimson markings on its yellow flowers.

DAPHNE. The only deciduous daphne commonly offered by nurserymen is *D. Mezereum,* an upright shrub (4 feet) with small purplish flowers before the leaves. Its berries are scarlet and ornamental. There is a white-flowered variety for those who are distressed by the almost-magenta flowers of the type. *D. Genkwa,* **Lilac Daphne,** is difficult to obtain, not reliably hardy, and sometimes dies for no apparent reason. It is, however, worth striving for by those who like the less common shrubs.

DEUTZIA. Easily-grown shrubs varying in height from 3 to 10 feet, deutzias are valuable for their many small flowers in spring.

D. gracilis. Grows to 3 feet or more, its many arching branches covered with white flowers in May. Can be used to make a delightful low hedge.

D. scabra. Strong upright shrub, 8 feet high; white flowers tinged with pink. Variety **Pride of Rochester** even stronger and may reach a height of 10 feet; flowers pink and white.

EUONYMUS. *E. alatus,* **Winged Euonymus,** has curious flat corky projections on the branches. It is grown mainly for its brilliant scarlet foliage in the autumn. Variety *compactus* is valuable for use as a hedge shrub.

EXOCHORDA, **Pearl-bush.** The common name comes from the globular flower buds. *E. Giraldii Wilsonii* grows to a height of 10 feet and has large pure white flowers in May. It needs a moist soil for best results.

FORSYTHIA, **Golden Bell.** Few shrubs can endure neglect and come up smiling in the manner of forsythia, though in severe winters with much sub-zero weather the flower buds, formed in the fall, may be killed. Forsythia is one of the easiest shrubs to force into bloom when branches are cut and placed in water indoors. This should be done after they have experienced a few weeks of freezing weather.

F. intermedia. About 8 feet high, the arching branches covered with yellow flowers in early April before the leaves appear. Variety *spectabilis,* flowers of deeper yellow, more densely disposed.

F. suspensa. Long slender drooping branches and rather pale yellow flowers. Can be trained as a vine on arches, pergolas, etc., reaching a height of 15 or more feet. Handsome when planted at the top of a high retaining wall and its branches allowed to trail down.

HAMAMELIS, **Witch-hazel.** These are interesting shrubs which produce their spidery flowers of 4 strap-shaped yellow petals either in late fall (*virginiana*) or late winter (*japonica, mollis,* and *vernalis*). They are valuable for planting in moist soil and will endure some shade.

H. japonica. Blooms in March and may reach 20 feet in height.

H. mollis. Most showy of all, but rather rare in gardens. Golden-yellow blooms may open in February if a mild spell is experienced.

H. vernalis. A winter-blooming native of the South.

H. virginiana. Native to the northeastern states; blooms in the late fall.

HIBISCUS, **Rose of Sharon.** The ordinary rose of Sharon (*H. syriacus*) has flowers of an unpleasing shade of purple and there are many garden lovers who dislike it. It is valuable for its August blooming, however, and there are varieties, both single and double-flowered, with unobjectionable coloring. Because of its habit of blooming on shoots of the current season it is commonly recommended to cut it back every spring. If this is done the result is long, strong shoots clothed with blossoms, but one destroys whatever claim the bush may have to a pleasing habit of growth. Unpruned specimens reach a height of 12 feet (Plate XXVIII). The following are among the varieties listed in catalogs: **Boule de Feu,** double red; **Joan of Arc,** double white; **Lady Stanley,** white tinted with rose; and **Paeoniflora,** white with a red center.

HYDRANGEA. Most of the hydrangeas are coarse, showy bushes bearing large compact clusters composed of many long-lasting flowers.

H. arborescens grandiflora, **Hills of Snow.** A rather straggly bush, up to 6 feet high, with snowball-like flower clusters in July and August. Needs a rather moist but well-drained soil, and partial shade. Cut back before growth starts in spring. Hardy in Ottawa.

H. macrophylla (*opuloides*). Source of the so-called "French" hydrangeas, much used for forcing by florists, also valuable for outdoor planting where winters are not too severe. Thrives near the seashore. Some varieties fail to blossom if cut back severely in spring. May be damaged by low temperatures, therefore on Long Island and northward it is safer to protect the canes in winter. (See Chapter XXVIII, WINTER PROTECTION.) Flowers of some varieties are pink in limy soils; blue in acid.

H. paniculata. Pyramidal heads of not-very-showy fertile flowers, intermixed with conspicuous sterile flowers with white sepals. In variety *grandiflora* ("Pee-gee" Hydrangea), fertile flowers entirely replaced with the sterile kind, making inflorescence more showy. Both kinds should have the shoots of the preceding year cut back to about two buds if large flower heads are required. Pee-gee hydrangea obtainable in bush form and also trained as a standard. Hardy in cold climates.

ILEX. *I. verticillata,* **Winterberry** or **Black Alder,** stands out among the deciduous hollies, by reason of its hardiness and brilliant display of red berries held through the winter. Both pistillate and staminate forms must be planted in proximity to ensure a crop of fruits. It grows 6 to 8 feet high, and requires a moist soil. *I. serrata* has smaller berries, produced in great profusion, but they are greedily eaten by birds almost as soon as they are ripe.

KERRIA. In regions where the winters are not severe, the green leafless shoots are attractive during the cold months. *K. japonica* has single, yellow flowers. The double-flowered form (*pleniflora*) is a little more vigorous, reaching about 5 feet. There is a lower-growing kind with leaves margined with silver.

KOLKWITZIA, **Beauty-bush.** I realize I am in a minority, but I simply cannot work up any great enthusiasm for this much-publicized shrub. I think its relatives, the weigelas, have greater value in the garden. Maybe I am prejudiced because of my intense dislike for the feeling of the hairy seed pods. Usually, after planting, one has to wait three or four years before it blooms. However, *Kolkwitzia amabilis* is hardy and of a graceful habit. Its pentstemon-like flowers, pink with yellow markings in the throat, are abundantly produced on the arching branches.

LESPEDEZA, **Bush Clover.** The shrubby lespedezas from Japan which are commonly used in ornamental horticulture behave as herbaceous perennials in severe climates because their stems are killed to the ground in winter. This does not prevent the production of a crop of flowers, because they are late bloomers and the flowers are produced on shoots of the current year.

L. japonica. White pea-like blossoms on a graceful shrub which becomes 3 feet high by flowering time (late September) if cut to the ground in spring.

L. formosa (Sieboldi) (Desmodium penduliflorum). Similar, but blooms a little earlier with reddish-purple flowers.

LIGUSTRUM, **Privet.** Some species are best known as hedge plants, but all may also be used in massed shrub plantings. The odor of the flowers is obnoxious.

L. amurense. **Amur River Privet.** Hardier than the California privet and should be used in preference in cold climates.

L. obtusifolium Regelianum, **Regel's Privet.** About 8 feet high, with spreading branches. Attractive in bloom with small racemes of not-too-ill-smelling white flowers. Bedecked in fall with clusters of small grayish berries.

L. ovalifolium, **California Privet.** So much used as a hedge plant that in some quarters "hedge" is believed to be its common name. Makes a handsome shrub 15 to 20 feet high with glossy foliage and white flowers with a sickening odor. May be killed to the ground during severe winters on Long Island.

L. vulgare, **Common Privet.** Hardy, with comparatively narrow, pointed leaves; not particularly symmetrical. Handsome, glossy, black fruits in clusters like small bunches of small grapes.

LONICERA, **Honeysuckle.** The bush honeysuckles are much in demand for mass planting. Their fruits are eaten by birds.

L. fragrantissima, **Winter Honeysuckle.** Flowers not showy but fragrant and come in February and March when anything in the way of outdoor blossoms is hailed with delight. Handsome foliage on a shapely bush 6 or more feet high.

L. Korolkowii floribunda. Bluish-gray foliage, small pink flowers and red berries. May grow 15 feet high and nearly twice as much across.

L. Maackii podocarpa. Another tremendous shrub, which assumes somewhat the same shape as the top of a "vase-form" elm. Flowers white; berries glossy, bright red and, with the leaves, remain on the bushes into November.

L. minutiflora. An upright-growing hybrid about 9 feet high with pale orange-colored berries.

L. pileata. Almost evergreen on Long Island. Low-growing (about 2 feet) with spreading branches and purple fruits.

L. tatarica, **Tartarian Honeysuckle.** Flowers fairly conspicuous and, in the type, bright pink, varying from white to rose-pink in varieties and hybrids. Fruits produced in summer, in some varieties red, in others yellow. Useful, well-known shrub growing up to 10 feet high, showy in flower and fruit and of ironclad hardiness.

PHILADELPHUS, **Mockorange.** *P. coronarius* is an old-fashioned shrub, up to 10 feet high, with fragrant, snow-white flowers. Some of the hybrids of this and other species are very attractive. **Atlas,** 8 feet tall, has large single flowers; **Avalanche** has semi-double fragrant white flowers on a bush 6 feet high; **Belle Etoile,** white flowers with a purple center; **Manteau d'Hermine** is comparatively dwarf, 2-3 feet; **Virginal** has semi-double flowers of pure white, approaching 2 inches in diameter, and appearing, not only in a grand display in June, but also on and off until frost.

PRUNUS. Besides the flowering trees, the genus containing the stone-fruits includes a number of showy-flowered shrubs. The Nanking cherry and flowering almond are much beloved by borers, and a close watch should be kept on the bushes so that the insects may be discovered and killed before they have done much damage.

P. maritima, **Beach Plum.** A rather unsymmetrical bush up to 10 feet high, valuable for seashore locations. Produces myriads of small white flowers in May, followed by purplish fruits which may be used for preserves.

P. tomentosa, **Nanking Cherry.** Small pink flowers changing to white in early May. Fruits, like small red cherries, ornamental (if left uneaten by birds), and said to make good wine; do not taste bad when eaten from the hand. May grow to 10 feet; hardy North.

P. triloba plena, **Flowering Almond.** Pompon-like pink flowers studded along the branches before the leaves appear. May attain a height of 10 feet, but if desired to keep it low, may be cut back a foot or so immediately after blooming. In England sometimes used as a wall shrub. May be obtained from nurserymen either as a bush or grafted on a tall stem to form a standard.

RHODODENDRON, **Azalea.** The deciduous kinds, both the species which are hardy, and the so-called "Ghent" and "mollis" hybrids, which are more often used for forcing, are quite showy. The hybrids are not commonly offered by nurserymen since the quarantine went into effect. Good forms when and if obtainable are: Anthony Koster, coccinea speciosa, Daviesii, Nancy Waterer, narcissiflora, Raphael de Smet. Soil should be the same as for evergreen rhododendrons, which see.

Among the best species, all natives of eastern United States, are:

R. arborescens. White, June, July. May grow to 18 feet.

R. calendulaceum, **Flame Azalea.** Orange and orange-scarlet, late May.

R. nudiflorum, **Pinxter-bloom.** Pink and fragrant, flowers in April or May. Good either in sun or partial shade.

R. Vaseyi. One of the best, with clear pink flowers early in May.

RHODOTYPOS, **Jetbead.** *R. tetrapetala (kerrioides)* is an unassuming little shrub, about 5 feet high, well able to take care of itself in the shrubbery and increase itself by self-sown seeds. It has pure white flowers in May, followed by seeds the size of small peas arranged in fours, and ultimately turning black and persisting all winter.

RHUS. *R. typhina,* **Staghorn Sumac,** largest and showiest of the American species, is effective when planted in semi-wild surroundings. Characterized by enormous pinnate leaves whose fall coloring is gorgeous, furry brown branches, and heavy conical clusters of velvety dark red berries, it may grow up to 30 feet, though usually is about half this height. The variety *laciniata,* which has deeply incised leaflets, is, if anything, even more striking and well worthy of a place in a large garden. (For *R. Cotinus,* the **Smoke-tree,** see *Cotinus coggygria.*)

RIBES, **Currant.** There are several species of *Ribes* used in ornamental plantings, notably *R. aureum* and *R. sanguineum.* The latter is a native of the Pacific Northwest and does not do any too well in the climate of Long Island. It is the showiest kind, with tassel-like clusters of red flowers.

ROBINIA. *R. hispida,* **Rose Acacia,** although a native of the southeastern states, is hardy into Canada. Growing about 8 feet high, it bears racemes of rosy-pink pea-shaped flowers in June and occasionally thereafter.

ROSA, see Chapter XV, ROSE GARDEN.

SORBARIA, **False Spirea.** These are shrubs closely related to *Spiraea.* Their handsome pinnate foliage and late-blooming habit make them valuable in the shrubbery.

S. Aitchisonii, is probably the best species for the garden. It grows 6-8 feet high with foot-long panicles of tiny whitish flowers. July-Sept.

S. sorbifolia, is very hardy, of similar appearance to the preceding but not so tall. It spreads freely by suckers. June, July.

SPIRAEA. In the genus *Spiraea* are some of the most satisfactory of hardy shrubs, which bear an abundance of minute white or rose-pink flowers in clusters. They require only good soil, sunshine, and plenty of moisture for a thrifty growth.

S. Bumalda variety **Anthony Waterer.** Flat-topped heads of rosy-pink flowers, reminiscent of those of the rose-colored form of the common milfoil, produced throughout the summer on a bush which reaches about 2 feet in height.

S. prunifolia plena, **Bridal Wreath.** Grows to about 7 feet, covered in May with clusters of double white flowers like tiny pearl buttons.

S. Thunbergii. About 3 feet high with slender erect branches and small white flowers in early spring.

S. Vanhouttei. Has already received too much boosting in the opinion of many, but is exquisite when growth is just beginning. Planted by itself will form a dense, slender-twigged bush 8 feet high and fully as much through, covered in late spring with innumerable white flowers. *Does not need pruning.*

STAPHYLEA, **Bladder-nut.** *S. colchica* is one of the most decorative of the bladder-nuts. The bush is shapely and grows to a height of 10 or 12 feet, bearing creamy-white flower heads in May.

STEPHANANDRA. No one gets excited about *Stephanandra,* but *S. incisa (flexuosa)* is used in great quantity by landscape architects. It is one of those plants which are indispensable but never obtrusive. Its flowers are of no account, but its small deeply lobed leaves blend well with the foliage of other plantings, and it is mainly used for facing down tall shrubs.

SYMPHORICARPOS. Grown largely for their ornamental fruits, most species of *Symphoricarpos* are also attractive in form and foliage. Native American plants, they are hardy North.

S. albus (racemosus), **Snowberry.** A graceful bush, about 5 feet high, the branches of which are bent over in the fall with their burden of white

fruits the size of small cherries. (I have a suspicion that this species and
S. Chenaultii are intolerant of acid soil.)

S. Chenaultii. A hybrid, habit rounded, 4 or 5 feet high, bearing small
foliage and spotted fruit. At a pinch it could be used to give the same effect
as box.

S. orbiculatus (vulgaris), **Indian Currant, Coral-berry.** Slender branches
clothed with small rose-red fruits in the fall.

SYRINGA, **Lilac.** I suppose there is no shrub more widely beloved than
the old-fashioned lilac, or "laylock" as it is called in some districts. Its
sweet fragrance, beautiful flowers, and cool foliage endear it to all. Some
of the named varieties of the common lilac, sometimes called "French"
lilacs because so many of them originated in France, have larger trusses of
bloom and present great variety in coloration, but do not entirely displace
Syringa vulgaris in our affections. There are a number of species which
have considerable garden merit. (See also DECIDUOUS TREES.)

Lilacs require a well-drained, rather rich soil, and an open situation. If
they fail to thrive it may be because the soil is too acid. Ground limestone
in liberal amounts (1½ pounds to a square yard) will correct this trouble.

S. chinensis, said to be a hybrid of *S. persica x vulgaris,* has lilac flowers.
Variety *Saugeana,* red-purple flowers, has larger and darker leaves.

S. persica. When well-grown, extraordinarily graceful with its slender
branches, small leaves, and loose clusters of rosy-purple flowers. Grows
8 to 10 feet high. White forms also known.

S. reflexa. One of the most attractive of lilac species and distinct from
any other. Flower clusters pinkish-lilac, and instead of being held erect
droop gracefully. More difficult to grow than common run of lilacs and
rather rare in catalogs. Worthy of a trial when obtainable.

S. villosa, **Late Lilac.** Almost a small tree, 12 feet tall, with rather coarse,
large leaves. Blooms usually toward the end of June.

S. vulgaris, **Common Lilac.** Reaches a height of about 10 feet and has
light purplish flowers.

The following is a selection from the several hundred named kinds:

White	Single—**Mont Blanc, Vestale**	
	Double—**Edith Cavell, Ellen Willmott**	
Pinkish-lilac	Single—**Lucie Baltet, Macrostachya**	
	Double—**Mme. Antoine Buchner, Pres. Fallières**	
Reddish-lilac	Single—**Mme. F. Morel, Congo**	
	Double—**Mrs. Edward Harding, Paul Thirion**	
Bluish-lilac	Single—**Bleuâtre, Pres. Lincoln**	
	Double—**Olivier de Serres, Emile Gentil**	

TAMARIX, **Tamarisk.** These are deep-rooting shrubs, graceful in habit, with plume-like growth and tiny pink flowers produced in such abundance that a bush in bloom looks like a pink cloud. Tamarisks are especially adapted for seashore planting, and may be trained as wall shrubs.

T. parviflora. Early blooming (April, May), with the flowers disposed along the branches in short spikes. Grows to 10 or 15 feet.

T. pentandra, **Summer Tamarisk.** Grows to 10 feet or more and blooms from July until late summer. Hardy in eastern Canada.

VACCINIUM, **Blueberry.** Those who have the right conditions—acid soil and a rather moist location—will find blueberries of considerable ornamental value, and no one needs telling how good they are in pies. They are now available in many garden varieties characterized by their large fruits. *V. corymbosum,* the **Highbush Blueberry,** has gorgeous red foliage in the autumn. It may attain a height of 12 feet.

VIBURNUM. Every garden should have at least a few viburnums. Some species are prized for their fruits and some for their abundant floral display. From the score or more of species and varieties commonly listed I consider the following most desirable.

V. Burkwoodii. A hybrid of the next species and *V. utile* is described as an "improved *Carlesii.*" It is partially evergreen.

V. Carlesii. Flowers fragrant, pink and white, produced in rounded clusters in early spring. A rather cantankerous shrub, which requires a well-drained sunny situation. Reaches up to 4 feet in height and about 6 feet in diameter.

V. dilatatum. One of the showiest of berried shrubs, with clusters of scarlet fruits produced in early fall and, as they are unpopular with birds, remaining on the bush well into winter.

V. tomentosum. Probably the handsomest viburnum, grown for its flowers, which are arranged in large clusters along horizontal branches, the outer circle of the clusters made up of sterile white flowers much larger and showier than the fertile ones in the center. Grows to 10 feet.

V. tomentosum sterile, **Japanese Snowball.** Fertile flowers replaced in this variety by sterile ones so that the inflorescence assumes the appearance of a snowball. Not so conspicuously horizontally-branching as *V. tomentosum.* Vastly preferable to *V. Opulus roseum,* the **European Snowball,** because not subject to the hordes of black lice which seem invariably to accompany the latter.

V. trilobum (americanum), **Cranberry-bush.** Although called cranberry-bush, is not the source of culinary cranberries. It is a native shrub about 12 feet high with large clusters of bright scarlet berries which are ornamental from August till spring.

VITEX, **Chaste-tree.** These shrubs are usually killed back from 2 or 3 feet to almost the ground line on Long Island, depending upon the severity of the winter, but this is of no great moment because the flowers are produced on growth of the current season, and the pruning necessitated by frost is good for them rather than otherwise. A well-drained, sunny position is desirable. As the chaste-trees are variable when raised from seed, it would probably pay some enterprising nurseryman to select the best forms and propagate them by cuttings.

V. Agnus-castus. Branching spikes of small lavender flowers produced over a long period in summer. Leaves grayish-green, divided like those of some Japanese maples. (See Plate V.)

V. macrophylla. Similar, with larger, greener leaves and flowers of deeper lavender-blue.

WEIGELA (DIERVILLA). Strong-growing and easily contented shrubs, the weigelas produce garlands of tubular flowers on last year's branches in May. Prune them by freely cutting the flowering branches for decoration indoors or by removing some of the older branches during the winter. French nurseries offer many horticultural forms, some with variegated foliage.

W. florida. The common old weigela, formerly known as *W. rosea,* is still worth growing; *W. florida alba* has white flowers.

There are many good garden varieties of weigela including: **Bristol Ruby,** a symmetrical bush about 6 feet tall with ruby-red blooms in June and July and intermittently until frost; **Eva Rathke,** mahogany-red flowers with conspicuous white stamens; **Feerie,** graceful and free-blooming with pale rose-colored flowers; **Othello,** deep red in bud, bright rose when opened; and *W. venusta* with rose-purple flowers.

YUCCA. Those who have seen the desert candles on California hillsides will want to grow *Y. filamentosa,* **Adam's Needle,** which makes spikes 6 feet high of pendent, creamy white, bell-shaped flowers in July. These are effective when seen against a dark background. The one defect to score against Adam's needle is its attraction for loathsome black lice which often disfigure the flower spikes. The sword-like foliage, about 2 feet high, has decorative value.

ZANTHORHIZA is included mainly to allow me to finish with "Z"! *Z. apiifolia,* **Shrub Yellow-root,** is a low shrub, 2 feet high, spreading by underground suckers. It is useful as a ground-cover under large trees.

CLASSIFIED LISTS OF TREES AND SHRUBS

EVERGREEN TREES

Large (50 to 100 feet)
  Abies concolor, White Fir
  Abies Nordmanniana

Cedrus libanotica (*libani*), Cedar of Lebanon
Pinus nigra, Austrian Pine
Pinus resinosa, Red Pine
Pinus rigida, Pitch Pine
Pinus Strobus, White Pine
Pinus sylvestris, Scotch Pine
Tsuga canadensis, Hemlock

Small (usually 20 to 30 feet)
Ilex Aquifolium, English Holly
Ilex opaca, American Holly
Juniperus chinensis, Chinese Juniper
Juniperus virginiana, Red Cedar
Thuja orientalis, Oriental Arborvitae

Spire-like or conical (50 to 100 feet)
Abies alba, Silver Fir
Abies homolepis, Nikko Fir
Picea orientalis, Oriental Spruce (slow-growing)
Picea pungens, Colorado Blue Spruce

Spire-like (up to 30 feet)
Chamaecyparis (*Retinospora*) *pisifera*, Sawara Cypress
Sciadopitys verticillata, Umbrella Pine
Thuja occidentalis, Arborvitae

Narrow (up to 30 feet)
Juniperus chinensis, Chinese Juniper
Juniperus virginiana, Red Cedar

DECIDUOUS TREES

Large (50 to 100 feet)
Acer rubrum, Red Maple
Acer saccharinum, Silver Maple
Acer saccharum, Sugar Maple
Aesculus Hippocastanum, Horsechestnut
Betula lutea, Yellow Birch
Betula nigra, Red or River Birch
Cercidiphyllum japonicum, Katsura-tree
Fagus grandifolia, American Beech
Fagus sylvatica, European Beech
Ginkgo biloba, Maidenhair-tree
Gleditsia triacanthos, Honey Locust
Liquidambar Styraciflua, Sweet Gum
Liriodendron Tulipifera, Tulip-tree
Magnolia acuminata, Cucumber-tree
Platanus acerifolia, London Plane
Quercus alba, White Oak
Quercus borealis (*rubra* of catalogs), Red Oak
Quercus coccinea, Scarlet Oak
Quercus palustris, Pin Oak
Tilia cordata, European Linden
Tilia tomentosa, White Linden
Ulmus americana, American Elm

Small (20 to 40 feet)
Acer Ginnala, Amur Maple
Acer palmatum, Japanese Maple
Acer pennsylvanicum, Striped Maple
Cladrastis lutea, Yellow-wood
Cornus florida, Flowering Dogwood
Crataegus Lavallei (*C. Carrierei*), Hawthorn
Crataegus Oxyacantha, English Hawthorn
Crataegus Phaenopyrum (*C. cordata*), Washington Thorn
Elaeagnus angustifolia, Russian Olive
Malus baccata, Siberian Crab-apple
Syringa japonica, Tree Lilac

Spire-like or conical (up to 100 feet)
Larix decidua (*europaea*), European Larch
Magnolia acuminata, Cucumber-tree

Narrow (40 to 80 feet)
Acer saccharum monumentale, Fastigiate Sugar Maple
Ginkgo biloba fastigiata, Fastigiate Maidenhair-tree
Populus alba pyramidalis, Bolle's Poplar
Populus nigra italica, Lombardy Poplar
Prunus serrulata Amanogawa, Japanese Cherry (30 feet high)

Flowering trees (40 to 80 feet)
Aesculus Hippocastanum, Horsechestnut
Catalpa speciosa, Western Catalpa
Cladrastis lutea, Yellow-wood
Paulownia tomentosa (*P. imperialis*), Empress-tree
Prunus serrulata sachalinensis, Japanese Cherry
Robinia Pseudoacacia, Locust
Sophora japonica, Chinese Scholar-tree

Flowering trees (20 to 40 feet)
Cercis canadensis, Redbud or Judas-tree
Chionanthus virginica, Fringe-tree
Cornus mas, Cornelian Cherry
Halesia carolina, Silverbell
Koelreuteria paniculata, Goldenrain-tree
Magnolia Soulangeana, Cup Magnolia
Magnolia virginiana (*glauca*), Sweet Bay
Malus (*Pyrus*), Flowering Crab-apples
Oxydendrum arboreum, Sorrel-tree
Prunus serrulata, Japanese Cherries (small varieties)
Sorbus Aucuparia, Mountain Ash
Styrax japonica, Snowbell or Storax
Syringa japonica, Tree Lilac

TREES FOR SPECIAL PURPOSES

Street trees (large)
Acer platanoides, Norway Maple
Acer saccharum, Sugar Maple
Platanus acerifolia, London Plane

Quercus borealis (*rubra* of catalogs), Red Oak
Ulmus americana, American Elm

Street trees (medium)
  Ailanthus altissima, Tree of Heaven
  Gymnocladus dioica, Kentucky Coffee-tree

Trees for wet soil
  Acer rubrum, Red Maple
  Betula nigra, Red or River Birch
  Larix decidua (*europaea*), European Larch
  Liquidambar Styraciflua, Sweet Gum
  Magnolia virginiana (*M. glauca*), Sweet Bay
  Nyssa sylvatica, Tupelo or Sour Gum
  Quercus palustris, Pin Oak
  Salix, Willow, in variety
  Taxodium distichum, Bald Cypress
  Ulmus americana, Elm

Trees for dry soil
  Betula populifolia, Gray Birch
  Juniperus virginiana, Red Cedar
  Phellodendron amurense, Amur Cork-tree
  Pinus Strobus, White Pine
  Pinus sylvestris, Scotch Pine
  Quercus borealis (*rubra* of catalogs), Red Oak
  Quercus coccinea, Scarlet Oak
  Quercus velutina, Black Oak

Trees to grow in shade
  Cornus florida, Flowering Dogwood
  Ilex opaca, American Holly
  Oxydendrum arboreum, Sorrel-tree
  Taxus cuspidata capitata, Japanese Yew
  Tsuga canadensis, Hemlock

EVERGREEN SHRUBS
3 to 10 feet
  Azalea (see *Rhododendron*)
  Berberis Gagnepainii, Barberry
  Berberis Julianae
  Buxus sempervirens, Box
  Chamaecyparis obtusa nana, Dwarf Hinoki Cypress
  Euonymus radicans vegetus, Creeping Euonymus
  Euonymus patens (almost evergreen)
  Ilex crenata, Japanese Holly
  Ilex glabra, Inkberry
  Juniperus chinensis Pfitzeriana, Pfitzer Juniper
  Juniperus communis hibernica, Irish Juniper
  Juniperus squamata Meyeri
  Kalmia latifolia, Mountain Laurel
  Leucothoë Catesbaei, Drooping Leucothoë
  Picea Abies (*excelsa*) *conica*, and other dwarf spruces
  Pieris japonica, Japanese Andromeda

3 to 10 feet (Cont.)

Pinus Mugo, Swiss Mountain Pine
Pyracantha coccinea Lalandi, Laland's Firethorn
Rhododendron (Azalea) *obtusum amoenum*
Rhododendron (Azalea) *mucronatum* (*R. ledifolium*)
Rhododendron hybrids, in variety
Taxus cuspidata, Japanese Yew
Taxus media Hicksii
Thuja occidentalis, Arborvitae, dwarf forms
Thuja orientalis, Oriental Arborvitae, dwarf forms

Usually below 3 feet

Arctostaphylos Uva-ursi, Bearberry (trailer, 6 inches high)
Berberis verruculosa
Buxus sempervirens suffruticosa, Dwarf Box
Calluna vulgaris, Heather
Chamaecyparis obtusa compacta, Dwarf Hinoki Cypress
Daphne Cneorum, Rose Daphne
Erica carnea, Alpine Heath
Hedera Helix, English Ivy (trailer, 6 inches high)
Hedera Helix conglomerata
Juniperus chinensis Sargentii, Prostrate Juniper
Juniperus Sabina tamariscifolia
Juniperus squamata Meyeri (kept low by pruning)
Mahonia Aquifolium, Oregon Grape or Holly Mahonia
Pachysandra terminalis, Japanese Spurge
Pieris floribunda, Mountain Andromeda
Pinus Mugo, Swiss Mountain Pine (kept low by pruning)
Rhododendron (Azalea) *Hinodegiri*
Taxus baccata repandens, Prostrate English Yew
Teucrium Chamaedrys, Germander
Thuja, Arborvitae, dwarf forms

DECIDUOUS SHRUBS

10 to 15 feet

Benzoin aestivale, Spicebush
Enkianthus campanulatus, Necklace-bush
Hamamelis virginiana, Witch-hazel
Hamamelis mollis
Hibiscus syriacus, Rose of Sharon
Hydrangea paniculata grandiflora, "Pee-gee" Hydrangea
Lonicera Maackii podocarpa, Late Honeysuckle
Lonicera tatarica, Tartarian Honeysuckle
Magnolia stellata, Starry Magnolia
Philadelphus grandiflorus, Mockorange
Photinia villosa
Rhododendron (Azalea) *Vaseyi*
Syringa vulgaris, Common Lilac
Viburnum tomentosum
Symplocos paniculata, Sweetleaf

5 to 10 feet
  Acanthopanax Sieboldianum (*A. pentaphyllum*)
  Acer palmatum, Japanese Maple
  Aesculus (*Pavia*) *parviflora*, Dwarf Buckeye
  Aronia arbutifolia, Red Chokeberry
  Berberis Vernae, Barberry
  Buddleia Davidi, Butterfly-bush
  Callicarpa japonica, Beautyberry
  Clerodendron trichotomum, Glorybower
  Cotoneaster racemiflora songarica
  Cornus stolonifera, Red Osier Dogwood
  Euonymus alatus, Winged Euonymus
  Forsythia intermedia spectabilis, Golden Bells
  Forsythia suspensa Fortunei
  Hydrangea arborescens grandiflora, Hills of Snow
  Kolkwitzia amabilis, Beauty-bush
  Lespedeza formosa, Bush Clover
  Ligustrum obtusifolium Regelianum, Regel's Privet
  Lonicera fragantissima, Winter Honeysuckle
  Myrica carolinensis, Bayberry
  Neillia sinensis, Tube Neillia
  Philadelphus coronarius, Mockorange
  Prunus triloba, Flowering Almond
  Rhododendron (Azalea) *arborescens*
  Rhododendron (Azalea) *calendulaceum*, Flame Azalea
  Rhododendron (Azalea) *nudiflorum*, Pinxter-flower
  Robinia hispida, Rose Acacia
  Rosa Hugonis, Father Hugo's Rose
  Spiraea prunifolia, Bridal Wreath
  Spiraea Vanhouttei, Spirea
  Stephanandra incisa (*S. flexuosa*)
  Viburnum tomentosum
  Viburnum tomentosum sterile, Japanese Snowball
  Viburnum Wrightii
  Vitex macrophylla, Large-leaved Chaste-tree
  Weigela candida varieties
  Weigela rosea

3 to 5 feet
  Abelia grandiflora, Glossy Abelia
  Berberis Thunbergii, Japanese Barberry
  Buddleia Davidi nanhoensis, Butterfly-bush or Summer Lilac
  Caryopteris incana, Bluebeard or Blue Spirea
  Cotoneaster horizontalis
  Cotoneaster horizontalis perpusilla
  Chaenomeles lagenaria (*Cydonia japonica*), Japanese Quince
  Deutzia gracilis
  Hypericum aureum, St. Johnswort
  Kerria japonica pleniflora
  Rhododendron (Azalea) *obtusum Kaempferi*

3 to 5 feet (Cont.)
  Rhododendron (Azalea) *yedoense* (*yodogawa*)
  Rosa rugosa
  Spiraea Bumalda
  Symphoricarpos vulgaris, Indian Currant, Coral-berry
  Viburnum Carlesii

SHRUBS FOR SPECIAL PURPOSES

Shrubs for dry soil
  Acanthopanax Sieboldianum (*A. pentaphyllum*)
  Berberis vulgaris, Barberry (except in wheat-growing regions)
  Cornus racemosa (*C. paniculata*), Dogwood
  Hypericum aureum, St. Johnswort
  Juniperus communis, Juniper
  Juniperus Sabina, Savin Juniper
  Lespedeza formosa, Bush Clover
  Myrica pensylvanica, Bayberry
  Prunus maritima, Beach Plum
  Rhus canadensis, Fragrant Sumach
  Rhus typhina, Staghorn Sumach
  Robinia hispida, Rose Acacia
  Rosa setigera, Prairie Rose
  Rosa spinosissima, Burnet Rose
  Symphoricarpos vulgaris, Indian Currant
  Viburnum Lantana, Wayfaring-tree
  Viburnum prunifolium, Blackhaw

Shrubs for wet soil
  Aronia arbutifolia, Red Chokeberry
  Aronia melanocarpa, Black Chokeberry
  Benzoin aestivale, Spicebush
  Cephalanthus occidentalis, Button-bush
  Clethra alnifolia, Summersweet
  Exochorda grandiflora, Pearlbush
  Hamamelis virginiana, Witch-hazel
  Ilex glabra, Inkberry
  Ilex verticillata, Winterberry or Black Alder
  Rhododendron (Azalea) *viscosum*, Clammy Azalea
  Rubus odoratus, Flowering Raspberry
  Salix caprea, Goat Willow
  Salix discolor, Pussy Willow
  Sambucus racemosa, European Red Elder
  Spiraea tomentosa, Hardhack or Steeple-bush
  Viburnum cassinoides, Withe-rod
  Viburnum dentatum, Arrow-wood
  Viburnum Lentago, Sheepberry

Shrubs to grow in shade
  Acanthopanax Sieboldianum (*A. pentaphyllum*)
  Benzoin aestivale, Spice-bush
  Forsythia in variety, Golden Bells
  Hamamelis, Witch-hazel

PLATE VI. (*upper*) *Magnolia stellata*—NARCISSUS SIR WATKIN NATU-
RALIZED ON BANK. (*lower*) KOREAN OR YODOGAWA AZALEA,
Rhododendron yedoense

PLATE VII. (*upper*) RHODODENDRONS. (*lower*) WISTERIA TRAINED TO
BUSH FORM BY PRUNING

Hydrangea arborescens grandiflora, Hills-of-Snow
Ilex glabra, Inkberry
Kalmia latifolia, Mountain Laurel
Leucothoë Catesbaei, Drooping Leucothoë
Ligustrum, Privet
Mahonia Aquifolium, Oregon Grape or Holly Mahonia
Pieris floribunda, Mountain Andromeda
Pieris japonica, Japanese Andromeda
Rhododendron in variety, Rhododendron and Azalea
Rhodotypos scandens, Jet-bead
Taxus, Yew
Viburnum dentatum, Arrow-wood
Vinca minor, Periwinkle (trailing)

Trees and shrubs for hedges: (See Chapter X, HEDGES).

VIII. FOUNDATION PLANTING

Foundation planting is the term applied to the special planting which is set in close proximity to the walls of the house. Unfortunately, one finds really good examples of it all too seldom.

Principles of foundation planting. As the connecting link between house and garden, foundation planting should be in harmony with the design of the dwelling and the type of planting on the grounds. If the architect of the house is available, it is a good plan to consult him, for the way the foundation planting is carried out may make or mar the appearance of his work. For example, if the house is low and rambling, the spire-like effects of such subjects as red cedars will make it seem insufferably squatty. On the other hand, if the house is high in proportion to its width, low rounded shrubs will make it look more than ever like a skyscraper.

When the rest of the garden is almost exclusively deciduous it is a mistake to use nothing but evergreens about the foundation, because the transition will seem so abrupt that the planting will fail in its purpose of linking the house with the garden.

The degree of formality of the planting adjacent to the house should depend somewhat upon the type of architecture. When both the garden and house are formal it would be obviously incongruous to make an attempt at naturalistic planting around the foundations. On the other hand, stiff little evergreens are decidedly out of place beside the front door of a rambling type of house.

Considerable restraint in quantity as well as style should be exercised in foundation planting. There should appear to be some contact between the house and the earth, but this cannot be seen if the foundation is entirely surrounded by bushes. A house with no vegetation around it looks bare and uninviting, but one should not go to the other extreme and completely smother the walls with planting—unless the architecture is so atrocious that the best policy is to keep it hidden. In such a case vines in abundance will be one of the mainstays.

Types of plant material. Although practically every type of plant material, except large trees, may be used in the planting around the foundations, one must be careful to select species and varieties which will really serve the purpose intended.

So often we see a foundation planting containing, apparently, one example of every evergreen from the nurseryman's stock. Such an incongruous mixture looks bad enough when new and the plants are at least in scale, but how unsightly it is at the end of five or six years, when the giants of the forest (such as hemlock, white pine, and spruce) have grown and grown, shutting off light from the windows and crowding out their slower neighbors!

Naturally dwarf plants, slow growers, or specimens which may be kept within bounds by annual pruning, should always be selected. In the first group are such subjects as *Daphne Cneorum, Pachysandra terminalis, Pachistima Canbyi.* In the second group: *Chamaecyparis squarrosa nana, Pinus Mugo,* and dwarf arborvitae. In the third group: yews of various kinds, California privet, and *Carpinus Betulus.* Extended lists of plants suitable for foundation planting follow on pages 118-120.

In order to have in mind a clear picture of the mature appearance of the trees and shrubs desired, make a scale drawing of the outlines of the house, then superimpose the outlines of the plants as they should appear in future years. If the sketch shows that some will not fit, they may be rejected in favor of others before the planting is started. A knowledge of the behavior of the plants you contemplate using and their ultimate size, shape, and characteristics is essential. While this may be gained from books and catalogs, it is better obtained from actual inspection of growing plants and inquiry about them. They may be observed around other houses or in botanic gardens or nurseries.

Grouping of subjects. As a general rule, the plants should be grouped at salient points rather than planted in a row or used as individuals. A distinctive plant on either side of a doorway may be appropriate, but repeated at intervals all around the house such specimens would look anything but pleasing. Plants suitable for flanking a doorway include boxwood, when a rounded shrub is required; spreading Japanese yew, where a broad deep green mass is wanted; rhododendron for a large rounded bush less formal than boxwood; upright Japanese yew which can be trimmed in pyramidal shape to harmonize with roof lines, or certain *Chamaecyparis* species, or a selection from the many varieties of columnar junipers which vary in ultimate height from a few up to 25 feet or more. Whichever kind is chosen, it should fit the character of the house both in point of size and habit of growth.

Groups of plants will probably be desirable at the corners and in angles formed by ells. While they may consist of either evergreen or deciduous subjects, or the two combined, the plants composing them should not be too dissimilar in size and texture of foliage. For example, the foliage of boxwood and of cranberry-bush is not a happy combination; whereas boxwood and firethorn admit of association. These groups, however, should be of material sufficiently dissimilar to give a pleasing outline through variation of height.

Leave the windows alone if there is any doubt about whether a planting on either side of them will, by framing them, improve the appearance of the house. In any case, planting around and under windows should be of such a nature that it will not cut off light and air.

Use of vines and wall-shrubs. The use of vines on the house is not nearly so prevalent in America as it is in Europe. There is a lack of knowledge here of the opportunities for beautification of houses by means of vines. But chief among the reasons for their comparative neglect are the wooden houses on which a growth of vines is inconvenient, and the difficulty of growing certain species because of the extra heat radiated from the walls in regions having a hot summer climate.

When the space available for planting against the house is too narrow for shrubs, vines may be used freely to soften the lines of the architecture. When there is a porch which is used as an outdoor sitting room, vines are essential to give some degree of privacy. For this purpose it is usually wise to utilize either annual vines or those which die to the ground in winter, so that sunlight is not shut out during the season when it is most needed.

If an expanse of unsightly foundation is exposed, either vines or additional shrubs should be set out. When there are only a few feet in height to be covered, the winter creeper (*Euonymus radicans*) is admirable, as it clings by itself to any rough surface. On the north side of a building English ivy serves a similar purpose. If an evergreen vine is not considered necessary, Japanese or Boston ivy, *Parthenocissus (Ampelopsis) tricuspidata,* is satisfactory. The variety *Lowii* is preferred when not much room is available, because it is not so rampant a grower.

There is no lack of vines or shrubs which may be used against the house. Among annuals there are moonflowers, morning-glories, the hyacinth-bean, balloon-vine, and wild cucumber-vine. Perennials which die to the ground in north temperate regions include the fast-growing kudzu-vine and the Madeira vine. Of woody vines there are *Actinidia, Akebia, Parthenocissus, Ampelopsis,* Dutchman's pipe-vine, bittersweet, silver lace-vine, clematis, honeysuckle, and wisteria. Vines clinging by aerial rootlets or by adhesive tendrils are the climbing hydrangea, English ivy, *Euonymus, Parthenocissus,* and *Campsis* (*Bignonia*). (See also Chapter IX, VINES.)

A number of shrubs have flexible branches which may be trained to serve the same purpose as vines. In this group are "climbing" roses, flowering quince, tamarisk, firethorn, matrimony-vine, *Forsythia suspensa,* and *Jasminum nudiflorum.*

Soil and planting. Apart from esthetic considerations, there are a number of purely practical matters in connection with foundation planting.

The soil close to the walls is likely to be full of builders' rubbish which should be removed before planting is started. Make up any deficiency with manure or topsoil and dig deeply so that there is a space of good soil 2 to 3 feet wide and from 1½ to 2 feet deep.

If the house is low with overhanging eaves, it is usually necessary to plant away from the walls in order that the plants may receive the benefits of rainfall and sun. When there are no gutters to conduct water from the roof it is advisable either to set plants far enough from the wall to be free of the drip line, or to install eave troughs. If, in the North, the house has a roof with a steep pitch, guards made of wires should be set along the eaves to prevent snowy avalanches from smashing the plants below; or else, during the dangerous period, the plants should be covered with slats or boards.

Subjects which have opposite soil preferences must naturally not be planted together. For example, large-flowered clematis on a trellis back of azaleas would be impracticable (without going to the trouble of providing separate soil compartments) because the clematis demands a soil rich in calcium carbonate, which is poisonous to the acid-loving azaleas. Similarly, the preferences of plants for sun and shade must be considered in the foundation planting.

A SELECTION OF MATERIAL SUITABLE FOR FOUNDATION PLANTINGS

(For Descriptions see Chapter VII, TREES AND SHRUBS.)

TALL (10 to 20 feet high). Trees have been chosen which are naturally of narrow habit or which may be kept in bounds by pruning, because there is usually no room for spreading trees in foundation planting. Except where otherwise noted, sunshine for at least half the day is desirable.

EVERGREEN

Chamaecyparis obtusa gracilis, Hinoki Cypress
Juniperus chinensis, Chinese Juniper
Juniperus chinensis columnaris (When a narrow, spire-like form is desired.)
Juniperus virginiana, Red Cedar
Juniperus virginiana Cannaertii (Does not like to be sheared.)
Pinus Cembra, Swiss Stone Pine
Pinus Strobus fastigiata, Fastigiate White Pine
Taxus cuspidata capitata, Japanese Yew (Will grow in partial shade.)
Thuja occidentalis, American Arborvitae
Thuja occidentalis fastigiata
Thuja occidentalis Wareana
Thuja Standishii, Japanese Arborvitae

BROAD-LEAF EVERGREEN

Magnolia grandiflora (May be trained as a wall tree. Not reliably hardy north of Washington, D. C.)
Pyracantha coccinea Lalandi (May be trained against the wall, or pruned annually to maintain desired shape and size. Not reliably hardy north of Philadelphia.)

DECIDUOUS

Carpinus Betulus, European Hornbeam
Cornus mas
Crataegus Oxyacantha, English Hawthorn (Double-flowered forms are preferred, in white, pink or scarlet. May be trained on wall or pruned annually to maintain desired shape and size.)
Magnolia stellata
Magnolia virginiana (Will grow when partly shaded.)
Malus floribunda Scheideckeri, Showy Crab-apple
Malus theifera
Oxydendrum arboreum, Sorrel-tree (Partial shade and acid soil desirable.)
Photinia villosa (Handsome red berries and red leaves in fall.)
Prunus serrulata Amanogawa, Flowering Cherry (Slender columnar habit.)

MEDIUM (3 to 10 feet high).

EVERGREEN

Chamaecyparis obtusa nana, Dwarf Hinoki Cypress
Juniperus chinensis Pfitzeriana, Pfitzer Juniper

Juniperus communis hibernica, Irish Juniper
Picea Abies Clanbrasiliana, Norway Spruce (A compact bush form.)
Picea Abies conica, Arrowhead Spruce (Low pyramidal form.)
Picea glauca conica, Dwarf Alberta Spruce
Pinus Mugo, Swiss Mountain Pine
Taxus cuspidata, Japanese Yew (Spreading form. Will grow when partly shaded.)
Taxus media Hicksii
Thuja orientalis elegantissima, Oriental Arborvitae (Foliage yellow in spring.)

BROAD-LEAF EVERGREEN

Azalea—see *Rhododendron*
Berberis Gagnepainii
Berberis Julianae
Buxus sempervirens, Box (Needs winter protection on Long Island, N. Y.)
Euonymus patens (Almost evergreen.)
Ilex crenata, Japanese Holly
Ilex crenata microphylla
Ilex glabra, Inkberry
Kalmia latifolia, Mountain Laurel (Will grow in sun or shade. Acid soil.)
Pieris japonica, Japanese Andromeda (Partial shade desirable.)
Rhododendron, in variety (Will grow in sun or shade but partial shade desirable. Acid soil.)
Rhododendron obtusum japonicum (Hinodegiri Azalea. Many other varieties of this type available.)

DECIDUOUS

Acanthopanax Sieboldianum (pentaphyllum) (Sun or shade.)
Acer palmatum, Japanese Maple, in variety
Azalea—see *Rhododendron*
Berberis Vernae
Chaenomeles lagenaria (Cydonia japonica), Japanese Quince
Euonymus alatus, Winged Euonymus
Forsythia intermedia (Will grow in partial shade.)
Hamamelis mollis, Witch-hazel (Blooms in January or February.)
Hydrangea macrophylla ("French" Hydrangea), in variety
Lonicera fragrantissima, Winter Honeysuckle
Philadelphus virginalis Virginal, Mockorange
Rhododendron (Azalea) *calendulaceum,* Flame Azalea (Partial shade and acid soil desirable.)
Rhododendron (Azalea) *molle* (Partial shade and acid soil desirable.)
Rhododendron (Azalea) *Vaseyi* (Partial shade and acid soil desirable.)
Rosa rugosa
Spiraea prunifolia, Bridal Wreath
Stephanandra incisa (Reddish-purple foliage in the fall.)
Syringa persica, Persian Lilac
Syringa reflexa (A lilac with pinkish flowers in drooping panicles.)
Syringa vulgaris, Common Lilac
Tamarix parviflora, Tamarisk (Plumy light green growth.)
Tamarix pentandra (Plumy gray-green growth. Both species may be trained as wall shrubs.)
Viburnum dilatatum (Noteworthy for its red fruit in early fall.)

Viburnum tomentosum (One of the handsomest of the viburnums.)
Weigela Féerie
Weigela venusta

Low (Usually under 3 feet high. Some varieties will need pruning to keep them low.)

EVERGREEN

Chamaecyparis obtusa compacta, Dwarf Hinoki Cypress
Juniperus chinensis japonica
Juniperus chinensis Sargentii (Requires a sunny position.)
Juniperus horizontalis plumosa
Juniperus Sabina tamariscifolia
Juniperus squamata Meyeri
Juniperus virginiana Kosteri
Picea Abies Gregoryana, Norway Spruce (Dwarf form.)
Picea Abies Maxwellii, Norway Spruce (Dwarf form.)
Pinus Mugo, Swiss Mountain Pine (May be kept low by pruning.)
Taxus baccata repandens, English Yew (Prostrate form.) (*Taxus* will grow well in partial shade.)
Taxus cuspidata densa, Japanese Yew (Shrubby form.)
Taxus cuspidata nana, Japanese Yew (Shrubby form.)
Thuja occidentalis pumila, Little Gem, American Arborvitae (Dwarf form.)
Thuja orientalis compacta, Oriental Arborvitae (Dwarf form.)

BROAD-LEAF EVERGREEN

Arctostaphylos Uva-ursi, Bearberry (Low-growing ground-cover. Needs sandy soil.)
Berberis verruculosa
Buxus sempervirens suffruticosa, Dwarf Box
Cotoneaster microphylla
Daphne Cneorum, Rose Daphne
Leiophyllum buxifolium (Needs a sandy acid soil.)
Leucothoë Catesbaei (Requires acid soil.)
Mahonia Aquifolium (Partial shade desirable.)
Pachystima Canbyi
Pachysandra terminalis (Low-growing ground-cover. Sun or shade.)
Pieris floribunda (Partial shade and acid soil desirable.)

DECIDUOUS

Azalea—see *Rhododendron*
Berberis Thunbergii minor, Japanese Barberry (Low form.)
Cotoneaster horizontalis
Deutzia gracilis
Hydrangea arborescens grandiflora (Grows well in shade. Keep down by spring pruning.)
Rhododendron (Azalea) *Schlippenbachii* (Partial shade and acid soil desirable.)
Viburnum Carlesii (May get up to 4 feet.)
Viburnum Opulus nanum, European Cranberry-bush (Dwarf form with smaller leaves.)

IX. VINES AND THEIR SUPPORTING STRUCTURES

Types and uses of vines. The word "vine" is applied to plants which have weak stems incapable of self-support. Their stems may trail on the surface of the ground or climb by attaching themselves to something stronger. In garden practice those in the first group are largely used as ground-covers, and those in the second group for furnishing walls, pergolas, trellises, fences, arches, etc. Some vines, such as Japanese honeysuckle, are adaptable enough to be used either as ground-covers or as climbers.

Methods of climbing. Vines occur as woody plants, both deciduous and evergreen, as herbaceous perennials, and as annuals. Their methods of climbing are interesting and varied. The English ivy and trumpet-vine climb by adventitious roots which attach themselves to any rough surface such as a brick or stone wall. The Boston ivy and Virginia creeper climb by means of adhesive disks which can cling to stone, brick, or wood. Sweet peas, grapes, and various gourds attach themselves to supports by means of tendrils, while clematis climbs with the aid of its leaf-stalks, which twine around any suitable support with which they come in contact. Under natural conditions, some roses support their long weak canes by means of the strong recurved prickles which catch on to the branches of the tree or shrub near which they are growing. Many climbers, like bittersweet, twine their stems around the nearest support.

There are also varieties of woody plants with more or less flexible branches which may be trained against walls in a manner resembling vines.

Selecting vines for special purposes (For descriptions see pages following). The methods by which vines climb have a bearing on their selection for particular purposes. Those which cling by means of adhesive disks or by aerial rootlets should receive first consideration when choosing subjects for wall embellishment. In this group are species of *Parthenocissus* (*Ampelopsis*), *Campsis* (*Bignonia*), *Euonymus, Ficus, Hedera, Hydrangea,* and *Schizophragma.*

Plants which climb by means of tendrils or twisting petioles are well adapted for growing on netted fencing or on brushwood, or for clambering among living trees and shrubs. In this group are species of *Cardiospermum, Lathyrus, Tropaeolum, Clematis, Cobaea,* and *Vitis.* The last three, which are strong-growing vines, may also be used on arches and pergolas.

The group which climbs by the twining of stems is a large one, and its members are adapted for a variety of purposes. They are happiest on comparatively thin vertical supports such as strings, slender poles, or fence pickets. Among the more important are:

ANNUALS: *Calonyction, Dolichos, Ipomoea.*

HERBACEOUS PERENNIALS: *Boussingaultia, Dioscorea, Pueraria.*

WOODY PERENNIALS: *Actinidia, Akebia, Aristolochia, Celastrus, Lonicera, Polygonum, Wisteria.*

Shrubs with long flexible branches are much used in England, where the practice of training them on walls enables the gardener to grow subjects which would not survive the winter if planted in the open. Shrubs of this type, of course, have to be fastened to the wall, usually by means of narrow cloth strips or leather shreds which are passed around the branches and then nailed to the wall. Specially made nails, which may be driven into wood, bricks, or mortar joints, may be used to hold the strips. There is also on the market a nail to which is affixed a strip of lead which is bent around a branch after the nail has been driven.

Skillful pruning is necessary to keep wall shrubs within bounds and to ensure floriferousness. Shrubs suitable for furnishing walls include *Tamarix, Cotoneaster, Pyracantha, Forsythia, Prunus triloba,* and varieties of *Crataegus Oxyacantha* and *Prunus Persica.*

Then there are roses, which, although not strictly climbers, are invaluable for furnishing pillars, pergolas, arches, and fences. See Chapter XV, ROSE GARDEN.

A point to remember when planting vines near the house is to provide a deep rich soil, which is often lacking around the foundations. Also, if there are overhanging eaves, the vines should be planted far enough from the walls so that they may receive the benefits from rainfall, unless you are prepared to make up by artificial means the lack of water from natural sources. See Chapter VIII, FOUNDATION PLANTING.

Alphabetical list of vines. Short descriptions and cultural directions for more than thirty vines, including clematis, sweet peas, nasturtiums, and morning-glories and their relatives, are given in the paragraphs below. The scientific names of the vines are given in alphabetical order, followed by the common name of each.

Actinidia arguta, **Tara-vine,** is a strong-growing species suitable for large pergolas, valued chiefly for its luxuriant foliage. Its white blossoms are pretty but not conspicuous, for they are usually hidden by the leaves. It · produces edible yellowish fruits, about 1 to 2 inches long.

Actinidia polygama, **Silver-vine,** a related species, has the property of attracting cats, which to the gardener is a dubious recommendation. It grows up to 25 feet and is valued for the silvery-white color exhibited by the young leaves of the staminate form.

Akebia quinata, **Five-leaf Akebia,** delights the eye with its rich clean foliage. It produces fragrant blossoms which, because of their dull color (purplish-brown and rosy-purple) and because they are partially hidden beneath the leaves, often pass unnoticed. This is a useful twining vine for fences and trellises and for covering tree stumps and rocks. It also has been successfully used as a ground-cover.

Ampelopsis brevipedunculata Maximowiczii (*A. heterophylla*), **Turquoise-berry.** This vigorous vine will sprawl, clamber, and climb by means of its tendrils over anything and everything within reach. Some call it a weed because it grows so luxuriantly and because (doubtless through the ministrations of birds) it has the habit of springing up in unexpected places. But even such detractors admit the beauty of its dark green foliage and its supremacy in the fall when the abundant berries, which change from lilac to verdigris to bright blue, are strikingly displayed on the leafless vines. It will grow in sun or shade and is useful when a vine is required that needs no attention beyond the curbing of its rampageousness. For other vines commonly known as *Ampelopsis,* see *Parthenocissus.*

Aristolochia durior (*Sipho*), **Dutchman's Pipe,** is a strong-growing vine, native in the eastern states, which climbs by twining. It gets its common name from the curiously shaped but inconspicuous flowers. It is grown for the beauty of its large rounded leaves, which will completely cover a trellis in a short time. It is, therefore, useful for pergolas and as a porch screen, seeming to thrive better when lime is added to the soil.

Bignonia—see *Campsis.*

Boussingaultia baselloides, the **Madeira-** or **Mignonette-vine,** is a tropical twiner which forms a tuberous root. Its stems, clothed with rather fleshy heart-shaped leaves, are capable of attaining 10 to 20 feet of growth in a season, but are killed to the ground by the first frost of autumn. It is suitable for covering porches, fences, and arbors. Its tiny white fragrant flowers are abundantly produced in longish racemes in late summer and fall. The tubers should be stored indoors during winter and planted out when danger of frost is past.

Calonyction aculeatum, **Moonflower.** Listed for convenience under the morning-glories, *Ipomoea.*

Campsis chinensis, **Chinese Trumpet-creeper.** Sometimes listed as *Bignonia grandiflora, Tecoma grandiflora,* or *Bignonia chinensis,* is a shrubby climber, with pinnate leaves and tubular scarlet flowers 2 inches in diameter.

Campsis radicans, **Trumpet-creeper,** is also known as *Bignonia* and *Tecoma.* It has tubular flowers of orange and scarlet, longer but less broad than the preceding.

The trumpet-creepers, including several varieties and a hybrid between the two preceding species, are valuable in the garden for covering walls, tree stumps, etc. They are, in general, quite vigorous and capable of climbing to a height of 20 feet or more, often by means of adventitious rootlets. They seem happiest in calcareous soil. Humming-birds are attracted by the showy flowers, which are produced from July to September. As the rootlets do not fasten the plant too securely, it is a good plan to pass a strip of leather over the principal branches and nail it to the support.

Cardiospermum Halicacabum, **Balloon-vine,** usually is grown as an annual which climbs to a height of about 10 feet by means of tendrils. It has light green divided foliage, inconspicuous flowers, and curiously inflated seed pods. Seeds may be sown in spring—either indoors and transplanted later, or in the position where they are to bloom.

Celastrus scandens, **Bittersweet.** This well-known vine, which twines its woody stem firmly around its support, is grown mainly for its showy clusters of orange-yellow fruits which opening display the crimson pulp surrounding the seeds. Failure of a specimen to produce berries is probably due to the plants bearing only male flowers. To be on the safe side it should be propagated by cuttings of specimens known to fruit. This bittersweet grows about 20 feet high and may be used for arbors, trellises, or pergolas, or allowed to scramble over low walls.

Clematis. A whole chapter or even a book could be written on clematis alone. The species range from rampant-growing, comparatively small-flowered kinds such as *C. paniculata* and *C. virginiana,* which are easy to grow, to the large-flowered hybrids such as Belle of Woking and Nelly Moser, which are inclined to be fastidious in their requirements. A deep, rich, and well-drained soil must be provided, with enough ground limestone mixed with it to make it alkaline. If clematis hybrids can be planted so that the roots are shaded and the tops are in the sunshine the chances of success are increased. I have seen them growing happily when planted on the north side of a low stone fence and allowed to ramble along the top; and also when planted in among climbing roses, or on the north side of shrubs and allowed to climb among them. I asked the late J. E. Spingarn, who knew more about clematis than anyone else in America, if he would make a selection of varieties for the beginner. He kindly responded with the following suggestions.

A SELECTION OF CLEMATIS FOR THE NOVICE IN THE UNITED STATES

"The wild species are especially valuable for trellises, pergolas, fences, old stumps and the like. Some are rampant and grow to 40 feet or more; others are slender vines not more than 6 or 8 feet high. I specially recommend, besides the Japanese clematis and *Clematis montana rubens,* the following species: *C. tangutica,* a slender, Chinese climber with bright yellow lantern-shaped flowers, which is hardier and handsomer than the somewhat similar *C. orientalis; C. texensis,* the finest of our native species, with scarlet to rose-pink urn-shaped flowers from June to frost, and a sight for the gods when in full bloom; *C. macropetala,* a very hardy plant with charming azure-blue flowers of striking and unusual shape; *C. Veitchiana,* with creamy bell-shaped flowers, not strictly hardy north of Philadelphia; *C. Kermesina,* with dark crimson flowers, sure to be a favorite when better known; and the species-like hybrid *C. Jouiniana,* with lovely lavender campanulate flowers and rampant as a weed. Every one of these is worthy of a place in any garden, and some of them may be used to drape boulders in the large rock-garden.

"Among the large-flowered hybrids, I suggest that the novice begin with the varieties easiest to grow, such as *Jackmani,* the most widely known of all, with violet-purple flowers; *Henryi,* with enormous white flowers; Madame Edouard André, with purplish red flowers; Ramona, with lovely blue flowers; and Gipsy Queen, with flowers of a richer purple than *Jackmani.* Of the other large-flowered hybrids now or soon to be available it is difficult to make a choice, since so much depends on one's color preferences; but I have no hesitation in recommending Prins Hendrik (azure blue), Nelly Moser (mauve with a red band down the centre of each sepal), Duchess of Albany and Countess of Onslow (both hybrids of *C. texensis,* with charming trumpet-shaped flowers of crimson and white), William Kennett (light blue), Mrs. Cholmondeley (light blue) and Belle of Woking (double-flowered pale mauve or silver-gray). All of these bloom on new wood except Belle of Woking."

Cobaea scandens, **Cup-and-saucer Vine,** is a tender woody perennial grown as an annual in the North. It climbs by means of tendrils produced at the tips of the leaves. Seeds should be started indoors and the seedlings planted out when danger of frost is past. It grows rapidly to a height of 10 to 20 feet. The flowers are large (1½ inches across), greenish-purple in color, and not particularly showy.

Convolvulus—see *Ipomoea.*

Cotoneaster. Few people think of cotoneasters as possessing qualities which would enable them to be used in place of climbers; and, of course, they are not really climbers, but some species may, when properly trained, be used for furnishing walls. I remember seeing, many years ago, in the Oxford Botanic Garden, *Cotoneaster horizontalis* forced to depart from its procumbent habit and grow upright by being trained on a wall, and I was impressed by the striking display it made.

Crataegus Oxyacantha, **English Hawthorn.** Garden varieties of the English hawthorn may be used for training on walls where they make an effective display of their white, pink, or scarlet double flowers in May. Neither this nor the *Cotoneaster* should be attempted except when time is available for the rather fussy work of training, tying, and pruning.

Cucurbita Pepo ovifera varieties, **Ornamental Gourds.** The culture of these plants has assumed the proportions of a fad. Their cultivation is essentially the same as that of cucumbers, except that they should be trained on some kind of support. See Chapter XXI, THE VEGETABLE GARDEN.

Dioscorea Batatas, **Cinnamon-vine,** climbs 10 to 20 feet by twining if given suitable support. A hardy perennial with an enormous tuberous root, it has shining, strongly ribbed, pointed, heart-shaped leaves and small clusters of cinnamon-scented white flowers. Small tubers are obtainable from seedsmen for spring planting.

Dolichos Lablab, **Hyacinth-bean,** is an annual, native to the tropics, capable of twining to a height of 20 feet. The flowers may be purple or white, but for decorative purposes they are somewhat eclipsed by the purple seed pods, which are broad, flat, and 2 to 3 inches long. The vine is good for twining on strings to form a porch screen. Plant seeds in the spring in the place where the plants are to grow.

Euonymus radicans, **Wintercreeper,** is probably the hardiest of the evergreen vines. It is invaluable for covering low walls or house foundations when a climber is desired which does not shoot up too quickly. It has rounded or oval leaves ½ to 2 inches long and clings by adventitious roots. *E. radicans vegetus,* the stronger-growing **Bigleaf Wintercreeper,** is prodigal in its production of pinkish fruits, which split in three parts to reveal the orange seeds inside, similar to its relative, the bittersweet. It is safest to obtain plants propagated vegetatively from fruiting specimens. The Wintercreeper will grow in sun or shade, but the leaves may be injured if exposed to sunshine in the winter.

Ficus pumila, **Creeping Fig.** This delightful plant is usually looked upon as a conservatory vine, but I recently saw a specimen which had survived the winter in a rock garden out-of-doors at Millbrook, N. Y. This would indicate that it is worth trying as a wall vine on the north side of the house in protected locations as far north as Long Island, N. Y. It clings closely by adventitious rootlets, the rather small leaves flattening themselves against the wall. Like the English ivy, in its arborescent stage it takes on an appearance different from the climbing form.

Forsythia suspensa and its variety *Fortunei* may be trained as wall shrubs. The species is charming also when planted at the top of a high retaining wall, from which its long flexible branches will drape themselves down the face.

Gourds—see *Cucurbita.*

Hedera Helix, **English Ivy,** is among the most valued of evergreen vines. It clings by aerial rootlets. Though adaptable to its surroundings and growing in either sun or shade, in the North it should be planted in a sheltered position on the north side of the house or wall, otherwise the leaves may be injured by winter sunshine. The variety *baltica* is reputed to be the hardiest form, surviving the winter as far north as Boston, but in my experience it is not so rapid a grower as the type commonly offered by florists. English ivy is as valuable as a ground-cover as it is as a wall vine.

Hydrangea petiolaris (*H. scandens*), **Climbing Hydrangea,** is handsome and distinctive in character, bearing flat-topped clusters of inconspicuous fertile flowers, surrounded by a row of conspicuous white sterile flowers, reminding one of certain of the viburnums. This plant may be distinguished from its relative, *Schizophragma,* by the four white bract-like sepals of the sterile flowers as compared with the single one of those of *Schizophragma.* Climbing by aerial rootlets, this hydrangea is capable of reaching a height of 80 feet.

Ipomoea, **Morning-glory.** In the seed catalogs, Morning-glory (*Ipomoea*), Moonflower (*Calonyction*), Cypress-vine (*Quamoclit*), and Bindweed (*Convolvulus*) are commonly listed together; so as a matter of convenience to the reader they are thus grouped here. The names of these genera are badly mixed in trade catalogs. Moonflower is listed as *Ipomoea,* the common morning-glory (*Ipomoea purpurea*) appears as *Convolvulus majus,* and so on. Good garden forms of morning-glories and their relatives include:

Heavenly Blue, a blue-flowered form of *Ipomoea tricolor,* which grows 10 to 20 feet. The roots should be confined in pots to promote early blossoming.

Emperor Morning-glory. This hybrid group is referred to *Ipomoea Nil* (*I. imperialis*), which grows from 2 to 8 feet high. The Japanese strains offer great color variations—white, blue, crimson, and purple, and flowers which are marbled and striated.

Common Morning-glory, *Ipomoea purpurea,* is offered in many varieties, both single and double.

Moonflower, *Calonyction aculeatum* (*Ipomoea Bona-Nox*), has fragrant white flowers 3 to 6 inches across, opening in the evening and closing before noon the following day. It grows 10 to 20 feet, but in the North it may fail to mature because of the short growing season.

Cypress-vine, *Quamoclit pennata,* has delicate, divided foliage and comparatively small starry flowers of crimson, white, or rose. It grows about 10 feet high.

For garden purposes all of the above may be treated as annuals. The seeds have hard coats (especially moonflower and the Japanese morning-glories), and germination is slow unless they are treated by filing through or notching the seed coats, or by soaking them in warm water for 24 hours.

Man-of-the-earth, *Ipomoea pandurata,* is a hardy perennial which makes enormous tuberous roots. It grows up to 12 feet and will thrive in dry soils.

Lathyrus odoratus, **Sweet Pea.** These delightful annual climbers are likely to be at their best when grown in a deep rich soil, in a region with comparatively cool summers, and in pure air. They are rather intolerant of city conditions, though they can be grown if care is taken to provide them with the right soil and if they are given an early start, to allow them to make a good root system before hot weather.

If you want to be especially good to sweet peas, prepare the ground by digging it 2 feet deep and mix with it decayed manure up to one third of the bulk of the loosened soil. When the vines are to be grown in rows for covering a fence, a trench 2 feet wide should be thus prepared. Bonemeal should be applied at the rate of 10 pounds to 100 lineal feet of trench—scattered over the surface and worked into the upper 6 inches of soil. Good underdrainage is essential.

For outdoor culture there are three methods commonly followed—late fall planting outdoors; planting under glass in February or March; and spring planting outdoors as soon as the ground is workable.

Fall planting is likely to be successful in climates where the winters are such that the seedlings come through without injury. In the vicinity of Philadelphia fall planting usually brings good results; in the vicinity of New York it is a gamble, with the gardener often on the losing end. The ground is prepared early in October and the seeds are planted 2 inches deep in November. When the ground has frozen to a depth of 2 or 3 inches the planting is mulched with 3 or 4 inches of light litter. This must be removed in the spring before it interferes with the growth of the seedlings.

Sweet pea seeds are delightful tidbits for rodents and some birds. They may be protected by coating them with red lead prior to planting. A convenient means of doing this requires the use of a tea-strainer, a candy-box lid, a pan of water, and a small quantity of dry powdered red lead. Place each batch of seeds in the strainer, immerse them in the pan of water, shake off the surplus water, and dump them into the lid of the candy box in which a little of the red lead has been placed. Shake the lid with a rotary motion, which coats the seeds with red lead. The powder adheres quite well to the moist seeds. Remove them, plant them, and proceed with the next batch.

To start the seeds indoors, the procedure to be followed depends on the equipment at hand. If a cool greenhouse is available, plant the seeds in mid-February in flats, spacing them 1 inch apart and covering with ¼ inch of soil. When the seedlings are 2 or 3 inches high, pot them singly in 2½-inch pots, or in threes in 3-inch pots. When they have formed new roots, remove them to a coldframe for hardening and, just as soon as the ground is workable, plant them outdoors where they are to bloom.

If nothing more elaborate than a coldframe is at your service, start about the beginning of March by soaking the seeds overnight in tepid water. Strain off the water, treat seeds with red lead, and then plant in 3-inch pots —3 seeds to a pot, and place in coldframe. When the seedlings are 2 or 3 inches high, harden them off and plant out at the first opportunity. No matter which method is used, if it involves growing them in pots, avoid allowing them to become pot-bound. If there should be danger of this before conditions are right outside, shift them into larger pots. Sweet pea seedlings, however, if they are properly hardened, will stand considerable freezing without injury and it is seldom that the soil conditions outdoors inhibit planting if the time-table given above is followed.

For outdoor spring planting, the soil should have been prepared the fall before. Just as soon as the ground is workable, make a trench 6 inches deep, scatter the seeds about 1 inch apart, and cover with 2 inches of soil. When the seedlings are of such a size that one feels sure they have survived the vicissitudes of infancy, thin them to 3 inches apart. A week or two later take out every other plant so that they finally stand 6 inches apart. As the plants increase in height, gradually fill in the trench.

If a sweet pea plant is allowed to trail on the ground, it seems to become discouraged and never makes the growth of which it is capable when it can climb from the start. Therefore, when the seedlings are 3 or 4 inches high, it is time to think of supports. In the early stages these may be twiggy growths stuck in the ground adjacent to the plants, but these will only take care of them temporarily. As final supports, brushwood (branches trimmed from trees or shrubs), strings, or bamboo stakes may be used. Brushwood perhaps has the least objectionable appearance. Placed on both sides of the row it should extend 4 or 5 feet above the ground, and should be lightly trimmed with hedge shears to "neaten" it. The trimmings can be stuck in the soil to help the seedlings in getting up to the permanent supports. If the location is windy, drive 2 x 2-inch stakes every 10 or 15 feet along the row and string a wire to which the brushwood may be fastened at intervals. Chicken-wire forms an efficient support but is not ornamental before it is covered with the vines. Two-inch mesh is satisfactory, and, of course, it must be supported by stakes about every 10 feet. If the peas are grown in clumps, a cylinder of netting supported by a single stake is sufficient.

If strings are used, 2 x 2-inch posts should be driven into the ground every 6 feet. Connect them with strips of 1 x 2-inch material, nailed horizontally at top and bottom. Knock 1-inch nails every 6 inches into these strips, allowing their heads to project ¼ inch. Starting at one end, connect the top and bottom nails with stout cord, zigzagging it up and down. Make a turn with the cord over each nail. The objection to the use of string is that it shrinks when wet (sometimes causing it to snap), while it lengthens and sags when it is dry.

Sweet peas climb by means of tendrils which occupy the place of the terminal leaflets. These tendrils clutch securely anything they touch, and this does not fit in with the schemes of those who grow sweet peas primarily for cut-flowers or for exhibition purposes. The tendrils in their blind reaching are just as likely as not to attach themselves to the flower stems, which makes it an exasperating job to cut the flowers. So the practice has grown up of cutting off the tendrils and training the vines by tying them with raffia to bamboo stakes (one stake to each plant), or of twining the vines around strings, if they are being grown for winter flowers in a greenhouse.

Lathyrus latifolius, **Perennial Pea.** Unlike the sweet pea, this species has no fragrance, but it is hardy, will grow almost anywhere, and it produces its sprays of rose or white flowers freely. Growing about 6 feet high, it is valuable for low fences, for sprawling over rocks, or in the perennial garden supported on brushwood.

Lonicera Heckrottii, **Everblooming Honeysuckle,** is believed to be a hybrid. It is free-flowering, blooming continuously from June to September with flowers which are yellow inside and rose outside. Since it is a sprawler rather than a climber, it may need assistance on a trellis or fence. Like the trumpet honeysuckle (below) it is subject to attacks by aphis.

Lonicera japonica, **Japanese Honeysuckle,** a potential weed, will grow almost anywhere and may be used as a ground-cover or as a climber. The fragrant flowers are white fading to yellow, and are freely produced during the summer. It is almost evergreen when the winter is a mild one.

Lonicera sempervirens, **Trumpet Honeysuckle,** one of the most valuable vines where it can be made to succeed, produces scarlet flowers from May to September. I have never had much success with it, and have a suspicion that it may require a calcareous soil.

Parthenocissus (Ampelopsis) quinquefolia, **Woodbine** or **Virginia Creeper,** has leaves of five leaflets which change to brilliant scarlet in the fall. It endures considerable shade and may be used as a ground-cover in woodland where, when opportunity occurs, it will climb trees.

Parthenocissus (Ampelopsis) tricuspidata, **Japanese** or **Boston Ivy,** perhaps the most popular vine for covering walls, has leaves which may have three lobes or be divided into three separate leaflets. It grows well in sunny situations and will also thrive in considerable shade. It will cling without aid to wood or masonry.

Parthenocissus (Ampelopsis) tricuspidata Lowii, the so-called **Geranium Creeper,** is not so rampant a grower as the species itself, and is therefore of value when the area to be covered is small. Its leaves are considerably smaller than those of *tricuspidata,* and are purplish when young, with red leaf-stalks and veins.

Polygonum Auberti, **China Fleece-vine.** This is one of the best-tempered of all vines and seems to endure almost anything—poor soil, neglect, city conditions and hard pruning. It produces its sprays of buckwheat-like flowers of white tinged with pink freely throughout the summer and fall. If given opportunity, it climbs to 20 or 30 feet.

Prunus triloba plena, **Double-flowering Plum,** may be trained as a wall shrub, providing a display of its double pink flowers annually if the shoots which have bloomed are pruned off immediately after flowering.

Pueraria Thunbergiana, **Kudzu-vine,** the most rapid-growing plant in the climate of northeastern United States, is capable of covering a fence or arbor in short order once it gets started. Although woody in mild climates, it is killed to the ground every winter in Brooklyn, but its roots survive and it comes up again as soon as the weather warms up. Its flowers are not conspicuous but it produces a mass of luxuriant foliage.

Pyracantha coccinea Lalandi, **Laland's Firethorn,** may be trained as a wall shrub, and indeed, it is almost necessary to do this in regions which experience much zero weather, for otherwise it is likely to be killed to the ground. It is grown largely for its foliage and for the abundant display of orange-red fruits.

Quamoclit pennata, **Cypress-vine.** Listed for convenience under the morning-glories, *Ipomoea.*

Tamarix parviflora, **Tamarisk,** whose masses of fine pink flowers in April or May transform the plant into a cloud of bloom, is a shrub which may be trained against a wall.

Tropaeolum majus, **Nasturtium,** is one of the most popular annual vines. The seeds may be planted on the compost pile where the plants will make it a thing of beauty during the summer and provide plenty of flowers for cutting; or it may be used to cover fences, trellises, or brushwood supports in the perennial garden. Seeds should be planted when the ground has warmed up in the spring in the positions where they are to bloom. The fly in the ointment, so far as nasturtiums are concerned, is the pesky black aphis to which it is subject. Spray with nicotine sulphate and soap solution just as soon as the pest is discovered.

Vitis Kaempferi (*V. Coignetiae*), **Glory-vine,** has glowing crimson foliage in the fall. It is a vigorous grower suitable for large pergolas or for covering a dead tree where its large heavy rounded leaves may be displayed to advantage.

Wisteria multijuga. Some varieties of this Japanese species of wisteria are said to produce flower racemes 3 or 4 feet long. I have never seen them this length, but there are named varieties now being offered by nurserymen which may live up to their reputation under proper conditions.

Wisteria sinensis, **Chinese Wisteria,** is the species most commonly seen. It is quite adaptable and can easily cover an area of 200 square feet; or, by suitable pruning may be made to develop either as a large bush or as a standard. There is a widely held belief that wisterias raised from seeds fail to bloom. This is not so, although plants produced vegetatively from free-flowering individuals, by cuttings or grafting, may come to the blossoming stage earlier. Plants which fail to flower may usually be induced to bloom the following year by pruning in summer, thus checking exuberant vegetative growth. The shoots of the current season should be cut back to within two or three buds of their point of origin at the time when they have nearly attained their maximum growth. If this does not result in blossoms the following year, the vine should be root-pruned by thrusting a spade in the ground close to the stem, in order to cut off a few of the strong roots.

Garden structures as supports for vines. The supports used for vines are many and varied, both in type and materials. The dwelling itself, if of brick, stone, stucco, or concrete, affords a climbing surface for those vines which cling by aerial rootlets and adhesive disks. If, however, the house is of wood, it is best to provide hinged or detachable trellises that can be let down when the house is painted. Hinged trellises are also a convenience when it is necessary to lay vines on the ground for winter protection.

Vine supports are best made of material which does not have to be painted, partly because of the inconvenience of removing the vines whenever they must be repainted, but also because wood that is allowed to weather naturally usually looks better than painted surfaces as a background for plants. The wood selected for garden structures should therefore be of a kind that resists decay, such as cedar, cypress, locust, oak, or chestnut (if the last is obtainable). If one can obtain weathered fence-rails from an abandoned farm they can be made into various attractive garden structures. It is said that soaking the wood in a 5-percent solution of copper sulphate adds to its life, but I have had no experience with this. Creosoting undoubtedly staves off decay, but creosote-treated wood may injure plants in its vicinity. Tests conducted by at least one of the Agricultural Experiment Stations indicate that certain water-soluble salts, such as zinc chloride, and other materials are effective in preserving wood, but the methods of application are not easy for the home gardener to put into practice. Charring, tarring, or setting wood posts in concrete, in spite of widely held opinions to the contrary, have not proved very effective measures to prevent decay of posts beneath the surface of the ground. Since decay ordinarily proceeds most rapidly where wood is in contact with moist earth, either naturally resistant woods, or concrete posts which are slotted to receive the horizontal wooden members of fences or trellises, or metal uprights and connections should be used for garden structures, or else one must become reconciled to periodical replacements.

Fences. Man-made enclosures for one's property may be of ornamental iron-work alone; of masonry and ornamental iron-work; of wood; of wire in various patterns designed for a pleasing appearance and supported on pipe frames; or they may be of a purely utilitarian style, such as cattle fencing. The last-named type is by no means beautiful and should be covered as quickly as possible with vines. If it is planned to paint the fence periodically, annual or herbaceous perennial vines should be used, because the dead stems are removed each year in either case, thus affording an opportunity for painting. If this type of planting is not acceptable, such shrubs as roses or forsythia may be tied to the fence, then unfastened and laid on the ground while painting is in progress. If painting is not contemplated, the vines may be selected on the basis of their appearance only. Personally, I think it scarcely pays to attempt to paint cattle fencing. If heavy galvanized wire is used, it may be expected to last ten or a

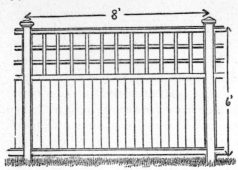

FIG. 17. Board and trellis fence

dozen years anyhow, and by that time you will probably want a different type of structure.

Except for the town garden, wooden fences are vastly preferable (Figs. 17, 18). In all cases, the style selected should harmonize with the surroundings. If the main object is to secure privacy, the fence may be made of closed pales, supported on stout posts (not less than 4 x 4 inches and spaced not more than 6 feet apart), and rails. A pleasing effect is gained when the pales are of cleft oak, western red cedar, or chestnut. Cleft pales have the advantage of being more durable than similar material that is sawed. Cypress boards of varying widths, lightly charred in a bonfire and then brushed with a steel brush to bring out the grain, are also effective. Attach the pales with non-rusting nails (galvanized iron, copper or brass) to avoid iron oxide stains.

If an open fence is preferred, the pickets may be spaced closely together or far apart, the distance depending on whether or not a barrier is required to keep animals in or out. The pickets may be of cedar or chestnut saplings to be informal, or of painted millwork if a fence of more formal character is demanded. In rustic surroundings the various types of woven wood fencing are pleasing in appearance and easy to install.

Trellises. The simplest pattern for a trellis is that of uniform squares arranged either diagonally or horizontally, the latter being generally preferable. Almost infinite variations in pattern are possible, but it is usually best to adopt one that is simple. Because of the somewhat flimsy character of the lath used (which may be from ¼ to ½ inch x 1½ to 2 inches), the trellis should be framed with heavier lumber for rigidity and neatness. (See Plates VIII and XVIII.)

Personally I have no use for the fan-shaped trellis, which is part of the stock in trade of every department store, but I recognize that it may have its advantage when a support is required for an individual vine, and when originality is not desired.

FIG. 18. Board fence and gate

Arches. For the purpose of gaining height in the garden when it cannot be done with a tree or shrub, arches are useful, but care must be exercised in placing them. An arch may be appropriate enough if used to span a walk or an entrance gate, but is entirely out of place when set in the middle of a lawn or flower bed. Arches may be made of metal with pipe frames—a durable sort of construction if galvanized, faithfully painted, and set in concrete—but arches of wood are more pleasing in appearance. Natural poles of larch, cedar, locust, etc., may be used in their construction, or oak or chestnut either rough-hewn or sawed. When the natural wood is used, the parts which enter the ground should be peeled. It might be worth while also to paint underground parts with asphalt paint in the hope that it may defer decay. When the surroundings demand something more elaborate, arches of millwork planed and painted may be used. As with all similar garden structures, arches should be of heavy enough construction (with uprights usually not less than 2 inches square) to avoid any appearance of flimsiness, and should be firmly set at least 18 inches in the ground. At the same time one should take care not to make them so massive that they are out of scale with the surroundings.

Pergolas. Usually the pergola is a series of flat arches connected longitudinally, often with additional cross-pieces on the "roof" between the uprights. It should seldom be used except for spanning a

FIG. 19. Arbor with seats

walk. With flower borders on either side, the pergola affords an opportunity to grow plants which appreciate shade during part of the day. Under some circumstances, the pergola may be designed to possess architectural value, and be constructed, in part, of masonry to harmonize with the character of the house. In such cases, the architect should be consulted before it is planned and erected. On the other hand, it may be very simple, designed mainly as a support for vines and to provide a shady walk between sections of the garden.

When the object in view is largely utilitarian (to provide support for vines or roses) uprights and cross pieces of 1½- or 2-inch galvanized pipe may be used, connected longitudinally with chains or with ropes first steeped in linseed oil. The pipes should be capped or filled with cement mortar to prevent the entrance of water, and should be set in concrete (make the forms by nailing four 6-inch boards together), which extends above the ground line and is beveled to shed water away from the pipe. Such a pergola, which in itself is not beautiful, should be covered as quickly as possible with vines to mask its construction. I have never seen any ill effects from tying roses or similar plants to metal supports, although there is an impression abroad that metal, owing to the facility with which it conducts heat, is inimical to vegetation supported by it.

In general, the pergola is built of heavier material than arches, but this, of course, is determined by the size of the structure. In a pergola designed to span an 18-foot walk, for example, the beams supporting the rafters (which in turn support the strips on which the vines are trained) should be of approximately 8 x 3-inch material, and the rafters 6 x 2 inches. The supporting posts, of course, are in proportion. These may be wood pillars or square posts, or be constructed of concrete or masonry. Such a structure would be entirely out of place in a small garden (Plate XVIII).

To span a walk of 5 or 6 feet, uprights formed of natural posts 6 inches in diameter at the base, with "beams" of the same size and rafters approximately 4 inches in diameter would be ample. If worked timbers were used, the uprights could be 6 inches square, the beams 6 x 2 inches and the rafters 4 x 2 inches, with slats 1 x 2 inches.

The uprights may be spaced from 6 to 10 feet apart and the space between may be either left open, or partially or wholly filled with lattice. If the pergola is flanked by flower beds, the space, naturally, will be left at least partly open. The head-room should be at least 7 feet.

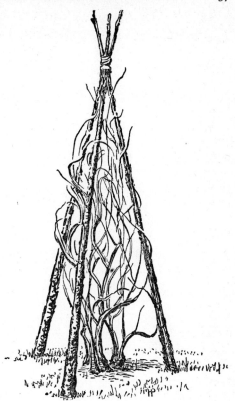

Fig. 20. Tripod

Arbors. Open-work structures, usually square, circular, or octagonal, designed to support the growth of vines which will shade the seats below, are known as arbors. As they are mostly used in the summertime, window-like openings should be left on all sides to allow the entrance of cooling breezes. Fig. 19 depicts a typical arbor.

Pillars and tripods. Useful for accent points in the garden, when well furnished with roses or suitable vines, pillars and tripods may be very decorative. From the standpoint of providing a suitable support for all classes of vines, a cedar post set 2 or 3 feet in the ground is admirable. The side branches should be left but cut back to 6 or 8 inches from the trunk. Tripods, made by setting three posts a foot deep in the ground in a circle 3 or 4 feet in diameter, bringing their tops together, are useful when a broader effect is desired (Fig. 20).

X. HEDGES

A healthy, well-grown hedge, when formed of the right material and occupying the proper position on the grounds, may comprise a beautiful part of the garden design. Even though hedges are sometimes planted for practical purposes such as a windbreak, a screen to ensure privacy, a barrier against animals, or to mark boundary lines, they may still be ornamental.

Selecting hedge material. There are many points to consider when choosing plants for use as hedges. They must be hardy and immune to insect and fungous pests. They must be naturally of compact symmetrical form or else of such a character that they may be pruned or sheared into the desired shape; and, further, they must be plants that are easily propagated, otherwise their price will be prohibitive.

California privet (*Ligustrum ovalifolium*) is the shrub most commonly used for a hedge in many parts of the country, largely because of its amenability to constant shearing and its comparative freedom from insect and fungous pests. I have become somewhat soured on California privet during the past few years because in the Brooklyn Botanic Garden it has been attacked and disfigured by thrips, and because the hedges which were kept closely trimmed were killed to the ground by the winter of 1933-34, although the untrimmed and lightly trimmed hedges of this species suffered comparatively little damage. But in spite of its defects there is little doubt that it will continue as the most popular hedge plant except in regions where the winters are so severe that it is killed to the ground every year. After all, there is no other shrub quite the equal of privet when all its qualities are taken into account. In addition to its immunity and its amenability, we must remember its ease of propagation (it is said that the cuttings for propagating purposes are made in some nurseries by running the shoots through a chaff cutter!); its adaptability to varied soil conditions; its rapid growth; and the ability to survive even though improperly transplanted.

But one does get tired of seeing almost nothing but privet, and, fortunately, there is no lack of other shrubs which may be used for hedges. Before deciding on the use of quick-growing but comparatively impermanent material like privet, the claims should be considered of such plants as beech (*Fagus*), birch (*Betula*), shingle oak (*Quercus imbricaria*); and the wayfaring-tree (*Viburnum Lantana*), as well as the evergreens, hemlock (*Tsuga*), Japanese yew (*Taxus cuspidata*), and arborvitae (*Thuja*). Even though the initial cost may be greater, and a few replacements may be necessary because of the failure of some individuals to survive transplanting, their permanency, beauty, and comparative rarity as hedges are sufficient to warrant their selection. But, before spending good money and labor on an expensive hedge, one should be reasonably certain that the species selected will thrive under the conditions of its future environment. Brief descriptions and requirements of the subjects listed below are given in alphabetical order on the pages following.

SHRUBS SUITABLE FOR HEDGES

1 to 2 feet high

Evergreen: *Berberis verruculosa, Buxus sempervirens suffruticosa, Chamaecyparis obtusa gracilis, Hedera Helix* (trained on a frame), *Taxus cuspidata nana, Thuja occidentalis* (dwarf varieties).

Deciduous: *Berberis Thunbergii minor, Deutzia gracilis, Spiraea* Anthony Waterer, *Viburnum Opulus nanum.*

2 to 5 feet high

Evergreen: *Berberis Julianae, Buxus sempervirens, Chamaecyparis pisifera filifera, Ilex crenata microphylla, Pinus Cembra, P. Mugo, Taxus cuspidata, Thuja occidentalis.*

Deciduous: *Berberis Thunbergii, B. Vernae, Chaenomeles lagenaria* (*Cydonia japonica*), *Deutzia Lemoinei, Euonymus alatus compactus, Hypericum aureum, Larix decidua, Ligustrum amurense, L. ovalifolium, L. obtusifolium Regelianum, Rosa rugosa* F. J. Grootendorst, *Spiraea Thunbergii, Stephanandra flexuosa.*

5 to 10 feet high, or taller

Evergreen: *Chamaecyparis pisifera* varieties, *Ilex crenata, Juniperus virginiana, Picea Abies, Pinus Strobus, Taxus cuspidata capitata, Thuja occidentalis, Tsuga canadensis.*

Deciduous: *Acanthopanax Sieboldianum* (*pentaphyllum*), *Betula populifolia, Euonymus alatus, Fagus grandifolia, F. sylvatica, Hibiscus syriacus,*

Ligustrum amurense, L. ovalifolium, L. vulgare, Lonicera fragrantissima, Quercus imbricaria, Rhamnus cathartica, R. Frangula, Spiraea Vanhouttei, Syringa japonica, S. Josikaea, S. villosa, S. vulgaris, Viburnum Lantana.

DESCRIPTIVE LIST OF TREES AND SHRUBS FOR HEDGES

Acanthopanax Sieboldianum (*pentaphyllum*) stands city conditions, is capable of thriving in poor soil and shade, and is hardy north to Massachusetts. It has light green, glossy leaflets. While not adapted for close shearing, it may be pruned just before growth starts in spring to keep it in shape and prevent it from growing too large.

Berberis Julianae will grow in sunshine or partial shade. It is fairly hardy and survives the winters of Brooklyn, although with some injury to its narrow lustrous leaves. A spiny shrub of upright habit, with yellow flowers and purplish fruits, it is probably not well adapted to shearing, but may be lightly pruned to keep it in shape.

Berberis Thunbergii, **Japanese Barberry,** runs a close second to California privet in popularity. Fairly good under city conditions and hardy in eastern Canada, it will grow in poor soil and stand partial shade. Since it varies considerably in the amount of fruits produced, asexual propagation (by layers, cuttings, or suckers) should be practised on heavy-fruiting individuals to increase the stock. It is so compact naturally that ordinarily it does not require shearing. Left alone it may ultimately form a broad rounded mass up to 6 feet in height.

Berberis Thunbergii minor is a low-growing form of the above, which by shearing may be maintained at a height of from 6 to 18 inches. Another variety of *B. Thunbergii* is the "truehedge columnberry." This is full of promise for those who desire a narrow, compact hedge. *B. mentorensis* is compact and semi-evergreen.

Berberis verruculosa, a low evergreen with small, spiny-toothed leaves, green with glaucous undersides, needs fairly good soil and a sheltered location. It is hardy in southern New England; does not need shearing, and grows to about 3 feet.

Betula populifolia, **Gray Birch.** In the collection of hedges at the Dominion Central Experimental Farm at Ottawa there is one of gray birch, planted in 1897. It is now 7 feet high and about 9 feet in diameter at the base and clothed with foliage from its top to the ground line. This is worthy of consideration for planting in sections where the bronze birchborer is not troublesome.

Buxus sempervirens suffruticosa, **Edging Box.** This is the variety much used for edging flower beds in England. It remains dwarf for a long time. Winter protection is considered desirable on Long Island.

Chaenomeles lagenaria (Cydonia japonica), **Flowering Quince,** which is hardy in Massachusetts, is worth considering by those who desire a hedge somewhat out of the common. It may be made compact by pruning. Its scarlet flowers are produced in spring before the leaves. Unfortunately it is subject to attack by scale insects.

Chamaecyparis obtusa gracilis is a compact pyramidal form of the Hinoki cypress, with rich, dark green foliage, which may be lightly sheared. It is said to dislike lime, and is hardy in Vermont.

Chamaecyparis pisifera filifera, a variety of the Sawara cypress, is an evergreen tree which may be maintained at the desired height by shearing, which causes it to develop a dense compact habit. At the Dominion Central Experimental Farm at Ottawa a hedge of this variety, planted in 1916, is now only a little more than 3 feet in height, having been kept low by shearing.

Deutzia gracilis is a compact low shrub which makes a delightful informal flowering hedge if left unpruned. As rabbits are fond of the twigs it may be necessary when newly planted to provide protection.

Deutzia Lemoinei is a hybrid between *D. gracilis* and *D. parviflora.* It has larger flowers and is a little more vigorous than *D. gracilis.*

Euonymus alatus makes a gorgeous display in the fall when the leaves turn rosy scarlet, and is interesting in winter because of its corky-ridged branches. It is easy to transplant and grows to 7 or 8 feet. A form offered by some nurserymen under the name *Euonymus alatus compactus* may be kept low by cutting back the growth of the preceding year before the new growth starts in spring. (Plate IX.)

Fagus grandifolia, **American Beech.** Probably the only reason this tree is not more widely used as a hedge plant is the uncertainty of the survival of every individual when transplanted. It is winter-hardy in Ontario.

Fagus sylvatica, **European Beech,** is perhaps even better for a hedge but it is not hardy so far north. When sheared in summer it retains most of its leaves throughout the winter—a valuable habit when a windbreak is required. Like the preceding, it prefers a well-drained calcareous soil.

Hedera Helix, **English Ivy,** may be trained to form a low hedge if a support is provided to which the long shoots may be tied during the first year or two. After the hedge is formed it may be clipped every spring just before growth starts. It is not reliably winter-hardy in exposed situations north of Long Island, N. Y.

Hibiscus syriacus, **Rose of Sharon,** may be allowed to grow naturally to make an upright hedge 10 to 12 feet tall. If a hedge of medium size is preferred, it may be kept down by cutting in late winter each year the growth of the preceding year to within one bud of its point of origin. As this shrub blooms on shoots of the current season, the pruning does not result in the loss of flowers. Sometimes it is subject to aphis attacks. It will stand city conditions and is said to be hardy in Montreal.

Hypericum aureum, **St. Johnswort.** This is a species which thrives in poor, dry soil. It naturally forms a broad compact hedge, not furnished, however, with foliage down to the ground line. Its brilliant yellow flowers, nearly 1 inch in diameter, are produced in July and August. Shear it lightly after blossoming to remove seed heads.

Ilex Aquifolium, **English Holly,** is considered by some to be even handsomer than boxwood in regions where it thrives. It is certain that a well-grown hedge of this species is impenetrable by man or beast.

Ilex crenata, **Japanese Holly,** is easier to grow than boxwood and just about as winter-hardy. In severe winters on Long Island, N. Y., the shoots may die back a foot or two, but it quickly recovers and, if not too often cut back, is capable of attaining a height of 12 to 15 feet in a sheltered position. It is easy to transplant.

Ilex crenata microphylla is a small-leaved variety of the above, said to possess greater hardiness. It is preferred for hedge purposes because it is naturally more compact. I have never seen any insect pests on these hollies.

Juniperus virginiana, **Red Cedar,** is a variable species and, when raised from seeds, many differences in habit of growth and color of foliage are to be expected. For this reason, if a hedge of uniform texture is desired, individuals of similar color and habit should be selected if the plants are collected in the wild; or stock propagated from cuttings or grafts of identical specimens should be used. Red cedar stands shearing and may be kept down to 4 or 5 feet or allowed to grow up to 30 feet. It is sometimes badly attacked by red mites.

Ligustrum amurense, **Amur Privet.** The hedges of this species which I have seen have not been so dense or well clothed with foliage as those of *L. ovalifolium,* but the Amur privet is much hardier.

Ligustrum obtusifolium Regelianum, **Regel's Privet,** is sometimes used for hedges, but my reaction on seeing them is that a shrub so naturally graceful is out of place when thus confined.

Ligustrum ovalifolium, **California Privet,** has already received mention on the first page of this chapter. When frequently trimmed, the size of the leaves produced on subsequent shoots is diminished until the effect at a distance is not unlike that of boxwood.

Ligustrum vulgare, **Common Privet,** is hardy and semi-evergreen. It has leaves which are narrower and more pointed than those of *L. ovalifolium.* If privet must be used for a hedge this species should receive the preference in regions of severe winters. It may be clipped, but if left to grow more or less naturally, it will provide a fine display of clusters of lustrous black fruits in the fall.

Lonicera fragrantissima, **Winter Honeysuckle.** I have never seen or heard of this species being used for a hedge, but to me it has many of the earmarks of a successful hedge plant. It is bushy, the leaves are not too large, and its fragrant flowers, produced in late winter, are an attraction. It might not be amenable to close shearing.

Picea, **Spruce.** Several spruces are adaptable for hedges, notably *Picea glauca (canadensis),* *P. Abies (excelsa),* *P. pungens,* and *P. pungens Kosteriana,* Koster's blue spruce. The species selected should be one which thrives in your particular locality. The spruces develop naturally into hedges which are comparatively broad at the base and narrow at the top. Although Koster's blue spruce is capable of growing into a dense and symmetrical hedge, consider long and carefully before employing it, and ask yourself if you constantly want to contemplate its alien blueness. Spruces are liable to bad attacks by red mites ("spiders") in hot summer climates.

Pinus Cembra, **Swiss Stone Pine,** is seldom seen in gardens. It is a pity that it is rather expensive, for its slow growth and beautiful foliage, somewhat similar to that of the white pine, make it an ideal plant for a low evergreen hedge.

Pinus Mugo, **Mugo** or **Swiss Mountain Pine,** is an extremely variable species. Matching plants should be selected in the nursery if they are to be used for hedges. It may be kept down to about a foot in height, or allowed to grow to 3 or 4 feet.

Pinus Strobus, **White Pine,** is one of the best when a tall hedge is required. It may be kept to a height of 6 or 8 feet, or allowed to grow much taller. This and *P. Cembra* give a gray-green effect.

Quercus imbricaria, **Shingle Oak,** forms one of the most successful hedges in the experimental planting at Ottawa. In twenty years it has attained a height and breadth of about 6 feet. The shingle oak has dark green oblong leaves which turn yellowish brown in the fall, changing to brown and remaining on the hedge all winter. It apparently does not object to being sheared.

Rhamnus cathartica, **Buckthorn,** is perfectly hardy as far north as gardens go. This and the following species should be looked upon as standbys for hedges in cold countries. The buckthorn has dull green oval leaves about 2 inches long. With occasional trimming it will make a dense hedge.

Rhamnus Frangula, **Alder Buckthorn,** has pointed oval leaves of dark lustrous green. It is probably preferable to the above as a hedge plant.

Rosa rugosa has many good qualities. Its dark foliage is handsome in summer and changes to orange and scarlet in the fall; its flowers are produced throughout the summer and are followed by large decorative red fruits; and it will thrive both in the city and by the ocean, where it endures the salt spray. It should not be clipped. **F. J. Grootendorst,** a hybrid rose of *rugosa* extraction, is equally useful and perhaps even more free-flowering.

Spiraea **Anthony Waterer** is a low-growing shrub with heads of small crimson flowers in summer. The only trimming needed is to shear off the flower heads when blossoming is over.

Spiraea Vanhouttei makes a graceful hedge up to 8 feet high if left unpruned. It is delightful in spring when the buds are unfolding on its myriads of twiggy shoots. The pure white flowers in crowded umbels follow to make a striking display. Under city conditions the leaves become somewhat rusty in appearance toward the end of summer.

Syringa, **Lilac.** Many of the lilacs are admirable for the production of tall hedges. If allowed to grow informally, a display of flowers may be expected, but if they are pruned severely to make a compact hedge their floriferousness will be reduced or become non-existent. *Syringa Josikaea,* the Hungarian lilac, *S. villosa,* and *S. vulgaris,* the common lilac, are all hardy and may be used in expectation of producing a beautiful hedge.

Stephanandra incisa (flexuosa) has gracefully arching branches and rather dense growth which adapts it for use as an informal hedge. The leaves are bright green, deeply lobed and serrate.

Taxus cuspidata, **Japanese Yew,** in one of its many forms will fill the bill to perfection when a rather sombre evergreen background is required. Its upright forms are capable of making a hedge 12 to 15 feet high, densely clothed with rich foliage. If a tall but narrow hedge is wanted, *T. media Hicksii* should be used. *T. cuspidata nana* and *T. media* are useful for forming low, broad hedges. The Japanese yew seems to stand city conditions better than any other evergreen suitable for hedge-making.

Thuja occidentalis, **Arborvitae,** occurs in many garden forms. In good, rather moist soil, it can be grown into a most attractive hedge. The dwarf forms may be used for low hedges, either sheared or left to grow naturally. The tall varieties, such as the type and varieties *pyramidalis* and *Wareana,* can be used when a height of 10 feet or more is required. *Thuja occidentalis* stands shearing without resentment and is hardy at Ottawa. For use south of Philadelphia, varieties of the oriental arborvitae (*Thuja orientalis*) seem to be preferred.

Tsuga canadensis, **Hemlock,** is one of the most ornamental evergreens for hedges when healthy and well grown, and it is hardy at Ottawa. Unfortunately it is sometimes capricious, and it is well to be sure that it thrives in the locality under the same conditions to which it will be subjected when planted as a hedge. It usually is at its best on a north slope.

Viburnum Lantana, **Wayfaring-tree,** is a change from the usual type of hedge shrub. It is capable of forming a tall, dense, rather broad hedge,

PLATE VIII. *(upper)* PERGOLA AND FENCE, TO SHOW DESIGN. *(lower)* THE SAME PERGOLA FURNISHED WITH ROSES

PLATE IX. HEDGES

FIELD MAPLE, *Ace*
campestre

ORNAMENTAL GRASS
Miscanthus sinens
(TALL), *M. sinens*
gracillimus (MEDI
Festuca ovina gla
(EDGING)

ROSE OF SHARON,
Althaea. MID-JUNE

CALIFORNIA PRIVET
(SEMICIRCLE) AND
Enonymus alatus c
pactus KEPT LOW B
PRUNING. THE BROA
EDGING IS ENGLISH

clothed with foliage down to the ground. The wrinkled leaves are about 3 inches long. It thrives best in a limestone soil.

Viburnum Opulus nanum is a dwarf form of the European cranberry-bush, seldom getting above 2 feet. It is useful, therefore, for a low hedge.

While I have not seen them tried, it is my guess that such species as *V. dilatatum* and *V. Wrightii* would be admirable for large hedges, providing a stunning display in fall and winter if left unpruned so that their brilliant, shining scarlet fruits may develop. *V. dentatum,* blue-black fruit, also may be used.

One is not restricted to trees and shrubs for hedge material. When space is limited it might prove desirable to utilize vines or rambler roses trained on a fence to serve the same purpose as a hedge.

In wet spots where the usual hedge subjects will not thrive, ornamental grasses such as *Miscanthus* and *Eulalia* may be used. (Plate IX.) For temporary hedges, such annuals as hemp (*Cannabis*), summer-cypress (*Kochia*), and summer-fir (*Artemisia*) are permissible.

Care of hedges. If the soil is naturally good, very little preparation is needed before planting a hedge except to dig in or plow in a dressing of manure; but if the soil is poor, it is advisable to make a trench 2 feet wide and deep, and fill it with good soil. If this cannot be done, the next best thing is to break up the ground 2 feet deep and incorporate a liberal quantity of well-decayed manure.

Planting. To ensure perfect alignment of the hedge, a line should be stretched along the space to be planted and a shallow furrow to be followed when planting made beneath it in the soil. If on a curve, the course should be laid out with the aid of a garden hose and similarly marked and followed.

The first hole should be made at one end of the furrow, taking out sufficient soil with a spade to accommodate the roots of a single plant without crowding. The soil for filling around the roots of the first plant can be taken from the space to be occupied by the second, and so on to the end of the furrow. It is essential that the earth around the roots be thoroughly firmed by tamping or by tramping.

The depth to plant is dependent upon the subjects being used. Privet, for instance, may be set 3 inches deeper than it was in the nursery; but the majority of plants, especially evergreens, should not be placed more than 1 inch deeper than they stood before.

No hard and fast rule can be laid down for the distance between plants. Specimens of privet are generally set 1 foot apart; Japanese barberry 9 inches to 1 foot; deciduous shrubs in large sizes, also ever-greens, 2 to 4 feet, according to size.

The time of planting depends upon the type of material used. Ever-greens may be planted in August or September, also in late April and May. Planting of deciduous shrubs for hedges may commence at the end of September and continue until the ground becomes frozen. Spring planting may start as soon as the soil is in workable condi-tion and continue until growth commences.

Shearing. Immediately after planting, most deciduous subjects should be pruned back severely to promote the formation of a bushy hedge with foliage down to the ground. It is a mistake to allow a formal hedge to increase in height too rapidly, as this tends to pre-vent it from acquiring the solidity and bushiness desired.

The amount of shearing required depends largely upon the taste of the individual. Many of the plants mentioned in the preceding list need little or no shearing; while, on the other hand, privet may have a clipping every few weeks if a very trim hedge is desired. It is usual, however, to shear privet about three times a year.

The hedge should be trimmed so that it is wider at the bottom than at the top; otherwise it is almost certain to become thin and ragged at the base because of insufficient light. It is feasible to clip hedges into various geometrical shapes, but a somewhat pyramidal form is most desirable as this shape lessens danger of breakage by snow.

Evergreen hedges such as arborvitae, red cedar, retinospora, and the yews may be sheared either before growth starts in spring or about the end of June or in July when the new growth has somewhat hardened; or, if the hedge is growing so vigorously that it seems likely to get out of hand, it may be sheared twice a year. Hedges of pine may be kept from increasing in height and bulk too rapidly and bushiness may be promoted by shortening the "candles" before the needles develop in spring. Hemlock, fir, and spruce should have the new growth shortened about the end of June, or in July.

After-care. A strip of soil should be kept cultivated on either side of the formal hedge as this enhances its trim appearance and keeps down weeds which might smother the lower branches and mar the solidity of the hedge. If leaves drift into the hedge during the winter they should be raked out in early spring in the interest of neatness. Thorough watering may be necessary during droughty periods. The application of fertilizer may or may not be desirable; if the hedge is making satisfactory growth leave well enough alone. A soil that is very rich may result in exuberant growth and, in consequence, necessitate too frequent shearing.

It is worth while to select the right subject for the hedge and to take pains to ensure that it is properly planted and cared for. A sickly and unkempt hedge is an eyesore, while an appropriate and well-kept one is beautiful.

XI. FLOWER BEDS AND BORDERS

Location and design. When planning beds for flowers, one should always keep in mind the general ensemble with a thought for the satisfaction brought about by a definite design in which the beds are related both to each other and to their surroundings. A cluttered lawn lacks the restfulness of a clear expanse of green. Flower beds, therefore, give the most pleasing effect when arranged along a walk, in groups to make a formal garden, or against a background of shrubbery. The size of the beds should be in proportion to the rest of the grounds, though seldom should they be less than 3 or more than 10 feet wide. Intricate geometrical patterns, which greatly increase the cost of upkeep, should always be avoided except in extremely formal gardens. Suitable plans are illustrated in Figs. 21 and 22. In Fig. 23 is shown a group of flower beds which are not satisfactory because the component parts are lacking in harmony of shape.

If a walk to be bordered by flowers is short, a rectangular bed on one or both sides of its entire length is appropriate. If it is long, groups of beds can be arranged, with spaces of lawn between them to break the formation and to provide easy access to other parts of the grounds. Variation in the shape of the beds will avoid monotony (Fig. 24).

Laying out the beds. When the time comes to lay out the beds a great deal of fun is in prospect in playing about with garden geometry. The tools necessary are several garden lines (mason's cord will do if regular garden lines are not available); a steel tape-measure (50 or 100 feet long, according to the size of the garden); a 10-foot measuring rod marked in feet and quarter-feet; and a quantity of marking stakes (of material 1 inch square cut into 8-inch lengths, with one end sharpened), and a mallet or hammer.

In laying out a series of beds such as are illustrated in Fig. 25, the first procedure is to find the center of the building or room on the axis of which the layout is to be made, and mark it on the wall near the ground level. From this mark measure off accurately an equal distance (about 10 feet) on either side along the line of the building and mark the two points with stakes. Take about 20 feet of wire or non-stretchable cord, form a loop at one end, and to the other attach a clothes-pin or something similar which is capable of making a mark on the ground. Slip the loop over one of the side stakes, stretch the line and strike an arc approximately on the axis. Move the line to the other side stake and strike an arc to intersect the first. Insert a stake with a nail driven in it to indicate the exact point of intersection.

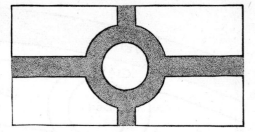

FIG. 21. Harmonious groups of beds

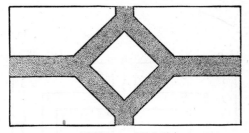

FIG. 22. Harmonious groups of beds

Now drive a stake at the central mark on the building, attach a cord and extend it so that it passes through the inter-section of the two arcs. This line will be at a right angle to the house and thus it indicates the axis of the house or

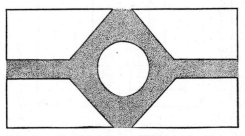

FIG. 23. Inharmonious groups of beds

room, and also the axis of the flower garden. As this line will serve as a base from which measurements are made in laying out the beds, it is important to do the work accurately. The marking stakes should be carefully driven in so that there is no danger of displacement before the work is completed.

The next step is by measurement to mark the points AA. Set off right angles at these points and locate by measurement the corners of the garden—BBBB. Right angles may be laid out by the method just described, or, if the nature of the terrain does not admit of this, by the

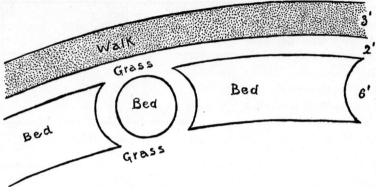

FIG. 24. Beds paralleling a walk

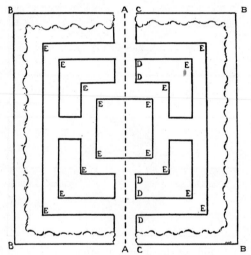

FIG. 25. To illustrate method of laying out beds

3-4-5 method indicated in Fig. 26. Here the right angle is made by measuring off any multiple of three, in feet or yards, along the base line from A and carefully marking it with a stake, B. (Each foot or yard is considered the unit of measurement.) From A describe an arc with a radius of four units and from B an arc with a radius of five units. Mark the intersection of the two arcs with another stake, C. A line now drawn from A to the intersection C will be at right angles to the base line. When the position of the corners has been determined, the accuracy of the layout may be checked by stretching lines diagonally across the square. If the work has been done accurately, each diagonal will be of the same length and the lines will cross exactly in the center. These diagonal lines will be an aid in locating the corners and angles marked E on Fig. 25. The rest is simply a matter of stretching lines and measuring to locate the other corners of the beds. Thus on

a line between CC it is possible to mark the corners D.
By moving the line the remainder may be similarly
marked.

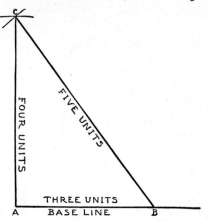

To lay out the design for the
beds shown in Fig. 27 the same
method is followed up to the
point of locating the corners of
the garden. To make the ellipse the following method
may be used: Stretch lines
lengthwise and across to divide
the plot into four equal parts.
With the intersection of the
lines in the center, indicate the

FIG. 26. Laying out a right angle by 3-4-5 method

desired length and breadth of the ellipse. From the point A measure
to the central line on either side of the intersection a distance equal to
half the length of the ellipse, and drive in stakes BC. Fasten a cord to
B, carry it around A to C and fasten. Remove stake A and place a
scriber (a short stake will do) in the bend of the cord and move it
around, thus marking on the ground the circumference of half of the
ellipse. Keep the cord taut all the time. When one side has been
marked, throw the cord over the stakes BC and do the other side. If
an oval is desired (that is, a true egg shape, broader at one end), it is
made by describing half an ellipse and attaching to it a semicircle with
a radius equal to half the short diameter of the ellipse (Fig. 27). This
is sometimes a desirable form for an automobile turn. The curved
edges of the corner beds in Fig. 27 may be laid out by making an
ellipse of larger size—in this case 8 feet longer and 8 feet wider.

It is usually quite simple to lay out beds of circular outline, or beds
in which one or more sides consist of segments of a circle. All that
is necessary is to find the center, drive in a peg, loop over it a cord
as long as the radius, attach a scriber and mark the outline. But when
the design of curved beds or borders does not correspond to any
definite geometric figure, the curves are best laid out on the ground
with the aid of a garden hose, which should be moved around until
it describes a curve pleasing to the eye and adapted to the space the
bed or border is to occupy.

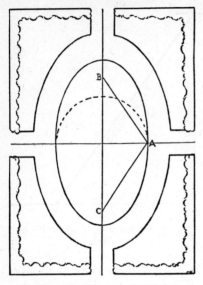

FIG. 27. Laying out elliptical bed. Dotted lines show how to attach a semi-circle to make an oval.

Digging the beds. The methods of soil preparation and improvement already outlined are entirely suitable for lawns, and usually for tree and shrub planting and for the vegetable garden. But when it comes to flower borders it is wise to be a little more meticulous in preparing the ground. English gardeners think nothing of trenching the ground 3 feet deep in order to provide a deep mellow bed of earth in which the plant roots may ramify and find more sustenance and moisture than in a shallow soil. Usually, however, it seems hopeless to expect American gardeners to acknowledge the wisdom of such thorough preparation; so, as a compromise, I am advocating double digging to ensure reasonably adequate soil preparation. First, however, one should know how to do single digging (Fig. 28).

But before any digging is attempted, the gardener should make sure that the soil is in the proper condition to be efficiently worked. If it is too wet, it will stick to the tools and the tilth will be damaged by puddling; while if too dry, its hardness will impede the work of the digging spade and fork.

The technique of digging involves the thrusting of the spade or fork vertically into the ground to the entire height of the blade of the tool being used. If the tool is thrust in at an angle, say of 45 degrees, it will not enter the ground deeply enough. Each spadeful of soil is turned upside down to reverse the position of the top and bottom layers, and, except when heavy soils are being thrown up to lie rough over winter, all lumps should be broken so that the soil is in fine tilth. A skillful digger can make the surface so fine that little or no subsequent raking is necessary. A wheelbarrow-load of manure should always be at hand to be applied evenly to the soil as it is dug, being

FIG. 28. Digging

spread at least 3 inches below the surface, especially when a seed bed is being prepared. (Some gardeners spread the manure over the surface before starting to dig, but if you object to manure on your shoes, the wheelbarrow method is preferable.)

Single digging. The simplest method of putting the soil in good shape for a border consists of first making a trench 1 foot wide and as deep as the spade or fork will allow when sunk vertically into the soil. The length of the trench is dependent upon the size and shape of the area to be dug. If it is a narrow border, the first trench should extend all the way across one end, and the soil removed should be carted at once to the other end, where it will be in readiness for filling the final trench. If the plot is wide—say, 20 x 40 feet—a convenient plan is to make a trench exactly half its width, throwing the soil of the first trench to the other side at the same end. Digging would then proceed as indicated in Fig 29, up one side and down the other, so that the soil from trench No. 1 will be available for filling trench No. 40.

Weeds and trash on the surface of the ground near the first trench may be scraped into the bottom, and several forkfuls of manure should then be scattered in the trench. This done, it is time to start to dig the second trench, thrusting the spade vertically into the ground and lifting the soil by bearing down with one hand and up with the other.

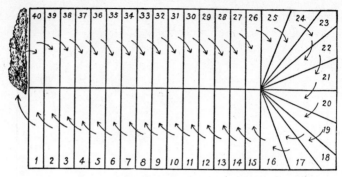

Fig. 29. Diagram of digging

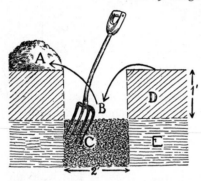

Fig. 30. Double digging: *A.* Soil removed in making initial trench *B;* *C.* Subsoil forked up and mixed with manure; *D.* Topsoil to be placed in trench *B; E.* Subsoil yet to be treated.

With a dexterous flick of the wrists the soil is turned top-side down over the trash and manure in the initial trench. Stabbing it with the spade or fork, combined sometimes with a beating motion, serves to break the lumps. Any large stones that are found are cast aside.

Trash and weeds are then dropped into the bottom of trench No. 2, and manure is thrown against the sloping bank of earth that has been formed when the soil was overturned into trench No. 1. The work thus proceeds until, when the last trench is reached, the soil from the first is thrown over the trash and manure in the bottom, and the job is finished.

Double digging. In double digging (Fig. 30), the initial trench is dug to a width of 2 or 3 feet to allow sufficient room to work the lower layer of soil. Manure is spread on this and then forked as deeply as possible into the ground. Then soil from the next 2- or 3-foot area is turned over into the trench to a depth of 5 to 6 inches and manure scattered on it. More soil from the second area is placed on top of this, leaving a trench comparable to the initial one. This in turn is filled with soil from the third area (after the subsoil has been manured and forked up) and so on until the end of the plot is reached, when the soil removed in making the initial trench is used for filling.

Style of planting. What to plant in these beds and borders is the next problem to solve. Spring-flowering bulbs may be used, plus tender bedding plants for the summer display. (See below.) Perennials are satisfactory subjects, especially for spring and fall bloom, while annuals hold an important place with their quick growth from spring-sown seed and their abundant flowering in midsummer. Each of these types of plants will receive special treatment in a separate chapter. For the present, therefore, we are concerned with the *style* to be followed in planting—that is, whether formal or informal; whether outdoor decoration or cut flowers for indoors may be more desired; whether the owner's preferences lean toward one group of colors, one dominant form of plant, or toward another; and whether there are sufficient funds available for replacements if certain formal styles of planting are considered.

The informal element. Formal beds ordinarily call for strictly formal planting, but so long as the design is not obscured by the growth of the plants, there is practically no limit to the methods of planting.

An interesting informal style for planting a formal garden was observed on one of the large estates in England. On the terrace were box-bordered beds of geometrical design, which were given a pleasantly informal touch by a solid groundwork of alpine forget-me-not, through which the flowers of the pink tulip Clara Butt appeared at irregular intervals as the result of deliberately haphazard planting.

Some years ago in England I was interested to notice what was then to me a novel idea in formal bedding. The scheme was probably dictated by reasons of economy, and consisted of perennials, annuals, and bedding plants, which furnished a series of formal beds in a public park. One bed, as an example, contained the following plants: perennials—double sunflowers, Shasta daisies, and *Erigeron speciosus;* annuals—cosmos and ten-weeks' stock; bedding plants—ageratum, snapdragon, and African marigold. Plantings such as this are suitable only in beds of considerable size, as the height of some of the subjects would be entirely out of proportion in beds less than 8 feet wide. But if properly planned such a planting is quite effective, and, by the use of spring-flowering bulbs which are later replaced with the annuals and bedding plants, it provides something of interest throughout the whole growing season.

A more common present-day method of planting formal beds is to form a groundwork of one or more low-growing plants, the monotonous flatness of which is broken by "dot" plants of greater height. A ground-cover of a bronze-foliaged, red-flowering variety of *Begonia semperflorens* interspersed with fuchsias grown as standards, with a border of dwarf lobelia, is a typical combination.

The trouble with formal planting is that if both a spring and summer display are desired, the contents of the beds must be changed at least twice annually. Thus after the summer bedding plants (set out in May or June) have been ruined by frost, they are removed from the beds and spring-flowering bulbs are planted. In climates where winters are not too severe, such subjects as pansies, English daisies, alpine forget-me-not, and rock-cress (*Arabis albida*) may be planted over the bulbs to form a ground-cover and provide bloom between the time of the passing of the bulbs and the setting out of the tender bedding plants in May or June.

In favored locations it is sometimes possible to leave the bulbs in the ground, but usually the results are not comparable to those obtained by setting out fresh bulbs every year. However, in a congenial soil and locality, bulbs may produce good blooms for several years in succession. The beds may, in such a case, be planted in spring with annuals or bedding plants for a summer display. Seeds of such plants as sweet alyssum, portulaca, *Phlox Drummondii,* or other long-blooming annuals may be sown in the beds toward the end of April; or in May bedding plants may be set between the rows of bulbs. This plan offers difficulty, however, because the soil cannot be properly tilled and because the bulbs are subject to injury when new plants are being set out. The unsightly ripening foliage of the bulbs also is a drawback, for it must be left until it has withered naturally.

Strictly formal style. The Elizabethan knot garden laid out at Hampton Court in 1924 offers some useful suggestions for formal planting which, by appropriate changes, might be adapted to an American garden. Interlacing ribbons of dwarf shrubs clipped to uniform size comprise the design of the beds in the Hampton Court garden. The type of pattern is illustrated in Fig. 31. Dwarf box, lavender, thyme, lavender-cotton, and savory are the shrubs used. For gardens in northern United States or in Canada, where thyme and lavender-cotton might not survive, *Berberis Thunbergii minor, Ber-*

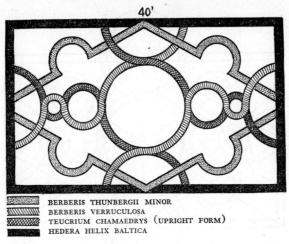

BERBERIS THUNBERGII MINOR
BERBERIS VERRUCULOSA
TEUCRIUM CHAMAEDRYS (UPRIGHT FORM)
HEDERA HELIX BALTICA

FIG. 31. Design for a "knot" garden

beris verruculosa, Hedera Helix baltica (trained and clipped), Teucrium Chamaedrys (the upright form), or the dwarf polyantha rose Eblouissant might be used as substitutes. The interspaces could be planted with a dwarf carpeting plant such as mother-of-thyme (Thymus Serpyllum and its varieties), Sedum acre, Antennaria neodioica, and such subjects. If a garden of this type were of considerable size, the shrubs forming the interlacing ribbons might be allowed to grow a foot or more in height, with Pachysandra used to fill the interspaces. A hardy formal garden may thus be established which eliminates the necessity of replanting twice annually. Trimming and weeding are the only tasks of maintenance demanded.

If more flowers are desired in a garden of this character, the groundwork of perennials may be omitted and bulbs, together with pansies, or English daisies may be planted for a spring display, to be followed by dwarf forms of Phlox Drummondii, verbena, lobelia, and sweet alyssum. The branches of the verbena and phlox need to be pinned to the ground to keep them from overtopping the smaller plants.

The Victorian style of carpet-bedding is now somewhat out of date, but if one wants to play with the idea, he may grow certain tropical and subtropical plants under glass and set them out when the weather is suitable. Scores of examples of what to raise and how to create a pattern may be found by referring to any of the old gardening books.

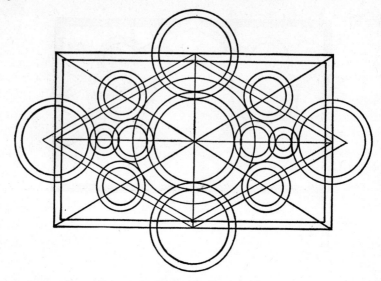

FIG. 32. Method of laying out Fig. 31

"Foliage" plants have always been especially in demand for carpet-bedding, because they function in the design from the time they are set out until they are brought indoors to avoid being frost-killed. Alternantheras are especially popular, because they are easily clipped into the bounds of the design. Dwarf flowering plants of long blooming habit have also been found useful, but the number of these is limited. Begonias, sweet alyssum, ageratum, dwarf lobelia, and dwarf forms of *Phlox Drummondii* can always be counted on to do yeoman service.

Laying out patterns in formal beds. When preparing to plant the more formal type of beds, especially those in which intricate designs are used, garden geometry once more comes into play (Fig. 32). The methods previously suggested, or modifications of them, will serve for laying out the main elements of the patterns. The plants which carry out the design must be set with mathematical precision. Marking sticks of various sizes, with teeth set at exact intervals, will help in spacing the plants evenly in exact lines. These markers may be made by inserting wooden pegs in holes bored in a stick 1½ inches square at the distances at which the plants are to be set. The teeth from broken wooden rakes serve admirably. In order to avoid too great a multi-

plicity of markers the teeth on
one side can, for example, be set
at 4 inches, on the opposite side
at 6 inches (Plate XXXI).

Before laying out the pattern
the bed must be raked level and
the surface carefully fined so that
the marks made when scribing
the pattern may be clearly seen.
When the main pattern has been
drawn the marker comes into
play to indicate the exact position
of the plants. One section is
marked at a time—using the

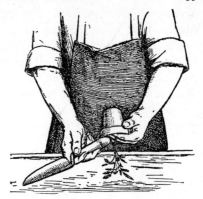

Fig. 33. Tap edge of pot with trowel
handle to loosen plant

marker by pushing the teeth into the ground; or, when curved lines
are being formed, by dragging it through the surface so as to make
grooves which parallel those of the main design. It is unnecessary to
say that this is a ticklish job which must be done carefully to avoid
obliterating lines which form other parts of the design. When one
section has been fully marked, planting should proceed, starting from
the center of the bed and working toward the edges. The actual planting is accomplished by making the holes for the roots of small material with a dibber, or using a trowel when the roots are larger. If the
plants are in pots they may be removed as indicated in Fig. 33. As the
plants are set in place, the soil must be made firm about their roots
by pressure of the fingers, and the surrounding earth should be carefully smoothed.

Methods of handling bedding plants. The tender bedding plants—
alternanthera, begonia, echeveria, lobelia, coleus, geranium, and the
like—are obtained by purchase from a florist or by raising them in
one's own greenhouse, afterward hardening them off in a coldframe
prior to planting.

The half-hardy and hardy plants—sweet alyssum, phlox, ageratum,
verbena, feverfew, etc.—may be started in a hotbed in March and
hardened off in a coldframe.

Certain hardy perennial plants used in bedding, such as *Arrhena-
therum bulbosum, Cerastium tomentosum, Veronica incana,* and

Sedum and *Sempervivum,* may be kept in the reserve garden until May or June when they are set in their summer quarters.

The extravagant use of "bedding out" plants has fallen into disfavor, and rightly so. It is expensive and does not begin to afford the possibilities for making an interesting and beautiful flower garden that are offered when the main standby is hardy material.

This brings us to a consideration of the hardy perennial garden, which itself requires a chapter.

XII. HARDY HERBACEOUS PERENNIALS

PLANNING AND CARE OF PERENNIAL GARDEN

The culture of hardy perennials is one of the most satisfying branches of gardening. But even the most rabid enthusiast must admit that a border or garden where the planting is strictly limited to this group is not constantly colorful. Unfortunately, many otherwise desirable perennials have only a short period of bloom; and others, such as oriental poppies, die down soon after flowering and leave distressing gaps in the planting.

What type of garden? There are several ways of overcoming the problem of avoiding a spotty effect in the perennial garden. One method is to arrange the spring, summer, and fall flowers in groups which form a definite pattern throughout the border; others are to make free use of annuals, bedding plants, and summer-flowering "bulbs" to fill the gaps; or to make segregated seasonal borders or gardens for spring, summer, and fall displays. The first two methods are applicable to both large and small properties; the last is practicable only where there is sufficient room for several flower borders or gardens, and desirable only when such gardens can be placed where they are not prominently in view during their off season.

If the principle of a mixed border is adopted, it is possible to contrive one that is colorful throughout the whole growing season. Hardy spring-flowering bulbs (which are really herbaceous perennials, though not often thought of as such) are largely relied upon for the early display. These are followed by spring, summer, and autumn-blooming perennials. Any gaps left by the early-blooming subjects are filled either by planting seeds of annuals in the place where they are to grow, or by setting out annuals or bedding plants which have been raised in greenhouse, hotbed or coldframe, and grown in pots or flats until time for their transfer to the border. There are almost no lengths to which one may not go in the provision of plants to fill bare spots. In many of the large show gardens it is part of the routine to grow this material in pots for the purpose of filling gaps in the flower garden.

Lilies, annuals, and bedding plants are sometimes grown to flowering size before they are set out for flower-garden display. It is questionable how far these extraneous aids to flower gardening are desirable. Certain it is that a greater sense of achievement comes when a constantly colorful garden is maintained without the aid of greenhouses and coldframes.

There are some plants, notably chrysanthemums, which are so complaisant that they may be dug from the open ground when they are about to bloom, and transplanted to another location with no indication of injury. If a piece of reserve ground is available (possibly in the vegetable garden), it is a good plan to grow there a selection of amiable subjects and transplant them to the flower border at the time when they are most needed.

In addition to the use of annuals and bedding plants, summer-flowering bulbs (the term being used in its broadest sense) may be planted in bare spots from the end of April to the beginning of July. The summer hyacinth may be set out in late April or early May; gladiolus from late April until early in July; dahlia and tuberose in late May or early June. The object of this interplanting is not only for the purpose of maintaining a constant supply of flowers, but also to eliminate the appearance of bare ground, which in itself is not beautiful and which may support weeds if not already occupied with garden plants.

Size and form of the perennial garden. The size and form of the perennial garden is, of course, dependent on the surroundings. It may consist of a series of related beds enclosed by a wall or hedge in a semi-formal layout, or of borders on one or both sides of a walk which may or may not have a background of wall, fence, hedge, or shrubbery.

I once knew an estate in England where the perennials were effectively displayed on the site of an old apple orchard. The trees were gnarled and picturesque, and, due to the removal of those which were too decrepit, did not appear to be planted in formal rows. A low hedge of boxwood enclosed this perennial garden (which was about 150 feet square), and access to the plants was gained by means of narrow walks of stepping-stones which meandered beneath the trees. The effect was delightful throughout the growing season, especially in the spring when the apple blossoms appeared in pinkish clouds above the perennials. Such a garden affords an opportunity to grow both sun and shade-loving plants in fairly close proximity.

I think, however, that the most effective perennial gardens are those consisting of a rather long border set in greensward with a backing of shrubs. The border should, of course, be in proportion to the size of the place. To get best results, it should not be narrower than 6 feet and, when circumstances permit, a width of 10 or 12 feet is preferable. Although a little shade is not objectionable, it is a mistake to place the garden where it is subject to invasion by roots of voracious trees such as the elm. If a border has to be placed in such a location, some provision must be made to prevent the tree roots from robbing it of water and sustenance intended for the flowers. The surest way to do this is to place a barrier of metal or concrete between the tree and the border, sunk in the ground sufficiently deep to prevent the roots from passing below it, and long enough to prevent them from passing around the ends. Another method is to dig a trench annually between tree and border, chopping off all the roots encountered—but this is not good for the tree and involves a great deal of work each year.

Making the planting plan. When about to make a planting plan for a flower border, obtain some paper which is marked in squares, and draw to scale the outlines of the beds or borders. Then with the aid of the plant lists following, the catalog of your favorite dealer in hardy plants, and a grain or two of salt to offset the sometimes too enthusiastic plant descriptions, proceed to make the plan. First, decide on the type of garden desired—whether strictly perennial, or mixed; whether seasonal or designed to carry on throughout spring, summer, and fall. The time of blooming, height, color, provision for succession of bloom, and texture of foliage must all be considered. The plants should be arranged so that the border does not present a monotonous slope from back to front. The skyline at the back should be varied, with the high and low spots maintaining a certain amount of balance. At intervals, tall and medium-height plants should extend toward the front of the border, forming bays in which plants of lower stature are placed.

Plants of one species or variety should generally be set out in groups containing from three to a dozen or more, depending on their habit and growth and the space available. For example, a single plant of viola would seldom be effective, but when six or more are planted together, they form a clump large enough to register. Moderate-sized plants, such as chrysanthemum, may be set out in groups of from three to nine specimens; while plants of strong bushy habit, such as peonies, make a sufficiently large mass when planted singly.

The groups of the various kinds should form irregular outlines, usually longer than broad, as indicated in the sample planting plans (Figs. 34, 35, 36). These plans are not intended to be followed exactly, and are included merely as suggestions.

In selecting the varieties, avoid using too many with an ephemeral blooming season—no matter how beautiful they are—and avoid including too many with poor foliage. Don't be disappointed if the result does not come up to expectations, for a garden is seldom perfect from the beginning. One advantage of dealing with annuals, perennials, and bedding plants is that if a mistake has been made it is possible to rectify it without much expense.

Planting and general care. The soil preparation for perennial beds and borders should be thorough. (See Chapter XI, BEDS AND BORDERS.)

Planting may be carried out in the fall or in the spring. Early-blooming plants are preferably set out in the fall, while late bloomers ordinarily may be planted in the spring without adversely affecting the current season's display of bloom. Holes should be dug large enough to accommodate all the roots without crowding. The soil should be carefully worked in among them and then compacted by pressure of the hands or feet. After planting, level off the soil with a rake so as to make a neat-looking job. If the planting has been done in the fall, wait until the frost has penetrated the ground an inch or two and then apply a protective mulch 2 to 6 inches thick, according to the severity of the normal winter in your region. This mulch should consist of light organic matter which will not pack so tightly as to exclude air. Strawy manure may be used, partly decayed leaves, or newly fallen leaves held in place with twiggy branches on top of them. Salt hay and peatmoss also make good coverings. I have a friend who mulches his flower border every fall with pine needles, with favorable results. Many gardeners are horror-stricken at the notion of using pine needles, believing that they are acid and very injurious. If they were left to decay and were then dug into the soil, they might cause considerable damage, but the practice is to remove them in the spring.

In applying the winter mulch, care must be taken to avoid smothering plants which have evergreen leaves. Foxgloves and Canterbury bells, if growing in sections where winter protection is needed, should

ANNUAL BORDER

Sweet Peas | Tithonia speciosa | Cosmos (late var) | Polygonum orientale | Helianthus cucumerifolius | Tithonia speciosa | Amarantus caudatus | Dahlia | Cosmos (late var) | Sweet Peas

Cosmos (early var) | Euphorbia marginata | Marigold Guinea Gold | Nicotiana affinis | Snapdragon (tall var) | Marigold Guinea Gold | Euphorbia marginata | Salvia farinacea | Tithonia speciosa

Ageratum (tall var) | Calliopsis | China Aster | Ageratum (tall var) | French Marigold | Anchusa | China Aster | Aretotis grandis | Snapdragon (tall var) | Pompon Dahlia

Sweet Alyssum | Phlox drummondi | Dimorphotheca | Marigold (dwarf) | Verbena | Petunia | Phlox drummondi | Sweet Alyssum | Nasturtium Golden Gleam | Snapdragon (intermediate var) | Ageratum (dwarf)

PERENNIAL BORDER

Helianthus orgyalis | Delphinium | Bocconia | Hardy Aster | Helenium | Hollyhock | Anchusa | Boltonia | Phlox | Pyrethrum | Hardy Aster | Delphinium | Lilium regale | Physostegia virginiana | Hollyhock | Helianthus orgyalis

Coreopsis grandiflora | Chrysanthemum | Madonna Lilies | Day Lilies | Peony | Anthemis tinctoria | Anemone japonica | Erigeron | Scabiosa caucasica | Rudbeckia speciosa | Chrysanthemum | Gypsophila | Salvia azurea | Coreopsis grandiflora | Peony

Eupatorium coelestinum | Iceland Poppies | Scilla sibirica | Arabis and Muscari | Campanula carpatica | Alyssum saxatile | Dianthus | Papaver | Delphinium chinensis | Eupatorium coelestinum

Nepeta mussini | Scilla | Geum | Crocus

T – Tulip | N – Narcissus

MIXED BORDER

Delphinium | Boltonia | Hollyhock | Delphinium | Hardy Aster | Hibiscus | Phlox | Delphinium | Helianthus orgyalis | Dahlia | Hollyhock | Hardy Aster | Helianthus | Delphinium

Day Lily | Lilium regale | Dahlia | Gladiolus | Antirrhinum | Anemone japonica | Rudbeckia speciosa | Day Lily | Lilium candidum | Phlox | Anemone japonica | Marigold guinea gold | Phlox | Dahlia | Day Lily | Shasta Daisy

Coreopsis grandiflora | Helenium | Peony | Ageratum | Verbena | Phlox drummondi | Marigold | Chrysanthemum | Shasta Daisy | Rudbeckia speciosa | Eupatorium coelestinum | Fuchsia | Coreopsis grandiflora | Peony | Marigold (French)

Aquilegia | Callistephus | Iberis sempervirens | Alyssum saxatile | Dianthus caesius | Heliotrope | Dianthus caesius | Eupatorium coelestinum | Iberis sempervirens | Phlox speciosa | Pyrethrum | Tunica saxifraga | Arabis | Ageratum | Lobelia | Alyssum

Nepeta

S – Santvitalia | T – Tulip | N – Narcissus | Alyssum | C – Crocus | PerSubsa | S – Scilla sibirica | Santvitalia | H – Hyacinth | G – Gladiolus

FIGS. 34, 35, and 36. Planting plans

have the mulch placed on the soil over their roots but under their rosettes of leaves, while their tops are protected by covering them with fruit baskets or evergreen boughs.

In the spring, the rougher portions of the mulch, if it is bulky organic manure, should be removed, while the finer residue is lightly forked into the surface soil. If salt hay or a pine-needle mulch has been used, it must be completely removed; if peatmoss, enough of it to avoid overloading the soil.

At this time, go over the border carefully and reset any plants which have been heaved out of the ground by the action of frost.

Throughout the growing season, the surface should be loosened 1 or 2 inches deep by use of a hoe (or your favorite cultivating tool) to kill weeds and to conserve moisture. Recently, doubts have been cast on the value of surface cultivation as a means of conserving moisture, but it is not likely that the practice will be abandoned for many years to come. Ordinarily, cultivation should be done after each rainy period, but not until the surface has dried enough not to stick to the tools.

Watering. During periods of drought, it is a great advantage if the flower garden can be watered. Whenever this is done, water should be applied in sufficient amount to wet the soil to the depth of at least a foot. Many amateur gardeners are considerably exercised regarding the correct time of day to water their gardens, having been told that plants never should be watered when the sun is shining. I have never seen any ill effects which could be attributed to their having been so treated, but the evening is the best time to apply water because it then has a chance to soak into the soil with less loss from evaporation than if applied in blazing sunshine.

Fertilizing. If the soil has been properly prepared, additional fertilizer during the growing season is not absolutely necessary. But, if it is desired to improve the size of the flowers of any particular specimens, the application of a quick-acting fertilizer as soon as the flower buds are formed will be beneficial. Use, for example, a 4-8-6 mixture made up of nitrate of soda or sulphate of ammonia to supply the nitrogen, superphosphate to supply the phosphoric acid, and sulphate of potash to supply the potash. The approximate amounts to supply the above proportions are: *for the nitrogen,* 26 pounds of nitrate of soda or 20 pounds of sulphate of ammonia, or 13 pounds of nitrate of soda plus 10 pounds of sulphate of ammonia; *for the phosphoric acid,* 53 pounds of 15-percent superphosphate; *for the potash*, 12½ pounds of sulphate of potash; and 9 pounds of sand for filler. Apply 2 to 3 ounces per square yard of soil surface. Many are wedded to the idea of stimulating plants by the use of liquid manure, but this to me has always seemed a laborious way of applying fertilizer.

Staking. Plants which are incapable of supporting themselves should be staked before they have fallen over by their own weight or have been toppled by the wind. Staking is a fine art and no one scheme of support is adequate for the variety of plants grown in the flower border. It is all too seldom that one sees a garden where the supports for the plants have been applied thoughtfully and intelligently in such a way that they are unobtrusive and the natural habit of the plant is left undisturbed. A common, but abominable, method of staking is to drive a broom handle into the ground alongside a clump of plants, pass a string around the clump and tie it to the broom handle.

Twiggy shoots of woody plants are invaluable for supporting herbaceous plants which are many-stemmed in habit. The twigs should be thrust into the ground about the plant to be supported before it has attained its full growth. As it grows, it will tend to lean outward and will almost completely hide the support. After the twigs are set in place, go over them with a pair of pruning shears and cut off the ends which project too far. The finer terminal twigs of the branches used will suffice for low-growing plants such as *Potentilla, Platycodon, Veronica Teucrium,* and so forth. For taller plants of heavier growth, such as *Coreopsis grandiflora, Gypsophila* and *Achillea ptarmica,* the stouter and older portions of the branches should be reserved. Therefore, twiggy branches which are suitable for such use should be saved from the winter prunings. A good plan to ensure a sufficient supply is to maintain a bush or two of California privet which may be cut down every winter to provide stakes for the following year.

Plants with a habit of growth like that of peonies can be supported effectively by placing over them a hoop, attached at the desired height to three or four legs. These supports may be purchased from almost any seed house, or may be contrived from material on hand. Delphiniums and similar plants may be supported by two tiers of hoops, or each shoot may be tied to a separate stake with raffia or soft string. Bamboo stakes are suitable for this purpose. Stout wire stakes of various sizes, with spiral turns in them, are useful for supporting individual shoots or flower stems. Remember, always, to maintain the natural shape of the plant. To this end, keep on hand stakes of various sizes. It is better to allow a plant to topple than to stake it in an unnatural position.

Prevention of seeding. Many plants will continue in bloom for a longer period if the flowers are not allowed to form seeds. So, unless seeds are required for increasing the stock of any special plant, faded flowers should be removed—if possible to do so without too much labor. A tidier garden also will result.

SELECTION OF HERBACEOUS PERENNIALS

Stock for planting in the perennial garden may be obtained by purchase of plants from nurserymen, by exchange or begging from friends, or by raising from seeds, cuttings, or division. (See Chapter XXVI, PLANT PROPAGATION.) Seeds should be obtained from reliable sources—preferably from dealers who specialize in seeds of hardy plants.

In the selection which follows, the intention has been to include only outstanding kinds of flowers, both commonly used ones and those which deserve to be better known. Personal predilections undoubtedly enter into a list of this kind. Thus, no achilleas are included because the kinds suitable for the perennial garden appeal to me as weedy plants of little value—except, perhaps, in special locations where difficulty is experienced in growing more desirable subjects in sufficient variety. Yet, in looking over several lists of "twenty-five best perennials," I find one or more varieties of *Achillea* included. Some plants of great merit are omitted because insects are too fond of them. *Valeriana officinalis,* for example, is almost always covered with lice while it is in bloom.

The catalogs of specialists in perennials should be consulted for more extended lists; also the tables showing height, spacing, etc., which follow this descriptive list. The months in which each perennial blooms are given in the descriptions below.

DESCRIPTIVE LIST

ALTHAEA, **Hollyhock.** It is difficult to know whether to class hollyhocks as annual, biennial, or perennial, as they partake of all three categories according to strain and the method of culture. Even a planting of annual or biennial varieties is likely to be perennial in character because of renewal by self-sown seeds.

A. rosea is the species from which the garden hollyhocks originated. Some varieties, **Palling Belle,** for example, do not exceed 4 feet, but in general they reach a height of about 8 feet. They are useful for the back of the border, for planting along fences, garage walls, etc. Single and double forms are obtainable in a wide range of colors. July and August.

ANCHUSA, **Bugloss.** These plants have coarse, unattractive foliage unpleasant to handle, but are indispensable because of the beautiful blue flowers produced over a long period.

A. azurea (*italica*). Several garden forms, including **Lissadel,** with intense blue flowers, and **Opal** whose name suggests its color. About 5 feet high; June-August.

A. Barrelieri. Dwarf (2 feet), with deep blue flowers in May and June.

A. myosotidiflora. Lacks the unpleasant foliage of the preceding kinds; now referred to *Brunnera,* which see.

ANEMONE. *A. japonica* blooms in September and October, and, in some sections is caught by early frosts. The flowers, 2 to 3 inches in diameter, are pure white with yellow centers on 2- to 3-foot stems. It prefers partial shade—and limy soil(?). This is one of the most attractive perennials either for garden display or cutting. There are several named varieties, some in other colors, which, to me, are no improvement on the type.

AQUILEGIA, **Columbine.** Ornamental foliage (when it is not marred by leaf miners) and graceful sprays of flowers in a wide range of color characterize the columbines. They will thrive in sun or partial shade.

A. caerulea, **Rocky Mountain Columbine.** Large long-spurred blue and white flowers. One of the most beautiful, but rather "miffy" under cultivation; and, because columbines hybridize so readily, difficult to get the true species. May and June.

A. chrysantha, **Golden Columbine.** Slender plant with graceful sprays of long-spurred yellow flowers. May and June.

A. glandulosa, **Altai Columbine.** Spurless flowers of sapphire-blue and white on 12- to 18-inch stems. Not easy to transplant to the open ground, except as a pot-grown plant.

A. hybrida. Almost every nurseryman has a "best" strain of columbine hybrids; almost always good. Great variety of colors, stems 2 to 3 feet high. May and June.

ARTEMISIA. **Wormwood.** Several species of this aromatic group of plants are useful for foliage effects in borders.

A. albula (**Silver King**), 2 to 3 feet high, has feathery sprays of white leaves which are useful for toning down flowers of harsh coloring and for separating warring colors. Its shoots may be cut, dried, and used for winter bouquets.

ASTER, Michaelmas Daisy. In Europe, especially in England, the native American asters are greatly valued for garden adornment and cut flowers, and some specialists in hardy plants list more than 100 named varieties in their catalogs. The majority of these varieties have been derived by selection and hybridization of *A. novi-belgii* (**New York Aster**), which has more than 80 named varieties ascribed to it, *A. novae-angliae* (**New England Aster**), *A. cordifolius, A. diffusus, A. ericoides,* and *A. vimineus.*

The fall-blooming asters vary in color from white to almost red and from pale lavender to deep purple. In size, they range from 1 foot in the case of **Snow Sprite** to the 6 feet or more of the **Climax** types. In habit, there are spreading kinds such as **Mauve Cushion,** and the upright-growing forms of the *novae-angliae* group.

American nurserymen, in general, list only a tithe of the varieties offered in the European trade, and restrict their offerings to the *Amellus, novae-angliae,* and *novi-belgii* groups. Following is a selection from the varieties available in this country:

A. Amellus varieties:

> **King George** (A.M., R.H.S.),* August. Bluish-violet rays and golden-yellow disk; individual flowers up to 3 inches in diameter.
>
> *Frikarti,* said to be a hybrid between *Amellus* and *Thompsoni;* large violet flowers with golden centers; 2 feet high; the variety **Wonder of Staffa** has lavender-blue flowers from early June until frost.
>
> **Mauve Cushion,** 1 foot, September to November. Forms dense cushions several feet in diameter. Flowers white tinged with purple. Said to be of Japanese origin.

A. novae-angliae varieties:

> **Harrington's Pink,** 4 feet. True deep pink, very lovely.
>
> **Mt. Rainier,** 3 to 4 feet. White with yellow disk.
>
> **Survivor,** said to be superior to Harrington's Pink.

A. novi-belgii varieties:

> **Beechwood Challenger,** 3 to 4 feet. Crimson-red, single, free-flowering.
>
> **Blue Gem,** 5 feet. Deep blue, semi-double, the best blue.
>
> **Climax,** 6 feet. Light lavender-blue. Individual flowers up to 3 inches under favorable conditions.
>
> **Gay Border Blue,** 5 feet. Blue with yellow eye; good for cutting.
>
> **Hilda Ballard,** 5 feet. Silvery mauve, large, double. Usually starts to bloom by middle of September.
>
> **Mt. Everest,** 3-4 feet. White, small eye.

* Award of Merit, Royal Horticultural Society.

Queen Mary, 3-4 feet. Rich blue, tinted with lavender. Flowers up to 2½ inches in diameter; pyramidal inflorescence.

Sunset, 3 feet. Pink, free flowering.

Snow Sprite, about 1 foot. Compact bushy habit with semi-double white flowers.

There is a series of dwarf perennial asters, ascribed to *Aster dumosus,* developed originally by workers for the British Imperial War Graves Commission as the result of a desire for a hardy dwarf edging plant for use in military cemeteries in France and elsewhere. These varieties never exceed a foot in height, and form attractive mounds of foliage which is almost obscured by the flowers when they come into bloom in late summer. Among the varieties offered by American nurserymen are the following:

Countess of Dudley, pink with yellow center.

Lavanda, lavender-blue, early.

Niobe, white, very dwarf.

To get best results with Michaelmas daisies, deep moist rich soil must be provided and annual division of clumps practised. The *novae-angliae* kinds will thrive in wet situations.

BRUNNERA. *B. macrophylla (Anchusa myosotidiflora)* grows about a foot high and in spring has deep blue flowers resembling forget-me-nots in graceful sprays. Will grow in sun or shade.

CAMPANULA, **Bellflower.** The campanulas suited for the perennial border are, in the main, of easy cultivation. Well-drained soil must be provided. Those listed below will grow in full sun but do not object to partial shade.

C. carpatica, **Carpathian Bellflower.** Grows 8 to 12 inches high. Foliage cool-looking; blue or white flowers, wide-open, 1½ inches in diameter. July to September.

C. lactiflora. The color of skim milk. Usually grows 3 to 4 feet high, but in favorable locations may reach 6 feet or more, as seen in Plate XI. June, July.

C. persicifolia. One of the most beautiful campanulas, but is weak-stemmed, therefore usually needs support. Grows 3 to 4 feet high. Flowers steel-blue in June and July. Variety *alba,* white. Best garden variety is **Telham Beauty** with enormous single clear-blue flowers. *Moerheimei* has semi-double white flowers. This variety should be propagated by division or cuttings rather than by seeds.

CERASTIUM. These creeping plants have to be watched lest they crowd out their neighbors. The old flower heads should be sheared off, after which the foliage—green or white—will be attractive for the rest of the season.

C. Biebersteinii. Makes dense mats of gray foliage which is almost obliterated by the pure white flowers in spring.

C. tomentosum, **Snow-in-summer.** Grown mainly for the effect of its almost white foliage; similar to the preceding but less rampant.

CHRYSANTHEMUM. In addition to the colorful fall-blooming chrysanthemums, which are described below, two familiar summer garden perennials belong in the genus *Chrysanthemum.* One is the "painted daisy" or pyrethrum; the other includes a varied group of white-flowered hybrids of *C. maximum,* known collectively as Shasta daisies.

C. coccineum. Often listed in catalogs under *Pyrethrum.* Characterized by divided foliage and showy, single or double blooms of crimson, lilac, pink, or white on 18-inch stems in late May and early June, with scattering flowers thereafter. Planting, and division (if necessary), should be done in spring. Good varieties are **Miami Queen, Robinson's Dark Crimson** and **Victory.**

C. maximum, **Shasta Daisy.** Glorified ox-eye daisies which bloom from June to September. Reputedly good varieties are: **Esther Reed, Mayfield Giant,** and **Silver Star.**

C. morifolium (hortorum). The so-called hardy chrysanthemums are close relatives of the greenhouse kinds seen in such abundance in the florist shops in the fall. As a matter of fact, some varieties are cultivated both outdoors and under glass. Although some of the "hardy" chrysanthemums are truly hardy, and will survive without protection the winters around New York, as a rule (with the exception of the new Korean and Arcticum hybrids), these are not the most attractive varieties. Therefore, to be on the safe side, the old plants are best protected over the winter. As chrysanthemums resent a heavy top covering in combination with wet feet, and show their resentment by dying before spring, placing a heavy mulch over them will not work. Some gardeners cover the plants outdoors with heavy waterproof paper, which will protect and keep excess water from their roots. I have found that the safest way to carry chrysanthemums through the winter is to dig up a few stock plants and plant them in a coldframe. From the stock plants, cuttings are made in February and March, rooted in sand, transplanted to flats of soil, and set out-of-doors in April. Better results, I think, are obtained by setting out new single-shoot plants from cuttings every spring. If no greenhouse or hotbed facilities are available for starting the cuttings, the old plants may be dug up in the spring as soon as the ground is workable. Shake the soil from their roots and cut off the strongest of the young shoots, with a supply of roots already formed. Plant these firmly in the soil, 1 foot apart, and water if the soil is at all dry.

As chrysanthemums are voracious feeders, spread a 2- to 3-inch layer of partly decayed manure over the soil after the roots have been removed late in the fall and dig it in deeply. When the young plants have become established the following spring, apply a complete fertilizer (about 5-10-5) to the surface soil at the rate of 3 pounds to 100 square feet. (See Chapter V, MANURES AND FERTILIZERS.) Another application 6 to 8 weeks later may prove of benefit.

When the young plants are 6 inches high pinch out the tips to induce branching. When these branches are 6 inches long, pinch out their tips, and continue this way until the plants are adequately bushy.

Disbudding is not extensively practised on outdoor chrysanthemums. If done, the flowers that are left will be somewhat increased in size, but they will never be comparable to those on greenhouse-grown stock. To obtain large flowers, it is necessary to select the right varieties and restrict them to one or two stems, allowing not more than one flower bud to develop on each stem. In disbudding outdoor chrysanthemums, the aim should be to thin out the buds so that a more symmetrical spray of flowers of increased size is produced. To do this, the weakest buds should be removed as soon as they are large enough to handle.

Most varieties of chrysanthemum need staking to prevent them from being toppled over by wind. If rather stout twiggy branches are thrust into the ground between the plants when they are about half grown, their subsequent growth will almost completely hide all vestiges of artificial support.

If it is possible to obtain a good strain of seed of early-flowering chrysanthemums, it is well worth while to plant them in a greenhouse or hotbed in late February and early March, putting the seedlings out in the open by the end of April. If planted in large masses they will provide a kaleidoscopic effect in the fall. For several years in the Brooklyn Botanic Garden we have had three or four beds, each containing around 250 plants of chrysanthemums raised from seeds. These beds have evoked more admiration from visitors than those which contain selected named varieties; this, in spite of the fact that in the seedling beds it is seldom possible to find individual plants worth naming and propagating vegetatively. Seedling chrysanthemums would produce a gorgeous effect if planted in large quantity in the foreground of shrubbery. (Plate XII.)

Following is a list of good varieties: The Arcticum and Korean groups are, in general, hardier than the rest. The "Cushion" varieties start to bloom in August and September, and are compact, dwarf, and broader than high; the "Decorative" types have double flowers of informal habit; flowers of the "Pompons" are more compact.

Varieties which especially appealed to me when seen at Bristol Nurseries last fall are marked *.

ARCTICUM HYBRIDS. **Allegro,** 2 ft., Oct., pink and coppery salmon, double;

Arctic Queen, 1½-2 ft., Oct., bronzy-yellow with salmon tints, single; *****Autumn Lights,** 2 ft., Oct., coppery-bronze; **Aviator,** 2 to 3 ft., Oct., coppery-red pompon; **Coral Sea,** 1½ ft., early Oct., salmon-rose and copper; **Good Morning,** 2 ft., early Oct., yellow, single.

CUSHION 'MUMS. *****Apricot Glow,** 2½ ft., **Dean Kay,** deep pink; **King Cushion,** coppery-bronze to dull red; **Lavender Lassie,** 2-2½ ft., **Major Cushion,** the best pink; **September Bronze,** good keeper; **September Gold,** golden-yellow.

DECORATIVE TYPES. **Algonquin,** 1½ to 2 ft., mid-Sept., yellow; *****Bokhara,** 2 ft., early Oct., rosy-crimson; **Joan Helen,** 1½ ft., late Sept., purple; **Magnolia,** 1½ to 2 ft., mid-Sept., pink, cream, and yellow tones; *****Olive Longland,** 2 ft., mid-Sept., apricot.

POMPONS. **Charles Nye,** 2 ft., deep yellow, compact; **Early Wonder,** 2½ ft., mid-Sept., blended pink; *****Fred F. Rockwell,** 2 ft., early Oct., bronze and orange-scarlet; *****Goblin,** 2 ft., mid-Oct., picoteed bronze; **Harbor Lights,** 2 ft., mid-Sept., creamy yellow; *****Irene,** 1½ ft., early Oct., small white; *****Judith Anderson,** 1½ ft., early Oct., deep yellow, button pompon; **Mme. Chiang Kai-shek,** 2 ft., early Sept., bronze; **Ruby Pompon,** 2½-3 ft., early Oct., ruby-crimson; *****White Wonder,** 3 ft., mid-Sept.

KOREAN HYBRIDS—doubles. *****Avalanche,** 1½ ft., late Sept., large-flowered white; **Burgundy,** 2½ ft., early Oct., wine red; **King Midas,** 2 ft., late Sept., yellow; *****Korean Princess,** 2 ft., Oct., red to pink, gold center, anemone type; **Lavender Lady,** 2½ ft., early Oct., lavender; **Mrs. Pierre S. Du Pont, III,** 2½ ft., early Oct., salmon-bronze, tinted pink; **Pink Radiance,** 2½ ft., late Sept., pink, shading to yellow at center; **Red Velvet,** 2 ft., early Oct., crimson.

KOREAN HYBRIDS—singles. **Crimson Splendor,** 2½ ft., Oct. 1st; **Louise Schling,** 2½ ft., early Oct., red; **Venus,** 2½ to 3 ft., mid-Sept., orchid-pink.

CIMICIFUGA, **Bugbane.** Members of this group are suitable in a large shaded border or in thin woodland. They are strong-growing plants bearing slender racemes of minute white flowers.

C. racemosa. Native plant, with divided foliage to a height of nearly 3 feet, and racemes of white flowers on stalks which may reach a height of 6 feet or more under favorable conditions. July and August.

C. simplex. Long racemes of white flowers in October. About 3 feet high.

COREOPSIS. *C. grandiflora* makes a sprawling clump 2½ feet high, with clear golden-yellow flowers. If prevented from seeding, it remains in bloom for several months, and is useful for cut flowers. There is a double-flowered form.

DELPHINIUM, **Larkspur.** The perennial delphiniums are among the most valuable plants for the hardy flower garden. It is somewhat of a struggle, however, to grow the hybrid kinds in regions with hot summer climates. The soil should be prepared by digging it at least 2 feet deep, mixing with it a layer, 6 inches thick, of thoroughly decayed manure. If the soil is the least bit acid, corrective liming must be done. Thorough underdrainage is absolutely essential. Young plants may be set out in spring or fall, spacing them 15 to 18 inches apart. In future years, as the clumps increase in size, the young shoots should be thinned if extra tall and strong flower shoots are desired. These thinnings, if cut just below the soil surface when the shoots are about 3 inches high, may be inserted as cuttings in sand in a greenhouse or coldframe. This affords a means of increasing the stock of desirable forms without disturbing established roots. Plants thus raised will bloom the following year. Other methods of propagation are by division of old plants in spring or fall, or by seeds, planted either as soon as they are ripe or during the following spring.

Delphiniums, especially when grown in uncongenial locations, are subject to various troubles caused by mites, insects, bacteria, and fungi. One of the most serious is brought about by the cyclamen mite, a pest almost invisible to the naked eye. The flower buds and leaves become distorted, blistered and blackened. Partial control may be effected by the removal, and destruction by burning, of infected shoots. Spraying at weekly intervals with a contact spray containing rotenone or pyrethrum, alternating with treatments of dusting sulphur is helpful.

The above measures will also control aphids or plant lice; "red spiders," responsible for stippled light-colored patches on the leaves which often ultimately turn brown; and thrips, which rasp the leaves and stems and cause the plants to become stunted.

Of the fungous diseases, among the most important is black rot, which causes yellowing of the lower leaves, followed by wilting and dying of individual stems or the entire clump. Sometimes the disease may be checked by drenching the crowns with a solution of bichloride of mercury—1 part to 2,000 parts of water. Badly diseased plants should be dug up and burned and the surrounding soil treated with the above deadly poison.

Canker manifests itself by elongated brown areas on the stems. The fungus ultimately enters the roots and kills them. Affected shoots should be cut off and destroyed by burning. Spray with Bordeaux mixture to prevent attack.

Mildew is sometimes bothersome. It forms gray patches on the leaves. Dusting the plants with dusting sulphur or spraying with Bordeaux mixture will keep it in check.

Bacterial diseases are leaf spot and crown rot. The former causes irregular black areas on, and some distortion of, the above ground parts of the plants. It is most prevalent in cool climates. Crown rot causes the leaf-stalks to turn black and become soft and rotten. Ultimately the crown is attacked and the plant dies. This disease is most severe in hot, humid sections. There is not much that one can do for plants affected by these bacterial diseases beyond promptly removing and burning the infected parts, and providing the best possible growing conditions.

Liquid manure applied at weekly intervals when the flower spikes are beginning to form will aid in increasing their size. If a second blooming is desired in the fall the flower spikes should be cut off when they are past their best and the plants fertilized. Some authorities recommend a yearly application of ground limestone to the soil in which delphiniums are growing.

In England, many named varieties of hybrid delphiniums are available. These are propagated by vegetative means. In this country, the more usual course is to raise them from seeds. Various strains are available, including the *Belladonna* type which grows to about 4 feet, with sky-blue flowers; the *elatum* types, which are capable of attaining a height of 6 feet; and the **Wrexham** or **Hollyhock** type, which produces tremendous more or less non-branching spikes with individual flowers nearly 3 inches across. The stems of these, under good conditions, may reach a height of 8 feet or even more. The color range is from white through pale blue, mauve and lavender, to deep purple. Many varieties exhibit opalescent coloring.

D. grandiflorum (*chinensis*), although a perennial, will bloom the first year from seeds sown in early spring. It has finely divided foliage and loosely branched flower spikes about 2 feet tall, the flowers being a deep, intense blue. There is also a white variety.

DIANTHUS. **Pinks.** The hardy pinks are valuable for the forefront of the perennial garden because of their low stature, abundant flowers and handsome foliage when not in bloom. Many species have a delightful fragrance. Some are suffruticose.

D. Allwoodii. A hybrid strain producing flowers on stems 6 to 12 inches high, from May to October. Named varieties differ in color and number of petals. Not winter-hardy in very severe climates.

D. barbatus, **Sweet William.** The best of the cluster-flowered pinks, bearing large heads of scentless flowers in many tones of red, also white and particolored. **Newport Pink** a good named variety. Though usually treated as a biennial, the sweet william is, under some conditions, a short-lived perennial.

D. latifolius, **Cluster Pink.** A supposedly hybrid group. **Beatrice**, pink, and **Silver Mine,** white, bloom from June until September.

PLATE X. BORDER OF PERENNIALS AND BIENNIALS

PLATE XI. *(upper left)* *Campanula lactiflora.* *(upper right)* DITTANY, *Dictamnus albus.* *(lower)* GLOBE-FLOWER, *Trollius europaeus*

D. plumarius, **Grass Pink.** Blooming in May and June, is worth growing for the glaucous, gray-green foliage alone. Many varieties with single or double fragrant flowers: **Bristol Jewel,** white and crimson; **Essex Witch,** pink; **Her Majesty,** double white; **Miss Gladys Cranfield,** rose-colored with crimson eye; **Old Spice,** salmon-pink, excellent for cutting.

DICENTRA, **Bleeding Heart.** *D. spectabilis* is an old favorite of early summer. The pendent deep-pink blooms on 3-foot arching stems, clothed with fern-like foliage, are distinctly decorative. It will grow in sun or shade.

DORONICUM, **Leopard's-bane.** Valuable for early spring bloom. The heart-shaped leaves are bright spring-green. The flowers are long-lasting when cut.

D. caucasicum, 2 feet, and *D. plantagineum,* 3 feet, are the kinds usually sold. Both have large clear yellow daisy-like flowers.

ERIGERON, **Fleabane.** *E. speciosus* and its varieties are best for the perennial garden, growing from 1½ to 2 feet high with lavender-blue flowers in June and July.

EUPATORIUM, *E. coelestinum,* **Hardy Ageratum,** has lavender-blue, ageratum-like flowers on branching reddish stems 2 to 3 feet high in September and October. The foliage is clean-looking. It will thrive in sun or shade and endure city life.

FUNKIA, see HOSTA.

GAILLARDIA, **Blanket-flower.** *G. aristata (grandiflora)* is one of the most useful perennials because of its long blooming habits. The flowers are yellow and red or orange and red, and are produced from May to frost above gray-green foliage. The plants grow to about 2 feet and are benefited by the support of twiggy branches stuck in the soil around them. They endure drought.

GEUM, **Avens.** *G. chiloense (coccineum)* and its varieties are long-blooming plants for moist well-drained soils. **Lady Stratheden** has double golden-yellow flowers; **Mrs. Bradshaw,** double flowers of scarlet. Both varieties grow from 18 inches to 2 feet.

GYPSOPHILA, **Baby's Breath.** *G. paniculata* variety **Bristol Fairy** is perhaps the best. Useful for garden display and cutting, it grows 2½ to 3 feet high and is covered in June and July with a cloud of small double white flowers on airy stems.

HELENIUM, **Sneezeweed.** Tall floriferous plants, the native sneezeweeds and their varieties are valuable for their bloom in late summer and early fall. They belong in the Composite family and have conspicuous rounded disks with toothed ray florets slightly reflexed.

H. autumnale superbum. About 5 feet tall with golden-yellow flowers. Variety **Riverton Beauty,** yellow flowers with dark disks; **Riverton Gem,** brownish-red; *pumilum magnificum,* a dwarf variety (2½ feet) with lemon-yellow flowers.

HELIANTHUS, **Sunflower.** Recent hybridization has brought many improved forms into the native sunflowers, which, being usually coarse strong-growing perennials, are suitable only for large gardens.

H. decapetalus (*multiflorus*). Several garden varieties blooming in August and September. **Bouquet d'Or,** double yellow, 4 to 5 feet tall; **Mrs. Moon,** single yellow. Usually need an occasional dusting with sulphur to keep down mildew.

H. orgyalis. Grows 8 to 10 feet high, with long narrow leaves gracefully recurving. Large single yellow flowers in the fall.

HEMEROCALLIS, **Daylily.** These are easily grown plants with long narrow leaves arising from the base and broad funnel-shaped flowers ranging from lemon to orange and, in the new hybrids, tawny-red. Dr. A. B. Stout of the New York Botanical Garden is responsible for originating a series of hybrids of much garden merit.

H. flava, **Lemon-lily.** Clear lemon-yellow lily-like flowers on stiff stems about 3 feet high, in May or June.

H. fulva, **Tawny-lily.** Strong-growing species about 4 feet high with orange-brown flowers.

Among the many garden varieties are the following: **Apricot,** 2 feet high, May and June; **Cinnabar,** brownish-red, yellow throat, 2½ feet, July and August; **Clarion,** pink, 3 feet, July; **J. A. Crawford,** apricot and yellow, 3 to 4 feet, July; **Lemona,** pale yellow, open at night, up to 5 feet, July and August; **Mikado,** orange and mahogany-red, 3 feet, July; **Ophir,** golden-yellow, 3½ to 4 feet, July; **Toreador,** red, 3 feet, July.

HEUCHERA, **Alum-root, Coral Bells.** The Heucheras have low tufts of leaves surmounted by small, bell-shaped flowers in sprays on slender stems up to 18 inches tall. They are useful for cut flowers and will grow in sun or shade. *H. sanguinea* has been productive of many named garden forms. Among them are **Perry's White; Pluie de Feu,** brilliant red; and **Rosa Mundi,** pink.

HOSTA (FUNKIA), **Plantain-lily.** Grown mainly for their bold foliage, plantain-lilies (which are known sometimes as daylilies) also have attractive flowers. They will grow in sun or shade, though a deep moist soil is essential for best results in sun. They are admirable for waterside planting.

H. lancifolia albo-marginata. Deep green leaves edged and striped with white. About 1 foot high, it is sometimes used as an edging plant.

H. plantaginea (*grandiflora*). Makes a tuft, 2 to 3 feet in diameter, of large pale-green grooved leaves, surmounted by fragrant snow-white flowers on 2-foot stems in July and August.

H. Sieboldiana. Mauve-purple flowers on 2½-foot stems; large gray-green leaves.

IRIS. The irises are among the most satisfactory of garden plants. The most popular group, the bearded irises, are thoroughly hardy and tolerant of a wide range of soils, provided they are well drained. They need sunshine. The season opens early with the dwarf kinds, which are followed in order by the intermediate group, then the tall bearded irises. For best results, these irises should be divided and reset every three or four years in August. The strongest rhizomes, each having about three growth-shoots, should be selected, the foliage shortened one half, and then the roots firmly set in the ground so that the top of the rhizome is just visible. Manure should not be used as a mulch, though it may be used sparingly when preparing planting places, if it is thoroughly decayed. Bonemeal at the rate of 4 pounds per 100 square feet is an approved fertilizer.

The slender Siberian irises and the showy Japanese types are both adapted for wet ground, especially beside streams and lakes, though they will also thrive under the ordinary conditions of the perennial garden. The Japanese irises do not grow well in limy soils. Peatmoss mixed with the soil is beneficial to them; its good effects are probably partly due to its increasing the water-holding capacity of the soil. Japanese and Siberian irises may be divided and transplanted with but little set-back in September or early spring.

Dwarf bearded irises grow from 4 to 8 inches high and bloom in April and early in May. The intermediate irises are, in general, about 2 feet high; while the tall bearded range from 2 to 4 feet, according to variety, and bloom in late May and June. The height of the Japanese and Siberian irises, which ranges from 2 to 4 feet, is greatly influenced by environmental conditions, and it also differs with the variety. The Siberian irises bloom in June, with the last of the tall bearded varieties. The Japanese come later, in July.

New varieties are constantly being introduced, some of them of such merit that they supersede older kinds. Catalogs of specialists should be consulted for up-to-date kinds. The varieties suggested in the lists below (supplied by Dr. G. M. Reed who had charge of the iris collections in the Brooklyn Botanic Garden) go back 10 to 15 years and are not expensive.

INTERMEDIATE: **Autumn Haze, Black Hawk, Chrysoro, Eleanor Roosevelt, Kochii, Red Orchid.**

TALL BEARDED: **Crystal Beauty, Dauntless, Golden Hind, Golden Treasure, Great Lakes, Gudrun, Imperial Blush, Indian Hills, Los Angeles, Rosy Wings, Summer Tan, Wabash.**

SIBERIAN: **Caesar's Brother, Gatineau, Kingfisher Blue, Papillon, Red Emperor, Snowcrest.**

JAPANESE: **Betty F. Holmes, Galathee, Ganymede, Koki-no-iro, La Favorite, Light in the Opal, Morning Mists, Nishiki-Yama, Rose Anna, Violet Beauty.**

LAVANDULA, **Lavender.** Although lavender is really a shrub, it is usually thought of as belonging in the perennial garden. It will survive sub-zero weather if planted in sandy well-drained soil in a sheltered location and protected by mulching. *L. Spica* (*officinalis* or *vera*) is the lavender used in perfumery. Its flowers are densely crowded in short spikes on long slender stalks in July and August. If not cut back, it ultimately forms a bush about 3 feet high. The **Munstead** variety is about a foot high.

LILIUM, see Chapter XIV, BULBS—summer-blooming section.

LIMONIUM, **Sea-lavender.** *L. latifolium* has large leathery leaves and produces many-branched flower sprays clothed with tiny lavender flowers. If the stalks are cut when at their prime, the flowers will retain their color when dried. It is especially suitable for very sandy soils at the seashore and will also grow in ordinary soil. July.

LINUM. *L. perenne,* **Perennial Flax,** has small narrow gray-green leaves and numerous slender 2-foot stems with sky-blue flowers (which close in the afternoon) in June and July.

LUPINUS, **Lupine.** The many varieties of *Lupinus polyphyllus,* and the hybrids which have been developed in England, produce showy spikes of pea-like flowers of many colors on plants up to 5 feet tall in gardens where they are happy. But they are temperamental and, frankly, I do not know the secret of growing them.

MONARDA, **Beebalm.** These North American herbs of the Mint family have delightfully aromatic foliage. They bear their flowers in terminal head-like clusters.

M. didyma. Deep crimson flower heads from June to August; 2 to 3 feet high; grows well in partial shade.

M. fistulosa, **Wild Bergamot.** Mauve in color; flowers slightly smaller.

NEPETA. *N. Mussini,* one of the most valuable members of the Mint family, has small grayish leaves and spikes of mauve flowers in great abundance in May, with always a few throughout the summer. It grows about a foot high and is capable of forming a patch a yard or more across.

PAEONIA, **Peony.** The widespread use of peonies in gardens is sufficient evidence of their adaptability to all kinds of climates and most kinds of soil. Best results are likely to be obtained when they are planted in deep well-drained rather clayey soils well supplied with plant foods, and when exposed to full sunshine. Their performance in regions where a cool temperature prevails at blooming time is likely to be more satisfactory than farther south, where the hot weather causes the blooms to fade too quickly.

The soil should be prepared at least 18 inches deep and bonemeal mixed with it—4 or 5 pounds to 100 square feet. Wood ashes at the same rate may be applied as a surface dressing in spring. If the soil is acid, it would be wise to use hydrated lime as a surface dressing at the rate of 5 pounds per 100 square feet, or twice this amount of ground limestone.

The preferred time for planting peonies is early fall—late September, or October—as new roots, which enable the plants to start off better the following spring, are formed at this season. At the time of setting out, the plants should not possess more than 5 growth-buds, or eyes. Peony plants may be obtained from nurserymen, either as divisions of the current season or as one-eye divisions which have been grown in the field a year or two to develop more eyes. The latter type, I think, is preferable.

The divisions should be spaced 3 feet apart and planted so that the eyes are 2 inches below the surface. Work the soil in among the roots and pack firmly by tramping.

In the spring, some of these divisions will attempt to bloom, but the wise gardener curbs his impatience to see what the flowers are like, and removes them in the bud stage, having in mind the future welfare of the plants.

Peonies are greedy feeders, so, to get best results, the fertility of the soil must be maintained by annual applications of decayed manure lightly forked into the ground, and surface applications of fertilizers such as bonemeal and muriate of potash.

Failure to bloom may be due to one or more of many causes. Too deep planting, disease (especially the botrytis blight or "bud rot"), attacks by root nematodes, lack of plant foods in the soil, and too much shade may be responsible.

To aid in controlling botrytis blight, and some other diseases of the peony, the foliage should be cut off just below the soil surface in the fall and destroyed by burning. There are many peony growers who believe that mulching the plants with manure in the fall favors the development of disease. Peonies are hardy, and it is not necessary to protect them with a mulch, so it is good policy to omit it if disease is feared. Plants infested with nematodes, as evidenced by gnarled swellings on the roots, should be dug up with the surrounding soil and burned.

Peonies planted in a lawn, or in the vicinity of trees, may fail to bloom because the grass and tree roots make too many demands on the fertility of the soil.

There is no evidence that the ants, which are so common on peonies in the spring, do any damage to plants or flowers—unless they happen to make a nest among the roots.

Following is a selection of moderately priced varieties. The lists of peony specialists usually carry the rating of the American Peony Society against the names of the varieties. These ratings can be used as a base for selecting additional varieties.

WHITE: **Avalanche, Festiva maxima, Mme. de Verneville** (fragrant), **Whitleyi major** (single, with conspicuous golden stamens).

PALE PINK: **Asa Gray, Baroness Schroeder, Octavie De May.**

PINK: **L'Etincelante** (single), **Mme. Geissler, Modeste Guerin, Mons. Jules Elie, Therese, Walter Faxon.**

RED: **Augustin d'Hour, Felix Crousse, Flag of War** (single), **Karl Rosenfield.**

DEEP RED: **Adolphe Rosseau, Monsieur Martin Cahusac, Phillippe Rivoire.**

PAPAVER, **Poppy.** While most of the poppies grown in gardens are annuals, two important perennials are included in this group, the one extremely delicate, the other almost blatantly showy.

P. nudicaule, **Iceland Poppy.** Refined flowers with silky petals of white, yellow, and orange on slender 18-inch stems, excellent for cutting. May to October. Not a long-lived perennial, therefore desirable to maintain the stock by raising additional plants from seed each year.

P. orientale, **Oriental Poppy.** Welcome in gardens only for its gorgeous scarlet flowers which, in some varieties, may approach 12 inches in diameter. Blooms for a short season, in May and June. Has coarse foliage which becomes unsightly shortly after the blooms have faded. Transplanting, if necessary, should be done in summer just as soon as the foliage has died down. Among named varieties are: **Beauty of Livermere,** dark red flowers of great size, 4 feet tall; **Mrs. Perry,** 6-inch flowers, orange and salmon-pink, 3 feet tall; **Perry's White,** white flowers, with a crimson blotch at the base of the petals.

PHLOX. The varieties derived mainly from *P. paniculata (decussata)* are the standbys of the perennial garden from July to September in locations where they can be made to thrive. With the exception of the white varieties, **Frau Antoine Buchner** and **Miss Lingard,** they do not seem happy under city conditions. Phloxes appreciate light shade in regions with hot summer climates. They are subject to attacks by mites ("red spider"), mildew, and an obscure disease which causes the lower leaves to die. These phloxes have such beautiful fragrant flowers, produced over a long season, that it is worth while to provide extra good cultural conditions, and dust them occasionally with dusting sulphur in the endeavor to overcome these bothers. A deep rich moist but well-drained soil is desirable.

Old flower clusters should be cut off to prevent seeding and to encourage the development of more clusters. If they are allowed to form seeds, these will fall to the ground and germinate. The seedlings are liable to crowd out the named variety; and, as they are likely to revert to the ancestral form, which has an unpleasing purplish color, they are unwelcome.

Divisions should be set about a foot apart and, if extra large panicles of bloom are desired, not more than three shoots should be allowed to develop from each root. When the plants are about 2 feet high supplementary feedings of liquid manure or a quick-acting commercial fertilizer should be given.

Phloxes may be propagated by division of the rootstock in fall or spring, by stem cuttings in early spring (as described under *Delphinium*), or by root cuttings. For these, take young string-like (not fibrous) roots from the plants in the fall, cut into lengths of 1½ inches, lay horizontally in a flat of sandy soil, and cover with ½ inch of sand. Keep the flat in a greenhouse (50°) and maintain the soil in a moist condition.

A selection of varieties follows: **Blue Boy,** nearly blue; **Caroline Vandenburg,** lavender-blue; **Charles Curtis,** sunset-red; **Columbia,** light-pink, longblooming; **Daily Sketch,** salmon-pink, crimson eye; **Mary Louise,** white, large flowers; **Miss Lingard,** white, starts to bloom early in June; **Van Beuningen,** salmon-red; **Widar,** violet, white eye.

PRIMULA, **Primrose.** Most of the primroses need to be fussed over to make them even partially happy in regions which have a hot summer climate. The following are the most satisfactory for the perennial garden.

P. japonica. One of the easiest kinds to grow, if only the soil is kept moist. Has lettuce-like leaves in rosettes, from the center of which the 18-inch flower stems arise, with whorls of flowers in tiers during late spring. There are various color forms. If you can obtain the crimson kind, my advice is to keep all others out of the garden. If they are admitted they will hybridize and the seedlings will exhibit a great range of disappointing colors.

P. polyantha, **Polyanthus Primrose.** Has flowers in bunches on 8-inch stems in early spring. Some are self-colored—white, yellow, or red; others, known as the gold-laced kinds, have dark-colored petals with a clearly defined margin of gold. Polyanthuses require the same cultural conditions as *P. vulgaris.*

P. vulgaris (acaulis), **English Primrose.** Grows about 6 inches high and has crinkled leaves and soft-yellow flowers. English nurserymen offer scores of varieties, ranging in color from white to red and from yellow to almost true blue. They should be planted in shade in a limy soil, well supplied with humus. Early spring.

PYRETHRUM, see *Chrysanthemum coccineum.*

RUDBECKIA. The well-known **Golden Glow** (*R. laciniata hortensia*) beloved by country folk and also, unfortunately, by large red lice, belongs in this genus. Of different style is *R. speciosa,* **Showy Coneflower,** an unrefined but useful plant to provide color in July and August, growing to 2½ feet tall. Its daisy-like flowers are brilliant yellow with brown disks.

SALVIA. This large genus of the Mint family provides many flower-garden subjects.

S. farinacea. Beautiful pale blue flowers on a plant of neater habit than *S. Pitcheri.* About 2 feet high.

S. Pitcheri (azurea grandiflora). Has an exasperatingly floppy habit, and spikes of entrancing blue flowers in August and September. Grows 4 feet tall.

S. Sclarea. Decorative leaves, large, broad, wrinkled, and white-woolly. Spikes 2 to 3 feet tall carry flowers of white, pink, or purple in July and August.

SCABIOSA, **Scabious.** *S. caucasica,* **Caucasian Scabious,** has lavender-blue flowers, 2 inches in diameter, on 18-inch stems from June to August. The hybrids originated by Isaac House and Sons of Bristol, England, have longer stems, a range of color from white to purple, and are excellent for cut flowers.

Shasta Daisy, see *Chrysanthemum maximum.*

STACHYS, **Woundwort.** *S. lanata,* **Bunnies' Ears,** has creeping stems, clothed with long oval velvety leaves, thickly covered with white hairs. It is sometimes used for edging perennial borders. The flower stems should be cut off before they fully develop.

TROLLIUS, **Globe-flower.** Relatives of the buttercups, the trolliuses have large flowers of incurving sepals which give them a globular appearance. They are happy in swampy ground, but will thrive in ordinary soil if it is not too dry. Most varieties bloom in May or June.

T. chinensis. Has curious-looking flowers with broad sepals and narrow petals of orange-yellow in July. Grows about 2 feet high.

T. europaeus. Garden varieties include **Orange Globe,** with flowers 1½ inches in diameter, and **Superbus,** lemon-yellow, both growing about 2 feet high; also **Goliath,** about 6 inches taller, with large deep orange flowers.

VERONICA, **Speedwell.** Veronicas are characterized by their small flowers which usually occur in close-set slender spikes.

V. maritima (longifolia) subsessilis. Spikes of small violet-blue flowers in August and September. The best veronica for the perennial garden.

V. Teucrium. Strikingly beautiful when covered with deep-blue flowers in June. Does not bloom, however, over a long period, and the 18-inch stems need support.

VIOLA. *V. cornuta* and its varieties are valuable plants for the front of the border. They thrive best in a deep rich soil and a cool summer climate, though there are some varieties which endure hot weather. **Jersey Gem** is one of these. It produces its large violet-blue flowers from May to August,

PLATE XII. *(upper)* CHRYSANTHEMUMS EIGHT MONTHS FROM TIME OF
SOWING SEEDS. *(lower)* *Bocconia cordata*—AN EXCELLENT
BACKGROUND PERENNIAL

PLATE XIII. (*upper*) BEARDED IRISES IN MASS PLANTING. (*lower*) CHRIST-MAS ROSE, *Helleborus niger*

sometimes blooming itself to death. Among other varieties worth growing are **Perfection, Purple Heart** and **Sutton's Apricot.**

TABULAR LIST OF PERENNIALS

The height and time of bloom, as given in the following tables, are approximate, and are influenced by soil and climate. The letter "s" appearing after the distance to be allowed between plants indicates that the plants are spreading and may be expected ultimately to exceed the space assigned them.

Name	Height	Distance apart	Color	Month of bloom	Remarks
ACHILLEA					
A. Millefolium roseum	2 ft.	1 ft.—s	cerise	6-7	Will thrive in poor soil.
A. Ptarmica, **Perry's White**	2 ft.	1 ft.—s	white	6-10	
ACONITUM, **Monkshood**					All parts of Aconitum
A. Fischeri	4-6 ft.	9 in.	blue	9-10	contain a poisonous al-
A. Napellus	3-4 ft.	6 in.	blue	7-8	kaloid. Dangerous to
A. Napellus bicolor	3½ ft.	6 in.	blue & white	7-8	grow them in garden where there are children.
AJUGA, **Bugle**					
A. genevensis	1 ft.	9 in.—s	blue	5-6	
A. metallica crispa	4 in.	6 in.			Grown for the metallic looking foliage.
A. reptans	9 in.	9 in.—s	purple	5-6	Will grow in wet or dry soil, sun or shade.
ALTHAEA, **Hollyhock**					
A. rosea and varieties	4-10 ft.	2 ft.	various	7-8	
ALYSSUM					
A. saxatile	1 ft.	1 ft.—s	yellow	4-5	Sun and well-drained soil.
A. saxatile compactum	1 ft.	9 in.	yellow	4-5	
ANCHUSA, **Bugloss**					
A. azurea (italica)	3-5 ft.	3 ft.	blue	6-7	Perennials with coarse
A. Barrelieri	2 ft.	1 ft.	blue	5-6	foliage and delightful flowers.
A. myosotidiflora, see BRUNNERA					
ANEMONE, **Windflower**					
A. hupehensis	1½ ft.	1 ft.	pinkish-purple	8-9	Partial shade.
A. japonica	3 ft.	1¼ ft.	various	9-10	Partial shade.
A. Pulsatilla	1 ft.	9 in.	purple	4-5	Requires limy soil.
A. sylvestris	1 ft.	9 in.—s	white	5-6	Cool soil and shade.
ANTHEMIS					
A. tinctoria kelwayi	1½ ft.	1 ft.	yellow	6-8	Soil need not be good.
AQUILEGIA, **Columbine**					Will grow in sun or par-
A. caerulea	2-3 ft.	1 ft.	blue & white	5-6	tial shade.
A. canadensis	1½ ft.	9 in.	yellow & red	4-5	

Name	Height	Distance apart	Color	Month of bloom	Remarks
Aquilegia chrysantha	3 ft.	1 ft.	yellow	5-6	
A. glandulosa	1 ft.	9 in.	blue & white	5-6	
A. sibirica	1 ft.	9 in.	blue	5-6	
A. vulgaris	3-4 ft.	1½ ft.	various	5-6	
ARABIS, **Rock Cress**					
A. albida flore pleno	6-9 in.	9 in.—s	white	4-5	Good in sunny location.
ARMERIA, see STATICE					
ARTEMISIA					
A. albula (**Silver King**)	2½ ft.	1½ ft.	white	all season	Grown for its white foliage.
A. lactiflora	6 ft.	2 ft.	white	8-9	
ARUNCUS, **Goat's-beard**					
A. sylvester	4-5 ft.	2 ft.	cream	6-7	Moist soil and partial shade.
ASARUM					
A. canadense, **Wild** or **Canada Ginger**	6-8 in.	9 in.	brown	6-7	Large kidney-shaped leaves; good groundcover. Flowers inconspicuous.
ASCLEPIAS					
A. tuberosa, **Butterfly-weed**	2-3 ft.	1 ft.	orange	7	Sometimes difficult to establish.
ASPERULA					
A. odorata, **Sweet Woodruff**	6-9 in.	9 in.	white	5-6	Small, fragrant, spreading plant.
ASTER					
A. Amellus	1½ ft.	1 ft.	purple	7-8	
A. cordifolius	4 ft.	2½ ft.	lavender	9-10	
A. **Mauve Cushion**	1 ft.	1 ft.—s	white, tinged purple	9-11	
A. novae-angliae varieties	4-6 ft.	2 ft.—s	purple	9-10	Excellent in swampy ground and for waterside planting.
A. novi-belgii varieties	1-8 ft.	1-3 ft.—s	various	9-10	
A. subcaeruleus	15 in.	9 in.—s	blue	6-7	
ASTILBE					Moist soil, sun or partial shade.
A. Davidii	3 ft.	1½ ft.	pink	7	
A. japonica	2 ft.	1 ft.	pink or white	6-7	
AUBRIETIA					
A. deltoides	6 in.	9 in.—s	pink & lilac tones	4-5	Benefited by partial shade when grown in hot climates.
BAPTISIA					
B. australis	4-6 ft.	2-3 ft.	indigo	6	Lupine-like flowers; handsome foliage.
BERGENIA					
B. cordifolia (Saxifraga cordifolia)	1 ft.	1 ft.—s	pink	4	Handsome large leathery leaves.

Name	Height	Distance apart	Color	Month of bloom	Remarks
BOCCONIA, Plume Poppy					
B. cordata	7-9 ft.	4 ft.—s	buff	7-8	Grown for its bold, gray foliage.
BOLTONIA					
B. asteroides	6 ft.	3 ft.—s	white	9	Useful in back of large border.
B. latisquama	4 ft.	2 ft.—s	pinkish	8-9	
BRUNNERA					
B. macrophylla (Anchusa myosotidiflora)	1-1½ ft.	1 ft.	blue	5-6	Sun or shade.
CAMPANULA, Bellflower					Species listed here will grow in sun or partial shade.
C. carpatica	8-12 in.	1 ft.	blue	7-10	
C. carpatica alba	1 ft.	1 ft.	white	7-10	
C. glomerata	1½ ft.	9 in.	blue-purple	6-7	
C. lactiflora	3-7 ft.	1-3 ft.	pale blue	6-7	
C. persicifolia	3 ft.	9 in.	blue	6-7	
C. rotundifolia	1-1½ ft.	9 in.—s	blue	6-10	
CENTAUREA					
C. macrocephala	2½ ft.	1½ ft.	yellow	7	Needs sunny location.
C. montana	1½ ft.	1 ft.	blue	5-7	Will grow in sun or partial shade.
CENTRANTHUS					
C. ruber, Red Valerian	3 ft.	2 ft.	red	6-7	Grows in old walls in Devonshire. Needs lime in the soil.
CEPHALARIA					
C. tatarica	7 ft.	4 ft.	yellow	7-8	Coarse growth, but useful for cut flowers.
CERATOSTIGMA, Leadwort					
C. plumbaginoides (Plumbago Larpentae)	1 ft.	1 ft.—s	blue with red bracts	8-10	Late in starting to grow in spring.
CHRYSANTHEMUM					
C. coccineum	2 ft.	1 ft.	crimson, white, lilac, pink	6	Pyrethrum of catalogs.
C. maximum varieties, Shasta Daisy	2-3 ft.	1 ft.—s	white	6-9	
C. morifolium (hortorum) (garden chrysanthemum)	1-4 ft.	1-1½ ft.	various	8-11	See descriptive list, p. 174.
C. uliginosum	4-6 ft.	2 ft.—s	white	8-9	Good in wet soil.
CIMICIFUGA, Bugbane					Graceful; useful for cut flowers.
C. cordifolia	5 ft.	2 ft.	white	8	
C. foetida	5 ft.	2 ft.	white	7-8	
C. racemosa	6 ft.	3 ft.	white	7-8	
C. simplex	2½-3 ft.	1 ft.	white	9-10	
CLEMATIS					
C. heracleaefolia Davidiana	4 ft.	4 ft.	blue	8-9	Coarse foliage.
C. integrifolia	1½ ft.	1 ft.	blue	6-7	Needs support.
C. recta	4 ft.	3 ft.	white	6-7	Needs support.

Name	Height	Distance apart	Color	Month of bloom	Remarks
CONVALLARIA, Lily of the Valley					
C. majalis	10 in.	6 in.—s	white	5	Can take care of itself, but better flowers are produced if the bed is replanted every few years.
COREOPSIS					
C. grandiflora	2½ ft.	1½ ft.	yellow	6-10	Valuable for its long-blooming habit and for cut flowers.
DELPHINIUM, Larkspur					
D. grandiflorum (chinense)	2 ft.	1 ft.	blue	6-7	
D. grandiflorum album	2 ft.	1 ft.	white	6-7	
D. hybridum (garden varieties)	4-8 ft.	2 ft.	various	6-7 & autumn	
D. nudicaule	1½ ft.	9 in.	red	5-6	Not easy to grow in all gardens.
DIANTHUS, Pink					Dianthuses in general need a well-drained, non-acid soil, and full sun. The fragrant flowers are useful for cutting.
D. Allwoodii	6 in.-1 ft.	9 in.	various	5-10	
D. barbatus	1½ ft.	9 in.	various	6-7	
D. caesius	8 in.	9 in.—s	pink	5-6	
D. deltoides	8 in.	9 in.—s	rose-pink	5-6	
D. latifolius	1½ ft.	9 in.	red	6-9	
D. plumarius varieties	1-1½ ft.	1 ft.—s	various	5-9	
DICENTRA, Bleeding Heart					
D. eximia	1 ft.	1 ft.	pink	5-9	Sun or shade.
D. spectabilis	2-3 ft.	2 ft.	pink	5-6	Best in partial shade.
DICTAMNUS, Gas-plant					
D. albus	3 ft.	2 ft.	white	6	
D. albus rubra	3 ft.	2 ft.	purple	6	
DIGITALIS					
D. ambigua	2½ ft.	1 ft.	yellow	6-7	These are perennial foxgloves.
D. ambigua Isabellina	3 ft.	1 ft.	tawny	6-7	
DORONICUM, Leopard's-bane					Will grow in partial shade.
D. caucasicum	1½ ft.	9 in.	yellow	5-6	
D. plantagineum	2-3 ft.	1 ft.	yellow	5-6	
DRACOCEPHALUM, Dragonhead					
D. Ruyschiana	1 ft.	9 in.	purple	6-7	
ECHINACEA					
E. purpurea	2-3 ft.	2 ft.	red-purple	7-8	
ECHINOPS, Globe Thistle					
E. Ritro	2-3 ft.	2 ft.	steel-blue	7-8	Grown for the bluish effect of the spiny flower heads and bracts.

Name	Height	Distance apart	Color	Month of bloom	Remarks
ERIGERON					
E. speciosus	1½-2 ft.	9 in.—s	lavender	6-7	
ERYNGIUM					
E. alpinum	2½ ft.	1 ft.	steel-blue	6-7	Striking foliage and unusual flower coloration.
E. amethystinum	2 ft.	1 ft.	bluish	6-8	
E. maritimum	1½ ft.	1 ft.	pale-blue	6-7	Handsome gray foliage. Will grow in seashore sand.
ERYSIMUM					
E. pulchellum	8 in.-1½ ft.	6 in.-1 ft.	orange	5	
EUPATORIUM					
E. coelestinum	2 ft.	1 ft.—s	blue	9-10	
E. urticaefolium (Fraseri)	3 ft.	1½ ft.	white	8-10	Will grow in dry soil in shade.
EUPHORBIA					
E. corollata	3 ft.	1 ft.	white	8	
GAILLARDIA					
G. aristata (grandiflora)	1½-2 ft.	1 ft.	yellow & red	5-10	Does not object to poor soil.
GALIUM					
G. verum	1 ft.	1 ft.—s	yellow	6-8	Tiny flowers in sprays good for cutting.
GERANIUM					Species listed here are showy but do not last long in bloom.
G. pratensis	2 ft.	1½ ft.	purple	5-6	
G. pratensis album	2 ft.	1½ ft.	white	5-6	
G. sanguineum	1 ft.	1 ft.	red-purple	5-6	
G. sanguineum album	1 ft.	1 ft.	white	5-6	
GEUM					These varieties do not thrive in poor, dry soils.
G. chiloense flore pleno	1½ ft.	1 ft.	red	6-9	
G. Lady Stratheden	2 ft.	1 ft.	yellow	6-9	
G. Mrs. Bradshaw	2 ft.	1 ft.	scarlet	6-9	
GYPSOPHILA, Baby's Breath					Benefited by lime in the soil.
G. paniculata, Bristol Fairy	2½ ft.	3 ft.	white	6-7	
G. repens	6-9 in.	1 ft.—s	white	5-7	
HELENIUM, Sneezeweed					
H. autumnale	4-6 ft.	1½ ft.	yellow	8-9	
H. autumnale pumilum	2½ ft.	1 ft.	yellow	8-9	
H. Hoopesii	2½ ft.	1 ft.	orange	6	
HELIANTHUS					Good for the back of a large border. Must be watched and prevented from smothering weaker plants.
H. atrorubens	3-6 ft.	3 ft.—s	yellow, reddish	9	
H. decapetalus (multiflorus)	4½ ft.	3 ft.—s	yellow	8-9	
H. orgyalis	9 ft.	4 ft.	yellow	9-10	
H. rigidus (scaberrimus)	3-6 ft.	4 ft.—s	yellow	7-8	

Name	Height	Distance apart	Color	Month of bloom	Remarks
HELIOPSIS					
H. helianthoides Pitcheriana	3-4 ft.	3 ft.	yellow	7-9	Rather weedy. Self-sown seedlings are liable to crowd out their neighbors unless removed.
H. scabra excelsa	3-4 ft.	3 ft.	yellow	7-10	
HELLEBORUS, Christmas-rose					
H. niger	1 ft.	1 ft.	white	winter	
HEMEROCALLIS, Daylily	1½-5 ft.	1-3 ft.	yellow, orange, red	5-8	See descriptive list, p. 178.
HEPATICA					
H. americana	4-6 in.	6 in.	white, pale blue, pink	4-5	Native woodland plant.
HEUCHERA, Coral-bells					
H. sanguinea and varieties	1-2 ft.	9 in.	red, pink, white	6-7	Will grow in partial shade.
HIBISCUS, Rose Mallow					
H. Moscheutos, hybrids	4-6 ft.	3 ft.	pink, crimson, white	8-9	Good for wet ground, though they will grow in ordinary soil.
HOSTA (FUNKIA), Plantain-lily					Best in moist soil and at least partial shade.
H. caerulea	2-3 ft.	2 ft.	blue	7-8	
H. japonica	1-2 ft.	1 ft.	pale lavender	7-8	
H. japonica albo-marginata	1 ft.	9 in.	pale lavender	7-8	Much used as an edging plant.
H. plantaginea	2 ft.	2 ft.	white	7-8	
H. Sieboldiana	2½ ft.	2 ft.	mauve	6-7	
IRIS					See descriptive list, p. 179.
JASIONE					
J. perennis	1 ft.	9 in.	blue	7-8	
KNIPHOFIA (TRITOMA), Torch Lily					
K. foliosa (Quartiniana)	2-3 ft.	1½ ft.	orange & yellow	5-6	Probably the hardiest.
K. rufa	2 ft.	1 ft.	yellow	6-9	Graceful, narrow leaves. Needs winter protection.
K. Uvaria (Pfitzeri)	3-4 ft.	1½ ft.	orange-scarlet	8-9	Needs winter protection.
LAVANDULA, Lavender					Really a shrub.
L. Spica (vera)	3 ft.	3 ft.	lavender	7-8	Well-drained soil and a protected, sunny position. If soil is acid, liming will prove beneficial.
L. Spica, Munstead variety	1 ft.	1 ft.	lavender	7-8	

Name	Height	Distance apart	Color	Month of bloom	Remarks
LIATRIS, Gayfeather					
L. pycnostachya	4 ft.	1 ft.	purple	7-8	
L. spicata	2-5 ft.	9 in.-1 ft.	purple	7-8	Needs moisture at root.
LILIUM, Lily					See "Bulbs," p. 248.
LIMONIUM, Sea Lavender					
L. latifolium	1½-2 ft.	1 ft.	lavender	7-8	Good for seashore planting.
LINUM, Flax					
L. flavum	1 ft.	9 in.	yellow	6-9	
L. narbonense	1½ ft.	1 ft.	blue	5-8	
L. perenne	1½ ft.	1 ft.	blue	6-7	Prefers a limy soil.
L. perenne album	1½ ft.	1 ft.	white	6-7	
LOBELIA					Growing naturally in wet soil, but will thrive in ordinary soil in partial shade.
L. cardinalis	3 ft.	9 in.	red	8-9	
L. siphilitica	2-3 ft.	9 in.	blue	8-9	
LUPINUS					
L. polyphyllus varieties	1-4 ft.	1-2 ft.	white & all shades of blue, purple & rose	6-7	
LYCHNIS					
L. chalcedonica	2½ ft.	1 ft.	scarlet	6-7	
L. Coronaria	2½ ft.	9 in.	cerise	6-7	Almost a biennial.
L. Haageana	1-1½ ft.	6 in.	orange to crimson	6-7	Not permanent in most gardens.
L. Viscaria	1-1½ ft.	9 in.	rose-pink	5-7	
LYTHRUM					
L. Salicaria	3-5 ft.	1½ ft.	red-purple	7-9	Particularly good in wet soil.
L. virgatum	2½ ft.	1½ ft.	red-purple	7-9	
MALVA, Musk Mallow					
M. moschata	2-3 ft.	2 ft.	pink or white	7-8	
MERTENSIA, Virginia Cowslip					
M. virginica	1-2 ft.	9 in.	blue	5	Best in shade. Dies down after flowering.
MONARDA, Bee Balm					
M. didyma	2-3 ft.	1 ft.—s	deep red	6-8	Will stand considerable shade.
M. fistulosa	3 ft.	1 ft.—s	mauve	6-8	
NEPETA					
N. Mussini	1 ft.	1½ ft.—s	mauve	5-6	
OENOTHERA					
O. fruticosa	1½ ft.	9 in.	yellow	6-8	
O. missouriensis	10 in.	2 ft.	yellow	6-8	Prostrate plant with flowers 4 in. in diameter.
PAEONIA, Peony	2-3½ ft.	3 ft.	white, pink, red	5-6	See descriptive list, p. 182.

Name	Height	Distance apart	Color	Month of bloom	Remarks
PAPAVER, Poppy					
P. nudicaule	1½ ft.	1 ft.	white to orange	5-10	
P. orientale	2-4 ft.	2-3 ft.	white, salmon, crimson	5-6	
PENTSTEMON					
P. barbatus, **Pink Beauty**	3½ ft.	1 ft.—s	pink	7-8	Useful for cut flowers.
P. barbatus, Torreyi	3½ ft.	1 ft.—s	coral	7-8	
PHLOX					
P. Arendsii	1½ ft.	9 in.	mauve & allied tones	5-9	A hybrid with several named garden varieties.
P. divaricata Laphami	1½ ft.	9 in.	blue	5-6	
P. paniculata	2-4 ft.	1 ft.	white, pink, red, purple	7-9	See descriptive list, p. 183.
P. suffruticosa, **Miss Lingard**	1½ ft.	1 ft.	white	6-9	Disease resistant.
PHYSALIS					
P. Alkekengi (Francheti)	2 ft.	1 ft.—s	red husks covering fruits	fall	Sun or partial shade.
PHYSOSTEGIA					
P. virginiana	3-5 ft.	1½ ft.—s	pink, purple or lilac	7-8	Spreads vigorously.
P. virginiana, **Vivid**	2 ft.	1 ft.	deep pink	8-9	
PLATYCODON, Balloon-flower					
P. grandiflorum	2 ft.	1 ft.	blue	7-10	Spreads by self-sown seeds.
P. grandiflorum album	2 ft.	1 ft.	white	7-10	
PLUMBAGO, see CERATOSTIGMA					
POLEMONIUM					
P. caeruleum	1½ ft.	9 in.	blue	5-7	
P. reptans	9 in.	9 in.—s	blue	5	
POLYGONATUM, Solomon's Seal					Flowers pendent on gracefully arching stems with 2-ranked leaves. Native species also available.
P. multiflorum	3 ft.	1 ft.	greenish-white	5-6	
POTENTILLA					
P. nepalensis	1½ ft.	9 in.	pink	6-8	
P. nepalensis, **Miss Willmott**	1 ft.	9 in.	red	6-8	
P. Warrensii	2 ft.	1 ft.	yellow	6-8	
PRIMULA, Primrose					Primroses in general require a cool, moist soil, and partial shade in regions having hot summer climates.
P. japonica	1½-2 ft.	1 ft.	crimson, rose, purple, white	5-6	

Name	Height	Distance apart	Color	Month of bloom	Remarks
P. polyantha	6-10 in.	9 in.	many colors, mostly in combination	4-5	
P. pulverulenta	2-3 ft.	1 ft.	crimson	6	
P. Sieboldi	10 in.-1 ft.	6 in.	white, rose, purple	5	
P. vulgaris (acaulis)	4-6 in.	6 in.	mostly yellow	4-5	
PULMONARIA					
P. officinalis (maculata)	6-12 in.	9 in.	purple	4	
P. saccharata (Bethlehem Sage)	6-18 in.	9 in.	reddish-violet	4-5	Handsome spotted foliage.
PYRETHRUM, see CHRYSANTHEMUM					
RANUNCULUS, Buttercup					Need wet soil for their best development.
R. acris flore pleno	1½-3 ft.	9 in.	yellow	5-8	
R. repens flore pleno	1 ft.	1 ft.—s	yellow	5-8	May become a weed.
RUDBECKIA, Coneflower					
R. speciosa	2½ ft.	1 ft.—s	yellow	7-8	
R. subtomentosa	3-4 ft.	1½ ft.	yellow	8-9	
SALVIA, Sage					
S. farinacea	2-3 ft.	1 ft.	blue	6-9	
S. Pitcheri (azurea grandiflora)	3-4 ft.	2 ft.	blue	8-10	
S. Sclarea	2-3 ft.	1 ft.	bluish, bracts white & rose	7-8	Biennial.
SAXIFRAGA					
S. cordifolia, see BERGENIA					
SCABIOSA					
S. caucasica	1½-2 ft.	1 ft.	blue	6-8	Good for cut flowers.
SCUTELLARIA, Skullcap					
S. baicalensis coelestina	1 ft.	9 in.	blue	7-8	Good in dry soil.
SEDUM					
S. Sieboldii	8 in.	9 in.	pink	9-10	
S. spectabile, Brilliant	2 ft.	1 ft.	pink	8-9	Worth growing for foliage alone. Rather stodgy, but indestructible.
S. spurium coccineum	6 in.	6 in.—s	red	7-8	Makes good edging, if restrained.
SIDALCEA					
S. candida	3 ft.	9 in.	white	6	
S. malvaeflora	2-4 ft.	9 in.	rose	6-7	
STACHYS					
S. lanata	6 in. (foliage)	6 in.—s	purple		Grown for its woolly foliage.

Name	Height	Distance apart	Color	Month of bloom	Remarks
Stachys officinalis (*Betonica*) *grandiflora*	1½ ft.	1 ft.—s	red-purple	6	
STATICE, **Thrift**					Good for edgings. Useful for seashore planting.
S. Armeria alba	6 in.	9 in.	white	5-6	
S. Armeria Laucheana	6 in.	9 in.	rosy-crimson	5-6	
S. Armeria, **Six Hills Hybrid**	6 in.	9 in.	pink	5-6	
STOKESIA					
S. laevis	1½ ft.	1 ft.	lilac-blue	7-8	
S. laevis alba	1½ ft.	1 ft.	white	7-8	
THALICTRUM, **Meadow-rue**					
T. aquilegifolium	3 ft.	1½ ft.	pinkish	6-7	Grown for its foliage.
T. dipterocarpum	4-6 ft.	1½ ft.	violet	8-9	Needs a cool, well-drained soil and partial shade. Difficult to maintain in many gardens.
T. minus	1½ ft.	1 ft.	greenish	6	Grown for its fern-like foliage.
TROLLIUS, **Globeflower**					Excellent as cut flowers. Needs a moist soil.
T. asiaticus	2 ft.	1 ft.	orange	5-6	
T. chinensis (*sinensis*)	2 ft.	1 ft.	orange-yellow	7	
T. europaeus and varieties	1½-2½ ft.	1 ft.	yellow & orange	5-6	
TUNICA, **Coat-flower**					
T. Saxifraga	8-10 in.	6 in.	pink	6-9	
T. Saxifraga flore pleno	8 in.	6 in.	pink	6-9	Less robust than species.
VALERIANA					
V. officinalis	3-4 ft.	1 ft.—s	pale pink	6-7	Subject to plant lice.
VERBENA					
V. canadensis	9 in.-1 ft.	1 ft.—s	red-purple	6-9	
VERONICA, **Speedwell**					
V. gentianoides	1½ ft.	9 in.—s	blue	5-6	
V. incana	1 ft.	6 in.—s	blue	6-7	Effective mat of gray foliage.
V. maritima (*longifolia*) *subsessilis*	3 ft.	9 in.	violet	8-9	
V. Teucrium	1-1½ ft.	1 ft.	blue	5-6	Several garden varieties available, ranging in height from 4 in. to 1½ ft., and of various colors.
VINCA					
V. minor, **Periwinkle, Trailing Myrtle**	6 in.-1 ft.	1 ft.—s	blue	5-6	Really a sub-shrub. Excellent ground-cover in sun or shade. Handsome shining foliage.

Name	Height	Distance apart	Color	Month of bloom	Remarks
VIOLA					
V. cornuta varieties, **Tufted Pansies**	6-8 in.	9 in.	white to violet, yellow and apricot	5-8	

HERBACEOUS PERENNIALS FOR WET SITUATIONS
(See also Chapter XVII, WATER GARDENS)

Descriptions of species marked with a star (*) will be found under the heading HARDY WATERSIDE PLANTS. Others, or their near relatives, will be found above in either the descriptive or the tabulated list.

Ajuga reptans
Aruncus sylvester
* *Astilbe* in variety
Boltonia latisquama
* *Caltha palustris*
Cimicifuga racemosa
Eupatorium purpureum
* *Hibiscus Moscheutos*
Hosta in variety
Iris, Japanese varieties
Iris pseudacorus

Iris sibirica
* *Lobelia cardinalis*
Lobelia siphilitica
Lysimachia Nummularia
* *Lythrum Salicaria*
* *Myosotis scorpioides*
Primula japonica
Ranunculus acris
Ranunculus repens
Trollius

HERBACEOUS PERENNIALS FOR DRY SOIL AND SUNNY LOCATIONS

Brief descriptions of these plants will be found in the tabulated list of perennials, above.

Achillea Millefolium roseum
Achillea Ptarmica
Achillea tomentosa
Alyssum saxatile
Anthemis tinctoria
Arabis albida
Asclepias tuberosa
Baptisia australis
Cerastium tomentosum
Coreopsis grandiflora
Dianthus caesius
Dianthus deltoides
Dianthus plumarius
Echinops Ritro
Euphorbia corollata

Gaillardia aristata
Gypsophila paniculata
Helianthus in variety
Iris, tall bearded
Iris ochroleuca
Linum perenne
Lychnis Coronaria
Oenothera fruticosa
Oenothera missouriensis
Papaver orientale
Phlox subulata
Sedum in variety
Sempervivum (See Chapter XVI, ROCK AND WALL GARDENS.)

HERBACEOUS PERENNIALS FOR SHADED SITUATIONS

Those marked with a star (*) are for deep shade. Descriptions will be found in the lists above or in other chapters indicated.

Aconitum in variety
Ajuga reptans
Anemone hupehensis
Anemone japonica
Anemone sylvestris
Aquilegia in variety
* *Asarum canadense*
* *Asperula odorata*
Astilbe in variety
Campanula carpatica
Campanula persicifolia
Campanula punctata
* *Cimicifuga* in variety
Convallaria majalis
Dicentra in variety
Digitalis purpurea
Doronicum
* *Epimedium* (See Chapter XVI, ROCK AND WALL GARDENS.)
* *Eupatorium urticaefolium*
Helleborus niger
* *Hemerocallis* in variety

* *Hepatica americana*
Heuchera in variety
* *Hosta* in variety
Lilium Hansoni
Lilium Henryi
Lilium Martagon
* *Lobelia cardinalis*
Lobelia siphilitica
Malva moschata
* *Mertensia virginica*
* *Monarda didyma*
Myosotis palustris (See Chapter XVII, WATER GARDENS.)
Phlox, most kinds except *P. Drummondii*
Physalis Alkekengi
Platycodon grandiflorum
* *Polygonatum multiflorum*
Sedum sarmentosum
Sedum spurium
* *Thalictrum* in variety
Viola in variety

XIII. ANNUALS AND BIENNIALS

ANNUALS, THEIR USES AND CULTURE

To the botanist, an annual is a plant which grows from a seed, produces its flowers, matures its seeds, and dies, all in one year. The gardener usually is not so strict, and places in the category of "annuals" many plants that are really perennials, such as snapdragons, four o'clocks, and ageratums, merely because it is more convenient and the custom to treat them as annual plants when growing them.

The place of annuals in the garden. One of the advantages of raising annuals is their comparatively low cost. In many cases it is possible to raise thousands of plants from a ten-cent package of seeds, a consideration which should appeal to those who are economically minded.

From a decorative standpoint, annuals are of great value because many of them have a long season of bloom and come in at the appropriate moment to provide a display of color after the early-blossoming perennials have passed. As cut flowers, they are almost indispensable. China asters, sweet peas, French and African marigolds, calendulas, calliopsis, zinnias, and larkspurs are a few of the many annuals which can be used to bring color and charm into the home during the summer and fall months. When the space available permits, it is a good plan to have a cutting garden where annuals and perennials may be grown, and freely cut when required without robbing the flower garden. This cutting garden might well consist of a few rows in the vegetable garden—possibly on either side of its main walk.

It is practicable, if the need arises, to make a garden of nothing but annuals (Fig. 34), though this is not recommended for several reasons. The chief drawbacks to the exclusive use of annuals are that they do not come into bloom until the growing season is well advanced, unless they have been started in the greenhouse, and they are not capable of supplying the height and bulk characteristic of trees and certain shrubs. But some of the annual plants are particularly well adapted to forming a temporary background in the garden. Suitable for this purpose and characterized by bold massive foliage,

are the castor-oil plant and the sunflower. Do not use the castor-oil
plant if there are children around who have the habit of tasting every
attractive thing they find. Its seeds are very poisonous, and the eating
of as few as three has been known to result in death. Hemp and cosmos
are tall-growing plants but their foliage is of finer texture. It is even
possible to make a rather attractive temporary hedge with certain of the
annual plants. The summer-cypress, *Kochia,* is excellent for this purpose, and so is the summer-fir, which appears in catalogs under the
somewhat cumbersome botanical name of *Artemisia sacrorum viride.*

Annuals also find a place as fillers among young shrubs which, if
set far apart to allow for future growth, are likely to give the planting
a spotty effect in its early years.

There are, of course, many annual vines which can be used to advantage in covering fences, arbors, and trellises, particularly where it
is essential that no sunlight be shut off during the winter and spring
months. Included in this group are the balloon-vine, with inflated
fruits which are a delight to children; the wild-cucumber-vine; the
hyacinth-bean, which has glistening red-purple seed pods; morning-
glories and moonflowers, and the ever popular sweet peas. (See Chapter
IX, VINES.)

Geographic origins. Practically the whole world has been drawn
upon to fulfill the desires of gardeners. The native origins of the
annuals alone which adorn our gardens make an interesting geo-
graphical study. The East Indies, for example, give us love-lies-bleeding
and the garden balsam. From China comes the almost indispensable
aster; from far-away Australia the Swan River daisy and the straw-
flower, the latter used in dried bouquets. Africa is the home of the
Cape-marigold and of the little lobelia, used for edging; Europe of
the snapdragon, stock, and sweet alyssum. The petunia comes from
South America, and our own country provides one of the most valuable of all the low-growing annuals in *Phlox Drummondii,* which
grows wild in Texas. Ageratum and cosmos come from Mexico, and,
although it does not sound reasonable, so do the "French" and
"African" marigolds.

Many of the modern annuals have been greatly improved by cross-
breeding and selection. Some of them tend to revert to less desirable
forms, and some annuals vary naturally; hence it pays the gardener to
buy a good strain of seeds from a reliable seedsman. When you come
to think of it, the amount that you pay for seeds of annual plants is as

nothing compared to the value of the time and labor spent in raising them to maturity.

Time for sowing. The time for sowing annuals depends on the class to which they belong. Many of the hardy annuals may be sown to advantage in late fall because this enables them to get an early start and form a root system which is deep in the ground before the advent of hot dry weather. In this group are such plants as larkspur, poppies (both field and Californian), cornflower, and portulaca. It is, of course, necessary to prepare the soil with just as much care as for spring planting. It is also advisable to mark the spot so that the plantings are not inadvertently dug up the following spring. Others of the hardy annuals, such as mignonette, sweet alyssum, and calliopsis, may be sown as soon as the ground is workable in early spring.

Starting annuals under glass. The half-hardy annuals may be started in seed pots or flats during March, either in greenhouse, hotbed, or coldframe. (See Chapter XXIV, COLDFRAMES AND HOTBEDS, and Chapter XXVI, PLANT PROPAGATION.) Another method of dealing with the half-hardy annuals is to sow the seeds outdoors when the ground has become warm and danger of frost is past—usually sometime in May. Then it is best to sow them in the place where they are to bloom, afterwards thinning the seedlings to the correct distance apart. Half-hardy annuals include the aster, petunia, castor-oil plant, marigold, and zinnia.

The tender annuals give the best results when started early in a greenhouse or hotbed. In this group we have begonia, ageratum and lobelia. Pansies, which ordinarily are treated as biennials, may be grown as tender annuals by starting the seeds in January or February in a greenhouse. If planting the seeds of tender annuals is deferred until it is warm enough to do so outdoors, the chances are that by the time they start to make a display, frost will come along and destroy them.

There can be no clear demarcation between the above groups, since a species which is considered half-hardy or even tender in Maine may be hardy in the Carolinas.

Planting annual seeds outdoors. Now let us turn our attention to the question of planting outdoors. It is assumed that the soil has been thoroughly prepared by the application of decayed manure and by digging. The next important undertaking is the making of a finely pulverized seed bed, which is done by raking the surface with an iron-toothed rake until all the lumps are broken and the soil is in fine tilth.

Small seeds such as those of poppy and portulaca are scattered on the surface of newly raked soil and the soil is raked again, quite lightly, to cover the seeds. Then the soil should be patted down gently to bring it in close contact with the seeds so that they may absorb the moisture necessary for germination. The extent of the patch should be indicated by marking its outlines with a groove made in the soil by a finger, rake handle, or trowel. It is just as well, also, to label the patch with the name of the seed planted. A common method of doing this is to fasten the empty packet to a stake and stick it in the ground.

Once a lady complained to me that her seeds had not germinated, though she had obtained them from a reputable dealer. With a flash of intuition I asked her how deep she had planted them, and when she replied "about a foot" I was able to tell her why they had failed. It is seldom necessary to plant any seeds more than 1 inch deep. A good general rule to follow in outdoor planting is to cover them with soil equal in depth to three or four times the diameter of the seed, so long as the depth does not amount to more than 1 inch.

For seeds that require ¼ inch or more of covering, scrape off a sufficient depth of surface soil with a trowel or the back of a rake, scatter the seeds, cover them with the soil that was removed, and pat it down.

Large seeds of plants which make strong growth, such as the sunflower and castor-oil plant, may be planted in hills spaced from 2 to 4 feet apart. With a trowel make a hole sufficiently large to accommodate three or four seeds. When the seeds have germinated, remove all but the strongest seedling in each group.

Those who live in the vicinity of large cities may experience considerable annoyance from English sparrows who seem to think that the seed patches were designed for their especial benefit. When sparrows take dust baths in a seed patch it usually means goodbye to any prospect of getting a good stand of plants. Pieces of chicken-wire netting laid on the ground will protect the plantings. The netting should be removed when the seeds have germinated, for by this time it has usually rained, so the surface is no longer loose and attractive to birds.

When annuals are to be raised in rows, as for cut flowers, it is convenient to make a drill or shallow trench with a draw-hoe or rake-

PLATE XIV. (*upper*) FLOWER BORDER OF ANNUALS. (*lower left*) ZINNIA, VARIETY FANTASY. (*lower right*) SALPIGLOSSIS

PLATE XV. *(upper)* POPPIES, SNAPDRAGONS, AND PERENNIAL PHLOX. *(lower left)* DIANTHUS, AGERATUM, AND SWEET ALYSSUM. *(lower right)* COSMOS, VARIETY ORANGE FLARE

head, plant the seeds in this drill and cover them as required. Although it is advisable when planting seeds to sow more than are required to produce the desired number of plants (in order to allow for accidents), one should not go to the other extreme and plant too thickly, because the removal of excess seedlings later will involve much work.

Handling of annuals. A certain amount of thinning, nevertheless, is an important operation, and one that is often neglected when annuals are being raised. Other important factors in the success of annuals are the hardening off of young plants that have been started indoors early in the spring and the prevention of seeding after the flowers have bloomed.

Thinning the seedlings. Soon after the seedlings have germinated, the work of thinning must begin. Preferably it should be done when the ground is wet and the sky is clouded. The seedlings to be discarded can then be pulled up with ease, and there is little danger of disturbing and injuring the roots of the plants that are to remain. The distance allowed between the seedlings is, of course, dependent upon the size and habit of the mature plants. Small varieties, such as the Virginian stock, may be eventually spaced at 3 to 4 inches; Shirley poppies, mignonette, and other strong growers ultimately will require at least a square foot of space. (See tabular list at the end of this chapter.) The operation of thinning should be spread over several weeks. The plants at first may be left from 2 to 6 inches apart, the distance depending on the character of the variety. Later, more plants may be removed so that those remaining stand at the required distance apart.

Thinning is really necessary to get the best results from annuals. It allows the plants sufficient room to develop into healthy, vigorous specimens without undue competition from their neighbors, and it aids in prolonging their season of bloom.

It is sometimes asked whether thinnings may be transplanted to other parts of the garden. This depends on the nature of the plant in question. Most of them may be transplanted without difficulty, but some, such as the field poppy, mignonette, and California poppy, are difficult to move with any degree of success.

Hardening off and transplanting. When annuals have been raised under glass in the greenhouse or hotbed, it is necessary to harden them by gradually exposing them to outdoor conditions (as explained in Chapter XXIV, COLDFRAMES AND HOTBEDS) before they are planted in the garden. If this precaution is not taken, they are likely to suffer considerable injury when suddenly moved from the sheltered, shaded conditions of indoor life and exposed to wind and glaring sunshine outdoors.

Pot-grown plants may be set out with little or no root disturbance and they will grow along without any check, provided the soil is firmly pressed around their roots at planting time and they are not allowed to suffer from lack of moisture. Although a dibber is sometimes used for making the holes for the reception of potted plants from 2-inch pots, it is better to use a trowel, which is stabbed into the ground and pulled toward the operator, thus making a hole into which the plant is placed. The trowel is then removed, and the soil pressed around the ball of roots with the fingers. If the plants are growing in flats (shallow boxes, 2 to 4 inches deep, of a length and breadth convenient to handle) the same method of planting may be followed, but it is desirable to exercise considerable care in removing them to avoid undue root injury. If the flats are made with one removable side, it is easier to get the plants out. After a side is taken off, it should be possible, with a mason's trowel, to cut the soil into squares, each containing a plant, and then to slide the trowel under each square of earth and transfer it to the ground without much root disturbance.

A moist cloudy day is preferable for transplanting from flats—even more so than when the plants are transferred from pots. If the soil is at all dry it should be watered thoroughly after the plants are set out. Leave a little depression in the soil at the base of each plant so that when the water is applied it will run where it will do most good. Should strong winds and bright sunshine make their appearance within a few days of transplanting, it may be advisable to shade the plants by placing berry boxes over them or by thrusting a shingle in the ground on the south side, tilting it toward the north so as to cast an effective shadow. These protective devices should be removed as soon as the plants have become established.

Prevention of seeding. The chief aim in life for an annual plant is to blossom and produce seeds, thus providing for the perpetuation of its species. When it has accomplished this task, its work is finished and it is ready to die. If, therefore, by removing faded flowers we prevent the plant from seeding, we can greatly prolong its period of bloom. This practice is thoroughly worth while when it does not become too arduous a chore. Sweet peas and pansies, in particular, are benefited by this care. Cutting the flowers for use in vases, of course, serves the same purpose.

Selecting annuals. In selecting annuals for the garden, the bulk of them should consist of the old established favorites such as snapdragon, phlox, zinnia, California poppy, petunia, and marigold—plants that may be relied upon to produce flowers over a long period. This does not imply that the newer introductions should be neglected. By all means, try them, but do not plunge too heavily until you are sure that they will behave well under the conditions characteristic of your own garden.

Following is a selection of the more important and worth-while annuals. The time of planting, distance apart, etc., are recorded in the more extensive tabulation which follows this descriptive list.

DESCRIPTIVE LIST OF ANNUALS

AGERATUM, **Floss-flower.** Valued for its long blooming habits, ageratum, if started early in the greenhouse, may begin flowering in May and continue until frost. The varieties range in height from a few inches up to 1½ feet. The color is generally powder-blue, but is sometimes deep blue and occasionally white or pink. **Little Blue Star** is a diminutive kind about 4 inches high. **Blue Perfection,** deep blue, 18 inches, and **Imperial Dwarf Blue,** 9 inches, are among the varieties listed by seedsmen. Ageratum is subject to attacks by mites ("red spiders") and white fly.

ALYSSUM. **Sweet Alyssum** is easy to grow and extremely free-flowering. If the plants get too straggly in summer, they may be sheared close enough to remove most of the seed pods. In a few weeks they will again be in full bloom. *A. Benthami* (which is now known to botanists but to few others as *Lobularia maritima*) grows about 8 inches high, is white and fragrant, and spreads to 2 feet. **Lilac Queen** is a compact form with pale rosy-lilac flowers and **Little Gem** is white, 3 to 4 inches high, spreading a foot or more.

ANTIRRHINUM, **Snapdragon.** The colorful spikes of snapdragon flowers with mouths that will open and shut, may often be seen growing on old walls in Europe, a choice which perhaps indicates a preference for lime. The cultivated snapdragons range in height from 6 inches to 3 feet. The dwarf kinds are suitable for edgings, the intermediates for bedding and flower borders, and the tall ones for the flower border. In sections where snapdragon rust is prevalent, the rust-resistant kinds should be used. Make selections from a seed catalog according to color and height desired.

ASTER, **China Aster.** To be correct, China asters should be listed under *Callistephus,* but as they are called asters in practically every seed catalog, that procedure is followed here for the convenience of the reader. By making a selection of early, midseason, and late varieties, and by starting seeds indoors in March and April and outdoors in May, one can have asters in bloom from late June until frost. They are long-lasting as cut flowers.

In some sections asters are subject to yellows, a mosaic disease transmitted by insects. When this is prevalent, it is wise to grow them in cheesecloth cages to keep insects away; or to give up the notion of growing them. Another destructive disease of asters is wilt. Strains are available which are resistant to this disease, and they should be preferred for planting.

As a general rule, the early-flowering asters are comparatively dwarf (12 to 18 inches), increasing in height in the midseason varieties, and rising to 3 feet in the late kinds. If only one type is to be grown, varieties should be selected from the midseason group. The "Princess" class, in which the central florets are almost quilled, is distinctive and good-looking. It is obtainable in various colors and, like the following, is wilt-resistant. The "Ostrich Plume" type, which produces flowers up to 6 inches in diameter, is excellent. For those who have a constitutional aversion to double flowers, the single types have a great appeal. Their flowers may attain a diameter of 5 inches, the disk florets yellow, and the color of the ray florets ranging from white to scarlet, and from pink to purple and dark blue.

CALLISTEPHUS, see note under ASTER.

COSMOS. This is one of the most useful of cut flowers. The tall late-flowering types in some sections may be caught by frost before they have an opportunity to develop their flowers, but many gardeners consider that they are worth raising for their foliage alone. If grown primarily for flowers, some of the dwarf early-flowering kinds should be planted as well as the tall late ones. There are double and crested varieties available, but it is doubtful if they are any improvement on the single-flowered kinds. The colors of cosmos range from white and pink to crimson. There is also a variety with orange flowers.

The **Sensation** types are superb for cutting, having flowers 4 to 6 inches across. They will bloom in ten weeks from the time of sowing the seeds and continue until frost. Single and double forms are available.

DIANTHUS, **Pinks.** The annual pinks are valuable for their extended season of bloom, which is prolonged if they are freely used for cut flowers. They may be obtained in both single and double forms in a wide range of colors, being especially rich in deep crimson tones. In some varieties, the flowers are curiously fringed.

DIMORPHOTHECA, **Cape-marigold** or **African Golden Daisy,** is well adapted for planting in sunny, rather dry situations. The daisy-like flowers in the type (*D. aurantiaca*) are golden-orange. The hybrids exhibit a range of color from white to orange and salmon.

ESCHSCHOLZIA, **California Poppy.** Although there are many new developments in color among the California poppies, it is doubtful if any surpass the old type with its flowers of egg-yolk yellow. These poppies have a long blooming season, and attractive feathery grayish foliage. Early sowing is necessary for best results; when convenient, it is desirable to plant in the fall so that a good root system may be formed before hot weather comes the following year. **Geisha** is among the best of the named garden varieties.

LOBULARIA, see ALYSSUM.

Marigold, see TAGETES.

MATTHIOLA, **Stock.** In sections having a cool summer climate, stocks are fragrant flowers of great merit. In hot regions, though they grow vigorously, they may fail to produce any flowers. The heavy spikes of bloom vary in color from white through many tones of pink and lavender.

Nasturtium, see TROPAEOLUM.

NICOTIANA. The white-flowered *N. alata grandiflora* (*N. affinis*) is particularly valuable for the moonlight garden because the flowers open at night and are deliciously fragrant. During the day, unless it is overcast, they look sad and wilted. *N. Sanderae* is a counterpart of the above except that the flowers are velvety-crimson. The white flowers of *N. sylvestris* (5-6 ft.) stay open all day.

PAPAVER, **Poppy.** The secret of success in growing annual poppies in regions with hot summers is to plant the seeds early so that the roots may be well developed before hot weather. They should be planted where they are to bloom, because transplanting either kills them or sets them back so that they are not much good. Thinning the seedlings must not be neglected —each plant should ultimately have at least a square foot to itself. Shirley poppies are variants of the field poppy of Europe, which is a bad weed in the grain fields there. They were noticed and perpetuated by the Rev. W. Wilks of Shirley Vicarage, from whence they receive their name. They are stunningly beautiful, having silken petals with clear colors ranging from white to scarlet. Various named varieties are available: **American Legion,** single, reminiscent of the "Flanders Field" poppies; **Cavalcade,** double flowers of orange-scarlet; and **Sweet Brier,** double rose-pink.

PETUNIA. Among the most valuable plants for the annual garden, petunias may be brought into bloom by June, by starting the seeds indoors in March. They will continue flowering until frost. The seeds should be barely covered, and thin sowing must be practised because the seedlings are very susceptible to attacks by damping-off fungi.

Petunias exhibit a great variety of size, form and coloring. The dwarf bedding varieties have comparatively small flowers on plants 6 to 8 inches high. The giant-flowered kinds grow about 1½ feet high and have flowers 4 or 5 inches in diameter, which may be ruffled, fringed or plain-edged, and single or double. The "Balcony" petunias have slender, more or less trailing branches which adapt them for use in window and porch boxes. These have flowers 2 to 3 inches across. The colors range from white to crimson, and light blue to deep violet. Some flowers are variegated and others are curiously veined with a color deeper in tone than the ground color.

PHLOX. The annual phlox, *P. Drummondii,* which is native in Texas, comes in a large range of colors, in dwarf varieties (about 8 inches) and tall ones (about 15 inches). Plants may be had continuously in bloom from June (if the seeds are started indoors in March) until frost by making additional sowings in mid-April and again about the middle of June. The tall varieties perhaps bloom more freely over a longer period. They may be made to serve the same purpose as the dwarf varieties in respect to height if the shoots are pinned to the ground with wooden or wire pegs as they elongate. The so-called "Star" varieties are not of much value.

Stock, see MATTHIOLA.

Sweet Pea, see LATHYRUS in Chapter IX, VINES.

TAGETES, **Marigold.** The French marigolds usually exhibit rich velvety red-brown markings on their flowers of clear yellow. In general, their flowers are smaller than those of the African marigolds and are produced on plants lower in stature (9 inches to 2 feet). But they are free-flowering and never out of bloom during the growing season once they have reached the blooming stage. The variety **Legion of Honor** starts to bloom when it is about 2 inches high and continues until frost, by which time it has attained a height of 9 to 12 inches.

The old type African marigolds were characterized by their foul odor and by flowers which reminded one of rubber sponges on sticks. The distasteful odor has been eliminated in some varieties (**Canary Bird, Golden Glow,** and others), and the shape of the flowers has been improved so that (in **Guinea Gold** types, for instance) they are almost gardenia-like in form.

Marigolds will thrive under a wide variety of conditions, including those prevalent in large cities.

TROPAEOLUM, **Nasturtium.** This valuable annual with vivid flowers of yellow, orange, or red is seen at its best in climates where the temperature seldom goes above 75 degrees. Nasturtiums, preferably, should be planted in a fairly sunny position, but they will thrive in shade. The tall climbing types may be used on trellises, and they are valuable for planting on the compost pile to mask it during the summer. The dwarf kinds are used for bedding and for planting in front of the flower border. The outstanding recent development in nasturtiums is the **Golden Gleam** type introduced a few years ago. In this class, which is semi-trailing, the flowers are semi-double and fragrant. These, like the rest of the nasturtiums, are valuable for cutting. Delightful arrangements may be made by using the flowers with their own foliage. Nasturtiums are subject to pernicious black lice which, if unchecked by a nicotine spray, completely ruin the plants.

VERBENA. In my early days, verbenas were commonly propagated from cuttings inserted in August, carried over winter in a greenhouse, and set outdoors in spring when danger of frost was past. Nowadays the usual practice is to raise them from seeds—a feasible proceeding because if a good strain is obtained, the progeny will largely be true to color and form. If a particularly fine specimen, exhibiting an advance in color, size of flower heads, and floriferousness, should show itself in a batch of seedlings, it would be worth while to perpetuate it by propagation from cuttings.

In addition to the large-flowered bedding verbenas in white, red, purple, and intervening tones, there are attractive dwarf forms listed in catalogs, such as: *V. erinoides,* which has finely divided foliage and purplish flowers, and *V. Mahoneti,* whose flowers are striped red and white. *V. rigida* (*venosa*) is an erect free-blooming kind with many small clusters of purple flowers of a rather distressing tone. There is a new variety described as having "pale mauve" flowers which is an improvement on the type.

ZINNIA. Some people abominate zinnias because they are acquainted only with those of harsh, crude coloring, with a dirty-looking center. These kinds, which can be reproduced almost exactly by taking an open, stubby pine cone and painting it a glaring red or yellow, do not have to be chosen, for there are varieties with pastel coloring, and form similar to that of "decorative" dahlias. The dwarf *Haageana* types are far removed from the usual conception of a zinnia. The "Fantasy" zinnias are much more informal than the older kinds. Zinnias are valuable because they are free-flowering and may be used for cutting. They are rather subject to mildew, which should be kept under control by the use of dusting-sulphur.

EXTENDED LIST OF ANNUALS IN TABULAR FORM

The tables indicate the height; the distance apart to plant—or to thin—the seedlings; the method of handling (whether seeds should be started indoors or out); the time of planting; the colors, and other observations. When both indoor and outdoor planting are permissible, the preferred method is starred (*). The times given are for the vicinity of New York City. In regions having longer or shorter growing seasons, the time should respectively be advanced or retarded.

Kinds considered the most valuable are marked with a dagger (†).

Name	Height	Distance apart	Method of handling Outdoors	Indoors	Colors and remarks
ABRONIA, Sand Verbena					
umbellata	9 in.	1 ft.	May		Pink. Good trailer for sandy soils.
ACROCLINIUM, see HELIPTERUM					
ADONIS					
aleppica	1½ ft.	6 in.	April		Red. Not very easy to grow.
† AGERATUM					Blue or white. Best started indoors.
dwarf	4-8 in.	6 in.	May	March *	
intermediate	9-12 in.	9 in.	May	March *	
tall	1½-2 ft.	1 ft.	May	March *	
† ALYSSUM (Sweet Alyssum, properly LOBULARIA)					White or lilac. Thin them gradually until they are correct distance apart.
compact varieties	3-4 in.	6 in.	April *	March	
spreading varieties	6-10 in.	9 in.	April *	March	
† AMARANTHUS					
caudatus (*cruentus*)	3-5 ft.	1-1½ ft.	April		Red, drooping, chenille-like.
tricolor	2-3 ft.	1 ft.	April	March *	Bold showy foliage of red, yellow, and green.
ANAGALLIS, Pimpernel					
arvensis, large-flowered blue, and scarlet	6 in.	6 in.	April & May		Good to carpet ground over spring-flowering bulbs.
ANCHUSA					
Blue Bird	1½ ft.	9 in.	May		Bright blue.
† ANTIRRHINUM, Snapdragon					Almost all colors and combinations except blue.
dwarf	6 in.	6 in.	April	March *	
intermediate	1½ ft.	10 in.	April	March *	
tall	3 ft.	1-1½ ft.	April	March *	
† ARCTOTIS					
stoechadifolia (*grandis*)	2-3 ft.	1 ft.	May	March *	Bluish-white. An excellent cut flower.
ARGEMONE, Prickly Poppy					
mexicana	2-3 ft.	1 ft.	May		Yellow or orange. Do not attempt to transplant. Good for sunny location and dry soil.
† ASTER (properly *Callistephus*)					White to crimson and purple. Watch out for wilt and "yellows."
early	1-1½ ft.	9 in.	May	March *	
midseason	2-2½ ft.	1 ft.	May	March *	
late	2½-3 ft.	1¼ ft.	May	March *	
BARTONIA, see MENTZELIA					
† BEGONIA					
gracilis varieties	1 ft.	1 ft.		Feb.	Pink, red, or white, good in partial shade.
semperflorens varieties	6 in.- 1 ft.	6 in.- 1 ft.		Feb.	

Name	Height	Distance apart	Method of handling Outdoors	Indoors	Colors and remarks
BRIZA, Quaking Grass					
maxima	1-1½ ft.	3 in.	April		May be dried for winter bouquets.
BRACHYCOME, Swan River Daisy					
iberidifolia	9 in.	6 in.	April to May		Blue, rose, or white.
BROWALLIA					
speciosa major	2 ft.	1 ft.		March	Purple, violet, and white. Partial shade.
CACALIA, see EMILIA					
† **CALENDULA, Pot Marigold**					Excellent cut flowers, all in tones of yellow and orange.
Chrysantha	2 ft.	1½ ft.	April		
Golden King	1½ ft.	1 ft.	April		
Orange King	1½ ft.	1 ft.	April		
Yellow Colossal	1½ ft.	1 ft.	April		
† **CALLIOPSIS**					Yellow and brownish-red. Tall varieties excellent for cutting.
dwarf	9-15 in.	6 in.	April		
tall	1½-2½ ft.	9 in.	April		
CAMPANULA, Bellflower					
Annual Canterbury Bells	2 ft.	1 ft.	April	March *	Blue, pink, or white. Bloom in late summer and early fall.
drabifolia (*attica*)	6 in.	6 in.	April		Blue and white.
ramosissima (*Loreyi*)	1 ft.	6 in.	April		Violet.
† **CELOSIA, Cockscomb**					
dwarf	1 ft.	9 in.	May	March *	Chiefly brilliant yellow, or red.
tall	2-3 ft.	1-1½ ft.	May	March *	
† **CENTAUREA**					
Cyanus	2-3 ft.	1 ft.	March		Blue, also pink, purple, white. Seeds may be planted in the fall.
CHRYSANTHEMUM					
carinatum, **Annual Chrysanthemum**	2 ft.	9 in.	April		Purple disk, rays white, yellow and red.
Parthenium, **Feverfew**	1-2½ ft.	9 in.	April	March *	White.
† **CLARKIA**					
elegans	2 ft.	9 in.	April		Pink. Excellent for cutting.
CLEOME, Spider-flower					
spinosa	3 ft.	2 ft.	April		Rose-purple or white, with long protruding stamens. Endures city conditions and partial shade.
COLLINSIA					
bicolor	1 ft.	6 in.	April		Purple and white.
CONVOLVULUS					
minor	1 ft.	6 in.	May		A dwarf morning-glory with flowers of various colors.

Name	Height	Distance apart	Method of handling Outdoors	Method of handling Indoors	Colors and remarks
† COSMOS					White, lilac-pink, crimson, also orange.
dwarf	3-4 ft.	2 ft.	May	April *	
tall	6-8 ft.	3-4 ft.	May	April *	
CYNOGLOSSUM, Hound's-tongue					
amabile	1½ ft.	9 in.	May		Blue.
DATURA					Poisonous to eat.
Metel (cornucopia)	3-5 ft.	2 ft.	late April	March *	Whitish, violet-tinged.
† DELPHINIUM, Larkspur					Either fall planting or early spring planting is essential for best results.
Ajacis	2½-3 ft.	9 in.	Oct. or		Blue, violet, pink, white.
Consolida	1½-2 ft.	9 in.	March		Blue, violet, or white.
† DIANTHUS					
chinensis varieties	1 ft.	6 in.	April	March *	Red and related tones, variegated and fringed.
DIASCIA, Twinspur					
Barberae	1 ft.	6 in.	May	March *	Rose-pink. A perennial which usually is treated as a half-hardy annual.
† DIDISCUS					
caerulea	2 ft.	9 in.	May	March *	Pale blue. Long-lasting as a cut flower.
† DIMORPHOTHECA, Cape-marigold					
aurantiaca & hybrids	1 ft.	9 in.	May	March *	Orange tones.
EMILIA, Tassel-flower					
sagittata (Cacalia coccinea)	1½ ft.	9 in.	May	March *	Small scarlet tassels.
ERAGROSTIS					
japonica (elegans)	1-2 ft.	6 in.	April		An ornamental grass with delicate sprays of bloom.
† ESCHSCHOLZIA					
californica	1 ft.	9 in.	Oct. or March		Orange-yellow, pale yellow, and reddish tones.
EUPHORBIA					
heterophylla, Annual Poinsettia	2-3 ft.	1 ft.	May		Does not resemble the Christmas poinsettia. Has green and scarlet bracts.
marginata (variegata), Snow-on-the-Mountain	2-3 ft.	1 ft.	April		Long-lasting as a cut flower. Upper leaves with broad white margins.
EXACUM					
affine, Arabian Gentian	9 in.	6 in.		Feb.	Blue. Unique appearance, and somewhat rare in gardens.

Name	Height	Distance apart	Method of handling Outdoors	Indoors	Colors and remarks
FELICIA					
Bergeriana	6 in.	6 in.	May	March *	Brilliant blue daisy-like flowers.
† GAILLARDIA					
amblyodon	2 ft.	9 in.	May		Brownish-red. Good cut flowers.
GILIA					
capitata	2 ft.	9 in.	Oct. & April		Light blue flowers in small heads; plant slender.
tricolor, **Bird's-eyes**	1½-2½ ft.	9 in.	April		Purple, lilac and yellow.
† GODETIA					Red, purple, and paler tones to white.
tall varieties	2-3 ft.	1 ft.	April		
dwarf varieties	1 ft.	9 in.	April		Thrive best in regions with cool summers. Will grow in partial shade.
GOMPHRENA, Globe Amaranth					
globosa	1-1½ ft.	1 ft.	May	March *	Usually bright purplish or white. Everlasting for winter bouquets.
Grasses (Ornamental)					
Briza maxima	1-1½ ft.	3 in.	April		
Eragrostis elegans	1-2 ft.	6 in.	April		
Pennisetum longistylum	2-3 ft.	1 ft.	May	March *	
GYPSOPHILA, Baby's Breath					
elegans	1½ ft.	6 in.	April & May		Sprays of white flowers, good for cutting. Plant at intervals of 3 weeks for succession.
† HELIANTHUS, Sun flower					
annuus	3-12 ft.	3 ft.	April		Yellow, or reddish. Useful for temporary background.
debilis (cucumerifolius)	4 ft.	2 ft.	April		Excellent for cut flowers.
dwarf varieties	1-3 ft.	1 ft.	April		
† HELICHRYSUM, Straw-flower					
bracteatum	2-3 ft.	9-12 in.	May	March *	Almost every color but blue. Cut and dry for winter bouquets.
HELIPTERUM, Everlasting					
Manglesii (Rhodanthe Manglesii)	1 ft.	6 in.	May		Pink. Good for dried winter bouquets.
roseum (Acroclinium roseum)	1½ ft.	6 in.	May		Pink. Good for dried winter bouquets.
HIBISCUS					
Trionum (africanus)	1-2 ft.	1 ft.	May		Large pale yellow flowers, dark at center.

Name	Height	Distance apart	Method of handling Outdoors	Indoors	Colors and remarks
† HUNNEMANNIA, **Tulip-poppy**					
fumariaefolia	1½-2 ft.	9-12 in.	May		Yellow. Excellent, long-lasting cut flower. Also fine for bedding.
IBERIS, **Candytuft**					
tall varieties	1 ft.	1 ft.	April		White, varying to rosy purple.
dwarf varieties	4-6 in.	4 in.	April		
† IMPATIENS					
Balsamina, **Garden Balsam**	2 ft.	9 in.	April		Usually rose or white. Will thrive in partial shade.
Sultani	2 ft.	1-1½ ft.		March	May be taken up in fall for use as a house plant. Tender perennial.
† KOCHIA, **Summer-cypress**					Small narrow leaves which turn dark red.
scoparia trichophylla	2-3 ft.	1-1½ ft.	April		Makes a good temporary low hedge.
† LATHYRUS					See Chapter IX, VINES, for details for culture.
odoratus, **Sweet Pea**					
dwarf varieties	8 in.	6 in.	Nov. or		
tall varieties	5-6 ft.	6 in.	March		
LAVATERA					
trimestris	2-3 ft.	1-1½ ft.	May		Deep pink or white.
LEPTOSYNE					
maritima	2-3 ft.	1 ft.	April		Large yellow flowers resembling *Coreopsis*.
Stillmanii	1½ ft.	9 in.	April		Blooms in 5 or 6 weeks from time of sowing seeds.
LINARIA					
maroccana	1 ft.	4 in.	April & May		Bright purple with yellow spot.
† LIMONIUM (STATICE)					
sinuatum	1½ ft.	9 in.	May	March *	Everlastings — cut and dry for winter bouquets.
Suworowii	1 ft.	6 in.	May	March *	Tiny rosy-lilac flowers in finger-like spikes.
LINUM					
grandiflorum rubrum	1-1½ ft.	9 in.	April		An annual flax with rich red flowers.
† LOBELIA					Lobelias prefer partial shade in hot climates.
Erinus, dwarf varieties	4-6 in.	6 in.		Feb. &	Bright blue or white.
Erinus, trailing varieties	4-6 in.	9 in.		March	Bright blue or white.
tenuior	1-1½ ft.	6 in.	May	March *	Bright blue or white.

Name	Height	Distance apart	Method of handling Outdoors	Indoors	Colors and remarks
LUPINUS					These lupines do not
dwarf varieties	1 ft.	1 ft.	April & May		transplant readily, so they must be sown in place and afterwards thinned.
Hartwegii	2 ft.	1-1½ ft.	April & May		Blue and rose.
mutabilis	2 ft.	1½ ft.	May		Violet, yellow and white.
LYCHNIS (VISCARIA), Rose of Heaven					
Coeli-rosa	1 ft.	6 in.	April or May		Obtainable in a large range of colors.
MALCOMIA, Virginian Stock					
maritima	4-6 in.	3 in.	April		Rose, lilac, white. Will thrive in partial shade.
MALOPE					
trifida grandiflora	2½ ft.	1 ft.	April		Rose-red mallow-like flowers, darker veined.
Marigold, see TAGETES					
MATTHIOLA, Stock					
bicornis	1 ft.	6 in.	April		Purple, night-blooming. Grown only for its fragrance.
incana, dwarf varieties	1-1½ ft.	9 in.	April	March *	Tones of rose and pur-
incana, tall varieties	2-2½ ft.	1-1½ ft.	April	March *	ple, also white.
MENTZELIA					
Lindleyi (Bartonia aurea)	1 ft.	9 in.	May		Yellow. Needs sunny position.
MESEMBRYANTHEMUM					
crystallinum, Ice Plant	6-8 in.	1 ft.	April		Grown only for its cool-looking foliage. Trailer.
MIMOSA					
pudica, Sensitive Plant	1-1½ ft.	1 ft.		March	Has interesting sensitive foliage, and tiny lavender pompon-like flower heads.
MIMULUS, Monkey-flower					
tigrinus	1-1½ ft.	9 in.	May	March *	Varied red and yellow. Grows best in wet soil, and/or partial shade.
Whitecroft Scarlet	8 in.	6 in.	May	March *	
† MIRABILIS					
Jalapa and varieties, **Four O'Clock**	1½-2½ ft.	1-1½ ft.	April	March *	Crimson, yellow, white. Endures city conditions.
NEMESIA					Pink, lilac, yellow, white,
dwarf varieties	9 in.	6 in.	May	March *	spotted.
tall varieties	1-1½ ft.	9 in.	May	March *	Nemesias do not thrive in hot weather.

Name	Height	Distance apart	Method of handling Outdoors	Indoors	Colors and remarks
NEMOPHILA					
insignis, Baby Blue-eyes	9 in.	1 ft.	April		Clear blue flowers. Will grow in partial shade.
† NICOTIANA, Flowering Tobacco					
alata (*affinis*)	2-3 ft.	1 ft.	April	March *	White.
Sanderae	2-3 ft.	1 ft.	April	March *	Red.
sylvestris	5-6 ft.	1½ ft.	April	March *	White.
NIEREMBERGIA, Cup-flower					
caerulea (often listed as N. *hippomanica*)	6 in.	6 in.		March	Blue perennial treated as annual
NIGELLA, Love-in-a-mist					
damascena	1½-2 ft.	9 in.	March		Blue; finely-cut foliage.
NOLANA					
atriplicifolia (*paradoxa*)	9 in.	1 ft.	April		Blue and white, yellow throat. Trailer.
PAPAVER, Poppy					
Rhoeas, Field Poppy	2-3 ft.	1 ft.	March		Red. Must be planted early.
PENNISETUM					
longistylum	2-3 ft.	1 ft.	May	March *	Ornamental grass much used for edging canna beds.
† PETUNIA					
dwarf varieties	6-8 in.	6 in.	May	March *	White to bright rose and
tall and trailing varieties	1-2 ft.	1 ft.	May	March *	purple.
PHACELIA					Phacelias grow best in
campanularia	9 in.-1 ft.	9 in.	April		partial shade in re-
ciliata	1 ft.	9 in.	April		gions with hot sum-
viscida	1 ft.	9 in.	April		mer climates. Flowers blue.
† PHLOX DRUMMONDII					
dwarf varieties	6 in.	6 in.	May	March *	White, magenta, rose
tall varieties	1-1½ ft.	9 in.	May	March *	tawny, purple.
† PORTULACA					
grandiflora	6 in.	6 in.	Oct. or April		Purplish-crimson, yellow, white. Good for a hot sunny position.
RESEDA, Mignonette					
odorata	6 in.	1 ft.	April		Grown for the fragrant
tall varieties	1-1½ ft.	1 ft.	April		flowers.
RHODANTHE, see HELIPTERUM					
RICINUS, Castor-oil Plant					
communis	4-8 ft.	4-6 ft.	May	March *	Excellent bold-foliaged plants for temporary background.
† SALPIGLOSSIS, Painted Tongue					
sinuata	2-3 ft.	9 in.	May	March *	Purples and yellows vari-egated.

Name	Height	Distance apart	Method of handling Outdoors	Indoors	Colors and remarks
† SALVIA *farinacea*	2 ft.	9 in.	May	March *	Blue. A perennial which may be treated as an annual.
patens	2 ft.	1 ft.	May	March *	Blue.
splendens	3 ft.	1 ½ ft.	May	March *	Scarlet.
splendens, **Welwyn**	3 ft.	1 ½ ft.	May	March *	The new pink "splendens."
splendens, **Zurich**	2 ft.	1 ft.	May	March *	Scarlet.
SANVITALIA *procumbens*	6 in.	9 in.	April		Yellow with purple center, long-blooming, suitable for edging.
procumbens flore pleno	6 in.	9 in.	April		Double-flowered.
SAPONARIA *Vaccaria*	1 ½ ft.	9 in.	April		Deep pink.
† SCABIOSA, **Pincushion-flower** *atropurpurea* varieties	2-3 ft.	1 ft.	April	March *	Purple, blue, mahogany, rose, white. Hummingbirds are fond of them.
SCHIZANTHUS, **Butterfly-flower** dwarf varieties	1 ft.	9 in.	May	March *	Orchid-like flowers marked with many colors. Rather fragile;
tall varieties	2-3 ft.	1-1 ½ ft.	May	March *	need a sheltered situation.
SENECIO *elegans*	1 ft.	6 in.	May	March *	Purple; yellow center.
SILENE *Armeria*	1-2 ft.	6 in.	April		Rose or white.
SOLANUM *integrifolium*	3 ft.	2 ft.		March	Grown for its orange-red fruits, useful for indoor decoration.
STATICE, see LIMONIUM					
Stock, see MATTHIOLA					
Sweet Pea, see LATHYRUS					
† TAGETES, **Marigold** dwarf varieties	8-12 in.	9 in.	May	March *	Yellow and deep red.
tall varieties	2-3 ft.	1 ½ ft.	May	March *	Brilliant yellow or orange.
THUNBERGIA, **Clock-vine** *alata*	9 in.	1 ft.	May	March *	Yellow with dark center. Trailer.
TITHONIA, **Mexican Sunflower** *rotundifolia* (*speciosa*)	6-8 ft.	3 ft.	May	March *	Coarse, but has spectacular, rich orange flowers in fall.

Name	Height	Distance apart	Method of handling Outdoors	Indoors	Colors and remarks
† TORENIA, **Blue-wings**					
Fournieri	9 in.-1 ft.	6 in.	May	March *	Blue and velvety purple. Sun or partial shade. Foliage turns reddish.
† TROPAEOLUM, **Nasturtium**					
dwarf varieties	10 in.	6 in.	April		Yellow, orange, and scarlet. Best in cool climates.
medium varieties	1½ ft.	1 ft.	April		
tall varieties	6 ft.	1-2 ft.	April		
URSINIA					
anethoides	1 ft.	6 in.	April	March *	Orange daisy-like flowers. Good annuals for sunny situations.
hybrids	2 ft.	1 ft.	April	March *	
VENIDIUM					
fastuosum	2-3 ft.	1 ft.	April	March *	Large orange flowers, dark-centered. Good, but finnicky annuals for sunny situations. Spectacular spiny-looking foliage.
† VERBENA					
dwarf varieties	6 in.	9 in.	May	March *	White, rose, purple, red.
tall varieties	1 ft.	1 ft.	May	March *	
VINCA					
rosea	1 ft.	9 in.	May	March *	Bright pink or white.
VIOLA, **Pansy**					
tricolor	8 in.	9 in.		Feb.	Usually treated as biennial, but seeds planted in greenhouse in February will bloom in early spring with varied purple, blue, yellow, or white flowers.
Virginian Stock, see MALCOMIA					
VISCARIA, see LYCHNIS					
XERANTHEMUM, **Immortelle**					
annuum	2-3 ft.	9 in.	April		Everlasting for winter bouquets.
† ZINNIA					
dwarf varieties	1-1½ ft.	9 in.	May	March *	Wide range of colors, especially in newer varieties.
tall varieties	3 ft.	1 ft.	May	March *	

ANNUALS WHICH WILL GROW IN SHADE

Most annuals require sunshine throughout the larger part of the day. Those listed below are among those which will endure considerable shade.

Begonia	Celosia	Impatiens
Calliopsis	Cleome	Lobelia
Campanula	Godetia	Malcomia

Mimulus	*Petunia*	*Tropaeolum*
Nemophila	*Phacelia*	*Vinca*
Nicotiana	*Torenia*	*Viola*

BIENNIALS IN THE OUTDOOR GARDEN

Biennials are plants which make part of their growth one year, bloom the following year, set seeds, and die. Many gardeners are chary of growing biennials because of the inevitable inconveniences of handling some of them; but many are so beautiful that it is worth while to endure the bother for the sake of the display they make when in bloom. Oftentimes, when grown in a suitable environment, biennials will solve the problem of their maintenance by reproducing from self-sown seeds. This occurs usually when they are grown under more or less naturalistic conditions, or where the growth of the plants or the nature of the terrain is such that it is difficult to use the hoe efficiently. For example, I know of a garden where every year the biennial alpine forget-me-not makes a sheet of blue, many yards in extent, because the plants are left alone to seed themselves. They are growing in a rock garden, where, because it is not convenient to use cultivating tools, the soil is left undisturbed and the seedlings have a chance to flourish. Everyone knows of patches of hollyhocks which persist year after year, mainly through self-sown seedlings which survive because they come up under the shelter of the parent plants. Foxgloves, when they are established under semi-wild conditions in thin woodland, may be expected to take care of themselves, but if grown in the flower border where cultivation is meticulous, they must be renewed by plants which have been started elsewhere on the grounds.

Methods of raising. Biennials intended for a formal garden must be grown up to a certain stage in the reserve garden and then planted in the situations where they are to bloom.

The usual method of raising biennials is to plant the seeds sometime during the summer, and transplant the seedlings, when they are large enough to handle, to good soil in the reserve or propagating garden. Space them from 3 to 6 inches apart, according to the ultimate size of the plants. Early in the fall, if they are being raised where they are perfectly hardy over winter, transplant them again— this time to the places where they are to flower. If they are not winter-hardy, however, as, for example (in the vicinity of New York), pansies, Canterbury bells, and wallflowers, they are not transplanted in the fall, but are left undisturbed, protected by a coldframe or a covering of some kind, and transplanted to their flowering locations in early spring. (For further details of seed planting see Chapter XXVI, PLANT PROPAGATION.)

Plants sometimes fail to conform strictly to the categories in which they are placed by botanists and gardeners. The pansy, which is usually considered a biennial, may be treated as an annual; yet, under some conditions, it will behave as a short-lived perennial. The same is true of hollyhocks, Canterbury bells, stocks and sweet william.

TABULATED LIST OF BIENNIALS

Following is a tabulated list of the more important biennials, showing height, final spacing, time of planting, and season of bloom:

Name	Height	Distance apart	Month to plant	Month of bloom	Remarks
ALTHAEA					
rosea, Hollyhock	4-10 ft.	1½-2 ft.	5-8	6-8	See also Chapter XII, PERENNIALS.
BELLIS					
perennis, English Daisy	6-8 in.	6 in.	5-8	4-5	A perennial which is treated as a biennial.
CAMPANULA					
Medium, Canterbury Bells	2-3 ft.	9 in.	6-8	6	Just about the most beautiful biennial. The
Medium calycanthema,					
Cup-and-saucer Bells	2-3 ft.	9 in.	6-8	6	Cup-and-saucer varieties have petal-like sepals.
Canterbury Bells, see CAMPANULA					
CHEIRANTHUS					
Cheiri, Wallflower	1-1½ ft.	9 in.-1 ft.	5-6	4-5	Wallflowers need a mild winter climate, and cool conditions for blooming.
DIANTHUS					
barbatus, Sweet William	1½ ft.	9 in.	5-6	6	Transplant to blooming position in late August, or leave in cold-frame and transplant the following spring.
DIGITALIS					
purpurea, Foxglove	3-4 ft.	1 ft.	5-8	6-7	Good for naturalizing in partial shade. When protecting them for the winter (in regions where this is necessary) be careful to avoid covering the leaves with anything that will mat down and cause the plants to rot.

Name	Height	Distance apart	Month to plant	Month of bloom	Remarks
Forget-me-not, see MYOSOTIS					
Foxglove, see DIGITALIS					
Hollyhock, see ALTHAEA					
Honesty, see LUNARIA					
LUNARIA *annua,* **Honesty**	2 ft.	9 in.	5-7	5	Will grow in shade. Needs winter protection in severe climates. Valuable for purple-flowers and silvery seed pods.
MYOSOTIS, **Forget-me-not** *alpestris* varieties	6-12 in.	6-9 in.	5-7	4-6	Often used to plant between spring-flowering bulbs. In regions of severe winters the plants are kept in coldframes and set out in spring. In mild climates they are set out in the fall after the bulbs are planted.
Pansy, see VIOLA					
Sweet William, see DIANTHUS					
VERBASCUM *olympicum,* **Greek Mullein**	4-6 ft.	3 ft.	5	6-7	The garden mulleins produce spire-like flower stalks of great decorative value. The hybrids such as the variety **Miss Willmott** do not come entirely true from seeds. They may be propagated by means of root cuttings.
phoeniceum, hybrids	2 ft.	1½ ft.	5	6-7	
VIOLA *tricolor,* **Pansy**	6-12 in.	6-9 in.	8	4-6	Prevention of seeding and liberal use of the flowers for cutting prolongs the period of bloom.
Wallflower, see CHEIRANTHUS					

XIV. FLOWERING BULBS

(INCLUDING CORMS, TUBERS, AND RELATED TYPES OF PLANTS)

Commercial growers and venders, as well as many members of the gardening public, have acquired the habit of lumping together all plants with fleshy underground parts under the general term "bulbs." As a matter of convenience, in this chapter, I shall follow this custom, even though it would be more correct to differentiate bulb, corm, tuber, and rhizome.

From the standpoint of cultural considerations, bulbs may be divided into four main groups—hardy spring-flowering; hardy spring-flowering for forcing; tender spring-flowering; and summer-flowering.

HARDY SPRING-FLOWERING BULBS

The hardy spring-flowering bulbs include such favorites as tulip, daffodil, hyacinth, squill, snowdrop, grape-hyacinth, and fritillary (all of which are true bulbs); also the crocus (a corm), and winter-aconite and some kinds of anemone, which have tuberous rootstocks.

The most important of these bulbs, in the sense that they are the most frequently planted, are tulip, daffodil, crocus, and hyacinth; although the others, popularly known as the "lesser bulbs," are coming into greater favor with the increase of interest in rock gardening. Not only are they valuable rock-garden plants, but some may also be used for naturalizing and some in the perennial border. All the hardy spring-flowering bulbs may be planted in the open ground; and many varieties may be potted and forced, either under glass or in the house, for indoor decoration.

All of these bulbs must be planted in the fall—not just a week or two before the spring display, as many innocent admirers seem to think!

How to use spring-flowering bulbs. When planted in the open, bulbs are chosen and handled according to their purpose, whether in formal beds, in the perennial garden, naturalized in grass or in thin woodland, or planted in the rock garden.

Planting in formal beds. For formal plantings tulips and hyacinths are preferred because their habit of growth lends itself to formal designs. Usually the early tulips are used in preference to the May-flowering kinds, because they ripen early and may be removed from the beds in good time to make room for the summer bedding plants.

Spring bulbs in the perennial garden. In the perennial garden, any of the hardy bulbs may be used, with the exception of the fussy, diminutive kinds, which are better suited to the rock garden. The early varieties of tulips, with some exceptions (Keizerskroon, for example), do not seem to maintain themselves from year to year so well as the later-blooming kinds, but the May-flowering tulips are excellent for permanent plantings and should be used freely, in clumps of from ten to fifty bulbs.

Most of the hardy bulbs may be expected to persist year after year if the soil conditions are to their liking and if they are not maltreated by having their foliage cut off before it has properly matured. Should the sight of their dying leaves be insupportable, the bulbs may be dug up with the roots attached and planted in an out-of-the-way spot, left until the foliage becomes dry, then taken up and stored in a cool dry place until they are ready to be planted again in the fall. This, however, is not so good for them as to allow the leaves to mature and die naturally without any root disturbance.

Bulbs for naturalizing. Daffodils, poet's narcissi, and forms of *Narcissus incomparabilis,* also crocuses, winter-aconites, snowdrops, and squills, are the bulbs best adapted for naturalizing in grass and woodland. If they are expected to thrive there permanently, the grass must be left uncut until the bulb foliage is ripened. Therefore, do not plant them where long grass will look unkempt. In selecting varieties choose the least expensive kinds. They are usually cheap because they are vigorous and quick to propagate—desirable qualities in bulbs which are destined to take care of themselves.

Bulbs for rock gardens. The "lesser bulbs" are preferred for rock-garden planting. In general, they should be of low stature, such as Siberian squills, grape-hyacinths, snowdrops, winter-aconites, bulbous irises of the *reticulata* type, small fritillaries, wild tulips, and the smaller narcissi. Often they can be placed so that their ripening foliage is masked in part by carpeting plants; or annuals suitable for the rock garden may be planted to hide the bare ground which is left after the bulb foliage has died down.

When and how to plant spring-flowering bulbs. As many bulbous plants resent the desiccation which results from being too long out of the ground, they should be planted just as soon as the bulbs become available. Lilies (which are described among the summer-flowering bulbs), trilliums, dogtooth-violets, winter-aconites, and narcissi belong in this class. On the other hand, tulips and hyacinths are more tolerant of waiting, and may be planted any time before the ground is frozen. But even these will be worthless if an attempt is made to carry them over unplanted until the following fall. Tulips may be held to advantage, however, until cold weather has arrived, because when planted too early they have a habit of starting growth and sending shoots an inch or two above ground before winter comes. If the season should be a severe one with no snow on the ground, they would be likely to suffer injury.

The manner of soil preparation—if any—and the method of planting are both contingent upon the place of the spring-flowering bulbs in the garden.

Preparation for planting in beds or perennial borders. The beds for bulb planting should be prepared by scattering bonemeal on the surface at the rate of about 5 pounds to 100 square feet, and following with deep digging. All of the books and all of the gardeners will tell you that fresh manure in proximity to the bulbs or roots results in utter failure. The good gardener prefers for bulb planting soil which was heavily manured in the spring for a summer crop, so that when the time comes to plant the bulbs in the fall the manure is mellow, thoroughly disintegrated, and well mixed with the soil.

If certain precautions are followed, however, it is possible to incorporate manure in the soil for bulbs just prior to planting. First, remove the upper 6 inches of soil. Then spread decayed manure on the soil thus exposed, fork it into the ground, level off the surface, cover with 1 inch of unmanured soil, place the bulbs in position and cover with the rest of the soil. By following this method the manure is kept down so that there is no chance of contact with the bulbs; and, by the time the roots reach it, the chances are that it has become innocuous.

Depth of planting and distance apart. The depth of planting is dependent on the kind of bulb. A good general rule is to cover with soil equal in depth to two or three times the diameter of the bulb. The exact depth, however, is not a matter of life or death, and if there is a variation of an inch or two from what is considered ideal, no appreciable harm will be done. In very sandy soil it is considered best to plant rather deeper than normal, and not so deep in heavy clay soil.

The distance between bulbs in formal plantings should be from 2 to 4 inches for the smaller kinds—squills, crocuses, and snowdrops. Tulips may be set from 5 to 7 inches apart—the lesser distance for early kinds and the small varieties of cottage tulips, allowing 6 to 7 inches for Darwins and Breeders. Hyacinths and narcissi should be spaced about 6 inches apart.

Planting technique. The methods of setting the bulbs are determined by the type of soil and the preferences of the planter. If the soil is friable a dibber may be used, as this makes for quick planting. A dibber for bulb planting may be bought from a seed store; or it can be made (this is more usual) by utilizing a broken shovel, spade, or fork handle, cutting it to a convenient size and pointing it. (Plate XXXI.) Drawbacks attending the use of a dibber are: (1) Unless the operator is careful to vary the depth of the hole according to the size of the bulb, small bulbs are likely to be planted at a greater depth than large ones, whereas if any difference is made it should be the reverse. (2) There is danger of the bulbs becoming "hung" in the hole with an air space below them. (Personally I don't think this is very serious.) (3) In wet clay soil the twisting motion used in making the hole may so puddle the soil that roots have difficulty in penetrating it.

Bulbs may also be planted with a trowel. One who is unskilled with this tool may experience some difficulty at first in spacing the bulbs evenly and in getting them all at the correct depth, but these are the only drawbacks to its use.

Another good method, though it involves the handling of considerable soil, is to remove from 3 to 6 inches of soil from the bed (the amount depending on the size of the bulbs), set the bulbs in place, and then return the soil. This is a scheme much used by commercial bulb growers. The technique followed is a modification of that used in digging. For example: Suppose a long bed is to be planted; the soil to a depth of 3 to 6 inches is removed from the width of the bed for a distance of 6 feet. The bulbs are put in place in this area and sufficient soil to cover them is taken from the next area of 6 feet, and so on to the end of the bed (Fig. 37). The planter must be careful not to upset the bulbs when covering them with soil. One advantage of this method, especially when planting formal beds, is that the bulbs may be placed with great exactitude. When the other methods are

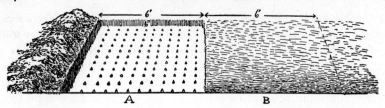

Fig. 37. One method of planting bulbs. Soil from *B* is used to cover bulbs in section marked *A*. See text.

used, the bulbs may be aligned by the marker described in Chapter XI, FLOWER BEDS AND BORDERS.

Treatment after planting. After the bulbs are planted, the beds should be untouched until the frost has penetrated an inch or two; then they may be mulched with 2 or 3 inches of light, littery, partly decayed manure. Salt hay (which is hay cut from the salt marshes), when obtainable, forms an ideal soil-covering for bulbs. This mulch is to prevent the frost from penetrating too deeply and to minimize heaving brought about by alternate freezing and thawing of the ground. In the spring before growth appears above the surface, all the coarser portions of the mulch should be removed. A manure fork is a handy tool for this purpose.

Planting in sod. When bulbs are to be set in grass to give the effect of a natural scene, a different technique is followed. A good plan is to scatter the bulbs more or less haphazardly on the ground and plant them where they happen to fall. Of course, they must be scattered with some reference to the general outline of the planting, which should be in drifts which are usually about two or three times as long as they are broad. (Plate XVI.) Similarly there should be some regard paid to the distance between them—which may vary from 3 to 18 inches.

For large bulbs a mattock (Fig. 122) is a good planting tool. It is driven into the ground as deeply as possible, a sod is pried up, from one to three bulbs are placed in the hole thus made, and the sod is returned. A crowbar is also effective but not, I think, equal to a mattock. When a crowbar is used for large bulbs, considerable jiggling is necessary to make the holes large enough, and these holes have to be filled with soil after planting is completed.

When planting small bulbs—winter-aconite, crocus, and snowdrop —in grassland, a spade is perhaps the best tool to use. It is thrust vertically into the ground to a depth of about 3 inches. Then the handle is depressed and the blade pushed horizontally to its full length under the surface. The handle is then lifted, the bulbs are spaced irregularly in the hole thus made, the spade is removed and the sod is replaced. Some of these plantings should be so close together that they almost touch; others may be from 1 to 3 feet apart.

Ordinarily, for naturalistic plantings in grass, no previous soil preparation is practised. If the soil is poor, however, a sprinkling of bonemeal mixed with the earth at the bottom of each opening will help the bulbs.

Planting bulbs in the rock garden. When planting bulbs in the rock garden it usually is not possible, because of the presence of other plants, to do a great deal in the way of soil preparation. Whenever possible the soil should be forked up to make it loose enough to facilitate planting. The rock garden bulbs, being comparatively small, can easily be planted with a dibber or narrow-blade trowel.

Selection of spring-flowering bulbs. The following are among the more important hardy bulbs. In some cases lists of varieties are appended, descriptions of which may be found in any standard bulb catalog. A far better method of selecting varieties is to visit a named collection in bloom in a botanic garden, public park, flower show, or commercial establishment; but this, of course, involves a wait of one year before one's own plantings may be seen in bloom.

ANEMONE. Varieties of *Anemone coronaria,* in blue, red, or white, and of *A. fulgens,* scarlet, are hardy south of Washington, D. C. They may be planted in well-drained rather sandy soil in September or October. For northern use, the tubers may be stored in a cool place over the winter and planted out in the spring. Varieties of the dainty lilac *A. nemorosa* and the blue-flowered *A. blanda,* are hardy kinds suitable for the rock garden. They should be planted 2 inches deep in woodsy soil in partly shaded situations.

CROCUS. For outdoor planting, corms purchased according to color are ordinarily used—the more expensive named varieties being reserved for pot culture. Crocuses look charming when naturalized in grass, being especially effective when grouped informally about the base of a high-headed tree which does not cast too dense a shade. In informal plantings the corms should be set with an average distance of 2 to 3 inches between them. Sometimes crocuses are used in formal beds to provide an early display which is followed later by tulips. In such cases the method of planting is to remove about 6 inches of soil from the area to be planted, put the tulip bulbs in place, cover them with 3 to 4 inches of soil, level it, place the crocuses in position, and cover them with the remaining soil.

CHIONODOXA, **Glory-of-the-Snow.** Among the most charming of the early spring bulbs, glory-of-the-snow is usually in bloom in early April. The ease with which it can be grown in the perennial border or rock garden in any reasonably good, well-drained soil still further commends it. I have seen it come up smiling from bulbs which had inadvertently been thrust about a foot deep when the border was being dug. Normally the bulbs should be planted 3 or 4 inches deep. There are several varieties available, usually less than 6 inches high, and all of them well worth growing. The commonest is *Chionodoxa Luciliae,* which is blue with a white center. There is a pure white variety and a pink one. *C. sardensis* has flowers of rich deep blue; variety *gigantea,* soft lavender.

ERANTHIS, **Winter-aconite.** This is one of the earliest of the spring flowers, showing color in February if the weather is at all favorable. It looks like a buttercup (on a stem 3 or 4 inches high) emerging from an Elizabethan ruff of glossy green foliage. It prefers partial shade and may be grown along the edges of shrubbery. The most successful plantings I have seen were growing in soil strongly impregnated with chalk. Liming is therefore recommended if winter-aconite is planted where the soil is the least bit acid. The rootstocks suffer if they become thoroughly dry, hence it is advisable to obtain and plant them early in autumn.

ERYTHRONIUM, **Dogtooth-violet.** This group of plants, predominantly American in origin, is probably better known, grown, and appreciated in England than here. The flower color in the genus ranges from white to yellow and from pink to rose. Blossoms are produced in April and May. In most species the leaves are mottled with reddish brown, purple, or white. In general they are plants of cool woodlands and should be given a shady spot and a moist but well-drained woodsy soil. Plant them 3 to 5 inches deep and mulch with an inch or two of decayed leaves. Varieties of *E. revolutum* such as *Johnsonii,* rose pink; *praecox,* creamy white and maroon; and *Pink Beauty* are among the best. The common adder's-tongue of eastern North America (*E. americanum*), which also runs into many forms, is well worth growing. The common name, dogtooth-violet, is a misnomer, for these plants are related to the lilies and have no connection whatever with violets.

FRITILLARIA. **Snake's-head, Guinea-hen-flower, Checkered Lily,** and **Mission Bells.** With such a plethora of common names, *Fritillaria meleagris* ought to be popular. For those who like the curious and unusual it is highly recommended. In April it produces slender 1-foot stems sparsely supplied with narrow leaves; topped with pendent, white to purplish, somewhat bell-shaped, more or less checkered flowers. I have seen it growing wild in meadows in England, but have had little success in attempts to naturalize it in grass here. It does, however, grow well when planted in the flower border or rock garden in well-drained soil.

GALANTHUS, **Snowdrop.** The pale drooping green-tipped blossoms of snowdrops form charming companions for the winter-aconite. Their blooms are displayed as early as February if the weather is mild. The bulbs should be planted rather thickly in groups, in sheltered, partially shaded spots. The groups may be from 2 to 10 feet apart and each should contain from ten to twenty bulbs placed on an average 2 inches apart. Leave them undisturbed and they will develop into clumps of quiet beauty. The giant snowdrop (*G. Elwesii*) is the variety usually preferred, although there are many who like the smaller *G. nivalis*.

HYACINTHUS. Varieties of *H. orientalis,* the common hyacinth, are among the most popular of hardy bulbs, especially in formal bedding, for which the comparatively cheap unnamed kinds, purchased according to color, are usually quite satisfactory. If planted in the perennial border and conditions are to their liking, they will persist year after year, and because of division of the bulbs will form clumps which are less formal in appearance than newly planted bulbs. They require a thoroughly well-drained soil. If it is at all heavy, a cushion of sand should be placed beneath each bulb at planting time. Set the bulbs 5 to 6 inches apart with at least 4 inches of soil over their tips.

H. azureus (often sold under the name *Muscari azureum*) much more closely resembles the grape-hyacinth (*Muscari*) than it does the garden hyacinth. Valuable for naturalizing in grass and for planting in the rock garden. For the summer hyacinth, see GALTONIA under SUMMER-FLOWERING BULBS.

IRIS. The bulbous irises are valuable spring flowers. There are many species available, but the only ones commonly seen in the gardens of eastern North America are the **Netted Iris** (*I. reticulata*) and the "English," "Dutch," and "Spanish" varieties, which are also used for forcing.

The netted iris has delightfully fragrant flowers of rich blue-purple and gold which are produced in April. Planted in a well-drained sheltered spot in the rock garden it will bloom year after year and the clumps will increase in size.

Next in order of blooming outdoors are the "Dutch" and then the "Spanish" bulbous irises. They both have a habit of starting into growth in the fall, with the result that their leaves are injured if the winter is severe. Defer planting them, therefore, until the last possible moment consistent with getting them into the ground before it becomes frozen and before they start to grow. Plant them 4 to 5 inches deep, and mulch with 2 inches of light organic matter. The "English" varieties are later-blooming, prefer a moist soil, and their bulbs should be planted as early as it is possible to obtain them. There is a wide range of color in the different varieties of bulbous irises, and the flowers are valuable both for cutting and garden display.

LEUCOJUM, **Spring Snowflake.** It is amazing that this delightful plant is not more widely grown, for, although it cannot be termed showy, a well-grown clump of *L. vernum* is charming, with its fresh green foliage interspersed with flower stalks, each bearing several drooping white green-tipped flowers. It should be planted in light, well-drained soil, making groups of six to twenty bulbs, spaced 3 to 4 inches apart, and set 5 inches deep.

MUSCARI, **Grape-hyacinth.** In general, grape-hyacinths are rugged bulbs, so well equipped to take care of themselves that some varieties, unless prevented from seeding, become nuisances in spots where they interfere with other plants. Naturalized along the edges of shrubbery or in thin shade under trees, their compact little spikes of flowers will provide a grand display of white and various shades of blue.

NARCISSUS. Here is a genus which is represented in gardens by a bewildering array of forms. A classification approved by the Royal Horticultural Society of Great Britain divides it into eleven main groups, but for our purpose perhaps the followng will suffice:

LARGE TRUMPET NARCISSI: The trumpet as long as or longer than the perianth segments. They may be yellow, white, or bicolored. Good varieties are: **Aerolite,** yellow; **Diotima,** yellow; **Golden Harvest,** golden yellow; **Imperator,** bicolor; **Lord Wellington,** yellow; **King Alfred,** yellow; **Mrs. E. H. Krelage,** white; **Robert Sydenham,** yellow; **Spring Glory,** bicolor; **Van Waveren's Giant,** bicolor; **Winter Gold,** very early.

MEDIUM TRUMPET NARCISSI: The trumpet from ¼ to ¾ the length of the perianth segments. This group is again divided into sections—Incomparabilis, Barrii, Leedsii, etc. If the flowers are colored yellow or yellow and red, they belong in the Incomparabilis group. Self-colored whites belong to the Leedsii section. In the Barrii section, with shorter trumpet or crown, the flowers may be either white or colored.

Good "Incomps" are: **Bernardino, Croesus, Red Cross, Sir Watkin.**

Good Barrii varieties: **Bath's Flame, Diana Kasner, Firetail, Lady Diana Manners, Mrs. Barclay.**

Leedsii varieties: **Crystal Queen, Daisy Schaffer, Gertie Millar, Hera, Lord Kitchener, Queen of the North, Silver Star.**

POET'S NARCISSI: The trumpet much reduced and described as a "corona"; perianth segments white; corona yellow rimmed with red. The variety *ornatus* is the first to bloom and is valuable for naturalizing in grass. Good garden varieties are: **Actaea, Glory of Lisse, Snow King.** The flowers of *poeticus plenus* are like those of a gardenia—when it can be induced to bloom—but, alas, in all too many gardens the flower buds blast. I have had it growing for years in my back yard, but never has a blossom opened, although the stock was obtained from a friend's garden where it bloomed profusely every year. It is said that heat and lack of moisture at the roots are responsible for its failure to bloom.

POETAZ NARCISSI: The result of crossing *N. poeticus* with *N. Tazetta* (the bunch-flowered, or polyanthus, narcissus). The latter is not hardy in our climate, but as a result of the cross a race of bunch-flowered narcissi has been produced which are hardy in the vicinity of New York. **Admiration, Cheerfulness** (double), and **Laurens Koster** are good varieties.

JONQUILS: Large trumpet daffodils often are erroneously called "jonquils." Actually, the jonquil is quite a different flower. *Narcissus Jonquilla,* which gives its name to the group, is a small plant with narrow rush-like leaves and clusters of small fragrant flowers of a rather aggressive shining yellow. Some of the hybrids are considerably larger than the type. **Campernelle, Golden Sceptre,** and **Orange Queen** are among the varieties most commonly grown.

Among the best varieties of narcissi for naturalizing are: **Emperor** (Trumpet); **Autocrat, Sir Watkin** (Incomp.); and **Conspicuus** (Barrii).

DOUBLE NARCISSI: There are many who do not like double Narcissi, but the following are not objectionable: **Daphne,** white scented; **Irene Copeland,** white and yellow; **Mary Copeland,** creamy white and orange; **The Pearl,** white and pale yellow; **Twink,** primrose and orange.

SCILLA, Squill. The earliest of all is the **Siberian squill,** *Scilla sibirica.* Tolerant of varied conditions, it grows 4 or 5 inches high, and is capable of providing sheets of intense blue when planted in masses in rock garden, flower border or grass. There is a pure white variety.

S. campanulata has large drooping bell-shaped flowers, in many-flowered racemes 1 to 2 feet high. A valuable plant for the perennial border, it is obtainable in white, blue, and pink. It will stand partial shade.

S. nonscripta (*nutans*), the **English Bluebell,** is the species which carpets the ground with a sea of blue in the Queen's Cottage grounds in Kew Gardens. It may be grown in the perennial garden or naturalized in partial shade where competition with grasses is not too severe.

TULIPA. The garden tulips may be divided into five main groups— Early, Cottage, Darwin, Breeder, and Parrot. Further division can be made on the basis of double-flowered kinds (found mostly among the earlies); hybrid tulips resulting from crosses between Cottage, Darwin, Breeder, and early tulips, to which various group names have been given; and "broken" or "rectified" kinds known as Rembrandts, Bizarres, or Bijbloemen. These last three originate mainly from the Cottage, Darwin, and Breeder tulips as a result of being infected with a virus disease which causes the colors to segregate; so that instead of being self-colored, the flowers are variegated with stripes, flakes and featherings of a dark color on a lighter colored background.

EARLY TULIPS, which bloom in April, are chiefly valuable for formal beds and forcing, though they may be used in the perennial border. Good varieties (color descriptions of which may be found, together with the height of the different varieties, in the catalog of almost any reputable bulb dealer) include **Albion, Coleur Cardinal, Keizerskroon, Pink Beauty.** Double varieties include: **Boule de Neige, Dante, Murillo.**

COTTAGE TULIPS. This group on the whole is smaller in stature than the Darwins and Breeders, and the flowers are less formal in shape. In some varieties the petals are incurved and the flowers long-egg-shaped in outline. In others the petals recurve. This group contains some of the most charming tulips for bedding, for planting in the perennial garden, or for the foreground of shrubbery. They blossom in May. Favorites are: **Advance, Barbara Pratt, Belle Jaune, Carrara** (by some classed as a Darwin) **Dido, Golden Harvest, Marjorie Bowen, Marshall Haig, Mrs. H. J. Pratt.**

DARWIN TULIPS, flowering in May, are, at the time of writing, the most popular of all. They are characterized by their large flowers of almost every color known in tulipdom, on stiff stems 2 to 3 feet high. They are valued for garden decoration and as cut flowers indoors. There are so many superlative varieties that it is difficult to make a selection. The following are kinds that appeal to almost everyone: **Aphrodite, Eclipse, Glacier, King George V, Mr. Farncombe Sanders** (noteworthy for its persistence and increase under ordinary garden conditions), **The Bishop, Yellow Giant.**

BREEDER TULIPS have immense blooms on tall strong stems. They run strongly to bronze and mahogany coloration—in some varieties rather sombre in tone—though perhaps not so dark as individual Darwin varieties such as **La Tulipe Noire** and **Zulu.** Frankly, I am not enamored of Breeder tulips, but can admire the following varieties: **Cardinal Manning, Cherbourg, Indian Chief, Louis XIV.**

PARROT TULIPS. This group has laciniated petals and fantastic coloring—such as crimson with black markings, or orange feathered with purple and green. Until the introduction of **Fantasy** the group as a whole was ignored except by those who liked a bizarre note in their garden. **Fantasy,** which is said to be a sport of **Clara Butt,** a famous old Darwin tulip which is still worth growing, has a strong stem and a large flower with somewhat incurving, laciniated petals which are deep rose on the inside. The outside is pink with apple-green markings. Many other varieties are available.

Considerable interest is now being shown in the "wild" or "species" tulips—called by some "botanical" tulips. The specific rank of some of them may be questioned, because there is a suspicion that they may originally have been garden forms. The smaller kinds are admirable for planting in the rock garden where conditions are more to their liking than in the border. The taller species, a selection of which follows, may be planted in the perennial garden if the soil is exceptionally well drained.

T. acuminata. Curious spidery flowers with petals of light yellow with red lines, more than 4 inches long but less than ½ inch wide. Grows about 18 inches high.

T. Greigii. Flowers of bright orange-scarlet on stems from 2 to 10 inches in height. Leaves undulated along the margins and marked with purplish blotches. Not easy to grow and prefers a hot, dry position.

T. Marjoletti. Although classed as a "wild" tulip, looks as though it has had previous experience in a garden. Flowers yellow with rosy-red markings on the outside. About 14 inches high.

T. praestans. Has scarlet flowers, produced up to eight on a stem. Fourteen inches high.

T. sylvestris. Sometimes offered in American catalogs as *T. florentina odorata.* One of the easiest of the wild tulips to grow. Golden-yellow, pointed flowers, sometimes two on a stem; grows to a height of 16 inches.

HARDY SPRING-FLOWERING BULBS FOR FORCING

Handling of bulbs for forcing. Almost any of the hardy spring-flowering bulbs may, with special treatment, be brought into early bloom indoors. The rules are fairly simple, but must be followed explicitly. Given sufficient opportunity to form roots while they are stored in their pots or pans in a dark cool place, the bulbs of tulips, hyacinths, daffodils, and other springtime subjects will provide a gay succession of flowers in the house while the outdoor garden is still covered with snow. The methods of handling them are outlined below.

Soil and receptacles. Spring bulbs intended for house culture or for forcing in greenhouses may be potted as soon as they are received in the fall. Any fairly good garden soil will serve for forcing bulbs, though one looks for better results if a rich loamy soil is used. If the soil is clayey it should be mixed with sand to give it the necessary porosity. The addition of ¼ of its bulk of leafmold will serve to lighten it and a 6-inch potful of bonemeal to each wheelbarrow load of soil will improve its fertility.

If the bulbs are intended for use solely as cut flowers, they may be planted in flats 3 or 4 inches deep, placing the bulbs with 1 inch of clear space between them, and deep enough to bring their noses just above the surface. When they are to be used for decorative purposes in the home or greenhouse they should be grown in pots or bulb pans. The size of pot chosen is decided by the size of the bulb and the number to be planted in each pot or pan. Tulips may be grown singly in 3- or 4-inch pots, but a better appearance is obtained if six bulbs are planted in a 6-inch bulb pan. Hyacinths are commonly grown as single specimens in 4- or 5-inch pots, depending on the size of the bulb, and are also quite satisfactory when from six to twelve bulbs are planted in bulb pans from 6 to 9 inches in diameter. Daffodils look better when several are planted together than when grown as single specimens.

Potting the bulbs. When potting the bulbs, place a piece of a broken pot over the drainage hole in the bottom of the pot or pan and follow with ½ inch of coarse ashes to aid the drainage. Then put in a handful or two of soil and pack down *lightly*. Rest the base of the bulb on this—if necessary adding sufficient soil to bring the tip of the bulb 1 inch below the rim of the pot. Put in more soil and press it down *firmly*, filling to within ½ inch of the rim. If the soil beneath the bulb is packed too firmly and the soil above is left loose, the chances are that the roots as they grow will lift the bulb out of the pot.

Treatment after potting. Assuming that the bulbs contain embryo flowers and have not been injured by overheating, the treatment given between planting and blooming time determines whether they will be a success or a failure. All hardy bulbs intended for forcing require a period of from six to ten weeks of low temperature (40 to 50 degrees) in order that they may develop a good root system before there is any appreciable top growth. Therefore they should either be stored in a bulb cellar where it is possible to maintain the required temperature, or placed outdoors in a plunge-pit (described below). The large growers of forced bulbs commonly use a cellar constructed solely for the purpose of storing bulbs for root production. They are then more accessible than when stored in a plunge-pit outdoors, when oftentimes it is necessary to break through 6 inches or more of frozen ground to get at them. It is sometimes possible to make a suitable place for the storage of bulbs in the cellar of the home by partitioning off a portion so that it is not heated by the furnace. In some houses there may be space in the attic which can be adapted to the purpose of bulb storage. When the bulbs are kept in this way they must be examined periodically and the soil must be watered if it becomes dry.

THE OUTDOOR PLUNGE-PIT. When the bulbs are stored for rooting outdoors, the usual practice is to dig a trench 1 foot to 18 inches deep and of a convenient width in a well-drained and easily accessible part of the grounds. In the bottom 2 to 3 inches of coal ashes are placed on which the pots or flats are stood. The soil removed in making the trench is now placed in between and over the pots of bulbs, mounding it up to shed excessive rain. When the frost has penetrated the ground 2 or 3 inches, a covering of straw, leaves, excelsior, old quilts, or "what-have-you" is put on to prevent the frost from penetrating any deeper. Freezing may not hurt the bulbs, but makes it difficult to dig out the pots and their contents without smashing them when the time comes to bring them indoors for forcing.

THE PACKING-CASE METHOD. If only a few pots of bulbs are to be forced and there is neither a bulb cellar available nor space in the garden for a bulb pit, a large packing case can be used as a makeshift. Place 6 inches of peatmoss in the bottom of the case and stand the pots of bulbs on it, leaving a clear space all around and on top for another 6 inches of peatmoss. Water the bulbs before you pack them away and stand the packing case in a shady spot. Cover with some kind of insulating material if the weather becomes very cold.

Time allowed for rooting. Some bulbs, such as Roman hyacinths and early tulips of the Duc van Thol type, will have formed sufficient roots in six weeks to permit of their being brought indoors for forcing; but it is safer to allow at least eight weeks, and preferably ten weeks, before bringing the other kinds indoors. If a succession of bloom is desired, take in a few pots or pans at a time. Do not bring them from the plunge-pit directly into the temperature of the average room, because this practice is almost certain to make the flower buds blast. Instead, give them a temperature of 50 degrees in a light room for a few weeks until the flower stems are developed, then bring them into a room in which a temperature of 65 degrees is maintained.

Other methods of culture. Certain hardy and tender bulbs which are brought into bloom indoors may be raised in fiber, in pebbles and water, or in water alone, as described below.

Bulbs in fiber. Instead of growing hardy forcing bulbs in soil, they may be grown in fiber, obtainable at most seed stores. Often when fiber is used the bulbs are placed in containers without drainage holes in the bottom. In this case great care must be taken to avoid waterlogging the fiber. Bulbs grown in fiber are cared for with greater ease when stored in a bulb cellar than in a plunge-pit outdoors.

Water culture. When growing hyacinths in the house, special vases called hyacinth glasses, which have a flange or shoulder, are sometimes used. Hyacinth culture by this method is easy enough if cool airy conditions for rooting can be provided. The bulb is placed on the flange or shoulder of the glass, which is filled with water just to the base of the bulb. It is then stored in a dark airy place at 45 to 50 degrees until the container is well filled with roots. The joker for city dwellers is to find such a place in a modern apartment. After the roots are well formed, bring the bulb into a light room with a temperature of 60 to 65 degrees when, if all goes well, it will bloom.

Pebble culture. While **Paper White** and **Soleil d'Or** narcissi, as well as the **Chinese Sacred Lily,** which is also a variety of the polyanthus narcissus, *N. Tazetta,* are really tender bulbs, they are used so extensively for indoor winter bloom in the North that it is most appropriate to treat them here. A bowl or container from 3 to 5 inches deep is half-filled with pebbles ranging from ¼ to ½ inch in diameter. Six Paper White or Soleil d'Or narcissi can be accommodated in a bowl 6 to 7 inches in diameter, while three Chinese sacred lilies are sufficient in a bowl of this size. The bulbs are placed on the pebbles and then more pebbles are dropped around them to hold them upright. Just enough water is poured into the bowl to reach the bases of the bulbs. The bowl is then stored in a cool airy place for three or four weeks, after which it may be brought into normal room temperature. The water must be replenished whenever it gets low. Paper White narcissi will stand almost any treatment, and some people are successful in blooming them even without first giving them a few weeks of cool temperature in which to form some roots, but they are likely to blast their buds if they are placed at once in a room of 75 to 80 degrees temperature.

Treatment accorded special groups. A few of the lilies may be forced into bloom in the house in spring, and lilies-of-the-valley make delightful small pots of bloom which may be enjoyed at almost any season.

Lilies for forcing. The lilies most commonly used for forcing are the **Easter Lily** (*Lilium longiflorum* varieties), *Lilium speciosum,* and the **Madonna Lily** (*Lilium candidum*). Of these, only the Easter lily is not reliably hardy outdoors in the vicinity of New York.

Although cold storage of lily bulbs has made it possible to have lilies in bloom at any season of the year, for the most part the bulbs are potted in the fall and brought into bloom sometime between Christmas and Easter.

The soil used should be a mixture of 2 parts loam, 1 part leafmold, 1 part thoroughly rotted manure, and 1 part sand. Place the bulbs singly in well-drained 5- or 6-inch pots, with about an inch of soil under them. Some gardeners make a practice of adding merely enough soil barely to cover the bulbs—filling the pots later with a 50-50 mixture of loam and decayed cow-manure when some growth has been made. If the bulbs are potted early (late August or early September) they may be placed in a shaded coldframe and covered with about 4 inches of partly decayed leaves. By the first of October they may be brought into the greenhouse and kept in a night temperature of 60 degrees and a day temperature of 70 degrees. With this treatment they may be expected to flower at Christmas. Later plantings may be kept in the coldframe until there is prospect of frost, when they should be brought indoors and kept in a night temperature of about 50 degrees for a week or two. After this the temperature may be raised 10 degrees. It will be twelve or thirteen weeks to flowering time, at a minimum night temperature of 60 degrees, from the time the bulbs are rooted.

Madonna lilies, which form roots from the base of the bulb only, should be planted nearer the top of the pot. An inch of soil over the bulb is sufficient.

Lilies-of-the-valley indoors. Although technically neither bulbs, corms, nor tubers, lilies-of-the-valley may be forced quite successfully if one obtains the right kind of "pips" (the name by which the resting buds with roots are known); but they cannot be brought into bloom unless the pips have experienced a period at a low temperature. For this reason retarded pips which have been kept in cold storage, possibly from the preceding year, are preferred. As they do not form any new roots, the kind of soil in which they are planted is immaterial. One large grower who flowers millions of pips every year uses sawdust. Almost anything that will hold moisture will do—sand, coal ashes, peatmoss, or fiber. When the pips are received from storage, shorten the roots to 4 or 5 inches by cutting them with a sharp knife. Pot them up so that they stand about an inch apart with the tips just above the surface. Water thoroughly and keep them in a dark place in a temperature of 70 to 80 degrees. Under dwelling-house conditions a good plan is to place them in a fairly tight box which has sufficient headroom for them to develop, because this will afford a more humid atmosphere about them. During the time they are in this high temperature they should be watered with tepid water. In three weeks they should be in bloom. Then bring the pots into the light and gradually reduce the temperature in order to prolong the life of the flowers.

Treatment of bulbs after flowering. Frequently I am asked: "What should be done with forced bulbs after they have finished blooming?" Generally speaking, they should be thrown away. Certainly they are useless for forcing the following season. Such bulbs as tulips, hyacinths, and the hardy narcissi, if they have been grown in soil, may be kept watered until the foliage has ripened naturally, and then be stored dry until the fall, when they may be planted outdoors. After a year or so they may recover sufficiently to produce flowers again. Plants grown in pebbles, the tender narcissi, and lilies-of-the-valley should be discarded, because for all practical purposes they are of no further use.

Selection of varieties. Not all of these bulbs are of equally easy culture. I would rank them somewhat as follows: Paper White narcissus and its allies, Roman hyacinth, early-flowering tulips, daffodils, lilies-of-the-valley, hyacinths, lilies. Crocuses are not any too easy to bring into early bloom, as they refuse to be hurried, and the flowers fail to develop if the plants are kept the least bit too warm.

In the selection of varieties, be guided largely by the catalogs of the bulb dealers who indicate the varieties best adapted for forcing. In general, the early-flowering group of tulips is easier to force than the Darwins and other May-flowering kinds. Following is a short list of good varieties not difficult to force.

CROCUS: **Kathleen Parlow,** white; **Maximilian,** lavender; **Enchantress,** blue; **Purpurea grandiflora,** purple; **Yellow Mammoth,** yellow.

HYACINTH: **L'Innocence,** white; **Lady Derby,** pink; **Myosotis,** light blue; **King of the Blues,** dark blue. (**Roman Hyacinths** are easy to force but should not be allowed to become frozen.)

NARCISSUS—Polyanthus varieties: **Chinese Sacred Lily, Paper White grandiflora, Grand Soleil d'Or.** (These should not be allowed to become frozen.) Hardy kinds: large trumpets—**King Alfred, Lord Wellington, Spring Glory, Van Waveren's Giant;** medium trumpets—**Firetail, John Evelyn, Queen of the North, Red Cross.**

Tulip: **Coronne d'Or,** double, gold and copper; **De Wet,** golden yellow; **Murillo,** double, rose-pink and white; **Keizerskroon,** scarlet, edged yellow; **Rising Sun,** yellow; **White Hawk,** long lasting.

In addition to the kinds mentioned above, grape-hyacinths, snowdrops, squills, etc., may be forced by using methods similar to those I have described.

TENDER SPRING-FLOWERING BULBS

The tender winter- and spring-flowering bulbs which will not stand freezing are potted in much the same way as the hardy kinds, except that they are usually not subjected to a cool period outdoors. A little more care should be given to the preparation and selection of the right kind of soil because these bulbs are capable of maturing their growth in pots, and if properly handled can be used again the following year. From winter to early spring is their normal time of blooming, so they are not forced into growth unnaturally as the hardy bulbs are when they are brought indoors. Following are some of the more popular of these bulbs which are suitable for cultivation by amateurs.

Amaryllis. This gorgeous flower of the genus *Hippeastrum,* perhaps better known under the name of amaryllis, has long been a favorite not only with gardeners who have greenhouses but also with those whose indoor gardening is restricted to a window ledge. Dormant bulbs of amaryllis are obtainable from the seed houses between October and April. They should be potted up singly, as soon as received, with the major portion of the bulb above ground. If there is a space of 1½ inches all around between the bulb and the side of the pot, the pot is large enough. For soil use a mixture of 3 parts loam, 1 part leafmold, 1 part decayed manure and enough sand to make the mixture porous. A level tablespoonful of bonemeal may be mixed with each 7-inch potful of soil. Keep the bulbs in a temperature as near 60 degrees as possible and be careful to avoid too much water. Normally the leaves are not produced until after the flowers. As soon as they appear keep the soil constantly moist. The plants may be placed outdoors during summer with the pots plunged in the ground. Before cold weather comes in the fall, bring them in and give them a rest by almost completely withholding water. When they show signs of activity, remove as much soil as possible from the surface without disturbing the roots and replace with new, rich soil.

Amorphophallus. A native of Cochin China, *Amorphophallus Rivieri* (which some botanists now are calling *Hydrosme Rivieri*) is variously known as umbrella arum, devil's tongue and snake palm. Its tuber, 4 to 8 inches in diameter, is capable of producing a flower even though it is not planted. The "flower," which is really a sheath, or spathe, surrounding a column on which numerous minute flowers are borne, is dark chocolate-maroon in color, with red dots, and grows on a stalk 2 to 4 feet high. How anyone can recommend this plant for culture in the home I cannot imagine (and yet it is done), for it has the vilest imaginable carrion odor, which it possesses in common with allied plants such as the "monarch of the east" (*Sauromatum*) which also is sometimes glowingly advertised for house culture. Tubers of these plants should be potted in rich soil in 10- or 12-inch pots, and watered freely when they start to grow. In May, or as soon as the weather becomes settled and warm, they should be planted in the garden. From each tuber a handsome, single, much-divided leaf is produced on a 4-foot stalk, the blade often being up to 4 feet in diameter.

Calla. Botanically called *Richardia africana* or *Zantedeschia aethiopica,* the calla, as can be seen by the shape of its "flower," is allied to the amorphophallus, but it has no objectionable odor. Dormant tubers are obtainable in the fall, when they should be potted just below the surface of rich soil in 5- or 6-inch pots. The soil as recommended for amaryllis but without the additional sand, will be suitable. Keep the soil moist, but not wet, until growth is well started, then water freely. In the spring they may be planted out-of-doors. In the fall they should be dug up and dried to ripen the tubers. The yellow calla (*Z. Elliottiana*) is a similar plant, except that its flowers are yellow and the leaves are spotted. It may be given the same treatment as the ordinary calla, except that the tubers should be thoroughly dried for a few weeks prior to planting.

Freesia. A popular bulbous plant native to South Africa, the freesia is grown in immense quantities in California to provide stock for greenhouse and home culture. Bulbs are obtainable in early fall, when they should be potted, six bulbs in a 5-inch pot, using the soil mixture advocated for amaryllis. If a succession of bloom is desired, batches should be potted up at intervals of about three weeks. The earliest lots may be started in a coldframe, but when the nights begin to get cold they should be brought indoors and kept in a temperature as near

50 degrees as possible. If grown in a dwelling they should be given the sunniest spot available; otherwise the stems will be so limp that it will be impossible to handle them. Water the bulbs sparingly until growth appears above the surface, then water thoroughly whenever the soil shows signs of becoming dry. When the shoots have attained a height of 6 or 8 inches, place thin bamboo stakes or stiff wires about 1 foot long in the soil around the edge of the pot. Connect these with a thread to form a support as the plants grow taller. When the foliage begins to turn yellow after the flowers are gone, gradually withhold water until the soil is completely dry. Keep the bulbs in this condition until fall, then repot them in fresh soil. Freesias have a delicious perfume and are admirable and long-lasting as cut flowers. Originally yellow, their arching sprays of bloom now are obtainable in white, pink, and violet.

Oxalis. Whenever I see this name I smile, for I once had a letter from a lady asking: "How shall I treat my Ox Alice?" *O. cernua,* a sprawling plant with yellow flowers, is the species to which the name **Bermuda Buttercup** is applied. *O. Bowiei* is a pink-flowered oxalis with somewhat fleshy, lush-looking leaves which, like those of most members of this genus, are shaped like those of clover. The bulbs of oxalis start into growth rather early, whether they are planted or not. As the shoots are brittle and liable to injury when the bulbs are potted, they should be obtained and planted as early as it is possible to get them. The floppy habit of the Bermuda buttercup adapts it admirably for use in wire hanging-baskets. (See in Chapter XIX the section on HANGING BASKETS.) A mixture of 2 parts loam, 1 part leaf-mold, and 1 part sand, with a sprinkling of bonemeal, will suit oxalis. If the soil is acid, add a tablespoonful or two of ground limestone to each peck of soil. This plant may also be grown in pots—six bulbs in a 6-inch pot.

SUMMER-FLOWERING BULBS

Some of the summer-flowering bulbs are hardy and should therefore be planted in the fall; others (such as *Tritonia*) will not survive the winter outdoors where low temperatures are experienced; and some (*Gladiolus,* for instance), even though they may be hardy, are handled to better advantage when dug in the fall and stored dry during the winter. The planting of certain kinds may be deferred till

July when convenience dictates. These are useful for filling vacancies left in the perennial garden by early-blooming subjects.

Special points in the culture of the summer-flowering bulbs (many of which are not true bulbous plants, though they are commonly spoken of as such) are given with the descriptions of the species, listed below.

ALSTROEMERIA. Forming an interesting group of tuberous-rooted plants, this genus is related to but vastly different in appearance from the daffodil. Alstroemerias are not commonly offered for sale by eastern dealers but are much grown in California—where in some quarters they are considered more or less as weeds. They bloom with great freedom during the summer and are excellent and long-lasting when used as cut flowers.

A. aurantiaca grows from 3 to 4 feet high. Ten or more large brown-spotted bright yellow flowers are produced in a cluster surmounting the leafy stem, which in itself is decorative. The tubers should be planted in the fall, 6 inches apart, at a depth which will allow 4 inches of soil above them. When the ground has frozen 1 inch deep, cover with a 6-inch mulch of straw or salt hay, which must be removed before growth starts in the spring.

Alstroemerias have the reputation of being tender outdoors north of Washington, D. C., but *A. aurantiaca* and a variety (*lutea?*) have survived for many years without any special protection in the Brooklyn Botanic Garden. Their successful cultivation outdoors seems to be a matter of protecting them for a few years until their deeply penetrating roots become thoroughly established, after which they will endure zero weather with impunity.

These plants are well worth a trial in regions where the temperature does not fall much below zero. They can be grown where the winters are very severe if the plants are dug in the fall and stored in a coldframe or cold cellar until the spring, then again planted outdoors.

Other species include *A. chilensis* and its hybrids in pink, rose, and orange tints, and *A. pulchella,* which is much smaller and has dark red flowers with brown spots and green tips.

AMARYLLIS. *A. Belladonna,* **Belladonna Lily,** is an interesting plant well worth growing if right conditions can be provided. It is reputed to be tender north of Washington, D. C. The type (there are several garden varieties) has rosy-red lily-like flowers, produced in late summer, usually when the plants are leafless, in umbels on a stout stalk 2 to 4 feet in length. Best success is likely to be attained when the bulbs are planted near the foundation of a south wall. A deep sandy loam is preferred and the base of the bulbs should be about a foot from the surface of the soil.

BEGONIA. The tuberous-rooted begonias, with their large brilliantly hued flowers, are admirable subjects for the outdoor garden if a partially shaded situation, sheltered from strong winds, can be provided for them.

The tubers should be started in March or April by placing them in flats or pots in a mixture of leafmold and sand, covering them with 1 inch of the mixture. Water sparingly until growth starts. After some growth has been made, they may be potted up separately in soil composed of equal parts of loam, leafmold, rotted manure, and sand. At least an inch of coarse ashes should be placed in the bottom of the pots for drainage. About the beginning of June the plants may be set out where they are to bloom, spacing them about 8 inches apart. Mulch the surface with an inch or two of leafmold, rotted manure, or peatmoss to aid in keeping the roots cool.

Before freezing weather arrives in the fall, dig up the tubers and store them in dry soil or sand in a cool room (50°) for the winter.

BOUSSINGAULTIA, **Madeira Vine.** See Chapter IX, VINES.

BRODIAEA. This genus, whose headquarters are in the Pacific states, has possibilities for gardeners in the East in sections where the winters are not too cold. Away from their native habitat they are sometimes intractable, but for those who are interested in growing plants which are not found in every garden, they are worth a trial. The species most frequently offered by eastern dealers are: *B. capitata,* 1 to 2 feet, lilac or lavender flowers in umbels; *B. coccinea,* **Floral Fire-cracker** (now called by some botanists *Brevoortia Ida-Maia*), 1 to 3 feet high, with brilliant red flowers tipped with green; *B. coronaria* (*grandiflora*), dwarf, up to 10 inches, large blue flowers; *B. ixioides,* usually about 1 foot high, with yellow flowers, produced in umbels on long slender pedicels.

Good drainage is important for these bulbs. They should be dried off after their growth has withered. Plant in the fall and mulch heavily with light littery material.

COLCHICUM, **Meadow-saffron** (sometimes erroneously called "autumn crocus"). Flowering in September and October, the meadow-saffron would be valuable in the rock garden were it not for the coarse heavy foliage produced the following spring. The large pinkish-lavender crocus-like flowers are showy. In the foreground of shrubbery the foliage is not objectionable.

Plant in August for September bloom, setting the bulbs 5 inches deep and 6 inches apart. The commonest species is *C. autumnale;* the best is *C. speciosum* and its variety *album.*

CANNA. Thirty or forty years ago, when the only varieties of canna were those with comparatively insignificant flowers, they were in great favor and often used for their bold foliage alone. Modern varieties exhibit a great improvement over the old kinds in range of color, increased size of blooms, and floriferousness, but they are no longer the fashion and are therefore to a large extent neglected. They are valuable for display in beds in public parks and on large estates, and useful for filling gaps in the background of flower borders of smaller gardens. They require a deep rich soil and plenty of water during the time they are actively growing.

When a greenhouse is available, the usual practice is to divide the rootstock into pieces, each having one or two growth shoots. This is done in late February or early March. The divisions are placed rather thickly in flats of leafmold in a temperature between 65 and 75 degrees. When growth starts they are potted separately in rich soil in 4-inch pots. A few weeks before the time comes for planting them outdoors, they are hardened off by placing them for 10 days or so in a cool greenhouse, followed by about 2 weeks in a coldframe. They may be planted in their summer quarters when danger of frost is past. Set them about 18 inches apart.

When the tops have been killed by frost, cut them to the ground, dig up the rootstocks without knocking all the soil from them, and store for the winter by packing them close together with a little peatmoss or sand between and over them in a single layer on the floor or a shelf, in a room having a temperature of about 50 degrees. Or they may be kept under a bench in a cool greenhouse. If neither cool room nor greenhouse is available, stand them on the floor in the coolest part of the cellar.

It is my impression that the modern canna is more difficult to carry over the winter than the old-fashioned kinds—but certainly it is more worth while to grow.

DAHLIA. So many people are in the habit of thinking of dahlias as bulbs that this chapter seems the logical place to treat them. Actually, the dahlia is a tuberous-rooted perennial, tender in the North, and cherished by male gardeners, who delight in growing enormous flowers which are practically useless, except to boast about.

The dahlia is valuable in the perennial border, both for its intrinsic merit and because it may be planted late (mid-June) to fill gaps left by early-blooming subjects.

It will thrive in a wide variety of soils, but usually does best in a rather sandy loam, well supplied with humus. Nitrogenous fertilizers should be used sparingly because they may induce a sappy, leafy growth. Dahlias are reputed to be benefited by liberal supplies of potash. This may be in the form of wood ashes at the rate of a half pound to a square yard; or ½ ounce of muriate of potash to the same area. A fourth to a half pound of bonemeal to a square yard will supply the necessary phosphoric acid, and probably sufficient nitrogen, if the soil is well supplied with humus. These fertilizers should be mixed with the upper 6 inches of soil prior to planting and after the ground has been dug at least a foot deep. Dahlias may be planted in the vicinity of New York between May 15 and June 15. When the object is the production of exhibition blooms the later date is preferred.

Stock for planting may consist either of divided rootstocks or of "green plants" which are produced by starting the tubers indoors, removing the shoots as they develop and rooting them in sand. After they are rooted, the cuttings are potted in soil in 3-inch pots. When dividing the rootstock care must be taken

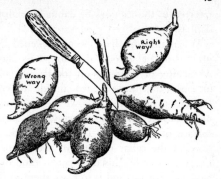

Fig. 38. Dividing dahlia clump

to include a growth bud (one is enough) with each division. Right and wrong methods of division are shown in Fig. 38. It is better to wait until the growth buds swell before dividing the roots.

The stakes for support should be set before the roots are planted. They should be stout enough (1½ to 2 inches in diameter) to support the plants firmly and should be driven into the ground at least a foot. The average dahlia requires a space about 4 feet square for proper development.

When planting root divisions make the holes from 4 to 6 inches deep depending on whether the soil is heavy or light. Lay the tuber horizontally in the hole, with the growth bud pointing upward, and cover with 2 inches of soil. When sufficient top growth has been made, the hole may be filled to the general level. "Green plants" should be set so that there is about an inch of soil over the ball of earth in which they are growing.

Keep the surface soil cultivated about 3 inches deep during the early part of the growing season. When fibrous roots start to form near the surface, cultivation should be shallower—not more than 1 inch deep. Water thoroughly during periods of drought so that the ground is wet to a depth of at least a foot. Usually, water need not be applied more often than once a week.

Thrips, leafhoppers, and aphids are inclined to be bothersome in many sections. Apply 3-percent nicotine dust during the hottest part of the day and repeat at weekly intervals.

Dahlias are subject to a disease, or a combination of insect trouble and virus disease, known as "stunt." Plants which are stunted, especially those which show mottling of the foliage with light and dark green areas, should be dug up and destroyed by burning.

When exhibition blooms are required, disbudding is practised for the purpose of developing large flowers on long stems unencumbered with lateral shoots and flower buds. Those interested in this phase of dahlia culture are referred to the catalogs of dahlia specialists or to books dealing solely with dahlias.

When the tops have been blackened by frost they should be cut to the ground and the roots dug up. This should be done with care to avoid wrenching or breaking off the fleshy roots. Preferably they should be dug in early morning, turned upside down and left exposed to sunshine (usually a sunny day follows the first frost) so that any water present may drain out of the hollow stems, and surplus moisture evaporate from the surface of the tubers. Toward the close of day bring them indoors and store in the cellar or attic in a temperature between 40 and 50 degrees. Every grower has his own pet method of handling dahlias in storage. Perhaps the best method is to place them in shallow boxes and cover them with sand or peatmoss. This tends to prevent extreme desiccation and provides a more even temperature in the vicinity of the roots. Some insist that the roots should be stored upside down, but this is probably not very important if water has previously been drained from the stems.

During the winter they should be examined periodically, and if the roots have begun to shrivel they may receive a light sprinkling of water; but if this practice is overdone, it will either cause them to rot or make them start prematurely into growth, which is almost as serious.

If they are kept in an unheated attic, a thought should be given to them on very cold nights and a quilt from the guest-room bed, or something similar, should be thrown over them as protection against freezing.

It is rather futile for me to recommend dahlia varieties. New varieties are constantly being introduced, so that a list is soon more or less out-of-date. However, the following list of excellent but not too expensive varieties has been compiled from various sources:

BALL DAHLIAS: **A. D. Livoni,** soft pink; **Leah Pearl,** pink and cream; **Marshall Kernochan,** carmine, prolific in blooming, said to be the "best red ball to date"; **Mary Helen,** deep canary yellow.

FORMAL DECORATIVE: **Bob White,** pure white, large flowers; **Dan'l Del Roi Albert,** purple, tipped white; **Fred Springer,** scarlet red; **Jersey's Beauty,** pink, an old variety but still popular; **Rose Fallon,** orange amber; **Sagamore,** orange, suffused red; **White King,** excellent for cutting.

INFORMAL DECORATIVE: **California Idol,** clear yellow, enormous flowers; **Ginger Rogers,** deep sulphur yellow; **Hunt's Velvet Wonder,** deep rosy magenta blending into true purple; **Jane Cowl,** warm buff and old gold blending to apricot and rose at the center; **Mrs. George Le Boutillier,** carmine red; **Sunrays,** clear buff, suffused apricot, reverse side of petals peach red; **Virginia Rute,** rich maroon or oxblood red; **Wachtung Giant,** deep amber yellow, suffused with orange cadmium.

SEMI-CACTUS: **All American,** mulberry rose, suffused salmon, base of petals yellow; **Edith Wilkie,** pure white, large blooms; **Golden Standard,** tan, amber and bronze; **Hilda Fioretti,** rose pink, blended deep rose, petals striped and tipped apricot yellow; **Lynn Fontanne,** vivid red with a few chrome yellow petaloids; **Miss Belgium,** bright orange, coral reverse, coral-pink center; **Son of Satan,** bright scarlet, large blooms; **Yellow Glory,** clear lemon yellow.

SINGLE: **Marshall's Glory,** cardinal red with white stripe in the center of each petal; **Newport Wonder,** rose pink with gold suffusion; **Pequot Yellow,** large clear yellow.

MINIATURE: **Baby Royal,** salmon pink shaded apricot with yellow at the base of the petals; **Bishop of Llandaff,** bright scarlet with a deep garnet center; **Fairy,** violet-rose, tipped with mauve; **Little Colonel,** soft pink, with primrose center; **Red Head,** fiery scarlet blooms on long stems; **White Fawn,** pure white.

POMPON: **Amber Glow,** coral and gold; **Clover,** white with a faint tint of pink; **Ebony,** dark black maroon; **Little David,** russet orange; **Little Edith,** primrose yellow tipped with bright carmine; **Morning Mist,** lavender.

EREMURUS, **Desert Candle, Foxtail Lily.** These are striking objects in the perennial garden when well grown. Some varieties, such as *E. himalaicus, E. robustus,* and their hybrids, are capable of sending up flower stalks to a height of 8 or 10 feet, clothed for a yard or more with hundreds of flowers of white, pink, yellow, and two-toned combinations, according to the variety. These flower spikes remind one of pointed Gargantuan bottle-brushes.

The fleshy roots should be planted in the fall, 2 to 3 feet apart and buried 5 inches deep. A rich well-drained soil and a sunny situation are necessary. Protect the roots over winter, in climates similar to that of the vicinity of New York, by a heavy mulch of straw, which must be removed very early in the spring, for growth starts long before it should in a climate such as ours. Because of this it is necessary, when frosty nights are anticipated, to protect the young leaves and flower spikes. Make a framework by sticking three or four bamboo stakes into the soil around the individual plants. Bend them over and tie the tops together. These will serve to support burlap or cloth in such a way that it protects the plants without actually being in contact with them.

GALTONIA. *G. candicans (Hyacinthus candicans),* **Summer Hyacinth.** A stately plant suitable for the perennial garden, the summer hyacinth sends up an open raceme of white flowers, individually somewhat like large snowdrops, on a stalk 3 or 4 feet high. Although it can survive the milder winters around New York, it is not reliably hardy, and the safest practice is to dig up the bulbs in late fall and store them in a cool place indoors. The bulbs should be set 1 foot apart and 6 inches deep.

GLADIOLUS. Its adaptability, ease of cultivation, range of color, and possibilities of use both for garden display and cut flowers, are among the reasons for the popularity of this genus.

Any good, well-drained garden soil will suit the gladiolus; follow the soil preparation recommended earlier in this chapter for bulbs in general.

The corms may be planted from April 15 until July 15. If a quantity is planted at intervals of two or three weeks, a succession of bloom may be maintained from June until frost.

If grown primarily for cut flowers, the corms may be planted 3 or 4 inches apart in rows 2 to 3 feet apart. In the perennial border they may be planted in groups of ten to twenty or more, spacing the corms 6 inches apart.

The depth of planting is dependent upon the type of soil. If it is sandy, they may be set 6 inches deep; if the soil is heavy, 3 or 4 inches is deep enough. One advantage resulting from deep planting is that the stalks are held firmly and are less likely to need staking.

Keep the surface soil cultivated during the growing season, and water thoroughly during droughty periods.

Although the gladiolus, if heavily mulched, can survive the winters experienced in the vicinity of New York, the best practice is to dig up the corms, store them under cover, and replant in the spring. They may be dug just as soon as the foliage becomes yellow or is killed by frost. Place in flats and keep them in a dry place until the tops become brittle. They may then be cleaned up by removing the tops, loose scales, and the withered corms of the preceding year. The cleaned corms, if there are only a few of them, may be placed in paper bags. The tops of the bags should be left open to admit air. When there are many corms to be cared for, they may be placed in shallow boxes or trays and stored in an airy cool room—40 to 50 degrees. They must be placed where they are out of reach of mice.

If the plants were infested with thrips during the growing season, fumigate the corms by placing them in closed paper bags with an ounce of naphthalene flakes to every hundred corms. Keep them in a temperature of about 70 degrees for three or four weeks, then open the bags, remove the remaining naphthalene, and store the corms in a dry place, as suggested above.

The following are varieties recommended by Humphrey F. Hedgecock, who says that they are available at a reasonable price and are good growers:

LARGE FLOWERING TYPE: *White,* Snow Princess, Surfside. *Pink,* Pink Picardy, Pink Paragon. *Rose,* Rosa van Lima. *Red,* Algonquin, Beacon. *Purple,* Purple Supreme. *Blue,* Blue Beauty, Rangoon. *Yellow,* Crinkle Cream, Spotlight. *Cream,* Leading Lady. *Lavender,* Elizabeth the Queen, Minuet. *Orange,* Capistrano, Lantana, Janet Lee. *Smoky,* Bagdad, Bolero, Vagabond Prince.

Small-flowered and miniature types: *White,* Snow Baby, White Butterfly. *Orange,* Orange Town, Orange Butterfly. *Yellow,* Fluffy Ruffles, Yellow Bird. *Pink,* Loveliness, Rosette.

LILIUM. The ideal time for planting lily bulbs is just as soon as possible after the bulbs are matured. This is usually when the leaves begin to wither. Sometimes the bulbs are not received from the dealer until the ground has frozen deeply. To give the bulbs proper care in such circumstances, mulch the soil early with a deep layer of straw or leaves to prevent it from freezing, so that the bulbs may be planted immediately after they are received; or, pot the bulbs or place them in a box in moist soil and store in a cold-frame until spring, then plant them (taking care not to disturb their roots) in their permanent locations. The first method is preferable.

A well-drained sandy loam plentifully supplied with humus provides the best rooting medium for most of the lilies. *Lilium superbum* will thrive under swampy conditions, but is also happy when planted in well-drained soil. Some lilies, such as *L. croceum, L. Henryi, L. regale,* and *L. tigrinum,* are satisfied in almost any reasonably good garden soil. Some varieties prefer a cool root-run, which can be provided by giving them a deep soil (at least 18 inches if possible) and planting them so that the ground over their roots is shaded. This may be accomplished by associating them with low-growing shrubs, over the tops of which their flower stalks may rise. The depths of planting has considerable bearing on success with lilies. Some varieties form roots from the base of the bulb only; others produce roots both at the base of the bulb and on the underground part of the stem. The first group should be planted about 4 inches deep, while the stem-rooters may have from 6 to 9 inches of soil over the bulb, depending on its size. Most of the firms specializing in lilies note in their catalogs the depth to which the various species should be planted.

One of the most promising lilies from the standpoint of garden value is *L. formosanum.* This is a white lily (somewhat like the Easter lily) which blooms from August up to frost. It is one of the easiest of all to raise from seeds, and it is possible to produce blossoming plants within six months of planting if the seeds are started in a greenhouse in February or March. This variety should be of special interest to those who have trouble with disease-ridden lilies, because of the opportunity it affords of easily raising disease-free stock which, if uncontaminated by association with infested lilies, may be expected to remain healthy.

Good *Lilium* species for the beginner are as follows:

L. canadense, **Meadow Lily,** is a native which is not particular as to soil. Growing about 4 feet high, it has broadly bell-shaped flowers in red or yellow with brownish spots. Plant 4 inches deep. June, July.

L. candidum, **Madonna Lily,** is worth taking a chance with. It may fail miserably, but if it does make up its mind to grow, it is wonderfully good, with its pure white flowers on stalks 3 feet high. The bulbs should be planted as early as obtainable, to give them a chance, before winter comes, to form their characteristic rosette of leaves. Plant 3 inches deep. June, July.

L. elegans. This and its relatives will thrive even in a city back yard. The flowers are held erect on stems from 1 to 2 feet in height. Plant 5 inches deep. June, July.

L. Henryi has yellow flowers with reflexed petals. Although it will grow in open exposures, the flower color is likely to fade in sunshine; therefore it is desirable to plant it in partial shade. In rich soil it may attain a height of 7 feet. Plant 9 inches deep. July, August.

L. regale, **Regal Lily,** has grown amazingly in popular esteem. The flowers are tubular, white with a yellow throat, with reddish markings on the outside. It grows normally 3 to 4 feet, but I have seen specimens up to 8 feet high. Plant 6 to 9 inches deep. July.

L. speciosum, **Japanese Lily,** is forced as a florist's flower, but is also excellent in gardens, growing about 3 feet high. The reflexed petals are white with crimson markings. Plant 6 inches deep. August, September.

L. superbum, **American Turk's-cap Lily,** grows 3 to 8 feet high. The flowers, with reflexed petals, are orange-scarlet and yellow with brownish spots. Plant 6 inches deep. August.

L. tenuifolium is a rather small (1 to 2 feet) narrow-leaved kind, with bright scarlet flowers, and is for some obscure reason called the **Coral Lily,** Its low stature makes it a valuable plant for the rock garden. Plant 4 inches deep. It probably is not a true perennial; therefore, in order to perpetuate it under garden conditions, seeds should be planted annually to maintain the stock. June, July.

L. tigrinum, **Tiger Lily,** has been a garden favorite for many generations, bearing numerous brown-spotted orange flowers horizontally at the summit of a sturdy leafy stem. Plant 6 inches deep. August, September.

OXALIS. The species most commonly used for outdoor planting is *O. rubra,* a native of Brazil, which produces its rose-colored flowers in great abundance throughout the summer. It is a neat tufted little plant, about 8 inches high, with attractive clover-like foliage. It can be used to advantage in the front of the perennial border or for edging a flower bed. It is sometimes winter-hardy in the vicinity of New York, but it is safest to dig up the plants in the fall and store them dry, without removing the soil

PLATE XVI. *(upper)* CROCUSES NATURALIZED IN LAWN UNDER TREE. *(lower)* POET'S NARCISSUS NATURALIZED IN GRASS

PLATE XVII. *(upper)* BULB PLANTING WITH DIBBERS. NOTE MARKER IN FOREGROUND. *(lower)* THE SAME GARDEN THE FOLLOWING SPRING. TULIP MR. FARNCOMBE SANDERS

which clings to them, in a frost-proof cellar or under the bench of a cool greenhouse. Set them outdoors 9 inches apart when danger of frost is past.

POLIANTHES. *P. tuberosa,* **Tuberose.** The waxy white flowers of the tuberose with their overpowering fragrance were in greater favor with our grandmothers than they are with the present generation. The bulbs should be planted in friable soil in the spring when danger of frost is past. Set them with 1 inch of soil over them and 6 to 8 inches apart. Dig the bulbs before cold weather comes in the fall, dry them, and store in a temperature of 60 degrees.

TRITONIA, **Montbretia.** When visiting Earlham Hall Gardens in England, I was much impressed by the gorgeous varieties of montbretia seen— many of them hybrids developed there. I made arrangements to secure a collection, but, I am sorry to say, I did not have much success with them; neither did a friend in another part of New York State. I am afraid our winters are too cold and our summers too hot for this group. Those living in milder climates than New York should by all means try them. A deep soil, well supplied with humus, is preferred. In sections where the winter is not severe (temperatures not lower than 20 degrees above zero), the corms may be planted in the fall 4 inches deep and 6 inches apart. In more rigorous climates they should be stored over winter in slightly moist leafmold in a temperature of 40 degrees, and planted out in the spring. The individual flowers are reminiscent of gladiolus, although usually slightly smaller, and are produced in branching sprays. Good varieties are: **Apricot Queen,** golden apricot; **Comet,** golden-orange and maroon; **His Majesty,** yellow shading to scarlet; **James Coey,** vermillion, suffused golden-orange; **Lady Wilson,** orange-yellow; **Red Knight,** vermillion and gold; **Star of the East,** orange-red.

Tuberose, see POLIANTHES.

XV. ROSE GARDEN

Whether one's "collection" consists of a single bush of old-fashioned yellow roses, a few ramblers on trellises, or a garden an acre or more in extent in which flowers of different types may be seen in bloom from June till November, roses seldom fail to bring delight to the garden owner who gives them a favorable site, appropriate soil, and the care from season to season which will keep them vigorous.

The place of roses on the grounds. Besides the species roses—those natural forms which have not been hybridized into varied color-tones and other qualities, as have the Hybrid Teas and Polyanthas, for instance—there are innumerable types of roses which can be adapted to many different garden purposes. The species roses are often most suitably placed in shrubbery plantings; the climbing types, including their horticultural varieties, on house walls, arbors, and fences, or used as ground-covers, especially on terrace slopes and banks along driveways. Both these and the sprawly semi-climbing roses may be effectively displayed in an informal setting where they are left to grow almost at will, as in the Rose Dell in the Royal Botanic Gardens at Kew in England. Here in a narrow valley with rather steeply sloping banks, the roses are allowed to scramble over the massive tree roots and stumps which serve, in part, to uphold the soil of the banks. During the blooming season this is one of the most popular of all the garden features at Kew.

The horticultural forms of bush roses (Teas, Hybrid Teas, Hybrid Perpetuals, Polyanthas, etc.) should be segregated in a rose garden, where they not only show off to best advantage, but are most easily given the care they require.

The site of the rose garden. A spot that is airy and yet somewhat protected from high winds should be selected for the rose garden. Perfect drainage of the soil is also essential. Light shade during part of the day is not objectionable—and, indeed, is preferable for some varieties. I have seen roses growing to perfection beneath widely spaced old oaks whose lowest branches were 30 feet from the ground and whose roots struck deep into the soil. But low-branched, shallow-rooting trees would rob the plants of too much light and nutriment.

Borders and beds. Posts connected with chains, a fence, or a series of trellises placed around the rose garden make an attractive enclosure and also provide the supports required for climbing varieties. The garden itself will look best if laid out rather formally, with a design of related beds which are usually long and narrow. (Fig. 39 suggests a desirable type of layout.) When beds are so wide that the gardener cannot reach all of the plants from the

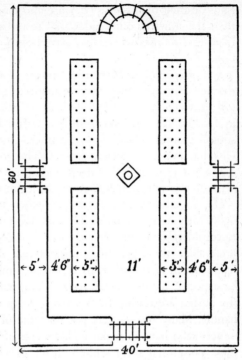

FIG. 39. Plan for rose garden

walk, both clothes and temper suffer. Narrow beds facilitate pruning, spraying, watering, fertilizing, and picking. Four rows of Hybrid Teas or Polyanthas set 15 to 18 inches apart or three rows of Hybrid Perpetuals spaced at 2½ to 3 feet should be the limit in each bed. The flatness of the planting may be broken at strategic points by posts or arches covered with climbing, rambler, or pillar roses, or by tree-roses, which are varieties budded on tall standards.

Planting and cultivation of roses. A thorough understanding of the requirements of roses, from soil preparation to winter protection, is helpful to the gardener. Fortunately, their needs are simple enough for any competent grower to provide for with ease; but if any step is neglected or inadequately performed, the rose garden may be a disappointment.

Which plants to choose. In most sections, field-grown roses, budded on strong-rooted understocks, will give better results than small cuttings on their own roots. They are also more likely to give satisfaction than the nineteen-cent "sidewalk" roses, which are bushes discarded from greenhouses where they have been forced for cut-flower production.

Soil preparation. Most roses prefer a rather heavy though well-drained loam, but they may be made to grow in almost any kind of soil provided it is enriched with liberal supplies of decayed manure—preferably that obtained from cow barns. Unless the character of the subsoil ensures good drainage, artificial drains must be provided. (See Chapter IV, SOIL IMPROVEMENT.) The soil should be prepared by digging it 18 to 24 inches deep, adding from 2 to 4 inches of manure; or, if this is not available, compost, leafmold or peatmoss.

Planting. Roses may be planted either in late fall and early winter or as early as it is possible to work the ground in the spring. There is considerable controversy as to whether fall or spring planting is preferable. My experience indicates that it is about six of one and half a dozen of the other. In very cold climates, spring planting might be expected to give better results. The main point is to plant while the bushes are resting from active growth and when the soil is fit to handle. Many rose dealers pot up some of their stock to sell to customers who have to make replacements after growth has started, but these pot-grown roses seldom thrive as vigorously as those planted when they are dormant.

Fall-planted roses should be cut back about one half and then mounded with soil. If it is possible to cover them completely, so much the better. On spring-planted roses all weak shoots should be entirely removed, and the remainder cut back to within 3 to 6 inches of the ground. It is a good plan to cover them also with earth, leaving it on until growth starts.

When planting, first trim bruised and broken roots. Make a hole large enough to accommodate all the roots comfortably. Build up the earth in the center, set the plant on this mound, spread the roots in all directions, as they lie naturally, cover them with soil free from lumps, and pack the soil firmly by stamping on it with the feet. The plant should be set so that the point of union between stock and scion (Fig. 40) is about 1 inch below the surface of the ground.

Mulching. During the growing season the surface soil must either be cultivated to form a dust mulch, or covered with a layer, 2 inches thick, of peatmoss or buckwheat hulls. We have tried all three methods in comparison and found but little difference in results. If any, it was in favor of the peatmoss mulch, but it should be pointed out that in some soils the constant use of peatmoss might result in making the soil too acid and too loose in texture. So far as acidity is concerned, this could be corrected with lime or by an annual application of wood ashes. One disadvantage attend-

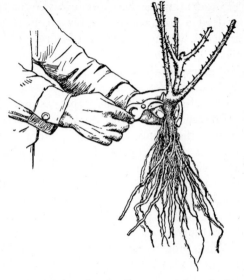

Fig. 40. Point of union between stock and scion

ing the use of buckwheat hulls is that birds, when hunting for stray kernels, scratch the hulls in every direction, and make the surroundings untidy.

Fertilizing. If the soil has been properly prepared, newly planted roses will not require any additional fertilizer during the first season. The fertility of established beds may be maintained by filling the trenches with cow manure after the plants are hilled up in the fall. Fork the manure lightly into the ground the following spring, taking care not to injure the rose roots. Then apply wood ashes at the rate of about 5 pounds to 100 square feet, and 2 to 2½ pounds of super-phosphate to the same area; or use 3 to 5 pounds of steamed bonemeal to 100 square feet in October. If the color of the roses is poor and the growth is not vigorous, cultivate dried blood into the surface soil in June at the rate of 1 pound, or a little more, to 100 square feet. Some growers apply 2 to 3 pounds of commercial fertilizer (4-12-4 or 5-10-5) in early August to help fall blooming. Do not try to force your roses to grow by giving them quick-acting fertilizers during hot weather; or later than August 10, because of the danger of stimulating sappy growth which will be unable to survive the winter.

Watering. Roses like cool weather and moist soil. During periods of drought, water them thoroughly so that the soil is wet to a depth of at least a foot. Cultivate, unless you are using a mulch of organic material, when the surface has dried sufficiently, and do not water again until the soil needs it—usually in about a week if the weather continues dry. The water should be applied to the soil and not to the foliage. Wet leaves afford opportunity for the germination of the spores of the dreaded black-spot disease.

Protection from pests. As soon as leaves form on the roses in the spring, the plants should be protected from black-spot and other fungous diseases by fungicides used either as sprays or dusts. I am well satisfied with the efficacy of Massey dust, which consists of 9 parts of finely divided dusting sulphur, and 1 part lead arsenate. It is obtainable mixed and ready for use under various trade names. The arsenic content poisons the leaf-eating insects, while the sulphur prevents fungous attacks.

When properly applied, Massey dust does not disfigure the leaves to any great extent. One should try to coat both surfaces of all the leaves with a thin film of the dust. It should be applied just *before* every rainy period—determined by consulting the weather forecasts and by exercising one's own powers as a weather prophet. Try to avoid dusting when the roses are at the height of their bloom, because the sulphur is likely to cause some discoloration of blossoms, but if the prevalence of fungi seems to warrant it, reconcile yourself to injured flowers in preference to defoliated and unhealthy bushes. During a normal season it usually is important to dust or spray on an average of every week or ten days. The prompt removal and destruction of affected leaves aids in combating diseases.

Bordeaux mixture is fairly effective in the control of black-spot, but has an objectionable appearance on the foliage. There are proprietary sprays which are good but more expensive than the Massey dust. Fermate, a synthetic fungicide is said to be very effective. Use as a spray or dust, following manufacturer's directions.

Before covering the roses for the winter it is a good plan to spray them with winter-strength lime-sulphur—1 part commercial lime-sulphur to 9 parts water. (See Chapter XXIX, GARDEN ENEMIES.) Do not allow it, however, to come in contact with painted supports or structures because it will discolor them.

Aphids are oftentimes bothersome on the young shoots and leaves. They should be sprayed with nicotine-soap solution before they become numerous.

Winter protection. In climates where the temperature gets down to nearly zero, winter protection is necessary, at least for most of the Tea and Hybrid Tea roses. If labor, soil, and lumber are available, the beds may be enclosed with a fence 1 to 2 feet high after the leaves have fallen. Then cover the bushes with a foot or more of soil, taking care to avoid breaking the branches.

Under conditions at the Brooklyn Botanic Garden it was found that hilling the bushes with earth taken from between the rows works satisfactorily, care being used to avoid injuring the roots. The trenches thus made were filled with cow manure. Around Christmas time the tops were further protected by covering them with salt hay or evergreen branches, preferably those of fir.

Acting on the assumption that Tea roses are less hardy than the Hybrid Teas, we hilled them up as just described, then built a tight board fence 2 feet high around the bed to keep off the wind. The overhead protection consisted of screens made of builder's lath nailed $\frac{1}{4}$ inch apart on $1\frac{1}{2}$ x 2-inch strips. This protection was so effective that we had fewer losses of Tea roses from winter killing than we did of Hybrid Teas.

Climbing varieties liable to winter injury (Gloire de Dijon, Emily Gray, Jacotte, etc.) should have a 3- to 6-inch mulch of manure placed over their roots. The tops may be removed from their support, if they are on a trellis, and bundled in cornstalks or straw. If growing on a pillar, it is not necessary to remove them before covering them. Another method, preferred where winters are more severe than around New York, is to untie the canes, bend them to the ground, and cover them with 3 inches of soil. From 6 inches to a foot of straw may then be placed on top.

Pruning. The main pruning of TEA, HYBRID TEA, and HYBRID PERPETUAL roses is done just as growth is starting in the spring. RAMBLER roses are pruned immediately after they have finished blooming. CLIMBING roses are pruned in the spring, although it is permissible to restrain the over-exuberant growth of climbing roses of the Van Fleet type during the summer if they are getting out of bounds.

In the case of TEAS and HYBRID TEAS, pruning may be severe or light according to the wishes of the owner (Fig. 41). If the object is the production of exhibition blooms, the bushes should be cut almost to the ground, only three or four canes being left on each bush and not more than three growth buds allowed on each cane. If the pref-

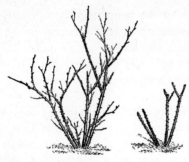

Fig. 41. Unpruned, and moderately
pruned H.T. rose

erence is for a number of flowers suitable for cutting, the pruning should be moderate, the canes being cut back just about one third, or down to six or eight growth buds. But if large quantities of flowers are desired for garden display, and there is no objection to short stems, pruning should be restricted to the tips of the canes, the removal of spindling wood, and, of course, all dead or diseased wood. In severe pruning the strength of the plant is concentrated in a few growth buds, which will result in long strong shoots and large flowers. When pruning is light, more growth buds are left, therefore more shoots develop, and the flowers are smaller in size but more numerous.

Most of the flowers are produced on shoots originating from canes which grew the preceding year; therefore, the pruner should aim at maintaining a supply of vigorous one-year-old wood, cutting out old branches which are not producing such wood.

Weak growers should be pruned severely to stimulate the development of strong shoots, which will be ideal for producing flowering shoots the following year. Strong growers should be pruned lightly—partly because severe pruning is unnecessary and partly because it would stimulate the production of shoots much too vigorous, and thus reduce the number of flowers.

In order to ensure a clean cut, the pruning knife or shears should be sharp. Do not leave any stubs. Cut close to a main branch; or, when a shoot is shortened, cut to within ¼ inch of a bud pointing in the direction you wish a shoot to develop. Usually this is an outside bud.

First cut out all dead wood and weak shoots originating near the base of the plant. Next remove any branches which show evidence of disease. Then cut out old branches which are producing nothing but weak shoots. Shorten the remaining canes by one third if your object is garden roses; by two thirds if exhibition blooms are desired.

Hybrid Perpetuals are pruned in much the same manner as the preceding kinds, except that, in general, they are not cut back so far. A narrow-blade saw may be necessary to remove very old branches.

In some varieties, the habit of making many strong shoots from the base enables us to cut out most, if not all, of the canes which have produced flowering shoots, and still have enough left to provide flowering shoots for the current season. The shoots that are retained may be shortened one third to one half; or, they may be left unpruned, bent over so as to form an arch, and held in place by tying their tips to pegs thrust into the ground. This procedure forces into growth buds which otherwise would have remained dormant, and results in the production of a large number of blossoms.

POLYANTHA roses should be pruned by the removal of dead wood. The bushes should be thinned each year by cutting out a few of the older branches at the ground line.

CHINA roses need very little pruning. Merely cut out dead wood, and branches which are no longer producing vigorous young shoots.

Before discussing the pruning of roses used for furnishing fences, arbors, arches, trellises, and pillars, it is necessary to define the types.

1. CLIMBERS. The official designation of the American Rose Society is "Large-flowering Climbers." In this group the flowers are comparatively large and produced few in a cluster. The superstructure consists of more or less permanent wood, and strong new shoots originate from the branches rather than from the base of the plant. Examples are Dr. W. Van Fleet, Emily Gray, Mary Wallace, and Mme. Gregoire Staechelin.

Strong-growing climbers may be pruned by shortening vigorous shoots in the growing season to keep them within bounds. It should be pointed out that roses of this type should not be planted where there is insufficient room for them to develop properly, because if it is necessary to cut them back severely every year, the result may be the production of few or no blooms. Further pruning consists of the removal of old worn-out branches in the spring. This last is the only pruning needed by the less vigorous climbers often used as pillar roses.

2. RAMBLERS. This is the small bunch-flowered group of roses, having relatively impermanent canes which are replaced by shoots originating from the base of the plant. This habit enables a typical rambler to be distinguished from a climber. There are some varieties in which the characteristics of the two groups are more or less combined. Examples of Ramblers are: Dorothy Perkins, Excelsa, and Hiawatha.

Rambler roses should be pruned immediately after flowering by removing all canes which have produced blossoms. The new shoots, originating from the base of the plant, should be trained in their place. Injured tips of these canes should be cut off in the spring.

3. CLIMBING HYBRID TEAS. These are vigorous mutations of Hybrid Teas which can be adapted for use as pillar roses. Examples are: Climbing Caroline Testout, Climbing Lady Ashtown, and Climbing Los Angeles. Only the old worn-out branches need to be pruned off in the spring.

A selection of roses for different garden purposes. In the suggestive lists of desirable roses offered below, three main divisions are noted: BUSH ROSES FOR BEDS, ROSES TO TRAIN ON SUPPORTS, and SPECIES ROSES. Brief descriptions are given of different types and varieties in each group.

BUSH ROSES FOR BEDS

TEA ROSES

Thirty years ago Tea roses were immensely popular, especially in Europe, but of late they have been largely supplanted by the Hybrid Teas. They have beautifully formed, sweetly fragrant flowers. Their value for garden use is lessened, however, by the weak stems which cause the flowers of many varieties to droop. They are not so resistant to cold as the Hybrid Tea varieties, and do not exhibit so wide a range of color.

Notwithstanding these defects they are beautiful and should be represented in every rose garden if the climate is not too severe for them. The following are outstanding varieties:

Harry Kirk, large creamy-yellow flowers which stand upright.

Lady Hillingdon, beautifully pointed buds and flowers of apricot-yellow.

Mme. Antoine Mari, worth growing for its shapely bush and handsome foliage. Pink buds opening to flowers of creamy-pink. Stems weak.

HYBRID TEA ROSES

At the present time Hybrid Tea roses, which are characterized by free-blooming habit and comparatively low stature, comprise the most popular of all groups. They give a great burst of bloom in June, followed by scattered flowers (usually of poorer form) during the hottest months, and flowers of wonderful quality (though not so many as in June) during the cool days of autumn. In favorable seasons good blooms are produced, in favored spots on Long Island, N. Y., as late as Thanksgiving. Considerable variation exists in size and habit of growth of the different sorts, and this must be taken into consideration when planting the beds. Some, such as those in the Radiance group, make strong bushes 3 or more feet in height; others, such as Château de Clos Vougeot and Rev. F. Page Roberts, tend to remain low and are somewhat spreading. Information on these points may be obtained from the catalogs of specialists—and by trial.

It has been said that the average life of a Hybrid Tea rose is three years. I believe it to be much longer, but it is true that some varieties need to be replaced every few years.

Following is a "baker's dozen" of Hybrid Tea roses which I consider good and reasonably sure to thrive. This is purely a personal selection and I realize that many favorites and many excellent new roses have been omitted.

Christopher Stone has, with me, taken the place of Etoile de Hollande, by many considered the best red rose. Vigorous grower.

Condesa de Sastago has coppery-red petals with golden-yellow reverse, fragrant and a good grower.

Crimson Glory has fragrant flowers of crimson shaded with deep red. It is difficult to decide between this and Christopher Stone.

Duquesa di Peñaranda, classed as a bicolor, is difficult to describe because its coloration is so varied. My impression is of apricot-pink, but see how it is described in rose catalogs!

Eclipse has flowers of clear golden-yellow. The narrow buds on long stems are especially distinctive.

Mme. Butterfly, although an old-timer, is still one of the best. Pink flowers of beautiful form.

Mme. Jules Bouche, perhaps the best white variety for conditions around New York. (Good white roses are scarce.) Faint tinge of pink in center of flower. Tall.

Mme. Leon Pain, an old rose (1904) but good; exceedingly floriferous. Buds salmon-pink tinted with orange; flowers fragrant; growth medium.

Katherine T. Marshall is exceptionally vigorous with large, fragrant, pink flowers on long stems suitable for cutting.

Peace, a bicolor with yellow petals edged with pink. Undoubtedly one of the best of the newer roses.

President Macia, slender buds and large pink flowers suffused with yellow at the base of the petals.

Signora, has long buds of burnt sienna, paling as the flower opens. Fragrant, and a tall grower.

Soeur Therese, an excellent rose with slender chrome-yellow buds marked with carmine, and large yellow flowers. Growth strong with excellent foliage.

HYBRID PERPETUALS

Except in regions where the winters are too severe for the cultivation of Hybrid Teas, the Hybrid Perpetuals are nowadays rather neglected. They are hardy, and capable of making bushes 6 or more feet in height, giving a great burst of bloom in June and often a few more flowers in the fall. Some of the newer varieties, owing to crossing with Hybrid Teas, have a tendency toward an everblooming habit.

The following are among the good varieties still obtainable from nurserymen:

Captain Hayward, scarlet-crimson, large, fragrant, not fully double.

Frau Karl Druschki, the handsomest white rose in existence, but lacking in fragrance.

Gloire Lyonnaise, white, very double large flowers, yellowish toward the center.

Mme. Albert Barbier, petals tawny-yellow with pinkish tints at the base and cream-colored tips. Has a tendency toward everblooming.

Paul Neyron, rose-pink, large, and fragrant. Sometimes "balls" (fails to open) in wet weather.

Prince Camille de Rohan, dark red, shaded with blackish maroon, good form, fragrant. Sometimes called "The Black Rose."

DWARF POLYANTHAS

This group is sometimes listed in catalogs under the absurd name "Baby Ramblers." If there is anything Dwarf Polyanthas do not do, it is "ramble"! The group is of mixed ancestry and in consequence there is great variation in the form of the flowers of the different varieties. All varieties agree, however, in their freedom of bloom, comparative dwarfness, ease of culture and habit of producing their flowers in clusters. In some gardens their hardiness, freedom of bloom, and the fact that they need not be renewed annually have impelled the owner to choose Polyantha roses is preference to geraniums for formal bedding.

Following is a selection of varieties:

Cameo, shell-pink and salmon, suffused with gold.

Carol Ann, salmon-orange, globe-shaped flowers in large clusters. Seldom grows more than 12 inches tall.

Cecile Brunner, tiny, perfectly formed buds of pink with a yellow base. Useful in miniature flower arrangements.

Chatillon Rose, bright pink flowers in large clusters. Showy and excellent for bedding.

Miss Edith Cavell, semi-double, rather small flowers of scarlet-red with darker shading.

Yvonne Rabier, white flowers, bright green foliage, and a compact habit.

"FLORIBUNDA" ROSES

The name "Floribunda" has been applied to a group of roses whose limits are somewhat nebulous. In general they are large-flowered clustered roses partaking of the characteristics of both Polyanthas and Hybrid Teas.

New varieties are constantly being added. The following are attractive:

Betty Prior is pink, with the outside of the petals a dark carmine.

Donald Prior, cherry red flowers almost four inches across.

Else Poulsen, rose-pink flowers of large size.

Goldilocks, golden yellow, beautiful in bud.

Improved Lafayette, red suffused crimson. Strong grower.

Permanent Wave, beautifully "waved" petals of cochineal-red.

Pinocchio, clusters of miniature hybrid tea blooms of soft pink.

Salmon Spray, salmon-pink, strong grower.

Summer Snow, pure white flowers.

World's Fair, dark scarlet, fragrant flowers.

CHINA ROSES

These are free-blooming kinds, but the flowers lack the form of the Teas, and the substance of the Hybrid Teas. They are not widely planted, but there are a few varieties which are excellent for use when a continuous display of color is desired. These are:

Fabvier, bright crimson with a few white markings on the somewhat ragged flowers. A dwarf bush with thin wiry twigs. An old variety—introduced over a hundred years ago.

Hermosa, a dwarfish but strong grower; foliage grayish green; flowers soft pink.

Hofgärtner Kalb, blooms freely even in hot weather. Larger bush than Hermosa (2½ feet); flowers bright pink and fragrant.

ROSES TO TRAIN ON SUPPORTS

The heights of the roses listed below are based on the performance of the varieties in the Brooklyn Botanic Garden.

STRONG-GROWING—capable of 15 feet or more

Dr. W. Van Fleet, pale pink flowers of good form, double.

Golden Climber, one of the best of the yellow-flowering climbers. Floriferous when established.

Mary Wallace, bright shining pink, double.

Miss Flora Mitten, pink, yellow stamens, single.

Silver Moon, white, single. Kills back in severe winters and is too large to protect easily.

MEDIUM-SIZE—10 to 15 feet

Alida Lovett, pink, double.

Coral Creeper, apricot-orange to pink. Good ground cover.

Bloomfield Courage, dark red, white center, yellow stamens; small, single.

Jacotte, orange-yellow, tinted copper-red, semi-double. Needs winter protection in Brooklyn.

Mary Lovett, white, double.

PILLAR ROSES—6 to 10 feet

Dream Girl, coral-pink and salmon; fragrant.

Dr. Huey, dark crimson-maroon, clustered, semi-double.

Le Rêve, bright yellow, tinted copper, semi-double. Subject to black-spot. Avoid heavy fertilization and pruning.

Orange Everglow, coppery-yellow, with everblooming tendencies.

Paul's Scarlet Climber, scarlet, large, double.

Prosperity, white, medium, rosette-like, double. Almost constantly in bloom from June until frost.

Star of Persia, bright yellow, large, semi-double. Subject to black-spot. Should not be heavily fertilized.

RAMBLERS—10 to 15 feet

Chevy Chase, rich crimson; resists mildew.

Dorothy Perkins, pink, double; subject to mildew.

Hiawatha, carmine, white center, yellow stamens, single.

Lady Godiva, similar to Dorothy Perkins but of stronger growth.

Sander's White, double, white rosettes; fragrant.

"FESTOON" ROSES

When roses are required for training on chains or ropes to form festoons, varieties with long flexible growths should be chosen. We have found **Lady Godiva** and **Excelsa** to be the most satisfactory for this purpose. The shoots should be twisted around the support so that the flower clusters are not turned topsy-turvy by their own weight.

HARDY CLIMBERS

In severe climates most climbing roses need winter protection. The late Dr. W. T. Macoun has reported that the following varieties "have proved among the hardiest and most reliable" (with protection) at Ottawa: **American Pillar, Crimson Rambler, Dorothy Perkins, Dr. W. Van Fleet, Euphrosyne, Evangeline, Hiawatha, Mrs. F. W. Flight, Tausendschön, Chatillon.**

CLIMBERS FOR MILD CLIMATES

In the southern states and along the Pacific Coast, gardeners are favored by being able to grow many varieties of climbing roses which are out of the question in northern gardens. These include the **Banksian** roses; the **Cherokee** rose, a native of China which has run wild from Georgia to Florida and Texas; and those in the **Noisette** group, including such famous **old** roses as **Gloire de Dijon** (this survives the winter in Brooklyn if pro-

tected), **Maréchal Niel,** and **William Allen Richardson.** The Climbing
Hybrid Teas also are excellent in mild regions. Such varieties as **Climbing
Lady Ashtown, Climbing Radiance, Climbing Richmond,** and **Climbing
Talisman** are fairly satisfactory in the vicinity of New York if protected dur-
ing the winter.

EVERBLOOMING CLIMBERS

Rose hybridists have for years been trying to produce everblooming
hardy climbers. **New Dawn,** a mutation of Dr. W. Van Fleet, and the first
plant to be patented in the United States, has everblooming qualities. **Prosperity,** as previously mentioned, is seldom out of bloom; and **Ceres,** a Pemberton rose, flowers more or less freely until stopped by frost, and might be
trained to serve as a pillar rose. **Climbing Summer Snow,** with pure white,
2-inch blooms is highly spoken of. Conflicting reports are current as to the
behavior of **Blaze,** which has been described as an everblooming Paul's
Scarlet Climber. Climbing Hybrid Teas and climbing mutations of Polyantha roses may under good circumstances exhibit a recurrent blooming
habit. Roses are temperamental, and their reaction is greatly influenced by
their environment. A rose which is truly everblooming in one garden may
be an utter failure in another.

SPECIES ROSES

The most popular of the "wild" or "species" roses is *Rosa Hugonis.* One
of the first to flower, it almost smothers itself with single, yellow blooms.
This free-flowering habit is sometimes its undoing, for it may fail to survive
the exhaustion brought about by producing the heavy crop of fruit which
follows. Unlike many roses, this species has handsome foliage and a shapely
habit.

But Father Hugo's rose is not the only wild rose that is worth growing.
The prairie rose, *R. setigera,* which is the last to bloom, is a vigorous
grower, and arouses admiration when its large blooms of deep pink are displayed on arching canes. Then there is the light crimson *R. rugosa* which
will thrive even on the seashore where it is exposed to salt spray. Its flowers
are fragrant and its fruits highly decorative.

One could write on and on of roses whose merits warrant them a
place in our gardens. Pages could be filled about *Rosa rubrifolia,* with
distinguished-looking glaucous foliage with a reddish tint; the diminutive *R. Roulettii* and its relatives—**Oakington Ruby, Pixie,** etc.—which
blossom while they are still small enough to be covered by a teacup;
the cantankerous *R. Moyesii,* a species with single blood-red flowers,
introduced from China by E. H. Wilson, and many others. Also there
are some groups resulting from the work of hybridists which I have

failed to mention—the Scotch roses including the **Altai Rose** (*Rosa spinosissima*) and, by all means, the old-time **Harison's Yellow** with semi-double yellow flowers, and a tough constitution. Then there are the Moss roses, the Cabbage, Damask, and French roses; the Penzance Briers, Lambertiana, Pemberton roses, and so on—all of which are interesting to the rosarian. Limitations of space prevent their treatment here: I must refer those of my readers who wish to specialize in roses to one of the many admirable books concerned wholly with this wonderful genus.

PLATE XVIII. *(upper)* ROSE GARDEN—OPEN ROOF PAVILION. ROSE, VARIETY MAX GRAF ON TERRACE BANK. *(lower)* PERGOLA AND METAL ARCHES

(*upper left*) ROSE, VARIETY DORO
THY PERKINS

(*upper right*) BED OF HYBRID TE.
ROSES. POSTS AND CHAINS TO SUF
PORT "FESTOON" ROSES

(*left*) ROSE, VARIETY CLIMBING LO
ANGELES

PLATE XIX

XVI. ROCK AND WALL GARDENS

ROCK GARDENS

Since the beginning of the present century, considerable progress has been made in rock garden construction, so that today in this country, as well as in Europe where the art is most highly developed, rock gardens may be seen which are artistically designed and properly adapted to alpine and rock plant cultivation.

Theory of rock gardens. The ideal rock garden is one capable of supporting a healthy growth of alpine and rock plants which, incidentally, are among the most attractive of hardy subjects. In order to display them in an appropriate setting and to provide conditions of culture approximating those under which they grow in nature, a rock garden is essential.

Apart from their value in providing a picturesque natural setting, the rocks perform several utilitarian functions. They help to keep the ground cool, they aid in promoting the efficient drainage which is so necessary, they conduct moisture to the roots of the plants, and they prevent, in part, the loss of moisture by evaporation. The rocks give shade and shelter; also, they hold up the soil, making a variety of contours possible in the garden.

One of the difficulties in growing alpine plants under lowland conditions is the extreme length of the growing season compared with what they experience when growing wild. In the vicinity of New York the period between the last frost of spring and the first frost of autumn is about 210 days; whereas, in alpine regions the growing season is about half this length. As long ago as 1857 the late Dr. E. Regel, in a paper on the Swiss alpine flora and the culture of alpine plants, advanced the theory that alpine plants require a much poorer soil in cultivation than under natural conditions. The reason given is that when alpines are planted in poor soil it slows up their rate of growth and in a measure compensates for the long growing season they experience in the lowlands. Whether or not Dr. Regel's theory is tenable, it is generally agreed that an over-rich soil is not good for alpine and rock plants under cultivation. It is apt to stimulate their growth so that they no longer possess the characteristic compactness which is one of their charms. Their consequent lushness of growth in a rich soil makes them likely to "damp off" during hot, humid spells in summer, or to die from the effects of winter.

Types of rock gardens. The forms that rock gardens take are numerous and varied, ranging from the many-pocketed structure made solely for growing a large collection of alpine and rock plants, to the purely landscape feature, in which the plants are incidental decorative material. The ideal lies between these extremes, consisting of a garden in which the rocks are arranged naturalistically, yet so placed that a reasonably large collection of plants may be cultivated.

A type that is satisfactory when the general surroundings permit is made in the form of a winding ravine. Such a garden affords every conceivable aspect—a perfect situation when dealing with the more capricious alpines.

Then there is the mound type formed by building up above the surrounding level over a central core made up largely of drainage material. This kind of a garden, because it dries out quickly, is more likely to be satisfactory in sections which have abundant rainfall evenly distributed throughout the growing season.

Some rock gardens consist of a series of raised rocky beds from 1 to 3 feet high with winding walks between. They are excellent when the main object is a collection of plants.

A sloping bank may afford opportunity for an interesting rock garden. If judiciously handled a rock garden can, in some instances, be effectively used in place of the usual turf of a terrace slope.

Semi-formal types of rock garden (Fig. 42) are appropriate if the house is formal in architecture and the garden has to be placed near it. In such cases the garden may consist of raised beds supported by almost vertical stone walls in which soil and appropriate plants take the place of cement between the stones. (See WALL GARDENS, below.) Walks of flagstone of random sizes with rock plants in the crevices look well in a garden of this type.

When the garden supplements existing rocky outcrops, it is important to keep the new construction in harmony. These outcrops may appear ideal as a nucleus for a rock garden (and sometimes they really are), but appearances are deceptive and the soil pockets in the vicinity of the rocks are often too shallow for the welfare of the plants.

Fig. 42. Semi-formal rock garden

The type of rock garden one chooses should bear some relation to the surrounding grounds and architecture. If the house is formal in design and the rock garden must be near by, it is a mistake to attempt to reproduce wild mountain scenery. But when the house and grounds are informal, especially if the plot has sharp contours, the acceptable style is a rock garden that partly imitates and also partly idealizes nature.

If the environment is level, a rock garden that rises abruptly above it looks entirely out of place. Under such conditions, a planting of shrubs may serve as a partial screen and also as a background for the rock garden itself. Diversity of contour may be obtained by excavating a winding walk and using the soil thus obtained to provide height along the sides.

Site and aspect. As a general rule the rock garden should be in the open where it is not subjected to the drip from trees or to competition from their roots.

Preferably the subsoil should be porous to permit the rapid drainage of surplus moisture. Special provision must be made for alpines which thrive in boggy situations.

No matter what the aspect of the garden may be, some rock plants can be found that will thrive in it. But in order to provide the varied cultural conditions demanded by a large collection of plants, it is well to arrange many aspects. When the bulk of the collection is of alpine plants, the garden should face, in the main, north or northeast. Although many of our choicest alpines are exposed to blazing sunshine in their native haunts, they appreciate a little shade during the hottest part of the day when grown in lowland regions of the temperate zone. This shade can be provided by the conformation of the garden and by large individual rocks.

The kind of rock to use. To keep the garden from seeming incongruous in its setting, the stone available locally should be used as a general rule, even though it may not be ideal for the purpose. The use of imported rocks may result in a better-looking garden *per se,* but if they introduce a jarring note they are inadmissible. The use of alien material is allowable when it is possible to build and screen the rock garden in such a way that it is seen as a unit without relation to the surrounding topography.

Weather-worn limestone of irregular shapes is perhaps the most pleasing material for construction and the easiest to work with. But weathered rocks of almost any kind can be used provided they are angular and blocky in form, of a neutral color, and of pleasing appearance. Stratified rocks, when they are not too thin, permit the construction of picturesque effects in the way of ledges, cliffs, and bold promontories.

The kind of rock that is commonly known as "tufa" is excellent, because of its porosity, cavities, and lime content, for certain groups of rock plants. Other things being equal, rocks are preferred which are porous enough to absorb considerable moisture, but which do not crumble when exposed to the weather. Glacial boulders may be used if they are of varied sizes and not too spherical in outline (Fig. 43), but they should be used sparingly. The general idea in mind when making the garden with boulders should be the simulation of a boulder-strewn slope such as one might expect to find on a terminal moraine. The worst kind of rocks to work with are small spherical ones. If these are the only kind available it is better to give up the idea of a rock garden.

Only in exceptional cases should more than one kind of rock be

Fig. 43. Boulder rock garden

used. It has many times been said, and it is worth repeating, that a rock garden should *not* be a collection of geological specimens.

Water in the rock garden. Although water in the form of cascade, brook, or pool is not absolutely necessary, it does add movement, interest, and attractiveness. Furthermore, in its immediate vicinity it affords opportunity to provide special cultural conditions for certain groups of plants. It should not, however, be introduced unless it can be done convincingly and with a natural appearance. A "spring," from the city water main, gushing from the top of a hill does not look natural.

Preliminaries to rock-garden construction. The first of the preliminary steps in the building of the rock garden is to remove the topsoil from the entire area. Grading, provision of drainage, and preparation of the correct soil must all be completed before the rocks and plants can be put in place.

Grading. With the modifications described below, the topsoil which is removed from the site of the rock garden will be the principal medium in which the rock plants will be grown. Therefore, for convenience in handling later, part of the topsoil should be placed on the walk and part on the outskirts of the rock garden.

The subsoil should then be shaped to make its contours roughly conform to the configuration which the rock garden is to assume. If the garden is being built on sloping ground it will probably be desirable to dig into the bank at selected points, and use the excavated soil to heighten near-by areas to obtain more rugged effects.

When the site is level the best plan is to make a little valley by digging out the area where the walk is to be and use the excavated material to gain height on the sides. It is then usually necessary to provide one or more drains at the lowest points to carry off surface water; otherwise, after a rainstorm the walks may be flooded knee-deep.

Drainage. If the subsoil proves to be naturally gravelly and porous, no artificial drainage will be necessary, but if it is impervious to moisture, provision must be made at once to carry excess water quickly away from the roots of the alpines. This should be done even though drainage is not so important in most parts of this country as it is in rainy England.

A 12-inch layer of cinders underneath the rock garden soil works admirably. Those, if possible, which have been exposed to the weather for six months or more should be used so that injurious compounds have had a chance to leach out. If cinders are not available, brickbats, small rocks, or similar material can be substituted.

Soil. The nature of the climate has an important bearing on whether one should lean toward porosity or retentiveness in making up a soil mixture. In a rainy section extreme porosity is desirable, but in a region of long periods of drought, a more retentive soil is preferred. In either case, if the more capricious alpines are to be attempted, the soil surface should be mulched with stone chips or fine gravel. This prevents moisture from collecting around the crowns of the plants (a condition which is likely to prove fatal in wet climates) and conserves the soil moisture in regions that are dry.

The soil should not be rich. It should be porous enough to let excess water rapidly drain away, yet at the same time it should be capable of holding sufficient water to prevent the plants from suffering from drought. If the topsoil is a fairly good garden loam, a mixture of 3 parts loam, 2 parts crushed stone ($\frac{1}{8}$ to $\frac{3}{8}$ inches), 1 part sand, and 2 parts humus will achieve the right conditions. The humus may be leafmold, swamp muck that has been kept high and fairly dry for two years, or granulated peatmoss which has, if possible, been exposed to the weather for a year or two before being used. If the humus is acid it should be neutralized by the addition of lime, except for sections of the garden devoted to acid-soil plants. About $\frac{1}{2}$ pound of

ground limestone to a bushel of humus will be near the amount required. By using the above mixture as a base soil it is possible, by the
addition of crushed limestone, acid peat, or sand in special sections of
the rock garden, to provide the right soil conditions for lime, acid,
and sand-loving plants, respectively.

The importance of soil reaction in respect to acidity and alkalinity
probably has been overestimated. Among alpine and rock plants,
some, such as *Arenaria groenlandica, Empetrum nigrum* and *Loise-
leuria procumbens,* are definitely lime haters. On the other hand,
such species as *Campanula Zoysii, Daphne petraea,* **Edelweiss,** and
most species of *Dianthus,* delight in a limy soil. But most alpine and
rock plants are reasonably tolerant and will thrive in a neutral soil,
provided that it is porous.

Moraine, or scree. A moraine or "scree," in rock gardener's parlance,
consists of a bed of stones, 2 feet or more deep, with or without a
small proportion of soil and humus, watered either from above or
below. One type of moraine consists of a watertight basin 2 feet deep
and of any convenient length and breadth, filled with a mixture made
up of 5 parts crushed stone ($\frac{1}{2}$ inch and smaller), 1 part sand, and
1 part sifted leafmold. Water is supplied during the growing season
through a pipe at the upper end and the surplus is drawn off by an
outlet at the other end *1 foot below the surface.* Another outlet is
necessary at the bottom of the basin to drain off all water during the
winter. The theory back of this practice is that during the growing
season there is a constant supply of cool water running through the
rooting medium, thus supplying the moisture and cool root-run in
which high alpines take delight; while comparatively dry conditions
are provided during the winter when the plants are at rest.

Many growers prefer not to bother with sub-irrigation in the
moraine and rely on rainfall or occasional overhead watering. In the
rock garden of the Brooklyn Botanic Garden a moraine of this type,
with the "soil" mixture described above, has been fairly successful.
Such plants as *Dianthus sylvestris, Campanula speciosa, Silene acaulis,
Arenaria stricta, Geranium argenteum,* and some of the encrusted
saxifrages have taken very kindly to this treatment.

Almost indefinite changes can be made in the character of the stony
mixture. It may be of limestone, sandstone, or granite, with varying
proportions of sand and humus. An experimenter in Ireland, using
dozens of different mixtures, found that pure limestone chips, includ-

ing the dust just as it came from the crusher, gave best results; whereas a neighbor five miles distant found that limestone and soil (3 to 1) was the most satisfactory mixture.

In order to give an air of verisimilitude to the moraine it could be built on a slope and made narrow at the top, broadening out more or less fanwise toward the base. A few flattish rocks placed here and there will serve as stepping-stones and help to mitigate the gravel-walk-appearance that is otherwise inevitable.

Constructing the rock garden. Before starting the actual work of putting the rocks in place it is helpful to study natural rock arrangements, not necessarily with a view to finding something to copy, but to get into the spirit so that a garden may be made which will be in harmony with nature.

After the subsoil is shaped up and the drainage material placed, about three quarters of the prepared soil should be spread over the site, the remainder being reserved for filling behind and between the rocks as they are put in position. Try to provide soil 2 feet deep in the planting areas.

Except when the rocks are small, tools will be necessary as an aid in moving them. One of the most useful is a two-wheel truck, such as that used by longshoremen. With one of these, and two planks on which to run it, large rocks may be moved with ease. Crowbars to use as levers and some chunky blocks of wood to serve as fulcra (wood being lighter to handle than stones of similar size) are also necessary. Iron pipes from 2 to 4 inches in diameter and about 3 feet long, make suitable rollers should their use be required. When the construction is extensive and very large rocks are to be handled, the aid of a derrick may be necessary.

Starting from the lowest point, place each rock on its broadest base, making sure that the soil beneath it is packed firmly. Sometimes it will be desirable to dig out soil to make room for a rock and sometimes a rock may stand free, while the space behind it is filled from the soil held in reserve. In general, from one half to two thirds of the rock should be hidden by soil, though occasionally an especially well-shaped rock may be allowed to lie on the surface.

Where the slope is gentle the rocks should be used sparingly, to build wide, sloping shelves on which plants may be grown. Concentrate the rocks where the grade is steepest—in some places leaving little more than a crevice for the plants.

PLATE XX. (*upper*) SCENE IN A BOULDER ROCK GARDEN. (*lower*) WALL
GARDEN IN CALIFORNIA PLANTED WITH SUCCULENTS

PLATE XXI. *(upper) Saponaria ocymoides. (lower)* PERENNIAL CANDY-TUFT, *Iberis sempervirens*

FIG. 44. Right way to place rocks   FIG. 45. Wrong way to place rocks

The rocks should tilt toward the soil so that rain may be conducted to the roots of the plants. (See Figs. 44, 45.)

When stratified rocks are used, place them so that the stratification lines all lie in one plane. As a general rule the strata should be slightly off horizontal. If placed vertically and the rocks are of a crumbling nature the effects of weather may cause them to disintegrate more rapidly than is desirable. Of course, if neighboring rock formations exhibit vertical strata, the rock garden should be made to correspond.

If the rocks are too small to gain the desired height when used singly, it is sometimes possible by careful matching to place several rocks together to give the appearance, when planted, of a single fissured rock.

Walks. Turf, gravel, or flat stones may be used for walks in the rock garden. Turf walks, although they are pleasing in appearance and suggest alpine meadows, present a problem in upkeep owing to the difficulty of mowing in proximity to rocks. The invasion of the planting areas by grass stolons is also a disadvantage. Gravel walks are permissible in gardens where there is considerable traffic, provided their color harmonizes with the general surroundings; but for most rock gardens, flat rocks interplanted with dwarf carpeting plants are to be preferred. In small gardens where the traffic is light, these walks may take the form of irregular stepping-stones with plants between them. Ample underdrainage must be provided to prevent puddles from forming during rainy periods.

Planting. Rock plants may be set out in early fall or spring. In general, in an established rock garden, hardy early-blooming subjects should be planted in the fall. Most of the nurserymen specializing in rock garden plants grow a good proportion of their stock in pots, so it is possible to obtain material that may be planted at any time without checking growth.

When planting, pack the soil firmly about the roots, taking care to leave no air spaces. When crevices between rocks are to be planted it is better to do so as the work of construction proceeds, because it is a difficult and tedious task to spread out the roots properly and pack soil around them in existing crevices. A natural appearance should always be the aim. Avoid setting the plants in straight lines. As a general rule, all the plants of one variety should be grouped together, rather than to spot them all over the rock garden. It may be desirable to depart from this practice when seeking the proper cultural conditions for a species known to be difficult.

Although the alpine plant enthusiast, as a rule, pays little attention to grouping plants with reference to their color values, being quite content with a kaleidoscopic effect so long as his plants are healthy, those who find pleasure in harmonizing color schemes have plenty of opportunity in planting the rock garden.

General care of the rock garden. In the spring, as soon as the frost is out of the ground and the winter covering has been removed, it is necessary to look over the garden and restore to the earth any roots that have been heaved out by frost. It is also a good plan at this time to apply a half-inch mulch of equal parts of stone chips and leafmold. Prostrate plants such as mountain avens and *Daphne blagayana* seem to benefit greatly from a mulch of this kind worked among their stems.

It is important that the plants do not suffer from lack of moisture during the spring. A drought in May when they are actively growing may seriously injure them.

A careful watch must be kept at all times for weeds. As it is seldom possible to use a hoe, weeding in the rock garden is largely a matter of finger-and-thumb work, combined with a hand fork or small cultivator to help remove the stubborn weeds and to loosen the surface soil. In connection with weeding, it should be remembered that the most beautiful plant may become a weed if it is growing in the wrong place; therefore, keep a close watch on the more exuberant rock plants and restrain them if they show signs of overwhelming weaker, choicer material.

Watering. Most alpines and rock plants require abundant water when they are actively growing. Some authorities recommend sub-irrigation by means of perforated water pipes but they are expensive to install and quite likely to get out of order. The simplest way to water the rock garden is by means of sprinklers throwing a fine spray. These should be left in one position long enough to soak the ground thoroughly. Some plants, such as the silvery-leaved milfoils and some of the more difficult high alpines, are likely to suffer from too much overhead watering. These should be segregated where water can be supplied through a short length of porous drain tile, or even an ordinary flower pot, permanently sunk in the ground beside them. A promising method of applying water that may solve the problem of watering the rock garden as a whole, as well as those plants which object to excessive water on their leaves, is by means of portable, perforated, flexible lead pipes, or cloth hose, from which the water may drip or ooze upon the ground in the vicinity of the plants.

Winter protection. In sections of the country where the rock garden is covered with a thick layer of snow all winter there is no need to worry about winter protection. It is in those regions where frost and thaw alternate that protection is needed—not to keep the plants warm; but to keep the ground frozen, to shade the plants from late winter sunshine, and prevent them from starting into a premature growth which may suffer from late frosts.

The kind of covering used must be light and of such a nature that it will not mat down into a soggy mass as a result of exposure to rain. Evergreen boughs, such as fir or pine, are the best possible covering. Salt hay, or oak leaves covered with twiggy branches to hold them in place, may be used if evergreen branches are not available. In localities where considerable rain is experienced during the winter it may be necessary to protect such plants as the silvery-leaved milfoils and any woolly-leaved high alpines from overhead moisture by placing a pane of glass over them on suitable supports.

Winter covering should not be put on until the ground has frozen sufficiently to stop all growth for the season.

Where rock gardens may best be made. If we except high mountain regions, the places in North America where rock gardens are likely to be most successful are Oregon, Washington, and British Columbia. In these sections the alpine plants that are considered ideal for rock gardens can be grown without much trouble. But many rock gardens, furnished with a large proportion of alpine plants, are in existence in the eastern states from Philadelphia northward. There is considerable interest in rock gardening in many of the southern states, and in the high-lying sections there is no reason why at least some of the alpine plants should not be grown. In the Middle West, particularly in Ohio, where there is a successful Rock Garden Society, rock gardening is in great favor, and fair collections of the more tolerant alpines are grown.

The cultivation of most high alpines is certain to be attended with almost insuperable difficulties except in regions having a low summer temperature and a growing season of 140 days or less.

However, rock gardens can be made and furnished with other than normal rock garden material. If one is fortunate enough to possess a wooded rocky ravine on his property, it can be developed as a charming wild-flower rock garden by using our native woodland flowers.

In some of the northeastern states, the rocky outcrops which are common could often be converted into pleasing landscape features by a judicious planting of such subjects as dwarf junipers and cotoneasters.

In Bermuda, where picturesque rock formations are plentiful, subtropical rock gardens could be developed with little expenditure of time and effort by planting suitable material to drape and embellish the rocks.

Unfortunately, the human race is prone to want "what is not," and garden makers, instead of making full use of natural features, seem to prefer to blast out the rocks and make a lawn if they live in a rocky region, and to import rocks at great expense to make a rock garden if they live on a prairie!

In my opinion, rock gardens should not be made in rockless regions, especially if the climate is not suitable for the cultivation of alpine plants. But there are many parts of the country where picturesque rock formations abound, and these may be appropriately embellished with available plant material.

Plants for the rock garden. Enough has already been said to indicate that the plants preferred for the rock garden are alpines or others which exhibit a dwarf or compact habit of growth.

In general, species which thrive as well in flower border or shrubbery as they do in the rock garden should be used with reluctance and looked upon as mere fillers, tolerated only until more suitable material is obtainable.

Bedding plants, such as begonia, pelargonium, petunia, heliotrope, and lantana, are absolutely taboo. Use annuals sparingly, resolutely avoiding commonplace varieties such as portulaca and sweet alyssum. The chief use of annuals in the rock garden is to cover the bare ground left by the dying down of early spring bulbs.

Dwarf evergreens may be planted with discretion to give accent and to provide some variety in height. If properly chosen and placed, they look in keeping with the rest of the plants. Evergreens are occasionally of value to hide errors in construction.

The importance of choosing the plants for the rock garden carefully cannot be overemphasized. If the wrong material is used, the rock garden loses its air of distinction and becomes merely a flower garden in which there are rocks.

The following plants, except where noted, will grow without overmuch coddling in the soil mixture previously described.

Except where otherwise indicated, the plants should be grown in open sunny situations. Light shade during the hottest part of the day is desirable in regions having high temperatures, except for those kinds whose indicated preference is for hot, dry situations. Following the alphabetical list of perennials, selections of flowering bulbs, of dwarf trees and shrubs, and of annuals are given.

Those recommended for beginners are starred (*).

ALPHABETICAL LIST OF ROCK GARDEN PERENNIALS

ACHILLEA. The species mentioned here thrive best in sunny situations and rather poor stony soil. All have the characteristic flat-topped cluster of flower heads.

A. ageratifolia. Gray toothed foliage; the flowers, on 8-inch stems, more daisy-like than in some other species.

A. argentea. Silvery leaves and flowers as above on 4-inch stems.

* *A. tomentosa.* Makes a mat of green woolly leaves. Flowers yellow on 8-inch stems.

AETHIONEMA. Plants of this genus are somewhat related to the candytufts, but are generally finer and softer in texture. Aethionemas hybridize freely. Exceptionally good forms should be propagated by cuttings of young shoots in summer. As they tend to be short-lived under cultivation, a few should be propagated every year. They require a sunny spot and well-drained soil, mixed with crushed limestone.

A. coridifolium. Sometimes sold as *Iberis jucunda.* Blue-gray glaucous foliage smothered with dense rounded clusters of pink flowers; 4 inches high.

A. grandiflorum. Graceful bush, 12 inches high, with loose spikes of pink flowers.

A. pulchellum. Drooping and much branched. Flowers rose-pink on stems about 8 inches high.

ALCHEMILLA. * *A. alpina* is grown for its beautiful five-fingered foliage, which is shining green above and silvery with silken hairs below. The flowers are dowdy and should not be allowed to form.

ALYSSUM. Sheets of yellow bloom followed by persistent masses of grayish foliage are provided by the perennial alyssums.

* *A. alpestre.* A prostrate grower with hoary foliage and yellow flowers produced over a long period in spring.

A. argenteum. Grayish leaves and golden-yellow flowers on stems 18 inches high.

* *A. saxatile.* Myriads of showy yellow flowers surmounting hoary leaves. A sprawly plant about 1 foot high.

ANDROSACE. Here is a group of attractive little plants related to primulas. The high alpine androsaces such as *A. helvetica* and *A. imbricata* are difficult to grow in lowland climates of the temperate zone. Best results are likely to be obtained by giving them moraine treatment (limestone or granite according to preferences of the species), or by planting them in rock crevices which can be sub-irrigated during the growing season.

A. carnea. Forms tufts of green foliage and heads of pink flowers on 2- to 3-inch stems. The amount of humus and stone chips in the soil should be increased. Light shade during the hottest part of the day is desirable.

A. lanuginosa. Makes long trailing shoots with silvery leaves and umbels of rose-lilac flowers in succession in late summer. Splendid when seen draping dark-colored rocks.

* *A. sarmentosa.* Foliage in rosettes, plant spreading by runners similar to those of strawberry. Flowers in pink umbels on 6-inch stems. Does well in the moraine, but will grow also in normal rock garden soil.

ANEMONE. Many of the anemones grow naturally in woodlands, hence these types prefer part shade in the garden.

* *A. hupehensis.* Of comparatively recent introduction, looks like a smaller edition of the Japanese anemone, with reddish-mauve flowers in summer. Part shade is desirable.

A. Pulsatilla (Pulsatilla vulgaris). Large erect rich purple flowers with masses of golden stamens, on short stems in spring, each flower surrounded by a lacy ruff of gray-green hairy bracts. Achenes, with long feathery styles, prolong attractiveness after blossoms have fallen. More in keeping with rest of rock garden plants if grown in poor soil with plenty of crushed limestone; in rich soils, grows too lush. Prefers sun.

A. sylvestris. White flowers on 8-inch stems. Needs a cool moist shady spot and plenty of humus in the soil.

AQUILEGIA. The columbines below will all grow in full sun, but seem to prefer partial shade.

* *A. alpina.* Large flowers of deep clear blue with golden stamens on 18-inch stems.

* *A. caerulea.* Flowers of lavender-blue and white on 1- to 2-foot stems.

* *A. canadensis.* Cinnabar-red and yellow. Height from 1 to 2 feet or more, dependent on soil. Plant in poor rocky soil for best results; becomes coarse and weedy-looking in rich soil.

* *A. flabellata nana alba.* Quite dwarf—about 9 inches high. Flowers white; leaves glaucous.

ARABIS. The masses of white flowers of the commonly grown species (*A. albida*) are quite indispensable in the rock garden. Other species provide interesting variation.

* *A. albida.* Gray woolly leaves and 8-inch spikes of white flowers. Double-flowered form preferable, because of its long blooming period. Often sold under the name *A. alpina.*

A. aubrietioides. Grayish hairy leaves in close tufts, surmounted by 6-inch spikes of pink flowers. Not very permanent.

A. Kellereri. Mat of gray foliage closely hugging the ground. Small white flowers. Best in the moraine or in very gritty soil.

* *A procurrens.* Makes a carpet of shining evergreen foliage, with foot-high racemes of small white flowers.

ARENARIA. When well established, the white flowers of these small subjects stud the plants with bloom.

A. balearica. Will sometimes cover soil and rocks with a quarter-inch carpet of bright green, dotted in spring with pure white flowers on 2-inch stems. Needs a cool moist well-drained spot and porous rocks over which to spread. Although sometimes a troublesome weed in English rock gardens, it is difficult to establish here.

* *A. grandiflora.* A trailing species with grayish leaves, and large white flowers. (In England I have seen it rambling happily through the walls—brick, laid without mortar—of a coldframe.)

ASTER. * *A. alpinus* has daisy-like purple flowers on 8-inch stems. There are many forms including a white one which is not so good, and the variety known as *speciosus,* which is very good indeed.

AUBRIETA. This genus forms one of the standbys in European gardens. When exposed to the hot sun of American gardens the flowering period is considerably shortened. Good varieties are: **Gloriosa,** rose-pink; **Lavender Queen; Crimson King; Dr. Mules,** dark purple; and **Moerheimii,** with gray foliage and pale pink flowers. These varieties must be propagated by cuttings or by division to keep them true to type. Many American nurserymen raise aubrietias from seed and offer them under color only.

CAMPANULA. This favored genus contains a large number of species suitable for rock gardens. Space does not permit mention of the dozens of fine kinds available.

C. caespitosa. According to Farrer, should be called *C. Bellardi*. It is also known as *C. pusilla*. A variable plant with quivering bell-shaped flowers on slender 4-inch stems. Has a habit of flowering itself to death. Plant in moraine or very gritty soil.

* *C. carpatica.* A strong and "easy-to-grow" kind. Stems 1 foot long, tending to flop, may smother any choice plant in their vicinity. Many forms, ranging in color from white to deep blue.

C. excisa. Violet-blue narrow bell-shaped flowers. Grow in moraine or in gritty soil free from lime.

C. garganica. Has a central tuft of leaves and spreading prostrate branches. Flowers flat and starry, ranging from white to slaty blue.

* *C. Portenschlagiana.* One of the easiest of the dwarf campanulas, and grows 4 to 5 inches high. Flowers violet-blue.

CYMBALARIA. Among the cymbalarias—miniature snapdragon-like flowers more commonly known as linarias—are some low-growing and trailing plants of special charm in the rock garden.

* *C. (Linaria) aequitriloba.* A trailer resembling the Kenilworth ivy, but much smaller in all its parts. Called by Farrer "a Tiny Tim of extraordinary charm." Admirable for planting in crevices.

* *C. (Linaria) pilosa.* Makes a mat of soft hairy foliage. Flowers lilac, striped with purple on upper petals, with white and yellow centers, from June to September.

DIANTHUS. Almost any of the dwarf pinks look well in the rock garden. The commoner kinds should be prevented from seeding, for otherwise there is certain to be a crop of self-sown seedlings which are liable to crowd out choicer plants.

D. alpinus. Perhaps the best of all the mountain pinks. Forms a mat of glossy green foliage, surmounted by rose-pink flowers of the size of a 50-cent piece, on 3-inch stems. Needs ample drainage, with a liberal supply of limestone chips in the soil.

* *D. caesius,* **Cheddar Pink.** Bluish foliage and fringed pink flowers, delightfully fragrant.

* *D. deltoides,* **Maiden Pink.** Forms dense mats of green foliage covered with an abundance of small deep-pink blooms.

D. neglectus, **Glacier Pink.** Grassy tufts of foliage and pink flowers with a satiny buff reverse, on 5-inch stems. A good plant for the moraine.

DICENTRA. * *D. eximia* has fern-like foliage and racemes of rose-pink flowers all summer long. It is native of western New York and the mountains southward to Georgia. It will grow in full sun, but prefers shade.

DODECATHEON. *D. radicatum* is a shooting star from the West, which in May sends up a flower stalk of about 14 inches, surmounted by a cluster of pale lilac-rose flowers. It needs light shade, a moist situation, and loamy soil.

DOUGLASIA. *D. Vitaliana* (sometimes sold as *Androsace Vitaliana*) forms flat mats of narrow greenish-gray leaves which at blooming time are almost completely hidden by the clear citron-yellow flowers. It should receive moraine treatment.

DRABA. Well adapted for crevice planting, the drabas grow preferably in limestone.

D. aizoides. Dense tufts of spiny-looking rosettes, with yellow flowers on stems 2 to 3 inches high.

D. olympica. Similar, with golden-yellow flowers on stems 4 inches high.

DRYAS. *D. octopetala* is a prostrate shrub, its branches clothed with tiny evergreen oak-like leaves. The 8-petaled flowers are creamy-white, on 2- to 3-inch stems, somewhat resembling those of *Anemone sylvestris*. It should be top-dressed in spring with a half-and-half mixture of leafmold and stone chips.

EPILOBIUM. * *E. nummularifolium* is a carpeting plant ¼ inch high with tiny round bronzy leaves. The flowers are insignificant. It is valuable for covering the ground where spring-flowering bulbs are planted.

EPIMEDIUM. * Herbaceous relatives of the barberries, epimediums have clean-looking ornamental foliage and quaint flowers in May and June. They prefer a moist well-drained soil, in partial shade.

E. alpinum rubrum. Leaflets with reddish margins, and red flowers. About 1 foot high.

E. macranthum. Flowers with long white spurs, red outer sepals, and violet inner sepals borne on 9-inch stems. Variety *niveum* has pure white flowers; *roseum,* white flowers tinged with rose; *violaceum,* violet spurs.

E. pinnatum. Flowers bright yellow with short red spurs.

ERINUS. * *E. alpinus* is a tufted plant with 3- to 4-inch stems of rosy-purple flowers. It is a biennial or short-lived perennial. Plant it in partial shade, preferably in a crevice. There is a form with carmine flowers and one that is white.

GENISTA. * *G. sagittalis* is a dwarf shrub which makes a mat of trailing branches with erect, curiously winged twigs, surmounted by yellow pea-like blossoms. It needs a hot dry situation.

GENTIANA. This genus contains some of the most valued of alpine plants. The most desirable species are sometimes difficult of cultivation, while the dowdy, weedy kinds, as usual, will thrive anywhere.

G. acaulis. Now divided into five or more distinct species. The segregate known as *G. gentianella* most* amenable to cultivation. Requires a deep rich well-drained soil and abundance of crushed limestone. Flowers enormous, of true gentian blue, arising stemless from a tuft of deep green foliage 1 inch high. Blooms in May.

* *G. septemfida.* Many forms, all among the most tolerant of the worthwhile gentians. Grows happily in well-drained but rather moist soil, in sun or partial shade. In August produces clusters of flowers of soft clear blue on rather weak 8-inch stems.

GYPSOPHILA. Here are mentioned two suitable rock-garden relatives of the common baby's-breath.

G. cerastioides. A dwarf tufted plant 2 to 3 inches high with white flowers marked with purple lines. From the Himalayas.

* *G. repens.* A trailing species with gray-green foliage and airy sprays of small white or rose-tinted flowers.

HELIANTHEMUM. * *H. nummularium* (sometimes sold as *H. vulgare* and *H. chamaecistus*). There are many garden varieties offered under such names as *grandiflorum, cupreum, tomentosum, venustum, roseum, stamineum, macranthum,* etc., all of which are good rock-garden plants in sections where the winters are not too severe. Their hardiness is dubious north of Philadelphia.

HYPERICUM. The weedy St. Johnswort of roadsides has a number of handsome relatives for the garden.

H. polyphyllum. Makes a tuft of slender shoots 6 inches long clothed with small bluish-gray leaves and topped with golden flowers.

H. reptans. One of the loveliest of the hypericums. Makes a trailing mat of vivid green with large golden flowers in succession throughout the summer. It comes from Sikkim, and sometimes winter-kills in the vicinity of New York.

IBERIS. * *I. sempervirens,* **Perennial Candytuft,** is a sprawling evergreen shrub, showy when its white flowers are displayed in May. An admirable plant for draping over large rocks. It should be lightly sheared after blooming.

IRIS. The small irises are choice plants for the rock garden.

* *I. cristata.* A dwarf species with creeping rhizomes. Leaves are pale green, about 6 inches long. Flowers pale blue on 3- to 4-inch stems. Does best in partial shade. White form that is very desirable.

I. gracilipes. Forms a tuft of narrow curving leaves and pinkish-lavender flowers on graceful stems. Give it a gritty soil with lots of humus, and partial shade.

I. tectorum. Rather large for the small rock garden. Makes strong clumps of leaves with bright lilac flowers on 18-inch stems. Plant in well-drained soil, in sun.

LEONTOPODIUM. *L. alpinum,* **Edelweiss.** This easily grown plant is reputed to be responsible for many alpine tragedies, when climbers have lost their footing in the endeavor to pluck its flowers. Its bracts, which look like gray flannel, are said to become white when planted in a soil that is rich in lime. It will grow in any well-drained soil.

LINARIA. *L. alpina.* A lovely plant, only a few inches high, with delicate gray foliage and flowers of violet and orange throughout the summer. Planted in gritty soil, it may usually be relied upon to perpetuate itself by self-sown seeds. For other species of *Linaria,* see CYMBALARIA.

MENTHA. * *M. Requieni* is a tiny creeper which hugs the ground closely. The small orbicular leaves emit a delightful fragrance when bruised. The violet flowers produced in late June are almost microscopic. This is a good carpeting plant for a moist spot.

NIEREMBERGIA. * *N. rivularis* is a low-growing plant spreading by underground stems. The flowers, almost 2 inches in diameter, 2 to 3 inches high, white, with a yellow throat, are produced from June until the fall. Since it sometimes fails to survive the winter outdoors around New York, portions should be dug up and kept in the coldframe over winter.

PENTSTEMON. There are many species of *Pentstemon* suitable for rock-garden planting, only a few of which are mentioned here. In general they require gritty soil and object to moisture during the winter. Many of them are not long-lived under cultivation, and it is a good plan to propagate a few every year so as to have vigorous young plants coming along to replace those that succumb to the effects of winter.

P. glaber. Glaucous bluish leaves, and flower spikes 1 to 2 feet high with large bright blue or purplish flowers.

P. heterophyllus. Green leaves, lance-shaped and linear. Flowers opalescent pink and rose-purple on slender stems 2 feet or more high.

P. rupicolus. A dwarf creeping species 3 to 6 inches tall, from the Cascade Range. Small blue-green leathery leaves and comparatively large red flowers. Needs a gritty soil and shade during the hottest part of the day.

P. unilateralis. Glaucous bluish-green leaves, and flowering stems 2 feet high or more, with the blue flowers arranged mostly on one side.

PHLOX. The low-growing and floriferous phloxes make excellent rock-garden plants.

P. adsurgens. A westerner with prostrate stems and glossy leaves. Flowers large, varying from white to deep pink or a combination. Sharp drainage and partial shade essential.

* *P. amoena.* A low, spreading plant with rosy flowers on 6- to 8-inch stems in early spring.

* P. divaricata. Blue flowers in clusters on 12- to 18-inch stems. Variety *Laphamii* and **Perry's variety** have a longer blooming season. Should be grown in light shade in soil well supplied with humus.

P. Douglasii. Forms a small tuft of narrow pointed leaves, with lilac or white flowers. Not easy to grow. In wet regions a well-drained gritty soil and protection from moisture during winter probably desirable.

* P. stolonifera. Makes a trailing mat of light green foliage; spreads by reddish runners which root as they grow. Flowers purple, in loose sparse clusters on 6- to 12-inch stems. Partial shade desirable.

* P. subulata. A well-known and easily grown species, ordinarily with magenta flowers in early spring, the color in some forms rather overwhelming. Varieties *lilacina,* pale lilac; *alba,* white; and **Vivid,** salmon pink, are unobjectionable.

PHYTEUMA. This genus of curious flowers with petals usually united by their tips is related to the campanulas. Only a few species are in cultivation.

P. hemisphaericum. Tiny blue flowers in almost globular heads on 3- to 6-inch stems above tufts of grassy foliage.

P. Scheuchzeri. Heads of blue flowers on slender bare stems 1 foot high.

POLYGONUM. *P. affine* is a trailing species from the Himalayas with attractive evergreen foliage which assumes bronzy tints in the fall. The deep pink flowers are produced from August to October in dense spikes on 6-inch stems.

POTENTILLA. Some of the cinquefoils, with their abundantly produced flowers looking like small single roses are excellent rock plants.

* P. nepalensis. A species from the Himalayas growing about 2 feet high with rose-crimson flowers produced from July until fall. Variety *Willmottiae,* dwarfer.

* P. tridentata. An evergreen about 6 inches high with deep green leathery leaves and small white flowers in summer. Either sun or shade suitable.

* P. verna. Makes a dense mat of foliage, with golden flowers in early spring on stems 3 to 6 inches high. Needs a sunny dry situation and stony soil.

PRIMULA. One of the largest alpine genera, contains hundreds of species suitable for rock gardens, but unfortunately many of them are difficult under cultivation.

* P. Auricula. Thick mealy leaves and yellow flowers with a ring of meal in their throats. Plant in partial shade, and mix crushed limestone in the soil. A very variable species.

P. Bulleyana. A strong-growing species, with leaves like those of Cos lettuce and red-gold flowers in candelabra-like tiers on 2-foot stems in July. Needs a rich damp deep soil and light shade.

P. denticulata. Rosettes of strong foliage and rounded heads of soft lilac flowers on 10-inch stems in early spring. Damp well-drained soil in sun or light shade best.

P. frondosa. Crinkly leaves, gray with meal on the undersides. Pink flowers in loose heads on 3- to 4-inch stems. Prefers partial shade.

P. japonica. A "lettuce-leaved" type with tiers of flowers on 2-foot stems. The color varies from white through magenta to deep crimson, which is best. Will grow well in full sun if soil is really wet; otherwise should be planted in partial shade.

PULSATILLA, see ANEMONE.

RAMONDIA. The ramondias are among the choicest alpine plants. They should be planted in rock crevices facing north, in deep peaty soil, with the rosettes flat against the rocks so that no water may lodge in the centers of them.

R. Nathaliae. Rosettes of glossy green leaves, flowers lavender-blue with 4-lobed corolla.

R. pyrenaica. Rosettes of dull green, with many rufous hairs. Flowers purple, corolla of 5 lobes.

SAPONARIA. *S. ocymoides* is a trailing species with myriads of pink flowers, valuable for draping rocks in full sun. It needs a well-drained soil.

SAXIFRAGA. There are hundreds of species and varieties of *Saxifraga* suitable for rock gardens, and such species as *S. Hostii* and *S. Aizoon* run into scores of varieties and hybrids. With the increasing interest in rock gardening in America, and more knowledge concerning their culture in our varied climate, considerably more than the sixty or so varieties now offered by specialists may be expected to be listed in their catalogs.

S. Aizoon. A species with lime-encrusted leaves, its varieties offering white, pink-spotted, or yellowish flowers. Gritty soil on a north slope, or the shade of large rocks desirable.

S. apiculata. A hybrid of the Kabschia group. Forms a cushion made up of innumerable tiny rosettes of evergreen strap-shaped leaves. Flowers of primrose-yellow in loose heads on 3- to 4-inch stems. Shade during hottest part of day. Use moraine soil with one third humus and plenty of water in early spring.

S. cochlearis. One of the encrusted group, with rosettes of reflexed, silvery leaves, and 6- to 8-inch sprays of pure white blossoms. Plant on north side of large rock in deep soil mixed with crushed limestone.

S. decipiens. A variable species, with many garden hybrids. Flowers of the type white, the hybrids varying from white to crimson. One of the "mossy" saxifrages, hence requiring partial shade and a deep gritty soil with one third humus. Small stones should be laid on the soil about the plants to conserve moisture and coolness in the ground. Keep a stock of young plants coming along—propagating them by taking off rosettes in August and inserting them in sand and humus in a shaded coldframe.

* *S. Hostii.* When happy, forms cushions made up of rosettes of silvery encrusted leaves. Flowers white on 12- to 18-inch stems.

* *S. Macnabiana.* A hybrid between *S. Cotyledon* and *S. Hostii.* Makes a 12- to 18-inch panicle of white flowers, speckled with crimson dots. One of the easiest of this group to grow.

S. moschata. A dwarf spreading "mossie" with many varieties ranging in color from creamy-white to red.

S. oppositifolia. Makes prostrate mats of tiny foliage with flowers that, in many varieties, tend toward magenta in color. Needs cool conditions, a stony soil, and lots of water in spring. In the vicinity of New York, I have never been able to grow it beyond the seedling state.

SEDUM. Small succulent plants bearing numerous minute flowers. Many of the sedums are admirably adapted to rock-garden use.

* *S. acre.* Dwarf with fat bright green leaves and golden flowers. Should be used with discretion, as it is, potentially, a pernicious weed, because any portion of the plant that is broken off and left lying on the ground is likely to form a new colony.

* *S. album.* An evergreen ground-cover with tiny sausage-like leaves and pure white flowers in July.

* *S. dasyphyllum.* One of the most delightful sedums. Has compact clusters of almost globular blue-gray leaves on 2- to 3-inch stems. Loose heads of white or rose-tinted flowers in summer. Will thrive in a shallow soil.

* *S. reflexum.* Makes mats of narrow fleshy leaves, with 8-inch stems surmounted by heads of yellow flowers in July.

* *S. sarmentosum.* Too vigorous and invasive a grower for the small garden. Trailing shoots are clothed with fleshy green leaves; flowers yellow.

* *S. sexangulare.* Has stems 2 to 3 inches high densely clothed with narrow cylindrical leaves. Flowers yellow.

* *S. spurium.* A trailing evergreen with flat leaves and pinkish flowers. Variety *coccineum,* more deeply colored, preferable.

SEMPERVIVUM. Rosette-forming succulent plants of great variety, often with attractively colored leaves and long-stemmed clusters of flowers. Sempervivums grow well in crevices of rocks. According to Correvon, Dr. Jordan of Lyon, France, claimed to have in his garden 6,000 different forms of *Sempervivum!*

* *S. arachnoideum.* Small rosettes are covered with woolly strands; attractive at all times and especially so when displaying its starry red flowers on 6- to 8-inch stems. (The size attained by this and other species is determined largely by the character of the soil in which they are growing. In

poor stony soil the rosettes are small, but increase in size if planted in rich porous earth.)

* *S. calcareum.* Bluish-green rosettes 2 inches in diameter; each leaf tipped with reddish brown. Flowers light red on stems up to 1 foot. A distinctive species.

* *S. Fauconnetti.* A small edition of *S. arachnoideum,* but not so cobwebby. In poor soils the rosettes may be not more than ⅛ inch in diameter.

* *S. soboliferum.* Globular rosettes with numerous pill-like offsets, attached by short slender threads which break and allow the offsets to roll away and form new colonies.

SILENE. The species of *Silene* mentioned here are attractive both in foliage and flower.

S. acaulis. Forms dense cushions of tightly packed rosettes of tiny pointed leaves. Plant it in the moraine. (I have seen plants collected from the Italian Alps with the foliage almost completely hidden by the rose-pink flowers, but it is a shy bloomer under cultivation.)

* *S. alpestris.* Forms low dense masses of shining green foliage and myriads of pure white flowers on branching stems 6 inches high. A grand plant for sun or partial shade.

* *S. Schafta.* Makes leafy tufts with rose-pink flowers produced over a long period in late summer and early fall.

THYMUS. * *T. Serpyllum* is a useful fragrant ground-cover for sunny situations, especially in calcareous soils. The flowers vary in color from white to rosy-purple, in heads on erect stems a few inches high. A distinct form known as var. *lanuginosus* with gray woolly leaves is desirable, although it apparently never blooms.

TUNICA. * *T. Saxifraga* is a tufted plant with airy foliage on thin, wiry stems which are surmounted by tiny pink dianthus-like flowers. It is in bloom from May to November and is especially valuable in poor soils in hot dry situations.

VERONICA. A rock garden scarcely seems complete without several veronicas, the species of which are varied in stature but almost unfailingly attractive, with bluish flowers usually in dense spikes.

* *V. gentianoides.* A strong-growing kind with low leafy tufts of glossy green foliage and foot-high spires of large pale blue flowers. Does best in fairly good soil.

* *V. incana.* Silvery-gray leaves and 8- to 12-inch spikes of small violet-blue flowers. Worth growing for foliage alone. Needs a dryish well-drained soil.

* *V. pectinata.* Forms prostrate mats of hoary deeply-toothed leaves. Grows well in partial shade. Occurs in blue and rose-colored forms.

* *V. repens.* A creeper barely ¼ inch high, with small egg-shaped glossy

leaves. Flowers pale blue, almost white, arising just above the foliage. A delightful, tolerant plant which, however, prefers partial shade and moist soil.

* *V. spicata.* A variable species, in general appearance similar to *V. incana,* but with green leaves.

* *V. Teucrium.* A handsome lush-looking plant with profuse spikes of large, rich blue flowers. Grows rather too large (20 inches) for the small rock garden. A form commonly sold as *rupestris* (probably referable to *V. Teucrium dubia*), preferred for rock-garden planting, forming low mats with spikes of flowers 3 to 4 inches high, from white to rose or deep blue.

VIOLA. * *V. cornuta* is an alpine pansy of which there are many garden varieties. The flowers, of pale violet, are produced throughout the summer. The variety **Jersey Gem** has violet flowers, while **White Jersey Gem** is pure white. A rich well-drained soil and partial shade are preferred for these violas.

FLOWERING BULBS FOR THE ROCK GARDEN

Many of the smaller-growing bulbs and related types of plants which are difficult to accommodate in the flower border find ideal quarters in the rock garden, and may with propriety be used there. *Colchicum, Crocus, Erythronium,* and other genera contain alpine representatives. Following is a list of kinds which are not difficult to grow. (For details of their culture see Chapter XIV, FLOWERING BULBS.)

CHIONODOXA. *C. Luciliae* and *C. sardensis* are among the first flowers of spring. They are beautiful and easy to grow.

COLCHICUM. *C. autumnale* and *C. speciosum* are valuable for their fall blooms. The foliage, which appears in spring, is coarse and unattractive.

CROCUS, spring-flowering: *C. biflorus, C. chrysanthus, C. Sieberi, C. susianus, C. Tommasinianus;* autumn-flowering: *C. speciosus* and its varieties; *C. zonatus.* (Fall-blooming crocuses, which are valuable because they bloom when rock-garden flowers are scarce, should be planted as soon as the corms are obtainable in August or September.)

ERANTHIS. *E. hiemalis,* **Winter-aconite,** is one of the earliest spring flowers.

ERYTHRONIUM. These should be planted in the shade, in well-drained soil, rich in humus: *E. americanum, E. revolutum,* and *E. revolutum Johnsonii.*

FRITILLARIA. The curious, checkered, pendent flowers of *F. Meleagris* are interesting and beautiful.

GALANTHUS. *G. nivalis,* the **Common Snowdrop,** and G. *Elwesii,* the **Giant Snowdrop,** are valuable for giving early bloom in partially shaded places.

LEUCOJUM. *L. vernum,* **Spring Snowflake,** is a dainty flower for early bloom.

LILIUM. The small lilies such as *L. tenuifolium* may be used to advantage.

MUSCARI. Among the best forms of **Grape Hyacinth** are *M. botryoides, M. botryoides album,* and *Muscari* **Heavenly Blue.**

NARCISSUS. Good rock-garden plants in this genus include *N. Bulbocodium, N. cyclamineus, N. minor, N. minor minimus* (which grows only 2 inches high), and *N. triandrus* and varieties. Strong-growing varieties of narcissus should be used in the flower border or naturalized in woodland or grass.

SCILLA. *S. sibirica,* when planted in masses, provides sheets of deep blue color.

STERNBERGIA. *S. lutea* has bright yellow goblet-like flowers in September. It needs a well-drained sunny sheltered spot.

TULIPA. Most of the small wild tulips may be used in the rock garden. The following are desirable species: *T. Clusiana, T. dasystemon, T. Kauffmanniana, T. linifolia,* and *T. patens (persica).*

DWARF TREES AND SHRUBS FOR THE ROCK GARDEN

CONIFEROUS

Chamaecyparis obtusa compacta
Juniperus excelsa stricta (Upright.)
Juniperus horizontalis Douglasii (Trailing.)
Juniperus squamata Meyeri (Spreading.)
Picea glauca conica
Pinus Mugo
Thuja occidentalis Ellwangeriana
Thuja orientalis Sieboldii

BROADLEAF EVERGREEN

Arctostaphylos Uva-ursi (A trailer, 4 to 5 inches high, needing a coarse, sandy soil.)
Berberis verruculosa
Cotoneaster Dammeri
Daphne Cneorum
Erica carnea
Euonymus radicans minimus (A low sprawly climber.)
Hedera Helix conglomerata (A dwarf semi-upright form of English **ivy.)**
Pieris floribunda (Needs a peaty soil.)
Rhododendron ferrugineum (Needs a peaty soil.)
Vaccinium Vitis-idaea (Needs a peaty soil.)

DECIDUOUS

Cotoneaster adpressa
Cotoneaster horizontalis (For large rock gardens only.)
Rosa Roulettii

ANNUALS FOR THE ROCK GARDEN

Annuals should be used with restraint. Their chief value is for covering bare patches left by the dying down of spring-flowering bulbs. Suitable species include *Androsace lactiflora, Ionopsidium acaule, Linaria maroccana, Nemophila insignis, Sanvitalia procumbens, Sedum caeruleum,* and *Sedum hispanicum.*

WALL GARDENS

Wall gardens are sometimes made standing free so that there are two faces available for planting. I must confess that I have seldom seen in the United States a really convincing wall garden constructed on this principle. The most satisfactory wall gardens are those which serve as retaining walls with considerable bulk of soil in back of them.

Wall gardens can be constructed to advantage where it is desired to support the earth of a terrace. They may be used to replace steep banks of turf, which are an abomination because of the difficulty of mowing and maintaining the sod in good condition. Retaining walls may be part of a formal rock garden, and if made on different levels, as suggested in Fig. 42, they may form a striking feature of the garden landscape.

How to construct a wall garden. It is sometimes said that a concrete foundation extending to below the frost line is a necessity in dry-wall construction. But I know of a boulder wall five feet high which has stood without shifting for eighteen years. It was made without any foundation other than the bare ground. The nature of the soil has considerable bearing on whether or not elaborate foundations are necessary. If you have any doubts as to the ability of your soil to support a dry wall, it would be well to provide a foundation extending below the frost line. This may be done by digging a trench and filling it with stones packed firmly, or by making a concrete foundation.

Although earth-filled walls intended for the reception of plants may be constructed perpendicularly, it is better to make them with a batter —each successive rock being recessed slightly from the one below— because the plants will be better situated to benefit from rainfall (Fig. 46).

The thickness of the wall at the base should be related to the height in the proportion of about one to two. Taper the wall, as the top does not need to be as thick as the base. Use a good proportion of your bulkiest rocks in the first course and fill in behind and between them with good soil packed firmly. Before proceeding with the next course, have on hand some small splintery pieces of rocks to serve as wedges. They will prevent the weight of the upper rocks from squeezing the life out of the plants you are to insert, and will also aid in making the wall stable. Planting should proceed simultaneously with the building. By so doing, it is easier to spread out the roots and pack soil around them in the depths of the wall, where they

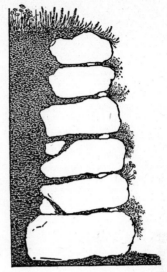

Fig. 46. Section through wall garden

are less likely to suffer from drought. Planting the crevices after the wall is finished is feasible, but it is an exasperating job productive of skinned knuckles, and when you are through you have the uneasy feeling that it has not been properly done, that you have broken many roots with your planting stick, and that you have left at least a few air pockets.

When spacing the plants, be careful to avoid planting a rampageous grower immediately above a choice but slow-growing "miff." In other words, don't plant *Cerastium tomentosum* near *Saxifraga longifolia,* or *Dianthus plumarius* immediately above *Geranium argenteum.*

Rock and alpine plants are occasionally used in England, planted in the copings of stone bridges, sometimes with highly successful results. I have seen one such planting in eastern North America that is fairly successful. When this type of wall gardening is attempted, "pockets" for the reception of soil should be left at intervals along the coping. These pockets should be at least a foot deep and have an outlet at the bottom to provide drainage.

A SELECTION OF PLANTS FOR THE WALL GARDEN

Achillea tomentosa
Ajuga reptans
Alyssum saxatile
Arabis albida
Arenaria montana
Artemisia glacialis
Campanula carpatica
Cerastium tomentosum
Cymbalaria muralis (*Linaria Cymbalaria*)
Dianthus, in variety
Erinus alpinus
Gypsophila repens
Helianthemum, in variety

Iberis saxatilis
Iberis sempervirens
Nepeta Mussini
Pentstemon, dwarf kinds
Phlox subulata
Saponaria ocymoides
Saxifraga longifolia
Saxifraga Macnabiana
Sedum, in variety
Sempervivum, in variety
Teucrium Chamaedrys
Thymus Serpyllum
Tunica Saxifraga
Veronica incana

XVII. WATER GARDENS

CONSTRUCTION OF POOLS

To many people the thought of water gardens conjures up visions of pools made of concrete or masonry, elaborately equipped with statuary and fountains; to others—a broad expanse of water with pondlilies floating on its surface and riparian plants at its margin. Another's fancy may turn to rippling brooks and shady pools with, of course, appropriate planting.

A water garden may be any of these—or it may be something even simpler. A successful pool for waterlilies may be contrived from washtubs which have outlived their usefulness in the laundry, by sinking them in the ground and disposing a few rocks picturesquely around their edges, placing 8 inches of good soil in the bottom and covering it with 1 inch of clean sand, then planting the lilies and filling the tubs with water. A few weeks later the result is charming.

Half barrels sunk in the ground serve a similar purpose. Two or more barrels grouped together with interplanted rocks around their edges make a delightful feature in the small garden. Or a battery of barrels may be grouped on a slope so that all are fed from the same source—a faucet which drips into the highest one. Connection between the tubs is made by half-inch lead pipes laid underground. Only a little water is required to replenish what is lost by evaporation and leakage. As a matter of fact, any considerable flow of water is undesirable, for waterlilies thrive best in a pool that is quiet and warm. Other aquatic plants, such as water hyacinth, will grow where the water is constantly flowing.

Making a concrete pool. It is not a difficult matter to construct a concrete pool (Fig. 47). To a cement mason it is, of course, just in the day's work; for the amateur who likes to putter around in old clothes and get some good exercise, it provides a fascinating diversion. The amateur mason perhaps had better not attempt a circular pool because the construction of the forms requires an experienced hand. But rectangular pools are comparatively simple except when a shelf

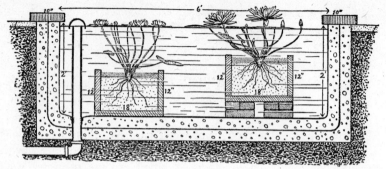

FIG. 47. Section through concrete pool. Tubs containing tropical lilies may
be raised as indicated.

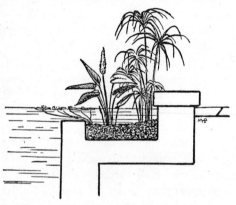

FIG. 48. Shelf for shallow-water plants

to accommodate waterside
plants is constructed (Fig.
48), but even this presents
no insuperable difficulties
to one who is fairly handy
with carpenter's tools.

*Excavation, forms, and
reinforcing.* First an excavation from 2 to 2½
feet deep should be made
to receive the forms. A
depth of 2 feet is sufficient
except where the water
will freeze more than 6
inches deep in winter; also it may suffice for small pools which can be
bridged with boards and covered with leaves or straw to keep the
water from freezing deeply.

When making the excavation, leave spaces free from heaps of soil
at each corner so that strings can be stretched to ensure alignment of
the forms (Fig. 50).

The thickness of the walls will depend on the size of the pool. In
small pools (about 6 x 9 feet), 6 inches is ample; for large pools (up
to 30 x 90 feet), the walls should be 1 foot thick at the bottom, taper-
ing to 9 inches at the top. The floor should be 6 inches thick.

Drive stakes of 2 x 4-inch lumber at 3-foot intervals along the lines
of the outside faces of the walls. These must be exactly in line and,

FIG. 49. Reinforcing rods set in excavation. Detail of fastening rods with wire.

if a large pool is being constructed, they should slope
inward toward the top; otherwise, they should be vertical.
Then nail 1 x 6-inch tongue-
and-groove boards of proper
length to the posts to make
the form for the outside of
the walls. Place ¼- or ½-inch
reinforcing rods about 18
inches apart to form a network on the bottom of the
pool, the rods being held off

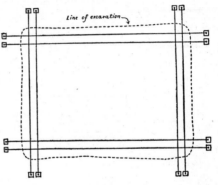

FIG. 50. Cords to align forms

the ground by bricks or rocks which are removed as the work of pouring the concrete proceeds. These rods are bent upward at right angles,
to reach almost to the top of the side walls. Hold them in place by
wiring them together at intervals (Fig. 49). The vertical rods in the
wall should be wired to two horizontal rods placed about 1 foot apart.
If more convenient heavy wire hog fencing may be used instead of
reinforcing rods.

It should be unnecessary to dwell on the importance of making the
tops of the forms absolutely level. The builder's skill, or lack of it,
will show up when the water is in the pool. The bottom of the pool
should slope slightly, but uniformly, to the drainage outlet at one
side or end. A fall of 6 inches in 100 feet is ample.

Outlet and overflow. The outlet should consist of a flanged and
threaded socket sunk ¼ inch below the level of the pool's bottom at

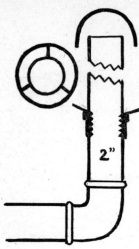

2"

FIG. 51. Overflow and drainage pipe

the lowest point. The socket is screwed to a pipe which passes through the concrete to an elbow joint which connects with a pipe leading to the sewer. This pipe must be trapped to prevent backing up of sewer gas. The fittings and pipe in the pool and concrete should be of brass.

Another brass pipe, long enough to reach to water level and large enough to take care of the overflow, is screwed vertically into the socket. It should be fitted with a brass strainer, or, better still, with a mushroom-shaped cover deep enough to extend ½ inch below water level (Fig. 51). Its diameter should be about 2 inches greater than that of the overflow pipe so that water may flow freely between its inside edge and the pipe. The object of these devices is to prevent leaves and other debris from entering the overflow pipe.

Mixing and pouring concrete. The concrete should be made up of 1 part fresh Portland cement, 2 parts sharp sand, and 3 parts half-inch crushed stone or gravel. Reject any bag of cement which has started to become lumpy, or trouble may develop later in the form of a leaky pool.

Spread the sand and gravel in layers on a mixing board or trough, place the cement on top, and mix thoroughly by shoveling before any water is added. Use enough water to make the mixture rather sloppy, and mix thoroughly with an ordinary garden draw-hoe, which is a valuable tool for this purpose. If a small pool is being constructed, it may be possible to shovel the concrete directly from the mixing board into the excavation, but on larger jobs a runway of planks for a wheelbarrow may be necessary. As the concrete is poured, work it in among the reinforcing rods with a hoe and true up the surface to conform with the desired slope. If at all possible, the entire floor should be poured at one operation. Before the concrete has set, the strip around the outside on which the side walls will rest should be scored with a wooden tool to make a rough surface. If it is proposed to apply a finishing coat of cement mortar (and this is a good practice), the whole surface should be roughened.

The next day the concrete will have set sufficiently to enable the form for the inside of the walls to be built on the concrete floor. All forms must be securely braced to prevent bulging when the concrete is poured, and this is particularly true of the form for the inside walls. A fairly tight joint is necessary between form and floor. Should there be any cracks, they may be filled with strips of wood cut to fit and wedged in place.

As the concrete is poured into the side-wall forms it should be thoroughly tamped with a stick or sidewalk cleaner (the tool used for clearing sidewalks of ice) to ensure that there are no air spaces. After the concrete has set, it should be kept wet for several days to prevent it from drying too quickly. This may be done by covering with straw, hay, or burlap sprinkled with water. It is advisable to finish off the interior of the pool with a plaster coat of cement mortar as insurance against leakage. If this is to be done, the inner forms should be removed and the mortar applied about twenty-four hours after pouring. Use 1 part cement and 2 parts sharp sand and apply the mortar with a plasterer's trowel after wetting the walls. Rounding the junction between the bottom and walls will facilitate the annual cleaning of the pool. The mortar may easily be shaped to a segment of a circle by using a half-gallon cider jug as a smoothing tool.

Pouring the concrete in one operation. The ideal way of constructing a pool is to make and install the forms so that all the concrete may be poured in one operation. This lessens the chances of leaks by eliminating the joint between old and new concrete. Setting up the forms so that both floor and walls can be constructed at the same time is a job which demands both skill and knowledge, and is best done by someone who is quite familiar with this kind of work.

Concrete pools without forms. Less expensive concrete pools may be made by excavating a depression of any desired shape with the sides sloping at an angle of about 45 degrees, reinforcing the bottom and sides with hog fencing which is kept off the ground with occasional bricks laid flat. The water line should be determined accurately, and marked, so that when the concrete is laid it may be carried to a uniform distance above it. The same type of overflow and drain pipes should be installed as in a pool made with forms. The concrete is mixed as previously described, but with less water, in order to obtain

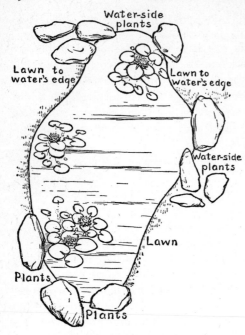

Fig. 52. Informal pool

a mix that will not run when placed on the sloping sides. Applied on both bottom and sides to a depth of 6 inches, the concrete is thoroughly tamped, then smoothed off with a mason's trowel. In the average climate such a pool, if carefully constructed, should be satisfactory, but I would not guarantee it in regions of severe winters.

Copings. There are various methods of finishing off the tops of the walls of concrete pools. If the pool is in a strictly formal setting, a coping of dressed stone may be used. If informal, the concrete may be masked by rocks of irregular shape and of various sizes, laid at intervals on the walls and here and there extending 2 or 3 feet into the surrounding ground (Fig. 52). These should be interplanted with waterside plants. (See the list on pp. 307-8.)

If the lawn is brought right down to the water's edge, the outside wall should be beveled so that the grass may grow up to the inside edge of the wall and the roots will still find sustenance (Fig. 53).

Clay-lined pools. Sometimes an informal pool which will be tight enough for all practical purposes can be made by lining a depression with clay. In such cases moist clay should be laid on the sides and walls to a thickness of

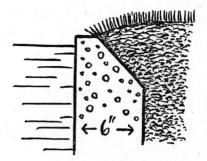

Fig. 53. Section showing bevelled top of wall

4 to 6 inches and thoroughly puddled by tamping or tramping. Usually, pools of this kind are formed by damming a little stream, and the overflow is taken care of by passing over the dam.

PLANTS FOR THE POOL AND ITS BORDERS

Among plants suitable for aquatic gardens, waterlilies, of course, will be the main standby for growing in the open water. Around the edge of the pool, those foliage and flowering plants which are especially suitable for wet situations will serve to form an attractive background and link the pool artistically with the rest of the grounds. Descriptions of appropriate plants—some of which may also be grown in the regular flower border—are given on pages 306-8.

Waterlilies. For garden purposes, waterlilies fall into two main groups: those which are hardy enough to remain out-of-doors throughout the year and the tropical kinds which will not survive frost. They require different handling in spring and fall, as described below. Sunshine is essential for all waterlilies.

Hardy varieties. Natural ponds and informal pools make a delightful setting for hardy waterlilies, though they are scarcely less effective when arranged in formal style. Several methods may be used in planting them.

Planting in natural pools. If the bottom of the pond is composed of good rich mud, no soil preparation is necessary. Simply tie a heavy piece of sod or a small rock to the waterlily rhizome or tuber and drop it into the water at the spot where you wish it to grow. The only precaution to be observed is to plant in water not over 3 feet deep, yet deep enough to prevent the roots from freezing. If there is no rich mud in the pool, at least a cubic foot of good soil should be provided to give the plants a start. This may be placed in a shallow wicker basket or fruit crate with the boards far enough apart to permit the roots to grow out between them. If the slats are too far apart to hold the soil, line the crate with a square of burlap. Plant the waterlily with the growing point barely below the surface of the soil, and slide plant, box, and soil into the water.

Planting in concrete pools. There are two methods of planting waterlilies in concrete pools, each of which has its advocates. One is to cover the bottom of the pool with 6 or 8 inches of soil, and the other is to place the soil in pots, tubs, or boxes. The first method is preferable for the welfare of the lilies, but in a large pool it has the serious drawback that, if it is necessary to wade into the pool to care for the lilies, the water becomes muddy. If a number of varieties are planted close together in a pool with a soil bottom they are almost certain to mix, sometimes to the detriment of the weaker varieties.

When conditions permit, prepare the waterlily soil a year in advance by making a compost heap of layers of a rather heavy loam and cow manure—two thirds soil and one third manure. If this is not possible, use heavily fertilized soil from the vegetable garden.

When the plants are grown in boxes, it is possible to exercise considerable control over their growth. By giving them a liberal root run, large plants are produced, while by restricting the roots, most varieties will be so reduced in size that they can be grown in a pool only 2 or 3 feet across. In general, however, the container should hold not less than 2 cubic feet of soil. The boxes may range in size from 18 x 18 x 10 inches for smaller varieties to 4 x 4 x 1 feet in the case of the strong-growing tropical kinds, or for large patches of the hardy types. (If one is ambitious to grow *Victoria regia,* the giant waterlily of the Amazon, which has leaves up to 6 feet in diameter, the box should be up to 8 x 8 x 1½ feet.)

For small boxes, the material used in construction may be cypress or pine boards 1 inch thick. For boxes 4 feet in diameter, it is better to use 1½- or 2-inch lumber. Such boxes will last indefinitely under water. Sometimes boxes of concrete are made when the pool is built to form an integral part of the pool, but once in place they can never be moved.

Hardy waterlilies may be planted at any time during the growing season, but are best set out early in April. Planting may be accomplished by draining enough water from the pool to expose the soil. Set the rhizomes or tubers in place with the growing point level with the surface. Cover the soil with an inch of clean sand, then refill the pool with water.

WINTERING HARDY WATERLILIES. The best, because it is the most natural, method of wintering the hardy waterlilies is to leave them and the water in the pool, taking precautions, however, to prevent the roots from freezing. Plants in large pools are not likely to freeze because they usually have sufficient depth of water over them. Small pools may be bridged with boards which are covered with hay, straw, leaves, or anything else which will keep out frost. Should fear be felt for the safety of the concrete if the water is left in the pool, it may be drained off, though I am not convinced that the concrete is any less liable to injury if this is done. If the lilies are grown where the winters are so severe that their roots will freeze, and it is not practicable to protect them by covering the pool, the water should be drawn off and the boxes of lilies packed closely together in one corner and covered 2 feet deep with leaves held in place by brushwood or wire netting. Care must be taken not to pile on the leaves so thickly that they start fermenting, or the results will be disastrous. While this method may protect the waterlilies, it does more harm to the boxes than five years under water undisturbed.

Tropical varieties. Greater size and fragrance and a color range which includes blue and purple are offered by the tropical waterlilies. They are highly prized subjects, therefore, in the aquatic garden, even though they require more care than the hardy sorts.

The soil and size of the boxes for planting recommended above for hardy waterlilies applies also to the tender varieties. It is the time and technique of planting which are different.

PLANTING. Not until the water is warm and settled hot weather is anticipated should tropical waterlilies be planted in the open. This is usually about mid-June in the vicinity of New York. Fill the boxes with soil, surface them with sand, and fill the pool with water several weeks before planting time so that the water may be warmed by the sun. Set out the plants by wading into the water and scooping a hole in the soil, with as little disturbance as possible, and inserting the lily previously removed from its 4- or 5-inch pot. Avoid burying the plants deeper than they were in the pots.

WINTERING. Carrying some varieties of tropical waterlilies over the winter is often quite a difficult matter, even when a greenhouse is available. Some kinds have viviparous leaves which produce young plantlets at the junction of leaf-blade and leaf-stalk. These young plants may be removed before cold weather comes in the fall, potted up, and stood in a sunny greenhouse in a tank with 3 inches of water over them. If a tank is not available, a 10- or 12-inch pot may be used. Make it water-tight by stopping up the drainage hole with a cork or rubber stopper, or by means of a layer of clay or cement mortar. Fill the pot up to within 3 inches of the rim with soil, set the plant in place and then fill the pot with water.

The varieties which produce tubers around the old crown may be carried over either with or without greenhouse facilities. When the old plants have been so injured by cold weather that they are no longer attractive, dig them up with as much soil adhering to their roots as it is convenient to carry. Stand them in a frost-proof room for a few weeks to ripen off. It is not necessary to water them. When the soil has dried out, conduct a search for tubers, which range in size from hazel-nuts to walnuts. If you are successful, place them in moist sand in a flower pot and cover with a pane of glass to keep mice out. In the spring, plant the tubers in 4- or 5-inch pots and stand them in a tank with 3 inches of water over them, placing the tank in a sunny spot with a temperature of 65 to 70 degrees. If this is not feasible, take a chance on planting the tubers in the pool toward the end of May.

If the variety does not produce tubers and there is no greenhouse in which the viviparous kinds can be cared for, the only procedure to follow is to obtain new plants in June from a specialist.

Pests of plants and pool. Waterlilies are not much bothered with enemies, fortunately, for the leaves are susceptible to injury from insecticides. The pool, however, is sometimes made unsightly by the growth of algae.

Insect pests. Aphids are sometimes bothersome. My favorite method of dealing with them is to knock them off into the pool with a strong spray of water from the hose. If fish are kept in the pool, as they should be to keep down mosquitoes, they will quickly gobble them.

Another pest is a leaf-miner (the larva of one of the midges—*Chirononus modestus*) which tunnels in the leaves, making marks which remind one of a Chinese laundry ticket. After struggling for years to control this "beast" by the use of insecticides, I finally hit upon a simple remedy, which consists of cutting off leaves showing signs of infestation as fast as they appear, and burning them at once. This may weaken the plants for a while, but they soon recover.

A pest which I have seen in other gardens, but which I have never had to combat, has a rather imposing name—*Hydrocampa proprialis.* The larva is quite a little navigator, for he cuts two pieces of leaf and attaches himself to them and goes floating off to pastures new. When he is feeding on a leaf, the little structure which he makes serves as a tent. Hand-picking from the leaves and scooping up the hardy mariners with a fish net and burning them aid in controlling this insect. It also has been recommended to place in the vicinity of the pool a pan of water with a film of kerosene on the surface. A lantern placed over the pan will attract the adult insects, which will flutter around and fall to their death in the kerosene-covered water.

Algae. When the growth of algae renders the pool greenish and foul-looking, possess your soul in patience for a while, if you can, and the water will probably clear up by itself. But if you cannot wait, prepare a saturated solution by stirring 2 to 3 teaspoonfuls of potassium permanganate in a gallon of water. Use 1 teaspoonful of the solution to each gallon of water in the tub or pool; or 1 gallon to 768 gallons. Only the youngest of baby fish will suffer, and the older fish don't seem to mind it at all. This is recommended by the Missouri Botanical Garden. Copper sulphate gives a more lasting effect, but may be considered too toxic for safe use by the amateur gardener. To determine the number of gallons of water in the pool, multiply the length by the breadth by the depth of water and convert the answer to cubic feet. Then multiply the answer by 7½ (the number of gallons in a cubic foot) and if you have figured correctly (something I can seldom do), you have the number of gallons of water in a pool. To get the cubical contents of a circular pool, multiply the square of the diameter by .7854, by the depth of the water.

Selection of waterlilies. The catalog of a waterlily specialist may prove confusing to a beginner because there are so many varieties from which to choose. Names of about 30 good varieties are given below.

For tub culture and very small pools, I would recommend the following small-growing, hardy varieties; *N. odorata minor,* white; **Joanne Pring,** a hybrid, pink; *N. tetragona,* white; *N. tetragona helvola,* yellow, believed to be a hybrid; and **Aurora,** which has flowers of several tones—first they are yellow tinged with red, then red-orange, becoming red the third day.

For pools of moderate and large size, the following are excellent: **Marliac White** and **Gladstone,** white; **Formosa, Morning Glory,** and **Pink Opal,** pink; **Attraction, Conqueror,** and **James Brydon,** red. Two-toned kinds are **Comanche,** apricot to red with orange stamens; **Sioux,** coppery-yellow to red; and **Paul Hariot,** yellow, changing to pinkish-orange to almost red. **Chromatella** is, I think, the best of the pure yellow varieties; **Sunrise,** also yellow, has larger flowers which open early in the season but they are not so freely produced.

The tropical waterlilies fall into two distinct groups—the day bloomers and the night bloomers. The day-blooming kinds are open from early morning till late afternoon, while the night bloomers open around 6 or 7

P.M. and remain open until about noon of the following day. The best time, therefore, to view a pool containing both groups is in the morning.

My favorite among the day-blooming tropical lilies is **Mrs. Edwards Whittaker,** which will produce abundant flowers nearly 1 foot in diameter, of lavender-blue, which pales as the flower ages; its variety **Marmorata** has leaves mottled with coppery-bronze. **Blue Beauty** has flowers of deeper blue. **General Pershing** is about the best of the pink forms; with **Mrs. C. W. Ward,** whose flowers are held high above the water, a close second. The new variety, **St. Louis,** brings the long-desired yellow coloration into the tropical lily pool, while **Mrs. G. H. Pring** is the best of the white-flowered day bloomers. **Peach Blow** is pink with a yellowish center; **Rio Rita** is deep pink; and **Sunbeam** is yellow.

If I were restricted to a half-dozen of the night-blooming kinds, I should select **Missouri,** a superb white; **Mrs. George C. Hitchcock,** deep rose-pink; **Emily Grant Hutchings,** amaranth-pink with large cup-shaped flowers; **Frank Trelease,** deep crimson; and **H. C. Haarstick,** rich red, bronze foliage.

Other aquatic plants. Besides the waterlilies, there are a number of other plants, some with attractive flowers, which either float on the surface or send their leaves and stalks of bloom above the water. Submerged aquatics may also be used in the pool if desired, though they add little if anything to its beauty.

In the lists of these other aquatics given below, the common names of the plants are given in alphabetical order, instead of the scientific names, as in other parts of the book, because the common names of these plants are usually more familiar to the average gardener. The scientific name follows the common name of each subject.

Shallow-water plants. There are several plants with more or less floating leaves which prefer to be planted in soil with only a few inches of water over it. These can be accommodated to perfection if the pool is provided with the shelf-like extension indicated in Fig. 48.

Floating Heart, *Nymphoides peltatum,* is one of the most vigorous in this group. It has small heart-shaped leaves and produces abundant, brilliant yellow, fringed flowers a little over an inch across. If planted in a shallow pond, this plant is capable quickly of taking complete possession of it, so it needs to be closely watched, and restrained if necessary.

Forget-me-not, *Myosotis scorpioides,* is a water-loving species whose dainty blue flowers are useful for pool decoration and for small flower arrangements when cut.

Parrot Feather, *Myriophyllum prosperpinacoides,* is grown only for its feathery, soft-green foliage, which is produced on trailing stems. That

PLATE XXII

TROPICAL WATERLILY,
VARIETY DAUBEN

HARDY WATERLILY,
VARIETY FORMOSA

JAPANESE IRISES

PLATE XXIII. *(upper)* WINDOW BOX PLANTED WITH WALLFLOWERS, *Cheiranthus.* *(lower)* PORCH BOX PLANTED WITH GERANIUMS, NASTURTIUMS, VINCA, WANDERING JEW

pestiferous insect known as the white fly is particularly partial to this plant.

Primrose Creeper, *Jussiaea repens,* is a sort of water vine which makes long trailing partially submerged streamers. It is related to the evening-primrose and produces a profusion of bright yellow flowers. It has to be carried over winter in the greenhouse.

Water-hyacinth, *Eichhornia crassipes,* is a great pest in some southern rivers where its growth is so rampant as to impede navigation. In the water garden its spikes of large lavender flowers are decidedly attractive. It floats by means of the swollen bases of its leaf-stalks, which are filled with air chambers. It may be grown in shallow water with its roots anchored in the mud or it may be left to float free in the water. It is killed by frost.

Water Snowflake, *Nymphoides indicum,* has detachable floating leaves which, if placed in shallow water, send down roots into the mud below. Like its relative, the floating heart, it has curiously fringed flowers which, however, are white. Not winter-hardy.

Floating plants. Though commonly recommended for water-garden culture, my reaction to floating plants is that, however beautiful and interesting they may be, they are messy-looking when floating free on the surface of the lily pool. Such plants as **Water-hyacinth** (above); **Water-lettuce,** *Pistia stratiotes;* and **Water Fern,** *Ceratopteris pteridoides,* may be confined in anchored wooden hoops. But such subjects as **Mosquito Fern,** *Azolla caroliniana;* **Duckweed,** *Lemna minor;* and **Salvinia,** *S. brasiliensis,* cannot be controlled by this means, for the first wind that comes along washes them out of confinement. I, for one, would never allow these plants in a lily pool. In a small tub where they are under control they are interesting and sometimes beautiful.

Submerged aquatics. In glass-sided aquaria where their beauty may be seen, submerged aquatics are excellent, but I have never been able to see the propriety of planting them in an outdoor pool. It is claimed that they absorb impurities and help to keep the water clear, but on this point I am somewhat skeptical. Those who insist on submerged aquatics will find the following vigorous if anchored in the mud at the bottom of a shallow pool: **Anacharis,** *Elodea canadensis;* **Fanwort,** *Cabomba caroliniana,* hardy north to Philadelphia if its roots are kept from freezing; and **Tape-grass** or **Eel-grass,** *Vallisneria spiralis.*

Tall-growing aquatics. Although the waterlilies will always be pre-eminent, there are other plants well adapted for growing in 6 inches to 1 foot of water. The first of these is the **East Indian Lotus,** *Nelumbo nucifera.* While not always successful as a tub plant, once it is established in a natural pond, its superabundant growth may become embarrassing. In the planting at the Brooklyn Botanic Garden, it was the custom to mow the outskirts periodically with a scythe to keep it from overrunning the lake completely. The importation of muskrats would quickly result in cleaning out a plantation should it become too obstreperous, for they are fond of its tubers.

The leaves of *Nelumbo,* which are like nasturtium leaves 2 feet in diameter, either float on the surface or stand from 2 to 5 feet above. The habit of holding its leaves high when grown in shallow water makes this lotus valuable in large pools where it can be made to thrive, because its height breaks the flatness of the view. The long banana-like tubers should be planted horizontally 2 inches below the soil in 6 inches or more of water, after the water has become warm. The clear pink flowers are fragrant, and the curious "pepper-pot" seed pods when mature may be used in winter bouquets.

Other erect plants which may be planted in shallow water include **Papyrus,** *Cyperus Papyrus,* which under favorable circumstances may grow 8 feet tall, with graceful tufts of long thread-like leaves at the top of the stalks; and the **Umbrella-plant,** *Cyperus alternifolius,* which grows 2 to 3 feet high with narrow shining leaves disposed like the ribs of an umbrella at the apex of each stem. Neither of these will survive the winter outdoors in the vicinity of New York City.

Waterside plants. Giving a naturalistic setting to the pool, plants which like moist situations for their roots may be grown at the water's edge. Supplementing the tender subjects in the pool itself, the **Garland-flower,** *Hedychium coronarium,* and several taro-like plants which are species of *Colocasia* (popularly called *Caladium*) may be used effectively. These plants produce fleshy rhizomes or tubers which may be carried over winter in a frost-proof cellar, storing them much the same way that one handles dahlias.

Among hardy plants for waterside culture are many beautiful flowering subjects, a dozen or so of which are described below. The first half of the list consists of plants which may or should be planted in mud; the others will grow near the water in any good garden soil. The list is by no means exhaustive, but will give the novice gardener a fair beginning for an attractive planting around a pool. Here, as above in the list of true aquatics, the plants are listed by their common names, the botanical designation following.

Arrowhead, *Sagittaria.* Some of the arrowheads have rather attractive white flowers and leaves which are decorative when not distorted by insect attacks. 1 to 2 feet.

Cardinal-flower, *Lobelia cardinalis,* grows sometimes with greater success in the ordinary moist soil of the perennial border, but it is also an ideal waterside plant, 2 to 3 feet high, bearing spires of purest red flowers in late summer and fall.

Cat-tails, *Typha latifolia* and *T. angustifolia,* have decorative value, but if not carefully watched and restricted, may easily get out of bounds. The better one to use is *T. angustifolia.* 4 to 6 feet.

Flowering-rush, *Butomus umbellatus,* has sedge-like leaves and umbels of pink flowers. I have a theory that it grows best in calcareous soils. 2 to 3 feet.

Iris. There are several groups of iris suitable for planting in the vicinity of water. The **Japanese Iris,** of which there are scores of desirable varieties, will thrive in shallow water, in wet ground, or in the soil of the perennial border. Good varieties are listed on p. 180.

The many garden varieties of the **Siberian Iris** (*Iris sibirica*) are delightful waterside plants with graceful, narrow foliage, and flowers which range from white to deep blue. Good varieties are listed on p. 180.

The **Blue Flag,** *Iris versicolor,* a native, is suitable for naturalistic waterside plantings. A good companion for it is **Yellow Flag,** *Iris pseudacorus,* an emigrant from Europe which has become naturalized in parts of New York and other northeastern states. Unless restricted, it is likely to become a nuisance, for it spreads freely by means of self-sown seeds. The seed pods should be cut off before they are mature. 2 to 3 feet.

Marsh Marigold, *Caltha palustris,* or, as they call it in England, **King Cup,** is a sort of glorified buttercup, handsome in early spring, with large shining roundish leaves and brilliant yellow flowers. The double-flowered variety is especially good. 1 foot.

Sweet-flag, *Acorus Calamus,* has no conspicuous flowers to commend it, but the foliage is attractive and fragrant. It is said that this is the "rush" used as floor covering in medieval times.

Water-plantain, *Alisma Plantago-aquatica,* reminds one of baby's breath when it displays its airy panicles of tiny white flowers. It will grow in partial shade if need be. 1½ to 2½ feet.

Other plants which are adapted to waterside planting, but which do not have to be planted in mud, include:

Hardy Asters, particularly varieties of the **New England Aster,** *Aster novae-angliae.* These are good for use in the vicinity of semi-natural pools. Good varieties are **Harrington's Pink,** 4 to 5 feet; and **Mt. Rainier,** with white flowers, 3 to 4 feet.

Astilbe, *Astilbe japonica* varieties, are much used by florists as forced plants for the Easter trade, but they are quite hardy. They produce feathery spikes of tiny white or pink flowers, closely resembling spireas. Good varieties are **Gloria,** deep pink, and **Queen Alexandra,** pink. About 2 feet high.

Creeping Charlie, *Lysimachia Nummularia,* is a prostrate ground-cover with good foliage, and yellow flowers produced from June to August.

Eulalia, *Miscanthus sinensis,* comprises a group of ornamental grasses of which there are many horticultural varieties. **Zebra Grass** has leaves barred with yellow; **Maiden Grass** forms graceful and elegant tufts; another variety is marked with white stripes. 3 to 5 feet.

Loosestrife, *Lythrum Salicaria,* provides a striking display of reddish-purple flowers. Originally a garden plant, it has escaped and run wild over swampy areas in New York State, thriving in abundance. Great variation exists in color and size of the flowers, and in looking over a wild patch it is possible to pick out many good forms which would serve well again for garden display. These should be dug up and propagated by division of the rootstock. 2 to 3 feet.

Meadowsweet, *Filipendula,* is another spirea-like plant. *F. hexapetala* has white flowers in loose flat-topped heads. There is a double-flowered form. 1 to 3 feet. A form of *F. rubra* sold by nurserymen as *F. venusta* has deep pink flowers in large panicles. 4 to 5 feet.

Rosemallow, *Hibiscus Moscheutos,* is a native plant which has been taken in hand by the hybridizers, who have produced improved forms with flowers 6 or 8 inches in diameter, ranging in color from white to crimson. These are produced on bushy plants with bold foliage. Rosemallows are late in starting into growth in the spring. 4 to 6 feet.

Royal Fern, *Osmunda regalis,* is capable of growing up to 10 feet when in a specially favored location. Its graceful fronds are very decorative. This and other ferns should play a large part in waterside plantings. Other desirable kinds are: **Cinnamon Fern,** *Osmunda cinnamomea;* **Hay-scented Fern,** *Dennstaedtia punctilobula;* **Interrupted Fern,** *Osmunda claytoniana;* **Lady Fern,** *Athyrium filix-femina;* **Maidenhair Fern,** *Adiantum pedatum;* and **Ostrich Fern,** *Pteretis nodulosa.* (See Chapter XX, section on FERNS.)

XVIII. THE CITY GARDEN

A really beautiful or flourishing city garden is seldom to be seen. It may be true that urban dwellers do not have a flair for handling living plants, but lack of design, poor soil preparation, and the use of unsuitable plant material are chiefly responsible for failure of gardens in crowded cities.

Good-looking and healthy gardens can be maintained on city properties if they receive a fair amount of sunshine. But it must be admitted that city gardeners face severe handicaps. Too often their garden is designed by an unimaginative building contractor. Enclosed by a board or picket fence, it consists of a rectangular plot of grass, surrounded by a concrete walk, which in turn is bounded by a flower border about 18 inches wide. Usually clothes-poles stand at each corner of the grass plot. Such a "design" (Fig. 54) positively prohibits a beautiful garden if left as it is; and it makes the area, already too small, appear smaller than it is. The only merits of this type of garden are the facilities it offers for hanging out the weekly wash.

First steps in improving the city garden. The first thing for the garden lover to do with a yard of this type is to remove the clothes-poles, saw them into firewood, and invest in one of those whirligig contraptions for clothes-drying which can be stored out of sight when not in use. An iron pipe may be driven into the ground to serve as a socket for the post of the drying-rack. A still better plan from the garden lover's point of view would be to send all the laundry out, so that the yard could be free every day of the week. Next, get rid of the concrete walks, and thus make the yard appear considerably larger. The disposal of the concrete may be a problem, and it may be necessary to pay to have it hauled away. In a pinch, some of the blocks might be broken up into pieces approximately 2 feet square and laid to simulate a walk of broken flagstones in the new design. As a general rule, substitutes should not be used for flagstones, but sometimes circumstances permit presentable-looking makeshifts.

If the yard is enclosed by a hideous high board fence, it would be

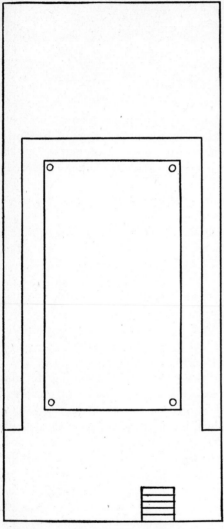

FIG. 54. Plan of typical city backyard

worth while to consider removing it and replacing it with a picket fence, which will have a more pleasing appearance and admit more sun and air.

A design suggested. A simple method of improving the appearance of a plot of this kind is suggested in Fig. 55. The walk is on the axis of the steps from the house to the garden and leads to a seat situated under an arbor. It passes along the flower border, giving easy access to the flowers, and from it the shrubbery on the opposite side of the garden may be viewed. If irregular flagstones are used, they are laid with crevices between, in which may be planted such dwarfs as creeping thyme and arenaria. (See PAVEMENT PLANTING, p. 510.)

Bricks are also appropriate for a walk, and are especially attractive when they become mellowed by weather and traffic. They should be laid with sand between them; then, when mosses make their appearance, the walk becomes really beautiful.

A gravel walk is satisfactory if laid on a well-drained foundation and if it contains sufficient binding material to hold stones on the surface. Loose stones are abominable to walk upon and injurious to the lawn mower when they are kicked upon the grass. (See Chapter III, WALKS.)

The grass plot promotes a feeling of restfulness and serves as a setting for the planting of shrubs on the west side of the garden. In its early stages, while there is room to spare, the shrub border may be enlivened in spring with groups of flowering bulbs, planted there the previous fall. Although the number of shrubs that will thrive under city conditions is limited, there are enough from which to choose to avoid monotony in their outlines.

The tree shown at the rear of the plot creates a point of interest. A flowering tree might well be chosen. Among small varieties that are adaptable to city conditions are Paul's scarlet haw-

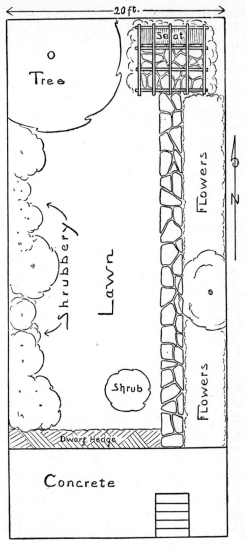

FIG. 55. A suggestion for improving Fig. 54

thorn, Japanese cherry, flowering crab-apple, and the pagoda-tree. If the aspect of the lot were reversed, a somewhat larger tree might be planted for shade. A catalpa graces my own disreputable yard, and although this tree has many failings it also has many good points to recommend it. It appeals to me because it is late in coming into leaf and it sheds early, thus allowing sunshine to enter the yard at a time when it is most needed. Its luxuriant leafage gives dense shade during the summer, and it can be trimmed to a high head to allow air circulation beneath its branches. The fallen leaves disintegrate quickly, so that their disposal is no great problem. When young it is a luxuriant, handsome tree—particularly attractive when displaying its large showy flowers. Its chief faults are that it is comparatively short-lived and its smaller branches are brittle and liable to breakage during summer storms.

To return to the plan—the arbor east of the tree balances the composition and provides a point of interest at the termination of the walk. A seat, a sundial, or a bird bath (for the benefit of English sparrows!) would serve a similar purpose in the design. If the situation is open, a small rock garden might be substituted, and a waterlily pool could be installed west of it and a little to the south. There are many clever garden designers who snort derisively at the idea of a rock garden in a city garden. But if made with restraint, as it should be, and with no attempt to reproduce mountain scenery, a city rock garden need not be inappropriate.

If the feature decided upon for the northeast corner lacks sufficient height and mass to balance the tree opposite, something must be done to eliminate the lop-sided appearance of the garden. Either a specimen shrub may be substituted for the tree, or another tree may be placed about half way along the east border. This will reduce the amount of space available for flowers but will give the desired balance to the composition.

Soil treatment and humus supply. The soil problems of the city gardener differ somewhat from those of the man in the country, because the soil of the city garden is likely to consist solely of that which was dug out when excavating for the cellar. Remembering that city conditions in general are far from favorable for the growth of plants, it is important to do all we can to improve this soil.

In crowded cities where adjoining houses are set wall to wall, there is often no access to the yard except through the house, and someone is likely to object vociferously to the carrying of stable or barnyard manure through the hallway to the garden. Substitution of the existing topsoil with real soil brought from the country presents the same objection; so the problem is to improve the physical texture of the soil by the addition of humus and to supply plant food without being execrated by the family or neighbors.

The humus supply should preferably come from decayed stable or barnyard manure, but if manure is ruled out, other sources for humus must be investigated.

Peatmoss. Most convenient is peatmoss in bales because it is tightly compressed into a compact package. When it is opened and broken up and the peat has absorbed some moisture, the bulk of one bale increases to twenty or more bushels, which is almost sufficient for the ordinary back yard. If the soil is sandy, however, or composed mostly of coal ashes, double this quantity could be worked in profitably during the initial preparation of the soil. Many brands of peatmoss, peat, and humus are on the market. The kind that is cheapest and most convenient to buy in the locality is usually the best to use. Many of these humus-forming products are quite acid. If the soil is already acid, therefore, the peat should be neutralized by the addition of lime before mixing it with the soil—except when rhododendrons and other acid-loving plants are grown. About ½ pound of ground limestone, or a smaller quantity of hydrated lime, may be expected to neutralize a bushel of the peatmoss commonly imported from Europe.

Tree leaves and garden refuse. Another source of humus supply— especially for subsequent use—is the leaves of street trees. It is a good plan to provide a large packing case or slatted crate which, screened from view, may be filled with leaves and garden trash. If each 1-foot layer is seasoned with a sprinkling of lime, its decay will be accelerated. There is conflict of opinion, however, regarding the use of garden refuse in the compost pile. The gardener thinks of plant debris as potential humus and nourishment for the soil, while the pathologist views it with alarm as a bed of disease. Personally, I am in favor of burning garden rubbish except when all other avenues to a humus supply are closed.

Fertilizers. Bulky, humus-forming materials other than barnyard or stable manure are deficient in plant foods. To supply this lack it is convenient to use one of the concentrated commercial fertilizers. One of approximately 5% nitrogen, 10% phosphoric acid, and 5% potash used at the rate of 3 to 4 pounds to 100 square feet will probably prove suitable. For a more extended discussion of soils and fertilizers see Chapters IV and V, SOIL IMPROVEMENT and MANURES AND FERTILIZERS.

I have seen excellent results in city back yards following the use of cattle manure which has been dehydrated and processed to kill weed seeds. Sold in convenient 50-pound bags, this manure supplies both humus and plant food. In the same class are preparations containing poultry manure mixed with peatmoss. The latter seems to act as a buffer, preventing the "burning" which often results from an overdose of poultry manure alone. A usual application of dehydrated cattle manure is 15 to 25 pounds to 100 square feet; of poultry manure with peatmoss, 6 to 8 pounds to the same area.

To discourage cats. A specter which haunts the dreams of the city gardener is the back-fence cat, who scratches up tender seedlings and raises havoc generally. It is said that 1½ to 2 teaspoonfuls of 40-percent nicotine sulphate in 1 gallon of water, sprayed around the garden, will make the area obnoxious to both cats and dogs.

Plants available for the city garden. Owing to dust, smoke, gas, and impure air, the number of plants which will thrive under city conditions is strictly limited, but there are enough to give variety. Conditions, of course, vary according to type and size of city. Generally speaking, the more congested the population the less favorable are conditions for plant growth. But a small city whose chief industry consists of chemical factories might have a more deleterious atmosphere than a city five times its size with innocuous industries.

A number of plants are reliable for a temporary display, but they may have to be renewed from year to year. If these plants were used on a large scale the cost of gardening with them might be prohibitive; but in a city garden one's requirements are modest in quantity, so their use may be recommended. This group includes practically all of the hardy bulbs which may be planted in the fall for a spring display. In some gardens they may be worth keeping over for a year or two, but in general they are best discarded when the flowers have faded. They should be replaced by summer bedding plants such as geraniums, begonias, and petunias. Supplementing the bulbs while they are in bloom are such subjects as pansies and English daisies, which remain for several weeks and are comparatively inexpensive. When these have become *passé,* summer-blooming "bulbs" such as gladioli and dahlias may be planted. Dwarf dahlias of the Coltness Gem type are preferable in the confined quarters of the city garden.

In the following list only those plants are included which have proved themselves capable of healthy growth in the residential sections of the borough of Brooklyn, which has a population of about two millions. Those which will grow under even more adverse circumstances are marked with a star (*). Most of them are described in Chapters VII, IX, XII, XIII, or XVI—TREES AND SHRUBS, VINES, PERENNIALS, ANNUALS, and ROCK GARDENS. References will be found in the index.

TREES

DECIDUOUS

* *Acer platanoides*, Norway Maple
* *Ailanthus altissima*, Tree of Heaven
* *Broussonetia papyrifera*, Paper Mulberry
* *Catalpa speciosa*
  Crataegus Oxyacantha, English Hawthorn
* *Ginkgo biloba*, Maidenhair-tree
  Gleditsia triacanthos, Honey Locust

* *Gymnocladus dioica*, Kentucky Coffee-tree
* *Magnolia denudata* and varieties
  Malus, Flowering Crabapples
  Morus alba, White Mulberry
* *Platanus acerifolia*, London Plane
  Prunus serrulata, Flowering Cherries
* *Quercus palustris*, Pin Oak
  Sophora japonica, Pagoda-tree
  Tilia cordata, Small-leaved Linden

SHRUBS

DECIDUOUS

* *Berberis Thunbergii*, Japanese Barberry
* *Calycanthus floridus*, Sweet-shrub
  Chaenomeles lagenaria, Flowering Quince
* *Forsythia intermedia*
* *Hibiscus syriacus*, Rose of Sharon
  Hydrangea macrophylla, "French" Hydrangea
* *Ligustrum ovalifolium*, California Privet
  Rhododendron calendulaceum, Flame Azalea
  Rose: Gruss an Teplitz

* *Salix discolor*, Pussy Willow
  Syringa vulgaris, Lilac
  Viburnum tomentosum

EVERGREEN

* *Chamaecyparis obtusa*, Hinoki Cypress
* *Chamaecyparis pisifera*
  Ilex crenata, Japanese holly
  Osmanthus ilicifolius
  Pachysandra procumbens
  Pieris japonica
  Rhododendron in variety
* *Taxus cuspidata*, Japanese yew
  Vinca minor, Periwinkle

VINES

WOODY

Hedera Helix, English Ivy
* *Lonicera japonica*, Japanese Honeysuckle
* *Polygonum Auberti*, China Fleece-vine
* Rose: Dorothy Perkins
  Dr. W. Van Fleet
  Emily Gray
  Excelsa
  Paul's Scarlet Climber

* *Wisteria sinensis*

ANNUAL

* *Convolvulus* in variety
* *Ipomoea* in variety

HERBACEOUS PERENNIALS

Lathyrus latifolius, Everlasting Pea
Dioscorea Batatas, Cinnamon-vine

PERENNIALS

Althaea rosea, Hollyhock
* *Chrysanthemum,* hardy varieties
Convallaria majalis, Lily-of-the-valley
Dicentra spectabilis, Bleeding Heart
Eupatorium coelestinum, Hardy Ageratum
Gaillardia aristata, Blanket-flower
* *Hemerocallis* in variety, Daylily
Heuchera sanguinea, Coral-bells

* *Hosta* in variety, Plantain-lily
Iberis sempervirens, Perennial Candytuft
Iris in variety
Phlox subulata, Moss-pink
* *Sedum acre*
* *Sedum spectabile*
Sempervivum tectorum

BEDDING PLANTS

Begonia semperflorens varieties
Bellis perennis, English Daisy
Dahlia in variety

Pelargonium zonale, Geranium
* *Petunia* in variety
Viola tricolor varieties, Pansy

ANNUALS

Lobularia (Alyssum) maritimum, Sweet Alyssum
Amaranthus caudatus, Love-lies-bleeding
* *Calliopsis* in variety
Celosia argentea cristata, Cockscomb
* *Cleome spinosa,* Spider-flower
Dianthus in variety
* *Euphorbia marginata,* Snow-on-the-mountain

Gaillardia, annual forms
Kochia scoparia trichophylla, Summer-cypress
* *Petunia* in variety
* *Portulaca grandiflora*
* *Mirabilis Jalapa,* Four o'clock
Ricinus communis, Castor-oil plant
* *Tagetes erecta,* African Marigold
* *Tagetes patula,* French Marigold
Zinnia elegans, Zinnia

XIX. ROOF GARDENS, WINDOW AND PORCH BOXES, VASES, HANGING BASKETS

The practice of growing plants in boxes offers splendid opportunities to those who are deprived of a real garden. Window and porch boxes have for many years been in favor as a means of brightening house fronts, but it is only recently that the inhabitants of skyscrapers have, with their roof gardens, been emulating the hanging gardens of the ancient Babylonians.

Principles of growing plants in containers. This type of gardening has limitations which are determined by the aspect, the quality of the soil, the size of the container, and the selection of plant material.

Soil requirements. The soil must be rich and bountifully supplied with humus. This is obvious when it is remembered that, in order to be effective, the boxes must be furnished with foliage and flowers quickly; and that, to achieve this end, the plants must be set close together. This results in tremendous root competition and, if there is not enough food for all, the plants cannot be expected to thrive.

A good general-purpose soil consists of 2 parts loam and 1 part decayed manure with a pint of bonemeal mixed with each bushel. As soon as the soil becomes filled with roots, supplementary feedings should be given. These may take the form of liquid manure made by mixing an ounce of complete commercial fertilizer (about 5-10-5) in a gallon of water, or by applying a level tablespoonful of the same fertilizer to each square foot of soil surface and cultivating it in. The boxes should be watered thoroughly a few hours ahead of applying the liquid manure. These feedings may be repeated as often as seems necessary—usually every four or five weeks. It is a good plan to maintain a mulch, 1 inch thick, of light organic matter on the surface of the soil to aid in keeping the roots cool and help to maintain fertility. This may consist of processed cattle manure, manure and peatmoss, or spent hops from a brewery.

Types of containers. Various receptacles are used, depending upon the means and taste of the individual, and the purpose for which they are intended. Old hot-water tanks (boilers) are sometimes pressed into service as porch boxes and are quite presentable when hidden by foliage. They are prepared for use by cutting a strip, equal to one third of the circumference, from the entire length of the tank, and by punching holes in the bottom to allow surplus water to drain away.

Then there are the so-called "self-watering" window boxes. These also are of metal, and are constructed with a false bottom, beneath which there is a water-holding compartment from which moisture is conducted to the soil above by capillarity. The great advantage of boxes of this type is that they eliminate the nuisance of water dripping from the drainage holes, which is the curse of ordinary boxes.

Window boxes or vases made of stone or concrete are heavy either to move or support, and they are bulky in comparison with the amount of soil they will hold. Terra-cotta containers are admirable, for they are thin, light, good-looking, and indestructible—except when they are dropped!

Wooden containers have many advantages. They are comparatively cheap, can easily be constructed to fit the available space, and are non-conductors of heat and cold.

To get good results, window boxes should be at least 8 inches deep and 10 inches wide—inside measurements. If a long space is to be filled, they should be made in units of not more than 3 feet each; otherwise when filled with soil, they are too heavy to move easily.

Cypress or white pine boards, which are 1 to 1¼ inches thick after both sides are planed, are best for wooden window boxes. Holes ½ inch in diameter should be bored 6 inches apart in the bottom board to allow for the escape of surplus water. Coarse material, such as that retained in the sieve when sifting manure or leafmold, should be placed in the bottom to aid drainage.

For roof gardens where large plants are required, the size of the containers should be increased in proportion. Butter tubs (disguised by paint) and regular plant tubs may be used for individual specimens of evergreens and small deciduous shrubs and trees. Sometimes it is practicable to make a continuous border of soil running around the available area. This may be from 2 to several feet wide, and, to make conditions really congenial for the larger-growing plants, should be from 18 inches to 2 feet deep. But before planning to deposit several tons of soil on the roof, find out whether the roof is strong enough to carry it.

Is it possible to use "permanent" plants? Material which does not have to be renewed every year would be the simplest and least expensive to use but, unfortunately, there are very few suitable plants which can live when their soil is frozen solid for long periods. The only ones I know which can be guaranteed to survive cold winters in vases or boxes without any protection are *Sedum spectabile* and *S. acre*. The first is an upright grower with dirty-pink flowers late in summer on stems which grow about a foot high under window-box conditions. *Sedum acre* is a low evergreen ground-cover bearing yellow flowers in summer. For other plants it is necessary to take steps to insulate the soil as much as possible against cold. This is scarcely practicable for window and porch boxes, but it is possible in the case of the tubbed trees and shrubs on roof gardens by moving them to the most sheltered location and placing them close together. Build a tight fence around them, 6 inches away and as high as the top of the largest tub. Fill the 6-inch space with peatmoss, hay, excelsior, or similar nonconducting material, and mulch the surface soil with decayed manure, partly decayed leaves, or peatmoss. Protect the tops of evergreens with burlap on suitable frames to shade them from sunshine and break the force of high winds, thus preventing the rapid transpiration from the leaves which causes them to look scorched at the end of the winter.

Roof gardens. It is usually good policy to combine permanent and temporary subjects in roof-garden plantings. The woody plants—tubbed trees, shrubs and evergreens—are used to provide the framework of the garden and to give an air of permanence to the composition. Annuals and bedding plants, set in boxes, tubs, or flower pots, or planted in front of the shrubs when a border of soil is available, will provide the necessary color.

Vines are often an important feature of a roof garden. By growing them on a suitable trellis, they will give height without occupying much space laterally. Also, a vine-clad trellis may sometimes screen an objectionable view or serve to ensure privacy. Perennial and woody vines may be planted if sufficient bulk of soil is available. When the soil containers are comparatively small, it is better to rely on annual vines—particularly the morning-glory and its relatives—which are likely to bloom more freely if their roots are confined.

The plants used in roof gardens should possess tough constitutions, especially under city conditions, where roof gardens are in greatest demand.

When there is a considerable bulk of soil in which roots can ramble, as in roof gardens where there is a border several feet wide and 18 inches deep, nearly all the plants listed as thriving in city gardens (Chapter XVIII) could be planted with fair assurance of success. The trees and shrubs suggested below are the kinds most likely to endure tub culture. There are probably many others which could be used. Whenever possible, the plants should be established in their tubs for a few months prior to exposing them to the rigors of life on a roof. This is especially true of the evergreens. It should be possible to find a nurseryman who will consent to tub the plants a few months ahead of the time they are to be used.

PLANTS FOR ROOF GARDENS

TREES

(These must not be expected to attain the stature of those growing in open soil.)

Ailanthus. This is almost certain to thrive if liberally fed.

Catalpa. The normally tall-growing forms may be used, also *C. bignonioides nana* (*Bungei*), in standard form, grafted upon *C. bignonioides.*

Ginkgo. This is so tolerant that it should do well almost anywhere.

Malus. The flowering crab-apples are worth a trial.

SHRUBS

Acanthopanax Sieboldianum. This stands smoke and dust, and thrives in shade or sun; therefore, it should be a good roof-garden plant.

Berberis Thunbergii. Valuable for its fall coloring and berries in winter.

Forsythia. Any of the commoner species may be used.

Ligustrum ovalifolium. The California privet is a great standby. The golden-leaved form will provide variation in leaf coloration.

Salix discolor. The pussy-willow is a tolerant back-yard plant, and should be able to survive the rigorous conditions of a roof garden if provided with plenty of water.

EVERGREENS

Chamaecyparis obtusa and *C. pisifera.* Both are worth a trial.

Hedera Helix. English ivy will probably need winter protection on an exposed roof.

Taxus cuspidata. The Japanese yew is the most tolerant of all the evergreens under city conditions.

VINES

Success with vines is more assured if they are provided with a good bulk of soil. Tubs, if they are used, should be at least 18 inches in diameter.

The morning-glories and related plants, listed under *Ipomoea* in Chapter IX, vines, may be used in roof gardens. The seeds may be planted where they are to bloom (first soaking them in warm water for 24 hours), or better still, because it lessens the time necessary to wait for flowers, set out young plants as soon as danger of frost is past. Support of some kind is necessary for them. If a permanent trellis is not available, a framework (as fancy as you wish) should be constructed, and vertical strings attached to it. If the plants are growing in a tub, a half-dozen bamboo canes, 6 or 8 feet long, may be stuck in the soil around the edges and the tops brought together and tied. This makes a practical and good-looking support. Other good vines for the roof garden follow.

Lonicera japonica. The Japanese honeysuckle normally starts into growth very early in spring. If possible, shade it to delay growth, with a view to avoiding injury by late frosts.

Polygonum Auberti does well in the city and thrives in exposed situations.

Rose. The varieties **Dorothy Perkins** and **Excelsa** are worth a trial.

Wisteria. A good city vine. The flower buds may winter-kill in exposed situations.

PERENNIALS

There is little gratification in using most hardy perennials as roof-garden plants, except for a few early-blooming kinds, those with good foliage, and varieties with a long period of bloom. In general, annuals and the bedding plants are more satisfactory for tub or box culture and are more constantly in bloom.

Pansies and English daisies, which under some conditions are perennials (but not in roof gardens), may be utilized by obtaining plants in March or April and using them for a spring display. The following perennials are worthy:

Chrysanthemum. Start with young plants and renew the soil every year. Feed them heavily.

Gaillardia. Prevent seeds from forming if you wish them to continue producing flowers.

Hosta (*Funkia*). Plantain-lilies are valuable for foliage even if no flowers are produced. Partial shade is desirable, and plenty of water required during the growing season.

Phlox subulata and varieties. These give a pleasing carpet of early bloom.

Sedum acre and *S. spectabile.* These two sedums will endure almost any trying conditions.

ANNUALS

Lobularia (Alyssum) maritimum. Sweet alyssum should be sown where the plants are to bloom.

Calliopsis. Either sow in place or set out young plants.

Celosia. Both the cockscomb and plumose types may be used.

Euphorbia marginata, **Snow-on-the-Mountain**. Sow in place.

Gaillardia. Sow in place.

Kochia. Sow in place, or set out young plants.

Mirabilis, **Four o'clock, Marvel of Peru**. Seeds may be sown in place; seedlings, raised in a greenhouse, may be planted; or the roots (which have been stored from the preceding year like those of dahlias) may be used.

Portulaca. Plant seeds in the fall or early in spring.

Tagetes, **French** and **African Marigolds**. The dwarf French marigolds are especially desirable because of their hardiness and free-blooming habits.

Zinnia. I am hesitant about recommending zinnias. Under some conditions, they are quite satisfactory; under others, apparently better, they fail to thrive. They are subject to mildew which, however, should not be so bothersome under the airy conditions of a roof garden.

BEDDING PLANTS

These (with exception of English daisies and pansies, which can be planted toward the end of March) should be set out as young plants when danger of frost is past. Among the most satisfactory are the following:

Begonia. The semperflorens type is the kind best adapted to roof culture.

Pelargonium, **Geranium**. These familiar plants are obtainable in considerable variety.

Petunia. The best-tempered and most accommodating of all roof-garden plants. There is a great range of colors and forms available.

BULBS

The hardy spring-flowering bulbs are not adapted to culture in small boxes when they are exposed to the winter on a roof. If it is possible to protect them by the method suggested for trees and shrubs one might bring them through the winter and have a good display in spring.

I have purposely been conservative in my suggestions regarding plant material for roof gardens. Practically all of the plants in the window-box lists may also be used, and doubtless there are many others.

Window and porch boxes. In order to ensure that window and porch boxes are constantly furnished with plants throughout the year, two or three complete changes of material are necessary. Starting in the fall, dwarf evergreens may be installed, with or without English ivy to trail over the front of the boxes. These plants, although capable of looking presentable throughout the winter, usually must be discarded in the spring. If they become bedraggled in late winter, they may be replaced about mid-March with early spring-blooming plants such as pansies and English daisies. These, in turn, may give way to more or less tender bedding plants (petunias, begonias, etc.) which continue the display until they are injured by frost, at which time they are replaced by evergreens.

If expense is a consideration, seeds may be planted in May directly in the soil of the window box. A selection of kinds adapted for this purpose is listed on p. 325. It should be recognized that when this method is adopted, the period during which the window boxes are attractive is not as long as when well-grown plants ready to bloom are set out.

Another inexpensive means of furnishing window boxes during the summer is to utilize the plants which, during the winter, have done duty as house plants. These often come in very handy, especially in shady locations, either used alone or in association with other plants.

PLANTS FOR WINDOW BOXES, PORCH BOXES, AND VASES

Except where otherwise noted in the lists below, all of the subjects suggested for window boxes are either greenhouse or house plants, or bedding material which should be set out as young plants when danger of frost is past. Following these lists are suggestions for window-box plants which may be raised from seed in the boxes themselves; also names of a number of evergreen plants for winter use.

FOR SUNNY SITUATIONS

Those marked with a star (*) will also grow in partially shaded situations.

More or less upright-growing plants

* *Ageratum,* either tall or dwarf, as conditions demand.

Callistephus, **China Aster.** Possibly less subject to the mosaic disease when grown in window boxes.

Centaurea gymnocarpa, **Dusty Miller.** The gray foliage shows up well against a dark background.

* *Coleus,* vari-colored foliage plants. Watch out for mealy bugs!

Lantana. A variety of colors may be obtained.

* *Pelargonium,* **Geranium,** in various color forms. The ivy-leaved varieties are excellent for drooping over the edges, in regions where they thrive.

* *Petunia*. These are among the best of all window-box plants.

Tagetes, **Marigold.** The French are more suitable than the African varieties.

Trailing plants to droop over edge

* *Asparagus Sprengeri*, **Emerald Feather.**

* *Hedera Helix*, **English Ivy.** Hardy if winter is not too severe.

* *Cymbalaria muralis* (*Linaria Cymbalaria*), **Kenilworth Ivy.**

* *Lysimachia Nummularia*, **Creeping Charlie, Moneywort.** This is a hardy perennial which might persist year after year if conditions were not too severe.

Sedum acre. Capable of surviving severe winters.

Nepeta (*Glechoma*) *hederacea variegata.* Though a hardy perennial, its ability to survive the winter in a window box is doubtful.

Thunbergia alata, **Black-eyed Clock-vine.** Many varieties are available, ranging from white to bright orange, with dark "eyes."

* *Vinca minor.* Although grown mainly for its foliage, the periwinkle-blue flowers are attractive in spring. It may be able to survive the winter even in a window box.

* *Vinca major* and *V. major variegata.* The former has large shining green leaves, the latter leaves variegated with creamy-white. Both are vigorous trailers. They need the protection of a cool greenhouse or coldframe during winter.

* *Zebrina pendula* (*Tradescantia zebrina*), **Wandering Jew.** Many forms exhibiting different leaf coloration are obtainable.

In addition to the above, various greenhouse "foliage" plants may be used for accent. *Cordyline* (*Dracaena*) *indivisa, Phoenix Roebelenii,* and *Sansevieria* are among the most popular. The two first named are especially good for use as center plants in vases. Quite often they are used in combination with trailing ivy-leaved geraniums, trailing lobelia, or one of the "floppy" types of petunia.

FOR HALF-SHADY SITUATIONS

Besides the above plants which have been marked with a star (*), the following, which prefer partial shade, may be used in window and porch boxes and vases.

Upright plants

Begonia semperflorens for flowers; *B. Rex* for foliage.

Chlorophytum (*Anthericum*) *elatum variegatum.* These plants have white flowers, but are grown mainly for their variegated foliage.

Fuchsia in variety. Small specimens may be used in window boxes. The stronger kinds are excellent in large vases.

Impatiens Sultani, **Zanzibar Balsam, Patient Lucy.**

Nephrolepis, **Boston Fern.**

Trailers

Hedera Helix, **English Ivy.**

Lobelia Erinus, trailing varieties. These, in regions with a cool summer climate, are among the most desirable and long-blooming of all window-box plants.

FOR SHADY SITUATIONS

All of the plants in the list immediately preceding this may be used, and in addition the following:

Ferns in considerable variety. Resistant types such as the **Holly Fern** and the **Boston Fern** should be chosen.

Palms, small varieties.

Peperomia maculosa. This is quite commonly used as a house plant and might enjoy a summer out-of-doors.

WINDOW-BOX PLANTS FROM SEED

The following plants may be raised from seed planted in April or May directly in the boxes. Those marked with a star (*) will do well in shade or partial shade.

Upright growers

Callistephus chinensis, **China Aster.**

Dimorphotheca aurantiaca, **Cape-marigold.**

* *Impatiens Balsamina,* **Balsam.**

Kochia scoparia, **Summer-cypress.** Foliage scarlet in fall.

Phlox Drummondii. Semi-upright, free and long-blooming. One of the best.

Tagetes patula, **French Marigold.**

More or less prostrate growers

Lobularia (Alyssum) maritimum, **Sweet Alyssum.**

* *Cymbalaria muralis (Linaria Cymbalaria),* **Kenilworth Ivy.**

Portulaca grandiflora, **Rose-moss.**

Thunbergia alata, **Black-eyed Clock-vine.**

* *Tropaeolum majus,* **Nasturtium.**

EVERGREENS FOR WINTER USE

Almost all evergreens of a dwarf type, or small specimens of larger-growing varieties, may be used in window boxes. It should be recognized that the use of these plants is expensive, as they seldom survive the winter and have to be discarded in the spring. The following upright kinds are desirable:

Biota orientalis, **Oriental Arborvitae,** and its horticultural forms.

Buxus sempervirens, **Boxwood.**

Chamaecyparis obtusa, **Hinoki Cypress.**

Taxus cuspidata, **Japanese Yew.** The dwarf forms are preferable.

The **English Ivy** is practically the only trailing evergreen available for use in severe climates. Those who live in regions where *Arctostaphylos Uva-ursi,* **Bearberry,** is plentiful may cut the long trailing shoots in the fall and stick them in the boxes so that they droop over the edge. They will remain in good condition until the spring.

Hanging baskets. When the plants they contain are flourishing, hanging baskets can be highly ornamental, suspended in porch and colonnade openings. They are most likely to thrive in regions of cool humid summers—or in a greenhouse. Elsewhere the difficulty of keeping the soil constantly moist becomes almost insuperable.

If the term "basket," however, is liberally interpreted to include the pottery, metal, and wooden containers which do not dry out so readily, and which sometimes are equipped with chains so that they can be suspended, hanging baskets may sometimes be used in hot dry situations. If provided with a water-tight saucer, the annoyance of water dripping on the floor is eliminated.

The most difficult feat in the management of the basket made of wire is the maintenance of soil moisture. In a greenhouse, or in situations where water may freely be sprayed from the hose without damaging the surroundings, it is simple enough, but when there are furnishings near by which are subject to damage by water, the idea of using hanging baskets had better be discarded, unless you are content with those of pottery or metal.

Most of the wire hanging baskets offered for sale are poorly constructed because, in the endeavor to supply an inexpensive article, the wires are spaced too far apart, and the soil is apt to sift between them. In an ideal basket, the wires are spaced not more than ½ inch apart.

In preparing them for planting, they are first lined with sheet moss, green side outward, obtained from rotting logs in the woods or from a concern dealing in florists' supplies. If the wires are widely spaced, an additional lining of heavy burlap should be placed next to the moss. The basket is now ready for the reception of soil, which must be packed down quite firmly to within about 3 inches of the rim. Put the plants in place, then pack more soil closely about them and finish off the surface so that it looks like a glorified soup plate, to facilitate watering. If bulbs are to grow through the sides of the basket it will be necessary to poke small holes in the burlap and place the noses of the bulbs where the shoots may find an exit.

The soil for hanging baskets and its subsequent fertilizing are handled much as in window boxes and plant vases.

The plant materials used are also of the same general nature. The best effect is often obtained by setting an upright plant in the center and surrounding it with trailers. For example: a small plant of *Phoenix Roebelenii,* a dwarf feathery-leaved palm, may be combined with a trailing lobelia; or either *Cordyline indivisa* or *Centaurea gymnocarpa* with *Lobularia (Alyssum) maritimum* or *Nepeta hederacea variegata.*

For greenhouse use, *Achimenes, Lachenalia,* and *Oxalis,* among the bulbous subjects, are commonly used.

The basket plants marked with a star (*) in the list below are most likely to be a success under outdoor conditions in summer.

Adiantum caudatum, a maidenhair fern with viviparous leaves, rooting and forming new plants at the tips.

Begonia Lloydii and other drooping kinds.

* *Ceropegia Woodii,* a small trailer with ornamental, fleshy heart-shaped leaves, good in hot dry situations.

Cyanotis kewensis, a small trailer clothed with reddish hairs.

Davallia bullata and *D. pentaphylla,* ferns.

* *Ficus pumila,* **Creeping Fig.**

Fittonia argyroneura, a tender foliage plant with small ovate leaves veined in white.

* *Nepeta hederacea variegata,* **Ground-ivy,** a hardy, rampant grower with small blue flowers.

* *Oplismenus compositus,* a grass better known to gardeners as *Panicum variegatum.*

Pellionia Daveaueana, a tender foliage plant with leaves of bronzy olive-green.

Piper nigrum, which produces the black pepper of commerce.

* *Saxifraga sarmentosa,* **Strawberry-geranium,** good in shade.

Schizocentron (Heeria) elegans, a tender mat-forming creeper with purple flowers.

Selaginella uncinata (caesia), a trailing fern-like plant, often incorrectly called *Lycopodium.*

* *Torenia Fournieri,* charming flowers of blue and velvety purple.

* *Zebrina pendula,* Wandering Jew, in great variety, good in shade.

XX. HERB GARDEN, FERNS, WILD GARDEN

HERB GARDEN

In recent years there has been a great revival of interest in the growing of herbs—employing the term in the sense of plants used as condiments, and for flavoring, garnishing, and scenting. Botanically, any plant is an herb which does not have a woody stem and which dies to the ground each year. Here the term will be given its popular meaning.

Herbs may be relegated to the kitchen garden or, if one chooses those which have some ornamental value, they may be grown in a formal or informal herb garden, designed and planted with decorative possibilities in mind, and included in the garden scene.

Ornamental herbs. Among the most attractive herbs for garden decoration are: **Balm,** *Melissa officinalis,* including a form with variegated leaves; **Borage,** *Borago officinalis,* an annual with blue flowers; **Chives,** *Allium Schoenoprasum,* which may be used as an edging to the beds; **Clary,** *Salvia Sclarea,* with handsome woolly leaves and fairly showy flowers; **Hyssop,** *Hyssopus officinalis,* with bright green foliage and bluish flowers; **Lavender,** *Lavandula Spica,* perhaps the most decorative of all; **Pot-marigold,** *Calendula officinalis,* well known, producing showy orange or yellow flowers; **Parsley,** *Petroselinum hortense,* the curly kinds being best for ornamental plantings; **Rosemary,** *Rosmarinus officinalis,* a shrub, tender in severe climates, bearing pale blue flowers; its variety *prostratus* quite ornamental; **Rue,** *Ruta graveolens,* with glaucous grayish foliage; **Sage,** *Salvia officinalis,* a sub-shrub, with gray wrinkled leaves; **Southernwood,** *Artemisia Abrotanum,* with much divided green leaves; **Tarragon,** *Artemisia Dracunculus,* which has narrow green leaves; and **Thyme,** *Thymus vulgaris,* a little shrub with tiny leaves.

An interesting blue and gray garden can be made by planting borage, hyssop, lavender, rosemary, rue, clary, and sage, cutting off the flower spikes of the last two.

Commonly grown herbs. Because herbs, which were the first plants to be cultivated in gardens, are known almost solely by their common names (at least, to the average gardener), in the alphabetical list below the common name is given first, immediately followed by the Latin, or scientific, name. The initial following the name indicates the type of plant: A—annual; B—biennial; P—perennial; S—shrub. The best method and time of year for propagation are indicated, then the distance between the plants after final transplanting or thinning, and a brief comment on the uses of each herb.

Name and type of plant	Method and time of propagation	Final distance apart	Uses
Angelica			
Angelica Archangelica B or P	Seeds—Fall or spring	2½ ft.	Tender leaf-stalks used as salad; roots and leaf-stalks candied.
Anise			
Pimpinella Anisum A	Seeds—Spring	6 in.	Seeds used for flavoring.
Balm			
Melissa officinalis P	Seeds—Mar., indoors Division—Fall or spring	1 ft.	Leaves used for flavoring.
Basil			
Ocimum Basilicum A	Seeds—Spring Seeds (for winter use) —Fall, indoors	9 in.	Leaves used for flavoring.
Borage			
Borago officinalis A	Seeds—Spring	1 ft.	Leaves and flowers used for garnishing and for flavoring beverages.
Camomile			
Anthemis nobilis P	Seeds—Spring	9 in.	Medicinal tea.
Caraway			
Carum Carvi A or B	Seeds—April, June	6 in.	Seeds used for flavoring.
Chives			
Allium Schoenoprasum P	Division—Spring or fall	Small clumps 6 in. apart	Leaves used for flavoring.
Clary			
Salvia Sclarea B	Seeds—May	1½ ft.	Leaves sometimes used for flavoring soups.
Dill			
Anethum graveolens A	Seeds—Spring	9 in.	Seeds used for flavoring pickles and vinegar.
Fennel			
Foeniculum vulgare B or P	Seeds—Fall or spring	1½ ft.	Leaves used for flavoring and garnishing.
Horehound			
Marrubium vulgare P	Seeds—Spring	1 ft.	Infusion of leaves used in making cough drops.

Name and type of plant	Method and time of propagation	Final distance apart	Uses
Hyssop			
Hyssopus officinalis P	Seeds or division— Spring	9 in.	The bitter leaves are sometimes used to "pep up" salads.
Lavender			
Lavandula Spica S	Seeds—Spring Cuttings—August	1½-2½ ft.	Used mostly in perfumery.
Mint			
Peppermint			
Mentha piperita P	Division—Spring	1 ft.	Leaves used for flavoring. (A moist soil is
Spearmint			
Mentha spicata P	Division—Spring	1 ft.	desirable.)
Parsley			
Petroselinum hortense B	Seeds—Spring	9 in.	Garnishing and flavoring. (Soak seeds before planting. Small plants may be potted for winter use indoors.)
Pot-marigold			
Calendula officinalis A	Seeds—Spring	1 ft.	Flowers used for flavoring and coloring.
Rosemary			
Rosmarinus officinalis S	Seeds—Mar., indoors Cuttings—July	3 ft.	Used for flavoring and in perfumery. (In severe climates where it is raised anew each year space the plants 9 in. apart.)
Rue			
Ruta graveolens P	Seeds or division— Spring	1½ ft.	Occasionally used as a flavoring, though I can't see how anyone endures it.
Sage			
Salvia officinalis S	Cuttings—Summer Seeds—Spring	2½ ft.	Leaves used for flavoring. (Needs well-drained soil.)
Savory			
Satureja hortensis A	Seeds—Spring	6 in.	Leaves used for flavoring.
Sweet Marjoram			
Marjorana hortensis P treated as an A	Seeds—Spring and early summer	6 in.	Leaves used for seasoning and garnishing. (Shade the seedlings.)
Tarragon			
Artemisia Dracunculus P	Cuttings—Summer Division—Spring	1½ ft.	Leaves used in salads and for flavoring vinegar.
Thyme			
Thymus vulgaris S	Seeds—Mar., indoors Cuttings—Summer	8 in.	The leaves are one of the most popular of flavoring agents.

Harvesting herbs. Leaves for flavoring may be used either fresh or dried. Usually they are gathered for drying just before the plants are ready to bloom, except in the case of biennials, when individual leaves are taken just as they are nearing their full size.

The shoots should be cut or the leaves gathered early in the morning, washed if necessary, and dried by tying them in small bunches and hanging them in a warm dry place or by spreading them in thin layers on paper. Placed on a shaded bench in an empty greenhouse they will dry rapidly. When thoroughly dry, the leaves are rubbed off and stored in tightly stoppered bottles so that the flavoring oils are retained as long as possible.

Plants of which the seeds are used should be gathered just before the seeds are ready to be shed, and spread in thin layers on paper to dry. When they are dry the seeds may be rubbed out. Dust and chaff may be removed partly by fanning and partly with the aid of fine sieves of various sizes. The cleaned seeds should be stored in stoppered bottles, both to retain the flavor and to preserve them from mice.

FERNS

Hardy ferns may be used effectively both in the wild garden and in the more domesticated parts of the garden.

Culture. Although we usually think of ferns as being shade-lovers —as most of them are—there are many which will thrive in the open sunshine provided there is a sufficient supply of moisture at their roots. Some of these sun-lovers will be found noted in the list below.

The soil for ferns in general should be friable and plentifully supplied with humus. A rather moist and sheltered location is preferred for most of them. If they are handled with care to avoid injuring the roots, ferns may be transplanted almost at any time, though preferably they should be moved in spring or fall when they are dormant.

Descriptive list. Below is a brief list of hardy ferns with their chief requirements.

Adiantum pedatum, **Maidenhair.** This is one of our handsomest native ferns. The best specimens I have ever seen were in gardens in British Columbia where they made luxuriant clumps 2 feet or more high. Maidenhairs should receive partial shade and a light rich moist soil.

Athyrium Filix-femina, **Lady Fern,** grows to a height of 2 to 3 feet, with elegant fronds. It is adaptable, but prefers a rich moist loam and partial shade.

Dennstaedtia punctilobula, **Hay-scented Fern,** spreads rapidly by underground rhizomes. It grows 1 to 2½ feet high and will thrive in sun or shade.

Onoclea sensibilis, **Sensitive Fern,** has less elegant fronds than those of the ferns usually grown for ornament. It needs wet soil and full sunshine, and grows 1 to 2 feet high.

Osmunda cinnamomea, **Cinnamon Fern,** may attain a height of 6 feet. The spore-bearing leaves are distinct from the sterile leaves and provide an effective contrast. It will grow in sun or shade, but demands moist soil.

O. regalis, **Royal Fern.** This species sometimes reaches a height of 10 feet, though more usually it is 3 or 4 feet high. It needs a rich moist soil and plenty of manure. It grows best in sunshine, but the soil must be wet.

Polypodium vulgare, **Rock Polypody,** is a small evergreen fern often seen growing wild over rocks. It needs a light moist soil and shade.

Pteretis nodulosa (*Onoclea Struthiopteris*), **Ostrich Fern,** may make fronds up to 6 feet in length when grown in a congenial position. It should be given deep rich soil in partial shade. Very handsome.

Pteridium aquilinum, **Brake** or **Bracken,** is mentioned here as a species likely to become a bad weed on account of its invasive underground rootstock. We have it running wild through a rhododendron planting where it was inadvertently introduced through the medium of the soil of balled-and-burlapped plants.

WILD GARDEN

The type of planting referred to here is not the kind of "wild" garden which consists of strong-growing exotic perennials planted and left to take care of themselves. Such a garden looks like that of a lazy man, unkempt and unattractive.

A true wild garden is made of native wild flowers in an informal or naturalistic planting. If you have the right conditions available, a wild garden can be one of the most beautiful parts of the grounds. Since many of our most attractive wild flowers grow with little sun, those who are fortunate enough to have a shaded ravine, some woodland, or even a few trees, may enjoy introducing such beauties as the trailing arbutus, shortia, galax, trillium, columbine, lady-slipper, spring beauty, hepatica, mountain laurel, and azalea—to name only a few of the many lovely plants available.

In an open meadow it is possible to plant asters and goldenrods in such a way that they look as if they came of their own accord. If the soil is sandy and poor you may be able to establish the bird's-foot violet and the orange milkweed (butterfly-weed). Or it may happen that you have the right conditions (a moist meadow) for the growth of the fringed gentian, and then, if you are able to solve the problem of raising it, there is a thrill in store for you. In wet places the purple loosestrife and the shrubby cinquefoil may be made at home without any difficulty, and a rocky bank affords an ideal situation for some of the native dwarf junipers.

Native wild flowers may be obtained for the garden by purchase from a nurseryman, by collecting plants in the wild, or by raising them from seeds or cuttings.

The easiest method, of course, is to buy the plants, and, if they are nursery-grown, they are more likely to succeed than those collected from the wild.

Collecting. If you collect your own plants, remember that in some states some of the choicest plants are protected, and it is against the law to dig them up. Also remind yourself that under no circumstances would you want to take home a plant if you were thus lessening its chances of survival as a wild species. Except in the hands of an experienced person, many plants will not survive transplanting from the wild.

One advantage, however, of doing your own collecting is that it makes you familiar with the situation in which the plant grows: this serves as a guide to the treatment to give it in your garden. If a plant is not easy to grow and you cannot nearly reproduce its natural conditions, do not attempt to transplant it. Although some wild flowers are tolerant of varied situations, it is generally wise to imitate the original environment.

When transplanting wild plants—as with "tame" ones—it is best to dig them up while they are dormant, and preferably with a ball of earth about their roots. If this is not practicable, dig them without breaking off more roots than necessary, and be sure to keep them constantly moist (with damp newspaper or moss) until you are able to plant them.

Propagating by seeds or cuttings. Raising wild flowers from seeds or cuttings is a fascinating hobby. Under controlled garden conditions it is sometimes possible to germinate more seeds from a given quantity and raise more plants than would be the case were they exposed to the hazards and competition of the wild.

A coldframe is helpful when starting the seeds, and essential when raising plants from cuttings. (See Chapter XXVI, PLANT PROPAGATION.)

Try to reproduce as nearly as possible the soil texture and the degree of acidity or alkalinity of the situation where the plants are growing wild. This is even more important after the plants have got beyond the seedling or cutting stage. A soil-testing set, obtainable from any large seed store, will aid in determining the acidity or alkalinity of the soil.

The home propagation of wildings gives one the heart-warming feeling that he is increasing native plants instead of denuding the countryside.

XXI. THE VEGETABLE GARDEN

The question is constantly popping up whether it is worth while to bother with vegetables on a small place. My neighbor in the country says: "Why bother to grow vegetables when you can buy them so cheaply from the peddler?" It is granted that not a great deal of money is saved growing one's own vegetables (if the cost of labor in caring for them is considered), but think of the quality of home-grown vegetables such as corn and peas compared with shopworn products! So if room can be spared in a suitable location, and labor is available, by all means have a vegetable garden.

Location and soil. It should be located in sunshine and far enough from large trees so that the vegetables are not robbed by the wide-spreading tree roots. Ideally, the site should be open to the south and sheltered from north and west winds to favor the quick maturity of the early planted crops.

The general soil preparation described in Chapter IV, SOIL IMPROVEMENT, will be sufficient unless you are fired with the ambition to shine as an exhibitor—in which case the soil should be double dug or even trenched and, if extra large and long parsnips and carrots are your hobby, 3-foot holes should be made with a crowbar, filled with extra-special sifted soil, and one plant only allowed to grow in each hole. These holes should be spaced from 6 inches to a foot apart in the row. If the soil is of an extreme type—either very sandy or a sticky clay—emphasis should be placed on crops adapted to the soil. Bush bean, beet, Swiss chard, tomato, and New Zealand spinach tolerate sandy soils. Potatoes will grow well in a sandy soil if it is properly fertilized. Cabbage and related crops—kale, etc.—thrive in a heavy loam, as do corn, parsley, parsnip, peas and rhubarb. Shallow soils are not well adapted to any of the crops in which the root is long, such as long beet, parsnip, carrot, and salsify.

Layout of the vegetable garden. Before planting the garden a plan should be made on paper so that the space available may be fully utilized and the ground occupied throughout the growing season. The plan on the following page suggests how this may be done.

North 60 feet		South

2 ft.
Corn ....

3 ft.
Corn ....

3 ft.
Corn ....

3 ft.
Lettuce ....followed by Tomato ....

3 ft.
Spinach (spring)..followed by ½ row Eggplant and ½ row Pepper

3 ft.
Potatoes ....

3 ft.
Potatoes ....

3 ft.
Peas (early)......followed by Cauliflower (fall) ....

3 ft.
Peas (early)......followed by Cabbage (late) ....

3 ft.
Early Cabbage....followed by Celery ....

1 ft. 6 in.
Bush Beans ....

1 ft. 6 in.
Bush Beans.......followed by Beets or Spinach ....

1 ft. 6 in.
Beets (early)......followed by Bush Beans ....

1 ft. 6 in.
Onions (sets).....followed by Beets or Turnips ....

1 ft. 6 in.
Carrots (early)....followed by Fall Spinach ....

1 ft. 6 in.
Onions (main crop) or Carrots ....

1 ft. 6 in.
Swiss Chard ....

1 ft. 6 in.
Parsnip, sown with Radishes ....

3 ft.
Rhubarb ....

3 ft.
Asparagus ....

3 ft. 6 in.
Asparagus ....

3 ft. 6 in.
Asparagus ....

4 ft.
Artichoke ....

2 ft.

NOTE: Two rows of spinach and two rows of lettuce may be grown in the spaces to be occupied later by eggplant and pepper, and by tomato. Similarly, two rows of onion sets may occupy the ground to be used later for growing beets.

It is, of course, intended merely as a suggestion and not meant to be followed exactly, although it does in the main follow the plan of an actual garden maintained for several years by the writer. The quantities and kinds of vegetables grown must, of course, be determined by individual preference. The following information giving the approximate amounts of vegetables that can be obtained from a row 100 feet long may help you to avoid planting in such quantities that you may be compelled to live entirely on beets or cabbage in order to avoid wasting the products of the garden! These figures, which are given merely as an approximate guide, are based on yields obtained from soil that is not exceptionally good. The amounts, of course, would vary according to soil, season, and care.

QUANTITIES OF VEGETABLES OBTAINED FROM A ROW 100 FEET LONG

Beets	60 bunches (5 to a bunch)	Onions (thinnings)	12 bunches (10 to 20 to a bunch)
Bush Beans (pods)	4½ pecks	Onions (for winter use)	30 pounds
Cabbage	50 heads		
Carrots (thinnings)	40 bunches (6 to a bunch)	Peas	5 pecks
		Parsnips	150 pounds
Carrots (for winter use)	85 pounds	Potatoes	2½ bushels
Cauliflower	50 heads	Swiss Chard	A row 20 feet long is sufficient for a family of five—more than sufficient for some families!
Celery	200 stalks		
Corn	180 ears		
Eggplant	120 fruits	Tomatoes (35 plants—staked and trained)	480 pounds
Lettuce	100 to 150 heads		

Directions for planting and care. In one of the large seed stores in New York I once overheard an old lady inquiring for lettuce seed. "How much do you want?" asked the clerk, and the old lady answered, "About a pound." The clerk, kindly but suspicious, asked how large a plot she intended to plant. "About 10 x 10 feet," she replied—so he sold her a 10-cent package. One *ounce* of lettuce seed is capable of producing around 8,000 plants; a pound could fill a garden the size of a large city block.

The following table indicates the approximate quantities of seed required to plant a row 100 feet long. The time to plant, depth of planting, and distance between and in the rows are also noted. The dates given for planting apply to a normal season in the vicinity of

New York; thus they are only approximate and must be modified in accordance with weather conditions, exposure, altitude, and latitude.

VEGETABLE PLANTING TABLE

Vegetables	Time to plant	Depth	Distance between rows	Distance in the row	Quantity of seed
Beans (pole) Beans (lima)	May 20 to June 20	1 in.	3-4 ft.	In hills 3-4 ft. apart, about 3 seeds to a hill	½ pint
Beans (dwarf)	May 10 to Aug. 1	1 in.	1½ ft.	4 in.	1 pint
Beets	April to Aug. 1	1 in.	1½ ft.	4 in.	2 oz.
Cabbages (early) Cabbages (late)	Feb. indoors; plants set out in March May in coldframe; plants set out in July	¼ in.	3 ft.	2 ft.	1 oz. will produce 2,000 plants
Carrots	April to July	½ in.	1-1½ ft.	3 in.	½ oz.
Cauliflower (early) Cauliflower (late)	Feb. indoors; plants set out in March May in coldframe; plants set out in July	¼ in.	3 ft.	2 ft.	1 oz. will produce 2,000 plants
Celery (early) Celery (late)	Feb. or March indoors; plants set out in May April outdoors; plants set out in June or July	⅛ in.	3 ft.	6 in.	1 oz. about 3,000 plants
Corn	May 10 to July 10	2 in.	3 ft.	1 ft.	½ pint
Cucumber	May 20	¾ in.	5 ft.	5 ft.	½ oz.
Eggplant	Mar. indoors; plants set out in late May or early June	¼ in.	3 ft.	3 ft.	1 oz. will produce 600 plants
Lettuce	April to Aug.	½ in.	1-1½ ft.	9 in.-1 ft.	¼ oz.
Muskmelon	May 20	¾ in.	6 ft.	6 ft.	½ oz.
Onion (seed)	April to May	½ in.	1-1½ ft.	4 in.	1 oz.
Onion (sets)	Mar. 15 to May 15	2 in.	1-1½ ft.	2 in.	1 quart
Parsley	April	½ in.	1-1½ ft.	6-8 in.	¼ oz.
Parsnips	April	1 in.	1½ ft.	6 in.	½ oz.
Peas (dwarf) Peas (tall)	Mar. 15 to May 15 and Aug. 1 to 20	3 in. 4 in.	2-3 ft. 4-6 ft.	2 in. 3 in.	1 quart 1 quart
Peppers	Mar. indoors; plants set out late May or early June	¼ in.	3 ft.	2 ft.	small package

Vegetables	Time to plant	Depth	Distance between rows	Distance in the row	Quantity of seed
Potatoes	April 15 to June	4-6 in.	3 ft.	12-18 in.	½ peck
Radishes	March to Sept.	½ in.	1 ft.	2 in.	1 oz.
Spinach	March and Sept.	½ in.	1-1½ ft.	4 in.	1½ oz.
Squash (bush)	May 20	¾ in.	4 ft.	4 ft.	½ oz.
Squash (running)	May 20	¾ in.	6 ft.	6 ft.	½ oz.
Swiss Chard	April	1 in.	1½ ft.	6 in.	1 oz.
Tomatoes	Mar. indoors; plants set out late May or early June	¼ in.	3 ft.	3 ft.	1 oz. will produce more than 1,000 plants
Turnips	April and Sept.	½ in.	1½ ft.	6 in.	½ oz.

How to plant. Before planting, the soil should be thoroughly raked to make a fine seed bed. Most of the crops will be sown in drills (shallow trenches) of suitable depth made with a draw-hoe or rake. A line should be stretched as a guide in order to make a straight row, which will give greater ease in cultivation. Scatter the seeds evenly in the drills, cover by raking fine soil over them and make it firm by patting with the back of the hoe or with one foot. It is a common practice to plant some vegetables in hills rather than in drills—that is, several seeds are planted in groups in the row. The space between the hills is usually equidistant in and between the rows. Corn, pole beans, cucumbers, squash and muskmelons are often planted this way.

When to plant. In the northern states the growing season is not long enough to get best results from such plants as tomato, eggplant, and pepper if seed-planting is deferred until it is warm enough to sow outdoors. Therefore such plants are started early under glass either in greenhouse or hotbed to afford a longer season. The plants are then set out when danger of frost is past. In order to conserve space in the vegetable garden, cabbage, cauliflower, celery, etc., are also usually started under glass or in a seed bed outdoors and the seedlings transplanted later to the garden.

It is usually worth while to take a chance and plant part of the crop of such tender vegetables as corn and tomatoes a little ahead of the time it is considered safe. These early plantings may be protected, should frost threaten, by covering them with berry baskets or with plant protectors obtainable from a seed store.

Thinning. When the young plants develop from seeds planted in the drills or hills, thinning is necessary to allow the remaining plants room to develop. The thinning may be done as soon as the plants are large enough to handle; or, in the case of some crops—beets, carrots, onions—it may be deferred until the thinnings are large enough to be utilized. When young beets are 6 or 8 inches high the tops make delicious greens; and carrots, pulled when they are of fingerling size, possess an incomparable delicacy of flavor. If thinning is thus deferred, however, the plants which remain do not develop into such good specimens as they would have done had the row been thinned much earlier.

Cultivation. When the garden is a going concern, cultivation is practised periodically to conserve moisture and keep down weeds. This should be done just long enough after a rain so that the soil is not sticky. The tools used may be hand hoes—either draw, or scuffle; wheel hoes; or—if the plot is large enough—motor cultivators. A little hand-weeding will also be necessary to remove weeds which cannot be reached with a hoe. Cultivation is well worth while to keep down robber weeds; to improve the appearance of the garden; and, by preventing seeding, to reduce the amount of weeding necessary the following year.

Mulch paper. Specially prepared paper, obtainable from seed stores, is sometimes used for mulching to eliminate the necessity of cultivating the soil. With some crops excellent results are obtained; with others the effect is not so good. When mulch paper is used the distance between the rows is determined by the width of the paper—it comes in rolls 18 inches and 3 feet wide. When used for crops that are planted in drills, it is placed between the rows. The same method may be followed with planted-out crops (cabbage, tomato) or the young plants may be planted through holes cut in the center of the strip of paper. A convenient method is to cut crosses in the paper at correct intervals, raise the four flaps thus made, dig a proper hole in the ground, set the plant in, make the earth firm around it, and fold back the flaps. The paper must be securely anchored by zigzagging twine or wire across the strips and fastening it to the ground with wire staples. Whether or not these wires and papers will occasion more annoyance than they are worth is for the individual to decide.

Cultivation of individual crops. Following are notes on the cultivation of the commonly grown vegetables.

Artichoke, Globe. A handsome perennial with massive grayish laciniated foliage and thistle-like flower heads, the globe artichoke is sometimes used as an ornamental plant in the flower garden. It is not thoroughly hardy and I have never found anyone who has had much success with it in north-eastern United States. In California it is so much at home that it has become a pernicious weed. It requires a deep sandy loam with perfect drainage; otherwise the plants will succumb during the winter. Seeds should be started indoors in February or early March, the seedlings potted up, and, as soon as danger of frost is past, set out 2½ or 3 feet apart in rows 4 feet apart. If conditions are favorable, a few of the edible flower heads may be produced the first year. As the seedlings are variable, desirable forms should be selected and propagated by means of the suckers which are produced at the base of the plants. These should be removed and planted in the early spring. In regions with severe winters the plants should be protected by mounding them with coal ashes or by covering them with a foot or so of leaves.

Artichoke, Jerusalem. This is a sunflower whose tubers, although generally used like potatoes, are lacking in starch and taste as nearly like nothing at all as can be imagined. Although usually cooked, they are perhaps best sliced raw and added to mixed salads. They are scarcely worth growing unless one has a cook of the variety that could "sauce up" such articles as an old pair of kid gloves and make them palatable. The Jerusalem artichoke will grow in almost any soil so long as it is exposed to sunshine. The tubers should be planted in spring 1 foot apart in rows 2 feet apart. It may be recommended for an out-of-the-way spot to form a screen (it may grow 12 feet high)—with the warning that it may develop into a troublesome weed.

Asparagus. One of the most delectable of vegetables, asparagus is slow in coming into bearing, because no stalks should be cut until two years after planting, and then only in strict moderation. The soil should be prepared by double digging and manuring to a depth of 18 inches. Then make a trench 14 inches deep, place in it 4 inches of rotted manure, pack it down and cover with 3 inches of soil. Now set out one-year-old plants, 18 inches apart (the trenches should be 3 to 4 feet apart), spread the roots carefully, cover with 2 or 3 inches of soil and make firm. As the plants grow the remaining soil should gradually be brought into the trench so that by the end of the growing season the ground is again level. If blanched asparagus is preferred the rows usually are made 6 feet apart to afford opportunity to obtain the soil needed for blanching. Soil from between the rows should be mounded over the plants in early spring to a depth of 6 inches or more and the shoots cut with an asparagus knife just as soon as they show their noses. Care must be taken not to injure undeveloped shoots when cutting.

To get best results from asparagus it is necessary to maintain the soil in a fertile condition. When growth starts in the spring apply nitrate of soda at the rate of 10 ounces per 100 square feet, making a second and third application during the cutting season if it seems necessary. When cutting ceases apply a complete commercial fertilizer—3 pounds per 100 square feet. In the fall cut the tops to the ground and burn them. Apply 3 inches of partly decayed barnyard or stable manure, which should be lightly forked into the ground the following spring. Some growers prefer to apply the manure when cutting ceases.

An asparagus bed may be started by planting seeds in rows 1 foot apart, thinning the seedlings to 3 inches, and transplanting them to their permanent location the following year. Or, as recommended above, one-year-old plants may be purchased, and, as this saves a year it is perhaps the best way for the home gardener to make a start.

Cutting may commence the third year, but should not extend over three weeks. When the plants are thoroughly established, cutting may be kept up for seven or eight weeks.

Bean, Broad or **Windsor.** This bean differs from the usual run of garden beans in belonging to a separate genus (*Vicia* instead of *Phaseolus*) and in being perfectly hardy. The seeds are used before they are fully mature. The broad bean should be planted early in the spring, 2 inches deep in rows 2 feet apart, spacing the seeds 3 inches apart in the rows. It requires a long cool season for its development, and does best in a rich, rather heavy, clay loam. It is subject to attack by a black aphis.

Bean, Lima. Since they are quite susceptible to cold, lima beans should not be planted until the weather becomes definitely warm—usually toward the end of May or the beginning of June in the vicinity of New York. The climbing type is commonly grown. Poles 6 or 8 feet high are first set in the ground 3 to 4 feet apart, then 4 or 5 seeds are planted around each pole. Lima beans require a sandy fertile loam for best results.

Bean, Snap. Both pole and dwarf varieties of snap beans may be grown. Although the pole beans bear over a longer season, the dwarf kinds usually are preferred because they produce a crop in shorter time and they require no supports. By planting at intervals of a few weeks a succession may be maintained. It must be admitted that the pole varieties possess one advantage: most of the crop may be harvested while standing up. The culture of the climbing types is similar to that of lima beans except that they are not quite so susceptible to cold and may be planted a week or so earlier. The scarlet runner bean, in spite of its strings, is the best flavored of all the beans grown for their pods. My experience with it shows that it is disinclined to set pods during the hot summer months, and that one has to wait until cool weather comes in the fall before anything fit for the table is produced. Meanwhile, it is worth growing for the decorative value of its flowers.

Bush beans may be planted at the beginning of May and at monthly intervals until August. I have obtained a crop from beans planted here in Brooklyn as late as August 15. The seeds should be covered with 1 inch of soil and spaced 2 inches apart, the seedlings later thinned to stand from 4 to 6 inches apart.

In both the bush and pole groups there are varieties which are grown for their seeds rather than for their pods. In some quarters doubts are expressed as to the wholesomeness for human consumption of the seeds of some varieties. The immature seeds of the broad bean are said to be poisonous under some circumstances, and it is reported that some forms of *Phaseolus lunatus,* from which the lima bean is derived, have brought death to livestock. The poison, however, does not occur in the garden varieties. Thousands have eaten quantities of both broad and lima beans without any ill effects. The ripe seeds of the scarlet runner also are said to be poisonous—but this bean is always eaten when immature.

Beet. The seeds may be planted as soon as the ground can be prepared in the spring. Beets prefer a rather sandy loam that is not acid. The rows should be from 12 to 18 inches apart and the seedlings thinned to about 4 inches apart. For the production of roots suitable for winter storage the seeds should be sown toward the end of June or early in July. If the soil is deep and light the long-rooted varieties may be used for this purpose.

Broccoli. A vegetable that deservedly has come into great favor in recent years, broccoli forms a head of closely massed flowers which should be cut when they are in the bud stage. If the plants are left in place after the first cutting they develop lateral branches each surmounted by a similar but smaller head which also may be cut and used. For the early crop, plant the seeds in a greenhouse or hotbed in March and set out the young plants 1½ feet apart in rows 2½ feet apart, after they have been hardened off in the coldframe. Later crops may be started in May and June by planting the seeds outdoors.

Brussels Sprouts. Like broccoli, Brussels sprouts is a close relative of cabbage, and like cabbage the plants are heavy feeders, requiring a deep rich soil. The treatment is essentially the same as that accorded late cabbage (below). They do not begin to produce until cool weather comes in the fall. Brussels sprouts are quite hardy and are not at their best for table use until they have experienced a few frosts. In mild climates the "sprouts" (miniature cabbages produced throughout the length of the stem, which may be up to 3 feet high) may be harvested throughout the winter.

Cabbage. For an early crop, young plants may be set out in spring from seeds planted the preceding fall, the seedlings having been wintered in a coldframe; or the seeds may be planted in greenhouse or hotbed in February or early March. Young plants set out in April are ready for use in June or July. The rows for early cabbage should be 2 feet apart, and the plants 18 inches apart in the rows.

For the fall crop the seeds are planted in a seed bed outdoors in May and the seedlings planted in rows, 3 feet apart with 2 feet between the plants, early in July.

The soil used for starting the seeds should be heavily limed a short time previously, in order to lessen the danger of attack from the fungous disease which causes club-root.

Although cabbage will succeed in a variety of soils, those which are calcareous, inclined to heaviness, and rich in plant foods are preferred. Surface dressings of nitrate of soda at monthly intervals at the rate of 10 ounces per 100 square feet are beneficial.

Carrot. Seeds may be planted at intervals of about six weeks from April to July to provide a succession of young carrots. The rows should be from 12 to 18 inches apart. If thinned to stand about an inch apart the seedlings may be left until they are the size of a finger before finally thinning them. These thinnings are delicious to eat. Carrots require a deep loamy soil for best results.

Cauliflower. Although closely related to the cabbage, cauliflower is more exacting in its requirements, and is not happy in sections with a hot dry climate. The seeds for the early crop should be started in a hotbed in March —the seedlings being transplanted 2 inches apart in flats when they have formed their first true leaf. When they are established, harden them off in a coldframe and plant 1½ feet apart in rows 2½ feet apart. To prevent wilting the leaf area should be reduced at transplanting time by trimming the large leaves about one half. The late crop should be started by planting seeds in May or June.

A rich friable soil, well supplied with organic matter, is required for cauliflower. This crop will not endure drought, so provision must be made for watering when the necessity arises; or the natural supply of moisture must be conserved by mulches of paper or littery manure.

Celery. Early varieties are started by sowing seeds in late February or March in a greenhouse or hotbed. The seedlings should be transplanted 2 inches apart in flats, transplanting again to 4 inches if they become too crowded. In May set the plants in the open ground from 4 to 6 inches apart in single or double rows 30 inches apart. When they have attained sufficient size, blanching is aided by placing foot-wide boards along either side of the row; or use cuffs of heavy wrapping paper tied in place with twine.

Another method of growing early celery, when a deep rich soil and plenty of moisture are available, is to set the plants 7 or 8 inches apart each way in beds of convenient length and breadth. Place boards along the edges of the bed to blanch the outside rows. The rest of the plants will blanch each other by the shade cast by their leaves. It is believed that celery crowded in this manner is more susceptible to fungous diseases.

Late celery is started by sowing the seeds in a coldframe, or outdoors as soon as the ground is workable. The seedlings are transplanted from 4 to 6 inches apart and allowed to grow along until they are planted in their permanent location in early July. Usually in the small garden it is planned to have late celery follow an early maturing crop, such as spinach or early peas. The late varieties make stronger growth than the early kinds and should be spaced 6 inches apart in rows 3½ to 4 feet apart. A usual method of blanching late celery is to mound the plants, as they grow, with earth taken from between the rows. To facilitate this practice celery is frequently planted in trenches 6 inches deep, but this is not advisable if the soil is shallow because it results in the roots having to forage in infertile subsoil. In the trench method, water is easily applied in the early stages of growth by running it from a hose into the bottom of the trench.

The cultivation of celery should not be attempted except where the soil is fertile and moist.

Celeriac may be grown in the same manner as celery, except that it is not blanched, and the rows are spaced 18 to 20 inches apart.

Chard, Swiss. The easiest to grow of all the pot-herbs and one of the most productive. Swiss chard (also called **Leaf Beet** or **Silver Beet**) is a variety of beet grown for its leaves and leaf-stalks. Unfortunately, to many it is not very palatable. The seeds are planted as soon as the ground is workable, and the seedlings, when they are 5 or 6 inches high, are thinned so that the remaining plants stand 6 inches apart. The thinnings may be used as greens—if you can find anyone who will eat them! Afterward, alternate plants may be removed and similarly used. For the rest of the summer the chard may be gathered by pulling off the outer leaves, or by cutting off the entire tops within 3 inches of the ground.

Corn. Because it is wind-pollinated, corn should be grown in compact blocks rather than in long single rows, in order to ensure setting of the kernels. It may be planted in hills 3 feet apart, planting 5 or 6 seeds in each, afterward thinning the seedlings to 3 plants in each hill; or in drills 3 feet apart with the plants thinned to stand 1 foot apart. Small-growing, early-maturing varieties may be planted a little closer together than this. In the vicinity of New York it is worth while to take a chance and plant as early as mid-April. If the first planting is killed by frost, not a great deal of harm is done, and if it comes through, one may eat home-grown corn much earlier. Succession of crops may be provided by planting an early variety every 3 weeks or so from April to July or by planting early, mid-season, and late varieties at the same time in May and in June.

Corn grows best in a rich fairly heavy soil. New hybrid corn varieties are much more productive than the "open-pollinated" or standard kinds, but there are many who are convinced that the kernels are not so sweet as those of old-timers such as Golden Bantam. The flavor of corn deteriorates rapidly after the ears are picked (since the sugar changes to starch), so it should not be gathered more than a half hour before the cook is ready for it.

Cucumber. They take up so much room that cucumbers probably should be raised only in a spacious garden. The seeds should not be planted until danger of frost is past. A good scheme is to dig holes a foot wide and 9 inches deep, 5 feet apart each way. Place a shovelful of decayed manure in each hole, return the soil and plant 10 or 12 seeds in each hill, thinning the seedlings to 4 or 5 after the insects have taken their toll. An early crop may be obtained by planting the seeds in berry boxes in a hotbed or cold-frame a month or 6 weeks ahead of the outdoor planting season. This and related crops—melon, squash, etc.—are resentful of root disturbance, so box and all should be planted, with a splinter or two broken off if necessary to allow the roots to emerge.

A sandy loam, well enriched with decayed manure, is suitable for cucumbers.

Eggplant. In the northern states it is necessary to start eggplants in a greenhouse or hotbed to lengthen the season of growth sufficiently to enable the plants to produce fruits. It is a good plan to transplant the seedlings from the seed bed to paper or earthenware pots so that no check to growth is experienced when the plants are set in their permanent locations. Eggplant is susceptible to cold; therefore, in the vicinity of New York, it is usually not safe to plant it out until the beginning of June. Plant 2 feet apart in rows 2½ feet apart. A warm light fertile soil is desirable.

Kale. A relative of cabbage, kale is cultivated in exactly the same way as late cabbage. It is hardy and therefore not adversely affected by frosts.

Kohlrabi. In order to obtain a tender palatable product, it is necessary to provide conditions which will enable kohlrabi to mature quickly. A heavily manured calcareous soil is desirable. Growth should be hastened by the application of nitrate of soda at the rate of 1 ounce to each 10 feet of row. Plant in rows 15 to 18 inches apart and thin the seedlings to 6 inches. Harvest when the swollen stems are about 2½ inches in diameter.

Leek. The seeds of leeks should be started in a hotbed, or in a seed bed outdoors in a sunny sheltered spot as soon as the ground is workable. Prepare for final planting by digging trenches 6 inches deep, 18 inches apart. Plant the seedlings 6 inches apart in the trenches when they have attained a height of about 6 inches. As growth progresses, gradually fill the trench with soil. In the fall, if the soil is rich and growth has been vigorous, it may be possible to increase the length of the blanched edible portion by earthing up the plants with soil from between the rows. Care should be taken to avoid getting soil in the axils of the leaves, because it is almost impossible to remove it by washing. Cuffs of heavy paper placed on the plants before mounding them with soil helps to avoid this trouble. The plants may be stored for winter use in moist sand in a cold cellar; or left outdoors in regions where the winters are not severe.

A deep rich soil is necessary for the production of worth-while leeks.

Lettuce. Demanding cool weather, lettuce can seldom be induced to "head" during the hot days of summer. The first outdoor sowing should be made as soon as the ground is workable. Not more than 20 feet of row (for the average family) should be planted at one time. Plant for succession at three-week intervals. The earliest crop may be started in the greenhouse or hotbed a month or so in advance of the time of outdoor planting. For the fall crop, plantings may be made in August.

The rows should be 1 foot apart with from 8 inches to 1 foot between the plants in the row, according to variety. A well-drained "quick" rich sandy soil is necessary for best results with lettuce.

Sometimes lettuce may be induced to head in hot weather by shading the plants with cheese-cloth screens made by tacking cheese-cloth on light wooden frames which are supported on stakes driven into the ground. When this method is practised it is convenient to grow the lettuce in beds 4 or 5 feet wide with the plants spaced 8 or 10 inches apart each way.

Muskmelon is cultivated in practically the same way as cucumber.

Okra may be treated just as you would corn, except that in the northern states succession plantings probably are useless.

Onion. Either sets or seeds may be used for raising onions. Sets are produced by sowing seeds thickly in poor soil and letting the plants mature as they stand. The result is a crop of small bulbs which are stored over winter and planted the following spring. They may be purchased in any large seed store. Sets should be planted in rows 1 foot apart, making furrows 2 inches deep for their reception. Place them 2 inches apart and cover them with soil. When sufficient growth has been made, alternate plants may be pulled out and used as scallions, leaving the others to mature. Sets are useful for producing an extra early crop.

For the general-purpose crop from seeds, sowing may be done as soon as the ground is fit to work, in rows 1 foot apart. The seedlings should be thinned to stand 4 inches apart. Those who like scallions may defer thinning until the stems are about as thick as a lead-pencil. The onions remaining, however, will not produce very large bulbs if this practice is followed.

To obtain superlative success with onions thorough preparation of the ground is necessary. Double-dig the soil in the fall and incorporate plenty of manure. In the spring cultivate the surface to make a finely pulverized seed bed. Light soils should be compacted by rolling before planting the seeds. Quickly available nitrogenous fertilizers applied when the plants have made a good start are valuable for this crop. Cultivation must be assiduously practised to keep down weeds. To produce exhibition onions of the Ailsa Craig type, individual specimens of which may weigh up to four pounds, start seeds under glass in February and plant the seedlings outdoors in April, in rows 18 inches apart, spacing the plants 6 inches apart.

Parsley. As the seeds of parsley are slow to germinate, often taking 4 or 5 weeks before the seedlings show themselves, it is a good plan to hasten germination by soaking the seeds in tepid water for 24 hours prior to planting in rows 1 to 1½ feet apart. The seedlings later should be thinned to stand 6 inches apart. Seeds may be started in the hotbed for an early crop. Parsley makes an attractive edging in the vegetable garden.

Parsnip. A crop of parsnips occupies the ground for the whole season. The seeds are slow in germinating, so the rows should be marked by sowing radish with the parsnip seeds to enable the soil between the rows to be cultivated without danger of injuring the parsnip seeds. The radishes are ready for table use before the parsnips have made much growth. Plant in early spring in rows 15 to 18 inches apart and thin the seedlings to 6 inches apart. Parsnips require a deep loamy soil.

Pea. Smooth-seeded peas may be planted as soon as the ground can be worked in the spring. They are not equal in flavor to the wrinkled varieties but are valuable for producing an early crop. The wrinkled or "marrowfat" kinds should be planted about 2 weeks after the smooth-seeded varieties.

Dwarf varieties may be planted 3 inches deep in double rows 6 inches apart with a space of 18 inches between each double row. These will not need any supports. The semi-dwarf and tall varieties may be similarly planted but the space between the rows must be increased to correspond with the height. These varieties must be supported, either with brush, chicken-wire netting, or stakes. In general, the taller the vine, the longer the picking season. Quite dwarf varieties may give only one picking. I think it a better plan, in regions with hot summers, to obtain successive crops by restricting the planting to semi-dwarf kinds; using an early variety such as World's Record, and a mid-season variety such as Lincoln planted a week later. Tall, late varieties are well adapted for localities where the summers are cool. Books and seed catalogs tell us that it is possible to raise peas in the fall by planting the seeds about the middle of August, but I must confess to consistent failures in my attempts to do this.

Peas do not like hot dry conditions at the root. Therefore it is considered a good practice to prepare a deep seed bed and plant the seeds deeply. One method is to open a trench 6 inches deep, plant the seeds and cover with 2 inches of soil. As the plants grow, the trench is gradually filled with the remaining soil.

A well-drained loamy soil of good moisture-holding capacity is suited for peas. Because they are legumes, with nitrogen-fixing bacteria accommodated in tubercles on their roots, it is not necessary to apply fertilizers rich in nitrogen.

Pepper. Treat peppers the same as eggplant except for spacing, which may be 15 inches, in rows 18 inches or 2 feet apart.

Potato. Early potatoes should be planted 4 inches deep, 15 inches apart, in rows 2 to 3 feet apart. Late varieties should be accorded more room— 18 inches by 3 feet—and planted 6 inches deep. The "seed" may consist of small whole potatoes (favored by many English growers); or the more common practice may be followed of using large potatoes cut into chunky pieces each containing two or three eyes. The soil should be cultivated to keep down weeds, and when the tubers are forming the plants should be hilled up to cover the tubers to prevent greening, and to aid in keeping the roots cool.

Potatoes are most productive in cool moist climates. The soil preferred is a well-drained fertile sandy loam. Many growers object to fertilizing directly with organic manure, preferring land to which a heavy application was made the year before, and making use of inorganic commercial fertilizers for the current season. Back of this practice is the belief that organic manures favor the development of disease. A complete commercial fertilizer rich in potash may be applied—25 pounds to 1,000 square feet, and worked into the surface soil after digging or plowing. A calcareous soil favors the growth of the organism responsible for potato scab, therefore lime should not be used except when the soil is excessively acid.

Pumpkin requires much the same conditions as cucumber. A common practice is to plant the seeds in the corn patch, in hills 9 feet apart each way.

Radish. Start the first planting of radishes as early as possible in the spring. For the average family, a row 6 feet long will be sufficient to plant at one time. Plant early varieties at two-week intervals until mid-May; then, if you are not surfeited with radishes, plant the summer varieties. About the end of July, winter radishes, which produce enormous roots (they may weigh up to 50 pounds) capable of being stored in sand for winter use, may be planted. The winter varieties should be given plenty of room—18 inches between the rows and 6 inches to 1 foot between the plants in the rows. Early radishes may be grown in rows 6 inches to 1 foot apart and thinned to 1 to 2 inches in the rows.

A "quick" light rich soil is necessary, because radishes are palatable only when they have been grown speedily.

Rhubarb. Deep, rich soil is required for the best development of rhubarb, which is a perennial. Plants may be set out in the spring or fall 3 feet apart each way. Cultivate to keep down weeds and to promote the production of a vigorous rootstock. Stalks may be pulled for use the spring following a season's growth. Although there are some who utilize the leaves as greens, this is a dangerous practice because some individuals are seriously poisoned by eating them. After the stalks have been harvested, the soil about the plants should be mulched with a 3-inch layer of partly decayed manure. Flower stalks should be pulled out as soon as they are visible, unless their use for indoor decoration is considered more important than a crop of rhubarb the following year.

The soil for rhubarb should be double-dug and a liberal quantity of decayed manure mixed with it.

Rhubarb varies in productivity when raised from seeds, hence desirable individual plants should be propagated by division when they are dormant.

It is possible to force rhubarb without much equipment. Roots should be dug in the fall, placed in boxes with soil around them, and left outdoors to freeze. In January or February they may be brought into the cellar. Leaves will then develop quickly.

Rutabaga, see **Turnip.**

Salsify. Sow seeds of salsify (also called **Oyster-plant** or **Vegetable Oyster)** in early spring 1 inch deep in rows 15 inches apart. Thin the seedlings to 6 inches. The roots may be dug and used in the fall; or stored in sand for winter use; or they may be left in the ground and used before growth starts in spring. In regions where the soil occasionally thaws, the roots may be dug at intervals during the winter.

The soil must be prepared at least a foot deep (deeper if possible) for the production of long strong roots, which are the edible portion of the plant.

Spinach. The seeds of spinach may be planted in September or early in spring in rows 1 foot apart, thinning the plants to about 4 inches. Quick-acting nitrogenous fertilizers are beneficial after the crop has made a good start. It must have a light but heavily manured soil and cool weather for its development.

Spinach, New Zealand. An entirely different plant, New Zealand spinach revels in hot weather. Seeds should be planted an inch deep in rows 2 feet apart. As the seedlings grow they may gradually be thinned (using the thinnings for greens) until the plants remaining are 1 foot apart. From now on the tender tips of the shoots may be picked off as required. The plants continue bearing until frost.

Squash belongs in the same family as cucumber and requires the same general treatment. The trailing kinds should be planted from 6 to 8 feet apart each way, and the bush kinds 4 feet.

Sweet Potato. A gamble in northern gardens, sweet potatoes are propagated by means of "sets" or "slips" obtained by placing small roots in sand in a hotbed. This stimulates the production of shoots which, when they are 6 to 8 inches long, are pulled off with roots attached. These young plants are the "sets" which are planted 12 to 18 inches apart on broad slightly raised ridges 4 feet apart, made by first plowing a furrow about 4 inches deep into which decayed manure is placed. A back furrow is then made on either side, which covers the manure and forms a ridge which is raked down to form a broad level area for planting.

Sweet potato succeeds best in a warm rich sandy soil.

Swiss Chard, see **Chard.**

Tomato. If accorded warmth and sunshine, tomatoes will succeed in almost any kind of soil. The seeds should be started in a greenhouse or hotbed in March, transplanted to flats or to paper or earthenware pots, and set out in the garden when danger of frost is past. They may be planted 3 feet apart each way, or 1 foot apart, in rows 3 feet apart. If the last-named method is adopted, the plants must be restricted to a single stem and supported on stout stakes at least 6 feet high. The lateral shoots are pinched out as soon as they can be grasped by finger and thumb, and the main stem is attached to the stake by broad tape to avoid injury. If planted 3 feet apart each way the plants may be allowed to develop naturally, but unless the plants are supported, or mulched with straw, this method results in some spoilage through the fruits coming in contact with the ground. Tomatoes do well under a mulch. Supports may be made by sticking four stakes in the ground around each plant and connecting them with barrel-hoops or twine, or a rack may be constructed by driving 2 x 2-inch stakes 6 feet apart on each side of the row, slanting them away from the plants. These should be connected with slats ($\frac{1}{2}$ x 1 inch will do) spaced about 9 inches apart. Cross-pieces connecting the stakes will help to keep the construction rigid and provide further support for the plants.

Turnip. For planting in spring, early turnip varieties such as **White Milan** are used. For fall use, yellow-fleshed types and the white strap-leaf kinds are commonly planted. The first group is sown in early spring—either broadcast, or in rows 1 foot apart, thinning the plants to 4 inches. The second group is handled in the same way except that the seeds are sown from the middle of July to the middle of August.

The **Rutabaga Turnip,** which is the best kind for winter storage, requires a longer period for development and more room in which to grow. The seeds should be sown about the middle of June, in rows 18 inches or 2 feet apart, and thinned to 6 inches.

A loamy soil, heavily manured, is preferred for turnips.

XXII. THE FRUIT GARDEN

Problems. There is no denying the pleasure and satisfaction that come from raising one's own fruit, but it is well to have one's eyes open before going in for any extensive planting. The following paragraphs are presented not with the idea of discouraging anyone from planting fruit trees and bushes, but merely to give the reader an inkling of some of the bothers with which the fruit grower may have to contend.

Pests. Unfortunately, most of the trees and shrubs grown for their edible fruit need to be sprayed rather frequently to keep them free from insect and fungous pests. Spray calendars released by Agricultural Experiment Stations recommend from five to ten applications of spray solutions throughout the year.

It is not easy to carry out spray programs of this nature without proper equipment—the purchase of which may not be warranted when only a small property is involved. However, when only a few fruit trees are grown there is perhaps less danger of their being attacked by insects and fungi in devastating numbers. If the neighborhood is possessed of a coöperative spirit, the spraying problem may sometimes be solved by means of a community spraying outfit purchased out of a fund provided by the beneficiaries.

Even if it is not possible to proceed with a full spray program as advocated by Experiment Stations and practised by commercial orchardists, it is worth while to plant apples, pears, peaches, and plums for their esthetic value alone. Under such circumstances, spraying only for pests which are likely to appear in the garden even without the fruit trees might be sufficient. There is always the chance that the trees will be reasonably free from troubles even though they are not sprayed.

In those sections where the cedar rust and the white pine blister rust run riot, it is sometimes necessary to decide whether apples are more important than red cedar and whether currants and gooseberries are worth more than white pine. The fungi responsible for the rust diseases of apples and of currants and gooseberries require another plant, called an alternate host, for the completion of their life cycle. In the case of apple rust, the alternate host is the red cedar; in the case of the white pine blister rust it consists of gooseberries and currants—especially the black currant. The elimination of one of the hosts in a locality is a means of combating the disease. No red cedars must be allowed to grow within one mile of apples, and no currants or gooseberries within half a mile of the white pine—and even this precaution may not give complete assurance of freedom from the diseases. Some authorities consider that spraying against these diseases is almost useless, while others believe it to be helpful.

Self-sterility. The prospective planter must remember that some varieties of apples, pears, cherries, plums, and strawberries are partly or wholly self-sterile and require to be cross-pollinated. Therefore, in order to get a full crop of fruit, another variety of the same kind, blossoming at the same time and possessing compatible pollen, must be grown in the vicinity. Nurserymen—or, better, the State Agricultural Experiment Station—can give such information.

Storage facilities. The selection of types of apples and pears for planting should be determined in part by whether or not storage facilities are available. If it is not possible to provide storage space where a uniform temperature of 35 to 45 degrees can be maintained throughout the winter, it is better to concentrate on varieties which ripen early and are ready for use during summer and fall; and let the commercial grower worry about providing fruits for winter use.

Help from Experiment Stations. Since directions and lists of desirable varieties vary in different states, the information is best obtained from the nearest State Agricultural Experiment Station, almost every one of which publishes bulletins covering the subject. Thus, it is easy for the reader to obtain, merely by sending a request on a postcard, detailed information on spray programs, varieties of fruit adapted to a given location, varieties suitable for cross pollination should those recommended require it, how and when to plant, prune, protect, and fertilize. It is important in each locality to choose fruits carefully, because it frequently happens that an otherwise desirable variety is adapted to only a limited range of climatic and soil conditions. In the case of annuals and perennials, not a great deal of harm is done if a variety not adapted to the location is planted, but with fruit trees it is exasperating, after a lapse of years, to find that they do not succeed in one's particular district.

Planting suggestions. Fruits may be used for garden decoration as well as for the value of their crops. Even an orchard may be partly made into an informal flower garden. Certain general practices apply to the handling both of the trees (or smaller plants) and the soil, no matter what the purpose of the fruits.

Soil preferences. While practically all fruits, subject of course to climatic limitations, may be made to grow in almost any kind of soil which will support vegetation, most of them have individual preferences for soil, in which they will produce a finer crop. Pears, blackberries, gooseberries, and currants will grow in a rather heavy soil which, however, must be well drained; apples, plums, quinces, grapes, raspberries and strawberries prefer a deep medium loam; peaches and cherries do well in a sandy loam, and strawberries also, if they are supplied with plenty of moisture while they are actively growing.

Mulching, cover-crops, and fertilizers. During the first year or two after planting, the soil over the roots of newly planted trees must either be mulched to conserve moisture and keep down weeds, or kept cultivated. It might prove desirable, especially in the case of unmulched trees, to water them during periods of drought. These measures enable the trees to get a good start. In commercial orchards sometimes a hoed crop is planted between the young trees. Another practice followed by some orchardists is clean cultivation over the entire area until about July, then planting a cover-crop which is plowed under the following spring. The cover-crop may serve the double purpose of checking late growth by removing water from the soil and of providing green manure when it is plowed under. Excessive applications of nitrogenous fertilizers to apples, pears, and quinces should be avoided, because of the danger of inducing sappy growth favorable to the development of fire blight.

Fruit trees for ornament. If fruit is cultivated primarily for its esthetic value, and not for the purpose of making a living, it is permissible to eliminate much of the meticulous attention to details of cultivation (which to the professional orchardist seem absolutely necessary), and endeavor to make the fruit garden or orchard as decorative as possible. One system of cultivation which tends in this direction is to plant the orchard to grass traversed with turf walks kept closely cut with the lawn mower. Daffodils or other bulbs can be naturalized in the grass of the unmown areas. The grass not occupied by bulbs should be mown occasionally with a sickle-bar machine and, unless tidiness is considered more important than the welfare of the trees, the cut grass could be allowed to lie where it falls to form a mulch. When the bulb foliage ripens, the remaining grass may be cut.

In recent years many city dwellers have purchased abandoned farms for use as summer homes or year-round residences. Often on these farms there is an old orchard which might receive the treatment suggested in the preceding paragraph. Usually, such an orchard will require some rejuvenational pruning which, if beauty is the prime consideration, will be directed toward developing the picturesque habit of the trees. Also a rather strenuous spray program may be necessary for a year or two if the trees are badly infested with insect and fungous pests. If the growth of the trees appears stunted, an application of fertilizer will help to bring them back to a normal rate of growth. If the orchard is in turf and the owner desires to maintain it thus, the fertilizer may be scattered on the surface, or applied by means of the perforation method described in Chapter VII, TREES AND SHRUBS. If the sod is to be plowed under, the fertilizer may be broadcast before plowing.

Fruit trees may be used in place of the trees usually planted when forming the garden landscape. When a broad tree, not too large, is required, the apple is excellent. And, incidentally, a well-fruited, red variety of apple is strikingly beautiful in the fall, as well as in the spring when its blossoms are displayed. Recently, I saw one such planted in the center of a carriage turn on a Long Island, N. Y., estate. With no other planting in its immediate vicinity, it stood out boldly and was extraordinarily effective. The crab-apples commonly planted to provide fruit for jelly are even more ornamental.

If a rather tall narrow tree is called for, consider the pear, which, with a little judicious pruning, may be made to assume the form of a rather narrow pyramid. Although the pear does not possess the decorative value of the apple, it has many claims to beauty. One of the most striking features in an English garden in which I once worked was a pergola of pear trees planted on both sides of one of the main walks. The trees were set about 2 feet apart and trained to single trunks on an iron frame which spanned the walk for a length of about 50 feet. Essentially, the trees were what the gardener calls single cordons, and the effect was that of a pleached alley. Of course, in addition to the regular winter pruning, considerable pinching back was necessary during the summer to keep the trees within bounds.

Still another example of an interesting use of fruit trees as decorative material is to be seen in the kitchen garden of one of the large show places in England. Here the vegetable garden is divided by two walks at right angles. At the point of intersection there is a pool and an ornamental wrought-iron rain-gauge. A row of dwarf fruit trees flanks the walks on both sides, with enough room between them and the edges of the walks for a border of herbaceous perennials.

Fruits on dwarfing stocks. Most fruit nurseries are able to supply apples and pears, in the more popular varieties, grafted on dwarfing stocks which reduce the stature of the trees and tend to bring them into bearing earlier. If you can be sure of obtaining trees which will remain uniformly dwarf, they are valuable for planting on small properties because they occupy less room and permit a greater variety to be grown.

Specific cultural directions. The fruits which form the major crops in temperate-zone gardens may be divided into the POME FRUITS (apples, pears, and quinces), the STONE FRUITS (peaches and nectarines, cherries, and plums), GRAPES, and SMALL FRUITS, most of which are popularly called berries. Simple directions are given below for the raising of each kind of fruit on the home grounds.

POME FRUITS

Apple. The trees should be planted where there is good air drainage to lessen the chances of damage from late frosts.

Age of trees for planting. One- or two-year-old trees are usually preferred for planting, except by those impatient souls who cannot wait the few years necessary to bring the trees to bearing age. There are some nurserymen who cater to this group by growing the trees in the nursery until they attain fruiting size, selling such trees, of course, at a greatly enhanced price. If immediate results are required and, if the pocketbook can stand it, bearing-age trees are worth planting, *provided* they are moved and planted without much damage to the root system. A properly cared-for apple tree may be expected to remain in bearing condition for 50 years. It is probable that a tree planted when it is 1 or 2 years old will give a better performance over this period than a tree planted when it is 8 or 10 years old, because the shock occasioned by transplanting is less, and the tree is better fitted to adapt itself to its new environment.

Time of planting. In regions of very severe winters or in exposed situations, spring planting is preferred for apples because it enables the roots to become established before they have to endure inclement weather. But planting may be done in the fall, not later than mid-November.

Distance between trees. The distance allowed between trees is dependent upon the character of the soil, the variety, and whether or not it is grafted upon a dwarfing stock. On rich land strong-growing varieties such as Baldwin and McIntosh are planted, as a general rule, 40 feet apart each way. In poor soil, 30 to 35 feet would be enough. Medium-sized varieties may be set 25 feet apart and those on dwarfing stocks 15 feet. There is another plan but, a few years after planting, it makes great demands on the strength of character of the owner. This is to plant twice the number of trees required, in order to get a larger crop in a shorter time, with a view to removing alternate trees before they interfere with the growth of the permanent individuals. But the grower must remember that it is just as unpleasant to uproot a healthy tree as it is to have a tooth extracted, unless he finds a ready customer for the trees, in which case he might find himself very much "in pocket" as a result of planting thickly.

Planting and pruning. The trees should be planted as described in Chapter VII, TREES AND SHRUBS. When pruning at transplanting time to compensate for loss of roots, have in mind the proper spacing of the branches which are to form, in the future, the framework or scaffold of the tree. These should be spaced as evenly as possible on the trunk and not closer together than 6 inches. If the leader is to be allowed to develop to a height of 9 to 10 feet, the scaffold limbs should be 8 to 12 inches apart. Shoots which leave the trunk at an acute angle should be cut off close to the trunk because if they are left they will form a crotch which sometime or other is almost sure to split. The height at which the head is formed is dependent upon the desires of the planter. It is easier to gather the fruit from a low-headed tree, but, on the other hand, it is easier to cultivate the ground beneath a high-headed tree and it affords better opportunity for planting ornamental shade-loving plants beneath it. Some orchardists consider that 30 inches is the most convenient height for the lowest limb of an apple tree.

Reams and reams of paper have been used in the discussion of pruning of apples and fruit trees in general. The attitude nowadays seems to be that once the head is formed not a great deal of pruning is necessary. Symmetry should be maintained by shortening shoots which show a tendency to outstrip their neighbors. Branches which cross and rub other branches should be removed; water-sprouts, which are weak succulent shoots often arising from trunk or main branches after severe pruning, should be cut off; and, if the branches are so thickly spaced that they prevent light from reaching the center of the tree or if they hamper the gathering of the fruit, they may be thinned. Apart from this, except in abnormal cases and the removal of dead wood if it occurs, no pruning is necessary.

Age of bearing, and failure to bear. The age of bearing is largely dependent upon the variety. If, at the expiration of 5 or 6 years, the trees fail to blossom, the owner should seriously think of initiating measures designed to bring about a bearing habit—except in the case of varieties such as Baldwin and Northern Spy, which may take 8 to 10 years to come into bearing. If the trees are growing vigorously the elimination of nitrogen from the fertilizing program, or the planting of a lawn or a cover-crop such as rye over their roots, will probably bring about the desired result. Root-pruning may, by checking exuberant vegetative growth, cause a tree to produce blossoms, but it should not be practised except when the preceding measures have failed. It is done by cutting off the roots encountered when digging a trench halfway around the tree 3 to 6 feet from the trunk (the distance depending on the size of the tree). If the tree still persists in its luxuriant vegetative growth, the other half of the root system should be pruned. Avoid pruning the tops while the trees are dormant when attempting to induce stubborn trees to bear.

Pear. The pear will grow on a variety of soils but, as previously noted, prefers those inclined to heaviness. The preceding cultural observations regarding apples apply also to pears except that, because of their pyramidal habit of growth, they may be set closer together—strong-growing varieties 20 feet apart, and the weaker kinds 15 feet apart.

Quince. While not nearly so popular as the apple and pear, the quince has its uses in the production of jellies and preserves, and is an interesting tree to grow. It may be trained either in bush form, which is preferable because of possible borer injuries, or as a small tree by restricting it to a single trunk in its early stages.

One- or two-year-old trees are preferred for planting in fall or spring. As quinces seldom attain a height in excess of 15 feet, they may be planted as close as 10 or 12 feet. Two or three trees are ample unless the fruit is grown for sale.

The quince is a surface-rooting tree and, in consequence, cultivation should be shallow to avoid injuring the roots. The necessary pruning consists of the removal of suckers and thinning the top if the branches become too crowded.

STONE FRUITS

Nectarine and Peach. Of these two by far the more important is the peach, although the nectarine, which is a smooth-skinned peach, is becoming more popular year by year. They require much the same methods of cultivation.

Shelter from prevailing winds is desirable, together with good air drainage, to lessen the danger of damage from late frosts. A rather sandy and well-drained loam is preferred. If space is limited, they may be set as close as 15 feet, but 20 feet is better.

Except in regions having mild winters, planting should be done in the spring. One-year-old trees should be used. The usual method of pruning at planting time is to cut off all lateral shoots and shorten the leader to 24 to 30 inches—a desirable height to develop the head. Pruning established trees may consist of cutting out some of the crowded branches to open up the center of the tree to air and sunshine. Large branches should not be cut, unless it is absolutely necessary. The flower buds of the peach, and consequently the fruits, are produced on the shoots of the preceding year; therefore, cutting back these shoots removes some of the flowers. This may be a good practice because the peach is prone to over-bear and cutting back is one method of thinning the fruit. Obtain a bulletin on peach pruning from your State Agricultural Experiment Station.

Cherry. Cherries are divided into two main groups—those with sweet fruit and those whose fruit is sour. These groups are again divided—the sweet cherries into the **Heart** and **Bigarreau** varieties, and the sour cherries into the **Duke** and **Morello** classes. Heart cherries have juicy, soft, sweet flesh produced on a tree pyramidal in outline. Bigarreau cherries are heart-shaped as in the preceding, but the flesh is firm and crisp and the tree is more rounded in outline. Duke cherries are smaller in size than the preceding. They are hybrids between the sweet and sour cherries and are more or less intermediate in flavor. The trees are inclined to be stocky with spreading branches. Morello cherries are small, dark-colored and very sour. In this country they are said to be susceptible to disease. They have slender flexible branches of drooping habit, which enables them to be easily trained as wall trees. In England they are frequently cultivated in this way and are in demand for planting on the north side of a wall because they will endure some shade.

Sweet cherries are difficult to grow. They are particular as to soil, demanding well-drained high ground which is light and rather sandy. The climate of the Pacific Northwest suits them admirably. They are not adapted to stand extremes of heat and cold. They may be set 20 to 25 feet apart. One- or two-year-old trees should be planted in the fall or early spring. Usually, they are pruned to start the head 2 or 3 feet from the ground. Very little pruning is desirable after the head has been formed and, as with the rest of the stone fruits, large branches should not be cut because large wounds are slow to heal, and because of the danger of causing gummosis—the exuding of sap from the tree.

Sweet cherries are subject to a multiplicity of pests, both fungous and insect, which is a great pity when we consider their ornamental value, combined with the delicious fruit which they produce.

Sour cherries are less "pernickety" and will grow on heavier soils. They should be set from 15 to 20 feet apart. Little pruning is necessary beyond opening up the center to light, except when they are grown as wall trees. Then, thinning out of the branches and "heading back" will be required to prevent the growth from becoming unwieldy. Much of this should be done during the growing season.

Plum. There are so many varieties of plums, differing greatly in their requirements, that it is difficult to treat of them briefly. They may be divided into three main groups, namely: varieties of European origin, those of Japanese origin, and varieties developed from native species. Some of the European varieties originated from *Prunus domestica,* a species of western Asia, and some from its variety *insititia.* Varieties of the type, *P. domestica,* are again divided into the prune group, the green-gage group, egg-plum group, and others. The *insititia* group includes the damsons and bullaces, which in general are small plums about the size of cherries, valued mostly for making preserves.

The *domestica* plums are superior in quality, but not so hardy as some of the derivatives from native species. They thrive in loamy soils and may be expected to bear well about 5 years after planting. They can survive the winter temperature of New York State.

The Japanese varieties will grow well in soils adapted to the growth of peaches. They come into bearing early and good crops may be expected 3 or 4 years after planting. Because of their early blossoming, they are subject to injury by late frosts.

Native varieties derived from *P. americana* and *P. nigra* are adapted for growth in regions having severe winters with low temperatures. Varieties of *P. Munsoniana* and *P. hortulana* will endure high summer temperatures. Plums of American origin are of little interest to growers in the northeastern states.

Although some plums are self-fertile, many require cross-pollination, and often the others are benefited by cross-pollination. Ask your State Agricultural Experiment Station to suggest varieties adapted to your location which will provide compatible cross-pollination.

One- or two-year-old trees are preferred for planting and they should be set 15 to 20 feet apart. Spring planting is best.

Prune at the time of planting to improve the shape of the tree, to eliminate branches which cross and those which form acute angles with the leader. During the first two or three growing seasons, stop "wild" shoots by pinching out their tips. Most varieties tend to bear more fruit than the tree should be allowed to carry if breakage is to be avoided and the best quality of fruit produced. Therefore, winter pruning is desirable to reduce the number of flowers produced. This should be followed up by removing, after the "June drop," all imperfect fruits and those which have been attacked by insects. Generally speaking, not more than one fruit should be allowed to develop on each spur, and spurs should not be closer together than 3 to 5 inches.

GRAPES

Except on the Pacific slope, where old-world grapes are extensively grown, varieties developed from native species are the main standby. *Vinifera* types and hybrids have been successfully grown in the northeastern states, but in general, they are less hardy and more subject to disease than the native varieties.

Grapes may be grown in almost any kind of soil provided it is well drained. Elevated ground and a southern exposure are preferred by most growers.

Supports. Supports usually are of posts 4 to 6 inches in diameter, spaced about 20 feet apart to accommodate two vines between two posts. The posts should be about 7 feet long and be driven into the ground 1½ or 2 feet. Two No. 9 wires are attached on the windward side of the posts, placing the first one about 30 inches from the ground and the second 60 inches. The end-posts must be securely braced. The wires are stretched taut with a wire stretcher. They are fastened around the end-posts and stapled to the intervening ones. Instead of a regulation support, the vines may be trained on an arbor or pergola, thus serving a double purpose—that of ornament and use.

Planting, training and pruning. One-year-old plants are set out in the spring, spacing them 8 to 10 feet apart, according to the strength of the variety. The plants should be cut back to two buds. Usually the first winter after planting they are again cut back to two or three buds. The vines may be allowed to trail along the ground the first year after planting.

There are many different ways of training grape vines. The four-arm Kniffen system, which requires the two-wire support described above, is perhaps the most popular in the East and Middle West. The second year after planting, if growth has been vigorous, the strongest cane is cut level with the first wire and tied thereto. The remaining canes are removed. Several shoots will develop from the top of the cane, two of which are to be trained along the lower wire. The following year (third) the strongest cane should be tied to the top wire and cut off just above it. Two of the next strongest canes should be selected, shortened somewhat, and tied to the lower wire. The remainder are cut back. The canes that are left should produce a fair crop of fruit. During the summer, two strong shoots from the top of the vertical cane should be trained along the top wire. The fourth year after planting, and subsequently, the arms which have carried the fruit-bearing shoots should be cut away and their places on the wires occupied by strong canes (one right and one left on each wire) which grew the preceding year. These should be shortened to six to ten buds and the remaining canes removed, except that a renewal spur should be left near the base of each of the retained canes. This is done by cutting four canes back to two buds. Whenever possible, they should be situated on or near the main trunk. The renewal spurs will produce shoots from which four canes will be selected at pruning time (early March) to carry the fruit-producing shoots of that year. Each of the buds left on the canes is capable of producing a shoot bearing one to four bunches of grapes. The amount of cutting back is determined by the strength of the vine—the weaker it is the more severe should be the pruning.

The above is only one example of the many systems of training.

Many novices are perplexed when the time comes to prune their vines. This is not surprising because the vines have a habit of not looking exactly like the diagrams in the pruning books. The important things to remember in pruning grapes are: (1) The shoots which bear the grape clusters originate during the current season from canes which grew the preceding year. (2) Arms which have supported fruit-bearing shoots should be cut away during the winter. (3) These arms should be replaced on the support by strong canes which developed the preceding year from near the head of the vine. (4) All remaining canes should be cut away, except for those which are cut back to form "renewal spurs."

This severe pruning keeps the vines within bounds and improves the quality of the fruit by reducing the number of bunches produced.

To avoid "bleeding" (which, however, is now regarded as not being very harmful) pruning should be done sometime during late winter (early March)—preferably on a mild day to ensure the comfort of the operator.

SMALL FRUITS

Unlike the preceding fruits, the bush berries have but little ornamental value, hence they are usually grown for purely utilitarian purposes. Unless they are raised in quantity sufficient to warrant an area to themselves, they should be relegated to the kitchen garden.

Blackberry. The cultivated blackberry prefers a heavy moist soil. The young plants, cut back to within 4 to 6 inches of the ground, should be set out in the fall, 3 to 4 feet apart, in rows 7 to 8 feet apart. Frequent cultivation is desirable. Little pruning is necessary until the bushes begin to bear, which will be during the second or third summer. From this time on, spindling shoots and all the canes which have fruited should be cut off at the ground line, and the remaining canes cut back about one third. The object of this is to produce a sturdy bush that will not topple to the ground when bearing fruit. Pruning should be done just before growth starts in the spring.

Raspberry. The raspberry adapts itself to a variety of soils but prefers a loam well supplied with humus, in a cool, moist, but well-drained location.

The plants should be set out in the spring. Spacing is determined by the system of cultivation. If the hill method is adopted, the plants are set 5 x 5 feet; if the solid-row system is used, they are spaced 3 feet apart in rows 7 feet apart. When the hill method is practised, stakes are set to each hill and the canes are tied to them. In the row system either the fruiting canes are cut off at a height of about 3 feet before growth starts, so that they need no support, or they are cut back about one fourth and are supported by stretching wires along the rows.

Black-cap raspberries differ from the red raspberries in possessing a non-suckering habit of growth. The usual method of training them is to pinch out the tips of the young growing shoots when they are about 30 inches high. This causes the cane to branch and stiffen so that it is self-supporting. The laterals should be cut back the following spring to from 6 to 12 inches.

It is the usual practice in pruning raspberries and black-caps to cut the fruiting canes at the ground line as soon as the fruit has been gathered. This allows the young canes (which will produce fruit the following year) room to develop, and exposes them to light and air so that their wood may properly ripen. If the canes which have fruited are not cut out during the summer, they must be removed before growth starts the following spring.

Currant. The red and white currants (*Ribes sativum*), the black currant (*Ribes nigrum*), and the gooseberry may act as hosts to the destructive white pine blister-rust. This fact should be taken into consideration before deciding to plant any representative of these groups.

Red and white currants are alike in habit of growth and similar in flavor, except that the latter are inclined to be less acid. Black currants have a distinct and peculiar flavor, and they have not made any great appeal to American palates as a dessert fruit, though jams and jellies made from them are moderately liked.

Currants delight in a rich moist soil. It is a good plan to mulch them in the spring with about 3 inches of partly decayed littery manure.

One- or two-year-old plants should be set in the fall, allowing about 4 feet between them. Prune by cutting out weak shoots and shortening those remaining one third. Subsequent pruning in the case of the red currant, which produces its fruit on spurs, should be directed toward maintaining about five main branches not more than three or four years old. This means that when the branches attain an age of three or four years, they should be cut off at a point near the base of the bush, thus allowing room for the more productive younger wood to develop. When currants are planted in rich soil, it may be necessary to shorten vigorously growing shoots in midsummer, especially during their early years, to prevent the bush from becoming leggy.

An English practice in pruning red currants is to cut back in midsummer all growth shoots which form among the spurs in the interior of the bush. Also, any wild-growing shoots on the exterior are shortened. In the fall the growth shoots among the spurs are shortened to 1 inch and the terminal shoots are shortened about one half.

Black currants bear best on one- or two-year-old wood. Therefore, when pruning cut out the older canes, especially those which show only a very short growth of young wood.

Gooseberry. I have yet to see an American-grown gooseberry worthy of being eaten from the hand. But it is possible to grow them so that they are acceptable for culinary uses, and those who share the Englishman's predilection for gooseberry "fool," tart, or pudding may be tempted to plant some.

Gooseberries delight in a heavy soil and cool growing conditions. The provision of a mulch on the soil over their roots as recommended for currants will help to keep the ground cool and moist.

They may be planted in the fall about 4 feet apart. Pruning consists of cutting out branches four or more years old and those which grow so low that their fruit may be spattered with mud during heavy rains. Nonbearing wood should be thinned to open up the bush to light and air and to make it easier to pick the fruit—a task which produces profanity under the best of conditions, and, if the bush is cluttered with unproductive spiny shoots, the effect on the picker is beyond mentionable words.

Strawberry. This delicious fruit will grow in a wide variety of climates and soils, but it prefers a cool growing season and a deep moist loam slightly on the acid side.

Some varieties of strawberries are pistillate (with no stamens), or bear so little pollen that for all practical purposes they are self-sterile. It is best not to plant such varieties, but if they are grown, at least one row of a perfect-flowered variety should be planted beside every three rows of the pistillate kinds to ensure pollination. Of course, both varieties must bloom at the same time.

Strong runners with roots may be set out in early spring; or, under garden conditions, new plants may be propagated as follows: As soon as runners start to form, 3- or 4-inch pots filled with soil are sunk into the ground in the vicinity of the plants. The tips of strong runners are layered in the pots and held in place with hairpins or something similar. When the pots become filled with roots, they are taken up, and the plants are removed and planted in a new bed. Such plants will produce fruit the following year.

There are several systems of growing strawberries. They may be planted 1 foot apart in rows 3 feet apart and all runners kept cut off. Large fruit is produced by this system, which allows weeding, cultivating, and mulching to be conveniently practised. Instead of removing all of the runners, a sufficient number may be left to form a matted row up to 2 feet wide. Although it is possible to maintain a strawberry bed for five years or longer, the first to third crops are usually the best. Therefore, it is well to have a bed coming along to take the place of the one to be discarded when it is no longer productive.

The beds should be mulched in the fall after the ground has frozen. The mulch may consist of strawy manure, straw or salt hay, the thickness dependent upon the severity of the climate. In the north central states, 6 inches of straw is thought to be desirable; in New York 3 inches is enough. In the spring the mulch should be loosened and, if it is too thick, enough should be transferred to the space between the rows to let the plants get through. When the plants start to bloom, the ground should be covered with a mulch of clean material (straw, salt hay, or pine needles) to keep the fruit from coming in contact with the soil and to prevent it from being spattered with mud during heavy rains.

XXIII. PLANTS IN THE HOME

Some garden lovers are not content to restrict their gardening activities to the outdoor growing season, even though they have no greenhouse facilities, and some have only houses or apartments in which to garden. Growing plants in the home offers an outlet for such enthusiasts, and I, for one, am in favor of it—if it is conducted with at least a modicum of sanity. Too many people become sentimental about their house plants and, because a particular specimen was a gift from Aunt Amelia, they continue to give it house room long after it has lost its beauty. Plants in the home are justified if they are decorative, if they are interesting, or if they are useful (such as herbs for culinary purposes). The curiosities belong in the spare room; herbs in the kitchen; while those in the decorative class should be relegated to the rubbish pile just as soon as they become unsightly. There is nothing more calculated to discredit house-gardening than the sight of a collection of woebegone and sickly plants, which have no prospect of ever regaining their health and beauty.

For many people, plants grown in glass cases (or bottles or jars), including aquaria, solve the problem of upkeep and satisfy the desire for indoor gardening.

POTTED PLANTS

Although the beauty of many potted plants is only transitory when they are brought into the home, there are many which will thrive year in, year out, if given reasonable care. A selection of these hardy ones is given on pages 371-3.

This chapter on plants in the home should be read in conjunction with Chapter XXV, GREENHOUSES, for information on potting soils, repotting, and the general principles of management of plants indoors. The section on forcing bulbs in Chapter XIV, FLOWERING BULBS, should be consulted for the methods of handling this group, which is well adapted for dwelling-house culture.

Difficulties of indoor gardening. The chief difficulty that has to be conquered in growing plants in the dwelling is the hot dry atmosphere of the average city home in winter. When the air is properly humidified, we discover that a temperature of 65 or 70 degrees is quite comfortable for ourselves, and that plants are also happier than in the normal apartment, where the temperature is kept around 80 degrees and the humidity like that of Death Valley. If there is no way of humidifying the air of the house as a whole, conditions can be made more tolerable for the plants—and the human occupants—by placing evaporating pans (which should be kept filled with water!) on the radiators, and by standing the potted plants in shallow water-tight pans filled with moist peatmoss or pebbles. If conditions are such that a daily light spraying with water may be given the plants, it is a great aid to the maintenance of the desirable humidity.

Other factors contributing to the failure of plants in the home are the presence of illuminating or cooking gas, insufficient light, the dust and impure air of large cities, and improper care.

Plants are far more susceptible to the ill effects of gas than are human beings, and it is important to ensure that there are no leaks, that the pilot light of the gas stove is not allowed to blow out, and that the gas is not turned on before someone is ready to light it.

Those who have attempted indoor photography realize that the amount of light in the house is far less than that outdoors; therefore the plants should be grown as near the windows as possible and on the sunniest side of the house.

There is little that one can do about the impure air of the city, beyond choosing resistant plants or those which can be grown in terraria (see page 376).

Dust, which clogs the stomata (breathing pores) and hinders the leaves from properly performing their functions, may be removed by wiping the leaves with a soft sponge wet with soapy water, or by placing the plants in the bathtub and spraying them thoroughly. But avoid the often recommended dose of castor oil. Applied to the soil it is harmful and, if smeared on the leaves, as is sometimes suggested, it may kill the plant by clogging its breathing pores.

Insect pests. The failure to detect insect pests and combat them immediately often wrecks the health of house plants or even claims their lives. Some of these pests, such as mites (commonly called "red spiders"), are quite minute and often the damage is done before their

presence is suspected. Close inspection at frequent intervals is necessary
and the aid of a magnifying glass is desirable. Spraying with clear
water is the best prophylactic measure I know of against insect pests.
The plants should be placed on their sides in the bathtub and the
leaves thoroughly sprayed, both upper and lower surfaces, with sufficient force to dislodge the insects but not with such vigor that the
leaves are torn. This should be done at least once a week.

Watering. The question I am most frequently asked is: "How
often shall I water my plants?"—to which there is but one answer: "As
often as they need it." No one can tell beforehand how often a plant
is going to require watering. This is determined by the character of
the species and of the plant in question, whether it is actively growing,
whether its pot is filled with roots, its vigor, the weather, the humidity
of the air, and the time of year. General principles to follow when
watering are:

1. Water thoroughly, standing the pot in a vessel of water if necessary, so that the ball of earth is wet through, and then refrain from
watering until the soil shows signs of becoming dry.

2. Plants which are actively growing and forming new shoots and
leaves may be watered freely.

3. Plants which have matured their growth and are resting should
receive only sufficient water to keep the leaves from wilting.

The water-tight jardiniere so often used to hold a flower pot is a
source of danger when water is carelessly applied. If it becomes partly
filled with water, the soil becomes waterlogged, air is driven out, the
roots decay, and the plant languishes.

Repotting. There is a widely held impression that repotting is a cure
for all the ills that plants are heir to, but this is far from true. The
plant's ill health may have been caused by any of the adverse factors I
have just mentioned, and repotting will not necessarily aid the plant to
recover. Sometimes the plant becomes sick because of waterlogged soil
brought about by insufficient drainage and careless watering. Repotting
into a larger pot is not a cure for this condition; in fact, it may ac-
centuate it. What should be done is to remove all of the soil from the
roots, washing it off if necessary. Then cut off all decayed roots and
transplant to a smaller pot, using gritty porous soil and giving drainage
particular attention. But when house plants get into an unhealthy
condition through waterlogged soil, usually the best plan is to throw
them away, because they are not likely, under house conditions, to

FOUR GOOD HOUSE PLANTS:

(*top left*) *Saxifraga sarmentosa.* (*top right*) BE-GONIA

BRAKE FERN (*Pteris*)

UMBRELLA PLANT

PLATE XXIV

PLATE XXV. (*upper*) LEAN-TO GREENHOUSE ATTACHED TO DWELLING.
(*lower*) GREENHOUSE WITH WORKROOM ATTACHED

Courtesy Lord & Burnham Company

survive the drastic root disturbance involved in cleaning off the old soil.

A plant needs repotting into a larger pot when it is growing vigorously and the pot is crowded with roots. Some plants, such as palms, pandanus, amaryllis, and nerine, do not object to being pot-bound; and, as there are obvious drawbacks to the use of large pots in the house, it is best to take advantage of this tolerance and keep the plants in comparatively small pots as long as possible. The required nutrients may be supplied by top-dressing with rich soil (first removing as much as possible of the old soil from the surface without disturbing the roots), or by the use of concentrated commercial fertilizers when the plants are actively growing. The amount to use is, of course, dependent on the size of the plant and the concentration of the fertilizer. A level teaspoonful of a 5-10-5 fertilizer supplied at intervals of five or six weeks will be about right for a plant growing in a 6-inch pot. Foliage plants such as ferns, aspidistra, and dracaena will be benefited by an occasional watering with a solution made by dissolving a teaspoonful of nitrate of soda in 6 quarts of water. Fertilizers must be applied with intelligence and the reaction of the plants should be carefully noticed. A sick plant in a waterlogged pot will not be benefited by an application of fertilizer, but a healthy one which has exhausted the available nutrients in its pot will perk up right away. It is better to err by giving too little fertilizer than by giving too much.

Occasionally, certain house plants grow so vigorously that they become too tall for the space assigned them. *Dracaena fragrans* and the ubiquitous rubber-plant are offenders, the former often losing its lower leaves so that it has the appearance of the famous "feather duster" palms of O. Henry. Such plants may be brought down to earth and made more presentable by means of the operation known as air-layering. (See Chapter XXVI, PLANT PROPAGATION.)

Displaying the plants. Transitory plants, whose decorative rôle is recognized as being only temporary, may be placed where they will be most effective, but bear in mind that they will last longer if kept away from radiators and as near as possible to the source of light.

Plants which we hope to make permanent occupants of the room should be placed near the windows. They may be displayed as pot plants on the window sill or on a plant stand, or they may be planted in the soil of an indoor window box constructed to fit the window space. A method which combines the flexibility of pot culture with the advantages of the more uniform moisture content of the soil of a window box consists of plunging the plants, still in their pots, in a window box filled with moist peatmoss. When this method is adopted, sickly plants can easily be removed and substitutions made; watering is needed less frequently because no evaporation takes place from the sides of the pots, and the air about the plants is somewhat moistened by evaporation from the peatmoss. The window box should be set on cleats in a water-tight tray to avoid the annoyance of water-drips on floor or rugs; or one may use the so-called "self-watering" window box, which has a water-tight receptacle at the bottom.

Culture of special plants. So many requests are received for specific directions for the culture of azaleas, cyclamens, and poinsettias as house plants that a few remarks on their proper handling are included here.

Azalea. The potted azaleas acquired at Easter are more likely to thrive as house plants than those obtained at Christmas, because they have not been unduly forced and because it is possible to place them outdoors within a few weeks, or just as soon as danger of frost is past. The pots should be plunged in the ground so that the soil does not dry out rapidly. A 3-inch layer of clinkers should be placed below the pot to keep worms from entering through the hole in the bottom and to provide drainage. The pot should be turned occasionally to discourage the growth of roots through the bottom. A partly shaded location is not amiss, but they should not be placed in dense shade or next year's flower buds may fail to form. The plants may be fertilized by applying tankage or cottonseed meal at the rate of a rounded teaspoonful to an 8-inch pot. Make two to three applications at intervals of 6 weeks. Water the plants during periods of drought. Before the first frosts of fall bring the plants indoors and keep them in a well-lighted room in a temperature as near 50 degrees as possible, watering them whenever the soil shows signs of becoming dry. When the flower buds are showing color, the plants may be brought into ordinary room temperature, though the flowers will last longer if kept cool.

Cyclamen. Though they are perennials, cyclamens which are kept over, even under greenhouse conditions, are not so satisfactory as those raised from seeds each year. They are therefore not very satisfactory as house plants. People who wish to make the attempt to preserve them through the summer for blooming the following winter should, if possible, keep them in a temperature between 50 and 55 degrees and maintain the soil in a moist condition until they have finished blooming. Shortly after this, the leaves will begin to turn yellow; the amount of water given should then be gradually reduced until the soil is fairly dry. Let them remain in this condition until August or September, when the corm should be removed, potted in new soil, and kept moist in partial shade outdoors. Bring them into the house before frost arrives, and keep them as near as possible to a temperature of 50 degrees.

Poinsettia. Usually received in full bloom around Christmas, poinsettias, under house conditions, start to deteriorate about the first of the new year. As soon as the leaves begin to turn yellow, gradually withhold water until the soil is quite dry. Store the plants, without watering them, in a temperature of about 60 degrees. When danger of frost is past, cut them down to a height of 6 inches and repot them in new soil. Place them outdoors in a sunny position and follow the same procedure suggested for azaleas. Bring the plants into the house before artificial heat is used in the fall and keep them in a sunny spot in a temperature of 65 degrees. Avoid exposing them to sharp fluctuations of temperature because this is likely to cause them to drop their leaves.

Selection of plants. Following is a list of plants which, given reasonable care, will thrive under house conditions. The common names are given first in alphabetical order.

FOLIAGE PLANTS

Common name	Scientific name	Remarks
Aspidistra	Aspidistra elatior	Will endure shade.
Baby's Tears	Helxine Soleirolii	Tiny moss-like creeper.
Blue Dracaena	Cordyline (Dracaena) indivisa	May be kept at 50° in winter.
Boston Ferns	Nephrolepis exaltata bostoniensis	Watch out for scale insects, and remove immediately.
Bowstring Hemp, see Snakeplant		
Cacti in variety		Need plenty of light, and careful watering in winter.
Chinese (or Japanese) Evergreen	Aglaonema modestum	May be grown in either water or soil.
Climbing Fig	Ficus pumila	Trailer for shade and cool temperature.
Dracaena	Dracaena fragrans	Tolerant of apartment house conditions.

Common name	Scientific name	Remarks
Dumb-cane	Dieffenbachia nobilis	Tolerant of apartment house conditions.
English Ivy	Hedera Helix	Trailer for shade and cool temperature.
Fern Asparagus	Asparagus plumosus	Climbing varieties need support.
Grape-ivy	Cissus rhombifolia	Good trailer.
India Rubbertree	Ficus elastica	Do not rub leaves with castor oil!
Kangaroo Vine	Cissus antarctica	Good for north window.
Nephthytis	Nephthytis Afzelii	Endures some shade.
Palms in variety	Howea, etc.	Rich soil and abundant moisture.
Philodendrons	Philodendron spp.	Will grow well in a north window.
Screwpines Common Screwpine Veitch Screwpine	Pandanus utilis Pandanus Veitchii	Has red spines and graceful leaves. Green leaves with white stripes.
Snakeplant	Sansevieria trifasciata Laurentii	Tolerant of apartment house conditions.
Strawberry-geranium	Saxifraga sarmentosa	Trailer, winter temperature 50°.
Succulents in variety	Byrnesia, Echeveria, Crassula, Kalanchoë, etc.	All need lots of sunshine and careful watering in winter to avoid getting soil too wet.
Wandering Jew	Tradescantia and Zebrina in variety	Trailer. Will grow in water for a long time.

FLOWERING PLANTS

African-violet	Saintpaulia ionantha	Best flowering plant for north window.
Apostle-plant	Marica Northiana	Beautiful iris-like flowers.
Azalea	Azalea indica	Peaty soil, winter temperature 50°.
Begonia in variety	Begonia Feastii Begonia semperflorens Begonia Thurstonii	Begonias grow best in a compost containing a good proportion of leafmold. Pots must be well drained.
Calla	Zantedeschia (Richardia) aethiopica	Needs rich soil and abundance of water when growing.
Camellia	Camellia japonica	Peaty soil, winter temperature 50°.
Cape-jasmine	Gardenia jasminoides	Flowers in summer. Cool in winter.
Chinese Primrose	Primula sinensis	Not worth keeping second year.
Christmas Cactus	Zygocactus (Epiphyllum) truncatus	Use gritty soil, partly decayed leafmold, and thoroughly decayed manure.
Flowering Maple	Abutilon hybridum	Prune in September.

Common name	Scientific name	Remarks
Gardenia	*Gardenia Veitchii*	Needs acid soil; moist air; night temperature in winter 60°.
Geranium in variety Horseshoe Geranium	*Pelargonium zonale*	Keep near 60° in winter.
Orchid Cactus	*Epiphyllum spp.*	See Christmas Cactus.
Patience	*Impatiens Sultani*	Keep near 60° in winter.
Shrimp Plant	*Beloperone guttata*	Pinch out tips of early shoots.
Spring-flowering Bulbs in variety, see Chapter XIV, FLOWERING BULBS		
Wax Plant	*Hoya carnosa*	Keep rather dry in winter.

Except where otherwise specified, loam with a small proportion of decayed manure should be used as potting soil.

TERRARIA

The use of wardian cases, which lately have been dignified by the application of the swankier term "terraria," adds considerably to the variety of plants capable of being successfully grown under house conditions. During the past ten years or so these aids to the house gardener have become quite popular, but they are by no means a new thing. About a hundred years ago the principle of growing plants in fairly tight glazed cases was discovered accidentally by Dr. Nathaniel Ward (hence the name "wardian" case), a London physician, who found the cocoon of a sphinx moth and, wishing to see the moth emerge from the chrysalis, placed it in moist earth in a glass bottle which he covered with a piece of tin. Much to his surprise, a fern and a grass appeared within a few weeks and grew successfully in the bottle for four years without any attention. They died during Dr. Ward's absence from home when the lid rusted, allowing water to enter the bottle and waterlog the soil.

The simplest form of wardian case for home use is a fish bowl. With moist soil placed in the bottom, the bowl is planted with suitable material and covered with a pane of glass, which maintains the humidity by keeping the moisture within. For more than nine months I had such a globe in my home. It was not watered during that period, and for three months during the summer received no attention whatever. As a result of this lack of attention, some of the plants died, smothered by their more aggressive neighbors, but those that survived were perfectly healthy.

FIG. 56. Home-made wooden terrarium

Home-made cases. There are many different types of cases designed for growing house plants. Some are merely glass domes with a receptacle for holding the plants; some look like miniature greenhouses; and some are more elaborate, equipped with electrical heating devices having thermostatic control. You may buy one of these ready-made cases or you may prefer to make your own. The construction is so simple that anyone apt in the use of tools will have little difficulty. First, construct a shallow box to fit the window or other space to be used. The box should not be less than 3 inches deep—4 or 5 inches is preferable—and should have half-inch drainage holes bored 6 inches apart in the bottom. Uprights from 9 to 18 inches high, made of 1 x 1-inch soft pine or cypress, with grooves ¼ inch deep on two sides are fastened at the four corners to hold the glass. The roof may be flat or peaked (Figs. 56, 57). It is, of course, much simpler to make a flat roof, for all that is required is a piece of glass cut to the right size which will rest on the uprights supporting the sides. The objection to a flat roof is the temptation that arises to use it as a table for holding books or magazines, and such treatment is, of course, detrimental to the plants in the case. If a peaked roof is made, the gable ends should be fashioned of similar 1 x 1-inch material with one groove, and the

Fig. 57. Terrarium with frame of brass strips

ridgepole with two grooves. The roof glass is held in place by pegs of wood or metal which extend through the gable ends and allow the lower edge of the glass to rest upon them. It is advisable to have two sets of holes on one side for the pegs so that the glass may be lowered ½ inch or so for ventilation at the peak, which is necessary when the condensation of moisture on the glass obscures the plants within the case.

A simpler case may be made by cutting glass to fit the plant box, pushing it down between the soil and the sides of the box, and binding the projecting edges with adhesive tape where they join (Fig. 93). This method necessitates a flat roof, made of a single pane of glass which may be tilted to give the necessary ventilation.

Soil. First, fill the plant box loosely with good earth. A mixture of 2 parts loam, 1 part leafmold, and 1 part sand, with a little thoroughly decayed manure, is satisfactory. If you cannot provide such a mixture, use good garden soil. Next, obtain a suitable selection of potted plants, turn them out of their pots, and plant them in the box, making the earth firm about their roots.

Selection of plants. The selection of the right kind of plants has an important bearing on the success of the wardian case. So far as possible, choose plants having the same temperature and moisture requirements—in other words, do not put plants from the north woods, such as partridge-berry and wintergreen, in the same case with plants whose native home is a tropical rain forest. Avoid geraniums and similar plants which are subject to disease under humid conditions; and also avoid plants which are specially adapted to dry conditions, such as many of the cacti and succulents. Plants that do not make too rapid a growth are preferable, for they do not so quickly outgrow their quarters. Among the suitable plants for a warm room are:

Adiantum cuneatum (Maidenhair Fern)
Aglaonema costatum
Anthurium Scherzerianum
Begonia, any of the dwarf varieties
Caladium, the small fancy-leaved kinds (for summer use)
Codiaeum in variety. (Croton. Suitable only for large cases, as they are fast growers.)
Davallia bullata (Squirrel's-foot Fern)
Davallia fijiensis
Dizygotheca (*Aralia*) *elegantissima*
Dracaena Godseffiana
Dracaena Goldieana
Dracaena Sanderiana
Fittonia Verschaffeltii and var. *argyroneura*
Maranta roseo-lineata
Philodendron cordatum
Selaginella Emmeliana
Selaginella Kraussiana and var. *Brownii*
Selaginella Martensii
Syagrus (*Cocos*) *Weddeliana*

In a cool room where the temperature hovers between 45 and 55 degrees, the following will be happy:

Acorus gramineus
Araucaria excelsa (which will quickly outgrow its quarters if only a small case is available).
Camellia japonica
Cyrtomium falcatum (Holly Fern)
Farfugium grande
Ficus pumila
Hedera Helix conglomerata
Mondo (*Ophiopogon*) *Jaburan vittata*
Pteris Wilsonii (Brake Fern)
Saxifraga sarmentosa

When it can be done without any danger of exterminating the native flora, collected plants from the wild may be used. Mosses and lichens of various kinds, partridge-berry, small ferns, etc., with a young spruce or fir to give the necessary height, may be worked up into attractive scenes in the cool-room terrarium.

General care. After the plants are set in the box, give the soil a thorough soaking with water if drainage holes have been provided, and set the box aside to drain. If it does not have drainage holes, great care must be taken to avoid waterlogging the soil. Apply only enough water to moisten the earth all through. After this preliminary watering, the chances are that no more water will be required for several months. Ward had plants growing for nine years without supplementary watering. The water that evaporated from the soil and that which transpired from the leaves condensed on the glass and thus returned to the soil. The frequency with which water must be applied is dependent upon the tightness with which the case is glazed. Do not water until the soil shows definite signs of becoming dry.

Much trouble will be saved if you make certain that your plants are free from insect pests before you place them in the case. Keep a close watch for insects and, if any make their appearance, promptly remove them by washing them off with soapy water on a soft sponge. Remove dead leaves from the plants and maintain a balance by judiciously pruning any of the plants that make too exuberant a growth.

So far, the place of the wardian case in the home has been discussed from an esthetic viewpoint only. It may also be used advantageously in the spring for starting seedlings of flowers or vegetables that are destined later to be planted outdoors; or for rooting cuttings in spring and summer.

Bottle gardens. Much in evidence at flower shows and in florists' windows during recent years, bottle gardens are a modification of the wardian-case principle. They may be constructed in almost any transparent glass container, from a gallon cider jug up to acid carboys with a capacity of 25 or more gallons.

Drainage. It is desirable to have two or three holes bored in the bottom of the bottle to allow surplus water to drain away. Almost any glazier should be able to do this. When setting the plants in the bottle, it is almost impossible to avoid spilling soil on their leaves. For appearance' sake, it is necessary to spray it off, and if there is no way for the surplus water to escape through the bottom, the soil may be waterlogged, to the detriment of the plants.

Planting. Soil should be placed in the bottom to a depth of from 2 to 6 inches, depending on the size of the bottle. The plants used, which may be selected from the list suitable for terraria, must be small enough to pass through the bottle's orifice. Usually, most of the soil must be knocked from their roots before they will pass through. Long tweezers and a long stick shaped into a spatula at one end are used in putting the plants in position and in planting them. A hole is scratched in the soil with the long-handled spatula, the plant is put in place with the tweezers, and the soil is scraped onto its roots with the spatula and patted down. The soil should be watered whenever it becomes dry, which will not be often because of the small opening through which evaporation may take place.

AQUARIA

When lack of humidity makes it difficult to grow plants in the home, the cultivation of water-loving subjects in an aquarium gives the indoor gardener a chance to defy the aridness of the atmosphere.

Many of the aquatic plants are beautiful in form and coloring and the arrangement of them in the aquarium on gently sloping banks of sand, with suitable accessories such as interestingly shaped rocks, offers plenty of scope for the artistic touch of the gardener.

Planting in an aquarium. The well-being of the plants demands the presence of fish unless they are set out in rich pond-mud, which has obvious disadvantages when used in the home aquarium. Undoubtedly, the best method is to plant in clean sand and rely on the waste products of fish and other animal life to provide the necessary plant nutrients.

A rather coarse sand is the best rooting medium. It should be washed thoroughly with clear water to remove dirt and debris before using it. Place a 1- to 3-inch layer in the bottom of the aquarium, forming it into the desired slopes and contours. Then put the small rocks in place and 2 or 3 inches of water. In order to avoid disturbing the sand, pour the water on to a piece of paper laid on the bottom of the aquarium or use a watering pot with a fine sprinkler. The aquarium is now ready to receive the plants, which should be set in place rapidly to eliminate any possibility of drying the leaves. First, take the rooted plants and spread their roots as much as possible. Then cover them with sand, taking care not to bury the crown of the plant—that portion from which the leaves arise. After the rooted plants are firmly fixed, those that are received from the dealer as unrooted cuttings may be set in place. The best way to do this is to put two or three shoots in a bunch and wind a piece of lead wire or lead strip around the base. Poke a hole in the sand with the fingertip and insert the bases of the cuttings. When all the plants are in place, fill the aquarium with water, taking care to pour gently so as not to loosen the plants from their moorings by disturbing the sand. In a few days the aquarium will be ready for the fish. Not being a "fish man," I will not presume to advise as to kinds and quantities of fish to use.

If you wish to add plants to an established aquarium, without removing any of the water, planting may be done with the aid of two slender sticks about 18 inches long. One should be forked at one end and used to hold the plant in place, while the other stick is used, first to scratch a hole for the roots, and then to push the sand over them.

Selection of plants. Plants for the aquarium may be divided into four groups: (1) those having submerged leaves, with their roots in sand or soil; (2) soil-rooting plants with floating leaves; (3) plants that float submerged in water; and (4) those that float mainly on the surface. It is in the first group that the most valuable plants for our purpose are to be found.

Soil-rooting plants with submerged leaves. For large aquaria, first consideration should be given to *Vallisneria*—sometimes called eel-grass or tape-grass. It has pale green translucent ribbon-like leaves which may attain a length of 2 or 3 feet. If planted at each end of the aquarium, the leaves will arch over and meet in the center, forming a beautiful frame for the ensemble. I have found this plant to be a vigorous grower which has to be weeded out occasionally to prevent it from monopolizing the aquarium.

Of similar habit, but not so rampant, are several species of arrowhead or *Sagittaria*. The giant arrowhead grows to a height of about 1 foot; the ribbon arrowhead is of moderate growth with narrower leaves; and the awl-leaf arrowhead is still smaller, with awl-shaped leaves about 4 to 6 inches long and well suited to the small aquarium. It may also be used to advantage in the foreground of large aquaria.

Entirely different in appearance is anacharis, *Elodea canadensis*. This has short leaves arranged in fours almost at right angles to the long trailing stems. When these stems reach an inconvenient length, the upper 6 inches or so should be nipped off and pushed in the sand to replace the older portions, which may then be discarded. This plant is known as ditch-moss, water-thyme and water-pest, in this country, as well as by several unmentionable names in England. One of the least offensive is "Babington's curse"—because a Cambridge professor of botany by the name of Babington is popularly supposed to have introduced it to the waterways of England where, in some places, it has become a considerable pest. All of the plants mentioned so far are good oxygenators—an important factor for the well-being of aquarium fish.

Another rooting plant, *Ludwigia,* is valuable for providing variety in form and coloration. The leaves are smallish, broad, and when grown in good light the undersides are reddish in color. When growing vigorously it needs to be pinched back occasionally in order to keep it within bounds.

The commonest and one of the most beautiful of plants offered for aquarium use is *Cabomba.* This has finely divided leaves, sometimes described as "fan-like." Unfortunately, it is quite brittle and if the aquarium contains obstreperous fish, it is likely to get broken.

Soil-rooting plants with floating leaves. There are not many suitable plants belonging in this group—those that root in the soil and float their leaves on the surface of the water. The water-poppy and the floating heart are worth a trial. Both have yellow flowers, those of the first having a brown eye in the center. I have had fair success with the floating heart when planted in sand, but better results are likely to be obtained with these plants if they are potted in rich earth and then submerged in the aquarium. The water snowflake, with white flowers, belongs in this group.

Submerged floaters. In the third group—those that float submerged in water—we have one of the most interesting of all aquatics—the bladderwort (*Utricularia*). This plant is partly carnivorous, and catches minute animals (which form part of its food supply) in bladder-like projections on the leaves. The bladderwort is in disfavor with some of the fish fanciers because they claim that it appropriates small animals to its own use which should go toward the sustenance of baby fish. But those who are primarily interested in plants can afford to ignore this drawback.

Surface floaters. In the fourth group we have those plants which float on the surface of the water. A few of these add greatly to the appearance of the aquarium but they should not be allowed to increase to such an extent that they monopolize the entire surface. *Salvinia* is one of the best of these floaters and thrives well under house conditions if the aquarium is covered with a pane of glass. When the light is scanty the small heart-shaped leaves are bright green; when grown exposed to strong light they become bronzy in appearance. A plant of similar habit is *Azolla,* sometimes called mosquito-fern because it was thought that its close matted growth might be of value in combating mosquitoes by preventing the larvae (which are aquatic) from breathing. The full beauty of this charming little plant is discernible only when viewed through a magnifying glass.

The water-lettuce (*Pistia stratiotes*) is one of the most striking of the floating aquatics, but it is not easy to maintain in a healthy condition. It forms a rosette of fluted pale-green leaves of velvety appearance. These leaves are plentifully supplied with air chambers which serve to float the plant. The flowers are small and inconspicuous, but observing them closely we see at once that the plant is related to the calla.

There are many other plants suited to aquarium culture but not all of them may be relied on to thrive, year in, year out, and some of them are only occasionally offered for sale by specialists.

General care. The aquarium does not involve a great deal of care. Sometimes green or brown algae make their appearance on the glass. They may be removed by scraping the glass with a safety razor blade in a suitable holder, or by rubbing it with a wad of steel wool. Snails are useful for keeping in check the growth of certain algae. The alga that makes masses of thread-like growths may be removed by twisting it around the finger or a rough stick. A reduction in the amount of light may be sufficient to discourage the growth of undesirable algae.

XXIV. COLDFRAMES AND HOTBEDS

Essentially, a coldframe is a bottomless box with a sloping glass top to shed rain and conserve heat. A hotbed is of similar construction, but is heated so that seeds can be started in it in very early spring. Fermenting organic matter, such as manure or leaves or a mixture of the two, is commonly used for heating hotbeds. Some of them are heated by flues or by steam or hot water pipes. In recent years, electricity has been successfully used.

If a suitable location can be found for them, coldframes and hotbeds are useful adjuncts to the garden, but they should always be placed where they will not detract from the garden picture.

Uses of coldframes. Coldframes are used for the planting of seeds before it is possible to sow outdoors, by which several weeks of growing time are gained; likewise, during the summer, for planting seeds of perennials and biennials, and for starting cuttings of woody and herbaceous material. They are also used for hardening off plants which have been started in greenhouse or hotbed, and finally, they afford a means of protecting, during the winter, plants which are on the border line of hardiness.

Seeds and cuttings. Seeds may be started in seed pots, seed pans or flats, or directly in the earth of the coldframe, and the resultant seedlings are later transplanted. If the first method is followed, 3 or 4 inches of the topsoil in the frame should be removed and replaced with coal ashes on which the pots and flats are placed. The ashes provide the necessary drainage and discourage earthworms from entering through the drainage holes. If the last method is followed, the topsoil is left in place, dug up and thoroughly raked to provide a finely pulverized seed bed.

Cuttings may be inserted during the summer months—substituting a rooting medium of sand, or sand and peatmoss, for the soil used for planting seeds.

Details of preparing seed beds, the methods of planting seeds, and the making and insertion of cuttings are described in Chapter XXVI, PLANT PROPAGATION.

Hardening off. The hardening off process is quite important, for by its neglect greenhouse or hotbed-grown plants may be so injured when planted outdoors that much of the gain anticipated from early planting is lost. The usual practice in hardening off is to place the plants in the coldframe and keep the frame rather close for a few days, raising the sash for ventilation only when the weather is warm, and closing it entirely at night. Gradually more and more air is admitted until after a week or ten days the sash can be entirely removed, both during night and day. The plants are then ready for planting outdoors.

Wintering plants in coldframes. A coldframe is a valued auxiliary for the winter protection of plants. Stock plants of "hardy" chrysanthemums which sometimes fail to come through the winter if left outdoors may be stored in the frame until it is time to take cuttings from them in February, or until the weather permits dividing and planting out. Similarly, seedlings and cuttings raised in the summer may be left in the frames until the following spring, if grown in a region where the winters are severe. Perennials and small shrubs such as *Nierembergia rivularis* and *Hypericum calycinum,* which are in danger of being winter-killed if left in the open, may be successfully carried over the winter in a coldframe.

The coldframe year. Thus, the coldframe year is divided somewhat as follows: In February, remove to the greenhouse hardy chrysanthemums which were stored in the frame during the winter. In March, start seeds of half-hardy annuals, both flowers and vegetables. In April or May, harden off greenhouse and hotbed-grown annuals and bedding plants. In June, July and August, start seeds of biennials and perennials, and insert cuttings of woody and herbaceous plants—all of which, if necessary, may be wintered in the frames. In November, December, January, and February use the frames for storing plants, removed from the garden, which need protection of a coldframe to enable them to survive the winter.

Management. One of the objects in using coldframes during the early spring months is to maintain the temperature with little fluctuation at an average which is higher than outdoors; therefore, proper attention to ventilation, and the conservation of heat acquired during the daylight hours is important. During sunny periods the temperature should, if possible, be prevented from rising above 70 degrees by opening the sash on the side opposite to the direction of the wind so that cold air does not blow directly on the plants. Wooden blocks should be used to hold the sash open. A convenient size for these blocks is 1 x 3 x 6 inches, which allows three different sizes of sash openings. When the temperature starts to fall in the afternoon the sashes should be closed to conserve the heat. If there is any prospect of the night becoming cold (40 degrees or lower), the frames should be covered with mats, straw, hay, or boards, to keep the cold out and the heat in.

In summer, when the object is to reduce the temperature about the plants, the glass of the sash is whitewashed and either lath or cheese-cloth screens are used, as described in Chapter XXVI, PLANT PROPAGA-TION.

Location of coldframes. The selection of the right location for cold-frames is important. From the point of view of getting the most value from their use, they should be placed on well-drained soil where they are sheltered from north and west winds and are open to sunshine. The frames should be placed with the high side to the north to receive the greatest benefit from sunshine. They should be easily accessible to avoid a long trip from the house in their daily care. In early spring, changeable weather may require regulation of ventilation several times a day; and if this chore necessitates long excursions in bad weather, it is likely to cause discouragement and neglect. A hose connection near by is very desirable.

Room must be left around the frames so that the sash can be easily removed when necessary. This space should be along the back or the front of the frame so that sliding the sash either backward or forward is a one-man job. Avoid a layout that makes the labor of two people necessary. All this is predicated on the assumption that the frames are furnished with standard sash, which is 3 x 6 feet, and too heavy for one person to handle with ease unless the frames are properly placed.

There should be well-drained walks around the frames to avoid mud in early spring when the frost is coming out of the ground. Coarse coal ashes are suitable for making these walks, laid to a depth of from 3 to 6 inches.

Construction of coldframes. The simplest coldframes can be made by setting up a 12-inch board on the ground to form the back wall and a 6-inch board for the front wall. The ends are made of a 6-inch board to which is cleated half of a 6-inch board cut diagonally length-

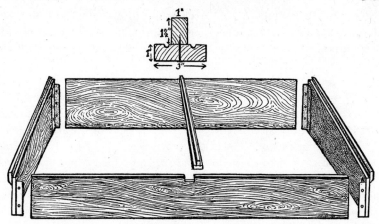

FIG. 58. Coldframe taken apart to show construction
—section of cross-tie above

wise to allow for the slope from back to front. If standard sash is to
be used such a frame should be 5 feet 11 inches wide, outside measurement, by almost any length made up of units of 3 feet (plus allowance
for the thicknesses of the divisions between sashes). A frame of the
above dimensions, however, does not allow sufficient headroom for
general purposes, and one with 9 to 12 inches of clearance at the front,
rising to 15 to 18 inches at the back, is generally preferable.

The back and front should be connected by cross-ties to add rigidity
and facilitate the handling of the sash. These ties should be dovetailed
into the walls so that they are flush with them, to avoid cracks which
might admit too much air. It is desirable to have a projection, about
1 inch wide, extending the whole length on each of the ties to separate
the sashes. A tie with this projection looks in cross-section like an in-
verted T (Fig. 58). Sometimes cross-ties are of T-iron fastened to the
walls with screws.

Coldframes may be purchased ready-made through large seed houses
and greenhouse construction firms, or they may be made on the place
in accordance with Fig. 58. The wood used in coldframe and hotbed
construction should be resistant to decay (cypress is good), and all
joints should be painted before they are assembled.

Uses of hotbeds. When seeds which require heat for germination
are to be planted very early in order to develop flowers or fruit before
the year is out, a hotbed may be used. After the heat has subsided (or

is turned off), the hotbed may serve as a coldframe for hardening off the plants. Some subjects may be grown to maturity in hotbeds.

My first experience with hotbeds was during a period when horses were abundant and manure was not so scarce as it is at the present day. In consequence we were prodigal in our use of it, and, instead of making a pit for the reception of the manure, we simply made a square pile 30 inches high, on which the frames were set. The manure extended for a distance of 3 to 4 feet on all sides of the frames.

Modern construction. Today the practice is to put the fermenting material in a pit 2 to 3 feet deep and the same length and breadth as the frame. The pit should be placed with the same regard for shelter, etc., as for coldframes. If the subsoil is not porous it is necessary to provide artificial drainage, for, if the manure should become waterlogged, fermentation will not proceed with sufficient rapidity to provide the necessary heat.

Wood-lined hotbeds. If the soil is of such a nature that a pit may be dug without the sides crumbling in, it is possible to manage without lining it—for a few years, at any rate. But if the soil is loose the pit should be lined with boards, concrete, brickwork, or stonework. Wood, of course, is not so permanent as concrete or masonry. To line a pit with boards, first dig it to the desired depth and of a width and length sufficient to accommodate the frame. The width of the excavation should be about 6 feet if a standard frame is to be used. The length depends on the number of sashes used. Cut vertical channels in the soil forming the sides of the pit to accommodate 2 x 4-inch stakes which should be driven 1 foot into the bottom of the pit and be long enough to extend to the surface. These stakes need not be closer together than 4 feet. They should be vertical and set in two parallel lines with their inside faces the correct distance apart—5 feet 11 inches (Fig. 59). The side boards, which should be at least 1 inch thick, are nailed to these stakes. The lumber need not be of first-class quality— pecky cypress is good. There are two methods whereby the ends may be formed. The one which involves the least amount of work is merely to slide the boards behind the end stakes and ram soil in back of them as the work proceeds to hold them in place; but it is better to supplement this by driving a 2 x 4 midway between the end stakes and nailing the boards to it (Fig. 60).

Concrete hotbeds. If the soil is not crumbly it is possible to make a concrete-lined pit with a form for only the inside of the wall, but much care is necessary to avoid caving in of the soil which acts as a form for the outside walls. Begin by digging the pit 6 feet 5 inches wide—and stretch cords to ensure exact alignment. Construct the forms to the required height (2 feet 6 inches), in sections which may conveniently be handled— usually in units 6 feet long. This is done by nailing boards to 2 x 4-inch cleats,

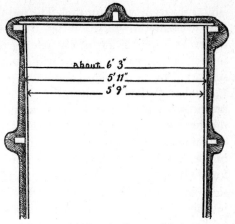

Fig. 59. Hotbed pit lined with boards

spaced 3 feet apart. Place the sections in the pit 4 or 5 inches from the soil face. Brace securely by stakes driven in the bottom of the pit along the line of the form, and by cross-ties at the top, taking care to line up the forms correctly and, with the aid of a mason's spirit level, to en-sure that they are vertical and level.

Make the concrete mixture of 1 part cement, 2 parts clean sand, and 4 parts broken stone or gravel—½ inch to 1 inch. Place the ma-terials in layers, with the cement on top, on a board or concrete plat-form. Shovel them over twice to get the components thoroughly mixed. Make a depression in the center, pour in water, and mix. Enough water should be used to make the mixture sloppy enough to be handled easily. Now comes the ticklish job of getting it into the forms without break-ing down the soil sides, and it is useful to remember that a strip of building paper placed against the soil face helps to prevent crumbling. Work the mixture in the forms by jab-bing it with a 2 x 1-inch scant-ling to eliminate air spaces. Fill up to the surface, and when the concrete has nearly set fin-

Fig. 60. Method of placing end boards

ish off smoothly with a trowel. The form should be left on for several days to allow the concrete to set. If the work is done in hot weather the exposed surfaces of the concrete should be prevented from drying too rapidly, by covering them with burlap bags, straw, or something similar, or by an occasional sprinkling of water.

Another method of constructing the concrete walls that might be practicable under some circumstances is to make a soil form by digging a trench as narrow as possible and 2 feet 6 inches deep with the outline and dimensions of the frame. The concrete is then poured in the trench. This eliminates all construction of wooden or metal forms. It is, however, difficult to dig such a trench and maintain the sides in a reasonably smooth condition, and it involves the use of just about twice as much concrete because it is practically impossible to dig a trench 2 feet 6 inches deep with a width less than 8 inches. When this form of construction is adopted, the pit is dug after the concrete has set. With both types the frame is placed on top of the concrete base with plenty of ashes heaped all around to cover the cracks between frame and base.

The construction of the frames themselves is similar to that described for coldframes earlier in this chapter.

When the soil is of such a nature that it cannot be used to mould the concrete, then forms of wood or metal must be constructed for both inside and outside wall faces. This form of construction involves a wider pit in order to have room to install the form for the outside wall. When it is necessary to provide forms for both faces one might just as well go a little further and carry the concrete up 6 inches above the ground level in front and 12 inches in the back and so do away with the necessity of using a wooden frame. In such cases make the forms so that the wall is 6 inches thick at the base, 4 inches at the top, with the inside face vertical. When the concrete has been poured, level off carefully. Before the concrete sets, place bolts, ¼ inch by 7 inches, vertically in the concrete so that they project 1¾ inches, and spaced 3 feet apart. Their purpose is to anchor a wooden sill of 2 x 4-inch material in which holes should be bored to receive the bolts. A tighter joint is possible if the sill is set upon a bed of soft mortar. If this plan is followed the anchoring bolts should project 2¼ inches from the concrete to allow for the thickness of the mortar. The top of the sill should be beveled to correspond with the slope of the frame

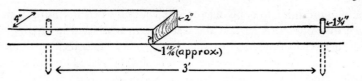

Fig. 61. Method of attaching wooden sill to concrete wall

from back to front (Fig. 61). Cross-ties of wood or iron are desirable
to facilitate the handling of sashes.

Heating the hotbed. Before winter sets in, the sashes should be put
on the frames, or you are likely to find the pit full of snow in early
March when you are ready to start using the hotbed. If fermenting
manure is to be used for heat, locate a good source of the material
during February, and obtain it two weeks ahead of seed-sowing time.
If electric heat is to be used, however, you presumably have no worry
except to turn the switch at the proper time before planting.

Putting in fermenting material. If fresh horse manure is scarce it
may be supplemented with tree leaves of the preceding fall in the ratio
of ⅓ leaves and ⅔ manure. A little over 16 cubic yards of organic
matter will be needed for a hotbed 12 x 6 x 2 feet. Turn the heap two
or three times at intervals of three or four days, throwing the outside
toward the center in order to get the whole mass heating evenly. When
it is nicely steaming place it in the pit in 6-inch layers at a time and
pack it firmly. The importance of packing the manure evenly cannot
be stressed too much. If it is not evenly packed all sorts of annoying
occurrences are likely to take place when it begins to subside, as undoubtedly it will. There will be mountains and valleys, making it
difficult to apply water evenly; some parts of the hotbed will be hotter
than others so that the seedlings will not develop uniformly; and if
the seedlings are in pots or flats, it will be difficult to find a level place
to receive them.

When the pit has been filled to a depth of 2 feet with fermenting
organic matter, place from 4 to 6 inches of sifted rich soil on the surface and pack it down lightly. This soil may be composed of 2 parts
sandy loam and 1 part thoroughly decayed manure or leafmold. Place
a hotbed thermometer in the manure, put on the sash and wait until
the temperature of the manure is down to 90 degrees, when the seeds
may be planted.

Some authorities recommend placing a 2-inch layer of straw over the manure prior to applying the soil, claiming that it ensures a more even distribution of heat. If the seeds are to be started in seed pots or flats, a layer of sandy soil of sufficient depth (1 to 2 inches) to afford a level space on which to stand them should be placed on the manure. See Chapter XXVI, PLANT PROPAGATION, for details of preparing seed beds.

Electrical heat. I believe that flue-heated hotbeds are not of much interest to the amateur gardener, and when it comes to using hot water or steam it is my feeling that one had better construct a small greenhouse in which it is possible to care for the plants in greater comfort than in a hotbed. But electrically-heated, thermostatically-controlled hotbeds possess advantages that should commend them especially to those who cannot be in constant attendance on the needs of the manure-heated hotbed. It is not possible to get best results from fermenting organic matter when only a small bulk of it is used, therefore when only a single-sash unit is in question, which often is quite enough for a small place, the electrically-heated hotbed would again seem to be preferable.

The pit may be made about 1½ feet deep, with from 8 inches to 1 foot of coarse ashes and clinkers placed in it for heat insulation and drainage. The ashes should be tamped down and covered with burlap to keep the soil (or sand if to be used for cuttings) from washing into the drainage. Then a 1-inch layer of soil is put in and the heating cable is laid. This consists of regular electric heating wire, covered with insulation and protected from moisture by a pliable lead or copper sheath. The cables ordinarily are designed to be used in 60- to 75-foot units connected to 115-volt circuits. One of these units is sufficient to heat a 6 x 6-foot frame. The cable is laid about 3 inches from the sides and ends and looped back and forth with the lines 6 to 7 inches apart in the intervening area (Fig. 62). This work and the hooking up of the thermostat should be done by an electrician. From 6 to 8 inches of soil are then placed in the bed and lightly tamped. Sometimes it is recommended first to place an inch of soil over the cable and then a layer of 1-inch chicken-wire netting before adding the remainder of the soil. The object of this is to protect the cable from injury when plants or soil are being removed from the bed.

When the wiring has been hooked up and the soil is in place and has been thoroughly watered, the current is turned on and left overnight. In the meantime a thermometer should be placed 2 inches deep

in the bed. The following day
the temperature is read and the
thermostat regulated. The soil
temperature should be maintained between 65 and 70 degrees.

More detailed information can
be obtained from State Agricultural Experiment Stations, manufacturers of electrical equipment, and seed houses.

Several advantages are claimed

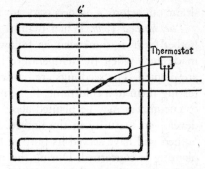

FIG. 62. Spacing of cables in electrically-
heated hotbed

for the electric hotbeds as compared with manure-heated beds. Because
of the automatic control, which gives a uniform temperature, the quality of the plants is improved. The rate of growth can be influenced
by raising or lowering the temperature. They can be used at any time
merely by turning a switch and therefore are available for rooting cuttings in late summer and fall. By shutting off the current, the hotbed
can immediately be turned into a coldframe, and the plants hardened
off without the necessity of moving them to another frame.

Handling of hotbeds. The remarks on ventilation and temperature
control for coldframes (above) apply with even greater force to hotbeds. Suggestions for the general care of hotbeds throughout the year
are given in the paragraphs below.

Management. Since the humidity in a hotbed is greater than that
in a coldframe, the seedlings are more exposed to damage from the
attacks of damping-off fungi (see page 423), unless the frames are
carefully ventilated to allow excess moisture to pass into the open air.
Extra precautions against loss of heat during the night and on cold
sunless days are very necessary, for in a hotbed the temperature maintained is higher, the hotbed is in use earlier in the season when outdoor
temperatures are lower, and the plants are as a rule more susceptible
to low temperatures. A common method of aid is to bank the outside
of the frames with manure in addition to covering the sash with mats
during the night.

Watering must be done with great care to avoid getting the soil too
wet, otherwise damping-off is almost certain to ensue. The plants
should preferably be watered in the morning so that any excess may

drain off before it is necessary to close the frames in the afternoon.

The hotbed year. When manure is used as a heating medium the hotbed year is somewhat as follows: In early March the hotbed is made and, when the temperature has sufficiently subsided, the seeds are planted. The seedlings are hardened off in April—usually by transferring them to a coldframe. If the manure is covered with soil, melons or cucumbers may be planted about the end of March and allowed to develop to maturity in the hotbed. Before they need much room the hotbed will have served its purpose so far as raising plants for outdoor planting is concerned. During the summer the hotbed (with the sash removed) will thus be occupied in raising a crop of melons or cucumbers. In the fall the manure and soil will be removed and used for fertilizing the garden, after which the sash is replaced and the frame is left idle, or used for storing semi-hardy plants, until it is time to start operations in the following spring.

When you are contemplating the installation of hotbeds and coldframes it is well to remember that the standard sash is heavy and, if you are not a husky, it would be advisable to use half-size frame and sash, or the "zephyr-weight" kinds.

XXV. GREENHOUSES

Gardeners who wish to prolong the season in which they may handle and enjoy plants which are growing and blooming will find the perfect answer to their desire in a greenhouse. Here they may raise an extensive variety of subjects which were denied to them outdoors, and all winter long they may have abundant flowers which they themselves have cultivated under the shelter of glass.

Site and equipment. Often greenhouses are separate units so located on the property that they become the focal point of garden activities. But sometimes it is possible to attach a greenhouse directly to the dwelling so that it may be heated by the house heating plant. It will be wise, however, to consult the architect first about how it will affect the good appearance of the building.

Many firms plan simple and good-looking greenhouses designed to form an attractive feature of the garden and usually provided with a workroom above a cellar which contains the heating boiler. Greenhouses have become more or less standardized in various sizes so that it is now possible to install additional units should one become so enamored of raising plants under glass that more space is soon required.

Location. Although there are plants which will thrive in a greenhouse against the north wall of a dwelling, it is preferable to provide any aspect but a northern one. If the greenhouse is a self-contained unit apart from the dwelling, it should be situated in the open, free from the shade of trees. Coldframes and hotbeds may with advantage be located in its general neighborhood, or abutting against its walls.

Humidity and ventilation. If the greenhouse is to be attached to the residence, be sure to have it provided with a floor which will not spoil if water is spilled upon it. It is necessary to increase the humidity of the air for most plants when they are grown indoors, and splashing water around on floors and benches of the greenhouse is an approved way of doing this.

Ventilation should not be forgotten. A greenhouse firm will know

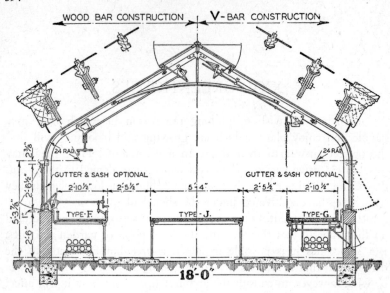

FIG. 63. Even-span greenhouse showing different types of construction, ventilation, and benches (Courtesy Lord and Burnham Company)

how to handle it, but beware of the contractor whose main activity is carpentry or structural ironwork and who is not familiar with the needs of greenhouse plants. Ordinarily, a 12- to 18-inch section of the roof, extending the whole length on both sides of the peak, should be made so that it can be opened to let in air without admitting rain. Ventilators in the side walls, underneath the benches, are desirable in addition to the roof ventilators (Figs. 63 and 64).

Greenhouse furniture. Greenhouses, like dwelling houses, need a certain amount of furniture and equipment. They should be piped for water and provided with threaded faucets for water hose on either side of each compartment so that watering and spraying may be done without much dragging of hose.

Benches or plant tables to hold soil for growing plants or on which to stand potted plants will be necessary. The type of bench installed will be determined by the method of cultivation proposed. If the plants are to be grown in soil on the benches (the usual method for cut-flower crops), the sides should be made from 6 to 8 inches deep to hold the soil. If pot plants are to be grown, the sides need not project above the bottom more than an inch or so to retain a layer of

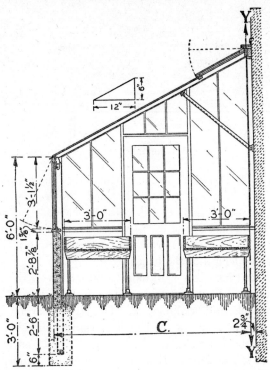

FIG. 64. Greenhouse. Typical straight eave lean-to section. (Courtesy Lord and Burnham Company)

pebbles on which the pots may rest. The pebbles are there to provide drainage and hold water, which, by its subsequent evaporation, maintains the humidity of the air.

Benches may be made of wood, of metal and wood, metal and slate, metal and hollow tile, or entirely of concrete. Of these the concrete is the most durable, but rather clumsy-looking if made in the usual wooden forms.

The most satisfactory bench for potted plants is one with pipe legs and an angle-iron frame on which slate slabs rest. Similar supports are at times used for benches in which the sides and bottoms are of wood. Benches made entirely of wood are seldom used, except in commercial establishments where appearances are of slight consequence and first costs are highly important. Wooden benches should be

Fig. 65. Portable potting bench

avoided whenever possible because when they start to decay they provide ideal habitations for wood lice and similar pests.

Benches for the reception of soil, whether of wood or concrete, must allow for the free passage of excess water. This is usually provided by cracks (¼ to ½ inch wide) which are spaced every 6 inches and ex‑ tend the whole length of the bench.

Except when there is a workroom connected with the greenhouse it is convenient to have a portable work table which may be used for potting, transplanting seedlings, etc. This table may be legless and rest on a cleared portion of the bench. A convenient size is 5 x 3 feet, with boards attached along the back and two ends, an arrangement which allows soil to be mixed on the table with less danger of spilling (Fig. 65).

Greenhouse routine. Routine work in a greenhouse consists of the following nine important chores.

Maintenance of humidity. This must naturally vary according to the kind of plants which predominate in the greenhouse. If cacti and succulents form the majority of its occupants, then the humidity is kept low; if, on the other hand, tropical plants from moist climates, such as ferns, bromeliads, orchids, marantas, etc., form the mainstay, the floor, sidewalls and benches should be wet down several times a day to provide the necessary high humidity. Usually the first job of the gardener when he enters the house in the morning is to "damp down," which means to spray the walks, walls, and the gravel on the benches. The amount of damping down necessary is dependent on the weather and the temperature. On a comparatively warm muggy day little is needed, but on a cold bright day in winter, when a great deal of artificial heat is necessary, and the air outdoors is dry, one should sprinkle frequently. On such days it is particularly important to wet thoroughly all evaporating surfaces just before closing for the night to maintain the humidity for as long a period as possible.

Maintenance of correct temperature. This also is dependent on the kind of plants grown, and varies from 40 to 45 degrees for violets to 65 to 70 degrees for what are known as "stove" plants. The temperatures given for greenhouse plants usually have reference to night temperatures—during the day they may be allowed to rise 10 or 15 degrees above the figure set for any particular house or compartment. The temperature requirements should be studied and interpreted with common sense. For example, in sub-zero weather, to maintain a minimum night temperature of 70 degrees might so desiccate the air of the house that the plants would suffer more than they would if the temperature were allowed to drop 5 or 10 degrees below the ideal minimum, because with the lower temperature it is possible to keep a higher degree of humidity.

Hot water should be the heating medium, except when the furnace is regulated and the temperature maintained by thermostatic control. Another exception is where the range of glass is so extensive as to necessitate the employment of a night fireman, when steam may be safely used. Many skillful gardeners still maintain that hot water is to be preferred in any case because the radiating surfaces, of necessity, must be more extensive, and consequently the heat is more evenly diffused.

Ventilation. Every day the ventilators should be opened if only to a mere crack, as fresh air is as desirable for most plants as it is for most human beings. Even on days when the outside temperature is little lower than that required in the house, and the temperature might be maintained without the use of fire heat if the ventilators were kept closed, the expert gardener likes to open them and use fire heat, because it promotes that elusive something which he calls a "buoyant atmosphere." Ventilation, especially in tropical houses, should always be accomplished by opening the ventilators on the side opposite to that from which the wind is blowing. In early spring when there are many days on which bright sunshine and heavy clouds alternate, much opening and closing of ventilators is necessary if an approximately correct temperature is to be maintained. Thermostatically controlled ventilators are available which obviate the necessity for constant attendance.

Watering. This is one of the most important operations in the routine work of the greenhouse and the one that is most often incorrectly performed. I have for many years been thoroughly convinced that more greenhouse plants are injured by too much water than by not enough, and unfortunately all too many plants are consistently overwatered. The prevalence of overwatering is due to the fact that when plants are watered with a hose, which is the usual practice in America, it is far easier to go through a greenhouse and water every plant, than it is to exercise discrimination and water only those which need it. Even if the gardener is reasonably careful throughout the week there is always a tendency on Saturday afternoon to slop water around recklessly to lessen the work on Sunday. When I was at the Royal Botanic Gardens, Kew, I was informed that any student using the hose for watering plants was subject to instant dismissal. I suppose the thought back of this regulation was that a man who is compelled to carry water laboriously in a watering can will water only those plants which really need it.

When a plant is suffering from lack of water it shows signals of distress in the form of wilting leaves, and if the gardener is sufficiently awake to supply the lack, it immediately recovers. But when a plant is overwatered great damage may be done to its root system before it shows any obvious distress, and it is a long time before the plant recovers, even if the over-wet condition is rectified.

There is no phase of gardening where close observation is more important than in applying water. Plants vary in their moisture requirements. Some species may be kept consistently wet throughout the year; others are happy if waterlogged during the time they are actively growing, but require to be dry at the root while they are resting. The calla is an example in this group. Many of the bulbous plants grown in the greenhouse, such as the eucharis-lily, while not tolerating a waterlogged soil, require plenty of water when they are growing, but merely enough to keep the leaves from wilting during the resting period. The texture of the soil, the condition of the drainage, the character of the weather, the amount of artificial heat, whether or not the pot is filled with roots, as well as the kind of plant in question, all have bearing upon the frequency of watering.

The correct practice is to go carefully through the greenhouse in early morning and water thoroughly any plants which need it. This is determined by the appearance of the soil, by the feel of it, and, if necessary, by tapping the pot with the knuckles. If the pot gives off a dull sound when tapped, the chances are that the soil is wet. If the pot "rings" the plant is likely to need water. After a few weeks of practice one soon gets to know the thirsty plants, and the work of determining which plants need water becomes easier. In the early afternoon another trip should be made to water the plants which have dried out during the day.

Spraying. Spraying plants with water from the hose is an effective means of maintaining humidity and of keeping insect pests in check. Spraying should not be done until the morning watering has been completed because of the likelihood of the surface soil in the pots becoming dampened and thus masking the need of the plants for water.

Discretion must be used in applying water to the tops of plants. Those in bloom may have their flowers injured if the water is applied too forcibly or too frequently. Plants with fuzzy leaves, such as *Gloxinia, Saintpaulia* (African violet), and other of the gesneriads, should be missed as far as possible because the hair on the leaves may become matted with water, thus causing the leaves to decay. Similarly, the very lacy forms of the Boston fern should be sprayed infrequently or not at all. When the outside air is damp and muggy, or if the house is below the required temperature, spraying should be omitted. Whether or not the plants should be sprayed just prior to closing the house for the night is determined largely by the weather and the time of the year. Ordinarily it is considered a bad practice to wet the tops of greenhouse plants when the temperature is falling, but if the air outside is dry and cold and considerable fire heat is necessary, spraying is justified. Also in the spring when many of the tropical plants are actively growing, afternoon spraying is beneficial. In general, tropical houses will require much spraying, and the need declines as the temperature falls.

Clear water properly applied is one of the most effective insecticides known. But to be of service it must be put on with sufficient force to dislodge the insects, and both upper and lower leaf surfaces must be reached. The finger of the gardener applied to the hose nozzle is used to direct the stream in a fine spray, up, down, and sideways so that all parts of the plant are reached. Merely spraying the upper surfaces in a gentle shower does little good beyond aiding in the maintenance of humidity. At the same time, care must be taken to avoid applying the water with such force that the leaves are torn.

Resting. Most plants require a period of rest. In temperate and arctic regions this is brought by a lowered temperature, although there are cases where the drought of summer is responsible, as for example in the case of the spring-flowering bulbous plants. In tropical and subtropical regions the resting period is coincident with a dry season and possibly with a lowered temperature.

In a book such as this it is impossible to indicate the methods of resting all the plants which are commonly grown under greenhouse conditions. In some cases methods are noted under the general cultivation of various species and groups at the end of this chapter. It is usually possible by close observance of the behavior of the different species to determine when it is desirable to give them a rest. When a tropical plant has been growing vigorously for from six to nine months it commonly indicates its desire for a rest by cessation of active growth and by yellowing and dropping of its lower leaves. In such cases we should recognize its need and reduce the supply of water to the roots (sometimes to the extent of completely withholding it), and give it a lower temperature. A good example is the poinsettia, which grows vigorously from late spring until early winter, when it blooms. Soon after Christmas its activities slow up and the gardener rests it by completely withholding water. The plants are stored under the benches, with the pots lying on their sides so that water cannot inadvertently be applied to the soil. There they remain dormant until May, when they are cut back to within 6 inches of the pot and watered. The plants soon send out vigorous shoots which are cut off when they are 4 or 5 inches long and inserted in moist sand as cuttings which, when rooted, are grown along to provide the flowering plants for the next Christmas. Another method, though not so good, which does not involve the rooting of cuttings, is to cut back the old plant, repot in new soil, and grow it along to flowering stage. The garden fuchsia is a plant which makes its growth and blooms during the summer months. It is rested by keeping it rather dry for three or four months during the winter. If it is kept constantly growing it becomes unhappy-looking and fails to bloom freely. Tender azaleas bloom in late winter and early spring. Coincident with blooming, or immediately after, the new shoots are produced which grow during the summer. The wood is matured and the plants are rested by a reduction of water supply and temperature in the fall and early winter.

The possession of a bulbous or tuberous rootstock usually is an indi-

PLATE XXVI. *(upper)* WORKROOM. *(lower)* INTERIOR OF LEAN-TO CON-
SERVATORY

Courtesy Lord & Burnham Company

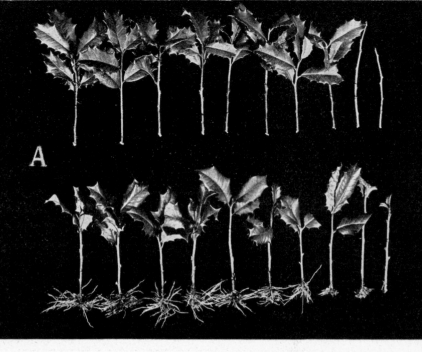

PLATE XXVII. ROOTING RESPONSE AFTER 5 WEEKS OF *Ilex opaca* CUTTINGS. A, BASAL ENDS IN TAP WATER (*top row*) FOR 54 HOURS, AND IN INDOLEACETIC ACID, 10 MG. PER 100 CC. (*lower row*), FOR 54 HOURS. B, SIMILAR TREATMENT WITH NAPHTHALENEACETIC ACID (*lower row*), 2 MG. FOR 4 DAYS. (*top row*) CONTROLS

Courtesy Boyce-Thompson Institute for Plant Research

cation that the plant is subjected in nature to a dry season during which it is dormant; this is a hint to the gardener to dry it off and let it rest when the foliage has matured.

Many plants fail to bloom properly if they do not have a resting period. When I was a journeyman gardener I came across an interesting example of this fact: A plant of *Napoleona imperialis,* a rare, beautiful, and interesting shrub from tropical Africa, had never bloomed, although it had years before attained sufficient size to warrant the expectation. It so happened that it became infested with a particularly stubborn species of scale insect which did not yield to any of the usual measures adopted for pest control. The gardener in charge decided, in desperation, to adopt the drastic remedy of withholding all water with a view to causing the plant to drop its leaves and with them the insects. This was done—and the insects were destroyed; but more than that, when the plant was again supplied with water it grew and blossomed profusely and was in better condition than ever. This story is not related with any thought of recommending such a measure as a general practice, but merely as an illustration of how a complete rest may influence a plant to blossom.

Repotting. Like watering, repotting should be done only when the plants need it. Seedlings and cuttings should be shifted into larger pots whenever those in which they are growing become filled with roots, otherwise their growth may be checked and the stems may harden so that it is only with difficulty that they will start into vigorous growth again. The usual practice is to promote them gradually to pots of larger size.

With subjects which have attained or are approaching their full size, especially if they are to be maintained in pots for years on end, the procedure is somewhat different. The object in these cases is to keep the plants in a healthy condition without recourse to pots or tubs of unwieldy size. This is done by repotting the plants once a year, usually when growth is beginning, in winter or early spring. If the plants have already attained dimensions as large as can be accommodated they are pruned, both top and roots, and reset in pots of the same size. Or they may be top-dressed by removing some of the old soil from the surface of the pots and replacing it with new soil.

With plants which possess a suitable habit of growth—*Aspidistra, Sansevieria,* many ferns, etc.,—the practice is to divide the plants annually (or as often as is desirable to prevent the roots from becoming too crowded) to avoid the necessity of transferring them to pots which are too large.

In many cases it is preferable to water the plants occasionally with liquid manure rather than to repot, either because the plants thrive better when their roots are crowded or to avoid the necessity of using pots or tubs too large to handle conveniently.

A preferred base for potting-soils is prepared by stacking layers of sod from a pasture with layers of manure—6 inches of sod and 3 inches of manure. This is left for a year, chopped with a spade into pieces about as large as a walnut (not, however, rejecting the finer particles) and mixed with sifted leafmold—2 parts of soil to 1 part leafmold, with sand added to give porosity if the base soil is clayey. Bonemeal may be added at the rate of a 5- or 6-inch potful to each wheelbarrow-load of soil. For plants which require an acid soil (azaleas, heaths, camellias, and such) equal parts of soil and acid peat are used, and the bonemeal omitted. For plants requiring abundant humus (begonias and some ferns) the supply of leafmold is increased to one half the bulk of soil. The presence in the potting soil of humus-forming materials such as partly decayed grass roots and leaves ensures proper aeration, because as the organic matter decays it loses bulk and forms tiny air spaces in the soil. Soil for potting seedlings, rooted cuttings and small plants should be passed through a half-inch sieve before using it.

When repotting, the plants are removed from their pots by turning them upside down, placing the fingers of one hand over the ball of earth to keep it from falling, and loosening it by tapping the rim of the pot on the edge of the potting bench.

Pots for repotting should be cleaned by washing them thoroughly inside. So far as the welfare of the plant is concerned it does not matter whether the outside is clean or not, except when they are to be used for orchids, when it is wise to wash the outside also to eliminate any growth of algae or mosses which would reduce their porosity.

New pots should be soaked in water for an hour or so, then dried before using them.

For large sizes drainage is provided by placing a piece of broken pot over the hole in the bottom and covering it with ½ inch to 2 inches of broken pots or coarse ashes. This should be covered with a thin layer of moss, or fibrous material from the potting soil, to prevent fine particles of soil from washing down and clogging the drainage material. A single piece of broken pot over the drainage hole will be sufficient in most cases for pot sizes up to 3 inches.

Press a handful or two of soil on top of the drainage material, then place the plant in the center of the pot, adding to or taking away from the soil in the bottom so as to bring the top of the old ball of earth far enough below the rim of the new pot to allow for watering. The amount of space at the top depends on the size of the pot—from ½ inch for 5-inch pots to 1½ inches for 12- or 14-inch pots. Steady the old ball of earth and the pot with one hand,

Fig. 66. Section of pot removed to show drainage, new soil and root-filled ball

and with the other pour in the new soil. Jar the pot on the bench to settle the soil and then pack it down with a potting stick of suitable size (for small pots a 6-inch wooden label is adequate) until it is of the same density as the soil in the old ball. The surface is finished off by pressing the soil down with the fingers (Fig. 66).

In potting cuttings and seedlings (where there is, of course, no ball of earth), the pot, with drainage provided, is one quarter to one half filled with soil, the plant is put in place with its roots spread out, and the pot is filled with soil, which is pressed down with the fingers. The pot is then jarred on the bench to level the surface soil and the job is done. It takes longer to tell about it than to do it.

Fumigation. In fumigation the glasshouse gardener has a weapon which is effective in the control of certain insect pests. It is good practice to fumigate periodically whether or not insect pests are obvious. The materials most commonly used in greenhouse fumigation are tobacco preparations and calcium cyanide. The various brands of tobacco preparations vary so much in the nicotine content that it is useless for me to give dosages, and reliance should be placed on the recommendations of the manufacturers.

In the old days, when cyanide fumigation was accomplished by the use of potassium cyanide dropped in a mixture of sulphuric acid and water, which resulted in the immediate release of deadly hydrocyanic acid gas, fumigation was a hazardous occupation. It also involved time-consuming preparations—hunting up earthenware containers; measuring out the correct proportions of water and acid; carefully mixing them; weighing the potassium cyanide; and wrapping it in paper before placing it in the acid and water, so that the release of gas was delayed until the operator had a chance to skip out of the house. Nowadays by the use of calcium cyanide the danger from inhaling the gas is lessened because it is given off more slowly and the introduction of the gas into the house is simplified—requiring only that the correct dose be measured and scattered on the moist greenhouse floor.

Although not so dangerous to use as potassium cyanide plus sulphuric acid, it should be recognized that calcium cyanide also is a deadly poison, both when ingested and when the gas is inhaled, and proper precautions should be taken. The practice at the Brooklyn Botanic Garden is to scatter the powder on the moist greenhouse floors after dark, then lock the houses with "keep out" signs on the doors until the morning, when it is quite safe to enter. The dosage for the general run of greenhouse stock is ¼ ounce of 40- to 50-percent calcium cyanide to 1,000 cubic feet of greenhouse space. Some plants, such as Wandering Jew, are liable to injury from this dosage, especially if the foliage is wet, so they should be covered with paper or removed before fumigating.

Shading. Although during the winter months all the available sunlight is required in the greenhouse, when the sun gains power in the spring it is necessary to temper its rays by shading of some kind. Personally, I much prefer to use removable shade such as that provided by wooden strips fastened together with wire and so constructed that the shades may be rolled up or down at will by cords and pulleys; or, failing this, scrim or similar material attached to a roller. The advantage of roll-shades is that on overcast days they may be removed —to the benefit of the plants.

Almost everyone has his favorite recipe for the type of paint-like shading which is applied directly to the glass. It usually consists of whiting or white lead (although I have seen plain mud used!) in water or gasoline, applied with a sprayer or paintbrush. A formula recommended by the Missouri Botanical Garden is made up as follows: water, 3 gallons; whiting, 5 pounds; cement, 6 pounds; powdered glue, ½ pound. Dissolve glue in hot water and add to the mixture just before spraying it on the glass. Keep mixture agitated. It must be used immediately. This shading gradually wears off, and usually by winter it has entirely disappeared.

Another shading recipe consists of white lead diluted with gasoline to the consistency of thin paint. It is applied to the glass with a large paintbrush and may readily be removed when required by brushing with a stiff dry brush. Disadvantages are the labor of applying and possibly the cost.

If time and labor available permit, it is a good plan to put on these shading materials in two thin applications rather than in one heavy one, because in the spring only a light shade is necessary, but when the really hot days are upon us it should be fairly heavy.

A possible solution of the shading problem, which may appeal to some, is to grow vines underneath the glass roof. If they are rested and pruned in winter, enough light will be admitted during the short days. They should be trained on wires held 8 to 12 inches from the glass, and extending from the eaves to the peak of the roof. Suitable vines for a house of intermediate heat are: *Allamanda Hendersoni*, with large satiny yellow flowers; *Antigonon leptopus,* **Coral-vine;** *Bougainvillea; Clerodendron Thompsonae (Balfouri)*; *Jasminum grandiflorum; Passiflora,* **Passion Flower** in variety; and *Stigmaphyllon ciliatum,* with clustered yellow flowers. They should be potted in 12- or 14-inch pots; or, if conditions permit, planted in the soil of the greenhouse, though the latter method is less satisfactory if their leafage is to be greatly reduced during the winter, because it is sometimes difficult to limit the water supply to the roots enough to cause the vines to go into the resting stage in late fall.

Selection of plants. What is grown under glass will, of course, be determined by the tastes of the owner. The greenhouse may be used: (1) as a sanitarium in which potted plants, debilitated by their use as decorative material in the home, may recuperate; (2) solely for the display of foliage and flowering plants in pots; (3) for the production of cut flowers; (4) in spring for raising seedlings, destined to grace the outdoor garden during the summer, or for rooting cuttings from June till fall, and (5) as a winter boarding-house for plants which could not survive the cold season outdoors. It may be devoted to one or to all of these purposes, but whatever use is made of the greenhouse, may I suggest that meticulous tidiness be insisted upon, for there is nothing more forlorn than a greenhouse littered with dirty pots, higgledy-piggledy flats, dead plants on the benches, and used plant stakes lying loose underfoot. Even when a greenhouse is employed in part for utilitarian purposes, it is possible for it to please with the beauty of neatness.

When only a single greenhouse without compartments is available, the choice of material is limited to that which will grow in the temperature which one decides to maintain.

Bulbs, shrubs, and herbaceous plants for forcing. Practically all of the hardy bulbs which are commonly forced for greenhouse decoration can be accommodated to perfection in an intermediate temperature. (See Chapter XIV, FLOWERING BULBS.) This will also serve for forcing various hardy shrubs such as azalea, flowering crab-apples, rhododendron, roses, spirea, lilacs, wisteria, and *Deutzia gracilis.* Herbaceous plants such as bleeding heart, delphinium, astilbe, forget-me-not, and many others may be forced into bloom in an intermediate house before their natural flowering period. Hardy shrubs intended for forcing may be grown in pots or, if they have a naturally compact root system or have been transplanted within two years, they may be dug from the open ground and potted or tubbed in the fall. Naturally, in selecting specimens for forcing, preference is given to those which will not take up too much room in the greenhouse.

Most hardy plants require a period of rest in low temperatures. For this reason it is useless to attempt to force them by bringing them into the greenhouse before the first of the year. In the meantime they should be stored in a temperature of about 35 degrees to keep them dormant. Unless very early bloom is desired, they should not be brought in until February. Herbaceous plants and shrubs are both handled in this manner.

Some typical greenhouse plants for benches and pots. In the following lists are a number of plants which will thrive in the temperature indicated above each column. In many cases the names appear in two columns and sometimes in three. An asterisk then indicates the temperature preferred. It will be noticed that a "middle of the road" policy in regard to temperature is best when it is desired to grow a large variety of plants and only one greenhouse is available.

Each list is followed by brief directions for cultivation of some of the more important subjects mentioned therein. In the first list (PLANTS COMMONLY GROWN IN BENCHES FOR CUT FLOWERS), plants which may also be raised in pots are preceded by the letter P. The kinds ordinarily raised from seeds are marked S; those grown from cuttings, C; by division, D; and by grafting, G; while the bulbous subjects (see Chapter XIV, FLOWERING BULBS) are indicated by B.

PLANTS COMMONLY GROWN IN BENCHES FOR CUT FLOWERS

45°-50°	50°-55°	60°-65°
S Calendula *	S Calendula	P, B Calla *
P, C Carnation	P, B Calla	P, B Easter Lily *
P, C Chrysanthemum *	C Carnation *	G or C Rose *
P, B Freesia	P, C Chrysanthemum	
P, S Gerberia	P, B Easter Lily	
S Mignonette *	P, B Freesia *	
S Schizanthus	P, S Gerberia *	
S or C Snapdragon	S Mignonette	
S Stock *	G or C Rose	
S Sweet Pea *	S or C Snapdragon *	
C or D Violet	S Stock	
S Wallflower *	S Sweet Pea	
	S Wallflower	

TREATMENT OF PLANTS GROWN IN BENCHES FROM SEED

Calendula, Pot Marigold. When sown in late July or early August calendulas are valuable because they start blooming just as the chrysanthemums are about over. The seedlings should be potted in 2½-inch pots and set 1 foot apart in the benches when the pots are filled with roots. Use sandy loam mixed with one fourth decayed manure. Pinch out all but one bud on each shoot if you want large flowers. The first-formed flowers are usually on short stems and may be discarded.

Snapdragon. Seeds are planted, or cuttings inserted, in June or July. The seedlings are transplanted to flats, and later to pots. Bring them indoors before there is danger of their being injured by frost. They may immediately be planted in a bench if one is available; if not, they may be kept in pots until the chrysanthemums are removed after flowering. Plant from 6 to 8 inches apart according to height of variety. Use sandy loam, on the alkaline side.

Stocks. The first planting should be made in July for November flowers, then at intervals of six weeks to provide for a succession of bloom. Otherwise the cultivation and soil for raising stocks are similar to those of snapdragon. Plant about 9 inches apart.

Sweet Pea. Seeds of the winter-flowering varieties of sweet pea are sown about the middle of September for February flowering. They may be planted either in pots to be transplanted later, or directly in the beds where they are to bloom. If the rows run north and south, space them 2 to 3 feet apart; if east and west, about 5 feet. Sweet peas require much headroom; consequently the central part of the house is preferred. Chicken-wire netting or strings are used for supports. Sweet peas grow best when planted in solid beds in deep loam with plenty of rotted manure.

Wallflower. Seeds are planted in May and the seedlings transplanted to an outdoor bed, spacing them 6 inches apart. In October the plants are carefully dug up and potted, or planted 10 or 12 inches apart in a raised bench containing sandy loam on the alkaline side.

TREATMENT OF PLANTS GROWN IN BENCHES FROM CUTTINGS

Carnation. Cuttings are made in February or March and when rooted are transplanted to flats or 2½-inch pots. About the end of April or first of May the young plants are set outdoors, 8 inches apart, in rows 18 inches apart. The plants should be dug up in August and planted in the benches, no deeper than they were when growing outdoors. Space them about 7 x 9 inches apart. Temporary shade is necessary until they have become established in the soil, which should be of loam with one fourth rotted manure.

Chrysanthemum. Cuttings are made in March from stock plants held over in a greenhouse or coldframe from the preceding year. When they have roots ½ inch long they are potted in 2½- or 3-inch pots. When these pots become filled with roots the plants are set in shallow benches (4 to 5 inches of soil), placing two-stemmed plants 9 x 10 inches apart. If grown to single stems, the less vigorous varieties may be planted 6 inches apart in rows 9 inches apart. Use loam with rotted manure, and apply liquid manure while growing.

Rose. Young plants, purchased from a specialist who propagates them by grafting or by cuttings, are set in the beds in June, planting them from 12 to 16 inches apart according to size of variety. Usually four rows are planted lengthwise of the bench. All flower buds are kept picked off until September. The plants are supported by means of wires stretched tautly along the rows about 3 feet above the soil. Galvanized wire stakes, to which the rose shoots are tied, are placed in the ground alongside each plant and fastened to the wire above. To a soil of heavy loam and decayed cow manure, additional food is supplied by a mulch of fresh or partly rotted cow manure.

FLOWERING PLANTS COMMONLY GROWN IN POTS

45°-50°	50°-55°	60°-65°
Acacia *	Acacia	Begonia *
Azalea *	Achimenes	Cattleya *
Calceolaria *	Azalea	Cypripedium *
Camellia *	Begonia	Easter Lily *
Cineraria *	Calceolaria	Gardenia *
Cyclamen	Camellia	Gloxinia *
Erica *	Cattleya	Hydrangea
Genista	Cineraria	Poinsettia *
Hydrangea	Cyclamen *	Saintpaulia *
Jerusalem-cherry	Cypripedium	
Oxalis	Easter Lily	
Primula (P. chinensis	Erica	
and obconica)	Gardenia	
	Genista *	
	Gloxinia	
	Hydrangea *	
	Jerusalem-cherry *	
	Oxalis *	
	Poinsettia	
	Primula * (P. chinensis	
	and obconica)	

TREATMENT OF FLOWERING PLANTS IN POTS

Achimenes. The tuberous rhizomes should be planted in light soil in early spring. Use about six to a 6-inch pot and cover them with an inch or two of soil. Their reclining habit of growth makes them valuable for use as basket plants. Place a row of rhizomes 3 inches apart about halfway up the basket and quite close to the side with their noses pointed outward. Then finish filling the basket with soil, and plant a further supply just below the surface. When the plants have finished flowering, water should be gradually withheld and the rhizomes stored dry, still in the soil in which they were growing, until the following spring. (See Chapter XIX, HANGING BASKETS.)

Azalea. "Indica" azaleas should be repotted immediately after flowering. Special azalea pots, which are intermediate in height between bulb pans and standard pots, should be used. Pay particular attention to drainage. Azaleas require an acid soil. Use a mixture of loam, acid peatmoss, and sand. If the loam is naturally acid, leafmold may be used instead of peatmoss. When the plants are established in their new pots and danger of frost is past they may be placed outdoors, burying the pots to their rims in coal ashes, peatmoss or soil. They must be watered whenever the soil shows signs of drying. Watch for lace bugs and spray with nicotine-soap solution if they make their appearance. Bring the plants into a cool greenhouse on the approach of cold weather in the fall.

Begonia. Tuberous-rooted begonias are valuable for providing summer bloom in the greenhouse. Start the tubers in early spring by planting them in flats in loose leafmold. When growth commences pot them in equal parts loam, leafmold, sand, and thoroughly rotted manure. Place plenty of drainage material in the bottom of the pots. In late fall withhold water and allow them to remain dry in the pots all winter. Tuberous begonias may sometimes be started from seeds in the greenhouse in January, with a temperature 60 to 65 degrees.

Winter-flowering begonias of the Gloire de Lorraine type (fibrous-rooted) are propagated from leaf cuttings, the stalk being inserted in sand at a temperature of 70 degrees. When shoots form, pot the young plants in 2-inch pots in equal parts of loam and leafmold with enough sand to make the mixture porous. As the pots become filled with roots, pot them in loam, partly decayed leaves, thoroughly decayed manure and sand. Keep them in a cool airy position (45°-50°) while they are in bloom.

Cineraria. To secure succession of bloom, seeds may be sown from the beginning of August to the end of September. Pot the seedlings in 3-inch pots and shift them into larger sizes as required. For first potting use equal parts loam, leafmold, and sand. For later pottings use two parts loam, one part decayed manure, one part leafmold. Final potting should be in 5- or 6-inch pots. Cinerarias should be kept as cool as possible, with a minimum of 45 degrees, throughout all stages of their growth.

Cyclamen. Seeds are sown in early fall in a mixture of equal parts of loam, leafmold and sand, and kept in a cool greenhouse. Germination is slow—sometimes it is two months before leaves show. Prick off the seedlings into flats, using the same mixture but half the quantity of sand. When sufficient growth has been made, pot into 3-inch pots, adding a little decayed cow manure to the soil mixture. Keep in a night temperature of 55 degrees. About the middle of May remove to a shaded coldframe. Shift into larger pots whenever the roots become crowded. Bring into the greenhouse before cold weather arrives and maintain a night temperature of 50 degrees. Be careful to avoid over-watering—especially when the plants are young.

Gloxinia. Summer is when the most abundant growth is made and the flowers are produced on gloxinias, which may be treated in much the same way as tuberous begonias. They are readily propagated by leaf cuttings during the summer, or by seeds sown in January or February. Avoid frequently wetting the leaves.

Hydrangea. The so-called "French" hydrangeas are valuable for spring decoration in the greenhouse. Cuttings may be rooted in late winter and later potted into 3- or 4-inch pots. Plant them outdoors during May in rich soil. About the end of September dig up the plants and pot them. Allow them to remain outdoors until they have experienced a few light frosts, then bring them indoors and store until the middle of January in a cool place (35°-45°)—preferably where there is at least some light. Start them in a temperature of 45 to 50 degrees and, after two or three weeks, raise the temperature 10 or 15 degrees.

Jerusalem-cherry. This relative of the tomato is grown for the beauty of its fruits around Christmas-time. The seeds should be removed from their pulpy covering and planted early in the year. Transplant the seedlings 2 inches apart in flats and later pot into 4-inch pots. As soon as danger of frost is past, plant them outdoors in good soil. Toward the end of August dig them up and pot them in 5- or 6-inch pots. Keep shaded for a few days, or until they become established. Bring them into the greenhouse (50°-55°) before frost.

Poinsettia (see page 400). Violent fluctuations of temperature should be avoided as they cause poinsettias to lose their lower leaves. It is also desirable that they should not be exposed to temperatures below 60 degrees.

Primula. The most important species for greenhouse use are *Primula chinensis, obconica, malacoides,* and *kewensis.* For winter flowering the seeds are planted from January to March in a temperature of 65 degrees. Prick off the seedlings in flats when large enough and, when they become crowded, pot them in 3-inch pots, using loam three parts, leafmold one part, rotted manure one part. For the next potting add a little bone-dust to the soil. Careful attention to setting the plants at the right depth in the soil is necessary in the case of the Chinese primroses. If set too deep they are likely to rot; if too shallow the plants will be wobbly and may be broken off at the ground line when they are being moved around. After they have passed the seedling stage, keep the plants as cool as possible. The winter temperature should be 50 to 55 degrees.

FOLIAGE PLANTS

45°-50°	50°-55°	60°-65°
Araucaria *	Araucaria	Ardisia *
Asparagus	Ardisia	Asparagus
Ficus pumila	Asparagus *	Aspidistra *
Pteris	Aspidistra	*Begonia Rex* *
	Asplenium (fern) *	Caladium *
	Caladium	Codiaeum (Croton) *
	Codiaeum (Croton)	Dracaena *
	Dracaena	*Ficus pumila*
	Ficus pumila *	Fittonia
	Nephrolepis (Boston	Nephrolepis
	Fern) *	Palms *
	Palms	Pandanus *
	Pandanus	Peperomia *
	Peperomia	Pteris
	Pteris (fern) *	Sansevieria *
	Sansevieria	

TREATMENT OF FOLIAGE PLANTS

With a few exceptions, this class of plants is more shade-enduring than most of the kinds grown for their flowers. Also, as may be noted on consulting the table on p. 411, most of them prefer a comparatively high temperature.

The following notes should aid the novice in caring for them.

Plants which spread by underground rhizomes or rootstocks may need to be divided at the time they are repotted to prevent them from becoming unwieldy. In this group are ferns, *Aspidistra,* and *Sansevieria.* Boston ferns in my experience, however, do not respond so well to division of the old plants. For this group a better practice is to raise new plants occasionally from the freely produced runners. This may be done by setting an old plant on a bench which contains soil, or by placing several 3- or 4-inch flower pots filled with soil near the old plant, and pinning a runner in each pot. When they have rooted, the runners may be severed from the parent plant and potted on as often as they require.

The screwpines (*Pandanus*) and most palms do not resent being potbound so long as soil fertility is maintained. This may be done by applying a commercial fertilizer to the soil every three or four weeks during the growing season. Use at the rate of a level teaspoonful to a plant growing in a 6-inch pot, scratching it into the surface soil. Or weekly applications of liquid manure during the growing season may be used. Prepare it by placing a bushel or two of horse or cow manure in a burlap bag and steeping it in a tub of water. Keep it in some place where it will not be offensive. Before using the solution, dilute it until it is the color of weak tea.

Begonia. Members of the Rex group of begonias are readily propagated by leaf cuttings. If the old plants become shabby, raise new plants this way, using only mature leaves. They will root and form new plants in shorter time if they are inserted during March and April. (See p. 440.)

Caladium. The "fancy" caladiums have leaves of extraordinarily delicate appearance, and in some varieties they are almost transparent. The tubers should be started in March or April, in a temperature of 70 to 80 degrees, placing them in flats of loose leafmold or peatmoss. Cover them 1 inch deep. When roots begin to form, pot the tubers in 3-inch pots, using leafmold three parts, loam one part, sand one part. For the next potting use equal parts of loam and leafmold with a little decayed manure and enough sand to give porosity. Keep the plants in a warm humid atmosphere and shade from bright sunshine. They make their growth in summer. When the leaves begin to die in the fall, gradually withhold water. When they have entirely died down, store the pots under a greenhouse bench in a temperature of not less than 60 degrees.

Croton. Bright sunshine is essential if crotons are to develop fully their brilliant leaf coloration. For this reason they should be given the sunniest position available. If the greenhouse has to be shaded for other plants during the summer it would be well to consider the possibility of placing them outdoors during the warm months.

Climbing Fig (*Ficus pumila*). As a wall covering, the climbing fig is admirable, clinging by adventitious rootlets and mantling the wall with small dark glossy leaves.

Another possible wall treatment in the greenhouse is to attach studding of 2 x 4-inch cypress every 3 feet and nail chicken-wire netting on it. Fill between wall and netting with fibrous peat or osmunda fibre, then plant it with ferns, selaginellas, *Peperomia, Fittonia,* and other foliage plants. It will provide a charming feature in your greenhouse.

XXVI. PLANT PROPAGATION

The multiplication of plants is one of the most fascinating branches of gardening, and the procedures involved are of absorbing interest to every plant lover. There is no lack of variety in the methods employed, for plants are propagated by means of seeds, spores, bulbils, cormels, tubers, rhizomes, division, runners, offsets, suckers, stolons, layers, cuttings, and budding and grafting.

Although plant propagation is an ancient art, it is only during comparatively recent years that scientific studies have been made in its theory and practice. Experimentation has brought a remarkable increase in our knowledge of how to propagate rapidly and surely plants which were formerly considered difficult.

PROPAGATION OF PLANTS BY SEEDS AND SPORES

To the botanist, seeds and spores are vastly different, but to the gardener they are akin because they are planted in much the same way and the final results are similar. Flowering plants bear seeds which may be used for reproduction, while ferns (and certain other lower forms) bear spores.

Flowering plants are produced from seeds more often than by any other means. Usually, the gardener has no difficulty in germinating seeds, provided they are given their requirements of air, moisture, and a sufficiently high temperature. These requirements are met, in outdoor planting, by covering the seeds with soil deep enough to keep them moist, but not so deep that they do not receive sufficient air or that the food stored in the seed is exhausted before the growing embryo reaches the surface. If the soil is heavy, planting must be avoided when it is wet, because working it then may puddle the soil, drive out air, and prevent the germination of the seeds. Temperature requirements are met by starting the seeds in greenhouse, hotbed, or coldframe, or by deferring planting until the ground has warmed up sufficiently in the spring. Many of the hardy annual seeds may be advantageously planted in late fall; they will then germinate in early spring when the temperature is right. This affords the young plants an opportunity to develop good root systems before hot weather sets in. (See Chapter XIII, ANNUALS.)

Raising trees and shrubs from seed. The seeds of many species of trees and shrubs require special handling, either to secure successful germination or to reduce the time between maturity and germination. Some seeds, such as willow, poplar, and certain species of maple, which ripen early in the year, are short-lived and must be planted immediately after they ripen. Many seeds, on the other hand, require an after-ripening period at comparatively low temperatures to ensure a successful stand. It has long been known that better results are obtained with the seeds of many trees and shrubs—also alpine and herbaceous plants—if they are planted in a coldframe in the fall. Oak and chestnut will not germinate if the seeds are allowed to become thoroughly air-dried. Either they must be planted as soon as they are ripe, or they must be stratified—that is, stored under cool conditions in a moist medium, such as peatmoss, sand, or soil, previous to spring planting.

The Boyce Thompson Institute for Plant Research at Yonkers, N. Y., has conducted numerous experiments designed to show the most efficient methods of handling difficult seeds with a view to securing satisfactory germination, and has published valuable data resulting from these experiments. The ideal conditions of temperature and time of stratification to ensure the breaking of dormancy by after-ripening have been worked out for a large number of species. I select from Professional Paper No. 15 by Dr. William Crocker, published by the Institute, the following as examples of the temperature and time effective for stratification:

	Best temperature (Fahrenheit)	Effective range of temperature (Fahrenheit)	Best time (days)
Abies lasiocarpa arizonica...	32°	32°-41°	30
Cornus florida	41°	32°-50°	120
Crataegus Oxyacantha	50°	41°-50°	365
Rosa canina	41°	32°-50°	270
Rosa multiflora	41°	41°-46°	50

These temperatures may be provided by placing the seeds in a refrigerator, first mixing them with peatmoss, which should be kept moist all the time they are under treatment. If a refrigerator is not available, satisfactory results are sometimes obtained by planting the seeds in the fall in a coldframe, mulching them with salt hay, or with snow as described on page 422.

Some species produce what the nurserymen call "two-year seeds," which do not germinate for a year or more after maturity. Instead of planting such seeds in the normal way, they are mixed with, or stratified in, a moist medium such as peatmoss or sand for a year before planting. Seeds in this group include some of the roses, hawthorns, *Cotoneaster*, and *Cornus*.

Seeds which have fleshy coverings, such as those of apple, holly, rose, *Magnolia, Berberis, Viburnum, Rubus,* etc., should have the pulp removed before they are planted or stratified. This is usually done by soaking them in water until the covering is soft and easily washed off.

Seeds that possess hard impervious coats—such as acacia, boxwood, camellia, honey-locust, and Osage-orange—may have their germination accelerated by soaking them in warm water for 24 hours prior to planting them.

Small seeds of trees and shrubs are best planted in flats or seed pans; large seeds may be planted in the open ground. The general procedure (except for those requiring special treatment, as described above) is the same as in handling perennial seeds (see page 417), except that the seeds of trees and shrubs are planted in February or March under greenhouse conditions; in April in the coldframe; or as soon as the soil is in condition, if open-ground planting is practised. Sometimes when dealing with rhododendron, dry sphagnum rubbed through a fine sieve is lightly sprinkled over the seeds to keep them moist.

The seedlings started in flats or seed pots are usually transplanted into individual pots, then when they become large enough, they are set in the open ground. (See method of handling cuttings, page 436.)

Seedlings of woody plants raised from seeds in the open ground are ordinarily left there for one or two years before transplanting (which is preferably done in the spring), the length of time depending upon the growth they have made.

Raising perennials from seed. Seeds afford the gardener a ready means of increasing his stock of *some* of the beautiful and interesting perennial plants—but it must be emphasized that not all may be satisfactorily increased in this way. Those which have been so highly developed by the plantsman and hybridist that they run to many different varieties do not, as a rule, come true from seeds, and hence are usually propagated by vegetative means (see **Division** and **Cuttings** pages 426, 432), except when the object is the production of new varieties. Included in this group are such plants as iris and phlox. Then there is another group, such as peonies and some of the lilies, which take so long to come to the flowering stage when raised from seeds that most gardeners prefer to leave their production from seeds to the specialist.

Time of sowing. August is the orthodox month for starting perennials. The theory is that seeds planted at this time will develop into plants which are large and strong enough to be set out in their flowering quarters in the early fall. Furthermore, by planting them as late as this, one is not bothered with their care during the hottest part of the summer. As a matter of actual fact, many of the seedlings started in August are not of sufficient size to withstand the winter in the perennial border without protection.

Personally, I much prefer to plant perennial seeds in May, usually in a coldframe. If the seedlings are transplanted to the open ground in summer and are not allowed to suffer from drought, by autumn they will make husky plants ready for their permanent site, where they will provide abundant flowers the following year.

Place of sowing. It is possible to make a seed bed in the open ground for the purpose of starting perennial seeds (also biennials), but this is not the best method of handling them, for drenching summer rains may cause the total loss of the seeds by erosion of the soil or may batter the soil until it becomes packed hard about the tender seedlings. The open ground may be all right for large-seeded plants, such as the marshmallow, gas-plant, and perennial pea, but for small-seeded kinds the protection of a coldframe is almost essential. The plants may then be easily protected from the heavy rains, also from intense sun and possible drought.

When a coldframe is used, it may be set on the ground and the seeds planted directly in the soil; or the seeds may be planted in flats or in seed pots placed on a bed of coarse ashes or sand in the frame. If a large quantity of one kind of seed is to be sown, it is perhaps better to use the soil of the coldframe directly. If, however, one wants a few plants each of many varieties, flats or seed pots should be used to enable each kind to receive the proper treatment day by day, for seeds vary in the rapidity with which they germinate, and while some with green leaves developing will be in need of sunshine, the laggards will still be in need of shade.

Soil and drainage. The kind of soil has an important bearing on the success or failure of the seeds. To get best results, it should be light,

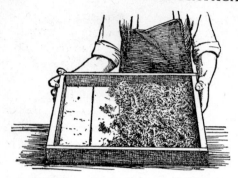

FIG. 67. Drainage material in flat

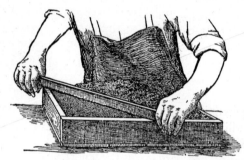

FIG. 68. Leveling soil with a lath

FIG. 69. Pressing down soil with a "float"

porous, and well tilled. If the seeds are to be planted in the soil of the cold-frame, it should be dug up to a depth of at least 6 inches, thoroughly broken up with a spading fork, and have sifted leafmold mixed with it, plus enough sand to make it porous. Then rake the surface with an iron-toothed rake, water it thoroughly, and allow it to stand for a week or so to settle before planting the seeds.

If your plan is to plant in seed flats or seed pots, the soil may consist of 2 parts good garden soil, 1 part leafmold, and 2 parts sand, the whole sifted through a half-inch sieve. About 1 inch of the coarse material which fails to pass through the sieve (with large stones or sticks discarded) should be placed in the bottom of the flats for drainage (Fig. 67).

Fill the flat with the prepared soil and strike it off even at the top by means of a piece of lath or something similar (Fig. 68). Press the soil down so that it is about ⅜ inch below the top of the flat (Fig. 69). A wooden float (Fig. 70) is a suitable tool for this purpose. Be careful to make the surface smooth and

level. The seeds may be planted in
drills or scattered on the surface.
Drills are conveniently made by pressing an ordinary desk ruler into the
soil to the correct depth (Figs. 71,
72). When planting in the soil of

FIG. 70. Detail of float

coldframes, the shallow trenches for the seeds may be made by pressing the edge of a lath into the soil to the required depth, or by scratching a straight line with a pointed stick, using a lath as a ruler.

In preparing the pots and pans, place a piece of broken pot over the
hole in the bottom and cover it with ½ inch of broken pots or coarse
ashes. Then fill the pot with sifted soil, struck off even with the rim,
and pressed down ⅜ inch with a circular tamper. This may be the
bottom of a flower pot, a tumbler, or a circular piece of wood with a
handle attached (Fig. 73).

Depth and thickness of planting seeds. It is impossible to lay down
any hard and fast rule as to the depth to plant seeds, but if you cover
them with soil equal in depth to the diameter of the seed, or a little
deeper in loose sandy soils, you will not be going very far wrong. The
seeds in the drills may be covered by running a thumb and finger on
either side of the row, afterward pressing the loosened soil down with
the float. When the seeds are planted by scattering (broadcasting)
them on the surface, a little additional soil may be shaken through a
fine sieve for covering the seeds. If a regulation ⅛-inch sieve is not
available, an ordinary flour sifter is an efficient makeshift. Some gardeners prefer to use sand for covering seeds.

If you are reasonably sure that the seeds are viable and likely to germinate almost 100 percent, be care-
ful not to plant too thickly. If you
plant the seeds thinly so that each
seedling has a chance to develop
without being too close to its neighbor, there is much less danger of
the seedlings succumbing to attacks
of the deadly damping-off fungi.

Watering and shading. After the
seeds are planted, the soil should
be thoroughly watered, whenever

FIG. 71. Making drills with a ruler

FIG. 72. Sowing seeds in drills

the soil shows signs of becoming dry, by means of a fine spray from a hose or watering pot. The seed bed or flat or row of pots should be completely shaded (but not airless) until the first sign of green appears above the soil. Light should then be admitted at once, but not too intense at first.

General care. When the seedlings have formed their first rough leaf, they should be allowed much more light. Gradually remove the shading until they are exposed to full sunlight.

Ample air should be admitted to the coldframe at all times, the purpose of the sash being merely to prevent washing from torrential rains.

When the seedlings have been up for a few weeks, the stronger-growing kinds may be transplanted to another part of the garden, spacing them 3 to 4 inches apart to allow plenty of room for development. If winter-hardy, they will be ready for their permanent locations in October. The weaker growers may, with advantage, be left in the coldframe until the following spring. After the first severe frost, salt hay or similar protective matter may be scattered over the seedlings and the sash put on. During very cold weather, the sash should be closed, and the frames banked with partly decayed leaves or manure.

Planting seeds in the open. If coldframes are not available, biennials and perennials may be started by planting them in a seed bed in the reserve garden or the kitchen garden, where they may be inconspicuously protected with screens.

Shading and soil preparation. Although shade is necessary in the early stages, sunlight is essential (except in the case of shade-loving plants) when the seedlings are beyond the baby stage, in order that they may develop a sturdy stocky growth. Therefore, the seed bed and the bed to which the seedlings are transplanted should not be in permanent shade such as that

FIG. 73. Tamper for seed pots

cast by trees and buildings. The soil should be raked until all surface lumps are broken; or the upper 2 or 3 inches may be sifted through a half-inch sieve. The seeds are planted in rows 3 to 6 inches apart, covering them with soil equal in depth to the diameter of the seeds. The depth of covering is less in this instance than it is in strictly open-ground planting (p. 200) because the needful moisture will be supplied by artificial watering, and the ground will be shaded, until the seedlings are well developed, by means of cheesecloth or lath screens, supported a foot above the bed on stakes driven into the ground and fastened so that they cannot be blown away.

Cheesecloth screens may be made by tacking heavy cheesecloth to wooden frames (1 x 2-inch lumber may be used) in units of suitable size for covering the area. It is a convenience in caring for the seedlings if the screens can be attached to their support with hinges on one side and door-hooks and screw-eyes on the other.

If lath screens are wanted, make the beds about 4 feet wide because this is the length of the ordinary building laths used. The laths are nailed ¼ inch apart on 1 x 2-inch lumber. Such screens are ordinarily heavy enough so that it is not necessary to fasten them down to prevent the wind from carrying them away. When the sky is overcast, it is beneficial to remove the screens. To prevent the surface soil from baking, it is a good plan to scatter dried bog moss, peatmoss, or similar light material between the rows. Another method of preventing the soil from over-rapid drying is to lay strips of burlap on the soil, but care must be taken to remove the burlap just as soon as the seeds start to germinate.

Seed-sowing in the greenhouse. When greenhouse space is available, perennials and some biennials may be raised by starting the seeds in January or February, growing them along in good soil with plenty of room so that they become good-sized plants capable of flowering during the current season if they are planted outdoors in April.

Handling special groups of plants. While certain groups of plants are handled in much the same manner as perennials, each has its special problems when raised from seeds or spores. Those of biennials, rock plants, greenhouse plants, and ferns are treated below.

Biennials. Biennials are started in much the same way as perennials. The seeds are planted, preferably in coldframes, during the summer. The seedlings are transplanted when large enough and spaced from 3 to 6 inches apart, depending on the ultimate size of the plants. In the fall, if they are being raised in a region where they are perfectly hardy over winter, they are again transplanted, this time to the positions where they are to flower. If they are kinds which are not thoroughly winter-hardy, as, for example, pansies, Canterbury bells, and wallflowers, in the vicinity of New York, they are not transplanted in the fall but are left undisturbed, protected by a covering of some kind, and transplanted to their flowering locations in early spring.

The method of protection is dependent on their susceptibility to winter injury in the particular location. For example, a common method of growing pansies is to plant the seeds in rows 3 inches apart in a coldframe in July or August. When the seedlings have developed sufficiently so that they may be handled easily, and before they are injuring each other by crowding, they are transplanted to rich soil in another coldframe, spacing them from 3 to 6 inches apart. When the ground has frozen about an inch deep, a light scattering of salt hay should be placed over the plants and the sash placed on the frames. Ventilation must be given on all warm days, and during severe weather the plants should receive additional protection by covering the sash with boards, mats, or salt hay.

Rock plants. The seeds of most rock plants germinate readily if planted in a cool greenhouse or coldframe in March. Some kinds apparently need a period of after-ripening at low temperatures to ensure a good stand. Seeds of this nature may be planted in the fall and left outdoors. A plan that is followed successfully in England, which would probably be equally successful here, is to sow the seeds in late fall or early winter and place the seed pots or flats in a coldframe that is filled with snow as soon as snow is available. When the snow has melted, the seeds are brought into a slightly heated greenhouse, when germination usually is prompt. Those kinds which mature their seeds early may be planted as soon as they are ripe.

Greenhouse plants from seed. For subjects to be raised entirely under glass, seeds usually are sown in flower pots, pans, or flats. The soil used, and the technique of planting, are essentially the same as described for perennials.

Under greenhouse conditions, no attempt should be made to cover very fine seeds (petunia, begonia, gloxinia, etc.) with soil. Instead, scatter them on the surface of the prepared soil, press them in with the tamper, and then cover with a pane of glass resting on the rim of the pot to maintain sufficient moisture about them (Fig. 75). Watering should be accomplished by standing the pots in a vessel of water until it reaches the surface of the soil by capillarity. When the seeds have germinated, air should be admitted by tilting the glass and, after a few days, removing it entirely.

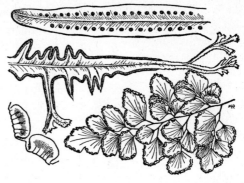

Preferably, seed pots and flats should be set in a propagating frame

FIG. 74. Various arrangements of spore-cases of ferns—*Polypodium, Pteris, Adiantum*. At bottom, left, sori of *Adiantum*, enlarged.

within the greenhouse until the seeds have germinated; or, if they are placed on an open bench, they should be shaded by paper. When the seeds have germinated, the paper should be removed except during the hottest part of sunny days.

When seeds are started under glass, they are subject to attack by various organisms which produce the disease known to the gardeners as damping-off. The symptoms are shrinkage and decay of the stem at a point near the surface of the ground, and as a result the seedling topples over and dies. Usually, thin sowing, the use of a porous soil in well-drained pots and flats, and avoidance of over-watering and of too humid an atmosphere, are sufficient to prevent these attacks. But when damping-off is known to be prevalent, it is desirable to sterilize the

FIG. 75. One method of planting fern spores

FIG. 76. Method of sowing
fine seeds and spores

Fig. 77. Removing seedlings from flat

soil before planting. This is done by baking, by steaming, or chemically, by the use of formaldehyde solution (page 485), or proprietary chlorophenol mercury preparations used according to the directions of the manufacturer. Thoroughly soaking the soil with boiling water after it has been placed in the pots and leveled and tamped for sowing is a measure accessible to every gardener, and one that is usually effective. The seeds, of course, should not be planted until the soil has cooled. Attacks may sometimes be halted by light applications of dusting sulphur. Transplanting the unaffected seedlings also helps.

Ferns from spores. For many ferns spores afford the most convenient means of propagation.

It is important to harvest the fern spores at the proper time. This occurs when the spore cases are just about to open (Fig. 74). When sowing the spores, portions of fern leaf bearing ripe spore cases may be laid on the surface of the prepared soil. This allows the spores to drift out over the soil (Fig. 75). Or fronds with ripe spore cases may be placed in paper bags until the spores are discharged, when they may be sown in the same manner as fine seeds (Fig. 76).

The usual method is to sow them in shallow well-drained pans of fine porous earth, previously wholly or partly sterilized (see above). The pans are covered with glass and set in saucers of water. There should be no overhead watering until the prothallia (small flat plates of green tissue on the underside of which the reproductive organs are formed) are well developed. After fertilization of the egg cells has taken place and the sporelings have made a leaf or two, they are pricked out (transplanted) into flats of light soil, just as seedlings are handled.

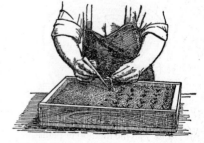

Transplanting small seedlings. When seedlings become crowded

Fig. 78. Transplanting seedlings

in the flats or seed pots, they should be transplanted—either singly in small pots, or spaced about 2 inches apart in flats. Prepare the flats as recommended for seeds, except that one part decayed and sifted manure may be added. Carefully remove the seedlings from pot or flat without injuring their roots (Fig. 77). Make a hole in the soil with a dibber, insert the roots, and gently press the soil firmly about them. The seedling should be set a little deeper than it was when growing in the seed pot (Fig. 78).

VEGETATIVE REPRODUCTION

It often happens that reproduction by seeds is not desirable, either because the characters we wish to perpetuate do not "come true" from seeds or because it is more convenient to propagate the plants vegetatively. Propagation without using seeds is carried out by various means —by bulbous structures developed on the plant, by runners and shoots of various types which arise from the crown of the parent plant, by cuttings of branches, leaves, or roots, or by budding and grafting. These methods are described in the rest of this chapter.

Propagation from bulbous structures. A reference to Chapter XIV, FLOWERING BULBS, will reveal the nature of the various structures that are included under the term "bulbs." In addition, a number of plants produce specialized organs, sometimes on the stem, sometimes around the mother bulb, which may be planted to produce new individuals.

Bulbils. Many of our bulbous plants propagate naturally by the division of the bulb into smaller bulbs or bulbils. The tulip, for example, when it has attained its maximum size (known as a "mother" bulb), tends to split up into a number of smaller bulbs. These may be planted about 3 inches deep, 2 or 3 inches apart in rows a foot apart, and, in the course of from one to five years, depending on the size of the bulbils when planted and the congeniality of the soil and climate, they will develop into flowering bulbs. In some cases the tendency to form bulbils may be accelerated by mutilation of the bulbs. This is the usual practice followed in commercial propagation of hyacinths. Either deep vertical cuts are made through the base of the bulb (*scoring*), or the base of the bulb is removed (*scooping*), exposing the base of the scale leaves which form the bulbs. This is done in the summer. By planting time in the fall, numerous small bulbils will have formed along the cut surfaces. These are planted, still attached to the mother bulb. They develop into mature bulbs in from three to five years.

Bulbils are formed on the aerial parts of several genera. Examples are the small bulbs formed in the leaf-axils of several species of lilies, or those formed in the inflorescences of "top" or "multiplier" onions. These may be planted in the same way as the bulbils produced on the underground parts.

Scaly bulbs such as those of lilies may be propagated readily by removing the outer scales and planting them in the same way that one would plant seeds—although they are really scale-leaf cuttings. Incidentally, it may be news to some that the green leaves of hyacinth and lily, if treated as cuttings, will develop small bulbils.

Corms and cormels. Popularly classed as bulbs, corms are bulb-like structures, but are solid throughout instead of being formed of scale leaves as in true bulbs. They increase in much the same way as bulbs by one or more corms being formed on top of the old corm. In addition, as in gladiolus, a number of tiny corms, known as cormels, may be produced around the base of the new corm. Cormels may be planted in essentially the same way as seeds. If properly cared for by transplanting when they become crowded, they will grow into corms of flowering size in from one to four years.

Tubers and tuberous roots. Familiar examples of subterranean tubers are potato and Jerusalem artichoke. Tubers afford a ready means of propagating plants that produce them—either planted whole or cut into portions, each possessing an eye from which a new plant will sprout. When the tuberous roots of dahlia are divided for propagating purposes it is necessary to cut them with a portion of stem attached to each root (Fig. 38).

Rhizomes. Rhizomes are underground, or partially underground stems, which, if cut into portions each bearing a growth bud, allow for rapid increase of plants producing them. Usually these divisions are made when the plants are dormant (canna, for example), but in the case of bearded iris many growers prefer to do this soon after the plant has bloomed.

Division. The methods of vegetative propagation just described may in some respects be considered as division. The term is more generally applicable, however, to rootstocks when they are forcibly separated by hand or by tools into pieces capable of propagation. Division is used as a means of propagation mainly with herbaceous perennials, although it can be adopted successfully with certain shrubs, such as some roses, spireas, and hydrangeas. In England it is employed to increase the stock of the dwarf boxwood used for edging.

Division is often accomplished by chopping the clump or rootstock into pieces of the desired size by means of a spade or mattock. This, however, is not a good method and, as a rule, better results are obtained by thrusting two spading forks (or hand forks if the plant is small) into the clump and prying it apart. The size of the division is dependent on the type of plant, quantity of stock available, and purpose for which the divisions are required. They may consist of single eyes, crowns, or buds, or several may be contained in each division. If the rootstock is divided into very small pieces it is usually advisable to plant the divisions in a sandy soil.

The operation is usually carried out when the plants are dormant, and, in the case of hardy plants, when the soil is workable. Peonies are commonly divided in early fall. Rock plants which bloom and make their growth early in the spring may be taken up and divided in late summer. Those which start into growth and bloom late in the season may be divided in spring. The divisions should be planted in soil that is more porous than that in which the parent plant is growing, and kept watered and shaded until new roots are formed.

Propagation by specialized shoots. Many plants give off specialized shoots which serve for the purpose of vegetative reproduction.

Runners. Slender shoots that run along the surface of the ground, at intervals forming buds which root and develop into young plants, are known as runners. The strawberry is propagated almost entirely by this means. Many alpine plants produce procumbent shoots which may be used to increase the stock. Sometimes the rooted runners are dug from the open ground. Sometimes the gardener plunges small pots filled with earth into the ground around the parent plants and pins the runners in them, so that when rooted the young plants may be transplanted without root disturbance.

Offsets. Essentially, offsets are similar to runners but have shorter stems. The houseleek is an example of a plant producing offsets. In some species of houseleek, as in *Sempervivum soboliferum,* the offsets are comparable to bulbils. Formed in the axils of the leaves, they fall off when mature, and, if growing on a slope, roll away to form new colonies. Offsets may be taken from the parent plant any time when they are mature; planted in pots or flats of sandy soil they will grow without any special treatment.

Suckers. Branches given off below the surface of the soil, growing erect and producing roots, as in the lilac and plum, are called suckers. They may be dug up with roots attached in either spring or fall. When using this method of propagation make certain that the tree or shrub you wish to increase is not grafted on a different variety, which would give rise to suckers of an undesirable type. The formation of suckers may be artificially stimulated in some subjects by root mutilation. This may be seen in the crop of suckers which arises when the roots of such trees as Lombardy poplars have been injured by spade or fork when working around them.

The terms "offset" and "sucker" are sometimes applied to the side shoots arising from screwpines, pineapples, and similar plants. In the pineapple these shoots are also called slips.

Slips. This is a term which is popularly applied to shoots of any plant that are pulled, or slipped off, and used as cuttings. The rooted shoots of sweet potato, produced by placing the tuberous roots in hot-beds and covering them with sand, are called slips, draws, or sets. With roots attached these are pulled from the mother root when they have attained a length of 6 inches. This is the accepted method of propagation of sweet potatoes, rather than by tubers as in the case of "Irish" potatoes.

Stolons and layers. A stolon is a branch given off above the soil level which, either by growing downward or of its own weight, comes in contact with the soil and takes root.

The term layer is applied to a shoot wholly or in part covered with earth to promote the formation of roots. Layering, on the whole, is a sure method of plant propagation, and does not demand much in the way of skill or equipment. In some cases, however, it is not so prolific as seeds, cuttings, or grafting. It may be successfully used with most woody plants that possess a habit of growth which enables their branches to be brought into contact with the ground.

PROPAGATION BY STOLONS. Shrubby plants that naturally take root by stolons are fairly common, among them forsythia, matrimony-vine, raspberry, dewberry, many willows, and several shrubby dogwoods. Stolons, when rooted, may be severed from their parent and transplanted to lead an independent existence. This should be done in spring or fall when the plants are dormant.

SIMPLE LAYERING. The usual method is to cut a notch in the stem about 18 inches from the tip of the branch which is to be layered. The

FIG. 79. Layering: *A*. Point where layer is severed from parent

branch is then bent down to the ground and the wounded portion is buried in a trench 2 inches deep. The layer is held down by means of a heavy stone or by pegging it with a forked stick (Fig. 79). As a general rule layers should be made in the spring. They will be rooted and may be severed from the parent plant in the fall and transplanted the following spring. With some plants, such as Japanese honeysuckle, layers will root and be ready for transplanting in less time than this; others (some rhododendrons and magnolias) may take longer.

SERPENTINE AND CONTINUOUS LAYERING. When plants form long flexible shoots, as in grape-vines and some roses, several rooted plants may be obtained from one shoot by using serpentine or continuous layering. By the former method the shoot is undulated and the lower loops covered with earth or buried in shallow trenches. In continuous layering the shoot is pegged down and covered lightly with earth throughout its length.

MOUND LAYERING. A convenient way of increasing plants of bushy habit is by mound layering. The stock plant is cut back a year before it is to be layered. This is done to promote the production of quantities of young shoots near the ground. The following spring it is layered by making a mound of earth over the center of the bush, thus covering the base of the shoots. In a year these shoots will be sizeable plants well furnished with roots. This is a method sometimes used to propagate currants and gooseberries.

AIR LAYERING. Trees or shrubs whose branches cannot conveniently be brought into contact with the ground may be propagated by air layering (or Chinese layering). A notch is cut in the branch, or the bark is girdled, at the point where root formation is desired—usually

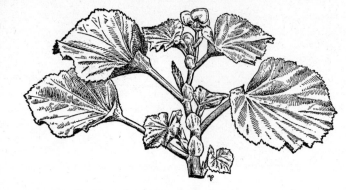

FIG. 80. Begonia shoot suitable for use as a cutting

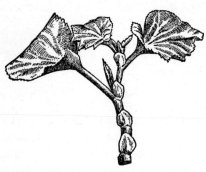

FIG. 81. Begonia cutting prepared for insertion

1 to 2 feet from the tip. A hinged layering-pot of metal, or one of pottery either cut in two longitudinally, or slotted on one side to the drainage hole, is then placed on the branch over the wound. The branch passes through the hole in the bottom of the pot, which is then filled with soil to be kept moist until sufficient roots are formed, then the rooted branch is severed and planted as a separate plant. Layering pots may be improvised by breaking ordinary flower pots into approximately equal halves and tying the broken portions together about the branch. You may be able to get the pot to break just right at the first attempt, but the chances are that two or three dozen pots will be ruined before one breaks to your liking! Another method is to form a cone of waterproof paper, thin sheet zinc, or rubber sheeting, about the branch to hold the soil. In a greenhouse, where humid conditions may be maintained, air layering is usually accomplished by wrapping the wound with a double handful of sphagnum moss, which is tied in place and kept moist by the spraying that the plants normally receive.

Air layering is a valuable means of propagating plants that are not easily or conveniently increased by other methods. It also offers a practical method of "bringing down to earth," without loss of leaves, leggy

FIG. 82. Geranium shoot suitable for use as a cutting

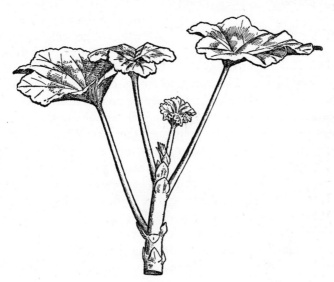

FIG. 83. Geranium cutting prepared for insertion

Fig. 84. Cutting herbaceous shoot below ground line

plants with bare stems and leafy tops. It is commonly applied to rubber-plants and to dracaenas of the "feather duster" type. Apartment-house dwellers whose dracaenas are touching the ceiling may use air layering to advantage.

Cuttings. The term *cutting* is applied to a portion of a plant severed from its parent and treated so that it may form roots and produce a new plant. Cuttings may be made of stems, leaves, portions of leaves, tubers (Jerusalem artichoke, potato, etc.), fruits (*Opuntia*), and roots. Stem cuttings are made either of growing shoots (softwood cuttings), of half-ripened wood, or of dormant shoots (hardwood cuttings).

Softwood cuttings. Plants of garden origin and species which seldom set seed are often successfully increased by means of softwood cuttings. Chrysanthemum, phlox, and delphinium are among the herbaceous plants that may suitably be propagated this way. While the operation usually takes place in early spring, any time during the growing season when young non-flowering shoots about 3 inches long are obtainable, softwood cuttings may be taken and inserted in sand (Figs. 80-83). It is believed that if the cut can be made below the surface of the soil, the cutting will root more readily (Fig. 84). Varieties of rockgarden plants, such as *Phlox subulata*, violas, and many others, may be handled in a shaded coldframe during June, July, and August.

Softwood cuttings of woody plants are usually made between the end of May and July 15.

Important factors in the success of cuttings made from growing shoots include not only the shelter, shade, and moisture provided, and the rooting medium but also the time and manner in which the cuttings are taken, the care that is given them until they are established as new plants, and often the use of special methods to induce root-growth.

PROPAGATING FRAMES. The humid atmosphere required by young cuttings may be maintained by placing individual cuttings under bell-jars, tumblers, or even preserving jars, and by shading and spraying as often as is necessary to keep them from wilting.

For large quantities of cuttings, a greenhouse, coldframe, or special propagating frame is needed. An ordinary coldframe can easily be adapted to serve the purposes of a propagating frame by providing a suitable rooting medium (see below), by painting the glass of the sash with whitewash, and by shading with lath or cheesecloth screens during the hottest part of the day.

ROOTING MEDIUM. The material used for the insertion of the cuttings has an important bearing on the results obtained. Formerly the commonest medium was clean, rather coarse sand. However, tests made by experimenters tend to show that while sand is the best medium for some varieties, a half-and-half mixture, by bulk, of peatmoss and sand gave best results with the majority of the plants tested, while peat proved to be the best medium for a few kinds. Vermiculite (expanded mica) is coming into wide use, and slag has been used successfully with some varieties. Coconut fibre refuse is sometimes used with good results in European practice. Many old-time gardeners prefer a porous soil mixture, surfaced with sand, in which to insert the cuttings. Some cuttings, such as oleander and willow, root readily in water.

Amateur gardeners should find considerable interest in experimenting with various media, time of insertion, etc. As an example of differences in behavior, I record the results of a little experiment with *Berberis verruculosa.*

Cuttings inserted	6 in sand	6 in sand and peatmoss
June 15	1 rooted, rest dead July 24	All dead July 24
July 25	1 rooted, rest dead Sept. 1	All dead Sept. 1
Aug. 14	6 alive but not rooted Oct. 3	6 rooted Oct. 3

As a general practice the frame should be prepared by putting a 2-inch layer of coarse sand in the bottom, covered with a 4-inch layer of a mixture of sand and peat in equal proportions, which must be firmly tamped down.

BOTTOM HEAT. It is desirable, but in most cases not absolutely necessary, to maintain the rooting medium at a temperature 5 to 10 degrees

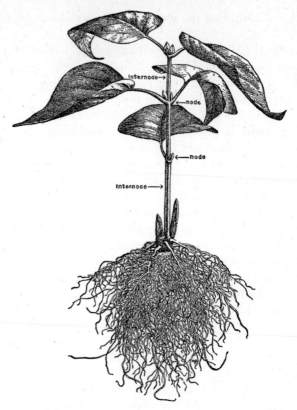

FIG. 85. Lilac—cutting inserted June 15. Drawing made
Nov. 8.

higher than the air surrounding the cuttings in order to stimulate root
action before top growth starts. This may be accomplished by heating
pipes, fermenting manure or leaves, or by electric heating cables beneath the cutting bed.

POSITION OF BASAL CUT. The position on the stem of the basal cut
sometimes is important. Older recommendations were to make the cut
just below a node, or to take the cuttings with a heel of older wood.
(Nodes are those points on the stem at which one or more leaves are
attached. The regions between are called internodes. (See Fig. 85.) A
heel cutting is a shoot pulled or cut off with a small portion of the
stem from which it grew, as shown in Fig. 86.) But some plants root

Fig. 86. "Heel" cuttings: *A. Melastoma, B. Metrosideros*

best when the cut is made midway between the nodes, and a few root best when the cut is made just above a node.

As a general practice the cut should be made below the node, about midway between it and the center of the internode, provided that this point is not more than ½ inch below the node. The cut should be slightly diagonal and made with a sharp knife or razor blade. When many cuttings have to be made it is a good plan to protect the thumb with a small piece of rubber hose attached as shown in Fig. 87. The size of the cuttings is dependent upon the character of the subject. Those of shrubs will average about 5 inches long; of herbaceous perennials, about 3 inches; and of most rock plants, about 2 inches. They may be inserted with the aid of a dibber and the rooting medium must be firmly packed about the base of the cutting.

In preparing the cuttings for insertion, no more leaves should be removed than necessary to prevent wilting. Usually the lower leaves of the cuttings are removed to facilitate insertion, but L. B. Stewart of the Royal Botanic Garden, Edinburgh, says: "The removal of leaves from the stems of cuttings is a practice to be condemned, as a great deal of time is wasted in cutting off the leaves; the cutting itself generally sheds them if they are not required."

FIG. 87. Thumb protected with piece of rubber hose

GENERAL CARE. After insertion, the rooting medium should be thoroughly soaked with water to settle it further about the cuttings. No more shade should be given than is necessary to prevent them from wilting. As a general rule in a coldframe the sash should be kept tightly closed, though ventilation may be desirable on hot days or if molds or other fungi make their appearance. The rooting medium must be kept constantly moist.

Dead and fallen leaves must be removed from the frame daily. When the cuttings have made roots from 1 to 2 inches long they should be removed from the propagating frame, carefully potted in sandy soil, and placed in a rather close shaded frame until their roots become established, when they may gradually be inured to the open air.

Usually the rooted cuttings are kept in pots plunged in ashes, sand, or peatmoss until the following spring, when they may be planted in the open ground. Early-rooted cuttings of vigorous hardy plants may be in condition to be set in the open ground during the current season.

USE OF CHEMICALS. Many investigators, both abroad and at home, have successfully used chemicals such as acetic acid, sucrose, and potassium permanganate to accelerate the rooting of cuttings, either by soaking the cuttings in the solution or by applying the solution to the rooting medium.

The work of Drs. Zimmerman and Hitchcock of the Boyce Thompson Institute for Plant Research indicates that any species of plants can be propagated from cuttings with the aid of root-inducing substances. The most effective compounds are indolebutyric acid and naphthaleneacetic acid. The basal ends of the cuttings are dipped in a powder impregnated with the compound, or placed in a water solution of the substances (about 1 inch in depth) for five to twenty-four hours (depending on the species and age of the tissue), then transferred to a rooting medium to be handled in the customary way. Apple, haw, blueberry and hazelnut cuttings, known to be difficult, then root readily. Plate XXVII shows the results obtained by treating cuttings of *Ilex opaca* (American holly) with growth substances.

Chemicals which promote root growth are now available under various trade names. If difficulty is experienced in rooting cuttings it may be worth while to try one of these growth substances by following the directions on the package.

CUTTINGS FROM FORCED PLANTS. Some plants which are difficult to root from cuttings may be successfully handled if the cutting wood is obtained from plants forced in the greenhouse. Examples are: *Acer* (Japanese maple), *Chionanthus* (fringe-tree), and *Daphne Cneorum*.

Dormant or hardwood cuttings. There are all stages of transition between honest-to-goodness softwood cuttings and hardwood cuttings. Many deciduous and evergreen plants root with facility from cuttings made from what the gardener calls half-ripened wood.

BROAD-LEAF EVERGREENS. As a single example of how cuttings of broad-leaf evergreens may or may not succeed, an experiment with holly is cited. At the Maryland Experiment Station cuttings of American holly taken on nineteen occasions, between June 19 and April 6 of the following year, gave best results between August 20 and the end of September. Of those planted on September 9, 100 percent rooted, and of those planted on September 22, 98 percent rooted. The percentage rooting dropped to 46 percent of the November 15 insertions and rose to 84 percent of the insertions of November 29.

CONE-BEARING EVERGREENS. Cuttings of certain quick-rooting coniferous evergreens, such as some varieties of retinospora and arborvitae, may be inserted during August in propagating frames outdoors, and left there until the following spring if carefully protected from winter injury. The more usual practice with conifers, however, is to root the cuttings under greenhouse conditions (at about 60° F.) from material of the current season taken between October and the end of the year. If possible, the cuttings should be gathered when they are not frozen. The kind of medium used has a great influence on the rooting of some coniferous evergreens. Tests made by some experimenters seem to indicate that peat and sand is not the ideal rooting medium for some types (yews, for example), which give their

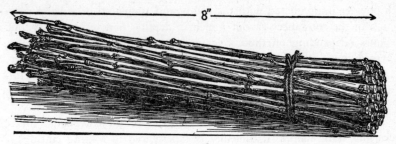

FIG. 88. Hardwood cuttings ready for storage

FIG. 89. Method of planting callused cuttings

best performance in either straight peat or straight sand, depending on the time when the cuttings are inserted. Coniferous evergreens of a resinous nature, such as pines, are extremely difficult to root from cuttings.

Convenience may dictate whether the cuttings are placed in flats or benches. The air about the cuttings should be humid, and they need protection from strong sunshine.

DECIDUOUS TREES AND SHRUBS. Cuttings of dormant wood afford an easy means of propagating some trees and many shrubs. The cuttings are made of firm wood of the current season, after the leaves have fallen, and are cut into lengths of 6 to 10 inches. Some shrubs, such as *Diervilla* and *Althaea,* are what the nurseryman calls "end growers," and of these only the tips of the shoots should be used. When the cuttings are made they are tied in bundles of fifty or a hundred, with the butts even (Fig. 88). They are then packed in moist sand, peatmoss, or sawdust and stored in a cool cellar (40°-45° F.) over the winter. If a suitable storage structure is not available they may be buried outdoors in sandy, thoroughly drained soil. By the time the ground is workable in the spring the cuttings are callused and ready for planting in nursery rows. The usual practice is to set them deeply with only the tips showing above the surface (Fig. 89).

Leaf cuttings. Although few plants are commercially propagated by leaf cuttings, many of the species commonly grown as house

FIG. 90. Leaf of *Begonia rex* with plantlets growing from vicinity of cuts

plants may be easily increased if the leaves are inserted in suitable media and given proper care. Succulent plants such as *Sedum, Echeveria, Bryophyllum,* and some species of *Kalanchoë* readily produce plantlets from leaves inserted in sandy soil. In the case of *Sedum* and *Echeveria,* mature leaves are pulled from the parent plant and

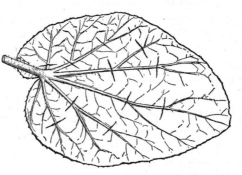

91. Leaf of *Begonia rex* with main veins cut preparatory to planting

the stem ends pressed into loose sandy soil. They root readily without any special treatment, the young plants coming from buds which originate at the base of the leaves. In *Bryophyllum* and *Kalanchoë* the leaf is laid flat on the surface of sand or sandy soil and weighted down with pebbles. The young plantlets are produced in the indentations along the margins of the leaves. These plantlets may even grow and produce roots while still attached to the parent plant.

Several kinds of begonia are habitually propagated from leaf cut-

FIG. 92. Piece-leaf cutting of *Begonia rex*

tings. In *Begonia rex* the entire leaf may be laid flat on the rooting medium and pinned down with hairpins, or weighted with pebbles (Fig. 90). When this method is followed the usual practice is to cut through the main veins just below the point where they fork (Fig. 91). Another method is to cut the leaf into V-shaped pieces each containing a good-sized vein (Fig. 92). These are inserted in sand, with the proximal point of the "V" down, in a warm propagating case. If a regular propagating case is not available, one may be improvised by cutting four pieces of glass, 9 inches to a foot wide, to fit the sides and ends of a small flat. These are placed vertically inside the flat so that their lower edges rest on the bottom. They are held in place by the weight of the sand in which the cuttings are inserted. The glass should project above the flat 6 to 9 inches. A fifth piece of glass is cut the same size as the flat, and rested on the upper edge of the side walls to form the roof. Such a case is fairly tight and serves to maintain the necessary humidity about the cuttings (Fig. 93). An aquarium can be converted into a propagating case by drilling holes in the bottom for drainage and providing a pane of glass to cover the top. Begonias of the Gloire de Lorraine group may be increased by taking entire leaves and inserting the petiole in the rooting medium. The same method is followed with *Peperomia, Gloxinia,* and *Saintpaulia.*

Sansevierias may be propagated by cutting the leaves into lengths of about 3 to 5 inches and inserting them (right end up, of course) in sand. The statement has been made that *Sansevieria trifasciata Laurentii* will not produce plants by this method. This is not so. It will produce new plants, but apparently they never

FIG. 93. Home-made propagating case

have the characteristic yellow stripe along the margin of the leaves.

Root cuttings. Many plants, both herbaceous and woody, may be propagated with ease by means of root cuttings. If greenhouse facilities are available the roots may be dug in early winter, cut into lengths of 1 to 3 inches, and buried ½ to 1 inch deep in flats of sand or of sand and peat. The thickness of the roots used is dependent on the subject —varying from ⅒ of an inch in the case of phlox to ½ inch or even more with some of the woody plants. Cuttings of the roots of hardy plants may be taken in the fall, stored in a cool place in moist peat or sand, and planted outdoors in the spring; or they may be made in the spring and planted immediately, though the former procedure is to be preferred. Plants commonly propagated this way include *Anemone japonica, Verbascum* (named hybrids), *Phlox* (varieties), *Aesculus parviflora, Clerodendron trichotomum,* and *Sophora japonica.*

Budding and grafting. These are the terms used to describe the operation of placing, or inserting, a portion of one plant (bud or scion) upon another plant (the stock) to unite them so that the scion is supported on the roots of the stock.

Why plants are budded or grafted. The reasons for adopting this procedure with certain plants, or groups of plants, are many. In some cases graftage is used to propagate plants which do not "come true" from seeds and which do not readily root from cuttings. Most of our fruit trees come in this group. Apples are budded or grafted on seedling apples or grafted on pieces of roots of older trees. Peaches are usually budded on seedlings of the "wild" peach; pears are budded on pear seedlings, or on quince stocks obtained from cuttings or layers, and so on.

Sometimes graftage is employed to modify the growth of the scion, as when apples are worked on Paradise stock and pears on quince stock, for the purpose of dwarfing them. Seedlings may be grafted on an old stock for the purpose of hastening their flowering or fruiting. Graftage may be employed when a plant does not make satisfactory growth on its own roots. For example, most of the Tea and Hybrid Tea roses are budded on stocks having a strong root system, and it is a common practice among nurserymen to bud or graft named lilacs on plants or cuttings of privet. This latter practice has been roundly condemned by some horticulturists who claim that lilacs should be raised from cuttings. It does, however, result in a salable plant in a shorter time, and, if grafted low down and subsequently planted deeply, so that the lilac may ultimately form its own root system, it is difficult to see any objection to the practice. In any case it is preferable to working named lilacs on seedling lilacs which are likely to sucker badly and choke out the scion.

Grafting and budding are also used when it is desired to produce a plant of special form, as when weeping trees (mulberry, elm, *Sophora*, etc.) are worked on a tall stock. Standard or tree-roses and umbrella catalpas are similarly produced.

Plants of trailing or weak habit of growth may be grafted on sturdy stocks so that their charms may be more effectively displayed. Crab-cactus is often grafted on *Pereskia,* and trailing forms of *Cereus* upon upright-growing kinds.

It is difficult, and perhaps impossible, to define the limits within which grafting can be done. Although it is reported that successful unions have been made between such distantly related plants as chicory and euphorbia, as a general rule there must be a close affinity between stock and scion to ensure a successful union.

There is much variety in the technique employed in budding and grafting. Limitations of space necessitate that only the more important methods be mentioned here.

Technique of budding. In budding, a single bud, with bark (and sometimes a portion of wood) attached, is inserted under the bark of the stock, usually when the cambium layer is active. The technique commonly followed is that known as T-BUDDING (from the shape of the cut in the stock), or SHIELD BUDDING (from the shape of the portion inserted). It is usually performed during the summer when the bark separates readily from the wood. Roses, apples, and peaches are among the plants propagated in this way. A shoot (bud-stick) is cut from the plant it is wished to propagate. The tip is cut off to reject immature buds. Then the leaves are cut off except for ½ inch of the stalk, which serves as a handle when inserting the bud. The buds are cut, with a sharp thin-bladed budding knife, starting about ½ inch below the bud (Fig. 94). Cutting toward the tip of the shoot, the bud is removed together with a thin sliver of bark and wood. Some operators prefer to remove the sliver of wood back of the bud; others leave it on (Fig. 95). A T-shaped cut is made through the bark of the stock, the two flaps of bark at the top of the T are raised and then the bud is slipped into the slit,·between the bark and the wood. If any of the bark to which the bud is attached projects, it is cut off

flush with the cross-arm of
the T (Fig. 96). After the
bud is inserted it is tied in
place with raffia, waxed
cloth strips, or woollen or
other soft string. Rubber
budding strips are coming
into use for holding buds
in place and are favorably
reported upon. If non-

Fig. 94. Budding—cutting the bud

elastic material is used for tying the buds, the ligatures must be cut, ten
days or two weeks after the bud is inserted, to prevent strangulation of
the bud by the tightening of the tie brought about by increase in diameter of the stock. The following spring all of the growth of the stock
above the inserted bud is cut off and any other shoots which may develop on the stock, excepting, of course, those which originate from the
inserted bud. Budding is usually performed on seedlings one to three
years old, but in the case of roses the practice is sometimes followed
of inserting buds at intervals along the whole length of strong canes
of older plants. These canes, after a few days, are then cut into sections
and treated as cuttings, or they may be layered. Lilacs may be successfully budded on unrooted cuttings of privet, which are then inserted
in suitable media for rooting; but this is not a common practice.

PATCH BUDDING is the method often employed when the plants to be

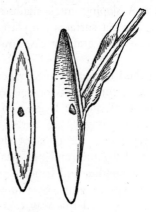

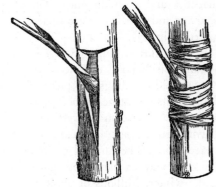

Fig. 95. The bud cut off and
sliver of wood (left) removed

Fig. 96. The bud inserted (left) and
tied (right)

operated on have thick bark, as in some nut trees. A rectangular piece of bark is removed from the stock, and a piece of exactly the same size, containing a bud of the variety it is wished to propagate, is fitted into the depression and tied snugly in place with strips of waxed cloth. A double-bladed knife with the blades set parallel about 1 inch apart, or a tool with four blades set in a rectangle about 1 x ½ inch is often used to facilitate patch budding. There are many other forms of budding but they are not commonly used. Flute, annular and whistle budding are variants of patch budding. Plate and H-budding are variants of shield budding. In CHIP BUDDING a mortise is cut in the stock and a chip of bark and wood containing a single bud is cut to fit the hole thus made. PRONG BUDDING is perhaps more nearly akin to scion grafting, in that a small twig is attached to the shield-shaped portion that is slipped under the T-cut of the stock.

Technique of grafting. Grafting is the application or insertion of a shoot (the scion), usually not more than one year old and containing one or more buds, to or into the stock. Union takes place in the cambial tissue, the layer which encircles the stem between the bark and the wood. In this area the cells are capable of dividing and forming new cells. This must be remembered when the stock and scion are of unequal size, for the scion must be so placed that, on one side at least, its cambium is in contact with that of the stock. Scion grafting is usually done in winter or early spring, when the scions are dormant.

The simplest form of grafting is the SPLICE GRAFT commonly used on roses intended for greenhouse forcing. A sloping cut is made in the stock and a similar one in the scion. The cut surfaces are placed together and tied. They are then placed in a close grafting case until united (Fig. 97).

WHIP GRAFTING (Figs. 98, 99) is the method frequently used when working on "whole" or "piece" roots—that is, entire roots of one- or two-year-old seedlings, or pieces of roots from mature trees. Long sloping cuts are made on both stock and scion. Tongues are made on both stock and scion by vertical cuts starting near the point of the diagonal cuts. Stock and scion are then fitted together and tied with waxed string. The finished grafts are tied in bundles and handled in the same way as hardwood cuttings. This type of grafting is done in the winter. Millions of apple trees are propagated this way every year. When a large number of grafts are to be made machines are used to facilitate tying.

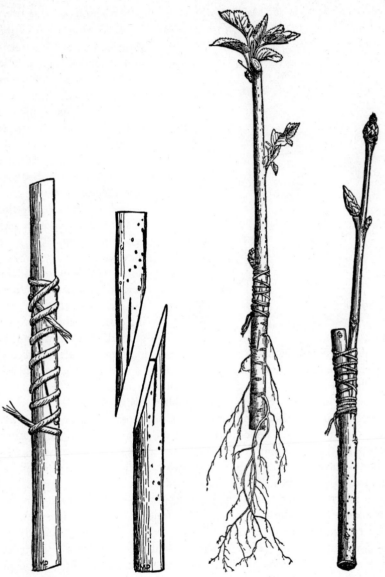

Left. Fig. 97. Splice graft. *Left center.* Fig. 98. Whip graft—positions of cuts. *Right center.* Fig. 99. Whip graft—weeping mulberry on "piece-root" of white mulberry. *Right.* Fig. 100. Side-graft—lilac on privet cutting.

FIG. 101. Veneer graft

The SIDE GRAFT (Fig. 100) is used a great deal in the propagation of evergreens and Japanese maples. The stocks used are seedlings or cuttings, two or three years old, with stems about the thickness of a lead pencil. They are potted in the spring so that they may be thoroughly established before they are brought into a cool greenhouse in the fall. Three or four weeks before grafting is to start they are placed in a warm-house (60°-65°) to induce new root formation. When the roots are actively growing the stocks may be grafted. A slanting cut is made, 1 to 2½ inches long, extending almost to the center of the stock. The end of the scion is cut to a long wedge shape and fitted in the cut on the stock with the cambium layers together. The scions are tied in place with twine or rubber strips. The pots are then plunged, almost horizontally, in moist peatmoss, sand, or sphagnum moss with the scion uppermost. Usually they are kept in propagating cases in the greenhouse. In about four weeks the stock and scion should have grown together, at which time less humidity is maintained about them, and about one third of the top of the stock is removed. In another four or five weeks the rest of the stock may be removed, or, in the case of difficult subjects, another third, leaving the remainder to a later date.

The VENEER GRAFT (Fig. 101) is a modification of the side graft. A piece of bark and wood is removed from the stock by a long diagonal cut (about 2 inches) and a shorter almost horizontal cut. The scion is cut to fit. The advantage of these types of graft over splice, whip, saddle, or wedge graft is that if union fails to take place, the stock is still available for the insertion of another scion.

The grafting of coniferous and broad-leaved evergreens, Japanese maples, magnolias, and tree peonies (these are usually worked on pieces of roots of herbaceous peonies) is usually carried out in greenhouses during the first three months of the year.

CLEFT GRAFTING (Fig. 102) is the method largely used in making over old fruit trees to new varieties. The scions of wood of the preceding season, 6 to 8 inches long, are cut wedge-shaped and inserted in a branch, preferably not more than 2 inches in diameter. The stock is cut off squarely and a cleft made with a grafting chisel in which the scions are placed with their cambium layers in contact with those of the stock. All exposed cut surfaces are then waxed. (Grafting wax is obtainable from any large seed store.) This work is done in the spring when growth is starting.

In all grafting work it is desirable that the stock be in a slightly more advanced stage of growth than the scion. Scions to be grafted on plants established outdoors may be held back by cutting them during the winter and holding them in a moist medium in cold storage, or by burying them outdoors in a cold shaded spot. In outdoor grafting all cut surfaces are covered with grafting wax. In some cases (nut grafting) the entire scion as well as cut surfaces may be coated with melted, but not too hot, paraffin wax.

FIG. 102. Cleft graft. All wounded parts must be waxed.

INARCHING, OR GRAFTING BY APPROACH. This practice is adopted when dealing with plants that are difficult to propagate or graft by the usual methods, or when it is desired to work a seedling on an older plant in order to hasten its flowering. In the first case the stocks are grown in small pots. They are then brought near the twigs that are to serve as scions, either by tying them to the branches of the plant to be propagated, by fastening them to a stake, or by standing them on a conveniently situated shelf or platform. A sliver of bark is removed from both stock and scion, and the two cut surfaces are brought together and

Fig. 103. Approach grafting—*Codiaeum* sp. carrying several varieties: *A*. Grafts of preceding year; *B*. Rooted cutting (removed from pot and ball wrapped in burlap to reduce weight) in process of being grafted by approach; *C*. Character of cuts.

tied. In this method of grafting the scion is not removed from the parent plant until it has united with the stock. When approach grafting is used for the purpose of hastening the flowering of seedlings the same procedure is followed, but in reverse, inasmuch as the seedlings (scions) are in small pots and are grafted upon a plant which has attained flowering size. Fig. 103 illustrates approach grafting.

The foregoing is merely a summary of the practices followed in plant propagation. It has not been possible to go fully into details. Those who wish to delve further into this fascinating subject should consult books dealing wholly with plant propagation.

XXVII. PRUNING ORNAMENTAL TREES AND SHRUBS

Contrary to a widely accepted belief, the vast majority of ornamental trees and shrubs do not require extensive annual pruning. Consequently, one is tempted to give the would-be pruner the famous advice that Mr. Punch gave to those about to be married: "Don't!" Much harm to plants may ensue when pruning-saw and shears are used by unskilled hands; and those who are ignorant of the "whys and wherefores" of pruning are advised to restrict their pruning to the removal of dead, diseased, and scale-infested branches. If this advice were generally followed we would not see so many forsythias mutilated by hedge shears in winter with consequent distortion of habit and fewer flowers the following spring; and there would not be so many tales of wisteria and "French" hydrangea failing to blossom because of too severe pruning in spring.

Purposes and methods of pruning. It must not be inferred from the above that pruning is altogether a bad practice. It is possible by pruning to aid the rejuvenation of sickly plants and assist in the control of insect pests and fungous diseases. Pruning may be used to correct faulty habits of growth, to maintain symmetry, and to bring about earlier blossoming. By reducing the number of growth buds on shrubs which produce their flowers on shoots of the current season, it is possible to develop larger flowers on longer stems; and pruning or shearing is almost always essential in the production of hedges and plants of special outline for use in formal gardening.

Following are some of the considerations that should actuate anyone engaged in pruning practices.

Dormant pruning. Severe pruning when the plant is dormant usually results in the production of strong vegetative shoots during the following growing season. The commonly accepted reason for this is that the food supply rising from the roots is concentrated in a few growth buds instead of being dissipated over a large number.

Severe pruning may be rejuvenational in its effects when properly

449

done and accompanied by feeding at the roots. Thus, old shrubs which are making poor growth may sometimes be given a new lease of life if they are cut almost to the ground. Lilacs, for example, usually respond to this sort of treatment (Plate XXVIII). It should, however, be recognized that such pruning is to be avoided as much as possible. In the case of shrubs whose flowers originate from wood of the preceding year, one year's blossoming is lost, and possibly two, if the vegetative growth induced by severe pruning is so strong that no flower buds are formed. Furthermore, it sometimes happens that such drastic treatment, by completely upsetting the balance between roots and top, brings about the demise of the plant. The ideal treatment for shrubs which tend to become decrepit with age is to maintain constant juvenility by the removal (annually, if necessary) of old worn-out wood. Among the common shrubs that are amenable to this treatment are *Philadelphus, Deutzia, Weigela,* and *Forsythia.*

Old devitalized trees may sometimes have their vigor renewed by cutting back up to one third of their top growth when they are dormant. A nice sense of judgment is necessary to ensure that enough is cut off to be of benefit, yet not so much that a thicket of sappy watersprouts is produced. In general, the cuts should be made close above branches pointing in the direction in which it is wished to have the tree develop.

Occasionally we have to deal with a tree which is well placed and vigorous, but which, because of neglect or just plain perversity, has developed a faulty habit, weak crotches, and crossing branches. Such a tree might well require the removal of half, or even more, of its top growth to bring it into a semblance of symmetry. To avoid the dangers of a lack of balance between top and root, it is a good plan either to spread the corrective pruning over several years, or to cut out during the winter about half of the wood that has been marked for removal, then, the following summer, check the over-vigorous growth by removing the remainder.

Summer pruning. When applied to shrubs which are making vigorous vegetative growth, summer pruning may, by checking their exuberance, bring about increased flower-bearing. This statement is not universally applicable, and observation and thought should be used before putting it into extensive practice. It may work very well with non-blooming wisterias if the long trailing shoots which are produced in early summer are cut back at the right time. If they are cut too soon, dormant buds start into growth; if pruning is deferred too long, nothing is accomplished beyond shortening the shoots. Observation must determine the correct time to cut back these shoots to within three or four buds of their point of origin. This should be done just before the shoots have attained their maximum length— usually in July. The theory is that the check to growth occasioned by the removal of growing parts at a time when food is still rising from the roots results in the conversion of growth buds into flower buds. If a vigorously growing wisteria persistently fails to bloom after summer pruning of the growing shoots, root-pruning should be resorted to.

In the case of highly trained fruit trees, summer pruning is necessary. These trees, which are in much greater favor in Europe than they are here, are trained in various shapes, usually against a wall. One of the simplest forms is the "cordon" which may consist of single or double "trunks" on which the fruit spurs are borne. These trunks may be trained horizontally, obliquely or vertically. There is almost always a tendency toward the production of an excessive number of side shoots, thus, in order to maintain the cordon in the correct shape and to encourage the formation of fruit spurs, it is necessary to prune the side shoots several times during the growing season by pinching out their tips.

Summer pruning of shrubs which do not have a definite season of growth, but which continue producing new shoots and flowers as long as weather remains favorable, belongs in a different category. If the flowers of everblooming roses such as China, Tea, and Hybrid Tea, are cut with long stems leaving only two or three growth buds on the shoot of origin, strong flower-bearing shoots will be produced from these few remaining buds. If merely the faded flowers are removed a greater number of flower-bearing shoots are likely to develop, but they will not be so vigorous. It all simmers down to the question of whether long-stemmed roses are desired for cutting or quantities of blooms are wanted for garden display.

Pruning trees and shrubs which blossom on old wood. Shrubs or trees which produce their blossoms on wood that is one year old or more cannot be extensively pruned when dormant without reducing the number of flowers produced the following spring. It does not necessarily follow that pruning this class in winter, or when dormant, is absolutely prohibited. Lilacs may be pruned when dormant without much loss of bloom if the parts removed are restricted to suckers and weak spindling branches; and, on occasion, branches bearing flower buds may deliberately be sacrificed in order that those remaining may have a better chance to develop. It is usually recommended to prune forsythias and other early-blooming shrubs immediately after flowering, but pruning can often be done to advantage during the winter, and the prunings may be forced into bloom indoors for use as cut flowers. As a general practice, however, it is better to prune these early-blooming shrubs which flower on old wood immediately after they have finished blooming. Pruning should consist of the removal of old worn-out wood (a thinning process) and correcting any irregularity of growth, always remembering that too little pruning is far preferable to too much (Plate XXIX).

Cutting the flowers with long stems for indoor use often serves, in part, the same purpose as regular pruning, and in some cases (lilac, for example) is an important means of preventing the plants from increasing too rapidly in height. If pussy willows are wanted with long whip-like growths, the shoots of the preceding year should be cut back to one or two growth buds, while if the "pussies" are wanted on short twiggy growths, extensive pruning should be avoided.

Some varieties of the so-called "French" hydrangeas apparently are only able to produce flowers from shoots which originate from near the tips of the canes of the preceding year. Therefore the rather common practice of cutting them to the ground every spring is to be frowned upon, for it usually results in strong vegetative growth and no flowers. Instead of being so drastic, pruning should be restricted to the removal of thin spindling shoots and to cutting back the tips of the canes to sound wood, if they have been injured by the winter. In regions which experience severe winters the bushes should be protected by covering them to prevent the canes from being killed by cold, with the consequent necessity of cutting them off at the ground line.

Pruning shrubs which blossom on new wood. Shrubs which produce their flowers on shoots of the current season may be pruned, often to great advantage, by cutting them back just as growth is starting in spring. Roses of the Tea, Hybrid Tea, and Hybrid Perpetual classes belong to this group. But because roses present special problems to the gardener, the entire question of pruning them is treated in Chapter XV, ROSE GARDEN.

The "Pee-Gee" hydrangea (*H. paniculata grandiflora*) may be pruned in late winter or early spring by cutting back the shoots made the preceding year to within one or two buds of their point of origin. This results in strong shoots bearing enormous panicles of flowers, but it also results in an ungainly plant and many of us think that more pleasing effects are obtained when this shrub is left unpruned or when the one-year shoots are cut back only lightly—say, about one third. Much the same treatment may be given to the rose of Sharon (*Hibiscus syriacus*), except that in this case the flowers are produced along the shoots of the current season instead of in panicles at the tips (Plate XXVIII).

When it comes to the summer-lilac (*Buddleia*) and shrubs of similar habit, it is possible to make out a good case in favor of drastic spring pruning. In the first place, in the climate around New York, the frost is likely to take the matter out of our hands by killing the tips almost to the ground so that, willy-nilly, the pruner must use his shears to rid the bush of dead wood. Secondly, in buddleia the shoots of the current season branch freely and flowers are formed on both lateral and terminal shoots; an abundance of flowers therefore develops on a shapely bush even after it has been severely pruned.

To produce brightly colored twigs. In shrubs which are grown for the effect of their twigs in winter, such as *Cornus stolonifera* and varieties of *Salix vitellina,* the brightest color is seen in the young twigs. Because of this it is commonly advised to cut back these shrubs severely just before growth starts in the spring. However, unless this heavy pruning is followed up in summer by pinching out the tips to stimulate free branching, the result is likely to be unsatisfactory because the long whip-handle growths are far less attractive than an abundance of shorter twiggy shoots. A better plan is to cut out annually old weak branches of poor color and shorten the strongest shoots.

Removing suckers from grafted plants. A close watch should be kept on grafted plants. If suckers arise from the understock, remove them promptly. In so doing cut them as close as possible to the parent stem so that no buds are left behind to cause trouble in the future. When suckers originate from below the ground level and it is not easy to cut them off, they may usually be removed by an upward and outward pull. After a few trials one develops a knack of doing this so that the sucker is removed and no buds are left behind. Grafted roses, rhododendrons, lilacs, and flowering almonds should be particularly watched for suckers.

Pruning to develop a compact habit. Removal of the tips of growing shoots promotes a compact twiggy habit because it usually results in stimulating the growth of buds which normally would have remained dormant. Light "heading in" of shoots of the preceding year, when the plant is dormant, serves a similar purpose. We make use of this principle in shearing hedges and in trimming to symmetrical outlines plants used in formal gardening. For the proper methods of pruning and shearing both evergreen and deciduous plants used for hedges, see Chapter X, HEDGES. Shearing should not be practised except when it is desired to produce plants having special definite outlines. Judicious shortening of exuberant growths which tend to spoil the normal symmetry of a species may, however, be practised to advantage. In special cases when it seems necessary to promote the production of a branch in a certain direction and it is considered undesirable to cut away any portion of the tree or shrub, a properly situated dormant bud may be made to start into growth by cutting a notch, extending into the sapwood, immediately above the bud. This partially interrupts the flow of sap toward the end of the branch: thus diverted, the sap finds an outlet by forcing the bud into growth.

A factor in the control of disease. Pruning may be an important factor in the control of insect pests and plant diseases. Shrubs and trees that are badly infested with scale insects should have the worst infested branches removed if this can be done without completely destroying the symmetry of the bush or tree. This pruning serves the double purpose of cleaning up a large part of the infection and of stimulating the growth of the remaining branches. Such pruning, of course, should always be accompanied by appropriate spray treatment. The removal of infected branches or the cutting out of cankers is an important part of the treatment indicated in the control of such bacterial and fungous pests as fire blight and apple canker. On the other hand, watersprouts and other soft sappy growth induced by excessive pruning are favorite feeding grounds for aphids, and are highly susceptible to attack by fire blight.

For methods of pruning newly transplanted trees and shrubs, see Chapter VII, TREES AND SHRUBS.

Technique of pruning. Because pruning leaves open wounds which may cause serious infection, the greatest care must be exercised when the work is being done. The style and the sharpness of the tools, the way each cut is made, and the use of protective measures to discourage disease are all important factors in the pruning of woody plants.

Tools. The tools used in pruning should be sharp, to make a smooth cut to which a wound dressing may be applied with facility. In the case of saw cuts it is sometimes advisable to smooth the surface with a plane or sharp knife, for a clean cut is believed to heal with greater rapidity than a jagged one. For small branches, a pruning knife skillfully used is probably the best tool, as its use involves a minimum of injury to the plant tissues. Pruning, however, can be done more expeditiously with pruning shears, and if these are kept sharp and carefully used, little damage to surrounding tissues will result. Long-handled lopping shears are used extensively in pruning shrubs where the branches to be removed are up to 1 or 1½ inches in diameter. In my opinion, however, branches 1 inch or more in diameter can be cut out more advantageously with a narrow-bladed pruning saw.

Position of the cuts. The cuts in pruning should be made just above a bud or buds pointing in the direction in which it is wished to have the bush or tree develop. When large branches are involved they should be removed by cutting close to and parallel with the axis of the parent branch or trunk. A wound that is close to an actively growing part of the tree or shrub will be quickly healed over by the development of callus tissue. If stubs are left, they will die because sap is not flowing through them. Decay will set in, and eventually it may extend into the living trunk far beyond the original dying stub.

When cutting out branches of considerable weight, grave injury to the tree may result if certain precautions are not observed. The first cut should be made about a foot from the point where the final cut is to be made and should be an upward cut from beneath the branch. Continue cutting until the saw binds. The second cut should be 2 inches nearer to the trunk and from the top of the branch downward. This results in the removal of the branch without any danger of slivering the bark of the trunk below. The stub which remains may now be removed with safety because it may be steadied with one hand while the few last cuts with the saw are being made (Fig. 104).

Wound dressings. Although in some quarters doubts are cast on the desirability of treating wounds (especially small ones) to prevent decay, the consensus of opinion seems to be that some protective substance should be applied, at least to the larger wounds. A wound

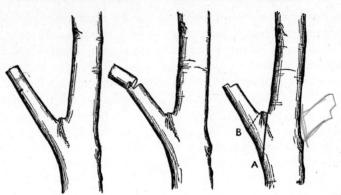

FIG. 104. Removing a large limb. Final cut at *A—not* at *B*.

dressing should inhibit the germination of spores of disease-causing organisms, prevent the checking (cracking) of the wood, and at the same time be non-injurious to the living tissue of the cambium, or growth layer, underneath the bark.

Experiments carried out by the United States Department of Agriculture, Yale University, and the Bartlett Tree Research Laboratories in collaboration, seem to indicate that the best material for this purpose is the Bordeaux paint developed by Dr. S. M. Zeller of the Oregon State Agricultural College. This consists of equal parts by weight of commercial dry Bordeaux mixture and raw linseed oil, applied with a stiff paintbrush. A drawback to the use of this material is the conspicuous and unsightly color changes through which it passes. A commercial preparation is now available for which it is claimed that the color of the material is "changed to meet the conditions of shade trees."

Both shellac and a thick paint made of zinc oxide and linseed oil are fairly satisfactory dressings that are conveniently obtainable by the average amateur gardener. Asphalt paints have been used with good results, and also coal tar, when kept away from the edges of the wound to avoid injury to the cambium layer. It has been suggested that rubber latex or melted beeswax be applied to the cambial region before the dressing which is designed to protect the wound.

Summary. Most of our ornamental trees and shrubs are not improved by annual or extensive pruning. Except in special cases, the natural shape of tree or shrub should be maintained as far as is possible.

It is important to know when and where flower buds are produced in order that pruning may not result in failure to bloom.

Pruning of the top to compensate for loss of roots at transplanting time is important.

Pruning is a lifetime study and should be carried out thoughtfully, with careful observation of results, so that errors may be avoided in future practice.

XXVIII. WINTER PROTECTION

In northern climates most gardens contain at least a few plants which need to be helped through the winter to enable them to survive. These weaklings are found among the "hardy" perennials, trees and shrubs, bedding plants, and summer bulbs. The degree of "tenderness," of course, varies with the location in which they are grown as well as with the inherent quality of the different species. There are some which cannot endure the faintest touch of frost, while others, on the border line of hardiness, can survive a normal winter, but are likely to be injured or even killed outright if the season is unusually severe.

This chapter deals with the subject in a general way. Winter protection as applied to special groups—perennials, roses, roof-garden plants, dahlias, gladioli, waterlilies, bulbs, and others—is discussed in detail in the chapters devoted to their cultivation.

Protecting perennials and bulbs. When a protective mulch is applied to the perennial garden or over the place where the hardy bulbs are planted (as described on pages 164 and 224), the main object is to maintain a more equable soil temperature. In other words, the mulch is designed to prevent, so far as possible, the alternate thawing and freezing of the soil, which results in serious injury, especially when shallow-rooting plants are heaved out of the ground. When mulching material consists of manure, it also serves to improve the fertility of the soil.

Mulches and winter coverings in general should not be put on until the ground has frozen, partly because of the danger of keeping the plants too long in a growing condition, thus rendering them susceptible to injury when really cold weather arrives; and partly because, if the covering is applied before field mice have selected their winter homes elsewhere, they may make their headquarters in it, and from this vantage point feast on the very plants you are attempting to safeguard.

Protecting woody plants. When protecting woody plants of doubtful hardiness, both roots and tops must be covered. Usually, it is unnecessary in the New York climate to put on covering before Christmas.

The most serious damage occurs to evergreen trees and shrubs during March when they are exposed to bright sunshine and drying winds. Both elements draw the moisture from the leaves; the roots are unable to replenish it because the soil around them is partly or completely frozen. Consequently, the leaves "burn" and die. Our endeavors, therefore, should be to prevent the soil from freezing too deeply, to shelter the plants from high winds, and to shade them from the sun. In some regions protection from snowfall also is essential.

The soil over the roots should be covered with from 2 inches to a foot of protecting material, depending upon the severity of the climate and the nature of the plant. The covering may be strawy manure, straw, salt hay, peatmoss, or leaves—the two last for rhododendrons and allied plants.

The type of covering applied to the tops of the plants is decided largely by the kind of material on hand and the character of the subject. Among the materials used are burlap, cut evergreen boughs, hay, straw, building paper, packing boxes, soil (especially when the plants can be laid down), and lath screens. Ordinarily, better results are obtained when the covering does not entirely exclude the air.

The erection of a temporary board fence on the windward side may be all the protection needed with the hardier shrubs. This is the method adopted on some of the Newport, R. I., estates to keep even such common deciduous subjects as California privet from injury by salt-laden winds.

Evergreens subject to "burning" may be protected by cutting boughs from common species of pine and fir, and either sticking them in the ground around the plants as a shade, or completely enveloping the plants and tying the boughs in place. Cut evergreens are the least unsightly of all the materials used for covering.

A common way of protecting valuable boxwoods is to erect a light wooden framework over them and cover this with burlap, which is tacked to the wood to keep it in place.

Lath screens, made by nailing ordinary building laths to strips of light wood the height of the subject to be protected, serve well against winter weather. Three of these screens placed in a triangle around a

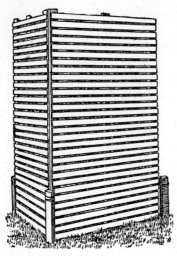

FIG. 105. Lath screens to shelter
plants from wind and sun

bush or small tree often give effective protection (Fig. 105). The screens should be wired or tied together at top and bottom to hold them in place, and in windy locations it may be necessary to drive stakes at each corner for anchors. I have had good success in protecting a Scotch broom hedge with a tent made by placing such screens in a row on both sides of the hedge, fastening them together at the top with wire. Short pegs driven into the ground at the base of the screens prevent them from spreading.

A fairly effective way of protecting trees and shrubs is to tie the branches in as closely as possible and then cover with burlap, which is sewn in place with twine and a sailmaker's needle. "French" hydrangeas may be protected in this way, or by the rather laborious method much used by Newport, R. I., gardeners, which involves the use of a topless and bottomless box placed over the plant and then filled with soil so that the canes are completely covered.

Instead of using burlap, straw or hay may be the covering material. The branches are first tied in rather closely, the hay or straw applied and held in place with cord. This, however, constitutes a fire hazard if careless cigarette smokers are allowed in the garden. Again, packing boxes with a few holes bored in them to provide ventilation may be placed over small and medium-sized shrubs. The trouble with all these methods is their unsightliness.

Protection from snow. In regions which experience heavy wet snowfalls, some protection against the danger of breakage is desirable. Evergreens with the habit of growth of the oriental arborvitae are especially liable to injury because the wet snow lodges between their branches and its weight causes them to split. Protection can be afforded by tying the branches together in the fall. A convenient means of doing this is to fasten a length of tape to a low branch and then wind it tightly in a wide spiral around the bush. A more elaborate method of ensuring snow protection is that sometimes used by the Japanese (Plate XXX). This has the merit of being decorative, but its installation is time-consuming, and probably too tedious an operation for American gardeners, who do not, like the Japanese, go to great lengths in the endeavor to make the winter overcoats of their plants presentable. Their covering is put on with great care, and if straw is used, as it commonly is, it is sometimes trimmed into designs.

This prompts the suggestion that Americans who wish to enjoy their gardens during the winter should either use nothing but really hardy material (so far as trees and shrubs are concerned), or take a leaf from the Japanese gardener's book and apply their protective measures in such a way that they are decorative (Plate XXX).

Bringing plants indoors for protection. In addition to the plants which are protected in place, there are those which must be brought indoors. In this group are the bedding plants which are propagated by cuttings or division, tubbed specimens employed for lawn or porch decoration, and various bulbs, corms, and tubers used for summer display.

Bedding plants. The method of handling bedding plants is determined by the quantity grown and whether or not greenhouse facilities are available.

Our grandparents used to carry pelargoniums (geraniums) over winter by digging them up in the fall, tying them in bundles and suspending them from the rafters of the cellar. But they had at their disposal an unheated but frost-proof cellar, with a dirt floor which gave off enough moisture to enable the plants to survive. The modern cellar with its heater and concrete floor is altogether too hot and dry for this method.

Those who have no greenhouse and wish to save a few tender plants (geraniums, coleus, etc.) should root cuttings in August, pot them into small pots and carry them over winter in the sunny window of a room where the temperature is kept around 60 degrees. An alternative is to dig up the old plants just before frost, cut them back at least one half, and keep them under the conditions described above for cuttings.

Two methods are followed when a greenhouse is available. Stock plants are dug up and potted in the fall, or cuttings are rooted in August. By the first method, any suitable shoots removed when cutting back the plants preparatory to potting them, as well as the young shoots produced later by the stock plants, are inserted as cuttings until enough young plants have been obtained for the following year. By the second method, the young plants rooted in August are usually cut back at least once during the winter, and the cut-off portions utilized as cuttings.

Tubbed plants. Such subjects as agapanthus, oleander, bay-trees, lemon verbena, and century-plants, grown in tubs and used for decorative purposes outdoors during the summer months, become a problem in the fall if one does not have proper facilities for wintering them. The ideal way to store them is in a greenhouse where the temperature is maintained between 35 and 40 degrees. Failing this, an unheated frost-proof cellar may be used, placing them where they receive the greatest amount of light. Sometimes it is possible to winter them in a deep coldframe if it is situated mostly below the ground on the south side of a heated building. The above-ground portions of such a frame should be banked with manure and plenty of material held near by to provide a frost-proof covering that can be placed on the sash during severe weather. Salt hay may conveniently be used for this purpose. It should be applied to a depth of 1 or 2 feet during cold weather and raked off so as to admit light when the temperature is above freezing.

Tender bulbs. Tender bulbs, corms, and tuberous roots are generally cared for by digging them up in the fall and storing them dry, either uncovered or surrounded with dry sand or peatmoss.

For most of them, a temperature between 40 and 50 degrees is preferable. Strictly tropical plants such as the tuberose and devil's tongue are comfortable in a temperature of around 60 degrees. Great difficulty is experienced in carrying over such plants as canna and dahlia if nothing but a hot dry cellar is available for storing them. If kept dry they shrivel and lose their vitality; if kept moist they start into growth far too soon.

Summary. Among the important rules to remember when giving protection to tender plants for the winter are:

1. Do not mulch the ground above their roots until freezing weather.

2. Do not apply so thick a covering that all air is excluded.

3. Evergreens need protection from winter sun and wind rather than from the cold.

4. Most of the tender bulbs and similar subjects suffer the least harm when stored in a temperature between 40 and 50 degrees.

5. If a greenhouse is not available, the tender bedding plants which are more or less actively growing during the winter are best cared for in a sunny window where a temperature of about 60 degrees is maintained.

XXIX. GARDEN ENEMIES

INSECTS AND OTHER ANIMAL PESTS

It is manifest that garden pests cannot be completely covered in a single chapter. But it is possible, by explaining the general principles of pest control, to provide a working knowledge that will, in most cases, enable the gardener to save his plants.

General principles of insect control. Insects may be divided into two groups from the standpoint of methods used for their control: SUCKING INSECTS, which obtain their food by piercing the plant tissues and sucking the sap, and CHEWING INSECTS, which bite off and eat portions of the plant. Broadly speaking, the first group is controlled by the use of insecticides which kill the insects when brought in actual contact with their bodies, and the second group by applying poison to the plant parts attacked, so that the insects, after eating, die of internal poisoning. Under some circumstances, both groups may be dealt with by subjecting them to a lethal gas, as when fumigation is practised in greenhouses or in portable tents outdoors. (See Chapter XXV, GREEN-HOUSES.)

Sucking and chewing insects may both be further divided into those which feed openly and those which feed under cover. While some attack plants more or less indiscriminately, others have preferences, such as for iris or rhododendrons, and these are given special mention in the descriptive lists below. Insects which feed out of sight, such as root lice, leaf miners, stem borers, and gall makers, are usually the most difficult to control.

The application of the correct remedial measures at the right time is of first importance. Usually, insects are more vulnerable at certain stages of their life, and the gardener must take advantage of this and apply his control measures at the proper moment. As examples: (1) The codling moth is assailable when the egg hatches and the larva begins to eat its way into the fruit of the apple or pear. Therefore, the orchardist applies a poison spray to his fruit trees just as soon as the petals fall, so as to catch the larva on its way to the interior, knowing that it is useless to apply the poison once the insect has gained entrance to the fruit. (2) Some scale insects which, because of their armor-like covering, are unaffected by insecticides at dilutions which are non-injurious to foliage are combated by spraying during the dormant season (when the plants are leafless) with concentrated solutions which at this period are not injurious to vegetation, but are toxic to the insects. Or they may be sprayed immediately after they have hatched from the eggs, at which time they have not developed their scaly covering and are, therefore, susceptible to insecticides at a concentration which is not injurious to foliage.

Methods of applying insecticides. The method by which insecticides are applied has an important bearing on their success. Spraying or dusting should, first of all, be thorough. When using a contact spray, the insects must be hit with it; when using a stomach poison, the parts attacked must be evenly coated. With many insects, particularly those with waxy or woolly coverings, the spray is more effective if applied with considerable force; therefore, a spray pump capable of developing good pressure is desirable. When applying stomach poisons (also fungicides), a nozzle capable of delivering a fine mist-like spray is preferred. The operator should endeavor to apply just enough spray to coat the leaves, and no more, because if the fluid starts to run, much of the poison will be concentrated at the tips of the leaves, whereas even coverage is the objective.

Insecticides and fungicides may be applied either in the form of dusts or sprays. Dusts have come into considerable favor in recent years, for they have the advantage of taking less time to apply, and, as they are usually received from the manufacturer ready for use, less time is lost in preparation. On the other hand, dusts are apt to be more expensive, because of the amount blown away during application. They sometimes cause serious discomfort to the operator by irritating the eyes and mucous membranes of nose and throat.

List of insecticides. Some of the more important of the insecticides (also fungicides) with dosages are listed below. *Before using them, note the precautions mentioned at the end of the list.*

There are many proprietary sprays on the market ready for use when diluted according to the directions of the manufacturer. In some of these pyrethrum-soap is the killing agent. Some contain derris extract (rotenone), and some are combinations of this with nicotine. Many of them contain the much publicized DDT, and some are

PLATE XXVIII. (*upper left*) LILAC. VIGOROUS GROWTH AS A RESULT OF SE-
VERE PRUNING IN WINTER. (*upper right*) SWEET BRIER
ROSE. THE DARK STEMS ARE "OLD WOOD." (*lower left*)
ROSE OF SHARON, *Althaea*. EFFECT OF SEVERE ANNUAL
PRUNING. CF. UNPRUNED BUSH. (*lower right*) ROSE OF
SHARON. NATURAL HABIT OF GROWTH

PLATE XXIX. *(upper)* FORSYTHIA BEFORE PRUNING. *(lower)* FORSYTHIA AFTER PRUNING WHICH SHOULD BE DONE IMMEDIATELY AFTER FLOWERING

"all purpose" sprays designed for use against fungous pests as well as chewing and sucking insects.

DDT gives promise of being exceptionally valuable against certain pests, and is especially useful against leaf-hoppers, gladiolus thrips, flea beetles, codling moth, oriental fruit moth, boxwood leaf miner, etc. It has its limitations however: for examples, it is not effective against Mexican bean beetles and some kinds of aphids; its use may result in an increase of mites presumably by killing their natural enemies; apparently it is injurious to some plants including squash and, to some extent, sweet corn; its poisonous nature will make gardeners chary of using it in the kitchen garden on vegetables shortly to be eaten until more is known of its effects. It is still being experimented with and my advice is to keep abreast of the information concerning it by perusing horticultural periodicals. Do not neglect to read the label on the container to make sure that it is designed for the purpose you intend to use it.

Proprietary insecticides are valuable to the amateur who wishes to avoid the bother of mixing his own. The following, however, are easy to prepare.

Sprays for sucking insects.

DDT

DDT powder (40 to 50%)   1 pound   Water   50 gallons

NICOTINE SOAP SOLUTION

Nicotine sulphate (40%)   ½ pint   Nicotine   1 teaspoonful
Soap (flakes or powder)   2 pounds } or { Soap   1 ounce (scant)
Water   50 gallons   Water   1 gallon

For aphids and other soft-bodied sucking insects.

SOAP SOLUTION

Laundry soap   ½ to 1 pound   Water   8 gallons

Useful against aphids.

MISCIBLE OILS

(Used mainly when plants are dormant.)

Several brands of miscible oils are on the market and are obtainable at large seed stores. They should be used according to the directions of the manufacturer. Usually, they are diluted 1 to 15 for use on dormant deciduous plants; 1 to 30 on dormant evergreens. Some manufacturers suggest the use of their product during summer at strengths varying from 1 to 100 to 1 to 200, but this involves risk of injury to foliage.

LIME-SULPHUR

Commercial lime-sulphur 1 part   Water 9 parts

Used as a spray against scale insects and eggs of aphids on dormant, deciduous trees and shrubs. Also as a fungicide.

Dusts for sucking insects. Nicotine, rotenone and pyrethrum—important ingredients of most dusts—quickly lose their insecticidal properties when exposed to the air. Therefore they should be stored in airtight containers.

There is a combination proprietary dust on the market in which nicotine is mixed with sulphur and lead arsenate. This is useful against aphids, mites, chewing insects and some fungous diseases. Dusts are available containing from 3 to 10 percent DDT. Some simple and effective dusts are described below. For rotenone, which is also a stomach poison, see *Dusts for chewing insects* below.

NICOTINE DUST

Nicotine may be applied in the form of dust—either as ground tobacco or as a nicotine extract mixed with hydrated lime which serves as a carrier. A 2-percent nicotine dust may be made as follows:

Nicotine sulphate (40%)   5 pounds
Hydrated lime   95 pounds

Place the ingredients in a tightly closed container with a half-dozen large smooth stones, and shake or roll until an intimate mixture is formed. Store in an air-tight container. Apply by means of a dust gun during the hottest part of the day. The temperature should be over 70 degrees for good results. For aphids, leafhoppers, thrips, etc.

PYRETHRUM POWDER

May be used undiluted or mixed as follows:

Pyrethrum powder ½ pound   Flour 1 pound

Mix thoroughly and keep in a tightly closed mason jar for two days before using. Useful in the control of ants and aphids.

DUSTING SULPHUR

Effective against mites ("red spiders") on evergreens, etc. Also used as a fungicide for the control of black spot on roses, mildew, and other fungous diseases.

Sprays for chewing insects. Some easily mixed and effective sprays to be used against chewing insects on both herbaceous and woody plants are described below.

LEAD ARSENATE

Lead arsenate (dry) 1½ pounds   Water 50 gallons

Standard for most chewing insects which feed openly.

TARTAR EMETIC

Tartar emetic	1 ounce
Brown sugar	2 ounces
Water	3 gallons

The above formula has been recommended as a remedy against gladiolus thrips on growing plants.

Dusts for chewing insects. Rotenone and pyrethrum (see *Dusts for sucking insects*) act as both contact and stomach poisons.

CRYOLITE (SODIUM FLUOALUMINATE)

Cryolite	1 part
Talc or flour	1 to 2 parts

Has been recommended for use against Mexican bean beetles. Use rotenone when pods begin to form.

LEAD ARSENATE

Lead arsenate 1 part   Hydrated lime or dusting sulphur 9 parts

With lime used against chewing insects; with sulphur against chewing insects and certain fungi.

ROTENONE

In the form of powder or spray, rotenone may be used when there is objection to an arsenical poison. However, it does not protect plants over so long a period. Follow manufacturer's directions.

Fumigation. Many kinds of insects which infest plants in greenhouses and coldframes may be killed by burning TOBACCO or NICOTINE EXTRACTS. Because the nicotine content varies with different brands, dosages as recommended by the manufacturer should be used.

CALCIUM CYANIDE offers an easy and effective means of ridding greenhouses of a variety of insect pests. The usual dose is 1 ounce of 40- to 50-

percent calcium cyanide (Cyanogas) to 4,000 cubic feet. See Chapter XXV, GREENHOUSES.

PARADICHLOROBENZENE (P.D.B.) gives off a gas which is fatal to peach borers. Use at the rate of about 1 ounce per tree. See PEACH BORERS, p. 482, for method of application.

Poison bait. When using poisonous baits take care to keep them away from children and domestic animals.

MIXTURE FOR CUTWORMS, GRASSHOPPERS, ARMY WORMS

White arsenic, Paris green, or Sodium fluosilicate   1 tbsp.
Wheat bran 2½ pounds; Molasses 1 cup; Water 1 pint

Mix dry ingredients; add molasses and water to moisten.

Since these baits are poisonous they should be used with care where they are accessible to children and domestic animals. Scattering the bait thinly and evenly in the vicinity of the plants it is desired to protect reduces the danger.

MIXTURE FOR ANTS

There are many effective proprietary ant poisons on the market—some using arsenite of soda and some thallium sulphate as the killing agent. These should be used in preference to making up your own mixture.

Precautions. Lead arsenate must not be used in combination with sprays containing soap, because water-soluble arsenic oxide is set free, causing injury to foliage.

When lead arsenate is used in combination with sulphur sprays, it is advisable to add 2 pounds of hydrated lime to each 50 gallons to check the liberation of free arsenic. Some Experiment Stations recommend the addition of 2 pounds of hydrated lime to each pound of lead arsenate applied without sulphur. Do not apply sulphur within a month of using oil sprays; sulphur is injurious to melons and cucumbers.

Most insecticides—cryolite, DDT, nicotine, lead arsenate, Paris green, calcium cyanide, corrosive sublimate, etc.—are deadly poisons and great care must be exercised in their use. They should be stored under lock and key; hands and equipment should be washed after using them, and precautions taken to prevent pets from eating foliage which has been sprayed with poison. I am greatly in favor of using non-poisonous insecticides—pyrethrum rotenone, soap—on fruits and vegetables shortly to be eaten.

Spraying and dusting equipment. For properties of about one acre, especially if fruit is grown or if there are fairly large trees to be sprayed, a sprayer holding about 50 gallons is desirable. These sprayers usually have a pump, operated by power, of sufficient power to allow the use of 50 feet of hose when necessary. Ordinarily, disk nozzles are used, capable of delivering the insecticide in tiny droplets (against sucking insects), or in a fine mist (when using stomach poisons or fungicides). The character of the spray is determined by the size of the opening in the disk. An extension rod up to 12 feet in length is desirable for reaching the tops of trees. If the trees are so large that they cannot be reached even when the extension rod is used, a nozzle throwing a thin solid stream may do the trick of reaching the topmost branches. This is predicated on the assumption that sufficient pressure can be developed to cause the stream to break up into fine particles when it reaches its destination. A nozzle set at an angle of 45 degrees and attached to an extension rod 4 to 6 feet long is useful when it is necessary to spray the under side of the leaves of low-growing plants.

If your spraying program does not warrant the purchase of a 50-gallon sprayer, the wheelbarrow type, holding from 15 to 20 gallons, is the next choice. Sprayers of this kind may be operated with 10 to 15 feet of hose, which gives a fair amount of mobility; they require the services of two people to get best results—one to pump and one to direct the nozzle.

For smaller properties, a compressed air sprayer, holding about 3 gallons, is fairly satisfactory. This may be the knapsack type or carried by means of a shoulder sling. They are not so convenient to use as those preceding, and it is difficult, under some circumstances, to apply the spray where it will do the most good.

Those whose gardening activities are restricted to a city back yard will probably find it possible to get along with a still smaller compressed air sprayer holding about a quart. Those of the air-atomizer type which give a continuous spray broken into a fine mist are preferable.

Machines for applying insecticides and fungicides in the form of dust have received much attention in recent years. Dusting large areas with the aid of airplanes has become commonplace. Power-driven machines are available for dusting large orchards; and small efficient dusters worked by a hand crank are satisfactory in gardens of several

FIG. 106. Crank duster

acres. A type which appeals to me is illustrated in Fig. 106. It has a flexible tube leading to the nozzle which enables the dust to be directed to any location desired. The amount of dust discharged is controlled by a slide opening. The dust is agitated by revolving brushes in the container and blown out by a propeller-type fan. The container holds about 5 pounds of dust.

There are numerous dust-guns and bellows-type dusters on the market suitable for use in small gardens.

Injurious insects. It is impossible even to mention all of the insects injurious to vegetation. The selection which follows has been made partly on the basis of the importance of the insect and partly with a view to giving examples of as many kinds of control measures as possible.

SUCKING INSECTS WHICH FEED OPENLY

APHIDS (Fig. 107). Plant lice of various species, more correctly called aphids, attack a variety of crops, including vegetables, flowers, trees, and shrubs.

LACE BUGS. These lacy-winged bugs attack azaleas, rhododendrons, hawthorns, elms, and other woody plants.

Both aphids and lace bugs may be controlled by the application of a summer-strength contact insecticide immediately after the insects are discovered. Some species of aphids on woody plants are susceptible to sprays applied when the plants are dormant. (See SCALE INSECTS, below.) If more convenient, proprietary contact insecticides may be used, though they may be a little more expensive. Those containing pyrethrum (which is non-poisonous to human beings) are effective against a variety of insects. Although the insecticidal qualities of derris root have been known for a century, it is only in recent years that much attention has been directed to rotenone extract of derris root, which is both a contact insecticide and stomach poison. When this becomes better known and more generally available, it may supersede some of the more commonly used insecticides. Pyrethrum and derris root may also be used in powder form against insects.

CHINCH BUG. While the chinch bug is considered primarily a grain and corn pest in the central states, during recent years it has attacked lawns in the East with devastating results. It does not succumb readily to the usual contact insecticide. I have tried nicotine sulphate and soap solution at double strength—using 100 gallons of spray on about 1,700 square feet of lawn—without any adverse effects on the chinch bugs. DDT applied to the lawn as a 3- to 5-percent dust shows great promise as a means of controlling this pest. Sprays containing pyrethrum, or the use of a 3-percent nicotine-sulphate-lime dust, at the rate of 7 pounds per 1,000 square feet, are said to be effective.

LEAFHOPPERS. A wide variety of plants, including asters, dahlias, and elms, are attacked by leafhoppers. As they are at least partly responsible for transmitting virus diseases which are injurious to the two first named, it is important to

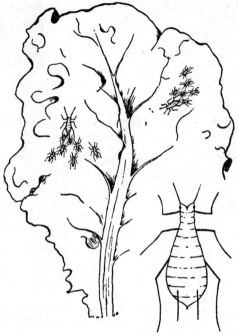

FIG. 107. Aphids

fight them. They are difficult to destroy because of their resistance, and because they jump when an insecticide is being applied. A 3-percent nicotine dust, applied during the hottest part of the day, is recommended against these insects. It may be necessary to use it at weekly intervals. Pyrethrum-soap spray is reported to be useful, and DDT in some instances is very effective. Bordeaux mixture is said to be a deterrent, but I have not seen any worthwhile results from its use. As most of the injurious leafhoppers pass the winter as adults hiding in garden trash, weed piles, etc., all debris should be cleaned up and composted or burned in the fall.

MEALY BUGS. Chiefly greenhouse pests in the North, mealy bugs attack a variety of plants. Fumigation with calcium cyanide is fairly effective, or they may be sprayed forcibly with strong nicotine-soap solution. There are various proprietary contact remedies which are satisfactory. When conditions permit, frequent spraying with water from the hose with sufficient force to dislodge the insects is a successful control measure. Outdoors, the umbrella catalpa is commonly attacked by a species of mealy bug. As soon as leaves have fallen, wash off insects and egg masses with a scrubbing-brush and water, then spray or paint with lime-sulphur solution 1 to 9.

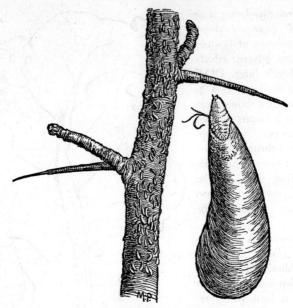

FIG. 108. Oyster shell scale—life-size on twig, and
enlarged individual

SCALE INSECTS. Oyster-shell scale (Fig. 108), San José scale, and scurfy scale attack a variety of trees and shrubs. The use of a miscible oil according to the directions of the manufacturer; or (on deciduous plants) commercial lime-sulphur, 1 to 9, applied when the plants are dormant, is recommended for scale insects. In some cases—for example, with the oyster-shell scale—it may be necessary to follow up the dormant treatment with nicotine-soap spray when the young scales are hatching—usually about the beginning of June. The use of a hand lens is an aid in determining when to apply the spray.

THRIPS (Fig. 109). These are intermediate in character between sucking and chewing insects so far as eating habits are concerned. They rasp the epidermis of a plant and then suck up the sap. Thrips attack a great variety of plants, including dahlia, gladiolus, and many greenhouse crops. Under greenhouse conditions, they may be kept down by fumigating with calcium cyanide (see Chapter XXV, GREENHOUSES), or they may be sprayed with contact insecticides. The gladiolus thrips has been a serious pest in recent years. It passes the winter on the corms, and various treatments have been devised to kill the insects during this period, including exposure to fumes of various chemicals and immersing the corms in corrosive sublimate solution. A remedy that is easily available is to place the corms in paper bags and sprinkle them with naphthalene flakes at the rate of 1 ounce to 100 corms. The bag should then be closed and kept in a temperature of 65 to 75 degrees for from three to six weeks. When growing plants are attacked they may be sprayed with an insecticide containing DDT.

WHITE-FLY. Primarily a greenhouse pest in the North, white-fly gets outdoors on plants which are started under glass. Ageratum, fuchsia, and tomato are among its favored food plants. These insects are easily killed by fumigation with calcium cyanide. When this is not possible, the problem of disposing of them is a little more difficult—not that they are immune to the ordinary contact insecticides—but because the adults fly away while the plants are being sprayed and return when the coast is clear. The use of a wide-angle nozzle delivering a fine spray will catch many of the adults on the wing; and, if the spray is applied to the under side of the leaves at weekly intervals for several weeks, the nymphs and the entire brood will be disposed of.

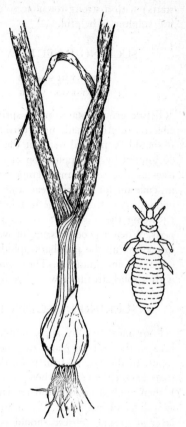

FIG. 109. Onion thrips (enlarged), and type of injury

RED MITES. Even though they are technically not insects, red mites (which are commonly called red spiders) are included here. Dormant treatment is effective in killing the eggs of some species on deciduous trees. On evergreens and deciduous plants during the growing season, a thorough but not heavy application of dusting sulphur is effective. This should be put on before the mites have done much damage.

CYCLAMEN MITES. Attacking delphiniums, cyclamen mites cause the condition popularly known as "delphinium blacks." This trouble was formerly ascribed to a combination of mites, fungi, and bacteria. Removal of infested shoots and leaves and weekly sprayings (beginning when growth starts) with a strong rotenone solution plus alternate treatments with dusting sulphur is helpful.

SUCKING INSECTS WITH SPECIAL PREFERENCES

EUONYMUS SCALE	PINE-LEAF SCALE
PINE-BARK APHID	TULIP-TREE SCALE

Before growth starts in the spring these pests may be sprayed with miscible oil solution made up according to the directions of the manufacturer. It should be pointed out that the leaves of evergreen conifers are liable to be injured by the application of oil sprays, and that the "bloom" on such trees as blue spruce may temporarily be removed. I have successfully used miscible oil for the pine-leaf scale without injuring the foliage and, in my opinion, it is worth while to take a chance on spraying evergreen conifers (as being the lesser of two evils) when they are infested with the above pests. When a good pressure of water is available, I have found it effective in controlling the pine-bark aphids, which appear as white cottony masses on trunk and branches. They should be washed off as often as necessary with a solid stream of water from the hose.

SUCKING INSECTS WHICH FEED OUT OF SIGHT

Root lice (woolly apple louse, aster root louse, corn root louse, etc.). Lice on the roots of plants may be controlled by the use of ground tobacco stems. In the case of fruit trees, the soil should be removed and the upper roots exposed over the whole area. A 3-inch layer of ground tobacco stems is then applied and the soil returned. The tobacco will serve as a fertilizer as well as an insecticide. When asters are infected with root lice a half-inch layer of ground tobacco should be cultivated into the surface; or, saturate the soil with nicotine solution. The corn root louse is combated by late fall plowing or digging, thus destroying the nests of the ants which are responsible for the nurture of the lice. The use of salty commercial fertilizers such as nitrate of soda and kainit is said to discourage root lice. Some species of root lice also attack the leaves and branches, and these should be met with contact sprays as directed above for sucking insects which feed openly.

Gall makers (spruce gall aphid, elm cockscomb gall, etc.). There are many kinds of gall-forming insects, many of which are plant lice and therefore included in the sucking group. With a few exceptions (grape phylloxera, for example), these insects are not of prime economic importance; therefore correct control measures have not been extensively studied. In general, they do not do a great deal of harm, although they make the

plants unsightly. An exception is the rose gall which causes rather attrac-
tive-looking pompons of moss-like texture to appear on rose stems.

Hand-picking and burning the affected leaves and stems comprise as
effective a remedy as any when it is possible to reach the branches. Spraying with miscible oil solution just before growth starts in the spring, at a
strength recommended by the manufacturer, is fairly successful against the
spruce gall aphid, but the glaucous covering (bloom) of the needles of
such trees as blue spruce is removed by a miscible oil spray.

CHEWING INSECTS WHICH FEED OPENLY

Insects such as BEETLES (Fig. 110), CATERPILLARS, etc., which eat the
leaves of plants are usually fought by the application of lead arsenate,
which obviously should be applied before the damage is done. Lead arsenate is poisonous and should not be used on fruits or vegetables which are
shortly to be eaten, unless the poison can be completely washed off before
using them. Pyrethrum or rotenone may be used on comestibles instead
of the more poisonous arsenate. Hellebore used to be specific against various
sawfly larvae such as the currant worm and the grape, pear, raspberry, and
rose slugs; but rotenone or pyrethrum sprays or dusts are more easily
obtainable and probably just as effective.

ASIATIC BEETLE, ASIATIC GARDEN BEETLE, JAPANESE BEETLE. All of these
beetles feed more or less openly as adults, and under cover in the larval
stage. When the larvae occur in large numbers, they are injurious to lawns,
which may be grub-proofed with lead arsenate, applied at the rate of 10
pounds to 1,000 square feet. This will make the lawn immune to injury
for several years. As an aid in securing even distribution of the lead arsenate, it should be thoroughly mixed with about 25 times its weight of
moist (not wet) sand or sifted soil. Application may be made any time
when the ground is not frozen or sopping wet. Do not forget that lead
arsenate is a deadly poison. Animals likely to eat the grass must be kept
away from the lawn until the poison has disappeared from the foliage. The
injury occasioned by the larvae is only part of the story—the adult beetles
also are destructive to a variety of trees, shrubs, and herbaceous plants.
Their foliage may be protected by spraying it with lead arsenate (powdered) 10 ounces, wheat flour 6 ounces, water 10 gallons (mix flour with
cold water to make a thin paste before adding it to the arsenate and water).
Trees and shrubs such as magnolia, boxwood, and rhododendrons, which
may be injured by arsenicals, should not be sprayed with the poison;
neither should fruits which are shortly to be eaten. For these a spray of
hydrated spray lime 2 pounds, aluminum sulphate ½ pound, water 10
gallons, may be used. First dissolve aluminum sulphate in 1 quart of water.

FIG. 110. Potato beetle—eggs, larvae, and adult

Whitening the leaves with this may repel the insects in light infestations.

Unfortunately, the feeding habits of the Japanese beetle (also, incidentally, of the rose chafer) are such that spraying is not effective in preventing them from eating their way into the hearts of flowers, such as roses. The open blooms may be protected by covering them with mosquito netting or buds may be cut and brought indoors to open. When the infestation is light, hand-picking is a good remedy. The beetles should be thrown into a can containing kerosene, or subjected to gasoline vapor by putting them in a closed container with gasoline. Sprays containing DDT are effective against the adults; and various proprietary poisons and repellents are available.

Thousands of Japanese beetles may be caught in specially devised traps suitably baited. Traps and bait may be obtained from seedsmen, hardware stores, etc., in infected areas. The traps should be suspended 3 or 4 feet from the ground in full sunshine well away from the vegetation it is desired to protect. They must be emptied of beetles at least every two days, and the container washed whenever it becomes soiled, so that there are no extraneous odors to mask that of the bait. It should be pointed out that more beetles may be attracted by the bait than are actually caught. If only one or two gardeners in an infested community make use of traps, their gardens may suffer more than those of neighbors who do not use traps, because many of the beetles attracted by the odor of the bait are uncaught and remain to feed on the surrounding vegetation. As a long-term project (effects usually are not visible until 3 years after application), the introduction of the parasitic milky disease to lawn areas is helpful. Spores are obtained from seed stores under various trade names.

ROSE CHAFER. This gangling beetle feeds openly on the leaves of a number of plants (including grape and alder) and also bores into the flowers of roses, peonies, and others. It is resistant to both stomach and contact poisons. The application of lead arsenate to the foliage of the plants attacked may be partly effective; and possibly the grub-proofing of lawns may reduce its numbers. Hand-picking and the protection of special plants by screening them with mosquito netting are probably the best remedies. Hand-picking may be facilitated by knocking the beetles into a funnel-shaped collector leading to a can of kerosene.

Grub-proofing of lawns as described above is also effective in reducing the numbers of other pests, part or all of whose life cycle is spent underground, though it may not entirely prevent damage if the adults are strong fliers, because they may enter the garden from untreated surroundings. Among the pests which commonly lay their eggs in grass-land and whose larvae feed on grass roots are the bumbling beetle, variously known as cockchafer, June bug, or May beetle, and the click beetle whose larvae are known as wireworms. Earthworms are destroyed by the lead arsenate treatment. It is not recommended that lead arsenate be applied to flower borders; therefore, when they are infested with soil pests of this type, other measures should be adopted. Digging or plowing the ground in the fall is an effective aid, as it upsets the domestic arrangements of these pests, exposes some of them to be consumed by birds, and brings some near the surface to succumb to the effects of winter. Frequent cultivation of the surface throughout the growing season also helps to reduce their numbers— chiefly by physical violence. Some of them (wireworms for example) may be trapped by impaling pieces of carrot or potato on thin sticks and burying the bait 2 or 3 inches under the surface of the soil. The baits, located by the sticks, should be examined daily and the larvae congregated on them destroyed. Small areas unoccupied by plants may be sterilized by steam or chemicals. The first method probably will not be convenient or worth while in small gardens, but carbon disulphide (inflammable!) may be poured into holes a few inches deep, situated 1½ to 2 feet apart, ¼ ounce to each hole.

BAGWORM (Fig. 111). This curious insect attacks a variety of trees and shrubs but its favorite food seems to be arborvitae. It spins itself a silken bag, intermixed on the outside with fragments of stalks and leaves of the host plant. The female lives, produces her eggs, and dies without ever leaving the bag. Hand-picking in winter and destruction of the bags containing eggs is a good method of control. Maybe, after a little experience, it would be possible to distinguish between those which contain eggs and those which were the residence of the gentlemen bagworms; and thus save time by paying no attention to the latter, for they are innocuous. Spraying the plants with lead arsenate is an effective remedy if applied as soon as the eggs hatch. It is necessary to watch closely to discern the young insects because of their habit of attaching fragments of the host plant to the out-

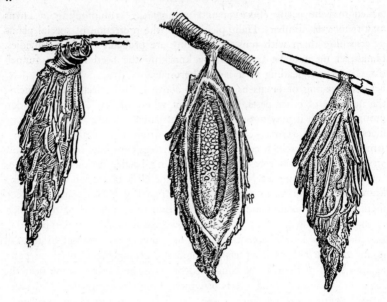

Fɪɢ. 111. Bagworm—larva feeding, "bag" cut open to show eggs, cocoon in winter (life size)

side of their homes. This makes them inconspicuous, especially when arborvitae is the food plant, because the cut-off portions retain their greenness for some time.

CANKERWORM and TUSSOCK MOTH. It has already been said that the usual practice in combating caterpillars is to spray their food with poison, but in a few instances, when the female of the species is wingless (as in the cankerworm and tussock moth), it is possible to prevent attack, when trees are the victims, by means of a barrier over which the larvae and adult females cannot pass. The barrier may consist of a band of sticky material, 6 inches wide, such as tree tanglefoot. This may be applied to a band of heavy wrapping paper tied tightly around the trunk. A barrier of fluffy cotton will serve the same purpose. It should be at least 6 inches wide and overlap 2 inches. It is tied with string an inch from the bottom and the upper part is then folded down loosely over the string. Under city conditions, these cotton bands become unsightly with dirt after a day or two.

The larvae of the tussock moths pupate on the tree; therefore it is essential to be sure that the tree is free of them and of the eggs before applying the barrier in May. The frothy-looking egg masses are easily seen and may be removed in winter or early spring.

Cankerworms (also known as inch worms, loopers, measuring worms, or span worms) pupate in the ground, and a band kept sticky from October 1 to the end of December and during April and May, will prevent many of them from getting on the trees. Or arsenate of lead may be sprayed on the foliage.

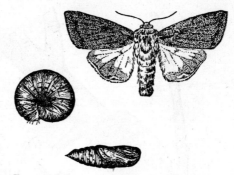

CUTWORMS (FIG. 112). The larvae of several species of

FIG. 112. Cutworm—adult, larva, and pupa

moths, cutworms attack a variety of plants by eating through the stems close to the surface of the ground. They are especially partial to zinnias, beans, corn, and potatoes. When the infestation is severe, several measures must be put into force to get the better of this pest. Crops which are set out as young plants (such as cabbage and tomato) may be protected by wrapping the stems loosely in stout paper at planting time. Cutworms may be trapped by laying on the ground near the plants pieces of board or shingles under which they will congregate. The traps must be examined daily and the worms killed. Another way of overcoming cutworms is by use of poison bait scattered liberally in the vicinity of the plants subject to attack. This method should be used only when the bait is not accessible to children, birds, and domestic animals. The bait may be obtained ready for use from seed stores or it may be made in accordance with the formula on page 468.

FLEA BEETLE. Several species of small beetles which are characterized by their ability to jump are known as flea beetles. They attack potato, grape and other plants. When it is necessary to use Bordeaux mixture as a fungicide, it usually acts as a deterrent to flea beetles also; otherwise the plants should be sprayed with lead arsenate, or with rotenone.

TENT CATERPILLAR. Recognizable partly through its predilection for wild cherry, the tent caterpillar may be combated from late fall to early spring by clipping off and burning the dark brown egg masses, which form almost complete belts around the twigs (Fig. 113). The tents should be destroyed in spring by breaking them up with a kerosene-soaked rag tied to the end of a long stick. This is better done in early morning when the caterpillars are in the nest, and before they have attained much size. They may also be killed by spraying their food with arsenate, but the measures outlined above will usually be found less expensive of time and materials.

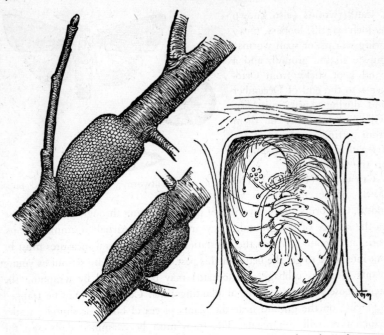

Fig. 113. Tent caterpillar—two views of egg masses; and embryo in egg (much enlarged)

CHEWING INSECTS WITH SPECIAL PREFERENCES

APPLE WORM or CODLING MOTH. The caterpillar which is the cause of wormy apples and pears is known in the adult stage as the codling (or codlin) moth. The adults lay eggs in the flowers, and the caterpillars tunnel into the fruit. This pest is "get-at-able" when it starts to eat its way into the fruit; therefore, the trees should be sprayed with a stomach poison immediately after the petals have fallen, and, in the case of bad infestation, again after a three-week interval.

ASPARAGUS BEETLE. Because of the nature of the crop, it is impracticable to spray with lead arsenate for the asparagus beetle adults which eat the asparagus shoots and disfigure them with their long cylindrical eggs which project horizontally. The larvae of the asparagus beetle are slimy and slug-like. A few shoots in each bed should be allowed to grow, while the remainder are cut close. When the beetles have oviposited on the trap shoots, they should be cut and burned. Follow this procedure for as long as the beetles are laying their eggs. If the whole bed should become badly infested by larvae, they may be killed by dusting them with nicotine dust, or by brushing them off with a stick on a hot dry day.

ASTER BEETLE. Several species of blister beetles feed upon the flowers of asters. Hand-picking and dropping the insects into a can of kerosene or protecting the plants by covering them with mosquito netting are good remedies; or they may be sprayed with rotenone.

MEXICAN BEAN BEETLE. This pest is the black sheep of the ladybug family. It eats away the softer portions of the leaves, skeletonizing them, and making them look like torn, worn-out lace. Because the bean foliage may be injured if arsenicals are used and because of the danger of poisoning if they, or cryolite, are applied at a time when the beans are almost ready to pick, the use of rotenone is recommended.

CHERRY MAGGOT. The larvae of two species of flies infest cherries while they are in process of maturing. The foliage may be sprinkled with sweetened lead arsenate to serve as a poison bait for the adult flies. This should be put on as soon as the flies appear. The cherries must be washed before eating to remove any residue of the poison. Rotenone should be used, preferably, instead of the arsenate once the cherries begin to form.

ELM-LEAF BEETLE. The adult of the elm-leaf beetle attacks the leaves in spring, causing shot-holes. The larvae appear a little later and eat the under sides of the leaves. Spray with lead arsenate as soon as the beetles commence feeding, with the object of killing as many adults as possible, thus reducing the number of eggs laid. When the eggs begin to hatch, spray again—paying particular attention to getting the poison on the under side of the leaves.

PLUM CURCULIO. A certain snout beetle, a little less than ¼ inch long, which feeds on unopened buds and young leaves of various fruit trees, is known as the plum curculio. When the fruit has set, the beetle cuts a slit in which an egg is deposited. The egg hatches in a few days and the larva eats its way into the fruit. Spraying with lead arsenate is sometimes satisfactory, but in the case of the peach is attended with danger of injuring the leaves. Enquire of your State Agricultural Experiment Station for formula adapted to your locality. When the infestation is a bad one a sheet should be spread on the ground and the trees jarred every morning, starting at the time the trees are in bloom, causing the beetles to fall on the sheet, from which they may be gathered and destroyed. All fallen fruit should be destroyed to lessen the infestation the following year.

CHEWING INSECTS WHICH FEED UNDER COVER

The most important of the chewing insects which feed under cover are borers, which eat their way into plant tissues. They attack both woody and herbaceous plants and also fruits. Our efforts to get the better of these pests must be largely along preventive lines. Those borers whose habit it is to gain entrance to the trunk of a tree at or near the surface of the ground can be controlled by covering the trunk to prevent the adults from ovipositing. Attacks of peach and apple borers may thus be prevented by placing a cylinder of wire mosquito-netting around the trunk to a height of 2 feet above the surface of the ground. A clear space of 1 inch should be left between the trunk and the netting—filling the opening at the top with cotton, and hilling up with soil at the base to prevent the entrance of the adults. Building-paper wrapped and tied around the trunks will serve the same purpose. Spraying the trunk and the lower part of the main branches with lime-sulphur or Bordeaux mixture acts to some extent as a deterrent; and DDT may be an effective repellent.

If insects have already gained entrance to a tree or shrub, the holes should be located and probed with a thin flexible wire to kill the borers. Or a few drops of carbon disulphide may be squirted into the hole and the opening plugged with putty or chewing gum. A spring-bottom oil can is a suitable tool with which to apply the carbon disulphide. Again I repeat the warning that this chemical is inflammable and explosive.

Below are described some specific borers and other pests which feed where they cannot be seen.

PEACH BORERS. Paradichlorobenzene (P.D.B.) crystals applied to the soil around the trunk between September 1 and October 15 will eliminate peach borers. About 1 ounce of the crystals should be applied in a ring, the inner edge of which is 2 inches from the trunk. Cover with a shovelful or two of soil and pat down smoothly. Do not use on trees less than three years old. See also the two paragraphs preceding.

HERBACEOUS BORERS. Borers also attack the stems of herbaceous plants, notably dahlias. A close watch should be kept on the plants and, at the first sign of wilting, the presence of a borer should be suspected. If discovered early in the season—say, not later than mid-July—the plant may be cut down to the ground with the expectation that it will grow again and produce blooms by early fall. The borer in the cut-off portion should, of course, be located and destroyed. Attacks later in the season may be dealt with by slitting the stem longitudinally at the point where the borer is operating, and killing it.

A correspondent claims that if ragweed is allowed to grow in the vicinity of the dahlia bed the borers will attack it in preference to the dahlias. I pass this along for what it is worth. Many will consider the remedy worse than the disease. In the interest of hay-fever victims, the ragweed should be cut and burned before it sheds its pollen.

The general procedure in combating borers of this type is to destroy them as soon as they are noticed by cutting and burning infected stems; or by the method outlined above, and by being careful to burn all crop residues in which they might hibernate.

IRIS BORER. The moth responsible for the iris borer lays its eggs in the fall on the iris leaves or on the ground in or near the clump. In the spring the eggs hatch, the larvae climb onto the leaves, enter them, and start burrowing toward the rhizome, where they do most of their damage. A thorough cleaning up and burning of all iris leaves in the fall will destroy most of the eggs. Another method is to burn over the plantations in late winter, either by means of a blow torch or flame thrower, or by scattering inflammable litter over the beds and setting fire to it. It requires nice judgment to make the fire sufficiently hot to destroy the eggs and at the same time not so hot that it injures the irises. Apparently, the practice of replanting iris every three years in August helps to keep the borer in subjection, because of the opportunity it affords of discarding and destroying infested rhizomes.

SQUASH-VINE BORER. Wilting of the vines of squashes and related plants—pumpkins, gourds, etc.—is a symptom of the squash-vine borer. A longitudinal slit should be made in the stem and the borer killed. Then the shoot should be layered by making a shallow trench in the soil and burying the wounded portion. By so doing new roots will be formed, and the vine has a good chance to recover. In sections where infestation is severe, it is a good plan to plant summer squash as a trap crop, as early as practicable, and delay planting the more valuable winter squashes until the latest possible date consistent with the expectation of obtaining a crop. The moths will lay their eggs on the summer squash, which should be destroyed by burning before the larvae leave the vines at midsummer to pupate. Spray or dust young plants with rotenone, especially base of stems.

CORN EAR-WORM, TOMATO WORM, or COTTON-BOLL WORM (Fig. 114). This pest, the larvae of one of the noctuid moths, feeds on corn kernels in the ear, or burrows into the fruit of the tomato, or enters into cotton-bolls. It pupates in an earthen cell, therefore fall digging or plowing results in the death of large numbers by breaking up many of these cells. Inject ¼ teaspoon treated mineral oil (obtainable with applicator from seed stores) about 5 days after the silks first appear. All corn ears should be picked before the kernels are ripe; and those considered unfit for human consumption, because of the presence of the worms, should be destroyed by feeding to stock or by burning. When tomatoes are attacked, the only remedy is the removal and destruction of infested fruit. A planting of corn in the vicinity is likely to lessen the injury to the tomato crop because the insect prefers corn to tomatoes.

CUCUMBER STRIPED BEETLE. The adults of the cucumber striped beetle, which also attack melons and other relatives of the cucumber, eat the young leaves, while the larvae infest the main roots. Young plants may be protected by screening them with mosquito netting. Ground tobacco scattered

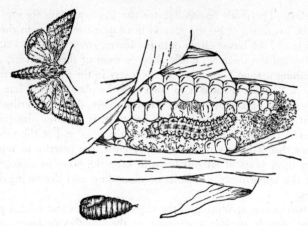

Fig. 114. Corn ear-worm—larva, adult, and pupa

freely on and around the plants acts as a deterrent. The leaves may be dusted with rotenone and talc—not sulphur. When the crop has been gathered, the vines should be dug up and burned, thus destroying any larvae in the roots.

LEAF MINERS. These are usually the larvae of small flies which lay their eggs in the leaves of the host plant. The eggs hatch and the larvae tunnel between the upper and lower surfaces of the leaves, causing markings which in many cases have a resemblance to Chinese writing. A number of ornamental plants are attacked by leaf miners—notably the columbine and waterlilies—and vegetables such as beet, Swiss chard, and spinach. It has been my experience that, in most cases, best results are obtained by picking off and burning the affected leaves. This, of course, should be done just as soon as the activities of the insects are discovered. Spraying with nicotine-soap solution at first sign of an attack is sometimes effective. At the end of the growing season (or earlier if a vegetable crop has been rendered unfit for consumption) the above-ground portion of the plants attacked should be destroyed by burning.

BOX LEAF MINER. The adult midges of the box leaf miner emerge from the leaves in late May. The bushes should be sprayed thoroughly every second day for two weeks, starting from the time the insects begin to depart from the leaves. Use nicotine-soap solution to which molasses has been added at the rate of 1 pound to 10 gallons of spray solution. Some investigators report that DDT applied just before the flies emerge from the leaves (usually about mid-May in the vicinity of New York) gave 100 percent control. Another observer says it is not satisfactory.

ANTS. Although it is seldom that ants attack plants, indirectly they may do a great deal of harm by nurturing plant lice and scale insects, and by disturbing the soil about the roots of plants when they construct their nests. When it is possible to find the nests, the whole colony may be destroyed by the use of carbon disulphide. Poke several holes into the nest with a stick and pour into each hole from 1 to 3 teaspoonfuls of carbon disulphide, fill the holes with earth and cover with wet burlap to keep the fumes in. Since a spark from pipe, cigar, or cigarette is sufficient to ignite the fumes of carbon disulphide—*no smoking* while it is being used. If there is no well-defined nest use one of the proprietary ant poisons.

Animal pests other than insects. Besides the insects described above, there are numerous common animal pests of plants, ranging from microscopic eel-worms, which do great damage, to four-footed creatures such as rabbits and moles. How to get rid of a few of these garden enemies is described below.

EELWORMS OR NEMATODES. These are microscopic worms which gain entrance to plant tissues in some cases through the stomata or breathing pores. They are commonly found infesting the roots of a large variety of plants where they make galls or swellings which interfere with the plants' life processes, causing them to become stunted and in some cases to die. Some kinds infest leaves of chrysanthemum, fern, and other subjects, dwarfing and distorting and sometimes killing the plants. Others, such as the phlox eelworm, make their home in stems.

Nematodes are difficult pests to dispose of. Those infesting leaves may be checked by frequent spraying or dusting with nicotine, although if only a few plants are affected it is better to destroy them by burning.

In the case of the root-infesting nematodes, the soil also is infested and the usual remedy is to discard the plants and sterilize the soil. Under greenhouse conditions, this may be done most readily by steam, but outdoors chemical sterilization is resorted to by using formaldehyde solution at the rate of 1 gallon of commercial formaldehyde to 50 gallons of water. Loosen the soil and apply 2 quarts to each square foot of surface. Cover with canvas or burlap for 24 hours. As soon as the soil is dry enough to work, it should be forked up to aerate it, and planting should be deferred until there is no longer any odor of formaldehyde. Larvacide (tear gas) and DD mixture are other soil fumigants. Follow manufacturer's directions. Dormant roots and bulbs of some plants (for example, chrysanthemum, peony, daffodil) may be placed in hot water (120° Fahrenheit) for half an hour, for the purpose of killing the nematodes infesting them.

EARTHWORMS. In spite of their value as tillers of the soil, earthworms are a decided nuisance when they occur in such numbers and sizes that their casts disfigure the lawn and smother the grass beneath them. The arsenate of lead treatment designed to grub-proof lawns will also eliminate earthworms.

Another means of killing them is to use mowrah meal. This is almost startling in its efficacy—one sees myriads of earthworms popping up to the surface and expiring within a few minutes after it has been watered in. Mowrah meal is the residue cake obtained after the expression of oil from the seeds of *Bassia latifolia*—the mohua-tree, a native of India. It is spread at the rate of 15 to 30 pounds to 1,000 square feet, with sufficient water applied to wash it into the soil. The dust is irritating to mucous membranes, so provision should be made to protect eyes, nose, and throat during its application. It loses strength with age, therefore only fresh meal should be used.

Corrosive sublimate is effective, but so poisonous that the dead worms must be immediately swept up and disposed of to avoid the danger of killing birds which might eat them. Use 2 ounces, dissolved in 50 gallons of water, to 1,000 square feet, followed by thorough watering to wash it into the soil.

Proprietary vermicides are obtainable from most large seed stores and may be used according to directions on the container.

Earthworms in flower pots may be dealt with by soaking the soil with lime water. It may be obtained from a drug store or made by stirring one pint of freshly slaked lime in 2½ gallons of water. As soon as it clarifies, it is ready to use. It should not be applied to acid-soil plants.

RABBITS. The first reaction when cotton-tails are seen hopping across the lawn in the twilight is "How cute!" But when they girdle our favorite fruit-trees by gnawing off the bark, nibble to the ground newly planted small shrubs, and take toll of the vegetable garden, their cuteness is likely to be forgotten.

A method of protecting woody plants is to spray or paint them with something distasteful to the rabbits. Commercial aloes at the rate of 1 pound to 4 gallons of water have been recommended for this purpose. This has proved fairly successful at the Brooklyn Botanic Garden. Also, lead arsenate sprayed on plants subject to attack has provided some measure of protection and has, on occasion, resulted in dead rabbits. Among the "nonpoisonous" repellents, which may be used in the vegetable garden if desired are: dried blood (preferably the so-called "soft" type) dusted thinly on the plants; and aluminum sulphate 4 tsp., hydrated lime 5 tbsp., water 1 gallon, sprayed on. If a dust is preferred, use: powdered alum 2 tbsp., wheat flour 4 cups. Mix well and dust on to cover the plants thoroughly. Always wash vegetables before eating if these repellents are used!

Fruit trees may be protected by placing wire screens around their trunks extending well above the anticipated snow line.

If you don't like to use these remedies in the kitchen garden you could install a rabbit-proof fence; or resort to shot-gun or a .22 rifle if shooting does not conflict with local laws.

MOLES. In Nature's scheme of things the mole is a beneficent animal who cultivates the ground and rids the soil of many obnoxious insects. The farmer can afford to look upon him with tolerance, but in the garden where he mars the lawn and tunnels through the bulb beds he is decidedly *de trop*.

There are dozens of methods of killing moles; and, as is so often the case when there is a multiplicity of remedies, not one is likely to be entirely satisfactory.

Traps are good but they must be properly set. Many of the runs made by moles are mere foraging tunnels, used only once. The traps must be set in runs which are in frequent use. These may be located by closing a section of each run, by pressure with the foot or otherwise, and noting the ones which are repaired.

If you are blessed with patience and the hunting instinct, you may catch a mole or two by keeping a close watch on the area where they are operating. When the surface soil is seen to heave as a result of a mole's progress through it, thrust a spade in the ground behind the mole and throw him out on to the surface. Then a sharp slap with the back of the spade will finish his activities.

The use of chemicals which give off a lethal gas has in some instances been attended with success. Calcium cyanide may be used by placing a teaspoonful in each burrow at 5-foot intervals. Close the opening, made when inserting the poison, by covering loosely with soil. Paradichlorobenzene may be similarly used, placing it every 6 to 10 feet. Carbon disulphide at the rate of a teaspoonful every 5 feet also is effective. As the last named is inflammable and the others poisonous, take precautions when using them.

The old car may be made to serve an additional purpose by using it to asphyxiate moles with carbon monoxide. Attach one end of a garden hose to the exhaust with electricians' tape and insert the other end in a main run. Let the motor run for about 20 minutes.

There are dozens of other alleged remedies for moles, ranging from steak and strychnine baits to the placing of castor beans in the runs. I rather hesitate to recommend poison baits because of the danger of their being snapped up by children and domestic animals.

SLUGS and SNAILS. Wherever there are constantly moist conditions in the garden and greenhouse, slugs and snails are likely to appear and take their toll of seedlings and young shoots and leaves. These pests are particularly troublesome on the Pacific Coast. They may be fought by means of poison baits; or by hunting them at night with a flash light to make them visible,

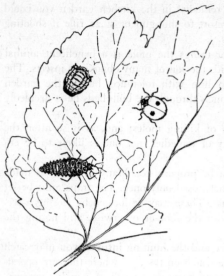

FIG. 115. Ladybug—pupa, adult, and larva (enlarged)—the latter devouring an aphid

and an old pair of scissors to snip them in two. It is helpful to dust freshly-slaked lime (if the plants are not acid-lovers), or proprietary slug-powders, in the vicinity of the plants attacked. Light sprinklings of powdered alum have also been recommended. Poisoned baits, especially those containing met-aldehyde are very effective. Garden debris, in which the slugs hide, should be cleaned up—paying special attention to fallen leaves in dank corners.

Beneficial insects. This chapter would not be complete without some reference to beneficial insects, of which there are many more kinds than most gardeners realize. There are, for example, the larvae of the LACE-WING FLY (*not* the lace bug) which voraciously devour plant lice and similar insects. The adults of one of the commoner species are beautiful pale green insects with semi-transparent wings and golden eyes. The eggs are laid in clusters on thin hair-like stalks—reputedly to prevent the larvae from eating each other.

The LADYBUGS, in general, also are carnivorous, both adults and larvae feeding on aphids and scale insects. Most people are familiar with the general appearance of the adult ladybug—their knowledge dating from childhood when "Ladybug, ladybug, fly away home" was an everyday chant during the summer. But not so many are acquainted with its larvae, pictured in Fig. 115. These often are strikingly colored—some of them lavender with red spots.

TACHINA FLIES, similar in appearance to the blue-bottle fly, are in part parasitic upon caterpillars and cutworms. The adult lays one or more eggs just back of the caterpillar's head. The eggs hatch and the maggots bore into the caterpillar's interior, feeding at first on non-essential organs. Their aim is to avoid killing the caterpillar before it

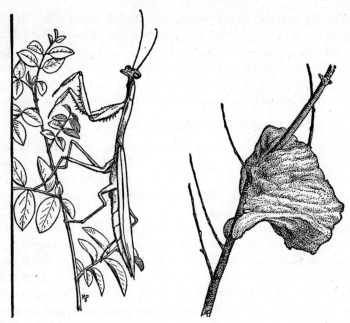

FIG. 116. Praying mantis (half-size)

FIG. 117.—Praying mantis—egg mass (full size)

has provided sufficient food to enable them to attain full size. When the maggots are mature they become less discriminating and eat the vital organs also, thus finishing their unwilling host. When cutworms and caterpillars are noticed with little white eggs on their anterior segments, they may as well be allowed to go their ways unmolested.

Various caterpillars, notably the tomato worm, are often seen covered with tiny white or yellowish silken cocoons projecting more or less at right angles to the caterpillar's body. These belong to a small parasitic wasp, the larvae of which take such toll of the caterpillar's strength that it dies instead of going through with its metamorphosis.

The PRAYING MANTIS (Fig. 116), rather fearsome in appearance, also is carnivorous, and probably accounts for the destruction of many noxious insects in the course of the season. Latterly they have become quite plentiful in the vicinity of New York and, owing to being featured in newspaper stories, are now fairly well known to the general public. The egg-masses (Fig. 117) are rather conspicuous during the winter and, of course, should not be destroyed.

CALOSOMA BEETLES, DIGGER WASPS, and WHEEL BUGS, which respectively attack the larvae of the gypsy moth, white grub, and various insects, are among those which may be considered friends of the gardener. It is worth while to try to get acquainted with these and other "good fairies," partly because their life histories are a source of interest, and partly to enable us to avoid killing them, in mistake for pests.

SOME DISEASES OF PLANTS [1]

Ornamental plants are subject to many diseases which may be very destructive. For the most part they are caused by living organisms such as fungi and bacteria; others are due to a virus, the exact nature of which remains unknown. Unfavorable conditions surrounding the plants may be the direct cause of injury.

Insects and diseases. Insects, in addition to causing direct injury to plants, are also important factors in the spread and development of diseases due to fungi, bacteria, and viruses. Iris root rot is much more destructive when the iris borer is present in the plantation. Brown rot of the peach and plum depends primarily on the occurrence of the plum curculio. The Dutch elm disease is supposed to depend upon certain beetles for the spread of the causal organism. Fire blight of the pear and apple is widely distributed by bees and other insects. The virus diseases are dependent upon insect carriers, since species of aphids and leafhoppers are mainly responsible for the spread of the virus from one plant to another.

The influence of environment. An adverse environment is frequently the primary cause of injury to growing plants. Many of the troubles encountered are directly traceable to some unfavorable condition. Sometimes it is a deficiency of an essential food material such as nitrogen, potash, or phosphorus, as in the case of potash hunger of potatoes. Unfavorable water relations are the cause of the bitter pit of apple and the blossom-end rot of tomatoes. Tip burn of potatoes and other plants is due to high temperature, while low temperature results in frost injury and winter sun scald. Manufacturing and industrial processes may produce injurious gases which escape into the air. Illuminating gas in the soil is especially disastrous to shade trees. Perhaps one of the most important factors in growing plants in the city is the contamination of the air from the chemical factories, automobile exhausts, and street gas

[1] By Dr. George M. Reed.

mains. It is difficult, of course, to diagnose a specific trouble unless all the conditions are known.

Environment also plays a part in the diseases caused by fungi and bacteria, since they are responsive to such factors as moisture and temperature. Moisture is particularly important, since it is necessary for the germination of the spores of the causal organisms of disease. Temperature not only has a direct influence on the disease organisms, but also affects moisture conditions. The shading of plants frequently favors a particular disease, partly through influencing the moisture conditions. Root rots are known to be favored by lack of proper aeration of the soil, which may be due to excessive moisture. Epidemics of many diseases develop in certain years when the external factors are particularly favorable. The occurrence of a wet season or a wet period is frequently disastrous to particular crops because the disease organisms concerned are especially favored.

Agents of disease. The most important organisms or agents which directly cause diseases of plants are fungi, bacteria, and viruses, the fungi and bacteria both belonging to a lower order of the plant kingdom, while the viruses are not yet clearly understood.

Fungi. The fungi are familiar as molds on bread and fruit and also as mushrooms. There are, however, many thousands of different kinds of fungi, some of which cause serious diseases of plants. Some of the widely grown crops are attacked by many different diseases, only a few of which, however, are particularly serious. Rusts, powdery mildews, rots and wilts are, for the most part, due to specific fungi.

Bacteria. Many of the most important human diseases, such as typhoid fever, diphtheria, and tuberculosis, are caused by different kinds of bacteria. Bacteria, as well as fungi, are responsible for the decay of plant and animal materials. It is less generally known that many plant diseases are also due to bacteria, such as the fire blight of pear and apple and the iris rhizome rot.

Viruses. Some of the most serious diseases of ornamental plants are caused by a virus, the exact nature of which is still unknown. The effects of the virus, however, are specific and well defined, and they can be studied just as accurately in the laboratory and greenhouse as diseases caused by bacteria and fungi. Many of the most important troubles of plants are due to a virus, such as peach yellows, China aster yellows, many potato diseases, mosaic of lily, narcissus, and other plants.

Methods of control. The basic principle in controlling plant diseases is the application of preventive measures. Individual plants are frequently too far gone for curative measures to be applied when the diseased condition is once recognized. Tree surgery, however, is useful in the control of the various decays of woody plants. In such cases it is possible to prolong the life of an individual tree by special methods.

Successful control is based on a knowledge of the causes of the disease. When the trouble is due to a living organism it is essential to know its full life history. Further, if the various factors of the environment which influence the development of the disease are known, it may be possible to apply successful preventive measures. Many methods have been utilized which are effective to a greater or less extent.

The use of disease-free seed and propagating material. Many plant diseases are definitely known to be spread by means of contaminated seed of the host plant and such diseases can be prevented by proper seed treatments. Some seed-borne diseases, however, cannot be successfully treated in this way and it is necessary to secure seed that has been harvested from a disease-free crop. This procedure is especially applicable to some important vegetable diseases, such as cabbage black rot and black leg, bean anthracnose and mosaic, and pea blight.

Many plants are propagated by cuttings, and diseases may be spread in the divisions. Several important diseases of the potato are carried on seed tubers, which may be prevented by using material obtained from a disease-free crop. Some virus diseases, such as lily and narcissus mosaic, can be largely avoided by using clean propagating material.

Crop rotation. Several plant diseases are caused by organisms which persist in the soil and, to some extent, these may be overcome by changing the crop from year to year. Crop rotation, of course, has other specific advantages and is more or less universally practised in good agriculture and horticulture. Some specific diseases which are avoided by suitable rotation are club root of cabbage, the wilt diseases of peony and China aster, and the crown rot of delphinium.

Modification of environal factors. Wherever a particular disease is strongly influenced by the physical or chemical condition of the soil, an obvious remedy is a change in the soil relations. Aeration of the soil is often effective. Frequently the application of a suitable fertilizer stimulates the plants in such a way that they grow well and escape serious injury from a particular disease.

Soil treatment. On a limited scale, the application of methods of treating the soil is possible. Damping-off diseases are quite prevalent in the seed bed, and their prevention is by the use of a formaldehyde drench or dust or the application of heat by means of steam or hot water. (See pp. 424 and 485.) Such a method, however, is not feasible on any large scale out-of-doors.

Roguing. The removal of diseased plants when recognized early is effective in preventing the further spread. Some virus diseases are kept in check by this procedure. It is necessary, however, to remove the infected plants when the first symptoms are observed.

Removal of the alternate hosts. Many plant parasites, especially among the rusts, have an interesting and complex life history involving two distinct hosts. One stage of the cedar-apple rust occurs on the cedar tree, resulting in the formation of galls which become very conspicuous in April, when they swell up in moist weather. The spores produced in these cedar galls are carried over to the apple in April or early May and result in discolored areas on the apple leaves and sometimes on the fruit. Some of the ornamental crabs are disfigured by the rust on the foliage. Spores produced on the apple leaves are later carried back to the cedar, where infection again takes place, resulting in another crop of cedar galls. The full life cycle requires two years. Sometimes hundreds of the gall-like structures may be found on a single cedar tree, and in some apple-growing regions the rust is a limiting factor in production. Control is most easily effected by the removal of one of the hosts. Naturally, in the apple-growing regions, it is the red cedars which are cut out. They must, however, be removed for at least the distance of about one mile. On a limited scale, spraying the apples in the spring at the proper time is effective.

The white pine blister rust requires the white pine and currants or gooseberries in order to complete its life cycle. For several years an active campaign has been carried on for the destruction of the latter in order to preserve the valuable white pine.

Removal of weed hosts. The disease of a cultivated plant may also occur on weeds which are growing adjacent to it. The cucumber mosaic in some sections has rendered the cultivation of this crop unprofitable. In addition to the cucumber and related crops, the wild-cucumber, milkweed, catnip, pokeberry and ground-cherry are hosts for the same virus disease and the eradication of these is an important step in the prevention of its spread. The virus which causes China aster yellows also occurs on a large number of other plants, from which it may be carried by the leafhopper to the China asters.

Removal of dormant stages of disease-producing parasites. Most of the parasitic fungi live over the winter in a dormant stage and, on the return of favorable conditions in the spring, produce new spores which serve to establish the organism the following season. Sanitation measures which result in the destruction of the dormant stages are advisable. The iris leaf spot, the peony wilt (see p. 181), and many other diseases are effectively controlled in this way. The infected leaves, branches, and fruits of various plants harboring the dormant stage should be gathered in the fall and burned.

Repelling insect carriers. The diseases which are dependent upon insects for their spread may be kept in check by eradicating the insect carriers. This method is especially applicable for the control of the virus diseases which are carried by aphids and leafhoppers (which see in the first section of this chapter). China aster yellows has effectively been brought under control by growing the plants under cloth which has a sufficiently fine mesh to keep out the leafhopper. Incidentally, it has also been discovered that this method of growing asters and other plants results in an improvement in the quality of the crop.

Spraying and dusting. The most generally useful procedure for preventing plant diseases is the application of chemicals in the form of sprays or dusts, and wherever crops are grown commercially the most important diseases are combated in this way. Spraying or dusting is as much a regular procedure in growing many crops as any other operation.

In commercial plant growing the application of chemicals has proved to be very successful. The operations are carried out on a large scale with adequate equipment and the materials are applied at the right time. The grower knows that year after year certain diseases are sure to be present and each season he applies the chemicals on a definite schedule for their control. The problem in the small garden is different and the operation of spraying or dusting plants often proves inadequate because of the lack of suitable equipment, as well as the failure to time the application properly.

Many chemical substances have been used in attempts to control plant diseases. Bordeaux mixture has proved to be one of the most successful sprays for plant diseases.

Bordeaux mixture is composed of copper sulphate and lime. Different proportions are used for the control of diseases of various plants.

In recent years many synthetic organic fungicides—Dithane, Fermate, and many others—have been produced which are of great promise. For information concerning these and for the identification of specific diseases and their control you should enquire of your State Agricultural Experiment Station.

Next to Bordeaux mixture in value are certain sulphur compounds. Lime-sulphur, in one form or another, is extremely useful as a spray for many diseases. The commercial concentrate may be purchased and used according to directions, or a home product may be made by boiling lime and sulphur. In recent years sulphur dusts have come into use and for certain diseases are extremely successful. There are several advantages in using the dust as compared with the spray.

Usually an insecticide is combined with the fungicide when the latter is used in the form of a liquid or as a dust. Thus injurious insects and plant diseases are controlled by the application of one mixture. Powdered lead arsenate may be added to Bordeaux mixture as a stomach poison for chewing insects. As a contact insecticide for the control of sucking insects, nicotine sulphate may be added.

It is necessary to emphasize the fact that spraying and dusting are preventive and not curative measures. A point to remember in all spraying or dusting operations for the control of plant diseases is that thoroughness is absolutely essential. In the course of a season a suitable spray or dust must be applied at definite intervals.

Utilization of resistant varieties. Plants vary in their susceptibility to particular diseases; hence one method of overcoming the ravages of disease is the utilization of varieties which are resistant. Practically all crops are being studied with a view to obtaining varieties which are not subject to serious maladies, and success has been obtained in many directions. One of the difficulties, of course, is that while resistant types or varieties are known, they are often less valuable because of undesirable qualities such as poor foliage, inferior flowers, or low yield in the case of vegetables and cereals. It is undoubtedly true that the average grower prefers to take a chance on complete loss of a desirable variety by disease rather than to grow a poor substitute. There are, however, some notable cases where the introduction of resistant types has proved successful. The development in Wisconsin of varieties of cabbage resistant to yellows is an excellent example. Varieties of beans resistant to anthracnose and mosaic have also been developed. Recently snapdragons resistant to rust have become known, and wilt-resistant China asters are available.

Some important diseases of ornamental plants. It is impossible even to list the diseases of ornamental plants. A few of the more important ones may be mentioned, however, with suggestions as to the best methods of control.

Rusts. There are two important rusts of herbaceous garden plants, the one on hollyhock and the other on the snapdragon. On the hollyhock the light brown to darker pustules appear on the leaves and stems, especially on the under side of the former. In severe cases, plants are defoliated, resulting in making them unsightly as well as more or less dwarf, and preventing the vigorous development of flowers. The most effective means of control is the removal of diseased parts in the fall of the year. All infected leaves and stems should be removed and burned. New plants should be grown from seed and the seedlings carefully watched for the appearance of the disease. Dusting with sulphur is also somewhat effective, but repeated applications of the dust must be made during the growing season.

Snapdragon rust occurs as reddish brown to almost black pustules on the leaves and stems. In severe cases defoliation results and practically no flowers are produced. This rust is not seed-borne and hence may be controlled by using only plants grown from seed. If cuttings are made, great care must be observed not to take them from infected plants. In recent years a number of new snapdragon varieties have been developed which are resistant to rust, and the propagation of satisfactory resistant types may largely solve the problems of this destructive disease.

Powdery mildews. The powdery mildews are characterized by a white or gray growth, usually on the surface of the leaves of various plants. They also appear on the young branches and sometimes on the fruits. There are a large number of different kinds of powdery mildews and the greatest variety of plants are attacked. For the most part they are rather superficial parasites and rarely do any serious damage except to cause an unsightly appearance.

The powdery mildew of the rose, however, is a very serious disease. It appears at about the flowering time and causes dwarfing of the shoots and a blasting of the flowers. Fortunately, the rose mildew can be kept in check by dusting with sulphur and the successful control of

PLATE XXX. *(upper left)* YUKI-YOKI. A JAPANESE METHOD OF ENSURING
PROTECTION AGAINST BREAKAGE OF BRANCHES BY SNOW.
(lower) YUKI-YOKI IN ACTION. *(upper right)* A JAPANESE
METHOD OF PROTECTING PLANTS BY ORNAMENTAL STRAW
COVERINGS

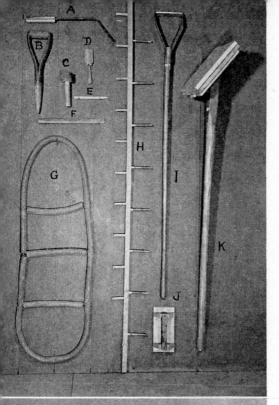

PLATE XXXI

HOMEMADE TOOLS: (A) WEEDER; (B) DIBBER; (C) TAMPER; (D) TOOL CLEANER; (E) DIBBER FOR SEEDLINGS; (F) POTTING STICK; (G) CARRIER FOR BALLED AND BURLAPPED PLANTS; (H) MARKER; (I) SCUFFLE HOE; (J) FLOAT; (K) SOD TAMPER

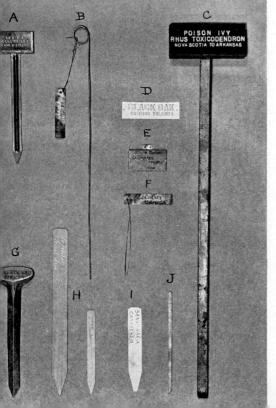

LABELS: (A) STAMPED LEAD IN HOLDER; (B) THIN COPPER, WIRE STANDARD; (C) STAMPED LEAD, WOODEN BACK, IRON STANDARD; (D) STAMPED ALUMINUM; (E) PORCELAIN; (F) THIN COPPER—WRITTEN WITH STYLUS; (G) ZINC; (H) PAINTED WOOD, WRITTEN ON WITH PENCIL; (I) ZINC; (J) STAMPED LEAD

the black-spot disease of the rose (Chapter XV, ROSE GARDEN) also results in the prevention of the powdery mildew.

The perennial phlox is commonly severely attacked by powdery mildew. Usually, however, it comes on rather late in the season. Less injurious powdery mildews occur on the sweet pea, zinnia, lilac, dahlia, and chrysanthemum.

Leaf spots. A large number of leaf-spot diseases occur on ornamental plants. Sometimes they do extensive damage, resulting in defoliation, hence the dwarfing of the plant and consequent production of poor flowers or fruit. In many cases no effective methods of control are known. In general, however, the diseased parts should be removed and destroyed. In the fall of the year, especially, a thorough cleaning up may result in keeping them in check.

Rots. There are a large number of different rots occurring on ornamental plants. One of the most common diseases of the iris is the bacterial soft rot of the rhizome. Sometimes this is very destructive, practically wiping out the entire plantation. It is particularly severe in crowded plantings, especially where the iris borer is established, and the destruction of the latter is a step in control. It is necessary, however, to reset the plants in new well-drained soil in order to control the disease. The addition of gypsum and some other substances is also effective in keeping down the soft rot.

A crown rot occurs on the delphinium, aquilegia, and some other plants. Sometimes extensive damage is done. The only effective methods of control are the removal of the diseased plants and their destruction. New plantings must be started in an area free from the invading organisms. Drainage and aeration of the soil are necessary. Sometimes a slightly infected plant may be successfully treated with some fungicide.

Blights. There are several diseases of ornamental plants that come under this descriptive name, and they are caused by many different organisms. The peony blight is the most common destructive disease of this plant, the stems, buds and leaves being infected. The shoots are attacked in the spring and suddenly wilt and fall over. Some stems may develop further, but the buds turn black and dry up. Under favorable weather conditions the causal fungus fruits abundantly, covering the diseased parts with a felty brown coat. The only effective method of control is the removal and destruction of the diseased parts. In the fall they may be cut off at the ground level and burned. To some extent the application of Bordeaux mixture or dusting with sulphur in the early spring is effective.

Wilts. Many ornamental plants suddenly show evidences of wilting. These wilts are due to various causal organisms and may appear in the early seedling stages or in older plants. Common wilts occur on the China aster and chrysanthemum. Usually the wilt organisms live in the soil and spread from there to the plant, and so rotation of the plants is one way of keeping wilts in check. Wilt-resistant varieties of China aster have been obtained in recent years.

Mosaic diseases. There are many virus diseases which are recognized as particularly important on ornamental plants. Well-known illustrations are the yellows of China asters, mosaic diseases of the lily, narcissus, iris, petunia, and many others. Dahlia stunt, in part at least, is due to a virus.

Practically all of these are distributed by aphids or leafhoppers (which see), and consequently an effective method of keeping them in control is the elimination of the insect carrier, which, in the case of China asters, is successfully done by using cloth tents. Methods effective in various cases, however, include the use of resistant varieties and of disease-free material for propagating purposes.

XXX. TOOLS AND LABELS

TOOLS

Gardening is made easier and more enjoyable by the possession of the right kind of tools for the job in hand. This does not necessarily mean that the owner of a small place has to invest in them heavily. Those which he purchases he can select with thoughtfulness and care, choosing kinds which fit his hands and suit the work they have to perform. Other tools a handy man can fashion for his own use from material at hand. For example, pieces of strap iron can be bent and fastened to wooden handles to make efficient cultivating and weeding tools. Plate XXXI illustrates some home-made tools.

A good gardener takes care of his tools. He puts them away clean and dry when he is through with them, and wipes the metal parts with an oily rag. A good gardener has a place for his tools and keeps them there when they are not in use. This place may be a corner of the cellar or workroom; or a regular toolhouse in the case of large establishments. It is *not* a waste of time to care for tools properly. They last longer, are easier to use, and may be found when they are wanted. The careless gardener wastes more time looking for tools than the good gardener spends in taking care of his and putting them away where they belong.

Tools for tilling the soil. Every gardener needs certain tools for tilling the soil—notably a spade, a spading fork, and rakes. The essential ones and their uses are described here.

Plow. When large areas are to be prepared for planting, a plow is necessary. If the subsoil is hard and impervious, a subsoil plow should follow in the furrow to break it up. This tool does not turn the soil but merely loosens it (Fig. 118).

Spade. The most important tool in the gardener's array is his spade. Since it can be used for a multiplicity of jobs, it should be selected with an eye to the principal tasks, and at the same time be of a weight and shape to fit the user. Spades made with a face of hard steel, backed with softer steel, are excellent for use in stoneless ground, for the cut-

499

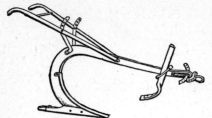

Fig. 118. Subsoil plow

ting-edge always remains sharp; but in stony ground the two layers of steel are sometimes jarred apart and the tool is then useless, so, on the whole, an even-tempered spade is best.

Spading fork. Ranking next to the spade is the spading fork, which is useful for digging, especially in heavy soil, and almost indispensable for lifting bulbs and potatoes; and in transplanting trees, shrubs, and large herbaceous plants. It serves as an efficient substitute for a manure fork in establishments too small to warrant the purchase of the latter.

Harrows. Before plowing is started in sod land it is a good plan to chop up the sods and work manure into the upper layer by means of a DISK HARROW. This may also be used after plowing to help make the surface fine. SPIKE or SPRING-TOOTH HARROWS are all that are necessary to fit friable soil for the vegetable garden. To get a fine tilth on the surface a SMOOTHING HARROW (Fig. 119) as described in Chapter VI, LAWNS, is just the thing, or a CHAIN HARROW may be used.

Rakes. For small areas the iron-toothed rake is the tool used for fining the surface soil. The number of teeth should correspond to the size of the areas to be worked and the strength of the user. The rake is an important tool, for it can be used in making drills, covering seeds, cultivating, and raking leaves and trash. A wooden rake is handy in the garden for cleaning up leaves, etc., but it is not indispensable.

Cultivating tools. When the garden is an acre or more in extent, especially if there is a large vegetable garden, a small MOTOR CULTIVATOR is of great value. Some of these are dual-purpose machines, to which a lawn mower may be attached. In smaller gardens, if vegetables are grown, a WHEEL HOE is a great help—though it does take considerable "steam" to push one if the ground is at all hard. For still smaller vegetable gardens and for cultivating in flower beds and around shrubs, HAND HOES are neces-

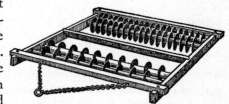

Fig. 119. Smoothing harrow

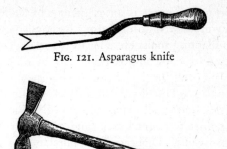

FIG. 121. Asparagus knife

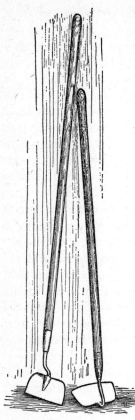

FIG. 122. Mattock

sary. These are of many types. My favorite is the kind of SCUFFLE HOE illustrated in Fig. 120. It is an efficient cultivating tool and may be used for throwing up the soil around the edges of flower beds, cutting turf edges, etc. For general garden use the scuffle or thrust hoe has many advantages over the COMMON or DRAW HOE (Fig. 120). It leaves the surface soil smoother and tidier; the operator does not have to walk upon his finished work; and it is adaptable to a wider range of uses. The use of a draw hoe is almost entirely restricted to the vegetable garden and to crops in rows, though it is useful for making drills and

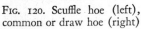

FIG. 120. Scuffle hoe (left), common or draw hoe (right)

mixing concrete. The operator walks forward when using this tool (he walks backward when using a scuffle hoe) and unsightly footprints are left on the loosened earth.

The width of the hoe should be such as to fit it for its special work. For all-around use 6 inches is the best width.

For close cultivating and weeding among the flower clumps and in the rock garden, a HAND CULTIVATOR or WEEDER is useful. These are of many types and are usually illustrated in the back pages of the seed catalogs, from where one should be chosen which seems to fill the gardener's own particular needs. I have found a three-tined HAND FORK, and a WEEDER with three steel claw-like prongs most satisfactory. An

ASPARAGUS KNIFE is an excellent tool for loosening perennial weeds in lawns, as well as for cutting asparagus (Fig. 121).

Planting tools. Here again the spade is the most valuable tool. It is used for trees, shrubs, perennials, bulbs, and, at a pinch, even for small plants. But for the latter a more efficient tool is the TROWEL. This should be of good-quality polished steel, with a sharp cutting edge. For seedlings, and small plants, DIBBERS of various sizes should be used. These are merely pointed sticks and may easily be fashioned by anyone who can whittle. Dibbers, either purchased or made from broken spade or fork handles (Plate XXXI), may be used for planting bulbs. A MATTOCK (Fig. 122) is excellent for making holes in sod when planting bulbs for naturalizing. (See Chapter XIV, FLOWERING BULBS.)

Lawn tools. The most important piece of equipment for the lawn is the LAWN MOWER. When a large area (more than ¼ acre) has to be mowed, a motorized mower, either gasoline or electric, should be obtained if at all possible. When costs have to be closely watched it might be worth while to consider a combination motor cultivator and lawn mower. Good hand lawn mowers range in price from about $20 up to $75, or more, for the best putting-green mowers. Cheap machines usually are unsatisfactory because they are hard to push, soon wear out, and are not able to do a good job. In selecting a mower get one adapted to your strength—don't be tempted to buy an 18-inch one if your "horse-power" does not permit you to push it easily through heavy grass. Single-wheel LAWN TRIMMERS are handy for cutting grass along the edges of flower beds and in places which cannot be reached by an ordinary mower.

When bulbs are naturalized in grass, tools capable of cutting long grass are a necessity. These may be a motor lawn mower equipped with a SICKLE BAR, a farmer's HAY MOWER, or a SCYTHE. If the area is small a GRASS HOOK may be used. There is a tool for cutting long grass, recently put upon the market, which is handled like a golf club. "Golf-widows" might find such a tool a capable instrument for interesting their husbands in gardening.

A ROLLER is a useful tool in lawn- and walk-making and for consolidating the lawn in spring, but it costs a good deal, is bulky to store and is not used more than once or twice a year, as a rule. The best plan to follow if your place is small is to borrow from a neighbor or rent one from the hardware store. Wide rollers should be made in sections to facilitate turning, and on all rollers the edges should be rounded.

In city back yards, often inconvenient of access to a roller, and for very small gardens, a TAMPER may be made to do all the work expected of a roller. The tamper may be bought or may be home-made from a 1-foot length of 2-inch plank (Plate XXXI).

There are machines for cutting and lifting sods, which are used on golf courses and large estates where patching and resodding are part of the routine. SOD-CUTTERS of half-moon shape and SOD-LIFTERS are helpful when cutting sods for lesser jobs; but a sharp spade skillfully used is an efficient substitute.

There are other lawn tools which are useful but not indispensable—such as seed and fertilizer distributors, sod perforators, etc. Any dealer in garden tools will be more than glad to explain their advantages.

Watering equipment. Hose of fairly good quality should be purchased in lengths of 25 or 50 feet. Cheap hose is likely to kink, wear out quickly, and become a general nuisance. The usual size is ¾ inch because it is not too heavy to haul around and it delivers sufficient water for ordinary purposes. A HOSE-REEL is handy for caring for the hose and storing it tidily when it is not in use. The kind which permits the hose to be attached to the faucet while sufficient length is unreeled to take care of the job in hand, has many advantages.

An adjustable HOSE-NOZZLE (costing about 50 cents) throwing a solid stream or a fine spray at the will of the operator is the only sprinkling device necessary in a small garden. A HOSE-HOLDER (costing about 35 cents) holds the hose in any position so that it may be left to water any desired area thoroughly. LAWN SPRINKLERS may cost from $1.50 to more than $30, depending upon how elaborate they are. The kind purchased will be determined largely by the size of the area to be covered. PORTABLE SPRAY-HEADS to be attached along a hose at intervals of 8 to 15 feet (depending upon water pressure available) have much to commend them. They afford an opportunity of finding a use for short lengths of hose which may be connected to make a flexible irrigating system.

When a greenhouse or hotbed forms part of the gardening equipment, a WATERING-POT is essential, because it is almost impossible to water fine seeds with a hose. The kind chosen should have a long spout, a very fine and a coarse rose, and hold 8 to 10 quarts.

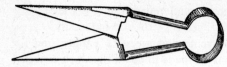

FIG. 123. Grass shears

Shears and other cutting tools. When long stretches of hedge have to be clipped, shears which work on the same principle as the hay mower are great savers of time and labor—if they are motor-driven. I have never been able to get along with those worked by hand or by turning a crank. The ordinary scissors-principle HEDGE SHEARS are satisfactory for small hedges and for lightly shearing certain types of evergreens, but they are not adapted for pruning trees and shrubs. For this work PRUNING SHEARS should be used. These are of various types. Some prefer those in which the cutting blade is pressed on to a bed of softer metal. I like the "parrot-bill" type with two cutting edges and "alligator-tail" spring. Others prefer the kind which has one thin cutting blade, and one comparatively thick so that the shears work on a sort of half-scissors principle. Whichever kind is selected, the cutting blade should be kept sharp. For cutting large branches from the base of old shrubs, long-handled LOPPING SHEARS are useful. GRASS SHEARS are used for cutting grass in places which the lawn mower cannot reach. Get the kind with a bend in the shank so that the operator does not have to skin his knuckles every time he uses them (Fig. 123). EDGING SHEARS OR BORDER SHEARS are used to trim the overhanging grass along the edges of walks and flower beds. These have long handles so that the user may operate them while standing upright. Do not get the kind equipped with a wheel. They cost more and the wheel is useless and in the way.

Other cutting tools should include a PRUNING KNIFE with a strong sharp curved blade and a handle that affords a comfortable grip; and a BUDDING KNIFE to be used when making cuttings, gathering flowers, and, of course, for budding and grafting. These knives should be kept sharp. If the garden program includes making over fruit trees by grafting them to more desirable varieties a GRAFTING CHISEL is necessary.

Carrying tools. The WHEEL-BARROW is the most important

FIG. 124. Trug basket

carrying tool in the moderate-sized garden which does not necessitate the use of a truck. The garden barrow with removable sides is the handiest. The tire should be broad, or pneumatic, to lessen danger of injury when the loaded barrow is wheeled on to the lawn. "Tray" barrows of steel, or the more expensive magnesium, are useful for mixing and transporting mortar or concrete, and for hauling soil.

If the garden area is so small that a wheelbarrow is unnecessary, a CARRYING BASKET is useful. I was brought up on the English TRUG-BASKET (Fig. 124) and still think it is the most desirable type for garden use. It can be used for carrying soil, fertilizers, vegetables, flowers, weeds, and trash.

A gadget devised by George Bishop, outdoor foreman of the Brooklyn Botanic Garden, is a great aid when transporting balled and burlapped trees and shrubs. Consisting of a framework of #12 wire, covered with pieces of old hose, it is easily made by anyone who has the hose the wire, and a pair of pliers (Plate XXXI).

LABELS

The ideal label has not yet been invented, and having struggled with the label problem for more than 35 years, I am convinced that it never will be. Each one suggested has some defect. Either it is too expensive, not durable, illegible, too conspicuous, easily lost, or injurious to the plant.

Labels undoubtedly detract from the garden picture and therefore should either be eliminated as far as possible or be inconspicuous, except when they serve an educational purpose in botanic gardens and public parks.

Labels are essential when plants are raised from seeds. For those which germinate within a few months the ordinary 6-inch, painted wooden labels are satisfactory. These are written upon with a soft lead pencil, or with India ink. When a pencil is used the writing is more legible and longer-lasting if the label is rubbed with a rag dipped in white paint and written on while the paint is still wet. Seeds which take a year or more to germinate need labels more permanent in character. These may be made from pointed strips of zinc about 6 inches long and ¾ inch wide. They are first lightly sandpapered and then written upon with a quill pen, using for ink a 10-percent solution of platinic chloride; or muriatic acid which has been allowed to stand on copper clippings for two months in a stoppered glass container; or one of the numerous preparations obtained from dealers in garden supplies.

Aluminum labels may be momentarily dipped in a 20-percent solution of caustic soda to roughen them and then written with ordinary lead pencil. These are said to be excellent and long-lasting.

In the outdoor garden the necessity for labeling may be largely eliminated by making maps showing the location of the more or less permanent occupants of the garden. Merely a list of the plants set out, kept up to date with mortalities recorded, is a great aid in enabling the owner to keep track of his specimens.

For trees and shrubs. Thin copper labels, written with a stylus and attached to the branches by copper wire, are valuable for labeling trees and shrubs. Such labels are long-lasting and are unobtrusive—too much so, at times, for they are difficult to read and sometimes difficult to find. During the pruning season they are often completely lost, if they happen to be attached to branches that are cut off. As an aid in locating them they should be attached to the same relative position on each tree or shrub. Always place them on the north side, for example, and then it will not be necessary to hunt around all the points of the compass in order to find each one. To lessen the danger of injury to a branch by constriction when a label is fastened in place, it should be attached with a large loop, thus allowing room for the branch to expand, and it should never be fastened to the main leader of the tree. The use of lead wire, which is much softer than copper wire, is another means of avoiding such damage.

Instead of attaching the label directly to the tree, it may be fastened to a wire stake, bent into a loop at the top and thrust into the ground near the plant.

If the names on trees and shrubs are meant to be read by the passer-by, it is possible to get practically everlasting labels made of metal cast with raised letters, or of porcelain with the name fired in the glaze. Permanent easily-read labels may be made at home by stamping the name with metal dies on rectangles of sheet lead. The depressions are filled with white enamel paint and the rest of the label may be blackened by running over it a rubber roller smeared with printer's ink. These labels are fastened with screws to quarter-inch wooden blocks which are either nailed directly on the tree trunk or fastened to a metal standard which is thrust into the ground. This is the type of label used, in part, in the Brooklyn Botanic Garden.

For perennials outdoors. The plants in the perennial garden may be satisfactorily designated by zinc labels with the shanks grooved to be pushed into the ground. These are inscribed with one of the indelible inks mentioned above. Another method is to use a label holder of the type illustrated in Plate XXXI, slipping in a rectangular label made of lead, zinc, celluloid, or waxed paper. I have already described the methods of marking on zinc and lead (pages 505-6). India ink is used for writing on celluloid (which may be white, green, or any other color), which is then varnished, thus making a fairly permanent label. When paper is used it should be thick and of good quality. After the name is written, the label is held with tweezers and immersed momentarily in hot paraffin. Such labels are not very permanent. Copper labels fastened to a wire stake, as described for trees, are also useful in the perennial garden. They are likewise excellent for dahlias, for they may be fastened to the dahlia stakes during the growing season and to the roots in storage, and they are likely to last as long as the plants are kept.

In the rock garden. Yet another problem is presented to the labeler in the rock garden. Except in a public rock garden, conspicuous labels are definitely out of place. The labels used in the rock garden of the late Ellen Willmott are unobtrusive and fairly satisfactory. The name is abbreviated and stamped with a small die at the top of a zinc strip. For example, *Saxifraga oppositifolia* will be rendered "Sax. opp." These labels are stuck in the soil near the plant and almost flush with the surface. Their great defect is the difficulty of finding them in a hurry. There is a firm which stamps lead strips to order with the name of any plant, and these labels are satisfactory for rock plants. One amateur alpine-plant specialist labels his plants by painting the name in black on small light-colored rocks. The aluminum labels previously mentioned are satisfactory in the rock garden.

When writing on labels of the stake type the name should always be kept toward the top so that it is not obscured when thrust into seed pot or ground. When writing lengthwise, therefore, always start the name at the top.

For multiple quantities of plants. In order to avoid the necessity of labeling every pot in greenhouse or coldframe, when there may be anything from two to a hundred of one variety, an understandable system of using only one label to a variety should be adopted. The best method, I think, is always to start each row of pots, left to right, from

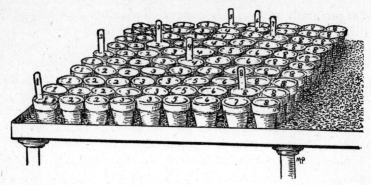

Fig. 125. Diagram illustrating method of making one label serve
many plants

the front of the frame or bench and place the label in the first pot of
each variety, as illustrated in Fig. 125. The same system can be followed in labeling plants in rows in the nursery or reserve ground.

A glance through the advertising pages of horticultural periodicals
and the back pages of seed catalogs will disclose many other kinds of
labels. I have mentioned only those which to me seem the most meri-
torious.

XXXI. ODDS AND ENDS

GROUND-COVERS

In the lexicon of the gardener, a ground-cover is a low-growing plant used, as the name implies, for covering the ground. Ground-covers have already been mentioned in Chapter VI, LAWNS, for planting under trees where grass will not grow; in Chapter II, GRADING, for use on terrace banks; and in Chapter XIV, FLOWERING BULBS, for carpeting the bare ground during and after the blooming period of bulbs.

It remains to suggest a few other uses for them and, for the convenience of the reader, to tabulate the kinds most in demand.

In England, ground-covers such as viola and mignonette are often used in the rose garden to hide the bare soil when the roses are sparsely planted. I do not recommend them for this purpose because they are in the way when it is necessary to fight what J. Horace McFarland, President Emeritus of the American Rose Society, euphoniously calls "bugs and bothers."

Beneath the trees in thin woodland, planted ground-covers in variety may add interest to the forest floor. On exposed hillsides they may help to prevent erosion as well as serve the purpose of hiding the ground.

Most satisfactory are those which will thrive without over-much attention. The perennials, low shrubs, and creeping vines in the following list (indicated by P, S, and V) belong in this category.

Those marked with a star (*) will grow in sun or shade. Those marked with a dagger (†) must have shade for best results. The remainder prefer sun.

* *Ajuga reptans* P
* *Akebia quinata* V
* *Arctostaphylos Uva-ursi* V (sandy soil)
* *Arenaria verna caespitosa* P
† *Asarum canadense* P
  Calluna vulgaris S
* *Convallaria majalis* P
† *Cornus canadensis* P (in northern or mountainous regions only)

* *Cotula squalida* P
* *Dennstaedtia punctilobula* P (a fern)
† *Epigaea repens* (subshrub)
* *Euonymus radicans* varieties S
† *Gaultheria procumbens* S
* *Hedera Helix* V
  Helianthemum nummularium S
  Juniperus S (dwarf spreading varieties)

Leiophyllum buxifolium S (sandy soil)
* Lonicera japonica S
* Lysimachia Nummularia P (especially good in wet places)
Mazus reptans P
* Pachysandra terminalis (subshrub)
† Parthenocissus (Ampelopsis) quinquefolia V
Phlox subulata P

Sedum acre P
* Sedum sarmentosum P
† Taxus canadensis S
Teucrium Chamaedrys (subshrub)
Thymus Serpyllum (subshrub)
Veronica filiformis P
Veronica Teucrium rupestris P
* Vinca minor (subshrub)
* Zanthorhiza apiifolia S

PAVEMENT PLANTING

The growing of plants between the stones or bricks of paved areas is known as pavement planting. If done with restraint it may give an air of mellowness and age to the garden, but if overdone it results in making the garden look untidy, and becomes intensely irritating to the visitor, who, instead of being able to enjoy the garden in comfort, is constantly occupied in looking for a place to put his feet.

The plants should be able to endure the inadvertent trampling which is inevitable in a garden walk. Varieties possessing this quality in a high degree are *Festuca ovina glauca, Arenaria verna caespitosa,* and *Tunica Saxifraga.* Sometimes sedums and sempervivums are recommended for this purpose but it occurs to me that such fleshy-leaved plants might have the same effect in the garden as a banana peel on the sidewalk. Almost any dwarf plants with leaves not easily bruised can be used, and those such as *Thymus Serpyllum* varieties and *Mentha Requieni,* which are fragrant when stepped upon, are especially delightful. Good subjects, besides those above, include *Achillea tomentosa; Alyssum montanum; Antennaria neo-dioica; Arenaria verna caespitosa; A. purpurascens; Bellis rotundifolia; Cerastium tomentosum; Dianthus,* dwarf varieties; *Erinus alpinus; Mazus reptans; Potentilla tridentata; Silene alpestris; Veronica repens;* and *V. Teucrium rupestris.*

Some garden owners like to grow grass in flagstone walks, even though landscape architects often frown upon the practice, declaring that grass makes the crevices too conspicuous. One of the best grasses for this purpose is Chewing's New Zealand fescue. It must, of course, be mown or clipped occasionally.

In order that the plants may succeed when planted between flagstones or bricks there must be some penetrable connection with the soil below. If the flags or bricks are set in concrete there is not much chance for plants to thrive between them unless cracks develop. A walk planned to accommodate pavement plants should be laid on a sand bed overlying soil. To lessen the necessity for weeding it might be well to lay the unplanted portions of the walk on a concrete base.

WEEDS

The frequent use of hoes and cultivating tools is one of the most potent factors in keeping down weeds in cultivated ground. Even such tenacious perennials as Canada thistle and bindweed succumb if their tops are chopped off below the ground line several times during the growing season.

The importance of preventing weeds from seeding is indicated in the old saying, "One year's seeding makes seven years' weeding." Therefore, every endeavor should be made to prevent weeds from seeding. In the cultivated areas use the hoe freely before the weeds have a chance to bloom. If the lawn is infested with dandelions, cut off and gather the flower heads with a dandelion rake (obtainable from large seed stores) so that no seeds are sown to increase the crop. Various methods for combating crab-grass in lawns are described in Chapter VI, LAWNS.

When weeds infest areas not devoted to plant-culture—drives, walks, etc.—other methods may be adopted. A blow-torch or flame-thrower is effective, particularly if used when the weeds are young and tender. There is no objection to operating a blow-torch in the vicinity of cultivated plants if it is used with care. In addition to killing weeds, it may be instrumental in destroying slugs, also eggs of injurious insects. One big advantage that the blow-torch has over chemical weed-killers is that its use does not poison the soil. There are, however, situations where chemicals can be used to advantage in fighting weeds—for example, in gravel walks which are difficult to hoe, although if the poisons are applied to excess over a long period there is a possible danger to trees and shrubs in the vicinity. The superintendent of one of the large public parks in Connecticut recently told me that trees near the park roadways were suffering from the effects of repeated applications of calcium chloride, used, not to kill weeds, but to prevent dust. However, if care is taken to apply just enough poison to kill the weeds (once a year should be enough) the chances are that near-by trees and shrubs will not be harmed.

Herbicides may be obtained, with directions for use, from any large seed store; or sodium arsenite may be used at the rate of 1 pound to 6 gallons of water. Apply it on a hot day through a fine rose on a sprinkling can, using just enough to wet the foliage thoroughly. Sodium arsenite is a deadly poison and must be handled as such. The vessel used in applying it and the hands of the operator should be washed after use, and any animal likely to eat the poisoned foliage must be kept away.

Hot brine is an effective herbicide, and has the advantage of being non-poisonous. It is made by dissolving 1 pound of salt in 1 gallon of hot water.

Atlacide, at one time inaccurately called calcium chlorate, used in spray or powder form, is an effective weed-killer but is destructive to clothes and leather shoes. Under very hot and dry conditions vegetation and clothes sprayed with it may constitute a fire hazard. It may be used at the rate of about 2 pounds in $1\frac{1}{2}$ gallons of water per square rod; or, as a dust, $\frac{3}{4}$ to $1\frac{1}{2}$ pounds to 100 square feet.

A new selective weed-killer, known as 2, 4-D, (2, 4-dichloro-phenoxy-acetic acid), a constituent of a number of proprietary herbicides, in many ways is a wonder worker. It is deadly to most broad-leaved weeds in lawns—dandelions, plantains, etc.—does not injure grass to any appreciable extent; and is extraordinarily effective against bindweed. It is also recommended for killing poison ivy, but there are some who prefer ammonium sulfamate (sold under the trade name Ammate).

HOW TO BUY SEEDS AND PLANTS

After a little experience, few gardeners need to be told how to go about obtaining seeds, bulbs, and plants; but the novice, I have learned, often has not the faintest idea where to buy any material or equipment for the garden. These unfortunates may be seen purchasing flower and vegetable seeds at the grocery or hardware store, and inquiring for nursery stock of their local florist.

In most large cities there are one or more universal providers from whom practically everything horticultural may be obtained; seeds, bulbs, bedding and greenhouse plants, trees, shrubs, fertilizers, and tools. Most of these firms issue catalogs and conduct a mail-order business in addition to selling goods through regular retail channels.

When only the usual trees, shrubs, and perennials are needed, a local nursery is often the best source of supply, because individual specimens may be selected, and freshly-dug material may be immediately delivered.

There are dealers who specialize in trees and shrubs, bulbs, herbaceous perennials, rock-garden plants, and so on. Some restrict themselves even more rigidly and deal only in roses, peonies, dahlias, or irises, as the case may be. Gardeners whose interests are confined to a special plant group should endeavor to get in touch with firms dealing in that specialty, for usually it is from them that rarities and the best stock can be obtained.

The novice can locate these various sources of plant material in several ways. He can join a garden club, horticultural society, or a special plant society and inquire of his fellow members. He can scan the garden pages of the local newspaper and the advertising columns of periodicals devoted to horticulture.

By joining plant societies the garden lover can broaden his knowledge and intensify his pleasure in gardening through meeting congenial people. By subscribing to one or more garden journals he is enabled to keep in touch with the latest horticultural developments.

The Horticultural Department of any State Agricultural Experiment Station or the nearest Botanic Garden will also aid the gardener who writes to inquire where certain groups or species may be obtained.

The gardener who is interested in unusual plants will often discover novelties in the advertising columns of foreign horticultural magazines found in the local public or horticultural library. The catalogs of several English seed houses are especially rich in rare rock plants and perennials.

My advice to the beginner is to be assiduous in collecting catalogs, which, except for some of the more blatant, are mines of information as well as aids to buying.

XXXII. THE GARDENER'S YEAR—A FEW REMINDERS

The calendar of gardening activities suggested below is based on conditions around New York City. In regions with a longer or shorter growing period, gardening practices should be modified to accord with the season. The gardener's time-table is more elastic than that of the railroads, and is much influenced by weather conditions.

Reference to the index will reveal the pages on which the subjects below are treated in earlier parts of the book.

January

Inspect the garden occasionally and apply protective measures if the bark of trees and shrubs is being eaten by rabbits and mice. Rabbits may be caught in box traps baited with apple or carrot.

It is not too late to apply winter covering to evergreens if it has not already been done.

Carefully shake the snow off small evergreens to lessen danger of breakage if winds become strong.

Vines and maples (which "bleed" if cut too late in winter) may be pruned on mild days.

Proceed with dormant spraying if the shade temperature rises above 45 degrees.

Save all the wood ashes from the open fireplace, to be cultivated into the soil in April.

Bulbs for forcing may be brought indoors from the plunge-pit at intervals of two or three weeks for succession of bloom.

Toward the end of the month cut branches of early-flowering shrubs, such as forsythia and Japanese quince, to force in water indoors.

Retarded lily-of-the-valley pips may be forced into bloom in about three weeks from the time of potting them.

Look over dahlias and other "bulbs" in storage and cut off portions which show signs of decay.

Gladiolus corms should be similarly inspected. If they are molding, dust with sulphur and remove to a drier place.

A good indoor job at this season is to look over tools carefully, oil them if necessary to prevent rusting, grind shears, and paint the wheelbarrow. Any dental work on the wooden rake should be done now rather than when the rake is needed.

Alpine seeds (if you have any on hand) may be planted now. Place the pots or flats in a coldframe and then fill frame with snow.

When the leaves of poinsettia begin to turn yellow, gradually withhold water from the roots and store them dry until spring.

If a greenhouse is available, seeds of pansies and many perennials may be sown with the expectation that they will bloom during the current season.

February

Seeds of begonia, lobelia and other bedding plants may be started in the greenhouse now if early bloom is desired. Seeds of perennials and the annual Canterbury bells also may be sown.

Toward the end of the month plant seeds of sweet peas in a coolhouse. Celery, cabbage, and onion intended for an early crop may be started.

Hardy plants for forcing which have been stored dormant may be brought into a cool greenhouse now. Continue bringing in bulbs from the plunge-pit.

Rhubarb, dug up and "boxed" in the fall, may be forced in the cellar.

Branches of early-flowering shrubs, cut in February, will bloom more readily when placed in water indoors than those cut early in January.

Bring stock plants of chrysanthemums indoors and make cuttings when the shoots have sufficiently developed.

Continue to watch out for damage by mice and rabbits.

Locate a source of supply of manure for hotbeds.

If you have any quantity of seeds left over from last year count out fifty or one hundred of each kind and test their power of germination by placing them between moist blotters in a warm room. If they germinate freely you may use the remainder for planting and save on your seed bill.

Study the seed catalogs and make out your order for the current season. Try a few novelties each year.

March

Look over stored roots and bulbs. If gladiolus corms show any signs of infestation with thrips fumigate with naphthalene flakes or immerse them in corrosive sublimate solution.

Hotbeds may be started about the middle of the month, and tender and half-hardy seeds planted therein.

Harden off sweet peas in the coldframe so that they may be planted outdoors by the beginning of April.

If weather is mild, partially remove the cover from the bulb beds.

When frost has left the ground look over the perennial border and the rock garden and reset any plants heaved out of the ground by frost.

Mulch the rock garden with equal parts stone chips and sifted leafmold.

Fruit trees, as soon as the buds start to swell, may be grafted with scions which were cut in the fall and kept dormant in a cold place.

Finish up the pruning of hardy trees and shrubs. Vines and maples will "bleed" if cut now, but most authorities believe that this does not harm them.

If frost leaves the ground early, and it dries up sufficiently, the manure mulches over the roots of trees, shrubs, and perennials may be lightly forked into the ground.

Lime may be applied (if considered necessary) after the manure is forked under.

If soil conditions are right, sweet peas and other hardy annuals may be planted.

Rose bushes should be planted as early as possible, but do not attempt it if the soil is wet and sticky.

Continue with dormant spraying on fine days.

The lawn should be raked and rolled in order to level inequalities caused by freezing.

Toward the end of the month there is a chance that the soil will be in the right condition so that bare spots in the lawn may be seeded; or a new lawn may be planted, if this was not done in the fall.

Coldframes, used for storing plants over winter, should be opened up on mild days.

Pansies, English daisies, and other bedding plants in coldframes should have the mulch of salt hay removed from them.

Pruning Hybrid Perpetual, Hybrid Tea, and Tea roses may be started at the end of the month if the weather seems favorable.

An early crop of rhubarb may be obtained by covering a clump with a tall fruit basket and mounding this with fresh manure early in the month.

Start tuberous begonias indoors.

Any trees which are not growing vigorously should be fed with a complete fertilizer high in nitrogen.

The wet heavy snow which we sometimes get in March is likely to damage evergreens, especially if its fall is followed immediately by freezing weather and wind. Therefore, it should be shaken from the branches of specimen evergreens before it causes breakage.

April

Sow seeds of hardy flowers and vegetables outdoors.

Drain and clean the lily pool before the lilies start to grow. Plant hardy waterlilies now.

Finish pruning roses. Prune forsythias and other early-blooming shrubs when the flowers have faded.

Rake and roll the lawn if it was not done last month.

Apply a fertilizer when the grass blades are dry.

Harden off, in the coldframe, seedlings which were started in the hotbed.

Dig up and reset chrysanthemums and hardy asters which have wintered outdoors.

At the end of the month plant out rooted cuttings of chrysanthemum which were started indoors and hardened off in coldframes.

Start planting deciduous trees and shrubs.

Plant evergreens toward end of month.

Evergreens such as arborvitae and yew which need pruning may be cut back just before growth starts. It is safer not to cut into wood more than one year old.

Dormant spraying may be done up until the time the buds begin to swell.

Just as soon as there is room available, plant melon and cucumber seeds in the soil of the hotbed for an early crop.

Gladiolus corms may be planted for early flowering.

The wood ashes saved from the open fireplace may be spread on the surface soil (50 pounds to 1,000 square feet) and cultivated in.

All winter covering should be removed by the middle of the month.

May

Plant seeds of half-hardy and tender flowers and vegetables outdoors.

Tender bedding plants—cannas, geraniums, elephant's ears, begonias, etc.—may be planted outdoors when danger of frost is past.

House plants, after their winter indoors, will be looking forward to a summer vacation. Get them outdoors as soon as it is safe to do so.

Quite often a minor drought is experienced in May. Be prepared to water newly planted trees, shrubs, evergreens and bedding plants; and also established rhododendron plantings should they seem to need it.

Strawberries should be mulched with straw, salt hay or pine-needles to keep the fruit from being spattered with mud.

Seeds of biennials and perennials for flowering next year may be planted toward the end of May.

Peonies should be watered with liquid manure or receive an application of a quick-acting complete fertilizer.

The side flower buds of peonies never amount to much, so they should be pinched off when they are about the size of buckshot, leaving but one flower bud to each stalk. This practice throws all the strength into the terminal bud and results in a larger flower.

As soon as full-sized leaves have developed on the rose bushes, start dusting with Massey dust to control black spot and leaf-eating insects.

Don't let the weeds get ahead of you: keep the hoe busy.

Supply the necessary supports to weak-stemmed plants before they are toppled over.

Cut lilacs freely for indoor decoration and try to shape up the bush as you do so. Often this is all the pruning lilacs need beyond the removal of suckers.

Plant gladiolus corms at intervals of two or three weeks for succession of bloom.

June

Just as soon as early crops are harvested in the vegetable garden, plant for succession.

Tropical waterlilies may be planted this month. Around New York not much is gained by planting them before June 15.

Continue to apply Massey dust to rose bushes before every rainy period. This must be kept up until the fall.

Pinch out the tips of growing shoots of chrysanthemums until they have attained the required bushiness.

Dahlias may be planted up until about the middle of the month.

Sheared deciduous hedges should be trimmed before the new growth hardens sufficiently to make it difficult to cut.

A supplementary feeding of a concentrated complete fertilizer should be given to any perennials which seem to need it.

Insects are liable to become troublesome now. Watch for them and apply remedial measures early.

After the "June drop" the fruits of apples, peaches, plums, etc., should be thinned if they stand too thickly on the branches.

Biennial and perennial seeds may be planted.

If you have a vacant coldframe, why not try your hand at propagating shrubs from softwood cuttings? From the last of May until August is a suitable time.

Remove flower heads from lilacs and rhododendrons in the interests of tidiness and to conserve the plants' energies.

Continue to cultivate the surface soil and thus kill weeds.

Set out celery plants in the vegetable garden and do not fail to water them thoroughly if the soil is dry.

Cut the long grass among naturalized bulb plantings as soon as the bulb foliage is withered. The "hay" may be wet down and stacked in a pile to decay and form humus.

July

Weed-killers may be applied with advantage to walks, drives, and poison ivy during this month.

Prevent annuals from seeding if you want to prolong their season of bloom.

Keep a close watch for borers and deal with them promptly.

Crab-grass will soon be making its appearance in the lawn. Take measures to prevent its increase.

Set out plants of late cabbage and celery. Plant seeds of beans, beets, and corn (early in the month) for succession.

Lawns should not be cut too closely during hot weather. Raise the cutting blades of the mower ½ inch or so if necessary.

Look over the trees and shrubs to make certain that guy-wires and label fastenings are not cutting into the bark.

If you are planning to plant next fall any of the less common bulbs, send your order to your dealer now.

Last call for planting gladiolus corms! They cannot be held unplanted beyond the middle of this month.

The spray barrel will probably be kept busy now.

Cuttings of shrubs and of some of the rock-garden plants may be inserted in a close, shaded coldframe.

Rambler roses should be pruned as soon as they have finished blooming. If the supports need painting it should be done immediately after the roses have been pruned and before the new shoots are tied up.

Wisterias which do not bloom should have their growth checked toward the end of the month by cutting back to three or four buds the long trailing shoots of the current season.

Delphiniums should be cut back to just below the flower spikes to prevent seeding. These cut-back plants will bloom again in the fall.

Shear formal evergreen hedges. The deciduous hedges will probably need another clipping at this time.

Continue watering and cultivating whenever necessary.

Take notes of any changes you wish to make in your plantings. Really, this should be done throughout the whole growing season, but until now perhaps you have been too busy.

August

Cut and dry everlastings and store them in large paper bags for use in winter bouquets.

If lilies have to be transplanted, do it as soon as the foliage dies down.

Plant seeds of pansies for next year's bloom. This is the last call for planting seeds of biennials and perennials. If you have new seeds of delphinium plant them now.

Bearded irises should be divided and transplanted if the clumps are crowded.

Plant autumn crocuses and Virginia cowslip, also Madonna lilies if the bulbs are available.

Make cuttings of bedding plants for next year's display, or for use as house plants during the winter.

Cut out raspberry and blackberry canes which have fruited.

Set out pot-plants of strawberries.

Study the bulb catalogs and order bulbs for fall planting, if you have not already done so.

Plant evergreens toward the end of the month.

Start the new lawn at the end of the month if the weather is favorable.

Plant beans, beets, lettuce, peas, and spinach. An early maturing variety of bush bean may be planted as late as August 15 with a fair chance that beans may be picked before frost.

September

Apply paradichlorobenzene to peaches and other trees attacked near the ground line by borers.

The last shearing of deciduous hedges should be done early in the month.

Plant evergreens, eremurus, and daffodils.

If it seems necessary, divide and replant oriental poppies, bleeding heart, and Japanese irises.

Transplant crowded lilies, and plant new bulbs as soon as they become available.

Plant peonies, and fertilize established plants—they make new roots at this season.

Transplant biennials to their winter quarters.

This is probably the best time to seed a new lawn, and to fall-fertilize established lawns.

Plants intended for house decoration in winter should be potted and brought indoors so that they may become partly adapted to their environment before artificial heat is used.

In localities where early frosts are experienced it is worth while to have on hand covering material—wrapping paper, newspapers, old sheets, etc.—to protect tender blooming plants. If they are enabled to escape the first frost they may continue in good condition for several weeks.

If there is any idle ground it can be planted to winter rye or hairy vetch, or both, for a cover-crop, to be turned under for green manure next spring.

Gather squashes and pumpkins after the first frost and store in a dry cool frost-proof place.

October

Cover-crops may still be planted.

Start to make any necessary changes in the perennial garden by transplanting plants which have finished blooming.

Plant deciduous trees and shrubs.

Plant hardy spring-flowering bulbs.

Dig up and store for winter dahlias, gladioli and other tender plants.

Dig up and set in pots or tubs herbaceous plants and shrubs intended for forcing.

Pot up bulbs for forcing.

Order roses for planting in November.

With an auger obtain a sample of soil from a depth of about 18 inches, and, if it is at all dry, thoroughly water all evergreens.

Drain all irrigation pipes so that there is no danger of their being burst by water freezing in them during the winter.

Clean, oil, and store lawn mowers. Paint any garden structures that need it.

Spread manure on the soil over the roots of trees and shrubs.

Make hardwood cuttings of trees and shrubs.

Make root cuttings of phlox, Japanese anemones, and other plants.

Bring under cover a sufficient supply of potting soil for winter use.

Harvest root crops of vegetables (except parsnip and salsify, which are improved by freezing) and store in sand in cool cellars.

November

Continue planting hardy bulbs, also deciduous trees and shrubs.

This is a good time to plant roses. After planting, hill them up with soil.

Make certain that climbing roses are securely attached to their supports.

Mark, with easily seen labels, bulb plantings and late-starting plants in the perennial garden, so that they may be avoided when forking under the manure mulch in early spring.

Put the lily pools to bed for the winter.

Take a chance on sowing sweet pea seeds in positions where they are to bloom.

Clean up and burn all debris which may harbor injurious insects.

Gather and burn bagworm cocoons and tent-caterpillar egg-masses.

Bring garden furniture under cover if it has not already been done.

Protect trees and shrubs from mice and rabbits.

Dig up stock plants of chrysanthemums and store in a coldframe.

If deciduous trees and shrubs are badly infested with scale insects, spray with a dormant spray solution now, and again in the spring just before growth buds open.

Apply protective mulches on the perennial garden after the ground has frozen an inch or two.

Stratify seeds of trees and shrubs. Remove the fleshy covering from such seeds as apple, magnolia, barberry, etc., before stratifying them.

Make and store hardwood cuttings.

Make and insert cuttings of evergreens in the greenhouse.

If you have an idle coldframe sash, place it over the plantings of Christmas-rose (*Helleborus*) to protect the flowers from the weather. Support it 18 inches above the ground by means of heavy stakes driven into the ground.

December

By this time, in all probability, it will not be too early to cover those plants which need winter protection.

Any tools not likely to be used during the winter should be cleaned, and any parts likely to rust should be oiled.

If your spray barrel is a wooden one be sure it is filled with water to prevent the wood from shrinking and developing leaks.

This is a good time to start pruning dead and dangerous limbs from trees. These should be burned in case they harbor insects and diseases. The wounds made in sawing off the limbs should be protected by painting them.

For the next three months keep an eye open for egg-masses of the tussock and gypsy moths (dab them with creosote), tent caterpillars, and for the cocoons of bagworms; and deal with them when a convenient time arrives.

Take a final look around the garden to make sure that all debris is cleaned up and burned.

If you are planning to make over unsatisfactory varieties of pears and apples by cleft-grafting, gather the scions you propose to use, pack them in moist moss, and bury them in a cold spot to keep them dormant.

This is a good time to grub out poison ivy. If you burn the roots and branches be careful to do so in an out-of-the-way spot. The smoke is dangerous.

It is not too late to take cuttings of evergreens and deciduous shrubs, preferably on a mild day when the wood is not frozen.

Cut brushwood to be used next year as supports for garden peas, sweet peas, and other plants. If it is placed in even windrows with the tops weighted by a plank, the branches will assume a more or less fan-shaped form adapted for staking plants in rows.

Gather up surplus Christmas trees from vacant lots and use them for sheltering and covering plants which need winter protection.

Inspect the stored bulbs and roots and treat them according to their needs.

Bring in bulbs from the plunge-pit or from cold storage and force them into bloom indoors.

But the gardener's year does not end on December 31, any more than it starts on New Year's Day. Seeds may be planted from April to October—and from November to March. Cuttings are made that new plants may be grown from one's choicest specimens; bulbs are planted for bloom both in the house and outdoors. Shrubs are pruned, sometimes to give finer blossoms the following year; soil is re-dug and fertilized to give the garden greater splendor. Every week brings its tasks—and every day its joys to the gardener. It is the pleasure that comes from work that keeps men gardening—and it is hoped that this book has served to make the work lighter, the pleasure greater, and the results more certain.

INDEX

The specific and garden names in the Descriptive Lists are in alphabetical order and are not accorded separate entry in the index. Generic names, however, are entered. See Lists, descriptive.

Neither the generic nor specific names in the Classified and Tabular Lists are in the index. See Lists, classified; and Lists, descriptive.

All common or English names are entered.